Praise for

Rewiring Regional Security in a Fragmented World

"*Rewiring Regional Security in a Fragmented World* captures the variety of security challenges and the diversity of conflict management practice across the regions. Featuring regional voices, this timely and innovative volume will help students and practitioners grasp the global conversations taking place on conflict and security issues. The editors are surely correct to conclude that we live in an age where security is divisible but collective action is more necessary than ever."

—**Martti Ahtisaari,** former President of Finland, Nobel Peace Prize laureate, founder and chairman of the board of Crisis Management Initiative

"The seasoned team of Crocker, Hampson, and Aall once again train their laser beam on a subject of pressing actuality. They have gathered a high-powered array of regional and other experts to show that not only is the global machinery creaking for managing conflicts and crises created in and for another era but that the world is poorly, or at best disparately equipped, at the regional level, to handle threats old and new. Despite this disheartening diagnosis at a time of resurgence of armed conflict and violence, the editors see grounds for hope in the emerging trend toward 'collective conflict management,' surely no peacemaker's dream. Rewiring is an urgent call to attention."

—**Alvaro de Soto,** former UN Under Secretary-General and Senior Fellow, Ralph Bunche Institute, Associate Fellow, Geneva Centre for Security Policy

"A world war is unlikely. That's the good news. The bad news is that regional conflicts are not disappearing. Indeed some are getting worse. Hence, they deserve greater study. This volume captures well both the challenges and opportunities of regional conflict management. The globally diverse voices in this book give it a special edge. Chester Crocker and his team have done the world a great service with this valuable resource."

—**Kishore Mahbubani,** Dean, Lee Kuan Yew School of Public Policy, National University of Singapore, author of *The New Asian Hemisphere: the Irresistible Shift of Global Power to the East*

"The book includes a broad and sweeping review of regions, their security problems, and organizations to deal with them by a series of knowledge-able and recognized experts. The editors have provided an enlightening and groundbreaking overview of both the state of the regional role in secu-rity around the globe and how regional security approaches might be made more effective in collective conflict management. A must read for anyone interested in this major topic of growing importance."

—**Thomas R. Pickering,** former Under Secretary of State for political affairs and Ambassador to the United Nations

Rewiring Regional Security

Rewiring Regional Security in a Fragmented World

Chester A. Crocker,
Fen Osler Hampson,
and Pamela Aall, editors

UNITED STATES INSTITUTE OF PEACE PRESS
Washington, D.C.

UNITED STATES INSTITUTE OF PEACE
2301 Constitution Avenue, NW
Washington, DC 20037
www.usip.org

Printed in the United States of America

The paper used in this publication meets the minimum requirements of American National Standards for Information Science—Permanence of Paper for Printed Library Materials, ANSI Z39.48-1984.

Library of Congress Cataloging-in-Publication Data

Rewiring regional security in a fragmented world / Chester A. Crocker, Fen Osler Hampson, and Pamela Aall, editors.
  p. cm.
  Includes index.
  ISBN 978-1-60127-070-2 (pbk. : alk. paper)
  eISBN 978-1-60127-101-3
  1. Security, International.   2. Regionalism (International organization)
3. Conflict management.   I. Crocker, Chester A.   II. Hampson, Fen Osler.
III. Aall, Pamela R.   IV. United States Institute of Peace.
  JZ6005.R44 2011
  355'.031—dc22

                                                          2010052942

Contents

Illustrations

Figures

Tables

Foreword

Recent decades have seen a remarkable growth around the world in the number and variety of institutions dedicated to conflict management and local security concerns. Perhaps the strongest growth has been in regional organizations. These institutions come in many sizes and shapes. Some have been established to address very specific problems, such as the US-Mexican Merida Initiative against trade in illegal narcotics. Others, such as the African Union, operate at the broadest regional levels, incorporating economic and social development issues as well as collective security imperatives.

In assessing these regional efforts, it is important to understand that conflict management goes far beyond the capabilities of individual institutions and states. Different regions have different requirements for dealing with discord and violence. Some, like Europe and the US, have long histories of elaborate defense alliances which require members to work within a strategic framework, standardize their weaponry, and scale up their interoperability. Other regions avoid confrontation and use long habits of cooperation to promote security, as illustrated by the Southeast Asian dedication to the "ASEAN-way."

What does this rise in regional conflict management capacity mean for international security? Are regions—through their dedicated organizations or through loose coalitions of states, regional bodies, and nonofficial actors—capable of addressing the array of new and emerging security threats? What does a "regionalization" of security cooperation mean for the international community, and especially the United Nations? Should the United Nations be strengthened or revitalized? Or should it continue the recent trend of subcontracting conflict management initiatives to regional organizations?

To address these questions, we need a fresh understanding of regional threats as well as an assessment of approaches to counteracting them. And we need a better grasp of existing regional security and conflict management capacities, and of the links between the security and conflict management fields.

This volume is designed to foster understanding of the mosaic of regional security challenges and conflict management responses in all their complexity. It explores not only formal regional institutions, but also the informal cooperation (or for some regions, lack thereof) that can grow out of a culture of regional security cooperation and the conflict management tradition.

For this effort, the editors of this volume have drawn together an impressive array of scholars and practitioners to provide a region-by-region analysis of security challenges and conflict management capacity. These experts are credible and diverse, coming as they do from Africa, the Middle East, Europe, Russia and Central Asia, South Asia, Southeast Asia, East Asia, South America, North America, Central America, and the Caribbean.

Editors Crocker, Hampson, and Aall are uniquely qualified to help bring us this fresh understanding. They are the joint editors or authors of no fewer than seven books covering related issues published by the U.S. Institute of Peace Press—including *Herding Cats: Multiparty Mediation in a Complex World*; *Leashing the Dogs of War: Conflict Management in a Divided World*; *Taming Intractable Conflicts: Mediation in the Hardest Cases*, and its companion volume, *Grasping the Nettle: Analyzing Cases of Intractability*. These volumes join many other Institute-sponsored studies on conflict management topics, including John Paul Lederach's *Building Peace: Sustainable Reconciliation in Divided Societies* and I. William Zartman's *Peacemaking in International Conflict*; and case-specific studies by practitioners such as Ahmedou Ould-Abdallah's *Burundi on the Brink: A UN Special Envoy Reflects on Preventive Diplomacy*, Princeton Lyman's *Partner to History: The U.S. Role in South Africa's Transition to Democracy*, and my own *Exiting Indochina: U.S. Leadership of the Cambodia Settlement & Normalization with Vietnam*.

Rewiring Regional Security explores new territory for the Institute by looking both intensively at specific regions and broadly across regions. It is a volume that transcends the often stove-piped studies of international relations, security, conflict management and resolution, and regional and area studies. In doing so, it offers a welcome complement to the Institute's Cross-Cultural Negotiating series that examines negotiation and other conflict management techniques inside and across nations. Books in this series explore the negotiating practices of China, Iran, France, and North Korea, among others, as well as studies of the impact of culture on Israeli-Palestinian and Indo-Pakistani negotiations.

We may have once thought that promoting international peace and security was simply a matter of powerful states willing to play a leadership role in world policing, and robust global institutions empowered to play an active role in conflict management. We now better understand that peace and security depend on a complex web of interrelationships between societies, countries, and regional and global actors. *Rewiring Regional Security* goes a long way to sharpening our understanding of these complexities. It helps us grasp the variety of regional institutions, perceptions, and policies in coping with security and conflict issues. Its central premise—that the growing regionalization of security organizations and activities is spawning an increasingly eclectic and improvised approach to handling conflict management in today's world—will likely be at the center of discussion and debate for some time to come.

Richard H. Solomon, President
United States Institute of Peace

Acknowledgments

Abook that attempts to scan the world's security threats and the world's regional capacity to address those threats owes acknowledgments in every corner. First, we would like to thank our authors, whose collective willingness to undertake this assignment and whose seriousness and creativity in addressing the issues lifted this book from the ordinary to the extraordinary. Second, we extend thanks to David Malone, Rohinton Medhora, and Gerd Schönwälder of the International Development Research Council, who supported the meetings that allowed us to bring authors together and to test ideas on other experts and who challenged us to achieve and maintain a comprehensive and rigorous approach throughout the project. Many thanks go to the University of the West Indies, Barbados, and the Geneva Centre for Security Policy for hosting the meetings of regional experts. We owe special appreciation to Carleton University's Center for Trade Policy and Law—especially Philip Rourke, Kevin Arthur, Chantal Blouin, Monique Moreau, and Doris Whitteker—for providing administrative support for the meetings and for the regional security and conflict management project in general, and to Carleton professor Christina Rojas for her substantive assistance.

The staff of the United States Institute of Peace's Academy for International Conflict Management and Peacebuilding also made invaluable contributions. Ethan Schecter, Andy Levin, and Annie Davies each in turn kept their eye on the ball and made sure that the editors did not drop it. Other Academy staff members provided suggestions and feedback, and helped in ways large and small throughout the four years of this endeavor. Many thanks go to the Institute's senior leadership—particularly Richard Solomon, Tara Sonenshine, and Mike Graham—for providing their enthusiastic backing and an open environment for the introduction and discussion of the ideas that came out of this project.

Finally, as always, USIP Press, under the leadership of Valerie Norville, worked its magic on this book. Our editor, Kurt Volkan, herded his cats—in the form of twenty-six authors—across seven continents with a light but firm touch that kept the book focused and moving forward. His knowledge of the field, deft editorial hand, management skills, and good humor made the experience a pleasure for all concerned. Many thanks also go to Marie Marr and Richard von Zimmer for the excellent design of cover and book, and to Kay Hechler and Michelle Slavin and their staffs for their contributions to the management and marketing of the book. The two peer reviewers were extremely helpful and provided excellent suggestions to improve the quality of the book. We are very grateful to the two of them for the time and effort they put into this project and hope they will recognize their contributions in the final product.

* * *

Carleton University gratefully acknowledges the support it received to hold two conferences in the support of this project at which a series of papers were presented by the contributors to this volume. This work was carried out with the aid of a grant from the International Development Research Centre, Ottawa, Canada.

Contributors

Pamela Aall is provost of the United States Institute of Peace's Academy for International Conflict Management and Peacebuilding, the Institute's education and training center for practitioners working in or on conflict. Her research interests include mediation, nonofficial organizations, civil-military relations, education and training, and the role of education in exacerbating conflict or promoting reconciliation. She is past president of Women In International Security, an organization dedicated to promoting women's professional advancement in the foreign affairs and security fields. She has also worked at the Rockefeller Foundation, the European Cultural Foundation, and the International Council for Educational Development. With Chester A. Crocker and Fen Osler Hampson, she has written and edited a number of books and articles on international conflict management, including *Leashing the Dogs of War: Conflict Management in a Divided World* (2007); *Grasping the Nettle: Analyzing Cases of Intractable Conflict* (2005); *Taming Intractable Conflicts: Mediation in the Hardest Cases* (2004); and *Turbulent Peace: The Challenges of Managing International Conflict* (2001). They are also series editors for the Routledge Studies in Security and Conflict Management.

Chester A. Crocker is the James R. Schlesinger Professor of Strategic Studies at Georgetown University's Walsh School of Foreign Service and serves on the board of its Institute for the Study of Diplomacy. From 1981 to 1989, he served as assistant secretary of state for African affairs. He chaired the board of the United States Institute of Peace (1992–2004) and continues to serve as a director of this independent, nonpartisan institution created and funded by Congress to strengthen knowledge and practice in international conflict. He is a member of the World Bank's Independent Advisory Board on governance and anticorruption and is a founding member of the Global Leadership Foundation. He consults as adviser on strategy and negotiation to a number of U.S. and European firms, and is a member of the Council on Foreign Relations, the International Institute of Strategic Studies, and the American Academy of Diplomacy. In addition to the series of books and articles coauthored and coedited with Fen Osler Hampson and Pamela Aall, he is the author of *High Noon in Southern Africa: Making Peace in a Rough Neighborhood* (1993).

Fen Osler Hampson, Fellow of the Royal Society of Canada, is the Chancellor's Professor and director of the Norman Paterson School of International Affairs, Carleton University, Ottawa, Canada. He is a member and former vice-chair of the board of directors of the Pearson Peacekeeping Centre and a member of the Board of the Parliamentary Centre and the Social Science Foundation Board of Trustees of the Josef Korbel School of International of International Affairs. He is the author/co-author of nine volumes and co-editor of twenty-five others. His latest books include *The Global Power of Talk: Negotiating America's Interests* (coauthored with I. William Zartman, forthcoming) and *Canada's International Policies: Agendas, Alternatives and Politics* (coauthored with Brian Tomlin and Norman Hillmer, 2007).

*   *   *

Gilles Andréani is a senior auditor in the Cour des comptes, an independent body that audits government programs, and an adjunct professor at Paris II Panthéon-Assas University, where he teaches international relations. Born in 1956, he has master's degrees in political science and law, and graduated in 1981 from the French school of government (École nationale d'administration). He has served in government since then, mostly in positions related to security policy. His latest position before his current one was head of the policy planning staff in the French Foreign Ministry, which he held twice, from 1995 to 1999 and again from 2001 to 2004. He previously was deputy head of the French mission to NATO (from 1993 to 1995), head of the disarmament division in the Foreign Ministry (from 1989 to 1993), and deputy head for studies in the Defense Ministry (1988–89). Parallel to his career in government, he has pursued teaching and research activities: he spent two years (1999–2000) at the International Institute for Strategic Studies as a senior fellow for international security and at the London School of Economics. Since 2001 he has taught international relations at Paris II. He joined the German Marshall Fund of the United States in 2009 as a transatlantic fellow. His research and teaching activities have mainly focused on transatlantic and European security issues.

Kwesi Aning presently serves as the director of research at the Kofi Annan International Peacekeeping Training Centre in Accra, Ghana, and on the World Economic Forum's Council on Conflict Prevention. He earlier served with the African Union as its first expert on counterterrorism, peace, and security and also with the United Nations Department for Political Affairs. He has taught at several universities around the world and serves on several editorial boards and has several publications to his name.

Oksana Antonenko is a senior fellow and the program director for Russia and Eurasia at the International Institute for Strategic Studies (IISS). She joined the IISS in 1996 as research associate. From 1998 to 2000, she was the director of the IISS research and seminar program on military reform in Russia and the Commonwealth of Independent States, focusing among other issues on foreign assistance to Russia for the retraining and resettlement of redundant officers. In 1999–2003 she headed a research and seminar program on Russia's regional perspective on foreign and security policy, focusing on Russia's relations with Europe, the South Caucasus, and Central Asia. In 2004–05 she worked on a research project on Russian-EU relations and coedited the book *Russia and the European Union: Prospects for a New Relationship*. In 2005–06 she facilitated track II meetings between Georgian and South Ossetian senior officials and experts with the aim of promoting conflict resolution in the Georgian–South Ossetian conflict. In 2006–07 she directed a research project on the Shanghai Cooperation Organization and security challenges in Central Asia. At present, she oversees research projects on NATO-Russia relations, regional strategy for Afghanistan, and Georgian-Russian dialogue on regional security challenges. She holds degrees from Moscow State University and Harvard University's Kennedy School of Government.

Chrysantus Ayangafac is currently a democracy and governance officer at the Department of Political Affairs, African Union Commission. Over the past nine years, he has conceptualized, initiated, and managed a range of programs and projects in the areas of governance, human security, conflict prevention, and international diplomacy. He has been widely published on diverse subjects in the fields of international relations, conflict, and integration. He is frequently called upon to advise national, multilateral, and bilateral institutions on Africa-related policy and regularly engages with policymakers and diplomats from around the world on human rights, governance, conflict, and postconflict reconstruction and integration in Africa. He is associated with several nongovernmental and academic institutions within and outside Africa and is an alumnus of the U.S. Department of State's International Visitor Leadership Program on Conflict Prevention and Management. He is fluent in English and French and holds a master's degree in international relations from Wits University and is currently pursuing a PhD in international relations.

Alyson J. K. Bailes served as a British diplomat for more than thirty years, specializing in politico-military and European issues, before resigning to take on the post of director of the Stockholm International Peace Research Institute from 2002 to 2007. She is now an adjunct professor at the University of Iceland in Reykjavik, teaching security studies and continuing to work in research projects on the European Union and NATO, arms control, new security concepts, and Arctic affairs, among others.

Raúl Benítez-Manaut is a professor and researcher at the North America Research Center of the Universidad Nacional Autónoma de México (UNAM). He was public policy scholar at the Latin American Program at the Woodrow Wilson Center of Washington in 1998 and 2003. In 2001, he was a visiting professor at the Institute for Latin American Studies, Columbia University and he served as professor at American University's School of International Service in 2006–07. He is lecturer of political science and international relations at UNAM, from where he holds a PhD in Latin American Studies, and the Instituto Tecnologico Autonomo de Mexico. He has taught as a lecturer at the Facultad Latinoamericana de Ciencias Sociales in Chile, Argentina, Costa Rica, El Salvador, Dominican Republic, and Guatemala; the China Institute for International Strategic Studies, Beijing; the Institute for Developing Studies of Tokyo; the University for Peace in Costa Rica; the Interamerican Institute for Human Rights, Costa Rica; the Torcuatto di Tella University in Argentina; the National Defense University, Washington, DC; the Universidad de Valencia, Spain; Georgetown University, Washington, DC; New York University; the Canadian Foundation for the Americas, Ottawa; York University, Toronto; and the Carter Center, Atlanta. He has written numerous journal articles and book chapters on matters of hemispheric security, the Central American peace process, the civil war in El Salvador, national security, geopolitics, and the armed forces of Mexico. He is the author of *La teoria militar y la guerra civil en El Salvador* (1989) and coauthor of thirteen collective books on security, foreign policy, and armed forces. He has been a member of the Latin American Studies Association since 1987 and is a member of the International Studies Association.

Richard A. Bitzinger is a senior fellow with the S. Rajaratnam School of International Studies in Singapore, where his work focuses on security and defense issues relating to the Asia-Pacific region, including military modernization in the Asia Pacific and weapons proliferation. He was previously an associate professor with the Asia-Pacific Center for Security Studies, Honolulu, Hawaii, and has also worked for the RAND Corporation, the Center for Strategic and Budgetary Affairs, and the U.S. government. In 1999–2000, he was a senior fellow with the Atlantic Council of the United States. He holds a master's degree from the Monterey Institute of International Affairs and pursued additional postgraduate studies at the University of California, Los Angeles.

Jacobus Kamfer (Jakkie) Cilliers is the executive director of the Institute for Security Studies (ISS). He holds a DLitt et Phil from the University of South Africa (UNISA). He cofounded the ISS in 1990 and played an important role in the transformation of the South African Armed Forces and the institution of civilian control over the military in the period from 1990 to 1996. At present, most of his interests relate to the emerging security architecture in Africa as reflected in the developments under the banner of the Peace and Security Council of the African Union as well as to issues around African futures. He is an Extraordinary Professor in the Centre of Human Rights and the Department of Political Sciences, Faculty Humanities at the University of Pretoria. He also serves on the International Advisory Board of the Geneva Centre for Security Policy in Switzerland and as a member of the board of advisers of the Center on International Conflict Resolution, Columbia University.

Ricardo Córdova Macías is the executive director of the Fundación Dr. Guillermo Manuel Ungo in El Salvador. His areas of research and teaching interests include peace processes in Central America, security sector reform, elections, democratization, and political parties. He has authored several publications. Most recently, he coauthored *La contribución del proceso de paz a la construcción de la democracia en El Salvador (1992–2004)* (2009).

Chantal de Jonge Oudraat is associate vice president of the Jennings Randolph Fellowship Program at the United States Institute of Peace. Before joining the Institute, she was a senior fellow at the Center for Transatlantic Relations at the Paul H. Nitze School of Advanced International Studies, Johns Hopkins University, where she focused on transatlantic relations and global security issues. She has also served as codirector of the Managing Global Issues project at the Carnegie Endowment for International Peace in Washington, DC (1998–2002); a research affiliate at the Belfer Center for Science and International Affairs, John F. Kennedy School of Government, Harvard University (1994–98); and a member of the directing staff at the United Nations Institute for Disarmament Research in Geneva (1981–94). De Jonge Oudraat is a member of Women In International Security and served on its executive board (1998–2007) and as its vice president (2001–07). She received her PhD in political science from the University of Paris II (Panthéon).

Barry Desker is the dean of the S. Rajaratnam School of International Studies, Nanyang Technological University (NTU), and concurrently director of NTU's Institute of Defence and Strategic Studies. He was educated at the University of Singapore, University of London, and Cornell University. His research interests include the World Trade Organization, terrorism, and civil conflict in Asia, as well as regional economic and security issues. Most recently, he has been published in the *Washington Quarterly*, the *Australian Journal of International Affairs*, the *Cambridge Review of International Affairs*, *Survival*, *Internationale Politik*, *Contemporary Southeast Asia*, and *The Pacific Review*.

Anoushiravan Ehteshami is dean of internationalisation at Durham University and professor of international relations in the School of Government and International Affairs. He was head of the School of Government and International Affairs at Durham University (2004–09) and was vice-president and chair of the Council of the British Society for Middle Eastern Studies (2000–03). His many book-length publications include *Competing Powerbrokers of the Middle East: Iran and Saudi Arabia* (Emirates Occasional Papers Series, 2009), *Reform in the Middle East Oil Monarchies* (coeditor; 2008), *Globalization and Geopolitics in the Middle East: Old Games, New Rules* (2007), *Iran and the Rise of Its Neoconservatives* (with Mahjoob Zweiri; 2007), *The Middle East's Relations with Asia and Russia* (coeditor; 2004); *The Foreign Policies of Middle East States* (coeditor; 2002), *Iran's Security Policy in the Post-Revolutionary Era* (coauthor, 2001), *Iran and Eurasia* (coeditor; 2000), *The Changing Balance of Power in Asia* (1998), *Syria and Iran: Middle Powers in a Penetrated Regional System* (with Ray Hinnebusch; 1997), *Islamic Fundamentalism* (coeditor; 1996), *After Khomeini: The Iranian Second Republic* (1995), *From the Gulf to Central Asia: Players in the News Great Game* (editor; 1994), *Iran and the International Community* (coeditor; 1991), and *Nuclearisation of the Middle East* (1989). In addition, he also has some ninety articles in learned journals and edited volumes to his name. His current research revolves around five overarching themes: the Asian balance of power in the post–Cold War era; the "Asianization" of the international system; foreign and security policies of Middle East states since the end of the Cold War; the impact of globalization on the Middle East; and good governance and democratization efforts in the Middle East.

Meenakshi Gopinath is currently principal, Lady Shri Ram College, New Delhi, and founder and honorary director of Women in Security, Conflict Management and Peace, an initiative that seeks to promote the leadership of South Asian women in the areas of peace, security, and regional cooperation. Her publications include *Pakistan in Transition, Conflict Resolution: Trends and Prospects, Transcending Conflict: A Resource Book on Conflict Transformation* and *Dialogic Engagement*. She has also contributed chapters and articles in books and journals on Gandhi, the politics of Pakistan, conflict resolution, and gender and peacebuilding. In recognition of her contribution to the field of women's education, she has received several awards. She serves on the boards of several research institutes, non-governmental organizations, and educational institutions and has been a member of the National Security Advisory Board of India.

John Graham is chair (emeritus) of the Canadian Foundation for the Americas and is a member of the Friends of the Inter-American Democratic Charter (established by former US president Jimmy Carter). In the "Friends" capacity he has been involved in missions in Central America over the past five years and in Haiti in 2010. He was the first head of the Unit for the Promotion of Democracy in the Organization of American States (OAS). In that role he led a number of OAS election observer missions in Latin America, participated in OAS mediation in Guatemala, and was the principal international mediator in the Dominican Republic postelection crisis in 1994. He has been a senior adviser for the Americas to the International Foundation for Election Systems (IFES). His activities for IFES have included leading election advisory missions to Guyana and Haiti and heading a Technical Advisory Team for the 1998 elections in Paraguay. He was the Organization for Security and Co-operation in Europe's senior election officer in Bosnia-Herzegovina (based in Bihac) in 1996–97. In 1998 he was an OSCE Office for Democratic Institutions and Human Rights observer in Srebrenica. He is a former director general, high commissioner, and ambassador in the Canadian Foreign Service, with assignments focused largely within the Western Hemisphere. He is the author of numerous book chapters and articles, and his manuscript on the Dominican Republic electoral crisis of 1994, "Stepping Back from the Precipice," will be published in 2011.

Jürgen Haacke is senior lecturer in international relations at the London School of Economics and Political Science. His research focuses on the international relations and security of Southeast Asia, especially the role of the Association of Southeast Asian Nations (ASEAN), as well as the politics and foreign policy of Burma/Myanmar. He is the author of *ASEAN's Diplomatic and Security Culture: Origins, Development and Prospects* and *Myanmar's Foreign Policy: Domestic Influences and International Implications*. He is also the coeditor of *Cooperative Security in the Asia–Pacific: The ASEAN Regional Forum* (2010).

Monica Herz is an associate professor at the Catholic University of Rio de Janeiro. She is the editor of *Contexto Internacional*. She has a PhD degree from the London School of Economics and Political Science. She has published several articles and chapters on Latin American security and Brazilian foreign policy and has written three books: *Organizações Internacionais: histórias e práticas* (with Andréa Ribeiro Hoffman; 2004); *Ecuador vs. Peru: Peacemaking amid Rivalry* (with João Pontes Nogueira; 2002); and *Global Governance away from the Media* (2010).

Bassma Kodmani is the executive director of the Arab Reform Initiative and senior fellow of the Académie Diplomatique Internationale in Paris. She has authored and edited publications on Middle Eastern conflicts, political developments in Arab societies, and relations between political and religious authorities. Her latest book *Abattre les murs* (Breaking Walls) was published in France in 2008.

Adam P. Liff is a PhD candidate in political science at Princeton University. His past research affiliations include the RAND Corporation and the Japan Center for International Exchange. From 2006 to 2008 he was a MEXT research scholar affiliated with the University of Tokyo's Graduate School of Law and Politics. He is the author of numerous writings on Japanese and Chinese foreign policy and regionalism in East Asia. He holds a BA (with honors) from Stanford University, where he graduated Phi Beta Kappa.

Hilton McDavid is the director of the Centre for National Security and Strategic Studies and academic director of the MSc in National Security and Strategic Studies Programme at the University of the West Indies, Mona, Kingston, Jamaica. He is also adjunct professor of national security affairs at the National Defense University's Center for Hemispheric Defense Studies. He holds a doctor of science degree in engineering management from the George Washington University and is a graduate of the Center for Hemispheric Studies, National Defense University; the Canadian Land Forces Command and Staff College, Canadian Forces Staff School; and Mons Officer Cadet School, United Kingdom.

Nigel Quinney, president of The Editorial Group, has explored the interplay of culture, conflict resolution, and diplomacy for some twenty years. He is coauthor (with Richard Solomon) of *American Negotiating Behavior*, and has edited most of the volumes in the United States Institute of Peace's Cross-Cultural Negotiation series. A publisher as well as a writer and editor, he is a consultant to European and American think tanks, academic institutions, and multinational corporations.

Itamar Rabinovich is professor emeritus of Middle Eastern History at Tel Aviv University, Distinguished Global Professor at New York University, and Distinguished Visiting Fellow at the Saban Center, Brookings Institution. He is the vice chairman of the Institute for National Security Studies affiliated with Tel Aviv University and a member of the International Advisory Council of the Brookings Institution. He was Israel's ambassador in Washington and chief negotiator with Syria in the mid 1990s. His latest book is *The View from Damascus.*

Hitoshi Tanaka is chairman of the Institute for International Strategy at the Japan Research Institute and a senior fellow at the Japan Center for International Exchange. He has been a visiting professor at the Graduate School of Public Policy, University of Tokyo, since April 2006. He was deputy minister for foreign affairs of Japan until August 2005. He had previously served as director-general of the Asian and Oceanian Affairs Bureau (2001–02) and the Economic Affairs Bureau (2000–01); consul-general in San Francisco (1998–2000); and deputy director-general of the North American Affairs Bureau (1996–98). He was director for policy co-ordination of the Foreign Policy Bureau, political minister at the Japanese Embassy in London (1990–93), a research associate at the International Institute for Strategic Studies (1989–90), director for North East Asian affairs (1987–89), and director for North American affairs (1985–87). He has a BA in law from Kyoto University and BA/MA in philosophy, politics, and economics from Oxford University. He has contributed many articles to various newspapers and monthly magazines. His latest publications include *Purofeshonaru no Kosho-ryoku* (The Logic of Strategic Negotiation; 2009), *Gaiko no Chikara* (The Power of Diplomacy; 2009), and *Kokka to Gaiko* (The Nation and Diplomacy; 2005).

Paul D. Williams is associate professor in the Elliott School of International Affairs at the George Washington University, where he is the deputy director of the Security Policy Studies MA program. His research interests lie in Africa's international relations, international peacekeeping, and theories of international security. He is author of *War and Conflict in Africa* (2011) and *British Foreign Policy under New Labour, 1997–2005* (2005); coauthor of *Understanding Peacekeeping* (2nd edition, 2010); and coeditor of *The International Politics of Mass Atrocities: The Case of Darfur* (2010).

Part I

The Global Context

1

The Mosaic of Global Conflict Management

Chester A. Crocker, Fen Osler Hampson, and Pamela Aall

A serious question for the current security environment is whether the world has the right institutional architecture for managing conflict. The experience of the last twenty years has made clear that the challenges to global security cannot be easily grouped into a few big baskets such as proliferation of weapons of mass destruction (WMD), ethnic conflicts, chronic underdevelopment, and terrorism. There has been an expansion in the definition of security to include issues such as public health and environmental degradation, as well as more traditional national security concerns such as interstate rivalry and power transitions.[1] Moreover, there are new linkages between these different security concerns.

In reviewing current global institutional architecture and its capacities, it is important to understand and assess the role of regions and regional groups or institutions in conflict management. This assessment, however, is more easily suggested than done. There are many challenges, most obvious among them being that regions are not like countries. Most states have established borders, identifiable populations, and a political structure that not only governs but also provides national security, at least to the extent possible. Regions have no such uniform definitions. There is rarely complete agreement on membership, geographical outline, or included and excluded populations. With the exception of the European Union, there are few common governance structures. And regional security is more often threatened by conflict from within that region than from an external menace. Even if a common definition of a region existed, the world's regions are not modeled on some central template. They differ as to power structure, political-governmental cultures, types of security challenges, styles of negotiation, intergovernmental norms, and perceptions of what "security" actually means and the principal challenges to it. Assessing security challenges between and among global regions is complex, because there may be not only different security challenges but also different perceptions of the same security challenges.

At the same time, there has been a growing recognition that local, regional, and global security are closely linked. The conflicts in Bosnia, the Congo, and Afghanistan prove that community violence can flare up to engulf large territories, spread across borders, and engage the international community. Of particular importance in dealing with these conflict patterns are the evolving relationships between global and regional actors and organizations. The relative salience of global versus regional initiative, capability, and legitimacy is central to understanding basic trends and tensions in international security. A balance sheet of demand and supply in security capacity in various regions would clearly be useful as would an effort to review the implications of the global-regional interface. That is the goal of this book: to explore how different regions define challenges to their security, how each region addresses these challenges, and how regional security capacity links to global peace and security.

Changing Security Threats and Conflict Management Requirements

Traditional Views of Security

Over the past forty years, the world has seen significant changes in official and popular views of security threats and conflict management needs. When he wrote *Politics among Nations*, Hans Morgenthau defined security in national terms: as the expectation that through its "monopoly of organized violence," the state would protect the citizen and the institutions of the state.[2] In the succeeding years, expert circles generally framed security challenges as arising from the competitive power struggles between states, epitomized by the Cold War military and political confrontation between the Soviet Union and the United States. Generally speaking, the traditional view of security sees threats as emanating from outside the state. Within this traditional frame of reference, the most effective national strategy is to maximize the power of the state and build up its defenses and military capabilities in order to deter would-be aggressors. Balancing or "bandwagoning" strategies may also be in order to maintain the balance of power and stability of the international system.[3]

During the Cold War, there was little official interest in or priority given to conflict management—that is, the use of nonmilitary means such as mediation, "good offices," or preemptive diplomatic engagement to promote negotiated alternatives to violence and political upheaval.[4] Although nuclear deterrence was underpinned by diplomacy and the credible threat to use force, conflict management was generally viewed in unidimensional terms. The dominant powers in a bipolar international system sought to manage their conflicts in order to avoid a loss of face or strategic setbacks and to prevent their conflicts from escalating out of control. However, they had little interest in using the tools of negotiation, mediation, and preventive statecraft more broadly to promote institution building, good governance, development, and the rule of law in countries and regions that were politically unstable or threatened by other sources of strife.

The East-West conflict found expression in proxy wars—initially in Greece, then in Korea, Vietnam, southern Africa, Central America, Afghanistan, and other places—but, with the exception of Korea and Vietnam, these wars were generally limited in scale and scope. As the inconclusive result of periodic strife between Israel and its Arab neighbors demonstrated, managing these conflicts generally meant keeping the lid on and preventing escalation—in the view of many, a job that was performed best by powerful states. While lip service was paid to the role of international organizations, such as the United Nations, in resolving conflicts, it was clear that the ability to freeze or manage conflicts lay with the powerful states, not with international or regional organizations. The United Nation's conflict management potential was confined to those cases where there was some measure of East-West tolerance or consensus, and its actions consisted mainly of good offices, electoral support in decolonization processes, and traditional peacekeeping operations in consensual settings such as Cyprus, Israel-Egypt (Sinai Desert), or Israel-Syria (Golan Heights).

During these Cold War years, more interest in conflict management was shown by scholars, religious and secular activists, and others outside government who sought to popularize a very different discourse about national security. This discourse focused on the threat of nuclear annihilation either as a direct attack or as a consequence of a nuclear winter. Proponents believed that conflict management consisted of pushing their own governments toward arms control and then eventually nuclear disarmament, thereby reducing stockpiles and removing the weapons from national armories. Such activity by civil society actors gained some traction in a few Western countries; however, there was virtually none within the Soviet bloc.[5] Toward the end of the Cold War, civil society pressure played an increasing role in affecting popular attitudes in the West, but successes in U.S.-Soviet arms control and disarmament negotiations came as a result of official diplomatic efforts, which stabilized the nuclear balance and brought forth greater transparency and predictability in U.S.-Soviet relations, especially during the final two decades of the Cold War.

In the immediate post–Cold War period, the world's attention shifted from tracking superpower rivalry, counting nuclear warheads, and arguing over "Star Wars" (as President Ronald Reagan's Strategic Defense Initiative was called in the press) to witnessing the outbreak of civil war on nearly every continent—wars that habitually spilled over state boundaries to contaminate entire neighborhoods. Perceptions of security changed as a consequence of the upsurge in sectarian violence and a similar upsurge in attention to conflict management in the broadest sense, as distinguished from the goal of advancing the national security of the state against direct, external threats.

Global security was redefined in local and regional terms and the tasks undertaken to provide security widened to protecting civilians from massacre by their own governments and shoring up weak states threatened by struggles among factional militias. In a very real sense, security increasingly came to be viewed as divisible, which is to say that there was no shared sense that these civil or regional conflicts affected the core values and interests of the wider community of nations. The United States struggled with the increasing diversity of threat perceptions at the regional level in its own efforts to project power and influence. In some regions, such as the Middle East or Central America, it tried (not always successfully) to shape the regional security agenda by imposing itself and intervening directly in the decision-making processes of regional states. This has sometimes resulted in a single-lens approach that overwhelmed and distorted regional issues by simplifying their causes and dynamics—for example, by targeting illicit economies or terrorism and ignoring a host of other factors, such as historic grievances or ideological and religious differences.

Traditional Westphalian conceptions of state sovereignty have also been reshaped in the post–Cold War era. Through its case-by-case decisions and statements, the United Nations Security Council chipped away at arguments in favor of absolute sovereignty and expanded the perception of what is legitimate relating to preventive action undertaken by the United Nations. As early as 1991, actions mandated by the Security Council in Resolution 687 imposed a highly intrusive and complex regime of monitoring to prevent Iraq from producing weapons of mass destruction. Thereafter, council members tended to use the international peace and security threat that flows of refugees could pose to neighboring countries to authorize various kinds of preventive action. Such arguments were advanced, notably, in the early stages of the disintegration of the former Yugoslavia, in Somalia, Haiti, and East Timor, and in the council's deliberations regarding the overflow of refugees into Guinea from neighboring Liberia and Sierra Leone. In the 1990s there was a short interval of successful international peacemaking and peacebuilding interventions. The generally positive experiences in Mozambique, Cambodia, Bosnia, East Timor, Sierra Leone, Liberia, Northern Ireland, and elsewhere seemed to argue for a strong role for outside third parties, often identified simply as the "international community," in helping to settle internal conflicts and as guarantors to settlements between states.[6]

Despite this increasing interventionism, responding to violent humanitarian catastrophes occurring in the territory of sovereign states continued to pose an ongoing challenge. As with situations of extreme human rights violations, many internal humanitarian abuses were met with condemnation and sanctions by the United Nations. Some instances led to Security Council authorizations of remedial force. Many, however, did not lead to the express authorization of more vigorous enforcement action. For example, the United Nations and members of the international community grappled with the ramifications of the failures of political will and/or execution in the cases of Somalia and Rwanda. After these failures, debates about security policy in major Western capitals and UN headquarters tended to focus increasingly on the proper extent and limits of third-party conflict management. These discussions of limits and extent included such pressing issues as when was international intervention (humanitarian or otherwise) justified, what were the limits to sovereignty, and who was authorized to decide when these lines can or should be crossed.

As a consequence, at times other actors took things into their own hands. In some cases, internal conflicts met with a more robust response through unilateral military intervention undertaken by states or regional organizations without prior express Security Council authorization. In some of these cases, the United Nations might engage after the fact, playing an important post-intervention legitimating role, for example, by the post facto authorization of intervention, as occurred in relation to interventions by the Economic Community of West African States Monitoring Group (ECOMOG) in Liberia and Sierra Leone in the 1990s.

Expanded Views of Security

The past two decades made it clear that while an element of security is objective, for example, that an army is threatening your borders, another set of security issues is perceptual and identity-based or dependent on circumstances. These include, for example, threats to stasis, threats to a sitting government and its political constituency, and threats to a society, community, or a way of life. The growing realization that peoples, societies, and even entire polities can be put at risk by "threats from below" has expanded the discussion of security to include majority-minority relations, language policy, and similar matters. The outbreak of civil wars in many parts of the world in recent decades sharpened the understanding of the human costs of war and led to the development of the concept of human security.[7] Definitions of human security differ in detail and emphasis, but they converge on the main points: human security consists of physical safety, economic well-being, social inclusion, and the full exercise of fundamental rights and freedoms.[8]

As useful as this concept is, it brought questions about the international community's responsibility in recognizing and responding to violations of this human security.[9] The responsibility to protect norm (R2P) was strengthened with the adoption by the United Nations General Assembly of many of the principles outlined in *The Responsibility to Protect*,[10] particularly the notion that the international community, in particular the United Nations, had a responsibility to act in the face of internal atrocities when states themselves proved unwilling or unable to protect their own populations. Unfortunately, despite some clear successes in strengthening this general disposition among states and facilitating state compliance to theses norms, international and intrastate violence continued relatively unabated in many corners of the globe—Darfur, Somalia, the Congo, and elsewhere where the international community demonstrated a limited appetite to intervene. The reality was that politics all too often stood in the way of any kind of direct intervention after a conflict escalated beyond the point of no return, not least by the Security Council but also by other international and regional actors.[11]

Another area of concern, especially among students of international development, involved the relationship between globalization (in its various meanings) and human insecurity.[12] On one side of this argument, enthusiasts of globalization argued that the breakdown of national barriers to trade and the spread of global markets were processes that helped to raise world incomes and contribute to the spread of wealth.[13] Although there were clear winners and losers in the globalizing economy, the old divisions between the South and the advanced economies of the North were breaking down and making way for an increasingly complex architecture of economic power. There was more or less general agreement that the forces of economic globalization were transforming international politics and recasting relationships between states and peoples with important implications for human security: globalization was not only intensifying trade and economic connections but also accelerating the pace of economic and social change. Further, it was not just goods and capital that were exchanged across borders, but ideas, information, and people.

On the other side, globalization's critics argued that although some countries in the South gained from globalization, many did not and income inequalities between the world's richest and poorest countries were widening. They suggested that trade and investment flows were intensifying between those countries that could compete in the global economy while leaving behind those that could not. As income gaps and deep-seated social and economic inequalities widened in many countries, so the argument ran, so did the prospects for violence and civil strife.[14]

The attacks on Washington and New York of September 11, 2001, and other attacks in Europe, South Asia, and other areas, changed prevailing views yet again. Third-party conflict management—a more or less discretionary feature of Western foreign policy in the 1990s—was set aside, at least temporarily, in order to focus on a direct threat to national security. But, no longer was the enemy a foreign country: it was loosely connected bands of militant jihadist ideologues whose mission was to hobble the United States and to drive it out of the Muslim world. In the United States and among its key allies there was a partial return to the concept of global security focused on counterterrorism and coping with failed (or failing) states, viewed by many as breeding grounds for terrorists, dealers in weapons and drugs, and other international miscreants.[15] In the last few years, the immediacy of the September 11 attacks has receded and the challenges of reconstruction and security stabilization in Iraq and Afghanistan have become unavoidably clear. Western officials tend to perceive "hybrid" threats flowing from a potentially toxic mixture of proliferating technologies, weak state institutions, local conflicts breeding in "ungoverned spaces," criminal mafias, terrorist networks, and dangerous regimes prepared to offer them clandestine support.[16] In sum, direct security threats and the indirect threats that flow from "conflict management" challenges have converged.

Differentiated Views of Security

Defining security challenges is not the sole province of official institutions and political and military leaders. Popular attitudes also matter. However, it is not easy to capture changing popular views about international security and conflict management, and even more difficult to assess these views by region. A series of recent polls by the Pew Research Center and the Council on Foreign Relations of public opinion in different parts of the world attempt to do so. These polls underscore that there is widespread public concern around the globe about the spread of nuclear weapons, religious and ethnic hatred, AIDS and other infectious diseases, pollution and environmental problems, and the growing gap between rich and poor.[17] However, as many of these polls also revealed, publics in different countries assess and rate these dangers differently.[18]

For example, the November 2009 Council on Foreign Relations poll indicates that there are different attitudes toward the threat posed by terrorism in different parts of the world. In countries that have directly experienced terrorism, concern about terrorism was high: over 70 percent of respondents in Morocco, Bangladesh, Lebanon, Pakistan, India, and Turkey viewed terrorism as a very serious security concern. Similar concerns were found in Italy (73 percent), Spain (66 percent), France (54 percent), Peru (70 percent), and Japan (59 percent). Extrapolating from these country-based results, it seems that terrorism was seen as a primary threat in three regions—the Middle East, South Asia, and Europe. The U.S. respondents, however, seemed less concerned (with only 44 percent citing terrorism as "a very big problem"). Fourteen other countries—most of Africa, some of Eastern Europe, and China, as well as other Asian states, rated terrorism as a small problem or not a problem at all.[19]

Although views of al-Qaeda were largely negative worldwide, this was not the case in Egypt and Pakistan—both of which are key actors in the conflict with al-Qaeda. "In both of these countries, far more people have either mixed or positive feelings toward al-Qaeda (Egypt 20 percent positive, 40 percent mixed; Pakistan 19 percent positive, 22 percent mixed) than have negative feelings (Egypt 35 percent, Pakistan 19 percent). In addition, there are several other countries where negative views are less than a majority position: China (48 percent), India (44 percent), Indonesia (35 percent), Nigeria (42 percent), and the Philippines (42 percent)."[20]

Attitudes toward the threat of nuclear proliferation also differed. In a poll of nine countries, majorities in six viewed nuclear proliferation as a critical threat—Mexico (75 percent), Israel (72 percent), and the United States (69 percent). In South Korea, only 50 percent considered proliferation "critical" (this somewhat surprisingly low percentage may be explained by the fact that 40 percent of the Korean respondents did consider proliferation "important," indicating that 90 percent of the Korean respondents were in fact concerned about the issue). By contrast, 27 percent of the Chinese respondents considered the threat critical, 43 percent important, and 17 percent (the highest percentage of all polled countries) did not think that proliferation was important at all.[21]

A few years earlier the 2007 Pew Research Center polled informed publics in forty-seven countries on their ranking of what they viewed as global

Table 1.1 Countries Most and Least Concerned about Specific Global Dangers by Percentage of Population

Spread of nuclear weapons

Most concerned	*Least concerned*
Japan 68	Ethiopia 12
Israel 66	Kenya 16
Lebanon 57	France 21
Turkey 57	South Africa 22

Religious and ethnic hatred

Most concerned	*Least concerned*
Lebanon 74	South Korea 14
Britain 67	Argentina 16
Kuwait 66	Ukraine 17
Palest. terr. 64	Uganda 19

AIDS and other infectious diseases

Most concerned	*Least concerned*
Tanzania 87	South Korea 7
South Africa 83	Germany 9
Kenya 82	Japan 11
Ethiopia 78	Sweden 14

Pollution and environmental problems

Most concerned	*Least concerned*
South Korea 77	Ethiopia 7
China 70	Lebanon 13
Japan 70	Senegal 13
Sweden 66	Ivory Coast 14

Growing gap between rich and poor

Most concerned	*Least concerned*
South Korea 68	Kuwait 21
Kenya 61	Venezuela 26
Indonesia 57	Japan 28
Chile 56	Mexico 28

Source: Pew Global Attitudes Project, *Rising Environmental Concern in 47-Nation Survey,* 31

dangers (see table 1.1). Categories are not overlapping with the Council on Foreign Relations poll, but both polls do tend to confirm that it is hard to understand regional perspectives through polling on a country-by-country basis.

It is clear from this chart that the definition of security is as diverse among individuals as it is among nations. However, while there are occasional similarities among countries in the same region (Japan, China, and South Korea are all concerned about environmental degradation, for instance), at other points regional neighbors show distinct disparities in their threat perception. Almost 70 percent of South Korean respondents believe that the growing gap between rich and poor is a global threat, while less than 30 percent of Japanese do so.[22] Understanding how regions view security remains elusive.

Another element in the growing diversity of security concerns lies in the different perspectives of the North and the South. In recent years, the idea that reciprocity among states is the bedrock of multilateralism and the workings of international institutions has come under challenge from critics who point out that international institutions are dominated by the interests of Western countries in multilateral decision making. Many developing countries feel profoundly disadvantaged by global multilateral political, financial, and trading arrangements. They also believe that the normative principles and political architecture of the United Nations (especially the Security Council) and the Bretton Woods system are biased toward the interests and values of the most powerful states in the international system. Many developing countries have long felt that they have been disempowered by international institutions and have not received commensurate benefits from their participation in postwar, global, and multilateral economic, financial, and trading arrangements. Many developing countries also believe that the North has traditionally been the normative and legal trendsetter in international institutions, with the South being on the "receiving end" of those norms and rules.[23]

There are many ideas about what mechanisms and institutions should replace current systems of multilateral cooperation and governance.[24] The legitimacy and accountability deficits in multilateral institutions play out at two levels. At one level, many would like to see a better representation from the South in the major decision-making organs of the United Nations and global summitry via the G20 and the Bretton Woods system of institutions. These calls have intensified in the aftermath the 2008–9 international financial and credit crisis.[25] At another level, many would like to see a devolution of authority and responsibility for decision making to the regional or even subregional level by strengthening and empowering local actors to play a much greater role in managing their own economic and political affairs than they do now. Some would also like to see the creation of new institutions of global and regional governance that involve new kinds of partnerships between intergovernmental bodies and civil society that are centered on a commitment to advancing and promoting human security.[26] There are many different proposals out there to change the architecture and machinery of global governance. But, as Manuel Lafont Rapnouil observes, "The reform of the multilateral system today will be slow, gradual and probably disorderly. It is all the more important to have clear ideas and different possible horizons, and to anticipate the problems that may develop with major restructuring."[27] In other words, the prospects of a grand global concert of nations or organizations are slim in the short term.

Finally, the globe has had to deal with the fact that despite global, regional, and national efforts, violent conflict has not gone away. While the past decade saw a downward trend in the outbreak and lethality of warfare, this trend now appears to be reversing itself with wider implications for international security and conflict management.[28] This new upswing in the outbreak of armed conflict is coupled with the troubling persistence of conflicts in various parts of the world—for instance, Afghanistan and Pakistan, Sudan and its neighbors, Iraq, Iran, the Great Lakes region of Africa, the Horn of Africa, Kashmir-India-Pakistan, and North Korea. These intractable conflicts challenge the world's capacity to hold in check potentially devastating civil and regional threats to peace.[29] While international organizations and powerful states deal with major economic dislocations and front-page news, these intractable conflicts sap resources and destabilize regions, acting as low-grade infections in the global body politic.

Our Starting Point

The changing perception of security threats has created a global debate about how to respond to these threats. The American response to 9/11 reflected a traditional approach: the United States overthrew the Taliban regime in Afghanistan, a state which it associated with the terrorist attacks. The results have been mixed at best. A growing school of thought maintains that current security risks cannot be dealt with through use of force alone. This school emphasizes diplomatic approaches, the use of soft or "smart" power, indirect capacity-building activities to empower democratic or democratizing governments and their security forces, and developing leverage through multilateral initiatives—the traditional political tools of conflict management.[30]

During the 1990s, the fabric of international security became stronger and more globalized. Yet long-standing conflicts continued to burn and a number of low-profile conflicts seemingly received little attention from the international security institutions and powerful states. This may help to explain why, contrary to the apparent trend toward globalization, there is a growing demand in many of the world's regions for greater regional control or influence over how security challenges are defined and responses organized. In parallel with the growing demand, the supply of regional conflict management initiatives is also expanding. The reasons are not entirely clear. Regional actors may feel that they have a better understanding of the conflicts in their neighborhoods, and therefore a better chance at helping parties craft a solution. Another factor may be the selective attention to regional security issues by global actors, which may reinforce demands for greater regional control, actively encouraging regional actors to define their own priorities, create their own facts, and design their own mechanisms and norms. Today's security threats are often buried deep inside regions, and the fabric of security looks increasingly like a patchwork quilt.

A Gap in the Literature

In all of this debate, there have been few efforts to illustrate on a region-by-region basis the supply/demand balance sheet for security challenges and conflict management capacity. Starting with the premise that in this new world regional organizations are coming to play an expanded role in dealing with security threats and managing conflicts in their regions, this book offers a comparative perspective on the threats to security and conflict management as seen by regional actors around the world. Through this means, this book also intends to add to the understanding of global conflict management capacity and the "balance" between regional/local security initiatives and global ones. The project starts with the premise that it is essential to understand the regional dimension and its implications for security, and to get fresh assessment of the links between regional and global security.

Interstate cooperation in the twentieth and twenty-first centuries is marked by a proliferation in the number of organizations and international regimes that adhere to both similar and different multilateral norms and principles. No two regions have the same security culture or regional security architecture, and there are important differences in the way threats to security are weighed. Some regions of the world—Europe, for example—have developed a crazy quilt of regional organizations. In other regions, states have quite consciously avoided formal multilateralism. The lack of formal, de jure, regional, multilateral institutions in the Asia-Pacific region has both a normative and a domestic, political explanation.[31] As the dominant regional nations, China and Japan in particular appear to have a mixed attitude toward formal institutions.[32] Prevailing political norms at the national level have also been antithetical to liberal internationalism because of colonial legacies that favored "rule by law" instead of the "rule of law" and custodianship in state-society relations. In their international relations in the postwar period, many countries in the Asia-Pacific eschewed multilateral arrangements in favor of direct, bilateral economic and security ties with the United States (though this too may now be changing).[33]

While there have been a number of studies, done by regional experts, that have focused on security and conflict management in specific regions, as well as a number of comparative studies written by individuals or scholars in the United States or Europe, this book will take the less-traveled approach of asking experts from a wide range of regions to engage in a comparative study across regions. Based on their analyses and the project's global scope, we present a fresh review of regional threats, perceived threats, and policies, as well as new perspectives on how institutions intend to counteract them. Only when we understand the security challenges and local capabilities to meet those challenges *as determined within the regions themselves* will we start to be able to assess who can do what in global conflict management.

This project builds on the argument that in order to understand global security, it is necessary to have a firm grasp on regional security matters. Over ten years ago, David Lake and Patrick Morgan argued that (1) regions had become more salient as components of international politics; (2) the post–Cold War period offered an opening for more cooperative regional orders; (3) in order to understand regions, the analyst must recognize that some generalizations can be drawn from looking across regions as long as it is done with care—they are neither "little international systems" nor so unique that comparisons cannot be drawn; and (4) in dealing with these regions, powerful states must recognize that regions are different and require foreign policies tailored to those differences.[34] Similarly, Barry Buzan and his colleagues Ole Waever and Jaap de Wilde have asserted that security threats are increasingly regional rather than global, and that the identification of threats comes from within societies and states rather than from a global or out-of-region origin.[35]

At a minimum, the regional security literature appears to agree that there are four dimensions for analyzing conflict sources from a regional perspective. Following Muhtiah Alagappa, these are: (1) international (the regional impact of global systemic conflicts such as during the Cold War or, today, the confrontations surrounding militant Islamic threats to the status quo); (2) extramural (directed at constraining and channeling the influence and power of major powers); (3) intramural (addressing interstate tensions and challenges at the regional level); and (4) "domestic" (addressing the many internal security issues faced by states in a number of regions).[36] While contemporary study of regionalism is robust, as discussed in a recent survey by Robert Kelly, it is also replete with basic debates about the autonomy of regional initiative and action, the significance of regions as a valid level of analysis, the degree to which regions can be defined in narrowly geographic terms, the core ingredients of "regional security

DEBATES ON RSOS

complexes," the relevance of European-derived regional models for other parts of the world, the degree to which regional security organizations are capable of addressing constructively the real security challenges faced by developing societies, and the desirability of participation in regional security affairs by Northern states.[37]

Some analysts, to be sure, are highly critical of the notion of regionalized security, seeing it as weak or faulty because of the following concerns:

- From the point of view of the powerful Western states, regionalization is often ignored or dismissed as irrelevant. A sometimes unilateralist Washington has a habit of rejecting regionalization, except when the rise of regional strength coincides with its own interests. European countries are more positive about the potential of regional powers and intergovernmental bodies providing security to their neighborhood, but still step in when regional powers seem incapable of carrying out the task, as the French did in Côte d'Ivoire and British did in Sierra Leone in the last decade.
- Related to this set of attitudes is the assessment that only the states of the Atlantic community are wealthy and powerful enough to establish regional organizations up to the challenge of security management, and that all other regions do not have the wherewithal to manage their own conflicts.
- Supporters of global institutions, on the other hand, view regionalization as competition for the United Nations, sometimes leaching away precious resources and sometimes getting in the way of UN missions.
- Skeptics of the efficacy of regional response mechanisms point to the disparity in regional capabilities, noting that some regions are resource rich (in terms of both money and trained personnel) and that others are less well-off. This leads to a system in which some regions only get what they can provide for themselves, leading to a further fragmentation of global security standards and norms. And skeptics from within regions point out that regionalization raises the specter of regionally hegemonic behavior, creating a situation that would allow one country to dominate the region under the pretense of providing a more secure environment for its zone of influence.[38]

We take a different approach, questioning the notion of whether in today's world there is some centrally conceived plan or normative construct in which the dynamics of "liberal peace" are playing out in the regions.[39] We recognize the desire for greater levels of local ownership in security management in many regions. But we also recognize that this desire and capability to act on that desire vary from region to region. Whether the regions' autonomy and scope to organize their own security affairs are dependent on decisions and policies taken by a handful of world powers or whether the regions are increasingly marching to their own drummers is a core question to be explored.[40] Our project will test both of these propositions: first, that some distant "hidden hand" is determining facts on the ground and conversely, that "no one is in charge."

The book grows out of our interest in strengthening links between the security and conflict management fields. Observers of on-the-ground field operations in Iraq, Afghanistan, Sudan, Israel-Palestine, Korea, and the Philippines report evidence of these links on a regular basis. Among organizations dedicated to helping societies reknit themselves after conflict, there is a strong agreement that providing security—and a sense of security—is a crucial step in the rebuilding process. In the academic literature, however, the links between security and conflict management seem much fainter, and tend to cluster in the literature around how wars end.[41] One explanation for the paucity of contact between the security and conflict management fields is that they often focus on different levels of analysis and different vantage points. Security studies tend to focus on the global or international level, and address the security perspectives, policies, and needs of powerful actors. The consumer of security studies is more likely to be concerned with direct, physical threats and challenges. Conflict management literature, on the other hand, tends to focus on challenges and threats that arise because parties are in a conflict situation (for example, India and Pakistan or Israel and the Palestinians), and it looks closely at the local or case-specific level and at particular instruments of conflict response—for example, prevention, crisis response, mediation, peacekeeping, institution building, and post-conflict peacebuilding. Examining what is going on at the regional level in the delineation of security threats and conflict management capacity to address those threats may provide a fruitful means to uncover connections between the two fields.

There is a natural tension—both in terms of the analysis and the resulting prescriptions—between focusing on the regional manifestations of conflict phenomena and their global impacts and consequences. Such conflict-linked phenomena as arms transfers, technology proliferation, health pandemics, terrorist networks, criminal groups trading illicit goods, flows of refugees and internally displaced persons (IDPs), and mass violations of humanitarian law all illustrate the problem. Whether regional responses to conflict are at times more effective at conflict management than global—or externally directed—responses is a central question of the project. This question is far from theoretical—it addresses the very core of global and regional security concerns. Should the international community invest heavily in regional organizations, or should it try to bolster the United Nations, allowing it to plan a central organizing and legitimating role in regional/global conflict management? More profoundly, are there any institutions, whether international or regional, that can address a region's security concerns?

In order to examine these issues, more must be known about the extent to which regions are decoupling from the global security mechanisms and norms due to such factors as the weakening of global capacity for direct, coercive action and sustained political-diplomatic-political initiatives; the weakening of global political will to act; and the weakening of global legitimacy to act (wherein those with the greatest capacity may lack legitimacy, and those with the greatest legitimacy may lack capacity). These factors that diminish the global capacity to act stand in stark relief to other trends, such as the strengthening—in some regions—of regional capacity for conflict management, and—in some regions—of regional desires and will to act.

Structure of this Volume

In this book, we have globalized the discussion, asking experts and authors from across the world to help us understand the regional approaches. Together they provide us with insight into

- security threats and global or regional instabilities that are likely to affect security—local, regional, and global—over the next five years;
- the manner in which existing regional/subregional institutions, political authorities, and civil society are responding to these challenges;
- the conflict management and security gaps and how should they be filled; and
- the implications for statecraft—U.S. foreign policy, the United Nations, and other actors/institutions in the international system who have "world order" interests—of the continually evolving mix between regional security challenges and regional conflict management capacity.

The discussion is framed by three stage-setting chapters. Gilles Andréani provides an authoritative analysis of the global security and conflict management environment in which the regional conflicts play out. Paul D. Williams and Jürgen Haacke guide us through the maze of regional organizations across the world, providing frameworks to allow for a deeper understanding of these institutions' comparative strengths and weaknesses. Nigel Quinney's chapter asks provocative questions about whether it is possible to identify a regional conflict management culture, in the same way that past analysts have identified regional security cultures.

The heart of the book is formed by the regional chapters. These chapters provide excellent windows into several regions, at times looking at different levels of security threats and conflict management capabilities within the same region. Thus, Kwesi Aning's chapter on the role of illicit economies—drugs and gangs—in Africa gives an in-depth view of a particular issue, while Crysantus Ayangafac and Jakkie Cilliers analyze broad security threats challenging African peace and security and assess the ability of pan-African institutions to deal with them. The chapter on Mexico and Central America by Raúl Benítez Manaut and Ricardo Córdova Macías and Hilton A. McDavid's piece on the Caribbean pick up the theme of the destabilizing effect of transnational crime, an observation confirmed by John W. Graham's more broad-ranging chapter on the Americas. All three chapters also point out the security and conflict management role that the United States plays in the regions to its south. Monica Herz, writing about South America, focuses on the evolution of a conflict management culture in a region seemingly intent on establishing homegrown institutions to manage potential conflict on the continent.

As expected, the three Middle East chapters by Anoushiravan Ehteshami, Bassma Kodmani, and Itamar Rabinovich reveal very different perspectives on the threat perceptions between Israel and its Arab neighbors, but they also show differences within the countries concerned, further complicating the regional picture. Alyson J. K. Bailes's chapter on Europe and Chantal de Jonge Oudraat's piece on the trans-Atlantic community (which covers both the European Union and NATO) explore a European security approach based on the skillful exercise of multipolar soft power, while Oksana Antonenko's review of Russia and Eurasia paints a very different picture of a complicated security dance between a hegemonic power and its less powerful and highly dependent neighbors. While the South Asia chapter by Meenakshi Gopinath explores another region that is heavily dominated by one country, it also makes clear that the regional security conversation in South Asia is proceeding on two nonintersecting tracks—a contentious traditional security track and a potentially more harmonious human security one. China looms large in the chapters on Southeast Asia by Richard A. Bitzinger and Barry Desker and on East Asia by Hitoshi Tanaka and Adam P. Liff, but these chapters also disclose a region that is defining its own approach to internal conflict management (an adaptation of the "ASEAN way") and a growing consciousness of its international role.

The effort to understand regional perspectives is especially pertinent at a time of preoccupation and reappraisals in the United States, Canada, Britain, and other global security providers as a result of the heavy costs of the Iraq and Afghanistan conflicts and related instability in Lebanon, the Palestinian territories, and Pakistan, and the global order based on key bodies such as the UN system and the Bretton Woods institutions is challenged by old charters, outdated leadership roles, normative disharmony, and lumbering bureaucracies. At the same time, the global financial crisis that burst upon key capitals in 2008 quickly developed global economic implications and has raised basic questions about both global economic-financial-monetary governance and about the relationship between economic policy imperatives and the search for international security and stability. When it comes to arrangements for preventing conflicts and promoting peace, the world is not "flat," as characterized by Thomas Friedman.[42] Rather, it is characterized by every sort of landscape—rolling, flat, hilly, rocky, mountainous—some of them accessible and some still quite remote. The book will have served a useful purpose if it sheds greater light on the connections between different kinds of landscape—that is, the different levels of conflict management response to security threats, the regionally diverse definitions of security, and the reasons behind the divergent regional preferences for conflict management response. The succeeding chapters will examine this terrain, adding to our understanding of whether there is a global conflict management gap and whether regions— through their regional organizations or through a loose coalition of states and cultures—will help to close this gap.

Notes

1. Russel Howard, Reid Sawyer, and Natasha Bajema, eds., *Terrorism and Counterterrorism: Understanding the New Security Environment, Readings and Interpretations*, 3rd ed. (New York: McGraw-Hill/Dushkin, 2008); Paul R. Pillar, *Terrorism and US Foreign Policy* (Washington, DC: Brookings Institution Press, 2004).

2. Hans J. Morgenthau, *Politics among Nations: The Struggle for Power and Peace* (New York: Alfred A. Knopf, 1985), 526–33.

3. Kenneth Waltz, *Theory of International Politics* (New York: McGraw-Hill, 1979).

4. The definition given by Beyond Intractability captures a common understanding of the term: "Conflict management involves the control, but not resolution, of a long-term or deep-rooted conflict. This is the approach taken when complete resolution seems to be impossible, yet something needs to be done. In cases of resolution-resistant or even intractable conflict, it is possible to manage the situation in ways that make it more constructive and less destructive. The goal of conflict management is to intervene in ways that make the ongoing conflict more beneficial and less damaging to all sides. For example, sending peacekeeping forces into a region enmeshed in strife may help calm the situation and limit casualties. However, peacekeeping missions will not resolve the conflict. In some cases, where non-negotiable human needs are at stake, management is the most feasible step." See Brad Spangler, "Settlement, Resolution, Management, and Transformation: An Explanation of Terms," Beyond Intractability, www.beyondintractability.org/essay/meaning_resolution/.

5. There were also some East-West bridge-building exercises, such as the Pugwash conferences, that sought to limit the nuclear arms race and the Dartmouth process, which aimed at U.S.-Soviet joint exploration of negotiated solutions to conflict.

6. Chester A. Crocker, Fen Osler Hampson, and Pamela Aall, eds., *Herding Cats: Multiparty Mediation in a Complex World* (Washington, DC: United States Institute of Peace Press, 1999); Chester A. Crocker, Fen Osler Hampson, and Pamela Aall, eds., *Grasping the Nettle: Analyzing Cases of Intractable Conflict* (Washington, DC: United States Institute of Peace Press, 2005).

7. Fen Osler Hampson, *Madness in the Multitude: Human Security and World Disorder* (Oxford: Oxford University Press, 2001).

8. Report of the Commission on Human Security, *Human Security Now: Protecting and Empowering People* (New York: United Nations, 2003).

9. J. L. Holzgrefe and Robert O. Keohane, eds., *Humanitarian Intervention: Ethical, Legal, and Political Dilemmas* (Cambridge: Cambridge University Press, 2003).

10. International Commission on Intervention and State Sovereignty (ICISS), *The Responsibility to Protect* (Ottawa: International Development Research Center, 2001).

11. Madeline K. Albright and William S. Cohen, *Preventing Genocide: A Blue Print for U.S. Policymakers* (Washington, DC: United States Institute of Peace, 2009).

12. Jorge Nef, *Human Security and Mutual Vulnerability* (Ottawa: International Development Research Center, 2002); United Nations Development Program, *Human Development Report* (New York: Oxford University Press, 1994).

13. David Held, Anthony McGrew, David Goldblatt, and Jonathan Perraton, eds., *Global Transformations* (Cambridge: Polity Press, 1999).

14. As the World Bank reports, globalization is contributing to a rapid growth in average incomes across the globe. In the next twenty-five years, much of this growth will be concentrated in developing countries, but it will be accompanied by growing income inequality and potentially severe environmental pressures. And some regions, notably sub-Saharan Africa, are unlikely to be the beneficiaries of such growth. Growing income inequalities within countries will also contribute to civil unrest, especially in the world's poorest countries. See World Bank, *Global Economic Prospects 2007: Managing the Next Wave of Globalization* (Washington, DC, 2007).

15. Chester A. Crocker, Fen Osler Hampson, and Pamela Aall, eds., *Leashing the Dogs of War: Conflict Management in a Divided World* (Washington, DC: United States Institute of Peace Press, 2007). Monty Marshall at the University of Maryland offers a similar conclusion. According to Marshall, "the most troubling regional sub-systems in the Globalization Era are the regions constituted by the sub-Saharan African countries and the pre-dominantly Muslim countries, which stretch from Morocco and Senegal in the west to Malaysia and Indonesia in the east. The Lorenz curves for these two regions are roughly equivalent; income inequality among African countries is only slightly greater than income inequality among Muslim countries." It is also apparent that "although the general magnitude of armed conflict in both regions has diminished substantially since the end of the Cold War, the overall decrease in warfare in Africa has fallen more slowly than the general global trend." Muslim countries, however, "are the sole region [sic] where there has been an increase in armed conflict in recent years, possibly levelling, or even reversing, the general downward [global] trend." Monty G. Marshall, "Caveats to the 'Pacification' of the Global System: Global Report on Governance, Conflict, and Systemic Development" (paper, International Studies Association 2007 Annual Meeting, Chicago, March 1, 2007).

16. Robert M. Gates, "A Balanced Strategy," *Foreign Affairs* 88, no. 1 (January/February 2009): 28–40.

17. Pew Global Attitudes Project, *Rising Environmental Concern in 47-Nation Survey* (Washington, DC: Pew Research Center, June 27, 2007).

18. Pew Global Attitudes Project, *Rising Environmental Concern in 47-Nation Survey*; Council on Foreign Relations (CFR), "Public Opinion on Global Issues: A Web-Based Digest of Polling from Around the World," November 2009, www.cfr.org/thinktank/iigg/pop/index.html.

19. CFR, "Public Opinion on Global Issues," 41.

20. Ibid.

21. CFR, "Public Opinion on Global Issues," 46.

22. In addition, there is little consensus on who should deal with these wider problems. For instance, of the four countries most concerned about the spread of nuclear weapons (see table 1.1), Japan and Israel thought the United States should take the lead, while Lebanon felt that the United Nations should be the principal conflict management agency. A majority of respondents in Turkey, however, believed that Turkey itself should take the lead in reducing the threat of nuclear weapons.

23. Edward Newman, Ramesh Thakur, and Jorn Tirman, eds., *Multilateralism Under Challenge? Power, International Order, and Structural Change* (Tokyo: United Nations University Press, 2006); Ramesh Thakur, "Global Norms and International Humanitarian Law," *International Review of the Red Cross* no. 841 (March 31, 2001): 19–44, www.icrc.org/Web/Eng/siteeng0.nsf/iwpList182/8605528CB8A2EC1DC1256B66005FA42B.

24. Colin Bradford and Johannes Linn, "Reform of Global Governance: Priorities for Action," Policy Briefing no. 163, Brookings Institution, October 2007, http://www.brookings.edu/~/media/Files/rc/papers/2007/10global%20governance/pb163.pdf; Dries Lesage, "Globalisation, Multipolarity and the L20 as an Alternative to the G8," Global Society 20, no. 3 (2007): 343–61.

25. Joshua Partlow, "At Brazil Conference, G-20 Urges Swifter Action on Financial Crisis," *Washington Post*, November 10, 2008, www.washingtonpost.com/wp-dyn/content/article/2008/11/09/AR2008110902499.html.

26. Mary Kaldor, Mary Martin, and Sabine Selchow, "Human Security: A New Strategic Narrative for Europe," *International Affairs* 83, no. 2 (2007): 273; August Reinisch, "Securing the Accountability of International Organizations," *Global Governance: A Review of Multilateralism and International Organizations* 7, no. 2 (April–June 2001): 131–50; Peter Willetts, "From 'Consultative Arrangements' to 'Partnership': The Changing Status of NGOs in Diplomacy at the UN," *Global Governance: A Review of Multilateralism and International Organizations* 6, no. 2, (April–June 2000): 191–212; Inge Kaul, Isabelle Grunberg, and Marc A. Stern, eds., *Global Public Goods: International Cooperation in the 21st Century* (New York: Oxford University Press, 1999); Inge Kaul, Pedro Conceição, Ketell Le Goulven, and Ronald U. Mendoza, eds., *Providing Global Public Goods: Managing Globalization* (New York: Oxford University Press, 2003).

27. Manuel Lafont Rapnouil, "A European View on the Future of Mutlilateralism," *Washington Quarterly* 32, no. 3 (July 2009): 182.

28. Andrew Mack, ed., *Human Security Report 2005: War and Peace in the 21st Century* (New York: Oxford University Press, 2005); Joseph J. Hewitt, Jonathan Wilkenfield, and Ted Robert Gurr, *Peace and Conflict, 2010* (College Park, MD: Center for International Development and Conflict Management, University of Maryland, 2010).

29. Louis Kriesberg, *Constructive Conflict: From Escalation to Resolution* (Lanham, MD: Rowman and Littlefield, 2007); Chester A. Crocker, Fen Osler Hampson, and Pamela Aall, *Taming Intractable Conflicts: Mediation in the Hardest Cases* (Washington, DC: United States Institute of Peace Press, 2004).

30. CSIS Commission on Smart Power, *A Smarter, More Secure America* (Washington, DC: Center for Strategic and International Studies, 2007), http://csis.org/programs/smart-power-initiative/smart-power-report; Joseph S. Nye, Jr., *Smart Power* (forthcoming).

31. Christopher Hemmer and Peter J. Katzenstein, "Why Is There No NATO in Asia? Collective Identity, Regionalism, and the Origins of Multilateralism," *International Organization* 56, no. 3 (Summer 2002): 575–607.

32. There are other tensions that thwart the development of stronger institutions in the region. The voluntary multilateralism and institutional weaknesses of Asia-Pacific Economic Cooperation (APEC), for example, are due to "the on-going creative struggle between ambitious multilateralists and national sovereignty realists." In addition to the great power rivalries between China, Japan, and the United States, the broader regional framework for cooperation has been held hostage to the countries of Southeast Asia (Association of Southeast Asian Nations), which preferred their own "incipient sub-regional architecture" that is centered on the "Asian way" of informal agreements and consensual decision making. Richard Feinberg, "Voluntary Multilateralism and Institutional Modification: The First Two Decades of Asia Pacific Economic Cooperation (APEC)," *Review of International Organizations* 3, no. 3 (2008): 239, 246.

33. Yoichi Funabashi, "Keeping Up With Asia," *Foreign Affairs* 87, no. 5 (September/October 2008): 110–25.

34. David A. Lake and Patrick M. Morgan, eds., *Regional Orders: Building Security in a New World* (University Park, PA: Pennsylvania State University Press, 1997).

35. Barry Buzan, Ole Waever, and Jaap de Wilde, *Security: A New Framework for Analysis* (Boulder: Lynne Rienner, 1998); Stephen Walt, "The Renaissance of Security Studies," *International Studies Quarterly* 35, no. 2 (1991): 211–40.

36. Muthiah Alagappa, "Regionalism and Conflict Management: A Framework for Analysis," *Review of International Studies* 21 (1995): 359–87.

37. Robert E. Kelly, "Security Theory in the 'New Regionalism,'" *International Studies Review* 9 (2007): 197–229.

38. Michael Pugh and Waheguru Pal Singh Sidhu, eds., *The United Nations and Regional Security* (Boulder, CO: Lynne Rienner Publishers, 2003), 31–46.

39. Ibid.

40. Peter J. Katzenstein, *A World of Regions: Asia and Europe in the American Imperium* (Ithaca: Cornell University Press, 2005); Parag Khanna, "Waving Goodbye to Hegemony," *New York Times Magazine*, January 27, 2008.

41. Stephen John Stedman, Elizabeth M. Cousens, Donald Rothchild, eds., *Ending Civil Wars: The Implementation of Peace Agreements* (Boulder, CO: Lynne Rienner Publishers, 2002); Roy E. Licklider, *Stopping the Killing: How Civil Wars End* (New York: New York University Press, 1995); Barbara F. Walter, *Committing to Peace: The Successful Settlement of Civil War* (Princeton: Princeton University Press, 2002).

42. Thomas L. Friedman, *The World is Flat: A Brief History of the Twenty-first Century* (New York: Farrar, Straus and Giroux, 2005).

2

Global Conflict Management and the Pursuit of Peace

Gilles Andréani

Conflict management is an elusive and contradictory concept. As Clausewitz demonstrated, the essence of violent conflict is limitless escalation,[1] which seems to stand in contradiction to the idea of management of any kind. At best, some conflicts will be mitigated by intervention from outside, but it should be recognized that others will not. By their very nature, they will tend to burn on until the interplay of violence allows an undisputed winner to emerge and define the terms of peace.

Moreover, conflict management, as a set of policy instruments to solve or at least alleviate violent conflict, does not occur in a vacuum. Its effectiveness will vary according to the nature of the conflict at hand, and its chance of working will vary depending on the nature of the opponents and the structure of the international system. At no point in time have diplomats and politicians more genuinely searched for collective security, arbitration, and disarmament than during the interwar period. It is now obvious that neither the objectives of some of the key players—Nazi Germany, the Soviet Union, or militaristic Japan—nor the balance between these subversive forces and those that upheld the international order as it existed allowed for a reasonable chance to settle differences other than by war. If anything, the belief in conflict management made matters worse, by delaying this realization and weakening the resolve of democracies.

By contrast, the years from 1815 to 1914 remain relatively peaceful ones in history, at least in European history, even as war was then regarded as a legitimate way of settling disputes among states. Conflict management rested on customary diplomatic processes such as the "European concert" rather than on any dedicated instrument, or formal prohibition of war, but it proved on the whole extremely effective in preventing or managing conflict in Europe. Initially, under the concert system, the more powerful states were able to impose solutions on lesser players when conflicts erupted among them or to at least contain the conflicts. The 1848–1871 period saw a weakening of the concert system as a series of wars occurred among major European powers, but the system somehow reasserted itself thereafter. By and large, the 1815–1914 period saw conflicts limited in scope or time, and none degenerated into a general conflagration of the kind the Europeans had known in the centuries before and were to endure again in the thirty years thereafter.

Based on these examples, there are two conceivable ways of approaching conflict management studies: the first considers conflict as a disease and evaluates the kit of curative options available within the international system to address the problem; the second looks at conflict as a function of the international system itself and thus sees conflict not as a disease but as a reflection of the way forces are distributed among the system and of the quality of the relations among major players within the system. According to this latter view, there are features of the system that make it either more peaceful or more bellicose and its main actors, those on which the system relies, more prone to reducing tensions as they occur, or to making those tensions worse.

A good deal of the contemporary thinking on conflict management revolves around the former, "medical-kit" approach to the problem, and mainly addresses the relevance and efficiency of the various instruments available to solve conflicts and stabilize the situation once open violence has ceased. Valuable as it is, this approach needs to be preceded by an examination of the features of the international system. The efficiency of conflict management tools can be properly assessed only against that background.

In this regard, the post–Cold War period combines two noticeable features at the global level: first, an alignment of power, interests, and ideas of the major powers following the demise of Communism, which have reduced open tensions among them to an all-time low; second, an array of instruments to prevent war, limit it in scope and space should it occur, and stabilize the situation afterward, for which there is virtually no precedent. Which of these two factors is more relevant to the peace the world has by and large enjoyed for twenty years is an open question, but the facts are there: this is a period that has known a degree of peace unprecedented in world history.

But war and peace, as should be obvious, are not static quantities but the result of inherently changing interactions. The characterization of the present era as one of peace would be dangerously complacent if it missed the dynamic dimension of the problem. In this perspective, four main issues must be addressed: there are dangerous weaknesses and imbalances in the current configuration of the international system; the inhibition of the use of force has been relaxed; crisis management institutions, developed as they may be, present obvious deficiencies in terms of equality and legitimacy; extreme ideas, and the evolving nature of political violence, may challenge current conflict management arrangements in an unforeseen way.

An Era of Improved Peace

How best to characterize the international system after the end of the Cold War has been a question of scholarly debate and of political controversy. Was it temporarily unipolar, as suggested in the expression "unipolar moment"?[2] Is it multipolar today, as so-called emerging countries themselves tend to suggest? After the parenthesis of the Cold War, is the world witnessing a return to normalcy—that is, to power rivalry among a plurality of states? Or is the world seeing the emergence of a rule-based international system that, together with that of an international civil society, could lay the foundation of a global democratic governance? Are states still the masters of that system, or are nonstate actors more and more central to global problems (transnational criminal networks and terrorist groups) and solutions (nongovernmental organizations [NGOs] and global public opinion)?

An Exceptionally Favorable Alignment of the International System

The best answer so far to this debate was given by Pierre Hassner, who suggested that rather than choose among these various alternatives, one should regard them as together forming a "mixed international system," a system analogous to "mixed regimes" in the classical debate on the constitution of the city.[3] Political philosophers, notably Aristotle and Polybius, praised the mixed regime as the best possible one,[4] as it would combine the best features of monarchy, aristocracy, and democracy. Hassner observes that ever since the end of the Cold War, an international system has evolved that combines the hegemony of one (America's unipolar moment), the dominance of a few (multipolarity and the concert of powers), and a growing democratic component (equality of rights among nations, a rule-based system, and the emergence of global civic forces).

Indeed, from the perspective of war and peace, such an approach is especially helpful to dissipate the cloud of disbelief and mystery that still surrounds the relative peaceful state of current international affairs. Just as, according to Aristotle, mixed government is the best political system in that it combines the best features of different types of constitutions, so too perhaps is the current alignment of the international system the ideal one in that it allows the world to enjoy the concurrent blessings of imperial peace, peace through concert, and democratic peace.

The word "imperial" does not quite capture the nature of America's current international dominance, for it has historically been associated with a hierarchical organization of the world and with the forced subjection of other peoples by their imperial master(s), features that do not fit with either contemporary democratic values or the fact that the international system is now one of nation-states. In the real sense, the last empire was the Soviet Union, and it does not have a successor.

On the other hand, the term imperial peace is not improper when characterizing the stability that has gone along with America's exceptional superiority in military and political power since the end of the Cold War. The United States is not in a position to dictate peace to the world, but it is able to contribute to the preservation of global peace and stability in two ways: U.S. military dominance inhibits the conduct of countries that might otherwise be tempted to resort to force; and the United States' circle of formal alliances coincides with a zone of peace where its allies are less tempted to settle differences among themselves through violent means (a situation of "peace through empire" that existed during the Cold War in both superpowers' "imperial domains" and continues to be felt today under the umbrella of Pax Americana).[5]

Concurrent with this unique American "imperial" dominance, a form of global concert has returned. The most immediate effect of the end of the Cold War was not the birth of a multipolar world—that is, a global balance of power relationship among states of comparable stature and influence—but rather the creation of a situation in which the main powers, unequal as they were, could nevertheless cooperate to maintain peace and security and manage conflicts. Absent the bipolar competitive structure of the Cold War, the Security Council could at last function as provided for in the UN Charter; for the first time since the end of the Second World War and its immediate aftermath, a global concert was made possible again.

Who composes this concert is by no means settled. Although a central framework for consultation, the concert's perimeter does not strictly coincide with that of the five permanent members (P5) of the UN Security Council. In effect, it has been a concert of variable geometry that has assumed various configurations according to each crisis: the Contact Group on the former Yugoslavia, the Six-Party Talks on North Korea, the Quartet on the Middle East peace process, the four main Western allies and the

European Union on Iran, etc. The G8 (formerly G7) has also occasionally had a role to play in conflict management.

In substance, the effectiveness of these various frameworks and the ingenuity of their collective character have varied greatly. Although the Six-Party Talks has been an effective and balanced diplomatic framework and the Contact Group managed the crises in Bosnia and Kosovo, the Quartet has been little more than a symbolic and perfunctory body. Be that as it may, the fact is that the ability of the main states to consult and cooperate on international security issues, be it within the P5, or in ad hoc frameworks, has been brought back into existence as a result of the end of the Cold War, opening qualitatively new opportunities of international cooperation in the management of conflict.

In addition to the unipolar and concert components of the post–Cold War international system, democracy has made parallel progress over the last twenty years. What "democracy" means in the international system should be qualified, though, as it is inherently a much more unequal universe than domestic politics, and one where legitimacy is not bestowed directly by voters. In an international context, "democracy" can properly be equated on the one hand to progress toward the rule of law and the equality of states before it, and on the other hand to progress toward democratic values as a shared reference within the international community.

On these two fronts, democracy has indeed progressed since the end of the Cold War. First, the sense of national independence and equality among states has grown, and international society is more democratic as a result. Differences in status and dignity among states are increasingly resented and are tending to regress. Second, as the number of democracies increases, democratic values tend to permeate international processes more, owing, in particular, to the role of public opinions and NGOs, whose influence has increased in proportion. That does not automatically translate into a reduction of tensions: democracy and nationalism are complementary rather than contradictory developments. Both tend to foster a sense of sovereignty that resents the intrusion of others in one's own affairs, hence complicating conflict management. But along with democracy and nationalism, the principled rejection of the use of force and coercion—and the aspiration for a rule-based international system—have grown to support conflict management processes globally.

Between these three levels of the international system—the unipolar, the concert, and the international community—there is no spontaneous convergence of interests. To be sure, the leadership of the United States and/or the privileged role of the concert are resented by the wider family of nations. In addition, there are sharp disputes as to which countries the concert should actually comprise, as established second-tier countries, especially from Europe, are being increasingly challenged by "emerging" non-European countries. The United States will take a demeaning view of the concert, or specifically of the Security Council, should the concert fail to agree with it. The United States' unease with the wider collection of nations assembled in the United Nations is hardly new. This unease manifested itself under the Clinton administration, which promoted the "community of democracies" as a more valid expression of the common global good than the international community and which yielded considerable ground to the ideological attacks of the Republican Party against the United Nations during most of the 1990s.

Despite these attitudes, the United States has come around to accept that even the "pretense of concert" can carry added efficiency and legitimacy,[6] and the situation in Iraq has demonstrated that acting in isolation from world opinion and in defiance of the UN Security Council can come at a high price for the United States. On the other hand, neither the international community nor the concert of the few can ignore the United States, which remains key to solving most international security issues of concern to them. Beyond the inevitable tensions among these three levels, a degree of convergence remains preferable for each of them.

A New Wealth of Conflict Management

As the international system has evolved in a more peaceful direction, international resources of conflict management have grown in number and efficiency. Since the end of the Cold War, a growing number of institutions have developed a conflict management role, with the Organization for Security and Co-operation in Europe (OSCE), the European Union, and NATO having gone beyond their historical mandate to participate not only in the prevention and resolution of conflicts but also in peace operations. Furthermore, the European Union and NATO have done so outside the geographical limits of Europe, such as in the Democratic Republic of Congo (the European Union and NATO), Indonesia (the European Union), or Afghanistan (NATO).

The globalization of conflict management has also been reflected in the expanded role played by a number of countries: China has committed contingents to UN operations in Haiti and Lebanon; European countries have successfully contributed to the solution of conflicts far beyond their traditional sphere of interests; Norway made a direct contribution to the first agreement between Israel and the Palestinians in 1993 and to the 1996 peace accords in Guatemala; and both Norway and Switzerland contributed to a tentative truce between the warring parties in Sri Lanka in 2002.

A number of private organizations are devoted to the monitoring, mediation, or solution of crises and conflicts. The fraternity of Sant' Egidio, a Catholic prayer and charity community, developed its international mediation efforts in the 1990s, notably in bringing about a peace agreement in Mozambique in 1992 and in brokering a tentative agreement between the parties of the civil war in Algeria in the mid-1990s. It also intervened in Albania, Kosovo, Rwanda, Burundi, and the Democratic Republic of Congo. Other organizations include the International Crisis Group, which, since 1995, has developed a fact-finding, analysis, and policy recommendation capacity on crises and conflicts globally, and Mahti Ahtisaari's Crisis Management Initiative, founded in 2000, which played a central role in the 2005 agreement between the Indonesian government and the Free Aceh Movement.

In addition to an expanded number of conflict management actors, new international legal instruments have been developed that can have an influence on conflict prevention and resolution. Although international criminal courts, the International Criminal Court (ICC) proper, and ad hoc international tribunals were all created to deliver justice—not peace— they are expected to contribute to the deterrence of mass violence and to the healing of societies in post-conflict transitions. The increased reach of domestic courts as they repress crimes such as torture or slave trade under universal jurisdiction regimes can also make a contribution.

The abundance of instruments and institutions that contribute to conflict management is not always an unmitigated good. For example, in the crises that erupted in the former Yugoslavia from 1990 onward, the European Union, NATO, the United Nations, and the Contact Group all played a significant role (NGOs, other individual states, and the OSCE played a minor one), but coordination among them was limited, to say the least; conflicts frequently occurred among them; and none of them assumed a durable and clear leadership role throughout more than a decade of crises.

Despite the proliferation of contributors, and the expanded reach of an increased number of institutions, two main global players stand out in the field of conflict management, the United Nations and the United States. This characterization may seem unfair to two major organizations that have tried, over the last two decades, to assert their role in conflict management, NATO and the European Union. What justifies their omission from the list of main global conflict management players is not their limited geographical scope (both have intervened well beyond the boundaries of Europe, their statutory zone of action) but the two inherent limitations from which they suffer.

NATO is not able to command the two ends of conflict management, the application of military tools and the negotiation of a political settlement. While it expanded its military peacekeeping and peace enforcement activities, others such as the United Nations, the United States, or a combination of both, such as the Contact Group, mastered the political end of the conflicts in which they were involved. Such has been the case in Bosnia, Kosovo, and Afghanistan.

The European Union commands a larger array of political, civilian, and military instruments than NATO and does not suffer from the same limitation. It played a major role in consolidating stability as it enlarged throughout Europe, but this has been a regional rather than a global contribution to peace. The European Union has not been able to display the qualities of resolve and political consistency that could make it an alternative source of global leadership in conflict management. It has made use of its various instruments and significant resources in a haphazard and piecemeal way. It remains politically and militarily much weaker than the United States and lacks the global legitimacy of the United Nations. By default, then, the United States and the United Nations remain the two main global players in conflict management.

They are global in the sense that they are expected to play a role in basically every conflict everywhere. Should they abstain to do so, their absence would be conspicuous and resonate. More often than not, there is a political meaning to their nonintervention (e.g., the United States' refusal to allow the United Nations to play a role in the resolution of the Arab-Israeli conflict).

They are not on the same footing as other players, in that they bring unique resources to bear on the management of conflicts. There is no substitute for the United Nations' ability to take legally binding decisions and to bestow international legitimacy upon them. The United States leverages its unique resources, of which its military dominance is its most conspicuous resource but far from its only resource. It can thus intervene in crises in unique, nonmilitary ways, as it did between Turkey and Greece in the Imia-Kardak affair in 1996, between Morocco and Spain in the 2002 Persil islet dispute, and between India and Pakistan in 1999 and 2002 when those two countries came close to open war. In these instances, the United States' main asset was not of a military nature but of a political one: the countries concerned highly valued their relationships with the United States, giving the United States exceptional leverage as it sought to contain these crises.

Since the end of the Cold War, both the United Nations and the United States have enjoyed an increased freedom to intervene in conflicts and contribute to their resolution. The UN Security Council was able to function effectively once it ceased to be paralyzed by the rivalry between the two superpowers. Its peacemaking and law-making powers have expanded to include sanctions, preventive action, global counterterrorirism, and counterproliferation regulations. UN peacekeeping activities have expanded in scope in two waves: the first one coincided with the post–Cold War settlements of the late 1980s and early 1990s and the operations in the former Yugoslavia; the second with the large-scale operations in Africa of the late 1990s and early 2000s. In this context, the United Nations learned from the shortfalls of the previous wave and its operations have gained in strength and efficiency.

As the United Nations' ability to act expanded, the United States enjoyed a unique freedom of action during the 1990s. Its network of alliances, formal and informal, not only survived the Cold War but also grew to include former adversaries in Europe. Important countries that used to remain at a distance from the United States, like India, sought its friendship. Russia, albeit progressively frustrated by U.S. policies in Eastern Europe and the Balkans up to the early 2000s, maintained a privileged partnership with the United States and chose not to oppose its key interests. The European Union did not rise as an autonomous power, much less as one able or willing to challenge the United States politically or militarily. All that gave the United States an unprecedented ability to move forward any conflict resolution agenda it might have. In particular, it reigned over the Middle East peace process, and there is no doubt that it will again preside unchallenged over the peace process if and when it should resurface as a result of the efforts of the Obama administration.

September 11, 2001, initially reinforced these trends, as the international community gathered in solidarity with the United States and in rejection of the large-scale global terrorism that had manifested itself on that occasion. The Iraq War can be said to have reversed that trend to a significant degree, with open international distrust for the motives and the wisdom of that war and a clear lack of support for it in the UN Security Council. However, those countries who opposed the United States paid a price, which may inhibit them from openly challenging the United States in the future.

Being a state with an autonomous capacity to define its interests and act accordingly, the United States can overrule opposition to its views. The United Nations, by contrast, depends on the consent of the member states, and disproportionately on that of the United States, in order to raise an issue, make a decision, or implement it. The United Nations has an international mandate with regard to international peace and security, with corresponding legitimacy and legal resources. The United States plays a de facto central role in support of the current international order, but for other states, that role is both a source of concern as well as of reassurance. Its legitimacy can never be taken for granted. Saying that the United States and the United Nations are the two main global players in conflict management therefore conveys oversimplifications and must take into account the asymmetries of their respective roles. These asymmetries are of a complementary character, making commonality of purpose and proper articulation between the United States and the United Nations an essential condition of efficiency. In this way, the United States and the United Nations together should be regarded as the "central system" of global conflict management.

That is not to say that the other institutions and players mentioned earlier play no role in conflict management. As a matter of fact, they do, and they have scored significant successes in a number of instances. But vis-à-vis the United Nations and the United States, they are in a peripheral or "niche-market" position. They will act when the United States and/or United Nations is not actively involved but will only support or complement them if they are.

Fewer Conflicts, Fewer Victims: Conflict Resolution's Qualified Progress

The computation of armed conflicts and their victims is an issue in itself, with data varying to a considerable extent according to the source and the many conceivable definitions of "conflict" and "victim." For instance, "deaths in combat" do not equal "war deaths," a much wider category. As a result, the number of war deaths published by the World Health Organization (WHO) far exceed those of either the *SIPRI Yearbook* or the *Human Security Report*.[7] The latter two are based to a large extend on the same source: the Uppsala Conflict Data Program, which focuses on the "deaths-in-combat" category. The WHO's sources of data and methodology are different and include wider categories of victims with more indirect relationships to combat activities.[8]

Addressing these discrepancies would go far beyond the scope of this essay and the expertise of the author, while not necessarily adding much in substance. For despite striking differences in absolute numbers, the various sources converge to form a discernable trend: the numbers of conflicts and of their victims have markedly declined since the end of the Cold War, and even more so since the beginning of the 2000s.

According to the 2005 *SIPRI Yearbook*, there were on average 29 major conflicts worldwide per year in the years 1990–94, 24 in the years 1995–99, and 21 in the years 2000–04.[9] The downward trend has continued ever since:

17 in 2005, 17 in 2006, and 14 in 2007, according to successive updates of the subject in the 2006, 2007, and 2008 *SIPRI Yearbook*s. The decline has not been regular in time and place. Conflicts in Africa, for instance, have declined from a peak of 9 in 1990 to 4 in 1996, bounced back afterward to 11 in 1998–2000, and then declined again more or less steadily to 4 in 2007. It should be noted that while the number of conflicts has declined since 1990, it was not significantly lower right after 1990 from what it was, on average, during the Cold War: there were less than 30 major conflicts per year worldwide in the years 1946–1970, and only in the last 20 years of the Cold War did the number of major conflicts exceed that level, reaching a peak of 40 conflicts per year on average during the 1980s.[10]

The number of war fatalities, however, has declined more markedly than the number of conflicts: the average yearly figure for deaths in combat during the Cold War (1946–1989) was about 200,000. Ever since, that figure on average has been well under 100,000 per year, a decrease that would be even greater if deaths in combat were expressed as a percentage of world population, which has increased twofold since 1960.[11] The 1990s saw significantly more victims per year than the 2000s. By comparison, road traffic accidents are estimated by the WHO to cause 1.2 million deaths each year.

These figures are not meant to diminish the social, political, and human catastrophes that go along with war of any kind. They reflect only direct war fatalities and do not take into account the displacement of populations or the mistreatment and increased vulnerability to disease or crime that populations may suffer as a result of war. They also do not exhaust the ongoing debate on the changing character of war and mass violence. As absolute quantities, they may be well beyond the mark and reflect only a part of the current human consequences of war.

The trends, however, seem to be there: in the post–Cold War era, the total number of armed conflicts and fatalities has declined significantly. Beyond the quantitative data related to conflicts and their victims, three elements point in the direction of a structural recess of war after 1990:

- Protracted Cold War conflicts were settled in the early 1990s, the most notable of which were those in Cambodia, Angola, Mozambique, Nicaragua, and Afghanistan;
- Conflict resolution initiatives have grown in number: according to the Uppsala University Conflict Data Program, on average roughly 10 major conflicts have been settled each year since 1990;
- Conflicts have not been exacerbated by the divergent alignment of major powers: the major powers mostly sought to cooperate on the management of conflicts, or sometimes abstained from them, but

never acted at cross-purposes or deliberately upset the peace efforts of others. Even in the 1999 NATO air operation against Serbia, neither Russia nor China—both of which deeply resented the operation—actively supported Serbia. Indeed, Russia helped bring the crisis to an end. Similarly, both Russia and China may have views on Iran and on the contribution of sanctions to solve the ongoing nuclear crisis with Iran that are markedly different from those of the European Union or the United States, but they have not, up to now, positively frustrated efforts to solve the crisis. One may argue that China would stand in the way of meaningful sanctions and, even more so, of military action against Sudan, but it is fair to say that the West has only halfheartedly tried to address the Darfur crisis and that no one can safely predict that China would openly oppose a clear and resolute Western policy on the issue, should one materialize.

At any rate, the attitudes of major powers on crisis management today range from real convergence to managed differences, with tacit acquiescence and grudging neutrality in-between. That is a marked improvement over Cold War practices, where war by proxy was the rule and cooperation on conflict management the exception. That is perhaps the most important qualitative development to have improved conflict management since the end of the Cold War.

Fault Lines beneath the Surface

The twenty-year period following the Cold War's end thus appears in retrospect to have been noticeably more conducive to conflict management efforts than any twenty-year period since the failure of the Europe-centered international system at the outset of the twentieth century. That is a satisfactory consideration, but also a reason to move the investigation further: after all, an observer standing in the year 1913 could have satisfied itself on grounds not wholly different.

The twenty years before World War I had seen no direct conflict between major powers (with the exception of the 1898 Spanish-American War and the 1904 Russo-Japanese War, which had been rightly seen as peripheral and contained rather than central and contagious events). In more than thirty occasions between 1870 and 1914,[12] the European concert had been able to prevent potentially major conflicts through negotiation. Even the downfall of the Ottoman Empire, the event all feared most likely to ignite general war, had taken place most unexpectedly in 1912–13 and had been managed by a diplomatic process, the London conference, which did little to influence events on the ground but at least prevented the major powers from joining the fight. Or so they thought, since less than a year after this last success of the European concert, the World War I broke out.

That is not to suggest that the world is on the eve of anything remotely comparable: the alignment of hostile alliances, the military incentives for preventive war, and the imperial hubris that existed in 1914 are not present today to create a risk of general war. The foundations of world peace are today comparatively much more solid. Taken together, the international system remains peaceful, and its conflict management resources are abundant. But the circumstances that have allowed the last twenty years to be relatively peaceful should be put into a dynamic perspective. These circumstances are bound to change. Today's imbalances and dissatisfactions, although clearly not of such a magnitude as to upset peace, may lead to tomorrow's conflicts if left unattended.

Quincy Wright identified four main conditions of peace:[13] a certain balance of material forces, the realization of a system of law intolerant of violence except as an instrument of execution, procedures for moderating extreme opinions, and the accommodation of new issues in the world system. These thoughts have passed the test of time and remain valid criteria against which to evaluate the resilience of the current system and its ability to prevent or contain war in the future. The result of such an examination suggests that the relative peace our time is enjoying should not be seen as a given, but as an opportunity to consolidate the four features identified by Wright as key to the furthering of peace within the international system—especially in the face of three fault lines that presently underlie the system.

An Unbalanced Distribution of Responsibilities

The sharing of responsibilities within the "central system" of conflict management reflects the global distribution of power. As a result, it is too dependent on the West, and specifically on the United States. An obvious consequence is that it can do little to prevent or solve conflicts that the Americans themselves initiate. In the case of the 2003 Iraq War, lack of consent from its allies or opposition within the Security Council can be said to have made the war politically more expensive for the United States, but those countries that opposed the war could not and did not prevent it.

Nor can the system do much to manage conflicts in which the United States has an important stake and which, for one reason or another, it either does not choose to resolve or intervenes in a biased or unbalanced way. The Israel-Palestine issue comes to mind, as one for which no alternative to the United States exists to solve it, even as the United States' involvement suffers from two critical limitations: (1) for reasons of its own, the United

States may deem that the issue not warrant active engagement on its part, as demonstrated in practice during the eight years of the George W. Bush presidency; and (2) even when the United States is actively involved, its privileged relationship and deep affinities with Israel make it difficult for the United States to effectively steer the process, which as a result suffers from a constant risk of imbalance and bias.

Pre-2003 Iraq is also a case in point. One can argue that during the 1990s, a peaceful solution to the problem of Iraq's weapons of mass destruction was not out of reach. The fact is, however, that such a solution was never fully pursued: one reason may have been the incompetence of Saddam Hussein's regime, whose provocations did not give the UN-mandated disarmament process a chance. The other is that U.S. policy toward Iraq was dominated by other objectives, such as regime change or, at a minimum, the continued imposition of sanctions over the country as a deterrent measure as long as Saddam Hussein ran it. The "conflict management" objective (seeing to it that Iraq complied with the 1991 cease-fire conditions so as to lift sanctions and reintegrate Iraq into its international environment) was superseded by these other objectives and was never pursued as such by the United States.

Finally, the global conflict management responsibilities that fall upon the United States far exceed its attention span. One cannot ask it to simultaneously deploy equal analytical wisdom, political commitment, and leadership on issues as diverse and complex as Afghanistan, Cyprus, Kosovo, Azerbaijan, Georgia, Palestine, Colombia, Lebanon, Iran, Sudan, Somalia, and Pakistan, just to name some of today's most salient conflicts, active or dormant, where it has been involved and remains key to a solution. (Iraq was left out of the list as a problem of America's own making—one that has clearly detracted its attention from some of these places.)

Americans will argue, not without reason, that they are not to blame for a situation that is a reflection of their own power and of the relative weakness of others. In this respect, the absence of Europe as an alternative provider of leadership in global conflict management is the most conspicuous, since, together, the Europeans represent the second largest pool of military, economic, and political resources that could be mobilized in support of international security. The promises of the early 1990s have not been fulfilled in this respect. Notwithstanding the significant contribution to stabilization and conflict prevention that the European Union's enlargement provided on the European continent itself, the organization and its member states play virtually no role in the major crises mentioned above in Asia and the Middle East, except in support of or as a complement to the United States. Only in Africa (in Sierra Leone, Côte d'Ivoire, and the

Democratic Republic of Congo) have the Europeans, either individually or collectively, significantly improved the situation, each time in conjunction with the United Nations. In the two most desperate security situations there, Darfur and Somalia, they have consistently failed to act decisively, just like the United States. Seen from a global perspective, however, the main issue is not the imbalance between the United States and Europe, but the overwhelming Western dominance in the management of conflicts in which non-Western countries have a significant stake—whether they are the countries concerned or other powers that feel unduly marginalized by the current global security arrangements.

Specifically, Russia remains key to solving a number of conflict situations due to its status as a permanent member of the Security Council; its interests in a number of crises on its Eastern periphery, ranging from North Korea to Afghanistan; the direct stakes it has in developments in parts of the former Soviet Union, most importantly the Caucasus; and its role in the Balkans. Without going too deeply into a contested and complex issue, that of the relationship between Russia and the West since the end of the Cold War, it can be argued that Russia does not play the positive and recognized role that it should. Russia is in part responsible for the present situation, but so is the West. In retrospect, the West has gone too far in openly ignoring Russia's concerns in the Balkans and the Caucasus, and in sidelining it in European security structures, notably as a consequence of NATO's enlargement. Recognizing for Russia a proper stake in conflict management in Europe and beyond will be difficult, in the context of a more authoritarian and less pliant Russia and of a much more polarized relation with the West. It is nonetheless desirable in order to rebalance global responsibilities in that field.

As for emerging powers, China has shown an increased willingness to contribute to conflict management (it is now the second largest troop contributor to UN peacekeeping missions among permanent members of the Security Council). Its growing role should be recognized and encouraged. Beyond China, the key to rebalancing responsibilities in conflict management lies in involving other emerging powers. The reform of the Security Council could play a key role in this respect. While there are no expectations that the issue can be easily reopened after the failed attempts at reform in 1997 and 2005, reform of the Security Council would seem to be the most visible way to expand the circle of responsibilities in global conflict management.

At any rate, it is even more necessary today to give a greater stake to important countries, be they established powers like Germany or Japan, or on-the-rise ones, like India or Brazil, and to minimize the overwhelmingly Western character of global conflict management. Short of a formal reform of the Security Council, are other means available to that end? The expansion of the G7 into the G8 in the mid-1990s in order to better integrate Russia comes to mind as a possible precedent. In the context of the 2008 economic crisis, the G20 has come to reflect the growing role of emerging countries in global economic decision making. By contrast with the G8, whose purpose is first and foremost political, the development of a political and security agenda for G20 countries is not in sight. Nor would it necessarily be a welcome development, as a "political G20" would inevitably emerge at the expense of the Security Council and seal the failure of its reform. The conclusion of this debate, then, is that the enlargement of the Security Council has become an even more necessary development, one which would need to be actively encouraged by the United States.

A historical precedent of what would be required to give a greater stake to emerging countries in international security and conflict management comes from the post–World War II period. At a time when the United States was much more powerful relative to the rest of the world than it is today, it chose to empower others and international institutions rather than directly manage world security problems itself. The Cold War forced a reluctant United States to do just that, but fortunately, the Cold War broke out only after the international institutions conceived in that moment of wisdom had been created.

One can argue that the second moment of the United States' unchallenged supremacy in the twentieth century, the post–Cold War period, saw the country display less wisdom: its instinct remained to take matters into its hands, as it had done during the Cold War, rather than devolve them to international institutions and other players that it would chose to strengthen at the same time. If Europe and others are first responsible for the current limits of their global influence, it is also fair to say that the United States only reluctantly accepted to recognize added security responsibilities to either the Europeans or international institutions and emerging players.

No one cedes power voluntarily. Some, however, realize that consolidating international security structures and devolving responsibilities at a time of unilateral dominance, in order to make any rebalancing to come more predictable and safer, is not a bad investment. That is a realization that a post-Iraq America could make, albeit in circumstances less favorable than in the immediate aftermath of the Cold War.

An Unequal Regulation of the Use of Force

Conflict management processes and an effective inhibition against the use of force reinforce each other. Shared opinion that the use of force is not an acceptable way to conduct international relations gives legitimacy and credibility to conflict management; conversely, effective conflict management mechanisms reinforce prohibition against the use of force. Such a prohibition, to be effective, has to be reciprocal and of a universal character.

Ever since the end of the Cold War, the reverse has happened, and both the practical ability and the doctrinal latitude to resort to force have been subjected to a growing asymmetry worldwide. Far from presiding over a reciprocal, contract-based prohibition of violent conflict, the "central system" of conflict management has increasingly tended to look like a unilateral police system to enforce the views of the United States and its allies on the rest of the world.

On the one hand, military means, and even more so those useable in the current strategic context— that is, force-projection capacities—tend to be more and more the preserve of the United States, which spends about as much for its defense as the rest of the world, without, it should be observed, a related decline in the threat perceptions of the American people. They have prompted the United States to claim, post-9/11, an ever-increasing freedom in relation to the use of force, including options for preventive military action in anticipation of a possible convergence between the global terrorist and proliferation threats.

In addition, the Bush administration sought to free itself from binding arms controls, notably the Anti-Ballistic Missile (ABM) treaty, which it regarded as a legacy of the past, to the benefit of either informal processes of arms control or unilateral controls targeted toward proliferators such as the Proliferation Security Initiative. At the same time, it reaffirmed the essential character of two unequal treaties: the Nuclear Non-Proliferation Treaty (NPT) and the 1990 Conventional Forces in Europe (CFE) treaty, which by virtue of the strategic evolution in Europe had ceased to be a constraint for anyone but Russia. Arms control has virtually disappeared as a component of conflict management, notably from the Middle East peace process.

Parallel to what essentially amounted to a growing ability to use force and growing claims for an increased freedom to wield it, the West promoted doctrines that sought to overcome traditional legal constraints against unilaterally resorting to force in the face of extreme humanitarian crises. Well intended as they may have been, such doctrines—humanitarian interference and responsibility to protect—and their controversial implementation, such as in northern Iraq in 1991 and Kosovo in 1999, could only be perceived as adding to a pattern of growing contrast between the prohibition of the use of force as a universal and reciprocal commitment of the UN Charter and its selective relaxation to the benefit of the United States and its allies.

The global prohibition against the use of force has been weakened as a result. The Russians have used Kosovo as a precedent to justify their own unilateral recognition in South Ossetia and Abkhazia. The argument, disingenuous as it may seem, nonetheless raises serious questions about the wider impact of the decision of a majority of Western countries to recognize Kosovo in 2008. Proliferating states, like North Korea and Iran, have drawn arguments from the selective repudiation of arms control by the United States, as well as from the widespread perception that disarmament commitments are uneven, if not biased, and that they mostly benefit the West. All in all, one should well consider what would happen if everyone sought to determine as freely the conditions of their security, including their latitude to resort to force, as the United States and the West have done since the end of the Cold War.

It is the nature of the current distribution of power, and of the international responsibilities of the United States, that will lead the United States to resort in practice to force more than other powers. But the corrosive effects of its claiming a special right to do so are only too apparent. It has now become essential to combine this strategic fact with deference to the universal character of the legal constraints on the use of force and to restore a sense of universality and reciprocity in these constraints, as well as in arms-control commitments.

The Internal Contradictions of Democracy

Although wars, as a rule, occur much more often by design than by accident, political ideas and emotional dispositions play a significant role in bringing about violent conflict. On the eve of World War I, doctrines such as social Darwinism, militarism, and imperialism, as well as a sort of fin de siècle nihilism, saw violent conflict as both inevitable and a healthy manifestation of the true self of nations. In the thirties, democratic individualism was challenged by doctrines that valued the collective and authority, such as Communism and Fascism, and to which a war ethos was intrinsic. In both cases, competition among nations was exacerbated by these extreme ideas. They did not cause war by themselves, but they made the task of those who did cause war easier.

The post–Cold War period has seen nothing comparable, by way of a global doctrine that would rise in defiance of a seemingly hegemonic liberal democracy. Whatever ideas there are to challenge it are fragmented rather than universal. For example, political Islam, the neo-Confucian doctrines propagated under the heading of Asian values, and the rather inchoate neo-Bolivarian movements in South America each claim a right to live according to principles different from liberal democracy, the universal character of which they dispute. They do not pretend to replace it across the board. The mutual affinity of these various movements is virtually nil. They are mostly unorganized and control no state worth mentioning, with the exception of Iran (and even so, the question of how "extremist" the government of Iran really is remains a controversial one).

Political extremism today seems to take its strength from the internal contradictions of liberal democracy rather than from any force able to challenge this doctrine from outside. Two of these contradictions are directly relevant to our subject: that between the hierarchical structure of the international system and the democratic empowerment of communities affected by violent conflict; and that between the democratic principle of equality and the selective implementation of international rules.

Conflict management, to be efficient, requires a measure of inequality among nations. Countries will provide the resources needed for collective action either if they are forced to or if it is the price to pay to assume a privileged power status within the international system. Either option requires some hierarchy among states. Conversely, if those responsible for conflict management normally exert authority on others, in particular the parties to the conflict, they will stand a better chance of getting those parties to accept a settlement. Kenneth Waltz went so far as to suggest that those international systems where security was best achieved were those that relied on a small number of powerful states able to impose order on other states. The fewer the number of powerful states, and the more contrasted their power situation vis-à-vis the others, the better, argued Waltz (hence his liking for the Cold War's bipolar structure).[14]

Even if one would hesitate to unreservedly endorse Waltz's vision, the necessity for some hierarchical dimension to make conflict management effective contrasts with a growing need to develop the ownership of those most concerned with the conflict. The peaceful engineering imposed from outside upon bellicose regions will work less and less. The demonstrations of open and sometimes violent distrust against UN personnel, both in South Timor and Kosovo, two regions that owed their independence to intervention from outside and then turned against their liberators, bear testimony to this fact. So does the rejection of the Annan Peace Plan by Greek Cypriot voters.

The ideologically charged accusation of neoimperialism against Western-sponsored conflict management should not be lightly dismissed. Unjust in substance as it may seem, it reflects a growing demand for autonomy and dignity, an impatience with outside interference. It is an expression of a raw sense of democracy rather than a rejection of democratic values, even if it is perceived or labeled as such in the West. Extremism of all sorts can take advantage of such feelings, as witnessed in Iraq and Afghanistan. The inherent trade-off between the efficiency that hierarchy and power carry and the need to empower those caught in conflict—and often those responsible for it as well—risks becoming more and more acute and problematic for conflict management.

Another contradiction that breeds extremism is that between the egalitarian ethos that lies at the heart of democracy and the fact for all to see that equality hardly progresses on a number of fronts in our world. The perception of the international system as a deeply unequal one, where norms are selectively enforced, fuels accusations of double standards and hypocrisy, which deeply weaken the international system's legitimacy. In this regard, the failure to address earnestly the Israel-Palestine conflict resonates deeply, far beyond the Muslim world. For all those who harbor a sense of grievance with the current distribution of power in the world, including with the remnants of past colonial situations, which the fate of the Palestinian people unmistakably echo, there is a symbolic dimension to this issue that adds to its actual importance and makes it a test case of utmost significance for the integrity and legitimacy of the international system.

The New Dimensions of International Security

As history demonstrates, very little can be known at present about the exact nature of tomorrow's most pressing security issues, but the pertinent questions about tomorrow are a bit more clear. A first question pertains to the return of large-scale interstate war among technologically advanced countries. The trend has been one of decline of such "classic" wars: will that trend be continued? If so, will armed conflicts as they have been known in the recent past continue to evolve in the same direction, with an increasing prevalence of civil war over interstate war, an increasing ratio of civilian to military casualties in conflict, growing numbers of displaced persons as a result of war, growing numbers of conflicts borne out of greed rather than of political motives, and a growing breakdown of state authority as a result of armed conflict? All of these trends, assuming they are really new, which is still a matter for debate, would not only bring further change to the nature of war but also touch the current limits of the traditional concept of war—that is, an organized struggle among armed parties, at least one of which is a state or aspiring to become one.

Other changes are much less clear, since they would call into question that very definition of war: should we anticipate a situation where the breakdown in personal security becomes a much more intense problem worldwide than war and thus warrants new types of international responses? Will terrorism and organized crime grow enough in scope to effectively challenge the monopoly of states on large-scale violence? Will new types of organized violence reach such intensity as to obliterate the category of armed conflict as it has been known so far? What if technology, in particular in the field of biology, computer technology, or nanotechnology, empowered individuals to inflict large-scale damage and casualties on society? Finally, are there entirely new forms of human violence that the rapid change in technology, and in economic and natural conditions on the planet, could bring about?

To remain on the safe side, one should not dismiss interstate war, and its possible return on a large scale. To be sure, such wars remain a distinct possibility, one which the international system must continue to dissuade. One must at the same time acknowledge the changing character of conflicts and recognize that of all the forms of violence, classic interstate wars may not be that which will present human security and survival with the direst challenge in the future.

That is another way to say that no one knows what kind of armed violence will most challenge security, broadly defined, in the future. The world should recognize, however, that the existing international system, although constructed mostly to prohibit interstate war, has proved flexible enough to address wholly unforeseen contingencies, such as large-scale transnational terrorism. Developing that flexibility—and not losing the benefit of a diminished occurrence of classic wars—is, by default, the most prudent goal moving forward.

*   *   *

Global conflict management has not as bad a record to show since the end of the Cold War: there have been fewer armed conflicts and victims, a number of old conflicts have been solved, and there has been a greatly reduced expectation that major interstate wars can realistically take place. This is perhaps a function of greatly increased conflict management resources, but it is more likely a result of the deeper structural changes within the international system that took place as the Cold War ended. These changes have left the United States practically without peer rivals to challenge its military or strategic dominance. The international situation has been more stable as a result. Europe has been stabilized under the dual aegis of Pax Americana and European integration. The end of the Cold War gave the UN Security Council and the concert of major powers a vastly improved ability to intervene in the management of crises and conflicts—an ability the Security Council had never enjoyed since the United Nations' creation.

The West's attempts at managing conflicts have been generally supported by other players, including Russia and China, which may have occasionally slowed or frustrated the West's efforts but never positively opposed them.

At the same time, as conflict management benefited from the transformation of the international system, it inevitably reproduced its flaws: both are too American, too Western-dominated, and too unequal, and both have lost sight of reciprocity and the mutuality of obligations. As a result, they are poorly legitimate, and the United States and its allies did not use the long interval of peace and the unprecedented freedom of action they enjoyed after the Cold War to redress this situation.

More recent attempts to redress the situation have not been a result of a revolution but of appeals for a number of discrete steps, such as calls to enlarge the UN Security Council, to devolve more responsibilities to the European Union, to promote arms control as a genuine way to improve global security, to seek to reinforce the prohibition against the use of force, deploy more fairness and energy in the resolution of the Arab-Israeli conflict, and to recognize Russia's potential contribution to conflict management where it has interests and influence.

Although no item on this collective agenda is a lost cause, each item looks much more like an uphill struggle than it did at the beginning of the 1990s. In between, 9/11 and the policy choices made in reaction by the Bush administration have added another layer of difficult challenges. International atmospherics are more tense, national ill-feelings are more openly voiced, and global economic conditions are less conducive to ambitious cooperative schemes. Yet expectations that the international system can be made more just, more inclusive, and more legitimate are there. There remains an opportunity to bring together the two main conflict management resources of the post–Cold War era, the United Nations and the United States. The fault lines in the system have not yet turned into open divisions, and dissatisfaction with the existing international system has, so far, been more conducive to disengagement and cynicism than to open violence. There is still a chance to take the necessary steps before the existing fault lines become insurmountable and the world recedes into a new wave of major conflicts.

Notes

1. Carl von Clausewitz, *On War*, book I, chapter 1.

2. Charles Krauthammer, "The Unipolar Moment," *Foreign Affairs* 70, no. 1, special issue, America and the World (1990/91).

3. Gilles Andréani and Pierre Hassner, eds., "Justifying War? From Humanitarian Intervention to Counterterrorism" (New York: *Palgrave* Macmillan, 2009), 239–43.

4. Aristotle's *Politics*, book VII, and Polybius's *Histories*, book VI.

5. On "peace through empire," see Raymond Aron, *Peace and War: A Theory of International Relations* (Garden City, NY: Doubleday, 1966), part I, chapter 6.

6. The expression is borrowed from Coral Bell, "American Ascendancy—and the Pretense of Concert," *National Interest* 57 (Fall 1999).

7. The *SIPRI Yearbook* is produced by the Stockholm International Peace Research Institute and the *Human Security Report* was formerly produced by the University of British Columbia's Liu Institute for Global Studies in the Human Security Centre and is presently produced at Simon Fraser University's School for International Studies.

8. Etienne G. Krug et al., eds., *Report on Human Violence and Health* (Geneva: World Health Organization, 2002), 216–39.

9. *SIPRI Yearbook 2005* (Stockholm: Stockholm International Peace Research Institute, Oxford University Press, 2005), see in particular pp. 122–31 in appendix IIA and the chapter by Lotta Harbom and Peter Wallenstren, "Patterns of Major Armed Conflicts, 1990–2004."

10. Ibid.

11. Although these figures, both the SIPRI estimates and those from the International Institute for Strategic Studies (IISS) Armed Conflict Database, as published yearly in the IISS's *The Military Balance*, converge, they are, of course, very rough estimates rather than precise figures.

12. This computation was made by Jost Dülffer in *Im Zeichen Der Gewalt: Frieden Und Krieg Im 19. Und 20.* Jahrhundert (Cologne: Bohlau Verlag, 2003).

13. Quincy Wright, *The Causes of War and the Conditions of Peace* (London: Longmans Green, 1935).

14. Kenneth Waltz, "The Stability of a Bipolar World," *Daedalus* 93, no. 3 (Summer 1964).

3

Regional Approaches to Conflict Management

Paul D. Williams and Jürgen Haacke

The post–Cold War era has witnessed considerable renewed interest in how regionalism is affecting the structures and processes of international security.[1] Although some analysts suggest that regional dynamics remain less important than the global dynamics generated by American hegemony and the interplay between systemic factors and domestic political variables,[2] others have argued that region-level analysis is increasingly important for understanding contemporary security dynamics,[3] and others still have used regionalism as the backdrop to explore the increasing roles played by regional arrangements in security-related activities.[4]

This renewed focus on regions has both reflected and been driven by three interrelated processes. First, the nature of many contemporary security challenges has become regional in scope inasmuch as threats are rarely contained by state borders. Second, the UN Security Council's practice of adopting a broad interpretation of what constitutes a threat to "international peace and security" has resulted in a higher tempo of peace operations and other security-related activities, which, in turn, has required the United Nations to develop partnerships with a variety of regional and other institutions.[5] Third, in certain parts of the world, regional arrangements themselves have become more proactive in addressing security issues—often in light of Chapter VIII of the UN Charter, but not always. This "picture of growing regional empowerment," as Louise Fawcett refers to it,[6] has progressed to the extent that some analysts have concluded—perhaps prematurely—that efforts to cope with violent conflicts "will primarily involve arrangements and actions devised and implemented at the regional level."[7]

Despite this renewed interest in regional approaches to conflict management, several respected analysts have observed that "there has been surprisingly little theoretically informed comparative analysis of the phenomenon" and that "there is room for much more theory-guided, comparative empirical research on the subject."[8] Rather than defend or rebut the idea that the regional level of analysis is central to contemporary global security dynamics, the purpose of this chapter is to offer an analytical framework that highlights variation in conflict management practices and presents some theoretically informed comparative analysis in order to understand the conflict management roles played by intergovernmental regional arrangements around the world. In particular, we analyze two sets of related questions. First, what significance have different regional arrangements accorded to conflict management among their security challenges, and what approaches to conflict management have regional arrangements designed in response to those challenges?[9] Second, how can we account for the particularity of conflict management approaches?

In order to address these questions, this chapter first explores the extent and nature of regional variation in relation to conflict management. It also illustrates how regional arrangements around the world have developed their approaches to conflict management. In an effort to account for the differences that we find, the chapter then discusses four clusters of explanatory factors: the exercise of political power, domestic political variables, ideational factors, and collective capacities. Next, the chapter briefly examines some of the main consequences of this regional variation by discussing what might happen when a regional arrangement is either unwilling or unable to engage in effective conflict management. The chapter concludes by emphasizing three substantive issues that are likely to figure prominently in future debates about regional conflict management: democracy promotion, the use of force, and engagement with actors within civil society.

Dimensions of Regional Variation

Although some regional arrangements see their role almost solely in terms of economic development and integration, an increasing number now include explicit provisions for dealing with security challenges, including various types of conflict. Table 3.1 lists nearly thirty regional arrangements that have explicitly engaged in various security-related activities; many also have some ambition and/or record in conflict management. Clearly, however, these arrangements approach security and conflict management issues in different ways: they do not necessarily exhibit a uniform definition of security challenges or the sources of potential conflict, nor do they

Table 3.1   Major Regional Arrangements with Security Provision, 1945–2009

Region	Regional arrangement
Africa	• Organization of African Unity/African Union • Intergovernmental Authority on Drought and Development/ Intergovernmental Authority on Development • Economic Community of West African States • Southern African Development Coordination Conference/Southern African Development Community • Economic and Monetary Community of Central African States
Europe	• European Community/European Union • Western European Union • North Atlantic Treaty Organization • (Warsaw Pact) • Organization for Security and Cooperation in Europe • Commonwealth of Independent States • Collective Security Treaty Organization
Asia	• (Southeast Asia Treaty Organization) • Association of Southeast Asian Nations • South Asian Association for Regional Cooperation • ASEAN Regional Forum • Shanghai Cooperation Organization • Central Asian Cooperation Organization • Islamic Conference Organization
Middle East	• League of Arab States • (Central Treaty Organization) • Gulf Cooperation Council • Arab Maghreb Union • (Arab Cooperation Council) • Economic Cooperation Organization • Islamic Conference Organization
Americas	• Organization of American States • Caribbean Community • Organization of Eastern Caribbean States • The Southern Common Market
Australasia	• The Australia, New Zealand, United States Security Treaty • South Pacific Forum/Pacific Island Forum

Note: Names in parentheses indicate the arrangement is defunct, while arrangements followed by a forward slash indicate a name change.

subscribe to a singular belief on what approach to conflict management, if any, they should follow in response.

On the face of it, these regional variations might simply reflect the fact that different regions face different issues and challenges regarding conflict management. Yet, on closer inspection regions often confront many similar conflict situations. For example, to a greater or lesser degree, all regional arrangements face challenges raised by four broad types of political or armed conflict. First, there are *intramural* conflicts. These involve a dispute between two or more members of the regional arrangement. A second type of conflict, *intrastate*, occurs between the government of a member state and internal opposition groups. In the Uppsala Conflict Data Program intrastate conflicts are further subdivided into either civil wars, which are fought for control of an existing government, or state-formation/ secessionist conflicts, which are fought between a government and a territorially focused opposition group that is seeking to redraw the borders of the existing state.[10] Intrastate conflicts will be internationalized to a greater or lesser degree depending upon the extent of external support for one or more of the parties, which may well arise from ethnic ties.[11] Regional arrangements in contemporary Africa, for example, have had considerable experience in dealing with intrastate conflicts that cross national boundaries, chief among them have been the series of interconnected wars in West Africa (Liberia, Sierra Leone, and Côte d'Ivoire), the Great Lakes region (Burundi, Rwanda, the Democratic Republic of the Congo [DRC], and Uganda), Eastern Africa (Sudan, Chad, and the Central African Republic), and the Horn of Africa (Ethiopia, Somalia, and Eritrea).

A third type is what we call *wider regionalized conflicts*. This refers to those (usually interstate) conflicts involving a mixture of members of the regional arrangement and external parties. Examples would be the conflict between EU-members Greece and Cyprus and non-EU member Turkey, and the conflict over the Spratly Islands involving the People's Republic of China (PRC), the Republic of China (ROC), and claimants from the Association of Southeast Asian Nations (ASEAN): the Philippines, Vietnam, Malaysia, and Brunei Darussalam. Finally, *nonstate armed conflicts* are those where organized, collective armed violence occurs but where a recognized government is not one of the parties. Examples might include violent intercommunal conflicts or fighting between warlords and clans. Such conflicts may be largely contained within the territory of one member state or spill across the borders into others.[12]

Among the most widely debated contemporary issues related to conflict management has been how regional arrangements should approach the "responsibility-to-protect" (R2P) principle. As it was agreed in the United Nations' 2005 World Summit Outcome document, the R2P principle commits states to protecting their populations from genocide, crimes against humanity, ethnic cleansing, and war crimes.[13] If governments "manifestly fail" in this duty, outsiders are obliged to take "timely and decisive" collective action through the mechanisms available in Chapters VI–VIII of the UN Charter.[14] Despite the emphasis the UN secretariat has placed on the preventive and capacity-building elements of R2P, many governments continue to treat the principle as largely synonymous with a doctrine of humanitarian intervention (i.e., using military force to protect human rights without the consent of the host government).

To the extent that they have been faced with intrastate conflict among members that generate significant violence and deaths, regional arrangements around the world have adopted a variety of different stances.[15] First, there are organizations such as ASEAN, the Shanghai Cooperation Organization (SCO), the League of Arab States (LAS), and the Organization of American States (OAS), which refrain from initiating interventions to protect populations under the auspices of the respective grouping because their participants do not see such action as legitimate and have concerns about the potential implications. Second, there are those arrangements that, like the African Union, claim they would intervene in certain "grave circumstances" such as genocide if they possessed the necessary capabilities. Third, there are institutions, the Economic Community of West African States (ECOWAS), for example, which have already used humanitarian justifications for military intervention within their own region, even if the operations were conducted by a limited number of members. Finally, some institutions, most notably NATO and the European Union, have cited humanitarian justifications for using military force in crises beyond their own regional boundaries, such as in Operation Allied Force in Kosovo (1999) and Operation Artemis in the DRC (2003), respectively. Both operations generated distinctly mixed reactions.

While the R2P and humanitarian intervention are important issues, regional arrangements exhibit many other differences when it comes to conflict management. It is therefore important to map the extent and nature of these variations.[16] In particular, this chapter identifies five different dimensions of regional variation. These relate to the significance attributed in declaratory terms to conflict management; the relative emphasis accorded to conflict prevention, conflict mitigation, or conflict resolution in practice, as well as post-conflict reconstruction/peacebuilding; the institutional framework available to engage in conflict management; the techniques adopted and instruments employed; and the geographic scope of the arrangement's conflict management activities.

The Significance of Conflict Management

Not all regional arrangements explicitly list conflict management as one of their central tasks. Moreover, those that have done so go about it in different ways: while some focus on conflicts that take place within the membership, others also respond to conflict outside the membership. The European Union, for instance, emerged from the idea that political integration was a crucial means of preventing conflict between European powers.[17] It has been so successful in this regard that serious intermember disputes involving the potential for armed conflict have been almost entirely eradicated. As a result, the European Union is often described as a security community wherein threats have come to be primarily associated with external issues.[18] Moreover, judging by the desire to spread the *acquis communautaire*—the body of EU legislation that candidate countries must adopt to become members—the European Union clearly sees the expansion of liberal democratic and economic systems as beneficial to conflict management processes in the wider region.

ASEAN is usually viewed as a regional arrangement whose primary purpose is to strengthen mutual confidence among members. But it also enjoys a reputation of having helped maintain peace and stability in Southeast Asia, notwithstanding the existence of a plethora of mostly bilateral territorial disputes and political conflict and the absence of any tried and tested "ASEAN peace process."[19] Nevertheless, key legal documents of the association contain an explicit focus on the settlement of disputes, such as the 1976 Treaty of Amity and Cooperation and ASEAN's newly adopted charter (2008). Similarly, the ASEAN Regional Forum (ARF) has identified three stages of security cooperation: (1) confidence building, (2) preventive diplomacy, and (3) the elaboration of approaches to conflict. The latter is not being pursued in practice, however.

Despite the involvement of some regional arrangements in conflict management, there are only a few regional security arrangements that identify conflict management in relation to intrastate/internal issues as a political objective, let alone a priority. For instance, the SCO is one such organization that has prioritized the challenges posed by nonstate groupings pursuing terrorism, separatism, and religious extremism but has not yet focused on the many territorial or transnational issues that strain bilateral ties among its members.[20] In Africa, on the other hand, the continent's various regional arrangements have afforded conflict management in general and intrastate issues in particular a central role. The African Union's Constitutive Act, for instance, places a heavy emphasis on conflict management. The peaceful resolution of conflicts is one of the organization's foundational principles, and conflict management is listed as one of the central functions of its supreme organ, the Assembly of Heads of State and Government. ECOWAS has also devoted a considerable degree of attention to conflict management after identifying it as the major impediment to regional development and prosperity.

The Focus of Conflict Management

Conflict management is an umbrella term, defined here as action to promote the prevention, mitigation, and resolution of conflict, including initiatives devoted to post-conflict reconstruction. For our purposes, however, it is useful to examine the relative emphasis regional organizations place on these particular dimensions of conflict management. ASEAN, for example, has traditionally focused mostly on conflict prevention, especially on the basis of promoting shared norms about interstate conduct. In contrast, it has played a far less prominent role in collectively mitigating specific intramural conflicts. Even in the event of escalating bilateral conflict between members, the association has generally not visibly intervened, as illustrated by the grouping's silence with respect to gunboat diplomacy involving Indonesia and Malaysia in 2005 or the border skirmishes between Thailand and Myanmar in 2001–02. ASEAN's position is evolving, however. When the border dispute between Thailand and Cambodia over Preah Vihear erupted again in 2008, the association's other members not only publicly called for the situation to be addressed peacefully but ASEAN foreign ministers also offered to facilitate a diplomatic solution by establishing a Contact Group, because they recognized that the border dispute could result in the use of force and disrupt regional peace and stability. In the event, the resolution of this conflict has been left to the concerned parties. In a similar vein, the ARF has emphasized confidence-building and preventive diplomacy as the focal areas of security dialogue and cooperation. It has not normally taken to pursuing conflict mitigation strategies in disputes between two or more of its participants.

In West Africa, in contrast, conflict prevention has been a relatively recent area of concern. Traditionally, ECOWAS had focused on conflict mitigation and invested most operational effort into peacekeeping operations. It was not until early 2008 that the organization adopted its Conflict Prevention Framework. Among other things, this emphasized the organization's renewed declaratory focus on human security and the need to prevent intrastate as well as interstate conflicts.[21] Other regional organizations have also tended to focus more on the peacebuilding side of the equation. The European Union is a particularly notable example, having conducted more than twenty peacebuilding or security sector reform missions in several continents.[22]

The Institutional Framework

Regional security arrangements clearly do not pursue conflict management in the same manner. There are two important factors to differentiate here. First, regional arrangements differ in terms of the mechanisms or bodies that their participants vow to establish in order to undertake conflict management activities. Importantly, even where regional security arrangements actually pursue particular forms of conflict management with similar vigor, they may opt for quite different institutional frameworks. The second aspect is efficacy and concerns the question of whether this institutional framework actually affords the regional security arrangement the possibility to undertake conflict management in practice. For instance, the ASEAN countries agreed in 1976 to include in the legally binding Treaty of Amity and Cooperation a provision on the establishment of an ASEAN High Council that in particular circumstances was to adjudicate between claimants to a dispute. The ASEAN High Council has to this day not been established. In the same way, following the establishment of ASEAN-10, members formally endorsed the establishment of the ASEAN troika as an ad hoc body in order to address "urgent and important regional political and security issues and situations of common concern likely to disturb regional peace and harmony."[23] That framework too has not been invoked. Similar stories are evident in the Americas where the OAS has never applied its official Treaty on Pacific Settlement of Disputes (the Pact of Bogota, 1948) and in Africa where the Organization of African Unity's (OAU) Commission for Mediation, Conciliation and Arbitration never became operational after it was established in 1965.[24]

With the exception of some areas of the European Union's activities, regional arrangements usually adopt intergovernmental forms of decision making. This is hardly surprising given the emphasis most states place on retaining their sovereign independence. More specifically, when it comes to issues of peace and security, consensus seems to be the most common method by which regional arrangements take decisions. Importantly, consensus is not usually considered the same as unanimity: whereas the latter requires each member to express their explicit approval for a course of action—usually through a vote—the former requires only that members agree not to publicly voice their dissatisfaction with the chosen course of action. Examples of arrangements opting for consensus as opposed to unanimity would include the "silence procedure" adopted by NATO and the Organization for Security and Co-operation in Europe.[25] In ASEAN's case, the so-called ASEAN way, which also emphasizes consensus, has prevented a larger role for the grouping with regard to conflict management.[26] The European Union, on the other hand, requires unanimous support (expressed in the form of a vote) for some of its actions and positions taken under its Common Foreign and Security Policy pillar.

Decision-making procedures within regional arrangements also differ according to whether authority to take decisions related to conflict management is delegated to organs composed of subsets of the membership. One example of such delegated authority is the decision taken by the fifteen member states in ECOWAS to delegate authority on peace and security issues to the smaller Mediation and Security Council.[27] A second example is the decision taken by the African Union's fifty-three members to delegate authority in matters of conflict management to its Peace and Security Council. Comprising fifteen members, the council has made its decisions by consensus, although officially in the event of a deadlock it may exercise a vote requiring approval by a two-thirds majority. The reliance on consensus has not been entirely uncontroversial, however. In particular, it raised some difficulties when the African Union tried to formulate mandates for its peace operations in cases where one of the parties to the conflict concerned was also a member of the Peace and Security Council, as was the case in both the AU mission in Sudan (AMIS) and the AU mission in Somalia (AMISOM).

A related aspect of procedural variation is the extent to which a regional arrangement's members envisage the secretariat or commission playing a significant role in decision making. Regional arrangements vary significantly in the size of the bureaucracies they fund and in how significant and proactive a role they permit their secretary-general and other senior officials to play in conflict management. Other things being equal, regional arrangements with efficient bureaucracies will be able to oversee a wider range of conflict management activities than those that do not invest heavily in such personnel.[28] At one end of the spectrum are those organizations such as the European Union and NATO that invest in large, well-trained bureaucracies and which expect their senior officials to play significant roles in conflict management.[29] Other arrangements place more weight on senior officials. The OAS secretary general, for instance, is expected to bring to the attention of the General Assembly or the Permanent Council issues that might threaten peace, security, or the development of the member states. Similarly, the first head of the AU Commission, Alpha Konaré, was the former president of Mali and played an important role in exercising leverage on behalf of the AU Commission. Indeed, some analysts went as far as to suggest that "as the custodian of AU documents, as well as the maker and interpreter of rules, procedures and regulations, [the commission] acquired unlimited and overwhelming power."[30]

Finally, it is important to note that regional arrangements sometimes take decisions and actions that do not conform to their official procedures. The military enforcement operations in Lesotho (1998) and the DRC (1998) ostensibly carried out under the auspices of the Southern African Development Community (SADC), for example, were both launched by factions of the membership that ignored the organization's formal decision-making rules. A similar situation occurred in 1990 when the ECOWAS military operation in Liberia was deployed without following the organization's proper rules.[31]

Techniques and Instruments

Regional arrangements differ considerably over what instruments they consider to be most legitimate and effective for promoting peace and security. Indeed, as Paul Diehl has observed, "Even when common mechanisms [of conflict management] exist, the salience, operations, and strategies can vary tremendously across regions."[32]

Once a regional arrangement has decided to include a particular conflict on its agenda, it may choose to legitimize a range of possible responses. In some cases, the arrangement might engage in some form of collective action such as launching a peace operation or delegating a member state or a coalition of member states to take the lead in conflict management activities. Alternatively, the arrangement might endorse action taken by a coalition composed of a mixture of member states and external actors. In another setting, the arrangement's members may decide to contribute economic resources or personnel to initiatives led by an external entity such as the United Nations or a powerful state. If the regional arrangement sees itself playing a role in the response it may differ from other arrangements in terms of determining what constitutes the most appropriate instruments of conflict management in the case at hand.

The list of potential techniques and instruments of conflict management is considerable, including the use of military force, the imposition of economic sanctions, and the application of diplomacy and other confidence-building measures.[33] Regional security arrangements will naturally seek to draw on different instruments and techniques as appropriate to the specific conflict in question. Although relatively rare, regional arrangements have sought recourse to legal mechanisms to arbitrate disputes among their members. Within Africa, for example, a number of intramural territorial disputes have been submitted to legal arbitration, including those between Ethiopia and Eritrea, and Nigeria and Cameroon. While the former appears to have been unsuccessful, the use of an expert commission in the latter case does seem to have worked.

Arguably the most common conflict management technique used by regional arrangements is negotiation and mediation, although organizations differ over the extent to which these are best carried out bilaterally by individual members or collectively by representatives of the arrangement. For instance, in recent cases in which ASEAN members have accepted third-party involvement to address domestic conflict situations, they have relied on individual members (for example, Malaysia and Brunei) and even nonstate actors and international organizations rather than on the organization as a whole (for example, in the case of Aceh). By comparison, the African Union has in recent years tended to use both groups of el-

Table 3.2 Examples of Peace Operations Conducted by Regional Arrangements since 1990

Organization	Peace operations
African Union	Burundi (2003–04), Sudan (2004–present); the Comoros (2006, 2007, 2008), Somalia (2007–present)
Commonwealth of Independent States	Abkhazia, Georgia (1994–present), Tajikistan (1993–2003)
Economic and Monetary Community of Central African States	Central African Republic (2002–present)
Economic Community of West African States	Liberia (1990–99, 2003), Côte d'Ivoire (2002–03), Guinea Bissau (1998–99), Sierra Leone (1997–2000)
European Union (military operations)	Macedonia (2003–05), Bosnia (2004–present), Chad (2008–present), Democratic Republic of Congo (2003, 2006)
Intergovernmental Authority on Development	Somalia (2005) [authorized but never deployed]
North Atlantic Treaty Organization	Bosnia and Herzegovina (1995–2003), Kosovo (1999–present), Macedonia (1999–2003), Afghanistan (2003–present)
Pacific Islands Forum	Solomon Islands (2003–present)
Southern African Development Community	Lesotho (1998–99), Democratic Republic of Congo (1998–2002)

der statespeople to help mediate on its behalf and—in a more traditional manner—individuals to act as special envoys to a conflict.

Collective peacekeeping is a tool employed by a growing number of regional arrangements but nowhere near a majority. Understood as operations involving the deployment of foreign, uniformed personnel to support a peace process, it is clear that some regional arrangements see this as an important part of their conflict management role, whereas other arrangements do not.[34] Table 3.2 provides a list of regional arrangements that have undertaken collective peace operations since 1990.

Another related point of contention is whether regional arrangements should consider enforcement measures to be a legitimate tool of conflict management. Coercive instruments or sanctions come in three main varieties: diplomatic, economic, and military. In relation to military sanctions, some organizations, such as the OAS and ASEAN, have not attempted to develop mechanisms for the collective use of force, while others have worked hard to ensure that they are able to conduct military enforcement measures. Among the most prominent examples of regionalized military enforcement have been NATO's operations in Bosnia (1995) and Kosovo (1999), ECOWAS's interventions in Liberia (1990) and Sierra Leone (1997), SADC's missions in Lesotho (1998) and the DRC (1998), the European Union's Operation Artemis in the DRC (2003), and the African Union's Operation Democracy in the Comoros (2008). In sum, while some regional arrangements rule out the use of military force on principled grounds, others will consider it on a case-by-case basis.[35]

It is more common for regional arrangements to countenance the use of economic or diplomatic sanctions in certain circumstances, particularly when internal conflicts result in some sort of illegitimate regime change. The African Union, for example, has suspended members that have undergone an "unconstitutional change of government" from participating in the institution, as happened recently when military coups took place in Togo (2005), Mauritania (2005 and 2008), and Guinea (2008). Since the 1997 coup in Sierra Leone, ECOWAS has adopted a similar practice, most recently in relation to Togo (2005) and Guinea (2008). The Commonwealth has also suspended members from its councils following a military coup, as happened in Pakistan (1999) and the Fiji Islands (2006), or after fraudulent elections, as in the case of Zimbabwe (2002). SADC, on the other hand, refused to sanction Zimbabwe's ruling regime despite overwhelming evidence of fraud and intimidation in successive elections. Similarly, in Central Asia, the SCO has not envisaged imposing sanctions against one of its members. In the ASEAN Security Community Plan of Action of November 2004, ASEAN states made a declaratory commitment not to condone unconstitutional and undemocratic changes of government, a commitment that in effect equally favors the incumbents of the more democratic states and the region's nondemocracies. In any event, the organization stayed silent on the 2006 coup against Thailand's then prime minister Thaksin Shinawatra. Nevertheless, the 2008 ASEAN Charter broadly highlights participants' principled commitment to the rule of law, good governance, democracy, and constitutional government.

Geographic Scope

The final dimension of regional variation examines how the arrangement thinks about its role in relation to wider processes of global politics, specifically whether it sees itself playing a role beyond its borders. As noted earlier, some regional arrangements are developing common foreign and security policies that require "out-of-area" action. This trend is most pronounced with respect to the European Union and NATO, both of which have engaged in numerous conflict management activities beyond their borders, including military operations and economic sanctions. While the European Union's military missions have centered on the Balkans and the DRC, NATO's operations have focused on the Balkans and Afghanistan. Both organizations have also recently been involved in responding to piracy along the Somali coastline. These activities have been justified on various grounds, including self-defense, the need to respond to challenges of global significance, and the need to address security challenges as early and as near to the source as possible. Beyond the European Union and NATO, however, regional arrangements tend to confine most of their practical activities to their own regions (although they will often make statements on issues beyond their borders). This is certainly true for ECOWAS, ASEAN, and the SCO. One of the only exceptions is the African Union's recent claim that when its African Standby Force (ASF) is operational it might operate outside Africa. As one of the African Union's recent documents put it, "Nothing precludes the ASF from deploying outside Africa, either as a contribution to a UN force or as a rapid reaction capability."[36]

Sources of Regional Variation

As the preceding section indicated, there is considerable variation in how regional arrangements approach issues of conflict management. Yet, as Paul Diehl concluded, "differences in conflict management responses cannot be wholly or even partly explained by reference to the regional variation in threats [because] divergence across regions is greater with respect to responses than threats.... Even when similar threats exist, regions may pursue very different responses."[37]

Such differences can be explained with reference to four clusters of factors: the exercise of political power, domestic political variables, ideational factors, and collective capacities. In practice, these factors are clearly interconnected in complex ways. They are discussed separately here for analytical purposes only. In addition, it is important to point out that, to date, the literature has tended to neglect the role played by ideational factors, specifically what might be referred to as a shared security culture. This embodies the collective dispositions and habits of participants in the regional arrangement with regard to the promotion of peace and security. In particular, a security culture expresses a consensus about what conflict situations belong on the collective agenda and what practical approaches are the most appropriate responses to the challenge at hand.

Exercise of Political Power

One prominent explanation for how regional security arrangements behave revolves around the influence of extraregional and intraregional hegemons. In relation to the former, the extent of external penetration in, and foreign influence exercised over, the region in question will undoubtedly affect the organization's behavior.[38] In the contemporary era, the extent of external penetration and influence over different regional arrangements remains the subject of intense debates, particularly the extent to which regional arrangements are influenced by outside pressures such as U.S. hegemony or are shaped by the way in which regional members choose to "localize" external influences.[39] External influence may also affect a region's conflict management agenda in a variety of ways. Since the terrorist attacks of September 11, 2001, a particularly prominent example has been the debates within many regions over whether to pursue military solutions to particular domestic conflict situations, perhaps even involving the possible use of foreign forces.

The direction and nature of the responses developed by regional security arrangements may also be shaped by a local hegemon. This is an important consideration because many of the world's regions have coalesced around a local hegemon. Amitav Acharya and Alastair Iain Johnston, for example, concluded that "regional institutions in several parts of the Third World do reflect the interests and preferences (or at least contestations over such preferences) of regionally powerful actors."[40] In relation to conflict management, the presence of a hegemon will likely affect not only the range of issues that make it onto the regional arrangement's agenda but also the range of permissible responses. In West Africa, for example, ECOWAS has not played a role in addressing the conflict in Nigeria's Delta states. A similar situation was apparent in the Commonwealth of Independent States, which played no role in responding to the conflicts in the Russian province of Chechnya. Regional arrangements containing a local hegemon must therefore work out ways to engage with it. How this is done will usually have significant repercussions for the region's approach to conflict management.

Domestic Politics

Another common explanation for the behavior of regional arrangements can be located in domestic political variables within the region's states. One recent example is Benjamin Miller's "theory of regional war and peace." This claims to explain why some regions "are particularly war-prone, while others are so peaceful that war among the regional states has become practically unthinkable."[41] Specifically, Miller argues that

> the "state-to-nation balance" is the key underlying cause that affects the disposition of a region toward war. . . . It refers to the degree of congruence between the divi-

sion of the region into territorial states and the national aspirations and political identifications of the region's peoples. This balance also refers to the prevalence of strong versus weak states in the region. There is a state-to-nation imbalance when there is a lack of congruence between states and national identifications and at least some of the regional states are weak states.[42]

Miller's arguments chime with earlier literature that stressed the importance of domestic political variables, including state weakness, in understanding patterns of regional conflict management.[43] Acharya and Johnston, for example, concluded that domestic politics was the "most important common factor shaping institutional design" and that "the more insecure the regimes, the less intrusive are their regional institutions."[44] This point has been demonstrated well in relation to the Arab League, which was purposely designed to avoid producing cooperation and integration that could have weakened political leaders in member states.[45] To stop this from happening, the Arab League generally abstained from intervening in conflicts involving competing blocks of transnational coalitions.[46]

Another variant of this perspective can be seen in Etel Solingen's argument that the strength of domestic political coalitions can help explain institutional genesis, design, and effects in other regions beyond the Middle East.[47] In her view, "domestic politics provide more complete accounts of why institutions emerge, in whose interest they operate, when they are allowed to play a significant role, and why they may not be vital to—or a sine qua non for—cooperation."[48] Accordingly, a concern with regime security exhibited by participants in regional arrangements would thus not only reflect the dominant interests of domestic elites but also affect the nature of the norms, procedures, and capacity of the arrangements. Specifically, regions with a critical mass of weak states are likely to "generate regional international organizations that reinforce, not erode, sovereignty."[49] In Africa, insecure governments have clearly used regional arrangements to enhance their regime security.[50] Roy Allison has made essentially the same point with respect to Central Asia by highlighting the function of regional arrangements for the region's authoritarian governments as one of "protective integration"—that is, protective integration for the regimes concerned.[51] The implication for conflict management is simple: weak states governed by insecure regimes will design organizations that are reluctant to challenge state sovereignty, and the arrangements they construct will very likely favor quite limited roles in conflict management.

Security Culture

Conflict management variation also reflects security culture—that is, shared dispositions regarding particular approaches to protecting values. Culture is not solely confined to modes of thought but is also manifested in specific norms and practices. It therefore provides a structural ideational context wherein certain dispositions have become routinely expressed and certain behaviors have been taken for granted. This conception of culture is similar to Pierre Bourdieu's concept of *habitus*. Habitus sets structural limits for action and generates perceptions, aspirations, and practices that correspond to the structuring properties of earlier socialization.[52] A shared security culture also tends to take the form of common discourses that are themselves actualized in habitual practices.[53] That said, at times the elements of a shared security culture may be seemingly at odds with the formal declarations of regional security arrangements.

Dispositions and practices concerning the use of force are but one component of a broader security culture.[54] Adopting this broader perspective is necessary on the grounds that most if not all participants of regional arrangements now operate with a comprehensive understanding of security and consider a range of policy tools to address security and conflict. The dispositions associated with a particular security culture will depend on the regional arrangement in question, and its members are likely to differ about its role and the legitimacy and the likely efficacy of collective action.

A useful distinction may be drawn between a culture's central tenets and its operational assumptions.[55] Applying this distinction to security culture, the central tenets would involve shared basic assumptions about, for instance, the importance of particular referents of security (for example, region, state, regime, community, or individual), the significant dimensions of security (military, political, economic, and so on), the nature of the general political-security environment (benign or difficult), the causes of regional conflict, and the basic security purposes of the regional arrangement. Operational assumptions, on the other hand, will concern more practical questions about, for instance, whether particular issues should be understood as a security threat, how to determine the most appropriate relationship between the regional arrangement and its individual members in particular cases, and which policy instruments are likely to be the most effective, feasible, and legitimate in view of a particular conflict at hand. A security culture thus includes a set of ideas about certain (effective and legitimate) responses to challenges that delimit the range of appropriate options available to the regional arrangement. For example, ASEAN members do not consider the collective use of military force to intervene in interstate or intrastate conflicts to be an option, while members of the African Union or NATO might.

The existence of a security culture at a regional level implies what Alexander Wendt has called "interlocking beliefs," whereby actors not only share the same beliefs but also assume that other actors think as they do.[56] In practice, however, we are usually dealing with a "majoritarian conception of culture," which is able to accommodate a degree of divergence or occasional contestation, particularly in the event of threats to vital material or political interests.[57] For example, in the late 1990s, ASEAN states demonstrated the resilience of entrenched dispositions when Thailand was engaged in a series of debates about the concept of "flexible engagement." This concept broached the issue of whether ASEAN should significantly adapt its longstanding practice of noninterference in response to new transnational challenges, most immediately those spilling over from the conflict in neighboring Myanmar.[58]

As defined here, a regional security culture shapes both the dispositions of state leaderships and the *collective* action undertaken by regional arrangements. As John Duffield has argued,

> The overall effect of culture is to predispose collectivities toward certain actions and policies rather than others. Some options will simply not be imagined. Of those that are contemplated, some are more likely to be rejected as inappropriate, ineffective, or counterproductive than others. To be sure, culture is not deterministic. It may not and often does not precisely determine behavior. But it can significantly narrow the range of actions likely to be adopted in any given set of circumstances.[59]

We are therefore more likely to see gradual changes within regional structures rather than a sudden and radical break with the past. To take just two examples, the ARF's development remains heavily influenced by ASEAN's security culture despite efforts by some participants to push the forum in the direction of practical security cooperation.[60] In addition, although the African Union tried to break with tradition in some significant respects, it could not completely divorce itself from many of the norms and priorities of its predecessor, the OAU.[61] As a consequence, it is fair to conclude that once institutional designs are established, they "tend to linger and create a path dependency that shapes the response of institutions to future challenges."[62]

Insofar as there is a habitus relative to conflict management, security culture will shape the way regional decision makers perceive events, pressures, and conditions, and hence the choices that state leaderships make in the context of regional cooperation.[63] Security culture will thus help explain why a regional arrangement does or does not become involved in meeting particular categories of threats and how it might respond. A shared security culture at the regional level will also shape, and often limit, the behavioral choices of a regional arrangement and its participants through perceptions and aspirations regarding collective action in response to particular conflicts.[64] Security culture will help explain why regional arrangements adopt a "yes-we-can," "no-we-can't," or "don't-go-there" approach to particular conflict issues.

Collective Capacity

In addition to these other explanations, at a very basic level it seems obvious that certain types of conflict management require the availability of particular capacities and capabilities. For instance, regional peacekeeping would not unreasonably be linked to the existence of relevant coordinating mechanisms and a pool of military or civilian contingents trained for the purpose. The absence of collective capacity thus need not reflect a lack of political will or institutional design flaws, but in extreme cases regional peacekeeping efforts can hinge on the limited availability of financial resources.

Although at a fundamental level material factors are always related to the way actors think about their environment, material constraints can influence the choices exercised by regional arrangements in significant ways. As David Lake and Patrick Morgan have concluded, material constraints will generally "matter most in extremely 'tight' systems of constraints or over the long run."[65] Here it is worth identifying two types of material constraints: the overall level of the resources available to members and the size of the budget allocated to the regional arrangement. Both will have some impact on how the regional arrangement approaches conflict management issues.

First, the collective activities of regional arrangements will clearly be affected by the level of resources available to their members. Of particular importance here are levels of gross domestic product/gross national income, development, and political commitment to conflict management. Other things being equal, regional arrangements whose members have access to greater levels of resources will be able to take on a greater variety of conflict management tasks, unless such resources are made available by external parties.

This feeds into the issue of budget allocation. Just because members of a regional arrangement are endowed with resources, this does not mean they will necessarily bestow the regional arrangement with significant capabilities. Think, for instance, of the vast levels of wealth controlled by many governments in the Middle East and the limited budget available to the Arab League. Small organizational budgets are also evident in both the Americas and Africa. In 2008, for example, OAS members were expected to give the organization only $93 million.[66] Similarly, between 1993 and 2005, the OAU/AU Peace Fund received a total of only $68 million—a paltry sum as far as peacekeeping operations are concerned. In an attempt to secure a sustainable source of funds for the organization, the AU Assembly ruled that from January 1, 2006, 75 percent of its funds would be supplied by just five member states (Algeria, Egypt, Libya, Nigeria, and

South Africa), each of which now contributes 15 percent of the African Union's regular budget.

Resources and budgets are important precisely because they allow regional arrangements to develop capabilities in particular areas. Even with plentiful amounts of money it is impossible to conduct certain conflict management activities without the right sort of capabilities. To mediate effectively one needs trained mediators; to keep the peace one needs trained peacekeepers; to run projects efficiently one needs skilled managers; and so on. The critical issue here is whether the members of the regional arrangement actually endow the arrangement with relevant capabilities for conflict management beyond the costs of a basic bureaucracy. Assuming that they do, there is a choice: do the members try and develop shared corporate assets, or do they donate their own national capabilities to regional projects? The vast majority of regional arrangements tend to work with the latter model. This is not surprising given the relatively low levels of political integration exhibited by most regional arrangements, especially in the developing world.

Beyond Regional Arrangements

The variation among regional approaches to conflict management inevitably implies that while some regional arrangements address particular conflicts, others do not. This warrants a brief examination of how conflicts are addressed when a relevant regional arrangement chooses not to deal with them. In principle, there are three broad alternatives, at least as regards interstate and intrastate conflict: first, the conflict is addressed by parties external to the membership of the arrangement (involving the United Nations, major powers, global players, or nonstate actors); second, other regional arrangements, perhaps with partially overlapping participation, become involved; third, member states deal with the conflict themselves—for instance, either by using negotiations or other foreign policy instruments to settle bilateral issues, or by employing their security forces if the issue is intrastate. Significantly, in the third case, addressing conflict may also involve significant capacity building that is reliant in particular on major or middle powers with relevant interests. For example, the government of the Philippines has benefited from substantial capacity building from the United States and Australia that allows the country's armed forces to decide in its favor longstanding conflicts with insurgent and terrorist groups.

The United States has also been at the forefront of organizing bilateral or multilateral military training that allows regional states to foster their respective capacity to engage in the use of force against armed groups. The Ethiopian troops that ousted the Union of Islamic Courts authorities in Somalia in December 2006, for example, had received training and assistance from the United States before the campaign and enjoyed intelligence support and assistance from U.S. Special Forces during it.[67] Notably, this kind of conflict management should not necessarily be seen as being at odds with the regional security culture. Indeed, while security culture will influence the collective policies of regional arrangements, individual member states may well choose to pursue conflict management outside this institutional context—individually or with perhaps a small number of fellow members or even outsiders, particularly where vital interests are threatened.

Another important example of external capacity building for conflict management is the UN effort to establish a standby team of mediation experts to help address regional deficits. Although it is clear that the United Nations has been the most significant peacekeeping actor for several decades, it has recently started to explore ways to boost regional conflict management capacities, especially in Africa.[68] At the launch of the mediation standby team in early 2008, B. Lynn Pascoe, UN under-secretary-general for political affairs, said there were conflict-ridden areas of the world in which regional expertise was not enough to address entrenched problems and where specific expertise was needed. This UN initiative was designed to help fill such regional gaps. Consequently, decisions about where to deploy these experts will be taken by the United Nations in consultation with the relevant regional organizations.[69]

Conclusions and Prospects

This chapter has discussed how regional arrangements vary in the extent to which they engage with particular types of conflicts and identified five dimensions of variation in relation to regional conflict management. Such variation can be understood with reference to the interplay of four clusters of factors: the exercise of political power, domestic political variables, ideational factors (specifically, a shared security culture), and the level of collective capacities. Understanding the relative importance of these clusters will require more detailed empirical research of the sort provided in region-specific chapters in this volume. That said, we submit that where a shared regional security culture has developed among participants of a regional arrangement, a distinct approach to dealing with conflict will be evident. Such cultures may lead some arrangements to adopt a "yes-we-can" approach while others will argue "no, we can't." After all, not all conflict necessarily animates regional arrangements to resort to collective conflict management. This usually requires both the conflict to be perceived as a threat to regional security and consensus among participants that a collective response is warranted and legitimate. Accordingly, the existence of a regional security culture does not automatically imply that regional arrangements will always be the primary vehicle of conflict management.

Although predictions are inherently problematic, we suggest that three areas of debate in particular are likely to influence the future of regional conflict management around the world: the relationship between democracy and regional security; civilian protection and the R2P; and the involvement of civil society in conflict management.

The first issue is the place of democracy promotion and its relationship to issues of regional conflict management—specifically, to what extent have the participants of a regional arrangement internalized a shared understanding regarding the link between democratic governance and security as concerns conflict prevention or even conflict resolution.[70] While some regional organizations have endorsed the idea that democratic governance is an important dimension of conflict management, others remain skeptical of this idea and concerned about its potential ramifications. Clearly the European Union and NATO both hold liberal democracy as an important part of the criteria for membership. In contrast, most other organizations have not fully internalized a commitment to democracy and do not place great weight on the requirement of democratic governance structures in order to be better able to address regional security and conflict management. ASEAN is one such case.[71] That said, some regional arrangements have at least endorsed declarations that suggest there is an important relationship between regional stability and democratic forms of governance. Both the Inter-American Democratic Charter (2001) and the ECOWAS Protocol on Democracy and Good Governance (2001), for example, emphasize the positive correlation between democratic governance at home and regional security and stability.

A second area of substantive debate will revolve around whether and how to apply the R2P in practice. According to the UN secretary-general, the R2P rests on three pillars.[72] The first pillar refers to the responsibility of each state to use appropriate and necessary means to protect its own population from genocide, war crimes, ethnic cleansing, and crimes against humanity, as well as from their incitement. The second pillar refers to the commitment that UN member states will help each other exercise this responsibility. The third pillar refers to international society's collective responsibility to respond through the United Nations in a timely and decisive manner, using Chapters VI–VIII of the UN Charter as appropriate, when national authorities are manifestly failing to protect their populations from the four crimes listed above. To date, regional arrangements have adopted different stances on the R2P, ranging from solid support (for example, the European Union) to barely concealed hostility (for example, the Arab League). In practice, regional arrangements will continue to debate what situations fall under the R2P rubric, what constitutes an appropriate balance between the preventive and reactive aspects of the R2P agenda, and whether and how to protect civilians caught up in deadly intrastate conflicts.

A third important issue in debates about conflict management concerns the relationship between states and nonstate actors within the context of regional arrangements. Some regional organizations are clearly more statist in their mode of operation than others. That is, while some regions have encouraged associations within civil society to participate in their conflict management structures, others have remained exclusive forums for interstate dialogue. This debate will in turn inspire more discussion about whether intrastate conflict should occupy a more prominent place in the agendas of regional arrangements. Similar to the aforementioned issues, it will also invite discussion about whether particular security cultures should be reevaluated in light of whose security is to be protected.

Notes

1. Regionalism is a notoriously difficult concept to define. For useful discussions, see Andrew Hurrell, "Regionalism in Theoretical Perspective," in *Regionalism in World Politics*, ed. Louise Fawcett and Andrew Hurrell (Oxford: Oxford University Press, 1995), 37–73; Louise Fawcett, "Exploring Regional Domains: A Comparative History of Regionalism," *International Affairs* 80, no. 3 (2004): 429–46; and Andrew Hurrell, "One World? Many Worlds? The Place of Regions in the Study of International Society," *International Affairs* 83, no. 1 (2007): 127–46.

2. For the former position, see Peter J. Katzenstein, *A World of Regions* (Ithaca, NY: Cornell University Press, 2005). For the latter position, see Mohammed Ayoob, *The Third World Security Predicament* (Boulder, CO: Lynne Rienner, 1995).

3. See, for example, Barry Buzan, *People, States and Fear*, 2nd ed. (Hemel Hempstead: Harvester Wheatsheaf, 1991), 186–229; Louise Fawcett and Andrew Hurrell, eds., *Regionalism in World Politics* (Oxford: Oxford University Press, 1995); David A. Lake and Patrick M. Morgan, eds., *Regional Orders: Building Security in a New World* (University Park, PA: Pennsylvania State University Press, 1997); Björn Hettne, András Inotai, and Osvaldo Sunkel, eds., *The New Regionalism and the Future of Security and Development* (New York: St Martin's Press, 2000); Douglas Lemke, *Regions of War and Peace* (Cambridge: Cambridge University Press, 2002); Barry Buzan and Ole Wæver, *Regions and Powers: The Structure of International Security* (Cambridge: Cambridge University Press, 2003).

4. For example, Paul F. Diehl and Joseph Lepgold, eds., *Regional Conflict Management* (Lanham, MD: Rowman and Littlefield, 2003) and Paul F. Diehl, "New Roles for Regional

Organizations," in *Leashing the Dogs of War*, ed. Chester A. Crocker, Fen Osler Hampson, and Pamela Aall (Washington, DC: United States Institute of Peace Press, 2007), 535–51. The UN Charter does not define "regional arrangement." This chapter adopts the broad definition used by Hans Kelsen as "an international agreement entered into by some, not all, Members of the United Nations." See Hans Kelsen, "Is the North Atlantic Treaty a Regional Arrangement?" *American Journal of International Law* 45, no. 1 (1951): 162.

5. See, for example, Alex J. Bellamy and Paul D. Williams, "Who's Keeping the Peace? Regionalization and Contemporary Peace Operations," *International Security* 29, no. 4 (2005): 157–195; Paul F. Diehl and Young-Im D. Cho, "Passing the Buck in Conflict Management: The Role of Regional Organizations in the Post-Cold War Era," *Brown Journal of World Affairs* 12, no. 2 (2006): 191–202.

6. Fawcett, "Exploring Regional Domains," 441.

7. David A. Lake and Patrick M. Morgan, "The New Regionalism in Security Affairs," in *Regional Orders*, ed. Lake and Morgan, 5.

8. Alyson J. K. Bailes and Andrew Cottey, "Regional Security Cooperation in the Early 21st Century," in *SIPRI Yearbook 2006* (Oxford: Oxford University Press, 2006), 195–98. See also John S. Duffield, "International Security Institutions," in *The Oxford Handbook of Political Institutions*, ed. R. Rhodes et al. (Oxford: Oxford University Press, 2006), 650. One of the few attempts to do so focused on two questions: why do different forms of institutionalization develop in different regions of the world, and do such differences in institutional design influence the effectiveness of regional arrangements? See Amitav Acharya and Alastair Iain Johnston, "Comparing Regional Institutions: An Introduction," in *Crafting Cooperation*, ed. Amitav Acharya and Alastair Iain Johnston (Cambridge: Cambridge University Press, 2007), 2.

9. This chapter uses conflict management as an umbrella term to include attempts to prevent, mitigate, and resolve conflicts.

10. See the Web site of the Uppsala Conflict Data Program, www.pcr.uu.se/research/UCDP/.

11. Stephen M. Saideman, *The Ties That Divide: Ethnic Politics, Foreign Policy and International Conflict* (New York: Columbia University Press, 2001).

12. Some regional arrangements may also take a position on armed conflicts completely external to the region and not involving any members directly. Such external armed conflicts would form a fifth type of conflict, but they are not our primary focus here.

13. UN document A/Res/60/1, October 24, 2005, paragraphs 138–40.

14. See United Nations, *Report of the Secretary-General on Implementing the Responsibility to Protect*, UN document A/63/677, January 12, 2009.

15. See, for example, Jason Ladnier, *Neighbours on Alert: Regional Views on Humanitarian Intervention* (Washington, DC: Fund for Peace, 2003).

16. David A. Lake and Patrick M. Morgan, "Building Security in the New World of Regional Orders," in *Regional Orders*, ed. Lake and Morgan, 347.

17. Ole Wæver, "The EU as a Security Actor," in *International Relations Theory and the Politics of European Integration*, ed. Morten Kelstrup and Michael C. Williams (London: Routlegde, 2000), 250–94.

18. See Emmanuel Adler and Michael Barnett, eds., *Security Communities* (Cambridge: Cambridge University Press, 1998).

19. Michael Leifer, "The ASEAN Peace Process: A Category Mistake," *The Pacific Review* 12, no. 1 (1999): 25–38.

20. Anna Mateeva and Antonio Giustozzi, *The SCO: A Regional Organization in the Making*, Working Paper 39 (London: LSE Crisis States Research Centre, September 2008).

21. *ECOWAS Conflict Prevention Framework*, ECOWAS document Regulation MSC/REG.1/01/08, January 16, 2008.

22. See Bastian Giegerich, *European Military Crisis Management*, Adelphi Paper 397 (Abingdon: Routledge for the International Institute for Strategic Studies, 2008).

23. The ASEAN Troika, Terms of Reference, Bangkok, July 24–25, 2000, www.aseansec.org/3637.htm.

24. On the Pact of Bogota, see Monica Herz, *Does the Organisation of American States Matter?* Working Paper 34 (London: LSE Crisis States Research Centre, April 2008), 10. On the OAU's Commission, see C. O. C. Amate, *Inside the OAU: Pan-Africanism in Practice* (New York: St Martin's Press, 1986), especially 156–67.

25. Within NATO's North Atlantic Council and Military Committee decisions do not require a formal vote. If a state wants to object, it must write a formal letter to NATO's secretary general expressing disapproval. This occurred in February 2003 when Germany, France, and Belgium wrote to the secretary general objecting to the U.S. request that NATO begin planning to provide Turkey with defensive systems in the event of an attack by Iraq during the impending war.

26. See Mely Caballero-Anthony, *Regional Security in Southeast Asia: Beyond the ASEAN Way?* (Singapore: Institute of Southeast Asian Studies, 2005); Jürgen Haacke, *ASEAN's Diplomatic and Security Culture: Origins, Development and Prospects* (London: Routledge Curzon, 2003).

27. Nine member states sit on the ECOWAS Mediation and Security Council. It has a quorum when two-thirds of its members are present. Decisions are taken by a two-thirds majority vote of members present.

28. One recent study noted that while some arrangements are run with as few as twenty to fifty staff (for example, the Inter-governmental Authority on Development, or IGAD), others hire many thousands (for example, the European Union, which has 25,000 workers). *Capacity Survey: Regional and Other Intergovernmental Organizations in the Maintenance of Peace and Security* (Brussels: United Nations University–Comparative Regional Intergration Studies, 2008), 6.

29. On the importance of expert bureaucrats within the European Union and NATO, see, respectively, Jolyon Howorth, "Discourse, Ideas and Epistemic Communities in European Security and Defence Policy," *West European Politics* 27, no. 2 (2004): 211–34; and Robert B. McCalla, "NATO's Persistence after the Cold War," *International Organization* 50, no. 3 (1996): 445–75.

30. Samuel M. Makinda and F. Wafula Okumu, *The African Union* (London: Routledge Curzon, 2008), 51.

31. See Katharina P. Coleman, *International Organisations and Peace Enforcement* (Cambridge: Cambridge University Press, 2007), chapters 3–5.

32. Paul F. Diehl, "Conclusion," in *Regional Conflict Management*, ed. Diehl and Lepgold, 274.

33. See Chester A. Crocker, Fen Osler Hampson, and Pamela Aall, ed., *Leashing the Dogs of War* (Washington, DC: United States Institute of Peace Press, 2007).

34. For an overview, see Donald Daniel, Patricia Taft, and Sharon Wiharta, eds., *Peace Operations* (Washington, DC: Georgetown University Press, 2008).

35. An important and related legal issue is the fact that Article 53 of the UN Charter clearly states that regional arrangements may not use military force without the prior authorization of the UN Security Council. In practice, however, several of the operations conducted by ECOWAS, NATO, and SADC were carried out without the UN Security Council's explicit authorization.

36. African Union, *Harmonized Doctrine for Peace Support Operations*, AU document, October 2006, chapter 5, paragraph 12c.

37. Diehl, "Conclusion," 274.

38. See Buzan and Wæver, *Regions and Powers*.

39. For the former position, see Katzenstein, *A World of Regions*. For the latter position, see Amitav Acharya, "The Emerging Regional Architecture of World Politics," *World Politics* 59, no. 4 (2007): 629–52.

40. Acharya and Johnston, "Comparing Regional Institutions," 19.

41. Benjamin Miller, *States, Nations and the Great Powers* (Cambridge: Cambridge University Press, 2007), 1–2. This idea is most commonly discussed with reference to the concept of a "security community." See Adler and Barnett, eds., *Security Communities*.

42. Miller, *States*, 2.

43. See, for example, Ayoob, *The Third World Security Predicament*.

44. Amitav Acharya and Alastair Iain Johnston, "Conclusion," in *Crafting Cooperation*, ed. Amitav Acharya and Alastair Iain Johnston (Cambridge: Cambridge University Press, 2007), 259, 262. Acharya and Johnston identify five major features of institutional design: membership (that is, the number of actors allowed to participate); scope (that is, the range of issues that the institution is designed to handle); formal rules (that is, regulations governing how decisions are made); norms (that is, the formal and informal ideology of the institution); and mandate (that is, the institution's overall purpose).

45. Michael Barnett and Etel Solingen, "Designed to Fail or Failure of Design? The Origins and Legacy of the Arab League," in *Crafting Cooperation*, ed. Amitav Acharya and Alastair Iain Johnston (Cambridge: Cambridge University Press, 2007), 180–220.

46. Barnett and Solingen, "Designed to Fail or Failure of Design?" 214.

47. Etel Solingen, "The Genesis, Design and Effects of Regional Institutions: Lessons from East Asia and the Middle East," *International Studies Quarterly* 52, no. 2 (2008): 261–94.

48. Solingen, "The Genesis, Design and Effects of Regional Institutions," 289.

49. Robert E. Kelly, "Security Theory in the 'New Regionalism,'" *International Studies Review* 9, no. 2 (2007): 218.

50. Jeffrey Herbst, "Crafting Regional Cooperation in Africa," in *Crafting Cooperation*, ed. Amitav Acharya and Alastair Iain Johnston (Cambridge: Cambridge University Press, 2007), 129–44.

51. Roy Allison, "Virtual Regionalism, Regional Structures and Regime Security in Central Asia," *Central Asian Survey* 27, no. 2 (2008): 185–202.

52. David Swartz, *Culture and Power: The Sociology of Pierre Bourdieu* (Chicago: University of Chicago Press, 1997), 103. For applications of such a conception of culture as practice, see Peter Jackson, "Pierre Bourdieu, the 'Cultural Turn' and the Practice of International History," *Review of International Studies* 34, no. 1 (2008): 155–81, and Michael C. Williams, *Culture and Security: Symbolic Power and the Politics of International Security* (London: Routledge, 2007).

53. See Iver B. Neumann and Henrikki Heikka, "Grand Strategy, Strategic Culture, Practice," *Cooperation and Conflict* 40, no. 1 (2005): 5–23.

54. For a discussion of strategic culture, which focuses on questions related to the use of military force, see Alastair Iain Johnston, *Cultural Realism: Strategic Culture and Grand Strategy in Chinese History* (Princeton, NJ: Princeton University Press, 1995).

55. Johnston, *Cultural Realism*, 37.

56. Alexander Wendt, *Social Theory of International Politics* (Cambridge: Cambridge University Press, 1999), 159–60.

57. Christoph Meyer, "Convergence towards a European Strategic Culture? A Constructivist Framework for Explaining Changing Norms," *European Journal of International Relations* 11, no. 4 (2005): 529.

58. See Jürgen Haacke, "The Concept of Flexible Engagement and the Practice of Enhanced Interaction: Intramural Challenges to the 'ASEAN Way,'" *Pacific Review* 12, no. 4 (1999): 581–611.

59. John S. Duffield, "Political Culture and State Behavior: Why Germany Confounds Neorealism," *International Organization* 53, no. 4 (1999): 772.

60. Jürgen Haacke and Noel M. Morada, eds., *Cooperative Security in the Asia-Pacific: The ASEAN Regional Forum* (London: Routledge, 2010).

61. Paul D. Williams, "From Non-Intervention to Non-Indifference: The Origins and Development of the African Union's Security Culture," *African Affairs* 106 (2007): 253–79.

62. Acharya and Johnston, "Conclusion," 264.

63. See Colin Dueck, "Realism, Culture and Grand Strategy: Explaining America's Peculiar Path to World Power," *Security Studies* 14, no. 2 (2005): 195–231.

64. See Emmanuel Adler, "Seizing the Middle Ground: Constructivism in World Politics," *European Journal of International Relations* 3, no. 3 (1997): 330, 337; and Johnston, *Cultural Realism*, 35, 53.

65. Lake and Morgan, "Building Security in the New World of Regional Orders," 348–49. Some scholars identify the lack of such capacities and capabilities as an impediment to cooperation; see, for example, Fawcett, "Exploring Regional Domains," 443.

66. Herz, *Does the OAS Matter?* 26.

67. Jeffrey Gettleman, "The Most Dangerous Place in the World," *Foreign Policy* (March/April 2009), 68.

68. See, for example, United Nations, *Report of the Secretary-General on Cooperation between the United Nations and Regional and Other Organizations*, UN document A/63/228-S/2008/531, August 8, 2008; and *Report of the African Union-United Nations Panel on Modalities for Support to African Union Peacekeeping Operations*, UN document A/63/666-S/2008/813, December 31, 2008.

69. United Nations, press conference, New York, March 5, 2008, www.un.org/News/briefings/docs/2008/080305_Pascoe.doc.htm.

70. For a discussion of some of the issues this raises, see Acharya and Johnston, "Conclusion," 274–76.

71. Rizal Sukma, "Political Development: A Democracy Agenda for ASEAN?" in *Hard Choices: Security, Democracy, and Regionalism in Southeast Asia*, ed. Donald K. Emmerson (Stanford: Shorenstein Asia-Pacific Research Center, 2008).

72. United Nations, *Implementing the Responsibility to Protect*.

4

Culture Counts

A Diplomatic Perspective on Culture and Regional Conflict Management

Nigel Quinney

T he idea that something as fuzzy and impalpable as culture might affect how hard-headed diplomats deal with concrete subjects such as security is regarded with a good deal of scholarly suspicion. Indeed, the notion sometimes elicits academic ridicule. No less a figure than I. William Zartman, one of the leading scholars of international negotiation, contends that "culture is indeed relevant to the understanding of the negotiation process, every bit as relevant as [the] breakfast [the negotiators ate], and to much the same extent."[1]

Not everyone is so dismissive. A number of academics are coming to accept what many practitioners of diplomacy and conflict management have long considered to be self-evident—namely, that a nation's culture does have an impact on how it defines and defends its security. When one moves from the national to the regional level, however, doubts about the association between culture and conflict management grow. Even those scholars and practitioners who accept that culture helps shape approaches to regional security and regional conflict management are uncertain about what kinds of culture matter, to what extent they matter, and how they matter.

"Security culture" certainly seems to have an impact on policymakers—an impact that has received significant scholarly attention—but is it the alpha and omega of cultural influence? Are other, both broader and narrower cultures also at work: not only professional cultures and institutional cultures, but also the cultures of social elites, of individual nations, and even of entire regions? And if other cultures are in play, how is their influence transmitted into the conflict management decision-making process, what kinds of diplomatic expectations and policymaking calculations do they shape, and what kinds of conflict management practices do they encourage?

This chapter takes a modest step toward answering these questions by discussing the results of a series of interviews with practitioners about culture's role in regional conflict management. In doing so, the chapter applies an approach developed in a long-term, ongoing study of national negotiating styles conducted by the United States Institute of Peace, a congressionally funded think tank based in Washington, DC. The Institute's Cross-Cultural Negotiation (CCN) project zeroes in on traits displayed by government officials as they negotiate with officials from other states. Drawing on interviews with diplomats and policymakers, as well as published records and analyses of specific negotiations, the project teases out patterns in behavior among negotiators from the same state. These patterns, as a series of country-specific CCN studies make clear, are shaped not just by the interests of and the relationships between the states represented at the bargaining table, but also by the cultures (national, institutional, professional) that negotiators from a given country share. In other words, each nation has (or, more precisely, each nation's official negotiators display) a distinctive negotiating style, and this style is rooted in part in the nation's culture, which helps explains why that style persists.

If the CCN approach can tell us something about culture's impact on diplomacy at the national level, why could it not do the same at the regional level? If we analyze the attitudes and behavior of officials from within the same *region*, might we see not only attitudinal and behavioral patterns but also the influence of a shared regional culture (or cultures) on that behavior? Admittedly, the CCN project focuses on negotiation, not mediation or other forms of conflict management. However, officials carry over to mediation many of the same traits and tactics they use when they negotiate on behalf of their own country; some of these traits are accentuated, others are de-emphasized. Moreover, it requires no Herculean methodological effort to widen the analytical lens to examine not just negotiation but other forms of diplomatic interaction among officials.[2]

For the purposes of this chapter, eight interviews were conducted with diplomats with significant firsthand experience of regional conflict management. Given that the interviewees have worked either for governments or for regional organizations or for both, the scope of the inquiry was largely confined to attitudes and activities at the state level. That limitation, however, still left a very large area to explore.

As the reader will discover, the interviews did indeed cover a good deal of territory, thematically, historically, and geographically. There was also significant variation in the interviewees' assessments of how and how much culture shapes regional conflict management. But most interviewees were in no doubt that culture does play a role—usually a supportive rather than dominant one—interacting with other factors to produce regionally distinctive approaches. In regions comprising countries with similar cultures, culture tends to make communication easier, fosters a sense of shared identities and interests, and facilitates practical cooperation. This effect is often magnified in subregions, not only because cultural ties are stronger in smaller areas but also because cultural bonds reinforce the sense of unity among small and midsize countries that band together to combat the power of a culturally distinct hegemon. History as embodied and expressed in culture is a particularly powerful engine of regional cooperation.

The interviewees distinguished between various kinds of culture and reflected on their interaction. The professional culture of diplomats, for instance, is seen as assuming an increasingly global character that dilutes the impact of national culture in multilateral fora. This universalizing dynamic is itself tempered, however, not only by the enduring potency of national cultures but also by distinctive institutional cultures and regionwide cultural impulses. In some parts of the world, an institutional culture has helped to nurture a nascent regional culture; in other parts, the latter has profoundly sculpted (or stifled) the former.

The chapter is divided into six main sections. The first section sketches the nature of the CCN project. The second discusses some of the advantages and problems of applying the CCN approach in a regional, rather than national, context. The third distills the interviewees' observations on the kinds of cultures that influence regional conflict management and their interactions. The fourth spotlights what the interviewees had to say about shared regional histories, identities, and affinities (i.e., regional culture) shaping regional and subregional approaches to conflict management. The fifth offers two vignettes of specific regions using particular conflict management approaches. And the sixth suggests avenues for future research

Before launching into the chapter, a few definitions are in order. Our subject matter—conflict management, regions, and culture—however, inhabits a fuzzy definitional universe.

Conflict management is the easiest of these three terms term to define, but any definition must perforce be broad-ranging. In this chapter, "conflict management" is taken to mean any and all approaches, mechanisms, and other measures intended to prevent, manage, or resolve violent interstate and intrastate conflict.

Region defies a neat definition. Does one delineate a region by its geography, its history, its culture, its political or linguistic or other complexion, or by some marriage of two or more of these features? What looks to one observer like a self-evident, cast-iron example of a region can look like nothing of the kind from another observer's perspective. As Luigi R. Einaudi, the veteran U.S. diplomat who served as assistant secretary general of the Organization of American States (OAS) from 2000 to 2004 and as acting secretary general in 2004–05, remarks, "The Western hemisphere in many ways does not exist—or at least it exists so grandly that it is impossible to talk about it in gross terms." Even a much smaller geographical area, Central America, which seems "a world unto itself," is politically fragmented and "there's no traditional definition of what's in Central America."[3]

This fuzziness is not necessarily unwelcome, because it allows us to ask the same questions about the role of culture in a wide variety of regions, and thus to gain some comparative perspective. For instance, it may be instructive to explore whether culture is more likely to facilitate or impede conflict management in a region defined in large part by its shared culture and history (such as Latin America) than in a region defined largely by the existence of mechanisms for regional cooperation (such as the ASEAN [Association of Southeast Asian Nations] region). In other words, can a common culture compensate for a lack of conflict management machinery, and vice versa?

Culture is a crucial term to define, but a very elusive concept to pin down. As explained a little later in this chapter, this chapter adopts the CCN project's definition of "culture" as "human software"—that is, the beliefs, traditions, values, norms, and assumptions shared by a specific group.[4] This broad definition allows us to explore the influence and interaction of a wide range of cultures.

With these definitions in mind, let us now outline the aims, assumptions, nature, and findings of the CCN project.

The CCN Project

Drawing on the model of a pioneering study of Chinese negotiating behavior written in the mid-1980s,[5] in the early 1990s the United States Institute of Peace initiated a series of both conceptual and country-specific assessments on the theme of cross-cultural negotiating behavior. The CCN series is based on the premise that negotiating is the usual, if not always the preferred, technique of international problem solving, and that greater understanding of the dynamics of negotiating, greater appreciation of the cultural and institutional influences of a counterpart's behavior, and greater self-awareness will help make specific negotiating encounters more productive. The CCN project has so far produced more than a dozen book-length studies.[6]

The project assumes that at least five factors influence the conduct of any given negotiation:

- the issues at stake;
- the personalities of the negotiators (and the rapport between them);
- structural factors such as the institutional and decision-making framework;
- the geopolitical context, including the relationship between the parties to a negotiation; and
- the cultures involved.

Of these factors, the last three typically change incrementally and gradually, making it possible to assess their longer-term impact. However, while scholars have devoted a good deal of attention to analyzing the influence of structural and geopolitical factors, culture has attracted relatively little attention as an ingredient in diplomatic negotiation.[7]

Some scholars have entertained the notion of culture's influence only to dismiss it out of hand, rejecting it as an irrelevance to international diplomacy. More often, however, analysts have shown a reluctance to engage with such an elusive and amorphous concept as "culture." Contributors to the CCN project sought to define "culture" by building on the definitions and usages of the term developed in the twentieth century by anthropologists and political scientists such as Franz Boas, Margaret Mead, Ruth Benedict, and Clyde Kluckhohn. Kluckhohn, for instance, wrote that "culture consists in patterned ways of thinking, feeling and reaction, acquired and transmitted mainly by symbols, constituting the distinctive achievements of human groups, including their embodiments in artifacts; the essential core of culture consists of traditional (i.e., historically derived and selected) ideas and especially their attached values."[8] In this chapter, as in Raymond Cohen's *Negotiating across Cultures,* culture is understood to mean "human software . . . made up of ideas, meanings, conventions, and assumptions" shared by a particular group; as "a grammar for organizing reality, for imparting meaning to the world."[9]

The CCN definition of culture is not one-dimensional. As another author of a book from the CCN series, Kevin Avruch, rightly points out, there are multiple, overlapping subcultures, "generic" and "local," national and ethnic, social and political, and so forth. The CCN project pays particular attention to national cultures (i.e., cultural traits that are widely shared within a given country) and institutional cultures (in this case, the norms and behavioral predispositions inculcated and/or reinforced by government institutions, especially those concerned with foreign affairs). Professional cultures and political cultures are also considered pertinent. Any given negotiator will be influenced by his or her distinctive set of cultures; thus, no two negotiators are culturally identical.[10] As Jeswald Salacuse notes, "no negotiator is a cultural robot."[11] Even so, the authors of the CCN studies have concluded that the shared national background and institutional context of each country's negotiators exert a significant and recognizable impact on many facets of negotiating encounters.

Each of the country-specific volumes identifies characteristic patterns of behavior in the approach to and conduct of negotiation and other forms of conflict management. The areas where culture can make a difference during negotiations are numerous and diverse. Characteristic patterns of behavior are seen in such things as

- primary objectives (e.g., concrete gains vs. relationship building);
- degree of openness (e.g., back channels vs. public pronouncements and positioning);
- focus of argumentation (e.g., principle vs. pragmatism, rational vs. emotional);
- attitudes toward compromise (e.g., a useful route to win-win outcomes vs. a shameful abandonment of principles);
- use of threats and enticements (e.g., readiness to use, types used, balance between);
- the use of language (e.g., explicit vs. implicit, legalistic vs. impressionistic);
- attitudes toward time (e.g., urgent vs. leisurely, short-term vs. long-term perspectives);
- attitudes toward conformity (e.g., emphasis on discipline and hierarchy vs. focus on freedom of action and individualism); and
- use of hospitality (e.g., lavish and instrumental vs. meager and functional).

Each element in a national negotiating style may or may not be unique to a given country, but the combination of characteristics is distinctive and unique.

Applying the CCN Approach on a Regional Level

The CCN project has generated useful knowledge about how officials from nations with different cultures negotiate with one another. There is good reason to suppose that the CCN approach can also yield a better understanding of if, how, and to what extent culture influences concepts and practices of conflict management by different regions.

One reason to anticipate that such a venture might prove fruitful is the breadth of the CCN definition of culture, which allows us to examine a wider range of cultures than those typically analyzed by scholars of regional security. Much of that scholarship has focused, wisely enough, on the concept of *security cultures*, which Paul D. Williams has defined as "patterns of thought and argumentation that establish pervasive and durable security preferences by formulating concepts of the role, legitimacy and efficacy of particular approaches to protecting values. Through a process of socialization, security cultures help establish the core assumptions, beliefs and values of decision makers about how security challenges can and should be dealt with."[12] In other words, security culture is a culture of policymakers, rather than the wider public, and it focuses on issues of concern to policymakers, such as the legitimacy of states, the nature and limits of national sovereignty, appropriate responses to conflict, and so forth. Other members of society may or may not share some of the attitudes that form part of a security culture, but they did not acquire those ideas in the same way—by being socialized within a club of national or regional policymakers.

In examining the origins of a particular—African—security culture, Williams traces its roots back a long time and into ground beyond the walls of policymakers' gatherings. "The origins of this culture lie in the discourses of Pan-African identity articulated since the late nineteenth century, and its constitutive elements have been refined in the crucible of post-colonial international politics."[13] But this is still territory that most Africans do not inhabit or at least territory that they visit only occasionally and usually as tourists. And, of course, the same could be said about any continent: most Americans, for instance, rarely immerse themselves in a culture built around discourses of American identity and focused on security challenges.

The CCN understanding of "culture" substantially enlarges this analytical territory in two ways. In the first place, we can explore cultures that are much more expansive in terms of their content—that address not just issues related to the security of a state, such as "We should/should not compromise with State X on Issue Y," but also much more fundamental concerns, such as "Compromise is a good/bad thing to do." Second, we can examine a wide array of cultures—not just those cultures that are largely restricted to policymakers and diplomats but also cultures that such officials share with larger, more diverse groups, such as the citizenry of a particular nation or even a particular region.

While the definitions of "culture" embraced by the CCN project are certainly sufficiently broad to accommodate the idea of a culture that transcends national barriers, a host of questions present themselves about the nature, diffusion, and impact of regional culture. For instance:

- If a regional culture exists, does it exist equally strongly throughout a given region? If not, does the pattern of its distribution influence its impact upon regional diplomacy? (For example, if the regional minnows share cultural traits but the regional sharks don't, is culture largely irrelevant?)
- Is a regional culture made up of discrete national cultures that happen (for historical reasons, coincidence, etc.) to overlap, or do countries share a regional culture that is to some extent distinct from their national cultures?
- Do countries within a region see themselves as sharing a common culture? If so, to what extent does this perception fuel a recognition of common interests, such as regional security, and a readiness to act collectively to enhance that security?
- To what extent are regional cultural similarities trumped by—or accentuated by—other factors (e.g., national interests, structural factors) when countries contemplate regional security?
- Do countries share a conflict management culture?
- Which forms of regional security does a given region favor, and are those preferences rooted, at least in part, in regional cultural traits?
- Do diplomats and other officials within a region share a regionally distinctive professional culture? Or is their professional culture global rather than regional?

To explore at least some of the issues raised by these questions, and to test whether the CCN approach might open a new window on the subject of regional conflict management, we followed—albeit on a small scale—a favored CCN methodology and conducted a round of interviews with highly experienced practitioners.

Adhering to the CCN assumption that it takes the cultural "distance" of a foreign observer to perceive what is distinctive about a given culture or negotiating style, almost all of our eight interviewees are foreign observers—"foreign" in this case meaning individuals who are not themselves from the areas they were quizzed about in the interviews. These observers, however, are far from uninformed about those regions. To the contrary, each has extensive firsthand experience of the region (or regions) he or she commented upon. Moreover, each is familiar with conflict management/regional security practices and/or institutions within the region, with diplomats and other government officials from within that region, and with the wider societies within the region.

Given that perception of different cultures varies according to the culture of the perceiver, we sought to limit the possible range of perceptual difference by enlisting interviewees who themselves come from a limited cultural "pool." In the event, seven of our eight interviewees are serving or retired professional diplomats and the eighth has worked closely with diplomats as a conflict management practitioner. Their national cultural backgrounds are almost as similar as their professional backgrounds, for all but one are American, Canadian, or British (a trio of nations that, while hardly interchangeable culturally, nonetheless bear marked cultural family resemblances).

This seasoned octet—two of whom have the added distinction of being contributors to this volume—are Alyson Bailes, Chan Heng Chee, Luigi R. Einaudi, Chas W. Freeman, Jr., John W. Graham, Milburn Line, Richard H. Solomon, and Frank Wisner. (A brief biography of each interviewee is in the appendix of this chapter.)

Because of the nature of their professional backgrounds—diplomacy in the service of a government, and substantial experience in many cases of regional organizations—the interviewees paid much attention to the role of state actors and to conflict management as practiced by regional intergovernmental organizations. They had comparatively little to say about nongovernmental organizations and similar nonstate actors. (This means, of course, that our portrait of culture and regional conflict management is incomplete; it does not mean, however, that the portrait is inaccurate in what it does depict.)

Each interview ranged widely, the course of the conversation shaped by the interviewee's individual interests, expertise, and experiences. All the interviews, however, were structured, albeit loosely, around a framework of four deliberately general queries:

- On the basis of your firsthand experience dealing with Region X, do you think that the region exhibits patterns of diplomatic behavior that are (A) consistent and/or (B) distinctive? How would you characterize those patterns?
- If you do see some patterns in the diplomacy of Region X, do you think those similarities are rooted, at least in part, in a similar culture? If so, what kinds or levels of culture are involved (national, institutional, etc.)?
- Does Region X think that conflict prevention and management is a legitimate and/or realistic goal for the region? If so, what forms of

conflict management does Region X tend to favor when seeking to keep or restore peace and stability within the region?
- Do you see particular cultural traits mirrored in attitudes toward and/ or the practice of conflict management in Region X? What are those traits?

Reflecting their professional backgrounds, the interviewees focused on Southeast Asia, East Asia, the Arab world, Latin America and the Caribbean, and Europe; other regions, such as sub-Saharan Africa, largely escaped comment. For the same reason, the interviewees said much about mediation, negotiation, and conflict prevention but little about other forms of conflict management, such as military intervention and peacebuilding.

The rest of this chapter distills and discusses common themes in the interviewees' responses. However, while the interviewees' observations have inspired and informed what follows, no interviewee should be held responsible—individually or collectively—for specific analyses presented in the following pages unless he or she is quoted directly. It should also be stressed that while the interviewees agreed on many issues, they also disagreed, whether by a matter of degree or very substantially, on some other topics.

The Role of Culture

Overall, a Spur to Regional Cooperation

All the interviewees believe that culture plays a role in shaping regional cooperation among diplomats, though at least two feel its impact is significantly limited. Least convinced about culture's influence is Milburn Line, a veteran of international missions and projects to promote human rights, who contended that "the individual is often as important as cultural background" and that "the mechanics of negotiation are essentially the same" for diplomats, except perhaps lower-level officials with little experience of international interaction. "Most diplomats know the difference between interest-based and position-based bargaining," said Line, "no matter what their culture." The majority of interviewees, however, took a somewhat different view, seeing culture as having the power to influence the outlook of diplomats at all levels. That power might not itself be decisive, but it is nonetheless real and far from negligible.

The greater the degree of cultural affinity among countries, the more likely those countries are to cooperate and the more effectively they are likely do so. Diplomats from the same region are able to work together without having to adjust their behavior to accommodate their interlocutors; indeed, shared cultural traits tend to be more pronounced when diplomats from the same region are talking among themselves. Diplomats from Southeast Asia, for instance, treat each other with conspicuous politeness, restraint, and tact, acutely sensitive of each other's concern not to lose face. By contrast, diplomats from, say, the United Kingdom and the Netherlands will be very frank with one another, will laugh readily, and may even raise their voices from time to time, knowing that such behavior will not engender ill feeling and may well help foster camaraderie.

Culture is particularly influential in terms of diplomatic *style*. "One's style emanates from one's culture," as Frank Wisner, who has served as ambassador to four different countries during a distinguished career with the U.S. State Department, succinctly noted. And culture can be so deeply ingrained as to be tantamount to instinct and to shape fundamental aspects of conflict management such as attitudes to process and aims.

Yet, culture is by no means the only impetus toward regional cooperation; developmental commonalities may be more important than civilizational ones such as culture. And hard, practical interests are usually more important still. Chan Heng Chee, Singapore's ambassador to the United States since 1996, declared that "culture is not a major influence; it's a secondary influence—unless the country has not been on the international stage for a long time. Even then, Myanmar behaves as it does, not so much because it's Burmese but because the regime has particular interests. The military regime has been consistent in its behavior despite changes in military leaders at the top. They self-isolate and remain suspicious of the outside world for survival. Take the aftermath of Cyclone Nargis [which struck in May 2008 and was the country's worst natural disaster]: Myanmar didn't accept foreign aid at first, but not because it was Burmese culture at work but because it was a closed regime."

Nor are cultural similarities and sympathies usually adequate by themselves to effect a mutually agreeable settlement of a dispute that affects interests other than cultural ones. "More cultural affinity between the United States and Latin America would help spur cooperation, but it wouldn't change things substantially" because the asymmetry of power is much more important, observed John Graham, who served as Canada's ambassador to several countries in the region and was the first head of the OAS's Unit for the Promotion of Democracy.

Nonetheless, even the most pragmatic of diplomatic "realists" ignores culture at his or her own peril, for it is part of a larger equation: "To get something done," commented Einaudi about his many years working within the OAS, "you need to pay attention to both political realities and culture."[14]

Which Cultures Matter?

Culture has an impact—but which culture? The interviewees commented on the influence exerted by five kinds of culture: diplomats' professional culture (and the cultures of some other transnational professional groups); institutional culture (in the form of the mores, norms, and practices of regional organizations); elite culture (the culture of the social and political elites within a particular country or region); national culture (not only the culture shared by most of the population in a given country but also subsets of national culture such as a country's political culture); and regional culture (the culture shared by significant segments of the populations of multiple countries within a given region).

(Surprisingly, few interviewees mentioned "security culture," even in passing. Why? Perhaps because it is more of an academic construct than a practitioner's consciously apprehended set of ideas and values. Or perhaps, conversely, because it is so pervasive as to be all but omnipresent and thus not worth mentioning; like the air we breathe, it is vital but invisible and taken for granted.)[15]

There are, of course, significant overlaps between these categories. And, in line with the CCN project's embrace of the notion of each individual possessing multiple cultures, any individual diplomat is surely influenced in some way by all five categories.

Yet, as the interviews made clear, there is also a tension or even a contradiction between some of these cultures. A national culture, for example, may valorize a trait (e.g., unwavering adherence to principle) that an institutional or diplomatic culture may reject in favor of its real or seeming antithesis (e.g., a readiness to compromise). In this respect, the diplomat can be a battlefield on which cultures clash. One or two interviewees intimated that diplomats deal with this internal culture war by embracing one culture when negotiating an agreement with fellow diplomats and another culture when trying to sell that agreement back home. Other interviewees, however, saw diplomats—especially those that work within multilateral organizations—as culturally denationalized creatures, or at least as members of a globalized club of professionals who interact according to their own rules.

Diplomats' culture. Diplomats are not the only professional group whose members are drawn from multiple countries, who perform upon the regional conflict management stage, and who have developed a recognizable culture that is most pronounced when they interact with one another. Other groups include soldiers, international lawyers, representatives of NGOs, scholar-practitioners, officials from nondiplomatic ministries, and even business people.[16]

Diplomacy, however, is for obvious reasons the most pertinent of these transnational professions. Diplomats have long shared a professional culture that, say some, trumps national cultures.[17] Part of the reason for the strength of this culture, argued some interviewees, is that no matter what country they represent, diplomats have much the same goals, notably, to reach agreement with their counterparts, which in turn requires that they not offend or alienate their interlocutors. "I have been more conscious of intrinsic similarities among diplomats [from different cultures]," said Alyson Bailes, a veteran British diplomat with considerable experience in European security organizations. Even in hard negotiations, "certain rituals and niceties unite" the negotiators. "Diplomats tend to control themselves, to play a role ... they give you leeway, elbow room to explore your differences" without resorting to shouting or violence. Chan concurred: "Diplomats from all regions learn some diplomatic niceties and forms. In diplomacy generally, not just ASEAN, you try to say things in a way that doesn't show anyone up."

This concern with self-control is said to have been accentuated by the multifaceted process of globalization, which has not only encouraged economic and technological standardization but also fostered cultural conformity among diplomats the world over. Wherever one goes, one is increasingly likely to encounter a professional diplomatic culture that is English-speaking, Western-educated, suit-wearing, and soft-spoken. Compared to ten years ago, for instance, Chinese diplomats are far more proficient in English and at home in multilateral forums. "The essence of a good diplomat is to be self-aware, to change if need be," observed Bailes. "Your home country is changing more slowly in response to globalization, but you have to change more quickly. You've got to learn a new culture, but not go so far that you 'go native.' ... You can go native in two ways: embracing the local country, or embracing the diplomats' culture."

This modern culture of diplomacy would seem to have a mixed impact on regional conflict management practices. On the one hand, what the former Austrian diplomat Winfried Lang has described as a "negotiation culture"—whose features include a sense of the need to accommodate one's counterpart, a high regard for flexibility, and awareness of the need for efficient communication—makes diplomats readier and more able to settle conflict through negotiation and mediation.[18]

On the other hand, to the extent that diplomatic culture is truly global, it militates against regional difference in conflict management practices—at least insofar as culture shapes those practices. But is it really global? Historically, the culture of diplomacy spanned nations but it certainly did not span the globe. The diplomatic forms and practices developed in Venice, Milan, and other republics and duchies in northern Italy during the Renaissance were gradually embraced by most Europeans, but not, for instance, by the Ottoman Empire, which continued to regard the niceties and intrigues of European bilateral diplomacy as beneath its dignity. In eighteenth-century Europe, the culture of diplomacy was French-speaking and defined by elaborate forms of conduct and attire. It spread as far east as the Russian Empire, but it was rejected, in part, by the newly founded United States, which, for instance, disdained consular uniforms and the title of ambassador until 1893. The young Soviet Union similarly rejected the diplomatic conventions of the day.

Have we now reached the end of history in terms of diplomatic difference? Certainly, there is greater uniformity among diplomats today than a hundred or even twenty-five years ago in terms of dress and demeanor and proficiency in the lingua franca of English, but what about at a deeper level? Charles W. Freeman, whose long diplomatic career saw him serve as President Richard Nixon's interpreter in Beijing in the early 1970s and as U.S. ambassador to Saudi Arabia in the early 1990s, contended that "this worldwide [diplomatic] norm masks the fact that beneath the form there are very different styles, which have a civilizational basis." Bailes, while she emphasized the extent to which diplomats in multilateral settings adopt a "neutral" style, noted that, as a general proposition, "the underlying culture is different both from nation to nation and region to region."

Institutional culture. There is a substantial overlap between the culture of diplomats and the culture of the multilateral institutions—such as regional organizations—where they often ply their trade. After all, diplomats play a large part in determining the rules and norms of how these entities conduct their daily business. Especially in the case of a newly established organization (or, for that matter, a new national diplomatic corps, a number of which emerged from the wreckage of the Soviet Union), the individual diplomats who are posted to a fledgling entity have the opportunity to mold its culture profoundly.

Yet there is also a tension between these cultures insofar as diplomats working within—and especially those working *for*—well-established organizations with elaborate bureaucratic structures have to accommodate themselves to the prevailing culture. "The UN would hardly work if the diplomats did not arrive there with certain similarities and behavior and then learn a UN culture," commented Bailes. "Diplomats from different cultures adopt a third, neutral style. This is exactly what happens at the UN; it's what allows alliances between very different states to be formed."

The fact that institutional culture shapes, rather than merely being shaped by, diplomats is significant for our inquiry in two ways. First, it means that to the extent a global professional diplomatic culture exists, it is modified at the institutional level.

Second, different regional organizations are likely to modify it in different ways. "There is a different culture in Brussels, in Geneva, and so forth," said Bailes. This culture affects not only diplomats but also officials in nondiplomatic ministries, as well as the experts who advise them and the lobbyists who try to influence them. In regions with several regional organizations all working on conflict management, different institutional cultural identities feed competition among those organizations: "It is remarkable," Bailes remarked, "how competitive they may become with each other as a result of esprit de corps as well as objective demarcation problems, so that an EU employee's hope to 'score over' a NATO one, OSCE over the Council of Europe, and so on becomes a strong cultural influence detracting not just from their mutual cooperation but from a proper focus on local needs."

The impact of institutional culture among global and regional conflict management organizations is diluted, however, by their need to recruit outsiders for many of the missions they mount. As several interviewees pointed out, in many organizations, each mediation or peacebuilding mission is set up in an ad hoc fashion and must draw on the human resources available at the time or else enlist individuals from a variety of national governments. Milburn Line, who worked in the 1990s in Bosnia and Herzegovina with the Organization for Security and Co-operation in Europe (OSCE) and the Office of the High Representative, recalls that the attitudes of Americans and Europeans to performing their common task differed. The former tended to be "idealistic, seeking to stick to the letter of the peace agreement [they were implementing], believing that doing so was the only way to build sustainable peace." The Europeans, by contrast, tended to more realistic and, at times, flexible on how to comply with the principles of the agreement. Cultural dissonance of this sort is exacerbated in most cases of multilateral military intervention, the influence of the culture of the institution orchestrating the operation having to compete with the cultures of military contingents from perhaps dozens of participating nations.

Elite culture. The notion of a globalized, denationalized diplomatic profession may resonate in states with a highly meritocratic, carefully structured career path for its professional diplomats, but the idea seems less applicable to countries whose diplomatic corps, as well as whose policymaking cadres or classes, are drawn from the nation's social and political elites. In the latter case, diplomats are often more conscious of their shared social identity—and its attendant culture—than of their shared status as diplomats.

In much of Latin America, to take an example cited by several interviewees, diplomats are recruited from the ruling class, and it is the interests of that class, rather than of a country as a whole, that the diplomatic corps defends. "Old elites do not have the free run of the region they had twenty-five year years ago, but elites in Latin America still retain a surprising degree of political and financial power," commented Graham. "The centralizing, top-down culture imported with the conquistadores, while obviously much attenuated, still shapes perspectives on government and status." There are signs that the old guard in foreign policy may be giving way to a new, less socially privileged group, but "so far," observed Luigi Einaudi, "elites have defended themselves well against attempts to have more popular influence on policy."

In regions with culturally diverse social elites, the phenomenon of a socially elevated diplomatic corps might impede their interaction, but in Latin America the culture of the elite is similar throughout much of the region. As a consequence (and as discussed later in the chapter), Latin American diplomats have a reputation for clubbing together in global and regional forums, for networking among themselves to support or oppose different kinds of conflict management initiatives.

This is not to say that elite culture and diplomatic culture are necessarily at odds with one another. Historically, elites and diplomats have both been more likely to exhibit cosmopolitan tastes and transnational affinities than most of their socially subordinate, nondiplomat compatriots. This is changing as more and more "ordinary" people travel and work abroad and as the global informational revolution fosters appetites and appreciation for foreign cultures. Even so, elite and diplomatic cultures generally remain more open to ideas of international interaction and cooperation than do national mass cultures.

Of course, greater interaction does not always mean greater cooperation. For instance, in Europe until the end of World War I, as the British diplomat and author Harold Nicolson remarked, diplomacy was the preserve of a certain class of people, of men who "possessed similar standards of education, similar experience and a similar aim [and] desired the same sort of world."[19] The aristocrats and haute bourgeois who filled the upper echelons of the Victorian and Edwardian diplomatic corps had much in common culturally, but that did not prevent them from creating a system of hostile alliances and secret covenants that helped plunge their continent into the worst bloodbath in its history.

National cultures. The role of national culture was an issue that colored responses (explicitly or implicitly) to many different questions posed in the interviews. Most interviewees accepted that national culture—whether understood to mean the cultural traits shared by most of a country's people or by a country's political, professional, and institutional cultures—helps shape attitudes toward international cooperation in general and conflict management in particular, but many were unable or reluctant to offer generalizations about specific countries or specific illustrations of one or another national culture at work. Others, however, had no such qualms.

There was general agreement that national culture has its most pronounced impact on countries that have time-honored diplomatic traditions and that have been isolated from the rest of the world or have at least limited their exposure to foreign influences. Richard H. Solomon, who focused on East Asia during much of his long diplomatic career, described the hermit state of North Korea as embodying "traditional Korean culture in Technicolor," notably in its obsessive concern with foreign threats. Saudi Arabia, noted Freeman, "was never penetrated by the West, its [political and diplomatic] traditions are entirely indigenous and deeply rooted in a very rich culture, one that took shape in the seventh century."

Unlike Saudi Arabia, Egypt did not escape Western colonialism, but, said Wisner, Egypt's attitude toward conflict management reflects its own ancient, culturally rooted beliefs about dealing with its neighbors; the influence of Western-style concepts and assumptions is minor. Freeman echoed this observation about indigenous cultures outlasting colonial accretions or impositions. "There are indigenous traditions that are alive and well, and that in some cases are reasserting themselves. That's certainly the case in India, which is behaving more and more in accord with Indian traditions than with those it inherited from the Raj."

The enduring strength of national cultures can obstruct the trend toward the globalization of diplomatic culture. Most states in the Arab world, for instance, continue to adhere to the tradition of vertical policymaking hierarchies and have almost no foreign policy apparatus, noted Freeman. Foreign policy is conducted in an "entirely personalized" fashion, and the individual who directs his state's foreign affairs may do so for decades at a time. The net effect is to make Arab states resistant to those trends in diplomatic styles and practices that have a visible impact in many other parts of the world.

The fact that those trends have a distinctly Western flavor also inspires resistance. The model of a modern diplomat is very much a Western construct: as noted above, the exemplar of the global diplomat wears Western-style suits, is highly proficient in English, speaks in measured and largely unemotional tones, and believes that conflicts can be resolved through discussion and compromise. Within the rarefied, cosmopolitan confines of regional and international organizations such figures may be so common as to seem a natural part of the world's diplomatic landscape, but at the national level they can sometimes seem altogether more exotic and alien.

Instead of embracing newly emerging global norms of diplomacy, some countries take great pains to transmit their own traditions of statecraft from one generation to the next. According to Freeman, "A well-documented cultural tradition of statecraft in Arabic and other languages has a powerful impact on diplomacy," creating continuity despite the absence of an elaborate foreign policy machinery. Books written in Arabic on statecraft many centuries ago are still read; Freeman recalled seeing princes in Saudi Arabia reading ninth-century tomes on statecraft. Future and junior diplomats are mentored in and consciously exposed to this Arab tradition. Iran has a different tradition of statecraft (and a professional foreign ministry), but it too maintains that tradition by requiring its diplomats to study time-honored texts such as Kai Ka'us ibn Iskandar's tenth-century manual of statecraft, *The Qabus Nama* (A Mirror for Princes).

The process of cultural transmission in other countries is rarely so deliberately engineered, but—as the studies generated by the CCN study attest—national cultures nonetheless penetrate foreign policy mechanisms. It could, indeed, hardly be otherwise. Unless recruited from other countries (as some diplomats were by the newly independent Baltic states in the early 1990s), the individuals who make and implement a country's foreign policy have been immersed in that country's culture from birth, and can hardly shake it off when they enter the ranks of its diplomats. Furthermore, political pressures, media scrutiny, public opinion, and a host of other domestic forces work together to penalize individuals who behave in ways deemed disrespectful of the national culture, while training programs, mentoring systems, and policies for career advancement combine to encourage adherence to cultural norms. Moreover, government officials are only one vehicle for expressing a nation's approach to conflict management; nongovernmental organizations, for instance, play a growing role in this area in many countries.

For the purpose of this chapter, the key question about national culture is not how it is transmitted, nor how it shapes how a nation seeks to manage conflict, but if and how it influences conflict management in a concrete fashion at the regional level. As discussed in the next section of the chapter, national (and other types of) cultures are most influential when they resonate with other national cultures within the region, creating a sense of a common identity and bolstering an awareness of common interests.

Culture at the Regional Level

Culture in the Form of History

"Historical factors are generally more important than they're given credit for," commented Bailes, an observation with which all or almost all the interviewees concurred. "Historical factors," of course, is a broad category. But even when "history" is interpreted relatively narrowly to mean history as embedded and expressed in culture—to mean shared perceptions of historical events and developments, and those perceptions' influence on other elements of a shared worldview—the interviewees saw its influence as pervasive and extensive.

History can be a powerful engine of regional cooperation, even—or perhaps especially—when the shared historical experience that drives contemporary cooperation was one of domination. The territory occupied by former empires has proved particularly fertile ground for subsequent regional cooperation. Several reasons explain this.

In the first place, empires have imposed common languages, religions, political traditions, and economic systems within a given region, creating a practical, conceptual, and cultural lingua franca on which to build regional interaction. Latin America is a prime example: indigenous culture has, until recently, barely impacted the diplomacy of the region, which has displayed its lavish debt to the culture of the Spanish colonizers and their descendents.

In the second place, the experience of struggling to expel the colonizers has bred a sense of camaraderie and common purpose. Such a sense is part of the glue that holds together the otherwise very disparate states that make up the African Union.

Third, empires that required their subject states to participate in imperial governance (the British Raj, for instance), as opposed to empires that sought purely to subjugate their unfortunate subjects and exclude them from any and all positions of authority (the Belgian Congo provides a particularly bleak example), helped to school those states in the arts of multilateral cooperation. "In the former Soviet bloc," noted Bailes, "some states have been able to use multilateral tactics and strategies acquired when those states were obliged to work together in the Warsaw Pact and COMECON [the Council for Mutual Economic Assistance]. The Balkan states, however, didn't have this experience, hence perhaps some of their difficulties in adjusting to cooperation and democratic structures" since the end of Communist rule.

In the case of India, as Solomon noted, the experience of empire helped to create not only a culturally identifiable region but a surprisingly cohesive, democratic sovereign state out of an area that, before the British arrived, had no conception of itself as a distinct and viable political entity. Moreover, the experience of empire had an impact not only on India's internal organization but also on its external relations. Pre-Raj India was a subcontinental system of decentralized power, different language groups, and a host of other factors acting against the formation and expression of a common identity. As a consequence, the subcontinent never projected itself beyond its borders as, say, China and the Moorish empire did; not until the British arrived did a regional approach to managing power relations on the subcontinent and beyond emerge.

History can also encourage regional cooperation by inspiring a desire to avoid repeating the past. Of this, Europe is the exemplar. The European Union "is considerably ahead of the OAS in its approach to maintaining peace within its own region," said Einaudi, "because most EU members know war benefits no one." This lesson, however, as Solomon remarked, was not easily or swiftly learned: "Only recently has Europe learned to work together. Centuries of war have given way to a few decades of cooperation." Still, there is no doubting the sincerity of the commitment of the post–World War II generation in Western Europe to the idea of transforming a history of hostility into a cooperative future. "Certainly," observed Line, "the French postwar generation felt history impelled them to build ties with Germany" by means of mechanisms for first economic and later political cooperation. It should be underscored that this sentiment was not restricted to political elites; the French and German elites may have spearheaded the process of European integration, but they could only do so because they enjoyed the broad support of their publics.

The reverse dynamic can also occur. The United Kingdom has acquired a reputation for dragging its feet on European integration in part because, while its political and business classes are generally supportive of much closer ties with Europe, its public has evinced much less enthusiasm for building more institutional bridges between Britain and the Continent. British politicians have been wary of getting out too far ahead of the British public on this issue in case the public—mindful of the country's long history of keeping the Continent at arm's length—exacts retribution at the ballot box.

Yet, political elites need not always fear being brought to account by publics initially resistant to or uninterested in regional cooperation. In the case of ASEAN, as Chan explains, policymakers and diplomats may have been out ahead of their publics in terms of an interest in building regional ties, but they have to some extent pulled their publics behind them. "ASEAN had no historical sense of itself before the organization was formed," noted Chan. "Southeast Asia is a geographic concept. But now there is a regional system. The reality of a growing common Southeast Asian identity is creating a higher comfort level among the peoples of the region. ASEAN has stimulated the development of a regional culture. Only 1 percent of people in the region might have heard of ASEAN but ASEAN has helped promote a regional culture via ASEAN programs for youth, programs that have boosted inter-ASEAN tourism, and so forth. ASEAN has helped engender, especially in the region's urban areas, a modern Southeast Asian identity and more awareness of each other's culture."

In the case of ASEAN, a history of regional cultural diversity and of limited interaction between peoples may have created publics indifferent to, rather than hostile to, regional cooperation. In some other parts of the world, however, history, far from encouraging regional cooperation, has impeded it. In East Asia, for instance, culturally entrenched memories of centuries of foreign attack have left peoples and governments alike wary of outsiders. "The Koreans have had to try to defend themselves against repeated interventions by outside powers—the Chinese, Mongols, Japanese—and have developed a very violent confrontational approach to dealing with outsiders," said Solomon. "Other countries in the region also have that culture to some degree. Rather than being servile in their dealings with big powers, the Japanese and the Vietnamese, like the Koreans, have sometimes adopted tough, confrontational approaches to preserve their own systems, agendas, and cultures."

Latin American countries are generally less fearful of one another but not necessarily any more forgiving. In Latin American diplomacy, said Graham, "history occupies a larger place than in other areas." And in Latin America, "old wounds heal very slowly and in some cases are cherished by the culture and the politicians"—witness the continuing potency in Argentina of the issue of the status of the Falklands/Malvinas, and the longevity and bitterness of border disputes between Venezuela and Guyana or Chile and Bolivia. As recently as 2005, Bolivian foreign minister Juan Siles said Bolivia could not vote for Chile's interior minister José Miguel Insulza to become the OAS's secretary general because the loss of Bolivia's coastline to Chile in a nineteenth-century war was "one of the few open wounds" in the hemisphere.[20]

The confrontational approach in East Asia, it should be noted, has coexisted or at least alternated with a very different approach, albeit one with equally deep historical and cultural roots: deference.[21] For millennia, the Chinese "tribute system" regulated diplomatic interactions among the elites of East Asia. This highly elaborate system essentially demanded displays of subservience to Chinese authority by the leaders of regional states (especially Korea and Vietnam) in return for China recognizing their local authority, granting them trading rights, and bestowing other privileges. The system harmonized with Confucian philosophy and its concern for hierarchical but mutually respectful relationships. The system also encouraged—and rewarded—the spread of key elements of Chinese culture, such as written language, throughout the region.

Over time, the formal tribute system declined, but its influence has not disappeared. In China itself, explained Solomon, "diplomacy still retains a highly ritualistic character." "The Chinese," remarked Line, "still think of themselves as the Middle Kingdom, as the center of the universe, and they still bring [visiting dignitaries] and sit them down in this imperial setting—and they show it on TV, this audience-with-the-emperor scenario, this paying of homage."

In the case of the former tributary state of Japan, the collapse of the Qing dynasty in 1912 led Japan to seek to assert itself, but in the aftermath of World War II, when the United States assumed the role of regional hegemon, Japan was content to play the role of subordinate, even to the extent of allowing U.S. troops stationed in Japan to be tried by American courts for crimes committed in Japan. Today, however, with China ascending and the nature and scale of the future U.S. presence in the region uncertain, Japanese diplomats have explicitly stated that Japan wants to play the role of regional balancer between the two major powers.

As Japan's shifting stance indicates, history can and does shape how nations seek to maneuver within a regional security framework, but history rarely dictates and rarely trumps more concrete considerations. Bloody wars, horrific massacres, and unjust "peace agreements" in the nineteenth century "did terrible damage to the Balkans," as Wisner noted, "creating an I-win-you-lose attitude throughout the region." Even so, and despite the more recent atrocities of the 1990s, Wisner predicted that "regional cooperation will surely develop because there is an economic impetus for cooperation; the reality of geography backs it up. Some limited collaboration on technical issues is already occurring. And once the problem of sovereignty is sorted out, cooperation will take hold."

Affinities and Identities

Practical interests, as Wisner's observation about the future of cooperation in the Balkans highlights, can indeed drive cooperation despite cultural obstacles. Yet it is also the case that while nations with very different identities and cultures may have powerful, pragmatic reasons to work together (indeed, as the examples of Israel-Palestine and India-Pakistan attest, culturally dissimilar countries can have *the most to gain* from cooperation, because the issues that divide them can threaten their fundamental security, even their very existence), those differences tend to obstruct communication and collaboration. By the same token, countries with shared transnational identities find it much easier to talk with one another and are often—though not always—readier to work together.

This inclination is reinforced in cases where states share several different types of identity simultaneously. Most nations in the Caribbean, for instance, speak the same language, English.[22] Their historical experiences are similar: colonization, slavery, a peaceful transition to independence, and since then relatively stable democratic governance. And their political and popular cultures have been significantly shaped by their ties to Great Britain, ties that are still maintained in numerous ways, including via membership of the Commonwealth. "They form a distinct group in the OAS, and see themselves," said Einaudi, "as culturally separate not only from Latin America but also from the United States and Canada—but not so separate from Britain. There's a cultural identity that matters. They are more confident of dealing with the United States because of their unity and because of their Commonwealth ties, which make them feel they can draw on a yet wider tradition and wider group of countries. Their shared cultural base is very important; other small countries, in Latin America, have never been able to come together to cross the Latin vs. Anglo divide. There is clearly a cultural differentiation that matters in all these approaches."

A striking contrast to this English-speaking Caribbean club is provided in the shape of Haiti, whose idiosyncratic mix of cultures—political, popular, linguistic, and so forth—has helped to consign it to the margins of the region's diplomacy. One of the few times "the OAS has voted for economic sanctions was in the case of Haiti in the 1990s," commented Einaudi, "and many have suggested that they only voted for them then because they were dealing with a poor, black, French-speaking country outside the Latin sphere."

Even strongly shared identities, however, do not necessarily lay the foundations for close cooperation on the regional stage. "In the Arab world," noted Freeman, "two concepts transcend the nation-state: the Arab nation (relations between Arab states are called 'sisterly' and emphasize honor and respect); and the *umma*, the Islamic nation (which calls upon all Islamic countries to protect one another if they are attacked by non-Muslim states)." These concepts carry significant weight among the public in the Arab world and can prompt supportive diplomatic moves. Line, for instance, recalled that when he was working with the international community in Bosnia, one Egyptian ambassador was cooperative, constructive, and open-minded with the international community "except when the Bosniak [Muslim] side was being politically provocative," at which point he was more defensive of that side because he was "probably responding to the need to serve his own constituency, the wider Arab world." But when the interests of Arab states are at stake, and especially when inter-Arab rivalries are involved, policymakers and diplomats often tend to pay only lip service to notions of Islamic and Arab nations. One result is the spectacle of meetings of Arab leaders at which they publicly pledge themselves to cooperate for the common good while conspiring to ensure that little action toward that goal actually takes place. Diplomacy between Arab states "is *not* cross-cultural diplomacy," pointed out Freeman, but "ease of communication [which a shared culture facilitates] does not necessarily translate into ease of cooperation."

Subregions, Subcultures, and Size

Cooperation is often easier to achieve at the subregional rather than the regional level. There are at least three reasons for this. In the first place, geographically smaller, more compact units are likely (for all sorts of historical and practical reasons) to have culturally stronger ties, as the above-mentioned example of the "Caribbean club" testifies.

Second, these impalpable bonds can be bolstered by very practical advantages that clubbing together can provide. As in the case of Caribbean nations within the OAS, clubbing together is an extremely useful means of amplifying their power; "they know that their ability to exist as international players," noted Einaudi, "depends on their ability to cooperate with each other." As Graham explained, they are small in size but they are also numerous, and so "fourteen states with a total population of less than three million exercise disproportionate voting power" in the OAS, much to the irritation of far more populous members of the thirty-four–strong organization.

Interestingly, when the Caribbean nations see themselves, not as forming a subregion of a larger region but as composing a region all by themselves, they are less ready to work together. Like many modestly sized states throughout the world, the English-speaking Caribbean states "suffer from an exaggerated sensitivity about sovereign powers," said Graham. "There are enormous pressures in this collection of micro states to transfer some powers to a central body for reasons of economy and leverage. Local insular pride usually stands in the way. When the region was being given independence from the United Kingdom, a huge effort was made to create a West Indies federation. After a very short time, this failed, in 1962, and, with the exception of some subregional arrangements (such as CARICOM [the Caribbean Community] and the Organization of Eastern Caribbean States) has not been reinstituted."

States within other subregions within the OAS exhibit similar behavior: proud and prickly when dealing with one another but full of esprit de corps when dealing with other subregions or the region as a whole. "Each country in Latin America is very distinctive, yet the region's diplomats club together very much in international fora," commented Graham. "Although there are now two clubs [one centered around Venezuela, Ecuador, and Nicaragua, the other around Colombia, Chile, and Panama], they network very much among themselves." This subregional instinct explains why, for practical purposes, as Einaudi noted, "the management of the OAS is conducted on a subregional basis, with positions to be taken by OAS decided by a small committee made up of the United States, Canada, CARICOM, the Rio Group, and the Central American group."

A third reason for the strength of subregionalism—and for its association with size—is that it offers one way of combating the power of a regional hegemon. From Russia to China to the United States, regional hegemons tend to be territorial behemoths, far larger in size as well as power than their regional neighbors.[23] Such bruisers have less need to cooperate with their neighbors to advance their interests. Indeed, a hegemon may be able to dictate a region's conflict management practices or at least veto specific applications of specific practices. If it takes a lead, it expects other countries to follow it. And it will also often seek to decide which conflicts can be tackled by the region collectively and which it will handle itself, knowing that in bilateral encounters it can usually overawe, overwhelm, or otherwise overpower its counterpart with its unmatched and multifaceted arsenal of resources.[24]

Faced with a hegemon, especially one with a long history of meddling in the affairs of other states within the region, smaller countries band together in what Einaudi calls "multilateral trades unionism." There is strength in numbers. And that strength is greater when cultural bonds (which tend to be strongest within subregions) reinforce the sense of unity among the ranks of the midsize and small states. In the OAS, for instance, Latin American countries, with their shared historical experiences of actual or feared U.S. intervention, have traditionally formed a fairly tight bloc seeking to constrain U.S. power. "Fear of the United States is part of the glue that holds Latin American states together," remarked Graham. "In many Latin American countries," he added, "there is now a visible sense of pride in Castro staring down eight U.S. presidents." Canada, too, as Einaudi commented, is "culturally resistant" to U.S. domination, but Canada's resistance takes a very different form and valorizes different historical feats and figures than does Latin America's.

The OAS operates by consensus, which might be considered to reflect the region's readiness to cooperate and to do what the "club" as a whole favors, but which is in fact rooted in unpleasant memories of the United States' historical habit of dispatching its troops southward. Consensual decision making gives even a small country the power to stop anything.[25] As Einaudi noted, "In the OAS, military threats and sanctions are ruled out culturally largely because of the history of relations between Latin America and the United States." The last time the OAS approved military intervention was in 1965, "when the United States invaded Dominican Republic after arm-twisting the OAS, which sent token troops." Since then, other countries in the region have done what they can to ensure that any peacekeeping troops deployed in the region are UN forces.

The struggle between regional hegemons and smaller states can be a struggle not only over power but also over culture. All hegemons are, by definition, powerful, but each hegemon has its own culture, which shapes how it exercises that power, including in terms of preferred approaches to dealing with conflict within its region. Russia—with its tsarist and Soviet traditions—is not reluctant to unglove its iron fist, as Chechens and Georgians know all too well.[26] India presents a sharp contrast. India, as Wisner commented, "holds two modestly contradictory views: one is that India is indisputably the dominant power in South Asia; the other is that, despite accusations from their neighbors to the contrary, India goes to great pains not to throw its weight around. They don't often march soldiers up to borders, they don't tend to invade neighbors, they don't operate on the basis of territorial ambition." This self-restraint, argued Wisner, stems in part from a belief among India's elite that restraint is smart policy. Indians know they will not give in to threats; neither will their neighbors. Restraint in the neighborhood is borne out by India's experience. Even though they believe "that it is in the nature of the world that those who have power will use it to the detriment of the weak, force has not settled South Asia's differences."

The hegemon of the Western world, the United States, rarely intervenes militarily in the hemisphere these days and instead seeks other ways (mediated agreements, sanctions, and declarations of principles, for example) to pursue its goals. In part, this multifaceted approach reflects the multifaceted nature of U.S. culture: an ambivalence about negotiating with foreigners and a superpower's impulse to dominate coexisting alongside a businesslike appetite for striking mutually beneficial deals, a legalistic concern to stipulate and enforce rules, and a moralist's sense of self-regard and appetite for sermonizing.[27]

In part, too, it reflects the outcome of the encounter between U.S. culture and the cultures of other members of the OAS. "In the United States," argues Line, "we tend to believe in the law (as in the Constitution, in civil rights legislation, and so forth). But in Latin America, law has always been much more clearly a double-edged sword. Latin Americans have lived with the ambiguity of law long enough to see through it as an unblemished tool." Indigenous peoples such as the Mayans "usually only encountered the law when it was used to take their land from them." And even the political elites, at least those on the political left, "see the law as a tool but not necessarily a neat, clean one." This intersection of U.S. and Latin American views may help to explain why the OAS, in the realm of conflict management, tends to shy away from inflexible legal instruments—such as sanctions—but to gravitate toward activities that involve seeing rules and regulations within a local context—such as electoral observation.[28]

Two Vignettes of Culture and Conflict Management

This section presents vignettes of two regions and their characteristic approaches to collective conflict management. These are, it should be emphasized, no more than rough sketches. As might be expected, given the relative brevity of the interviews and the fact that each interviewee was free to focus on whatever regions and cases they wished to discuss, their observations tended to be impressionistic rather than sharply defined or highly detailed. Even so, these sketches do offer concrete examples of how culture interacts with a range of other factors to shape conflict management choices and behaviors. The first vignette describes a case in which an institutional culture developed despite the lack of a broader regional culture. The second examines the ways in which a broader regional culture has effectively neutered any institutional efforts to engage in conflict resolution.

ASEAN's Quiet Diplomacy

The "ASEAN way"—that preference for quiet, nonconfrontational, behind-the-scenes diplomacy to avoid or defuse conflict between states in Southeast Asia—is an instance of a conflict management approach that was *not* deeply rooted in national or elite cultures but that has become very much a part of the region's organizational culture.

Western diplomats, said Chan, have had "to try and adjust to what they see as the ASEAN style—a different style. ASEAN is seen as a talk shop. Americans, Australians, and Europeans want to come into a meeting, go through the agenda, identify the issues, talk about them, and come to some conclusions. When they started attending the ASEAN meetings, they found that that was not the case. And they were quite frustrated. At

ASEAN, there is a refusal to bring up issues that will cause confrontation. The culture is: First, talk and get a feel for things."

The roots of this ASEAN culture, however, lie not in the region's broader culture; indeed, the ASEAN way emerged as a pragmatic response to the lack of an overarching regional culture. "ASEAN's values and style—its disinclination to address sharp issues—is born of substance, of very different states not wishing to interfere in their neighbors' affairs and provoke ill will," explained Wisner. "ASEAN spreads over so many cultures, and such diversity makes it hard to deal with one another without deferential attitudes, without putting off difficult issues to the future; you need such an approach because you have little confidence in being able to work together to resolve problems because of the scale of cultural difference." Chan made the same point: In the late 1960s, when ASEAN was created, "Malaysia, Singapore, Indonesia were engaged in armed confrontation, and armed conflict was just below the surface with Burma, Thailand, etc. So we adopted the principle of noninterference. Noninterference has become part of our culture, but that has been based on our hard substantive interests, a desire not to step on each other's toes, a hard-nosed understanding of our history—a history of conflict. If you really want to get on as a regional grouping, you'd better adopt the principle of noninterference."

This culture has evolved during ASEAN's forty-odd years of existence. The organization has become a little more action-oriented and results-oriented, especially when it works with states outside Southeast Asia, as in the case of ASEAN Plus Three (which includes China, Korea, and Japan) and the East Asia Summit (a gathering at which India, Australia, and New Zealand join the ASEAN Plus Three countries). ASEAN has also on occasion suspended its principle of noninterference, as in the cases of East Timor and Myanmar. "But even then," as Chan remarked, "we did not say things in a way to shame and name our own members. Western countries still tear their hair and say, 'Look at Myanmar and how they're treating their people, how can you opt for noninterference?' But ASEAN would never do what the European Union, for instance, did when in 2000 it publicly condemned member-state Austria because its government included Jorg Haider's [far-right, anti-immigrant] party."

This contrast with the European Union is interesting, because Bailes, for one, sees significant similarities in the conflict management styles favored by ASEAN and the European Union. "A preference for step-by-step and fuzzy approaches (including solutions based on deliberate ambiguity and agreement-to-disagree) is quite common in Europe and Southeast Asia." The two regions "are most inclined toward non-zero-sum solutions and accordingly toward a kind of surface politeness ('rules of cricket,' avoiding loss of face by any party)," she said, attributing this preference in part to the two regions' "long-term multilateral experience."

Cultural diversity in Europe—especially Western Europe—is far less, however, than in Southeast Asia; "the scale of cultural difference," to use Wisner's phrase, is far more modest. Europeans have thus a better prospect of resolving the issues that divide them by discussing those issues directly and explicitly. The fear of "losing face" is also a good deal less acute in Europe than in Southeast Asia. As a consequence, sometimes—witness the protests over Haider's membership of the Austrian government—this means that disputes are aired publicly and the language employed is not always the most diplomatically restrained.[29]

Calming but Not Resolving Conflicts in the Arab World

While ASEAN has developed an organizational culture of quiet diplomacy designed to resolve nascent disputes, in the Arab world the broader regional culture encourages a noisier diplomacy designed to quiet but not to resolve conflict.

Egypt's diplomatic style is based on its long history and is distinct from that of its neighbors in various ways, such as a nonpredatory desire to avoid military confrontation and, as Wisner said, to "handle neighbors, even potential enemies, the way one would handle a very soft-boiled egg." In other respects, however, Egyptian diplomacy resonates with the region as whole, not least insofar as "Egyptians, unlike Americans but like most Arabs, believe that there are many problems in the world, that very few problems have solutions, and that most problems are to be managed, keeping your own interests clearly in mind." Wisner recounted a visit he received twenty years ago from a Syrian student who had been videoing street crime and confrontation in Cairo and in Detroit. He had come to three conclusions: First, when an incident occurs in the street in Detroit, everything becomes very quiet; in Egypt, it becomes very noisy, as everyone, bystanders included, starts yelling and pointing. Second, in Detroit everyone runs away from the two protagonists who are confronting one another; in Cairo, people run in and smother the protagonists, talking to them and trying to clam them down. Third, in Detroit, someone wins and someone loses; in Egypt, no one wins and no one loses. The same holds true at the national level in the region. When conflict between Arab states occurs, others rush in to try to calm the situation down but they do not expect to solve anything. The underlying friction between the protagonists "will not have changed one iota."

The League of Arab States, supposedly the expression of regional solidarity and the vehicle for maintaining peace within the Arab nation, has achieved very little in the area of conflict management despite having existed for more than sixty years. Occasionally, Wisner observed, its secretary-general will be used to call the parties to a conflict to settle down, but there "is no significant inter-Arab quarrel that was satisfactorily resolved by the Arab League. The advantage of the Arab League lies not in resolving conflicts but in providing one more forum for calming down the parties, for removing the steam from the kettle."

Freeman suggested that this lack of accomplishment, this record of inactivity, is not, in fact, a failure—not, that is, from the perspective of its member states. "The Arab League," argued Freeman, "does what it is supposed to do, which is to provide the lowest common denominator of Arab diplomacy. . . . Some Arab governments retain ministers whose principal function seems to be to go to the Arab League and make sure no decisions are taken." He attributed this attitude to political culture and historical experience. In the first place, the "vertical hierarchies" characteristic of political authority in Arab nations allow individual leaders to be profoundly self-serving and work to undercut cooperation in many areas. Second, smaller states know that "but for Persian, then Portuguese, and finally British imperialism, they would long since have been swallowed by Saudi Arabia or Iraq. So there's jealousy and wariness and vested interests to protect. And cooperation just doesn't come very easily. This is not nationalism in the European sense; it's tribal and familial rivalry as embodied within states."[30]

Bailes also pointed to a similar historical and cultural tradition, observing that the approaches of Middle Eastern entities display "elements of posturing for posturing's sake, of a preferred zero-sum culture and of hatred of the 'other' as an individual—not just what he/she stands for . . . perhaps reflecting a 'modern' or 'premodern' (as against 'postmodern') conception of statehood and identity."

Avenues for Future Research

These two vignettes are hardly definitive portraits. But they do suggest that culture influences regional conflict management, and that it can do so in a variety of ways and with a variety of results. If this is indeed the case, then the subject deserves closer inspection, especially in light of the fact that regions are increasingly trying to fix their own problems rather than letting outsiders try to do so—witness, for instance, Turkey actively mediating several conflicts in the Middle East, and the African Union and the Economic Community of West African States (ECOWAS) assuming greater responsibility for peacekeeping in Africa.

What might be done to acquire a higher-resolution image of the interplay of culture and conflict management at the regional level?

A first step might be to undertake a more extensive, more rigorous, and more focused round of interviews with diplomats and other practitioners. Borrowing an approach that has proved effective in the CCN project, one could enlist a group of, say, ten to twenty "foreign" diplomats with firsthand knowledge of the culture and the conflict management practices of a particular region to spend a day or two discussing a limited agenda of issues. The results of that discussion could then be shared with "indigenous" practitioners so as to confirm, refute, or refine the conclusions reached; among other advantages, this second step would help reveal the extent to which "foreign" and "indigenous" perspectives coincide and diverge.[31]

Other potentially fruitful avenues to explore in the diplomatic world include the following:

- "Cultural localitis": To what extent and by what process do diplomats take on the culture of the country or organization to which they are posted? Are some cultures more "contagious" for foreign diplomats? Are the cultures of some diplomats more resistant to localitis? Which culture and which type of culture (professional, institutional, national, etc.) takes precedence in particular circumstances?
- Abrupt identity shifts: How (asked Bailes) do diplomats deal, in cultural terms, with sudden shifts in the identity of the state for which they work? What happened to the Soviet diplomats who suddenly found themselves working for their native republics after the fall of the USSR? Did they abandon behavioral styles and values that were suddenly historically outmoded, and did they embrace new ones more in line with the interests and values of their new states?
- Language and culture: To what extent does language facilitate or frustrate diplomatic communication?[32] Are some languages better suited to transparent communication than others? Do some languages embody concepts particularly relevant to negotiation and mediation? Can a diplomat who is not fluent in a local language be fluent in its culture? Does the fact that some regional organizations adopt a nonnative lingua franca—ASEAN, for instance, conducts its business in English—create a linguistically level playing field or does it muzzle the kind of nuance available only in local languages (which have evolved to reflect local concerns)?

A second step would be to explore beyond the diplomatic arena. After all, as the chapters in this volume attest, conflict management is not the preserve of regional organizations, nor of the states that form those organizations, nor of the diplomats that those states dispatch to represent them at those organizations. This chapter has focused on diplomats, but a wide array of both state and nonstate actors—drawn from the ranks of the military, NGOs, civil society, the media, business, think tanks, academia, and so forth—play direct and indirect roles in regional conflict management, and each brings its own culture with it. To what extent do these cultures harmonize or conflict with one another? To what extent does one or more dominate particular areas of activity? Do they interact to produce a "neutral" or "third" culture?

A third step would be to look beyond the region. When a region turns to extraregional players for help in addressing its conflicts—and all regions do so on occasion, and some regions do so habitually—it effectively invites "foreign" cultures to enter the peacemaking fray. Is the result cultural pandemonium, with miscommunication and misunderstanding the order of the day? Or can a foreign actor break an impasse between local protagonists by offering a fresh perspective and a new set of prescriptions—a perspective and prescriptions rooted in the foreigner's own culture? Or do the outsiders arrive on the scene with their "globalized" culture and insist that their local interlocutors subscribe to it? And if the local leaders do so and reach an agreement, can they sell that agreement to their constituencies, who are steeped in the local culture, not in the culture of international diplomacy?

*   *   *

Determining how and to what extent culture influences a given region's preference for specific conflict management approaches is a Herculean task, perhaps a Sisyphean one. Culture is so deeply embedded within a regional environment, and embedded at so many levels (institutional, elite, national, regional, and so forth) of the regional architecture for conflict management, that it is difficult to deny yet impossible to quantify its impact. Methodologically, one cannot control for culture's influence as one might control for a variable such as the involvement/noninvolvement of a hegemon in cases of conflict management—one simply cannot remove culture from the equation. Yet, just because it is difficult to ascertain the precise role played by culture, that is no reason to disregard it.

Appendix: Biographies of the Interviewees

Alyson Bailes worked in the British Diplomatic Service from 1969 to 2002, ending as ambassador at Helsinki before retiring early to take up academic posts. She is familiar with the workings of the European Union, NATO, and the OSCE and has also served in China. One of her research interests is the comparative study of regional cooperation frameworks.

Chan Heng Chee has been ambassador of Singapore to the United States since 1996. She has also served as permanent representative of Singapore to the United Nations and concurrently as high commissioner to Canada and ambassador to Mexico. She was founding director of the Institute of Policy Studies and director of the Institute of Southeast Asian Studies in Singapore.

Luigi R. Einaudi is a U.S. educator and diplomat with significant experience in policy planning. He served as the U.S. permanent representative to the OAS (1989–93) and as special envoy for the Ecuador-Peru peace talks (1995–98). In 2000, Ambassador Einaudi was elected assistant secretary general of the OAS and served simultaneously as acting secretary general from 2004 to 2005.

Chas W. Freeman, Jr., has been a career officer in the U.S. Foreign Service, serving in India, the Middle East, East Asia, Africa, and Europe. His positions include ambassador to Saudi Arabia during the Persian Gulf War, director for Chinese affairs at the State Department, principal deputy assistant secretary of state for African affairs, and assistant secretary of defense for international security affairs.

John W. Graham is chair emeritus of the Canadian Foundation for the Americas and a member of Friends of the Inter-American Democratic Charter. He was the first head of the Unit for the Promotion of Democracy at the OAS, and in that capacity he mediated in the Dominican Republic and Guatemala, and led a number of election missions in Latin America. He also served as senior OSCE election officer for two cantons in Bosnia and as Canadian ambassador in four countries, including Guyana and Venezuela.

Milburn Line is the executive director of the Joan B. Kroc Institute for Peace and Justice at the University of San Diego. He has worked in international missions with the Office of the High Representative, the OSCE, and the United Nations in Bosnia and Herzegovina and Guatemala and implemented human rights projects funded by the United States Agency for International Development (USAID) in Colombia and Guatemala.

Richard H. Solomon, president of the United States Institute of Peace, formerly served in the U.S. government on the National Security Staff, directed the State Department's Policy Planning Staff, and was assistant secretary of state for East Asian and Pacific affairs and ambassador to the Philippines. He also headed the political science department of the RAND Corporation and was professor of political science at the University of Michigan.

Frank Wisner began his extensive diplomatic career in Algeria and Vietnam in the 1960s, and over the following three decades he served as U.S. ambassador to Zambia, Egypt, the Philippines, and India. He has also held the positions of deputy assistant secretary of state for African affairs, under secretary of defense for policy, and under secretary of state for international security affairs. He retired from government service in 1997 but accepted an invitation in 2005 to be Washington's special representative to talks on Kosovo's independence.

Notes

1. I. William Zartman, "A Skeptic's View," in *Culture and Negotiation*, ed. Guy Faure and Jeffrey Z. Rubin (Newbury Park, CA: Sage, 1993), 17.

2. Widening the lens in this fashion in the case of the CCN project (so it became the "Cross-Cultural *Interaction*" project) might well produce an overwhelming torrent of data, because the project does not limit the range of diplomatic subjects within its purview— everything from nuclear proliferation to economic cooperation to environmental protection. But here we face no such tsunami of material because we are looking only at one, admittedly multifaceted, subject: conflict management.

3. For instance, asked Einaudi, "Do you include Costa Rica [the only long-established democracy in the region] or Belize [the only country in the region whose official language is English]?"

4. Raymond Cohen, *Negotiating across Cultures: International Communication in an Interdependent World*, rev. ed. (Washington, DC: United States Institute of Peace Press, 1997), 12.

5. Richard H. Solomon, *Chinese Negotiating Behavior: Pursuing Interests through 'Old Friends'* (Santa Monica, CA: RAND, 1995).

6. Three of these volumes are conceptual studies: *Negotiating across Cultures* by Cohen; *Culture and Conflict Resolution* (1998) by Kevin Avruch; and *Arts of Power: Statecraft and Diplomacy* (1997) by Chas W. Freeman, Jr. The remainder focus on individual countries or specific bilateral negotiating relationships. In addition to Solomon's assessment of China, the country- and bilateral-specific studies include the following, all of which have been published by the United States Institute of Peace Press: Michael Blaker, Paul Giarra, and

Ezra Vogel, *Case Studies in Japanese Negotiating Behavior* (2005); Charles Cogan, *French Negotiating Behavior: Dealing with* La Grande Nation (2003); Daniel C. Kurtzer and Scott B. Lasensky, *Negotiating Arab-Israeli Peace: American Leadership in the Middle East* (2008); Dennis Kux, ed., *India-Pakistan Negotiations: Is Past Still Prologue?* (2006); John W. Limbert, *Negotiating with Iran: Wrestling the Ghosts of History* (2009); Jerrold L. Schecter, *Russian Negotiating Behavior: Continuity and Transition* (1998); W. R. Smyser, *How Germans Negotiate: Logical Goals, Practical Solutions* (2003); Scott Snyder, *Negotiating on the Edge: North Korean Negotiating Behavior* (1999); Richard H. Solomon and Nigel Quinney, *American Negotiating Behavior: Wheeler-Dealers, Legal Eagles, Bullies, and Preachers* (2010); and Tamara Cofman Wittes, ed., *How Israelis and Palestinians Negotiate: A Cross-Cultural Analysis of the Oslo Peace Process* (2005).

7. There is a good deal more literature on the role of culture in *business* negotiations. One of the few studies to focus on broad cultural patterns and *diplomacy* is Walter Russell Mead's *Special Providence: American Foreign Policy and How It Changed the World* (New York: Knopf, 2001).

8. Clyde Kluckhohn, "The Study of Culture," in *The Policy Sciences*, ed. D. Lerner and H. D. Lasswell (Stanford, CA: Stanford University Press, 1951), 86.

9. Cohen, *Negotiating across Cultures*, 12. In a similar vein, Tamara Wittes defines culture as "the product of the experiences of individuals within a given social group, including its representations in images, narratives, myths and patterns of behavior (traditions), and the meanings of those representations as transmitted among the group's members over time and through experience." Wittes, *How Israelis and Palestinians Negotiate*, 4.

10. See Avruch, *Culture and Conflict Resolution*, part II, 23–55. In a similar vein, Wittes emphasizes that the definition of culture she presents "allows, importantly, for individuals within a group to be differently situated by class, race, or other social attributes, such that identifiable subcultures can exist within a broader recognized culture." Wittes, *How Palestinians and Israelis Negotiate*, 4–5.

11. Jeswald W. Salacuse, "Implications for Practitioners," in *Culture and Negotiation*, ed. Faure and Rubin, 201.

12. Paul D. Williams, "From Non-Interference to Non-Indifference: The Origins and Development of the African Union's Security Culture," *African Affairs* 106, no. 423 (2007): 256.

13. Ibid., 278.

14. Einaudi added that the United States, particularly in multilateral forums, "often fails to appreciate this, and so opportunities for conflict resolution go down the drain."

15. Alternatively, perhaps the interviewees said little about security culture simply because they were not asked explicitly to comment on it.

16. "A similar globalized culture also exists at the higher levels of business organization," noted Bailes, "both because of the multinational structure of many key businesses and because of the commonness today of long lines of outsourcing and supply chains. One does not think perhaps of private-sector people as part of conflict resolution (or perhaps, only as negative contributors), but it is now common to accompany efforts for political and security solutions with 'funding' conferences and campaigns to draw in international investment."

17. Hedley Bull defines diplomatic culture as "the common stock of ideas and values possessed by the official representatives of States," which was developed over the course of centuries and which is an integral part of the "society of states." See Hedley Bull, *The Anarchical Society: A Study of Order in World Politics*, 3rd ed. (New York: Columbia University Press, 1977), 316. Geoffrey Wiseman makes an intriguing argument for its continuing relevance

in Wiseman, "Pax Americana: Bumping into Diplomatic Culture," *International Studies Perspectives* 6 (2005): 409–30.

18. Lang recognizes that "this negotiation culture is constrained . . . by national interests imposed by the respective government on its negotiators by means of more or less stringent instructions." Winfried Lang, "A Professional's View," in *Culture and Negotiation*, ed. Faure and Rubin, 46, 44–45.

19. Harold Nicholson, *The Evolution of Diplomatic Method* (London: Constable, 1954), 75–76.

20. Reported by Pablo Bachelet, "New Leader: 'Critical Time for OAS,'" *Miami Herald*, May 3, 2005.

21. How to explain this coexistence of confrontation and deference? One possible answer—which underlines the interrelationship between culture and power—is that smaller states have opted for one or the other approach after calculating the constellation of regional power at any given time: when multiple power centers exist, confrontation may be a realistic and successful policy option because the larger powers are devoting most of their energies to fighting among themselves; but when a single power is regionally dominant, deference is the only sensible approach if one does not wish to be crushed. The domestic political makeup of the tributary states may also have an impact on the decision to opt for confrontation or deference: autocrats are readier to submit to external powers as the price of enjoying uncontested domestic authority, whereas democrats and/or nationalists depend for their domestic authority on demonstrating a readiness to stand up to outside powers.

22. The impact of a common language was mentioned by several of the interviewees but none explored the subject in any depth.

23. In the Americas, Canada and Brazil are exceptions to the tendency for nonhegemons to be appreciably smaller than the regional hegemon; both countries, however, are in the second rank of influence within the OAS, not the third or the fourth. Africa is sui generis, having a number of very large countries, several of which are larger than the continent's putative hegemon, South Africa.

24. No hegemon is all-powerful, however, and it must sometimes look to other, less powerful nations to accomplish on its behalf what it cannot accomplish itself. In some instances, the hegemon's very power renders it powerless to act, because other nations are unwilling to expose themselves to asymmetries of power when dealing with highly sensitive issues. For example, the dispute between Colombia, Ecuador, and Venezuela was dealt with outside the OAS, via the Rio Group. Mediation would not have worked within the OAS, argues Graham, because "the U.S. would have been at the table, and the U.S. supports Colombia and has tense relations with Venezuela. . . . The chemistry wouldn't have been there with a U.S. presence."

25. Organizations that operate by consensus are vulnerable to paralysis—a moderate form of which has afflicted the OAS in recent years because of political tensions, especially those between the United States and Venezuela. Yet, consensus, when it is achieved, can be a powerful force in conflict management, in part because it can add a cultural and political impetus to a peace process. At the signing of the 1998 Peru-Ecuador peace accord (the negotiations for which Einaudi had played a prominent role in mediating), many regional leaders were in attendance to confer multilateral blessing. Similarly, in negotiating the future of the Panama Canal in the late 1970s with the United States, Panama drew support from its bigger neighbors, and when the Torrijos-Carter Treaties were signed, many leaders of OAS member-states attended the ceremony to give a public stamp of approval and make

it harder for either signatory (one a regional minnow but the other the regional hegemon) to go back on its commitments.

26. For a discussion of Russian culture and history and their impact on Russia's readiness to use force, see Schecter, *Russian Negotiating Behavior*, esp. chapter 1.

27. For a thorough discussion of these U.S. diplomatic traits, see Solomon and Quinney, *American Negotiation Behavior*, esp. chapter 2.

28. The OAS does use sanctions sometimes (against Haiti in 1992 and Honduras in 2009, for instance), but by no means enthusiastically or regularly.

29. As Bailes observed, "The EU states' internal arguments, whether held in EU council rooms or not, can be extremely vicious and . . . small as well as big states are capable of the most reckless and confrontational behavior at times." At other times, however, EU members seek not to vent their grievances but to sublimate their conflicts. "At a higher level," argued Bailes, "the European security experiment is all about sublimation of difference, national self-restraint, and the creation of at least some elements and levels of common identity—as shown by the fact that all the aforementioned national differences are displayed for the most part in smoke-filled rooms with not the faintest idea of ever erupting into physical violence."

30. Over the centuries, Arabs have developed two types of negotiation. One of these, *mufawadat*, is dedicated to building relationships, avoids expressions of overt anger, enables representatives of states to come together as equals to discuss in a dignified fashion issues of honor and mutual concern, and encourages magnanimous gestures. Raymond Cohen writes that *mufawadat* involves a "courtly exchange of views" and implies "discussions conducted in a serious, positive, and sociable atmosphere, with interlocutors consulting each other in an amicable way, putting forward constructive suggestions." This is quite different from the other kind of negotiation, *musawama*, which denotes the haggling one does in the bazaar, the objective of which is to get as much as one can from a transaction and then walk away. "If *mufawadat* suggests the dignified and high-minded discussions by statesmen of matters of principle, *musawama* suggests petty-minded haggling. In Arab-Israeli negotiations the representatives of Arab states, bitterly resenting having to negotiate over issues that they consider to concern national honor—land, justice, the rights of the Palestinians—often claim that while they engage in *mufawadat*, it is the Israelis who insist on *musawama*." Raymond Cohen, "Language and Negotiation: A Middle East Lexicon," http://www.diplomacy.edu/books/language_and_diplomacy/texts/html/cohen.htm.

The practice of *mufawadat* within the Arab League, however, does not seem to have yielded much in the way of "serious, positive," and "constructive" approaches to settling inter-Arab rivalries.

31. The results of the interviews conducted for this chapter suggest that diplomats are less likely to see culture as influential in their own regional neighborhood. The number of interviews conducted, however, is far too modest to permit any solid conclusions to be drawn about "foreign" vs. "indigenous" perspectives.

32. This inquiry would build on the pioneering work, cited earlier in this chapter, done by Raymond Cohen.

PART II

REGIONAL REVIEWS

5

African Solutions to African Problems

Assessing the Capacity of African Peace and Security Architecture

Chrysantus Ayangafac and Jakkie Cilliers

Speaking in front of the UN General Assembly in New York on September 14, 2005, Rwandan president Paul Kagame recalled the tragedy of the 1994 genocide in his country. "Never again" he noted, "should the international community's response be left wanting. Let us resolve to take collective action in a timely and decisive manner."[1] Events in Rwanda and the lack of response from the international community to halt the subsequent carnage and bloodshed are important to consider when reviewing the recent expanded role of African regional organizations in conflict prevention and management, for it is from these events that one can trace the origins of Africa's modern peace and security architecture.

National and regional security issues are inexorably intertwined in Africa. State weakness and the lapping of ethnic groupings across porous, colonially imposed borders determine the extent to which instability in one country affects neighboring countries and speak to the need for regional solutions to domestic challenges.[2] Consequently, the inception of the African Union in 2002 and its purported interventionist peace and security architecture appears to vindicate regionalization and multilateral security mechanisms as a viable policy response to Africa's complex security challenges.

Nevertheless, continuous conflicts in Chad, Sudan, and Somalia; the recent resurgence of coups in countries such as Guinea, Niger, Guinea-Bissau, and Madagascar; the manipulation of elections in Zimbabwe, Kenya, and Niger; and ongoing suppression in Darfur and Zimbabwe—all of which have contributed to mass migration and food crises—suggest that the African Union, despite some successes, is struggling with the continent's evolving security threats. Africa clearly has weak peacekeeping capacity, a situation compounded by the international community's reservations about substantively contributing to peacekeeping and post-conflict reconstruction in African conflicts zones.[3]

The case for developing and pursuing African regional security mechanisms has often been captured by the phrase "African solutions to African problems"—one intended to mobilize Africans to solve their problems. But this call is often as much a cop-out to rationalize inaction from the international community as it is a self-serving shield by African dictators such as Robert Mugabe and others to protect themselves from international scrutiny. Considering Africa's capacity constraints, is African conflict prevention, management, and post-conflict reconstruction a reality or merely rhetoric?

This chapter investigates this question by examining the African Union's capacity to address Africa's evolving security challenges. In so doing, it first analyzes Africa's security threats and the factors that might trigger and sustain them and then moves on to analyze the African Peace and Security Architecture (APSA)—the institutional expression of a vision according to which Africans assume greater ownership and responsibility for African insecurity—as a policy response to Africa's security challenges. It concludes with an assessment of the capacity of the APSA to respond to the continent's security threats.

Africa's Complex Security Threats

Although Africa's security threats are constantly evolving, state weakness continues to be the principal source of insecurity in Africa. The principal reason for the structural weakness of African states is a developmental and governance crisis that dates back to the colonial era and that was perpetuated during the Cold War.

Africa is a hugely diverse continent. Nominally divided into fifty-three states, it has security threats that vary from country to country and from region to region and that are largely informed by local dynamics and the strategies and interests of local actors. For its part, the African Union has adopted a conceptual approach to security that encompasses both the traditional, state-centric notion of security and the notion of security premised on the concerns of the individual.[4] At first glance the African Union seems to be making the argument that sovereignty is about the responsibility to citizens and that there must therefore be a positive alignment between regime security and human security. The reality is that the African Union has not lived up to the ethos of its human security agenda. For example, its position on the 2009 indictment of President Omar El Bashir of Sudan is captured by the old debate of peace versus justice, within which AU leaders comes down squarely on that of peace at the expense of justice—a stance in sharp contradiction to the concept of human security. So while on paper AU policy is often in line with international norms and standards that espouse democracy, respect for human rights, and equity, in practice it promotes regime security at virtually all costs.

Security Threats and the Failure of Development and Governance

Politics by definition functions in a context of scarcity: scarcity of resources, scarcity of power, scarcity of identity, and scarcity of status.[5] In the context of massive population growth, historically poor levels of development, and an ongoing process of state consolidation, violent conflict is invariably the outcome of the failure of development and of governance to regulate, reconcile, and harmonize differences. Africa's security and governance predicament, then, is an unfortunate result of the developmental trajectory upon which the continent has embarked.[6]

The March 2005 *Report of the Commission for Africa* found that Africa has experienced more violent conflict than any other continent in the last four decades.[7] Most of the world's armed conflicts now take place in sub-Saharan Africa and at the turn of the twenty-first century more people were killed in wars in this region than in the rest of the world combined.[8] Between 1960 and 1990, there were eighty violent changes of government in the continent. By the end of 1998, only 39 percent of forty-eight sub-Saharan African countries enjoyed stable political conditions and good governance, 23 percent faced political crisis and turbulence, and 38 percent were engaged in armed conflict or civil strife.[9] Yet generally unreported in a world where bad news sells, recent years have seen some improvements in stability in Africa. The Human Security Report Group, for example, recently recognized a reduction in open armed conflict in Africa. In 2006, the annual battle-death toll in sub-Saharan Africa was just 2 percent of that of 1999, and the number of conflicts had fallen by half.[10]

Key Threat Variables

Despite this improvement, intrastate conflict remains the major security threat on the continent. The nature and dynamics of future intrastate conflicts in Africa will be shaped by three important variables: manipulation of ethnic identity; competition over natural resources; and the regional character of African conflicts.

Ethnicity. Ethnicity is not a cause of conflict, but the fact that African conflicts are increasingly fought along ethnic lines speaks volumes of the role that the mobilization of identity plays in countries such as Kenya, Côte d'Ivoire, South Africa, Chad, Sudan, Zimbabwe, and the Democratic Republic of Congo (DRC).[11] Against a backdrop of deprivation and poverty, political elites in African societies have shown little restraint in manipulating people through ethnic prejudice. The political agendas of leaders are framed in ethnic and exclusionary terms even if at the risk of open armed conflict, with elections often reflecting the demographic strength of various ethnic groups. Thus, in the context of grinding poverty and weak democratic institutions unable to manage elite contests over the spoils of the state, the politics and economics of ethnicity will be a critical denominator in regard to decisions about who gets what and how and when it is gotten, especially in societies endowed with strategic natural resources such as fossil fuels and minerals.

Natural resources. The politics of resource allocation and resource distribution is at the heart of contemporary conflicts in Africa.[12] Much research has pointed to the positive correlation between the abundance of Africa's natural resources and the abundance of conflicts in Africa.[13] Since control of the state is synonymous with control of the economy (as small, formal economies generally gravitate around state largesse) and, by extension access, to control of natural resources, the nature of the African state is a critical factor in explaining instability on the continent.[14] Thus, in the absence of a viable alternative for wealth creation and accumulation, natural-resource abundance increases the stakes with regard to state control.[15]

The current massive population growth in Africa and the impact of climate change will exacerbate contests over access to and control of Africa's natural resources.[16] Beyond political grievances, the conflicts in the northeast of the Central African Republic (CAR) and Darfur began as competition over grazing land by local communities as a result of changing patterns of rainfall that was subsequently instrumentalized by political elites for their own agendas. Moreover, climate change will increase global competition for Africa's natural resources and in the process shape and influence domestic politics. This is not only a problem on land but also in its surrounding seas. According to André Standing, "As fish resources elsewhere are decreasing and the demand and value for fish is steadily rising, there is a growing dependence by foreign fishing fleets, particularly from the European Union and Asia, on gaining access to historically under-exploited waters of developing countries."[17]

If African states are a critical variable in explaining insecurity on the continent, what then explains their weak nature? African states are weak because of poor governance and the acute economic crises experienced by the continent until recently.[18] From the mid-1980s, the lack of development and the weakness of states have been accentuated by rising external debt, structural adjustment programs, the disengagement of Cold War patrons, and the advance of democratization. These factors combined to challenge the prevailing political order (political tradition grounded in patrimonial and inward-looking economic policies). In many cases, these changes disrupted the stability of African state formation, increased resource competition, and accentuated the unsustainable character of the postcolonial social system.[19]

All this has started to change in recent years. While freedom of the press, the rule of law, and government transparency remain weak, and while corruption is widespread at many levels of politics and the economy, literally all indices show strong improvements over the last decade. Until the setbacks due to the spike in food prices and the global recession of 2008–9, a large majority of African countries enjoyed rising levels of prosperity and stability and an increasing normalization of fragile state situations. Further, most elections have been peaceful. More than nineteen presidential and parliamentary elections were held in eighteen African countries in 2007, though they were often marred by low turnouts (Nigeria and Egypt) and abstention (Algeria). Incumbent heads of state are often reelected by wide margins, as are new presidents. Even in Zimbabwe, amid substantial intimidation and manipulation, the governing party has maintained a charade of electoral process—a facade that fellow dictators of a decade earlier would have dispensed with at an early stage.[20] However, this improvement in the institutional construct of governance should not mask the fact that patronage and informal networks, which at times are transnational, still dominate African politics.

Regional character of African conflicts. African conflicts often spill across state boundaries from one country to another. Beyond rivalry and enmity between heads of state, violent conflicts in Africa are of a regional and un-regulated character, reflecting the absence of effective governance across national territories. They also reflect the lack of capacity of some African states to regulate the number of weapons in society and to exercise the monopoly of violence over their territory. Hence, the government in Kinshasa had virtually no ability to control events in North Kivu province of the DRC (four hours flying time distant to the east), where a local warlord, Laurent Nkunda, set up an alternative administration in 2008 and maintained control for over a year before being dislodged and eventually captured by a combined UN-DRC force.

The regionalization of conflicts is also often used as a tactic to ensure political survival of particular elites amid general chaos and widespread regional disorder.[21] Thus, exporting instability is a strategy of alignment and realignment in the absence of strong democratic institutions to manage elite contestation. For instance, western Darfur and eastern Chad have become an extension of Sudan and Chad's domestic political arenas. In 1996 Rwanda exported its civil war to the eastern DRC, officially to ensure its security, but also to track down the perpetrators of the genocide who had sought refuge in the Kivu Mountains. The outcome was the transformation of the Great Lakes Region into a major conflict zone that at one point involved Rwanda, Burundi, Angola, DRC, Zimbabwe, Namibia, Uganda, and the Republic of Congo (RoC). Chad also exported its civil war to the CAR with the intention of destabilizing President Ange-Felix Patassé, considered to be the main financial backer and ally of political and military groups hostile to President Idriss Déby Itno of Chad.[22]

Exportation of conflict is also made possible by the fact that so-called national conflicts are socially and structurally linked to one another or to what Luc Sindjoun calls "affection-based politics."[23] This entails building political allegiances or ensuring political survival by tapping into the close relationships across borders. Rwanda established very close ties with Congolese rebel groups of Rwandan origin, also known as the *banyamulenge*." This large Rwandaphone community enables Rwanda to have an active say in Congolese politics. Similarly, the Zaghawa people living on both sides of the Chad-Sudan border serve as a corridor through which the two countries influence one another.

The incidence of interstate conflict has been heightened by access to and control of strategic resources against a backdrop of poor border delimitation, the discovery of natural resources such as fossil fuels that are close to or straddle borders, and the impact of climate change on mutually shared resources such as seas and rivers.[24] The evidence posits a worrying trend. Nigeria and Cameroon fought a low-intensity conflict over the Bakassi Peninsula, which is deemed to be rich in natural resources such as fish and fossil fuel; Gabon and Equatorial Guinea have been fighting over the Mbanie Island in the common territorial waters of both countries; and DRC and Uganda are contesting ownership over the disputed Rukwanzi Island.

Elsewhere, such as in the eastern DRC, alliances with private groups in mineral-rich areas have enabled the establishment of rebel fiefdoms where local warlords are able to maintain local control through the revenues generated from their illegal activities.[25] In this manner, important elites in Rwanda, Uganda, and other neighboring countries have illegally tapped the immense mineral wealth of the Congo.

The Rise of Africa's New Security Threats

Another direct consequence of the failure of development and governance as a conflict prevention mechanism—exacerbated by the weak capacity of Africa states—is the rise of what is popularly called "Africa's new security challenges."[26] These challenges either are consequential to intrastate conflicts or reflect the lack of capacity by African states to deliver on security.

The proliferation, circulation, and illicit trafficking in small arms and light weapons is one such security challenge facing the continent— although they are not recent phenomena. Arms proliferation is both a cause and consequence of armed conflicts in Africa. The availability of these weapons reduces the cost of initiating and sustaining a rebellion. The proliferation of arms and light weapons has resulted in the mushrooming of armed robbery and organized crimes such as drug trafficking, human trafficking, environmental degradation, the illicit exploitation of natural resources, organized crimes, terrorism, and money laundering.

The most common transnational crimes in African countries include motor vehicle theft, money laundering in overseas banks, the illegal sale of petroleum and petroleum products overseas, the production and distribution of counterfeit currency, the import and export of narcotic drugs, and the smuggling of precious minerals and firearms. Studies from Namibia show that Namibia serves as a transit route to the United Kingdom, South Africa, Angola, and Zambia for gold, diamond, and narcotics smuggling and shipping enterprises.[27] Recent attacks on commercial banks in Cameroon and attacks on the presidential palace in Equatorial Guinea show how powerful criminal gangs have become.

The increase of organized crime is a function of the inability of national security forces to curb crime, of the growing economic discrepancies and the correlated social fragmentation of populations, and of the expansion of urban slums and unemployment. For example, the lack of capacity of Guinea-Bissau's security apparatus has made the country's political and administrative institutional structures vulnerable to penetration by drug traffickers and other organized criminal networks. According to the UN Office on Drugs and Crime and the UN Office for West Africa, Guinea-Bissau has become an important transit point for drug traffickers. Since

2007, the West African region has seen almost forty tons of cocaine transit through its territory, most of it through Guinea-Bissau, destined for Europe and North America.[28]

The lack of capacity in African states to patrol their maritime territories has also led to the illegal exploitation of marine resources and the resurgence of piracy, especially along the Gulf of Aden and the Gulf of Guinea. The latest piracy statistics released by the International Maritime Bureau's Piracy Reporting Centre indicate a dramatic increase in attacks of piracy.[29] The potential cost of piracy in these regions is not hard to fathom considering the importance of key maritime routes to the global economy. However, while piracy might be of immense importance to the West, this might not be the case to certain African countries. In West, East, and Central Africa, the principal security threats posed by the lack of capacity to monitor territorial waters are illegal fishing and the exploitation of natural resources. The sheer scale of illegal fishing now threatens around 200 million Africans who rely on fish for nutrition and 10 million who rely on fishing for income.[30] According to the Department for International Development (DfID), the value of illegal fishing for sub-Saharan Africa is $1 billion per year—almost one quarter of the annual total value of reported African fish exports.[31]

Climate change is another "new" security threat facing Africa. Climate change is already compounding Africa's existing risk and might wipe out efforts to tackle poverty if more robust efforts are not taken to address the problem. Africa is particularly vulnerable to climate change because of its overdependence on rain-fed agriculture and its widespread poverty and weak infrastructure. The main longer-term impacts of climate change include changing rainfall patterns, which affects agriculture and reduces food security; worsening water security; decreasing fish resources in large lakes due to rising temperatures; shifting vector-borne diseases; rising sea levels, which affects low-lying coastal areas with large populations; and increased water stress.[32]

Bloody riots in Burkina Faso, Cameroon, and Guinea (Conakry) in early 2008 suggest that food security is becoming a major security concern. The prevalence of malnutrition within the continent varies by region. It is lowest in Northern Africa (4 percent) and highest in Central Africa (40 percent), with between 33 and 35 percent of the population in sub-Saharan Africa considered to be malnourished in any given year.[33] The cause of food security threats seems to be lack of entitlement to food rather than the short supply of food.

In addition to these threats, migration and the plight of refugees and internally displaced persons represent a security threat on two counts. First, while remittances to Africa now rival overseas development assistance, the brain drain constrains the ability of states to deliver services. The constant migration of African professionals, such as doctors and nurses, to Europe, the United States, and countries such as India has compounded the continent's fight against HIV/AIDS, tuberculosis, and malaria. Second, refugees and refugee camps can at times be sources of insecurity and can lead to competition for local resources.[34] More importantly, refugee camps can serve as a launching base for a rebellion, as the situations in eastern DRC and eastern Chad have shown. The Hutu refugee camps in eastern DRC were used as bases to attack the Tutsi-led government in Rwanda, and Chadian and CAR refugees along the Cameroon border have at times been accused of armed banditry. The refugee camps in Chad have in some instances been used to launch attacks in Darfur.

The Threat of Unstable Post-Conflict Situations

The recurrence of violence after negotiated peace agreements, such as in Liberia in 1997 and in the DRC in 2006 and in more recent years, suggests that the failure to consolidate peace and deliver quickly on human security in post-conflict societies is an emerging security risk in Africa[35]—a failure that the largest UN peacekeeping mission in the world (the UN Organization Mission in the DRC [MONUC]) is still struggling to resolve. Cessation of hostilities through the imposition of a massive peace operation that temporarily provides an (external) guarantee against infection does not amount to peace. Liberia, Sierra Leone, Burundi, the CAR, and Guinea-Bissau are still very fragile states. Against this background it should be evident that Africa's future stability will increasingly depend on comprehensive and robust post-conflict reconstruction and development efforts that deliver on human security and economic growth.

From an African perspective—at least with regard to the AU Policy Framework on Post-Conflict and Reconstruction—the orthodox approach to post-conflict reconstruction and development, premised on restoring the institutional facets of states as the "constituted repositories of power and authority within borders" and the "performers and suppliers of political goods," appears to be misplaced.[36] First, this policy approach is premised on the thesis that a state in the Weberian sense existed in the first place. Henri Boshoff, using the example of the DRC, argues that the appellation "post-conflict reconstruction" is a misnomer, considering it is premised on the fallacy that a state even existed there.[37] Indeed, there is overwhelming evidence that most of Africa's collapsed states never resembled a modern Western polity, the case of the DRC being a blatant example.[38]

Too much emphasis on institutional reconstruction is the function of a scholarly tradition that links African state failure to leadership failure, the structure of African states, and the dynamics of democratization in polarized societies.[39] The high mark of this approach is the espousal of democratization and good governance as remedies to post-conflict societies, but the key to sustained peace is perhaps more cogently based on security and sustained and distributed economic growth.

The problem is that there is no generally accepted theory of democratization to guide development and reconstruction, that democracy does not provide economic growth, and that good governance disappears together with the peacekeepers. International development institutions stress the promotion of human rights and democratic principles with the result that elections and electoral reform have become central in contemporary post-conflict reconstruction agendas, but with little apparent lasting effect. The resumption of violence after post-conflict elections in the DRC in 2006, in the RoC in 2003, and in Liberia in 1997 suggests that post-conflict elections reflect the military asymmetry of conflicts that preceded them—though it is important to note that there are, as always, exceptions, such as the 2005 Liberian election, which did produce substantial forward progress. Thus, most post-conflict elections within the context of reconstruction after a peace mission end up legitimizing a military victor or a powersharing arrangement and, in some instances, institutionalizing wartime alliances.

Moreover, the orthodox approach to post-conflict reconstruction also seems to be anchored in the idea that state failure is the result of a loss of monopoly over the instruments of violence and coercion by a government within a given territory. Thus, state reconstruction often largely consists of efforts to strengthen the security apparatus of African governments. After all, failed states are purported breeding grounds for terrorism and serve as a launching pad for piracy. Rather than focusing on improved security for the population, the subsequent assistance provided is focused on bolstering measures and systems geared toward countering threats to Western interests/countries and the "international system." The unintended consequence of this policy approach is that most of the invariably repressive regimes in Africa, such as the one in Chad, have been bolstered. In Mali and Niger, government cooperation with the United States on counterterrorism has heightened grievances among the Tuareg community, which is fighting for greater autonomy. Thus, the dilemma faced by Africans and the international community alike is that the reconstruction agenda amounts to recreating the structures and institutions that were instrumental to state collapse in the first instance.

At the height of its structural adjustment programs some decades earlier, the World Bank seemed to suggest that economic recovery and political stabilization in post-conflict societies is contingent on rebuilding and transformation of the state, particularly the creation of a market-based economy in which the state would withdraw from productive sectors and work in coalition with nongovernmental networks to deliver social services. There is ample subsequent evidence to suggest that the weakness of African states in subsequent years was exacerbated by these neoliberal economic prescriptions and resulted in substantive increases in insecurity, hunger, and deprivation.[40] As such, one could argue that the market-driven reconstruction agenda of the West can to an extent recreate the same environment and framework that exacerbated state failure during the 1980s and early 1990s. Rather than cherry picking, there is need for a comprehensive post-conflict reconstruction agenda that is grounded in reconstructing the social fiber of the state—even while accepting that future African development will necessarily be driven by the private and not the public sector.[41]

The African Peace and Security Architecture

The Policy Agenda

Much of the initial praise lavished on the African Union after its inauguration in Durban in 2002 was motivated not only by the fact that it represents the start of a new political, judicial, and economic vision for the continent but also by the prominence provided in its Constitutive Act, the New Partnership for Africa's Development (NEPAD), and the African Peer Review Mechanism (APRM) to the principles of human rights, democracy, and good governance and therefore to human security. These commitments permeate its Constitutive Act and key associated legal commitments, such as the Protocol on the African Union's Peace and Security Council (PSC). Thus, Article 3(g) commits the African Union to the goals of promoting democratic principles and institutions, and popular participation and good governance, and 3(h) to promoting and protecting human and peoples' rights in accordance with the African Charter on Human and Peoples' Rights and other relevant human rights instruments. Respect for democratic principles, human rights, the rule of law, and good governance and the promotion of social justice now constitute a principle of the African Union.[42]

Importantly, the African Union seems to have embraced the importance of constitutionalism in rejecting the unconstitutional transfer of power. For example, the African Charter on Democracy, Elections and Governance, adopted by the Assembly of the Union in January 2007, considerably reinforces the legal system governing the reaction of the African Union to unconstitutional changes of government. On the one hand, the charter adds to the definition of unconstitutional changes of government, as contained in the Lomé Declaration: "Any amendment or revision of the constitution or legal instruments, which is an infringement on the principles of democratic change of government."[43] On the other hand, it considerably toughens the sanctions to be applied in case of an unconstitutional change. In fact, in addition to the suspension of the country concerned, the charter provides for the following measures for perpetrators of unconstitutional change: nonparticipation in elections held to restore constitutional order and in any position of responsibility in political institutions of their state, and trial before the competent court of the African Union. It also allows the possibility of the Assembly of the Union to apply other forms of sanctions, including punitive economic sanctions, and to impose sanctions on any state party that is proved to have instigated or supported unconstitutional change of government in another state. It also forbids state parties from harboring or giving sanctuary to perpetrators of unconstitutional changes of government and calls for the signing of bilateral extradition agreements as well as the adoption of legal instruments on extradition and mutual legal assistance. By January 2010, twenty-nine member states had signed the charter and three had ratified it. Fifteen ratifications are required for its entry into force.[44]

This shift in policy or normative posture is remarkable considering that the Organization of African Unity's (OAU's) prior mechanism for conflict prevention, management, and resolution was singularly ineffective because of the steadfast adherence to the principle of sovereignty and noninterference by Africa's postliberation leadership.

Article 4(h) of the Constitutive Act that established the African Union in 2002 and Article 1(k) of the more recent Non-Aggression and Common Defence Pact would suggest sovereignty is contingent on a government's willingness and capacity to deliver on human security, within the framework of the responsibility to protect. However, practice contrasts strongly with the strong normative commitment to the human security agenda in recent years, for any number of African countries, including Zimbabwe (which was elected to serve on the Peace and Security Council from 2010), are in direct contravention of the provision to which the African Charter on Democracy, Elections and Governance intends to legally bind its participant states once in force.

In attempting to make sense of this discrepancy between pronouncement and implementation, it is important to note that the African Union and its peace and security architecture is the outcome of a broader debate on integration in the continent. First, the African Union and its economic initiative NEPAD is evidence of a robust and vocal democratic constituency within Africa's political economy. As Berouk Mesfin argued, "It is simply amazing just how quickly democracy has come to monopolize the political landscape in Africa."[45]

The Architecture

The APSA refers to a well-ordered blueprint and neatly assembled structures, norms, capacities, and procedures aimed at preventing, managing, and preventing conflict as well as mediating for peace. APSA represents a comprehensive approach to conflict prevention, management, and resolution. It gives operational expression to the agenda for a new culture of peace and security on the continent. The APSA is not a novelty. It marks an evolution of African attempts to solve its own crisis and is cognizant of changing global politics and realities. A number of institutions compose the APSA.

Peace and Security Council of the African Union. This is the African Union's standing decision-making organ for the prevention, management, and resolution of conflicts. It is a collective security and early-warning structure that facilitates timely and efficient response to conflict and crisis situations in Africa.[46] The functions and powers of the PSC are spelled out in Article 6 and 7 of the PSC Protocol, respectively, and the PSC legitimizes and coordinates all the activities of the other institutions of the architecture.

The PSC is composed of fifteen members elected on a basis of equal rights, among which ten serve for a two-year term and five serve for a three-year term. Following the principle of equitable regional representation and rotation, each of the five subregions designates its representatives to the council. Hence, Northern Africa elects two countries; Eastern, Central, and Southern Africa elect three countries each; and Western Africa elects four countries.[47] The chair of the PSC is held in turn by the members of the PSC in the alphabetical order of their names (in English) for one calendar month.[48] The successive chairpersons of the PSC, in consultation with the commission, elaborate an indicative program of work for a period of six months that is then considered by the PSC members. In addition, the next chairperson is supposed to prepare a monthly program of work in consultation with the commission within twenty days of assuming the chairmanship.

PSC meetings, generally speaking, are closed meetings in which invited guests may be admitted, but it can also hold open meetings. The PSC can hold three types of meetings: formal meetings, at the end of which a communiqué containing substantive decision is issued; briefing sessions, during which council members receive information but no decision is taken and after which a press statement is issued; and informal consultations, during which council members exchange views but after which no document issued.[49] PSC decisions are generally guided by the principle of consensus. However, in the event consensus is not reached, decisions on procedural matters are approved by a simple majority vote and substantive matters are approved by a two-thirds majority of members eligible to vote.[50] The provisional agenda of the PSC is determined by the chairperson of the council on the basis of proposals submitted by the chairperson of the commission and member states. The inclusion of any item in the provisional agenda may not be opposed by a member state.[51]

While the rules and procedure of the PSC attempt to break from the consensual approach of African diplomacy, in reality, African diplomacy is grounded in consensus and the need for unity. However, in certain circumstances, as in the case of sanctions on Mauritania, the PSC has broken with this tradition. Such examples are usually the result of assertiveness by the chairperson and his or her diplomatic skills. Despite the fact that APSA provides a sound framework through which the continent can engage conflict situations, there is still a degree of unpredictability and consistency in much of its engagements.

Continental Early Warning System (CEWS). This institution provides timely advice on potential conflicts and threats to peace and security in Africa to several key AU institutions, including the chairperson of the Commission, the PSC, and the Panel of the Wise. The CEWS is intended to support the development of appropriate response strategies by the African Union and its institutions. Consequently, the impact of the CEWS is contingent on the link between analysis and response—the challenge of translating early warning into early action.

Institutionally, CEWS consists of an observation and monitoring center—the Situation Room—located at the Conflict Management Division of the African Union, as well as observation and monitoring units of the regional mechanisms, which are to be linked directly to CEWS. The key elements of the CEWS framework have been defined around three iterative and interactive phases or steps: ongoing information collection and monitoring, conflict and cooperation analysis, and formulation of policy and response options.[52]

AU member states agreed to the framework for the implementation of the CEWS in December 2006 in Kempton Park, South Africa, with plans to operationalize CEWS by mid-2010.[53] Based on an open, networked system that includes an early-warning module, a substantial amount of conceptual work on indicators, systems, and processes has been concluded. In terms of data collection and management, CEWS introduced an automated data-gathering and -processing system (including but not limited to a sophisticated news-monitoring system); a news-trends tracking service; and a system of grading sources and reports. Greater use of African information sources has also been prioritized. The Situation Room has been tasked with information collecting and monitoring, and CEWS has also developed a strategic conflict-analysis framework, the staffing for which is currently in process.

Operationalizing CEWS has witnessed some challenges. As El Ghassim Wane, the head of the African Union's Conflict Management Division argues, successful implementation of CEWS demands ongoing training and capacity building (technical, analytical, operational).[54]

Panel of the Wise. This is an advisory, early-warning mechanism aimed at stemming conflict before it breaks out.[55] The panel is composed of five highly respected African personalities (one from each region) selected by the chairperson of the commission after consultation with the member states concerned.[56] The panel has adopted a draft work program, held its first two meetings, and is in the process of establishing a secretariat. Rather than engage in the hot conflicts and challenges that make banner headlines, the intention is for the panel to focus on "forgotten" and unresolved crises and the implementation of peace agreements. As such, the panel will work with civil society and complement the work of the PSC.

While commentators have questioned the secretive and closed appointment process of its members, which includes serving government officials and individuals of advanced age, the panel should provide another important building block in the evolving security architecture of the union. There is also a need for strong support structures to aid the panel. The panel has recognized the need of a dedicated secretariat that is expanded beyond one person. Additionally, there is a need for a mediation support unit to support the panel in its mediation efforts.

African Standby Force (ASF). As the most ambitious and costly component of the APSA, the ASF is aimed at preventive deployment and the provision of humanitarian assistance as a means to avert overt conflict. It provides the African Union with capabilities to respond to conflicts through the deployment of peacekeeping forces and to undertake interventions pursuant to article 4(h) and (i) of the Constitutive Act.[57] The ASF is intended for rapid deployment for a multiplicity of peace support operations that may include, inter alia, preventive deployment, peacekeeping, peacebuilding, post-conflict disarmament, demobilization, reintegration, and humanitarian assistance.

In a reversal of thinking at the international level, it has now become accepted that the African Union can and should deploy in advance of the United Nations in the African context—as demonstrated in Burundi when the African Union Mission in Burundi (AMIB) was followed by the UN Office in Burundi (UNOB) in May 2004, in Darfur with the deployment of the African Union Mission in Sudan (AMIS) in June 2004, and subsequently in Somalia with the deployment of the AU Mission to Somalia (AMISOM) in March 2007. The principal original purpose of the ASF—to prevent another genocide like Rwanda—provided the rationale for quick response capabilities and the capability to mount a mission to cover the early days of a conflict while the ponderous UN peacekeeping system lumbered into operational mode. Today, it is accepted that the African Union will deploy first, opening up the possibility for a UN follow-on multidimensional peace support operation. In this scenario, ASF forces will therefore be deployed into a situation as part of the peacemaking process at an earlier stage than UN forces would engage. They would thereby help to create the conditions on the ground that could lead to a comprehensive peace agreement and the deployment of UN forces. This was indeed the situation in Burundi with the African Union and United Nations, and with the Economic Community of West African States (ECOWAS) and the United Nations in Liberia, Sierra Leone, and Côte d'Ivoire. The exit strategy for ASF operations is therefore a transition to the United Nations—which could include the redesignation of ASF resources as UN contingents.

Military Staff Committee. Composed of the Chiefs of Defense Staff or their representatives (of the countries serving on the PSC), this committee advises and assists the council in all questions relating to military and security requirements.[58]

Peace Fund. This fund is composed of financial appropriations taken from the regular budget of the African Union, voluntary contributions made by member states and other sources within Africa, including the private sector (civil society and individuals), and donations made in appropriate fundraising activities.[59] It has also benefited substantially from support from the international community.

Regional mechanisms of conflict prevention and resolution. Clearly defined under Article 16 of the PSC Protocol, regional mechanisms, such as those of the Southern African Development Community (SADC) and ECOWAS, are part of the overall security architecture of the African Union, which has the primary responsibility for promoting peace, security, and stability in Africa. In this respect, the PSC and the chairperson of the commission are charged with harmonizing and coordinating the activities of regional mechanisms in the field of peace, security, and stability in accord with the objectives and principles of the African Union. To this effect, the African Union and the key regional mechanisms of conflict prevention and resolution signed a memorandum of understanding on peace and security in 2007 that serves to regulate their interaction—although effective coordination among them remains problematic.

Civil society. The PSC encourages nongovernmental, community-based, and other civil society organizations, particularly women's organizations, to participate actively in the efforts aimed at promoting peace, security, and stability in Africa. Such organizations are intended to compose an important component of the APSA and, when required, may be invited to address the PSC.[60] Despite this intention, African civil society engagement with the PSC is almost nonexistent. At the time of writing, only one African civil society group has briefed the PSC.[61] The PSC agenda is a closely guarded secret and is weakly disseminated. This has reinforced the perennial lack of participation from a broader spectrum of interested parties. Consequently, provisions of the protocol that call on interested parties to participate in PSC discussions can only be fully operationalized if the calendar and agenda of the PSC is made openly available.

United Nations. Within the context of Chapter VIII of the UN Charter and Article 17(1) of the PSC Protocol, the United Nations is a critical component of the APSA. The AU-UN relationship is based on shared responsibility and a division of labor. The African Union's recent experiences in Burundi suggest the emergence of a division of labor between the two, whereby the African Union will deploy a military mission to respond to immediate crises and to create conditions sufficiently stable for the UN Security Council to authorize deployment. Another example of this shared responsibility based on comparative advantage is the emergence of hybridization in peacekeeping in Africa (i.e., joint AU-UN missions)—a development that reflects the limited African capacity in peacekeeping and the imperative of local ownership.[62]

A practice is emerging whereby the African Union seeks the blessings of the Security Council for its intervention and decisions in accordance with the requirements of Articles 51 and 53 of the UN Charter. This practice is informed by three strategic realities: first, any AU decision backed by the Security Council legalizes AU engagement;[63] second, by seeking the Security Council's blessing, the African Union may be able to constrain the actions of more powerful global players; third, and most importantly, seeking the Security Council's blessing allows the African Union to seek material support from the international community through the African Peace Facility (European Union) and other sources whose support is contingent on operations being sanctioned by the Security Council.

While there has been collaboration between the African Union and United Nations in matters of peacekeeping, it has been ad hoc and unpredictable at best. For example, in the case of Sudan, the UN Secretariat provided unusually strong mission-planning support to the African Union for its operation in Darfur in 2004 via a special political mission—a novel approach by the United Nations.[64] As aptly suggested by one UN report, there is need for the Security Council to define the "role of regional organizations in maintaining international peace and security" and to clarify "the nature of the partnership" with emphasis on how to develop mechanisms to promote common understanding and effective coordination across the range of conflict prevention and conflict resolution activities.[65] With regard to resource mobilization, there is a need for predictability, sustainability, and flexibility in the financing of UN-mandated peace operations undertaken by the African Union, with a particular focus on the expeditious and effective deployment of well-equipped troops and effective mission-support arrangements. It is against this backdrop that the AU-UN panel on modalities for support to African Union peacekeeping operations was established in 2008 pursuant to UN Security Council Resolution 1809. The panel's so-called Prodi Report (named for its chairperson, Romano Prodi) recommended (1) the use of UN-assessed contributions on a case-by-case basis to support UN Security Council–authorized AU peacekeeping operations for a period up to six months and (2) the establishment of a multidonor trust fund as a financial pool for peacekeeping support.[66]

To date, little has come of these recommendations, which are largely aimed at seeking a more sustainable funding basis for AU missions. Additionally, the timeline of six months to transfer control of a mission is just too short.

Assessment of the African Peace and Security Architecture

The Political Will to Act

With regard to norm setting or policy pronouncements, the African Union has had an impressive record, though its rate of implementation is far from impressive. For example, in Burundi, the African Union, with enormous support from South Africa, has been able to stabilize the country and bring the warring factions to the negotiating table. AMIB, which was launched in 2003, was the first operation wholly initiated, planned, and executed by AU members. In this regard, it represents a milestone for the African Union in terms of self-reliance in effecting and implementing a peace operation. Throughout its period of operation, AMIB succeeded in deescalating a potentially volatile situation and in February 2004 a UN evaluation team concluded that the conditions were appropriate for the establishment of a UN peacekeeping operation in the country.[67]

In the Union of the Comoros, after several months of sanctions and mediation made no progress, a coalition of willing African countries—Tanzania, Sudan, and Libya—supported the Comorian Armed Forces to remove self-styled "president" Mohammed Bacar from power in the island of Anjouan in March 2008. The African Union did so at the request of Comorian president Ahmed Abdallah Sambi.[68]

The crises in Chad, Côte d'Ivoire, Darfur, and Somalia have, however, exposed the lack of political clout, adequately trained personnel, and the financial wherewithal in the African Union to engage in a complex crisis. In such instances, the African Union has largely made an appearance without the capacity to have a positive impact on the situation. The case of Darfur is a clear example of how a skewed mandate can leave a AU-UN mission unable to stabilize a situation. The case of Zimbabwe, meanwhile, demonstrates how African countries aid and abet the suppression of another country's people, in this instance by Robert Mugabe. Years of unwavering support to Mugabe's Zimbabwe African National Union–Patriotic Front (ZANU-PF) had delivered few tangible results for South Africa's purported quiet diplomacy and eventually the country staggered toward an imperfect agreement on September 11, 2008, that took several months before continued economic collapse led to its partial enactment early in 2009. Events in Zimbabwe appear, according to some, to portend a wider trend first evident in Kenya in January 2008, when regional leaders looked on with hardly a murmur as Kenyan leaders thwarted the popular will of their people through the manipulation of electoral processes and the constitution—albeit not through the barrel of a gun as had been earlier the case.[69]

The African Union has articulated Africa's interests in the international arena in select instances, as evidenced by the AU position on UN reform. Even the new concept of hybridization in peacekeeping in Darfur is a realization of the importance of African leadership and direction in peace missions in Africa.

By moving from noninterference to what is now called "nonindifference," the African Union adopted an approach defined by the responsibility to protect—a concept that was subsequently popularized by the UN General Assembly at the World Summit Outcome in 2005. Evidence of this commitment is further provided by the frequency of meetings of the PSC. By February 2010, the PSC had met more than two hundred and sixteen times and sought to improve its workings along the way. For example, a 2008 organizational audit of the AU Commission concluded with 159 substantive recommendations of which 10 related to the PSC—all of them were subsequently discussed and adopted at an extraordinary meeting of foreign ministers in Tanzania in May 2008 and are in the process of implementation.

Looking at the political significance of PSC decisions, the African Union has demonstrated a political will to speak out. The mere fact that Sudan was refused the chairmanship of the African Union in 2007 and that the African Union called for the creation of a national unity government in Zimbabwe following the Zimbabwean presidential run-off election held on June 27, 2008, speaks volumes of a greater AU political will to act where it would previously have not. Though the African Union, by calling for a government of national unity, stopped short of asking Mugabe to resign, it indirectly indicted his legitimacy as president and called into question the legality of his regime. Such an indictment on Mugabe was certainly groundbreaking considering the African Union's practice of shying away from questioning the legitimacy of African leaders and of viewing such matters as domestic affairs.

But having the will to act is not enough. Having the capacity to act is equally important.

The Capacity to Act

While the African Union has in numerous instances demonstrated the political will to act in conflict situations, it sometimes lacks the necessary will to undertake effective conflict prevention. Partly influenced by the political experience of South Africa, Africa's economic powerhouse, the African Union appears to favor power-sharing agreements rather than principle as the preferred conflict resolution strategy. Yet it is naive to assume that the African Union is able to engage substantively on its own with major regional conflicts, such as those in Darfur and Somalia or between Ethiopia and Eritrea—three conflict zones that are literally in the backyard of AU headquarters in Addis Ababa. What then explains the African Union's success in Comoros but its relative absence in the conflict in Chad and its ineffectiveness in Darfur and Somalia?

Institutional Capacity

The structure, design, and function of the APSA reflect the desire by Africa's leadership to develop an intergovernmental security mechanism aimed at coordination, not direction. Since AU member states are the principal agents of implementation, the African Union's effectiveness depends on the commitment and ability of its members to act. This commitment is, in turn, premised on the quest for regime (not human) security. For example, the African Union lacks an effective sanction regime to deal with recalcitrant states and leaders. Even where sanctions have been imposed, the commission lacks the capacity to evaluate and monitor implementation (though the PSC created a permanent subcommittee on sanctions in March 2009) and to force regional economic communities (RECs) to align their position with that of the African Union. For example, when François Bozizé overthrew an elected government in CAR in March 2003, CAR was suspended from the African Union but not from the Economic and Monetary Community of Central Africa, where President Bozizé was supported by member states with tacit encouragement from France.

Against this backdrop, some observations about the APSA in its internal decision processes are appropriate—an arena permeated by the national interests of member states. For example, the Permanent Representative Committee, where AU member states gather to engage with the African Union through their diplomatic representatives in Addis Ababa, is an arena of constant infighting between the commission and its members. Members often perceive the AU Commission as an extension of their own state civil service, limiting the space for independence in the commission's decision-making processes. This has heightened the managerial problems at the commission, which in turn has compounded the institutional constraints of the APSA. For example, an independent 2007 AU organizational review found that inadequate in-house leadership and weak management systems and coordination had resulted both in poor supervision in the commission, within and between departments, and low morale among staff. Few commissioners and directors can claim to have had a respectful and productive relationship.[70]

Clearly the APSA is still a work in progress. As a consequence, some of its institutions have not been fully developed. The secretariat PSC is run by just four staff. The CEWS needs more qualified personnel and technical expertise to operate optimally. The Military Staff Committee meets infrequently since national militaries are understandably reluctant to second their top staff to Addis Ababa, as they see such a move as detracting from national priorities.[71] The ASF is not yet fully operational, with only three regions—West, South, and East—having made progress with the establishment of the required capabilities. Further, the rise of piracy in the Gulf of Guinea and along the Horn have demonstrated the African Union's lack of naval capacity.

Perhaps most important, the absence of political convergence based on good governance has negatively impacted on the political and institutional capacity of the African Union to implement its stated human security agenda. Despite its rhetoric, the African Union remains a club of leaders rather than an assembly of Africa's people. Citizen engagement is weak, and the predominant view remains focused on elite and state security rather than human security. Although the number of democrats in Africa steadily increased through the mid-1990s, with numbers having remained constant thereafter, key leaders such as those in Libya, Cameroon, Gabon, Burkina Faso, Uganda, Egypt, Zimbabwe, Nigeria, Kenya, and Ethiopia have either not been elected or elected under dubious circumstances in which associated processes have been manipulated and often marred by substantial violence and abuse of state power. Thus, the will and willingness in Africa to engage with fellow leaders, many of whom share a common democratic deficit, is limited.

Peacekeeping Capacity

While AU peacekeeping missions have been able to stabilize certain situations and provide a first response, their capacity to sustain a long-term commitment has been limited. In principle, it has generally been accepted that the African Union can and should deploy in advance of the United Nations. There are two practical challenges to this approach, which do shed light on the capacity constraints faced by the African Union in peacebuilding.

The first challenge concerns the relationship between UN and ASF operations, which could lead to a severe and early depletion of ASF forces available for deployment elsewhere. While the potential full standby strength of the ASF comes to 25,000 troops and up to 980 military observers, the United Nations had 55,980 troops, 6,995 police, and 2,153 military observers deployed in MONUC, the UN Mission for the Referendum in Western Sahara (MINORSO), the UN Mission in Liberia (UNMIL), the UN Operation in Côte d'Ivoire (UNOCI), the UN Mission in Sudan (UNMIS), the UN/AU Hybrid Operation in Darfur (UNAMID), and the UN Mission in the CAR and Chad (MINURCAT) in January 2009.[72] As these numbers indicate, the redesignation of ASF forces as part of UN operations would quickly deplete the available ASF capacity—even at the theoretical ideal. This depletion could be exacerbated by the fact that African troop contributors would obviously choose deployment to better-paid UN missions over their commitment to the less-well-remunerated ASF missions. Given the disparities in resources available to the two types of missions, the ASF does not generally receive the same level of logistic and other support as that of UN missions.

The second challenge relates to handing over control to the United Nations, with its more restrictive entry criteria than the African Union. In the aftermath of a slew of challenging missions, the 2000 Brahimi Report on UN Peacekeeping Reform emphasized the importance of "there being a peace to keep" and stated that the United Nations should not deploy forces unless a binding and overarching peace agreement was first in place.[73] The result is a marked UN reluctance to assume a peacekeeping responsibility before a comprehensive agreement is in place—an unrealistic and impracticable condition in fragile states where numerous fractured armed groups compete for dominance. In addition, even after the United Nations has accepted a peacekeeping role, there are often extremely long delays in effecting the transition from an AU to a UN mission, as occurred in Burundi and Darfur.

A lack of capacity at the level of the AU Commission has also complicated progress, because in the absence of guidance from Addis Ababa, regions applied their own interpretation to the common road map that set out the way forward on the ASF. Today key arrangements in SADC and ECOWAS and in Eastern Africa regarding command and control, logistics, and planning differ from one another—a situation that complicates the deployment and use of forces from different regions. Hence SADC would like to authorize and control the deployment of the Southern Africa Development Community Standby Force under the authority of the SADC Summit, whereas the Eastern African Standby Brigade Coordination Mechanism (EASBRICOM) more appropriately sees its function as largely that of force preparation, handing force deployment over to the African Union.

In preparation for an expert working session in Algiers in January 2008, the AU Commission listed the following role-related challenges that future African peace operations will likely face:

1. The likelihood that the UN will stage robust operations or enforcement missions under Chapter VII of the UN Charter remains small for the foreseeable future. The African Union and the regional mechanisms will, therefore, continue to face the challenge of sum-

moning the political will and the capacity to plan and execute robust missions.

2. While some of the ongoing situations of armed conflict will remain a challenge for some time to come, emerging trends suggest that such incidents of large-scale armed conflict will gradually decline in Africa. However, situations of low-intensity conflict are likely to remain a challenge. While these situations do not necessarily pose significant threats to international peace and security, they do constitute a threat to stability and sustainable development in the affected countries (and surrounding areas). As such, situations of this nature will occupy the attention of the African Union and the regional mechanisms and will be the focus of conflict prevention and management.

3. An operational African peace and security architecture will therefore need to develop effective early response systems and effective support for mediation efforts through, for example, preventive deployment.

4. A standby force implies that it consists of several components, including, for example, military, police, and civilian dimensions. However, there has been more focus and attention on the military dimensions than on the other dimensions. Although the African Union has recognized this, there is a need for more targeted attention to rectify this shortcoming.

5. Training of future peace operations personnel (i.e., the ASF) must of necessity address the different dimensions of the challenges of conflict and post-conflict environments in which such persons will operate. This means that, in addition to disarmament, demobilization, and reintegration and security sector reform programs, more attention should be given to the civilian dimension, including to child protection, gender issues, human rights, civil affairs, economic recovery, and HIV/AIDS.

6. African organizations have not demonstrated the ability to mobilize the financial resources required to address post-conflict reconstruction, and development needs on their own. However, they can nonetheless set the agenda for external and other partners in terms of articulating priority approaches to peculiar needs of the targeted post-conflict environments. The AU policy on post-conflict reconstruction and development needs does articulate principles and approaches, and the ongoing process of developing operational guidelines will be particularly relevant in guiding the training of ASF personnel for future missions.

Operational Capacity

Funding. Any robust conflict management operation requires financial resources. However, the African Union's financial woes often stem not from a lack of funds (particularly from the donor community) but rather from the African Union's absorption capacity and the massive administrative burden that accompanies international assistance. The budget of the commission has already expanded severalfold in the last decade. In January 2009, the AU Summit approved a budget of $164.3 million for the year, consisting of $93.8 million in assessed contributions from member states and the balance from partner organizations. Although the organization is still faced with substantial membership arrears, member state contributions have tripled in recent years.[74] Seventy-five percent of the regular budget comes from Algeria, Egypt, Libya, Nigeria, and South Africa.

External funding has put the rhetoric of "African solutions to African problems" to a test. Overreliance on external funding does not only risk creating a dependency syndrome but it also limits the maneuvering space of the African Union to engender its own activities and impedes indigenous response capacity. For example, the capacity of some AU missions has been hampered by a lack of weapons, yet financial support, from sources such as the African Peace Facility, does not allow for the purchase of lethal weapons. The Prodi Report tried to remedy this situation by recommending an extension of assessed UN funding to AU missions—a recommendation that has sunk without a murmur.

Staffing. The AU Commission faces staffing problems in terms of numbers and quality. Despite the availability of funds, the commission was operating with only 60 percent of its planned 912 staff in October 2007. Some departments, such as the one for peace and security, had just thirty staff members and the PSC secretariat had just three staff. This situation is further compounded by high turnover, lack of training, and painfully slow recruitment. The African Union has lost some of its most competent staff, as it is unable to compete in an open labor market. Though one can overstate the issue of wages, there are legitimate complaints about the absence of a suitable working environment and professional development opportunities. Moreover, the cumbersome and slow recruitment process grounded in the commission's quota system has not helped matters. Lengthy decision-making processes have contributed to the use of short-term contracts to fill the transition period, but this has not solved the problem of institutional memory. The professionalism of AU staff has come under intense scrutiny. There are also accusations that some AU staff use generous travel allowances to boost their salaries and that unnecessary travel has further reduced their ability to carry out work in a timely manner.[75] The AU organization audit also mentions allegations of pressure by some members of the Permanent Representative Committee for the recruitment of their relatives or nationals.

Backroom services. The conferencing, finance, and human resource departments are basically swamped by their workload. As a result, basic services, such as paying serving peacekeeping troops on time, has proved to be difficult during the current mission in Sudan. Another constraint is office space, though China has offered to build a twenty-three-story building (set to be the tallest building in Addis Ababa) by 2011 at a cost of about $150 million. Germany has also promised construction of a new building that will accommodate the peace and security department.

Capacity of Regional Economic Communities

RECs play a critical role in conflict prevention, management, and resolution on the continent, as they are conceived as building blocks of the APSA, but the adoption of peace and security functions by regional organizations has met with varying degrees of success and begs the question as to whether such organizations are adequately equipped to address the myriad traditional and nontraditional security challenges that presently confront African states.[76]

In some instances, the African Union has deferred to the initiatives of RECs in a mechanical application of the building-block approach—deferring to the positions of regions on matters where problems are considered too difficult or problematic to deal with otherwise. Proponents of this policy approach argue that it is part and parcel of the concept of security complex and the need for local solutions to local problems. However, as the cases of Zimbabwe and Madagascar have shown, such an approach at times is also used as an excuse to continue with an ineffective policy option. Further, as the case of the Chad-Sudan relationship reveals, it invariably serves to cover a lack of will and capacity to engage with a crisis.

The RECs are at different levels of development and some, such as the Economic Community of Central African States (ECCAS) and the Community of Sahel-Saharan States (CEN-SAD), have hardly taken off. Some RECs remain operationally weak, and it is questionable whether they have the resources and political will needed to carry out their security mandate. In the case of Central Africa, member states have often looked to actors outside the region, such as the United Nations and other African states and regional bodies, than to themselves for support and assistance in responding to conflict.[77] Against this backdrop, Mark Malan argues that there is a danger at a structural level that regional security organizations may take on "utopian ideals and complex institutional mechanisms" at the expense of more manageable efforts toward resolving ongoing conflict.[78]

The relationship between RECs and the African Union is at the heart of where the priorities of member states lie. For example, RECs are beginning to ask questions about who should control the various standby brigades of the ASF as conceived. For them, the ASF should operate at the regional and not at the continental level. There is also the matter of competition for donor funding. Over the past few years, enormous resources have been put into the ASF, and now some partners are beginning to rethink this strategy, perceiving the RECs as being more capable of addressing security threats in their own backyard.

Capacity of Nongovernmental Organizations

The African Union's foundational documents, especially the Constitutive Act, the PSC Protocol, and the Statutes of the Economic, Social, and Cultural Council (ECOSOCC), provide ample space for participation by civil society organizations in conflict prevention, management, and resolution. For instance, the PSC's conclusions on mechanisms for the interaction between the PSC and civil society organizations (known as the Livingstone Formula) spells out the areas in which civil society can complement the capacity of APSA.[79] The question then is, do nongovernmental organizations have the capacity to do what is being asked of them?

There are areas where some African civil society groups have been able to complement the capacity of the APSA. There is certainly a shortage of analytical and research capacity at the commission. Some African civil society groups such as the Institute for Security Studies have been able to complement the capacity of APSA by providing member states of the PSC, especially the rotational chair of the PSC, with analytical research on their proposed agenda. Also, with regard to policy development, certain African civil society organizations have been solicited to do the background research for the formulation of certain policies. Research and training in the realm of peacekeeping is another area where the African Union is increasingly soliciting the help of civil society organizations. However, these engagements are mainly ad hoc, as most of these civil society organizations do not have any institutional engagement with the African Union.

Despite the complementary and support role that civil society can play, they are hampered by their lack of capacity to influence policy development and implementation. Capacity constraints faced by civil society organizations are numerous. African civil society organizations lack the skills and human capacity to influence the APSA—not to mention their

national policies. Lack of funding and the inability to attract qualified staff
is a problem. From an institutional level, civil society engagement with
the African Union is minimal and often not constructive. Many African
governments are inherently suspicious about the motives of civil society.
As such, questions about the motive and source of funding of civil society
have often become the rallying ground for anti–civil society advocates. For
example, as one eligibility criterion for membership in ECOSOCC, the
basic resources of a civil society organization shall be substantially (defined
as at least 50 percent) derived from contributions of the members of the
organization.[80] Similar to a number of African governments, most African
civil society organizations with the capacity to complement and enhance
the APSA are almost entirely funded from outside the continent. Ironically, the same partners that fund African civil society fund African states
and multilateral organizations. Some within the AU Commission further
perceive civil society as competitors rather than institutions that are aimed
at complementing the work of the African Union. Thus, while there is
ample space for civil society–AU engagement, the African Union is still
an exclusive club for African presidents. As a result, institutions such as
ECOSOCC and the African Citizens' Directorate are institutional watch-
men that guard the status quo.

Conclusions

While Africa's security threat will change over time, state weakness as a result of limited capacity and poor governance remains the principal source
of insecurity in Africa. However, there is need for the African Union to
start developing response mechanisms to address nontraditional security
threats. As a consequence, responses and capacity-building initiatives that
are anchored in the concept of human security and the need to enhance
the responsiveness of African states will be key in the future. Such responses should not be on the shoulders of the African Union, as the institution suffers from myriad capacity constraints, most notably a lack of
political capacity or will to act. To some extent, RECs are filling the capacity gap left by the African Union, but at the heart of the conundrum is a
reflection of the weakness of African states that still see regime security as
the primary objective in African international relations. For their part, the
African Union and key RECs such as SADC have shut the door on civil
society—a reflection of their narrow focus on state versus human security.

Clearly, the call for "African solutions to African problems" reflects the
justifiable need for greater African responsibility and autonomy in developing indigenous conflict prevention and management capacities. Rather

than a panacea, the APSA provides an opportunity (political and institutional) to engage and develop appropriate responses to Africa's future security threats. Regionalism is not synonymous with international disengagement or desertion. From an African perspective, regionalism is about a division of labor and the sharing of responsibilities premised on a range of partnerships that are composed of African regional arrangements and mechanisms, UN organizations and initiatives, and Africa's development partners.[81]

Rather than denigrating the APSA for its very apparent early weaknesses, it is imperative that its capacity be strengthened so that it can provide a credible opportunity for the continent to tackle its security problems. Often in examining the effectiveness of the African Union, one falls into the trap of measuring results—and of demonizing the African Union rather than engaging in a critical analysis of its capacity constraints.

Developing the capacity of the African Union is much more than a technical question. It goes beyond resource mobilization, planning, and execution of peace support operations. It is ultimately a political question that is anchored in the distribution of power both among states, subregional organizations, the African Union, and the United Nations, and within the United Nations between the General Assembly and Security Council. Since states are the foundation and RECs the building blocks of the APSA, one could argue that the APSA's capacity constraints are a reflection of the weakness of African states. Against this backdrop, APSA's institutional constraints can be traced to the nature of African politics and how Africa's political leadership perceives and conceives the APSA. A close look at the design and function of the APSA suggests that the architecture was conceived as a coordinating mechanism without the real potential or mechanism to breach state sovereignty. Thus, how the APSA impacts upon the domestic politics of AU member states is critical in ascertaining its capacity to effectively respond to conflicts. A strong APSA requires solid, functioning, and accountable national structures. As much as the APSA is no substitute for reforming the nation-state across Africa, it is also no substitute for regional integration and an appropriate contribution from the international community in general and the United Nations in particular.

Notes

1. Rwandan president Paul Kagame (speech, High-level Plenary Meeting of the Sixtieth Session of the General Assembly of the United Nations, September, 14, 2005, 5), www.unmillenniumproject.org/documents/WS05_rwa050914eng.pdf.

2. See Articles 5 and 12 of the AU Solemn Declaration on a Common African Defense and Security Policy, Abuja, 2005.

3. See Festus Aboagye, *The Hybrid Operation for Darfur: A Critical Review of the Concept and the Mechanism*, Occasional Paper no. 149 (Pretoria: Institute for Security Studies [ISS], August 2007); Alex Vines and Roger Middleton, *Options for the EU to Support the African Peace and Security Architecture*, Programme Paper (Brussels: European Parliament, February 2008).

4. Article 1(k) African Union Non-Aggression and Common Defence Pact, Abuja, 2005.

5. Dirk Kotze, "Issues in Conflict Resolution," *African Journal on Conflict Resolution* 2, no. 2 (Durban: ACCORD, 2002): 77–100.

6. See the New Partnership for Africa's Development (NEPAD) framework document, www.nepad.org/2005/files/documents/inbrief.pdf.

7. Commission for Africa, "Our Common Interest," in "Report of the Commission for Africa," March 14, 2005.

8. Jakkie Cilliers, "Hopes and Challenges for the Peace and Security Architecture of the African Union" (forthcoming).

9. Adebayo Adedeji, ed., *Comprehending and Mastering African Conflicts: The Search for Sustainable Peace and Good Governanace* (London: Zeb Books, 1999), 9.

10. Human Security Report Project, *Human Security Brief 2007* (Vancouver: Simon Fraser University, 5).

11. See Jane E. Holl, "Carnegie Commission on Preventing Deadly Conflict: Second Progress Report," July 1996, www.wilsoncenter.org/subsites/ccpdc/pubs/rept2/frame.htm; Robert Kaplan, "The Coming Anarchy," *Atlantic Monthly* 273, no. 2 (1994): 44–76.

12. See Jeremy Lind and Kathryn Sturman, eds., *Scarcity and Surfeit: The Ecology of Africa's Conflicts* (Pretoria: ISS, 2002).

13. Paul Collier and Anke Hoeffler, *On Economic Causes of Civil War* (Oxford: Oxford University Press, 1998).

14. Cilliers, "Hopes and Challenges."

15. Chrysantus Ayangafac, ed., *Political Economy of Regionalisation in Central Africa*, Monograph no. 154 (Pretoria: ISS, 2008).

16. Jakkie Cilliers, *Climate Change, Population Pressure and Conflict in Africa*, ISS Paper no. 178 (Pretoria: ISS, 2009).

17. André Standing, *Corruption and Industrial Fishing in Africa*, Issue no. 7 (Bergen: Anti-Corruption Resource Centre, 2008).

18. Jakkie Cilliers, *Human Security in Africa: A Conceptual Framework for Review* (Pretoria: Human Security Initiative, June 2004), www.africanreview.org/docs/humsecjun04.pdf.

19. Mark Duffield argues that the criminalization of African economies can partly be interpreted as adaptation to globalization and market deregulation. See Mark Duffield, "Globalisation and War Economies: Promoting Order or the Return of History," *Fletcher Forum of World Affairs* 23, no. 2 (1999): 19–36.

20. Jakkie Cilliers, *Africa in the New World Order—How Global and Domestic Developments Will Impact by 2025*, Monograph no. 151 (Pretoria: ISS, 2008), 117–18.

21. Yves Chouala "Regional Relations and Conflict Situations in Central Africa," in *Political Economy of Regionalisation in Central Africa*, Monograph no. 154, ed. Chrysantus Ayangafac (Pretoria: ISS, 2008).

22. Jérôme Tubiana, "The Chad-Sudan Proxy War and the 'Darfurization' of Chad: Myths and Reality," Human Security Baseline Assessment (HSBA) Working Paper 12 (Geneva: Small Arms Survey HSBA, 2008); Chrysantus Ayangafac, "Chad-Sudan Proxy Wars Could Lead to Overt Confrontation," *ISS Today*, June 5, 2008.

23. Luc Sindjoun, *La politique d'affection en Afrique noire. Société de parenté, 'société d'Etat' et libéralisation politique au Cameroun*, GRAP Occasional Paper (Boston: Boston University, 1998).

24. See Debay Tadesse, *The Nile: Is It a Curse or Blessing?* ISS Paper no. 174 (Pretoria: ISS, November 2008).

25. Jakkie Cilliers and Christian Dietrich, *Angola's War Economy: The Role of Diamonds* (Pretoria: ISS, 2000).

26. See the AU Solemn Declaration on a Common African Defense Policy and Security Policy.

27. N. Ebbe Obi, "Drug Trafficking, Money Laundering, and Political-Criminal Nexus in Africa" (paper presented at the annual meeting of the American Sociological Association, Atlanta Hilton Hotel, Atlanta, GA), www.allacademic.com/meta/p107613_index.html.

28. Peacebuilding Commission, "Background Paper on Drug Trafficking in Guinea-Bissau," www.un.org/peace/peacebuilding/Country-Specific%20Configurations/Guinea-Bissau/28.05.2008%20Background%20Paper%20Drug%20Trafficking.pdf.

29. International Chamber of Commerce (ICC) Commercial Crime Service, "Unprecedented Rise in Piratical Attacks," www.icc-ccs.org/index.php?option=com_content&view=article&id=306:unprecedented-rise-in-piratical-attacks&catid=60:news.

30. Andre Standing, "The Crisis of Marine Plunder in Africa," *ISS Today*, February 10, 2007.

31. DfID, "The Problem of Illegal Fishing," www.dfid.gov.uk/news/files/illegal-fishing-action-plan.

32. African Partnership Forum, "African and Climate Change," Germany 2007. See also the AU Eighth Summit Declaration on Climate Change, Addis Ababa, 2007, and Jakkie Cilliers, *Climate Change, Population Pressure*.

33. Angela Nwaniki, "Achieving Food Security in Africa: Challenges and Issues," UN Office of the Special Advisor on Africa, www.un.org/africa/osaa/reports/Achieving%20Food%20Security%20in%20Africa-Challenges%20and%20Issues.pdf.

34. Howard Adelman, "The Use and Abuse of Refugees in Zaire," *Refugee Studies Review* 1, no. 27 (2001).

35. See Jakkie Cilliers, "Consolidating Peace and Security in Africa," *African Security Review* 13, no. 4 (Pretoria: ISS, 2004): 117–22.

36. See Robert Rotberg, "The Failure and Collapse of Nation-States: Breakdown, Prevention, and Repair," in *When States Fail: Causes and Consequences*, ed. Robert Rotberg (Princeton, NJ: Princeton University Press, 2004).

37. Henri Boshoff, "An Analysis of the Violence in Eastern Congo" (paper presented at ISS public seminar series, Addis Ababa, 2008).

38. Mahmood Mamdani, *Citizen and Subject: Contemporary Africa and the Legacy of Late Colonialism* (Princeton, NJ: Princeton University Press, 1996).

39. Jeffrey Herbst and Greg Mills, "Africa's Big Dysfunctional States: An Introductory Overview," in *Big African States*, ed. Christopher Clapham, Jeffrey Herbst, and Greg Mills (Johannesburg: Wits University Press, 2006); Rotberg, "The Failure and Collapse

of Nation-States"; I. William Zartman, "Introduction," in *Collapsed States: The Disintegration and Restoration of Legitimate Authority*, ed. I. William Zartman (Boulder, CO: Lynne Rienner Publishers, 1995).

40. For an analysis of International Monetary Fund policies and their impact on conflict in the case of Côte d'Ivoire, see A. Koudio, *Debt of Cote d'Ivoire and Challenges of Poverty Reduction* (Abidjan: Ivorian Center of Economics and Social Research, University of Cocody, 2004); Rachel M. Gisselquist, "Economic Adjustment and Regime Change in Africa: Côte d'Ivoire in Comparative Perspective," Massachusetts Institute of Technology, March 21, 2001.

41. The African Union policy framework on post-conflict and reconstruction and development is the reference point for this. See Omano Edigheji, *A Democratic Developmental State in Africa? A Concept Paper*, Center for Policy Studies (CPS) Research Report 105 (London: CPS, 2005).

42. Article 4 of the AU Constitutive Act, Lome, Togo 2000.

43. Article 23(5) of the African Charter on Democracy, Elections and Governance.

44. Executive Council, "Ethiopia Report of the Chairperson of the Commission on the Prevention of Unconstitutional Changes of Government and Strengthening the Capacities of the African Union to Manage Such Situations," EX.CL/566 (XVI), Sixteenth Ordinary Session, January 25–29, 2010, Addis Ababa, 2–3.

45. Berouk Mesfin, "Democracy, Elections and Political Parties: A Conceptual Overview with Special Emphasis on Africa," ISS Paper no. 166 (Pretoria: ISS, 2008).

46. Article 2 of the Protocol Relating to the Establishment of the Peace and Security Council of the African Union, Durban, July 9, 2002.

47. See the African Union's Modalities for the Election of Members of the Peace and Security Council.

48. Rule 23 of the Rules of Procedure of the Peace and Security Council on the African Union; see also African Union, "Conclusions of the Retreat of the Peace and Security Council of the African Union," Dakar, July 5–6, 2007.

49. Rule 15 of the Rules of Procedure of the Peace and Security Council on the African Union.

50. Rule 28 of the Rules of Procedure of the Peace and Security Council on the African Union.

51. Article 8(7) of the PSC Protocol.

52. Conflict Management Division of the Peace and Security Department, ed., *Meeting the Challenge of Conflict Prevention in Africa Towards the Operationalization of the Continental Early Warning System* (Addis Ababa: African Union Commission, 2008).

53. Ibid.

54. Ibid.

55. See Jamila El Abdellaoui, *The Panel of the Wise: A Comprehensive Introduction to a Critical Pillar of the African Peace and Security Architecture*, ISS Paper no. 193 (Pretoria: ISS, 2009), www.issafrica.org/index.php?link_id=3&slink_id=8158&link_type=12&slink_type=12&tmpl_id=3.

56. See Article 11 of the PSC Protocol; African Union, Modalities for the Functioning of the Panel of Wise, Addis Ababa, 2008.

57. Article 13(1) of the PSC Protocol; also see Jakkie Cilliers, *The African Standby Force: An Update on Progress*, ISS Paper no. 160 (Pretoria: ISS, 2007).

58. Article 13(8) of the PSC Protocol.

59. Article 21(2) of the PSC Protocol.

60. See Article 20 of the PSC Protocol.

61. See the 2009 ISS brief to the Peace and Security Council on small arms and light weapons.

62. Aboagye, *The Hybrid Operation for Darfur.*

63. This is also in keeping with the African Union's "Ezulwini Consensus" on UN reform.

64. Victoria K. Holt, *African Capacity-Building for Peace Operations: UN Collaboration with the African Union and ECOWAS* (Washington, DC: Stimson Center, 2005), www.stimson. org/fopo/pdf/African_Capacity-building.pdf.

65. United Nations, "Report of the Secretary-General on the Relationship between the United Nations and Regional Organizations, in Particular the African Union, in the Maintenance of International Peace and Security," Document S/2008/186, April 7, 2008.

66. United Nations, "Report of the African Union-United Nations Panel on Modalities for Support to African Union Peacekeeping Operations," Document A/63/666 S/2008/813, December 31, 2008.

67. Tim Murithi, *Institutionalising Pan-Africanism: Transforming African Union Values and Principles into Policy and Practice*, ISS Paper no. 143 (Pretoria: ISS, June 2007).

68. The operation was in response to the appeal for assistance made by the Comorian government and in conformity with the decision adopted by the Assembly of the Union at its Tenth Ordinary Session held in Addis Ababa from January 31 to February 2, 2008. AU military engagement occurred despite the protestations of the most powerful and richest country on the continent and the lead negotiator on Comoros, South Africa, which continued to favor negotiations.

69. Cilliers, "Hopes and Challenges."

70. African Union, "AU Audit Report," 2007.

71. Vines and Middleton, *Options for the EU.*

72. Calculated from data provided by UN Department of Peacekeeping Operations, www. un.org/Depts/dpko/dpko/bnote.htm.

73. The Brahimi Panel on UN Peace Operations was convened by the UN secretary-general in March 2000 to "assess the shortcomings of the existing [UN] system and make frank, specific and realistic recommendations for change." The report of the panel, which was led by Lakhdar Brahimi, a former Algerian foreign minister, was submitted on August 21, 2000.

74. Executive Council, "Report of the Chairperson on the Activities of the Commission Covering the Period July to December 2009," EX. CL/565 (XVI), Sixteenth Ordinary Session, January 28–29, 2010, Addis Ababa, 143.

75. Vines and Middleton, *Options for the EU.*

76. See, for example, Christine MacAulay and Tony Karbo, "Up to The Task? Assessing the Ability of the Economic Community of Central African States (ECCAS) to Protect Human Security in Central Africa," in *Political Economy of Regionalisation in Central Africa*, Monograph no. 154, ed. Chrysantus Ayangafac (Pretoria: ISS, 2008).

77. Ibid.

78. Mark Malan, *The OAU and African Subregional Organizations—A Closer Look at the "Peace Pyramid,"* ISS Occasional Paper no. 26 (Pretoria: ISS, 1999).

79. African Union, "Conclusions on a Mechanism for Integration between the Peace and Security Council and Civil Society Organizations in the Promotion of Peace, Security and Stability in Africa," Document PSC/PR/(CLX), December 2008.

80. Article 6 of the statute of ECOSOCC, www.africa-union.org/ECOSOC/STATUTES-En.pdf.

81. See Article 17 of the PSC Protocol.

6

Identifying and Responding to Africa's Security Challenges

Kwesi Aning

A frican states are grappling with several difficult security challenges. Such difficulties result not only from the magnitude of the challenges themselves, but also from the lack of both state and institutional capacity to respond quickly and effectively to challenges. While armed conflicts have been the single most devastating security challenge for the African continent, new and emerging security challenges are being superimposed on them—what might be termed "old" challenges. Such "old" security challenges are the perennial armed conflicts between, for example, Chad and Sudan, and Ethiopia and Eritrea. These tensions are also underpinned by political violence, food insecurity, and the easy availability of small arms and light weapons and ammunition (SALW). The "new" challenges find nourishment in the "old," giving rise to opportunistic groups that threaten human, subregional, regional, and international security. While these challenges persist, they also create dangerous opportunities within which criminal entities can thrive. Transnational organized crime (TOC) groups are emerging in Africa that exploit the spaces created by such insecurities and engage in activities detrimental both to human and international security. Such activities include drugs, arms, and human trafficking, cyber crime, money laundering, and other activities that feed into the creation of financing opportunities for terrorists and other violent groups. It must be emphasized, however, that even in Africa there are wide variations in the levels of such occurrences, the manner in which these groups pose threats to particular states and regions, and in the ability of states and regions to respond to such threats.

This chapter discusses a broad range of new and emerging security challenges that affect and impact the survival of Africa's constituent states. It seeks to (1) understand the dynamics and mechanics of the narcotics trade and the manner in which it impacts the continent, particularly West Africa, which is now known as the "coke coast"; (2) identify and analyze the threat of cyber crime; and (3) examine the strategies for coping with and responding to these challenges within the broader framework of initiatives undertaken by the Economic Community of West African States (ECOWAS) and the African Union.

Africa's New and Emerging Security Challenges

Organized crime is considered one of the major threats to human security. It impedes social, economic, cultural, and democratic developments across the global, with disproportionate effects on developing and fragile states. The threat and challenges of organized crime in Africa in general and West Africa in particular is enormous because of the high presence of fragile states that serve as potential breeding grounds for such activities.

For West African states, one of the most serious challenges to state survival at the beginning of the twenty-first century is the influx of narcotics into the subregion and the impact of drug money on public, private sector, and community institutions. This kind of money has bought drug cartels friends in high places in West Africa, penetrating the highest political levels. In this respect, narcotics are by far the most attractive quick-money spoiler in the region. But drug money *coexists* with illicit money from other business. These flows have become so pervasive that the coastal fringes of this region, which through the years has shifted from slavery to pepper transportation to the West, is now popularly referred to as the "coke coast."[1] The scale of the drug-trafficking problem is massive and is gaining increased attention. According to the UN Office on Drugs and Crime (UNODC), "Alarm bells are ringing about the volume of cocaine transiting the region (roughly 50 tons a year). West Africa . . . has become a hub for cocaine trafficking . . . worth almost $2 billion a year. This is more than a drugs problem. It is a *serious security threat*."[2]

Because of the sheer volume of drugs being trafficked from West Africa to Europe and other parts of the world, the subregion has been carved out by narcobarons into two hubs, with Guinea-Bissau servicing a northern hub and Ghana servicing the southern hub.[3] But this is not just about these two hubs; this is also about the challenge that organized transnational groups are posing to West Africa's fragile states, particularly the threats that they potentially pose to democratic governance processes and institutions. Almost all the West African maritime states are experiencing an increase in drug seizures: Cape Verde,[4] Ghana,[5] Sierra Leone,[6] Guinea Bissau,[7] Liberia, Guinea, Nigeria, and Senegal are all major points of entry for cocaine in West Africa.[8]

In his work on the drug menace in West Africa and its linkages with Europe, Amando Philipe de Andrés writes:

> In the three years between 2005 and 2007, some 33 tons of cocaine has been seized on its way to Europe via West Africa. Prior to that time, seizures for the entire continent had already exceeded one ton annually. Something has shifted, recently and dramatically. Given the limited law enforcement capacities of many West African states, it is also likely that only a small share of the cocaine trafficked through these countries is detected. In fact, the circumstances surrounding the best documented seizures suggest that most are made by chance, and that, in many instances, the amount seized was much less than the amount trafficked. But despite this under-capture, seizures were over 60 times higher in the first three quarters of 2007 than they were in 2002. This would appear to be indicative of a dramatic increase in the underlying traffic.[9]

To put these figures in their proper context, the UNODC estimates that European cocaine demand is currently between 135 and 145 tons per year. Multiton seizures therefore represent a significant portion of total annual supply. For example, the 13 tons seized in and off the coast of West Africa in 2006 equaled about 10 percent of the total amount of cocaine consumed in Europe that year. Most of this massive amount was intercepted in just seven seizures—five at sea and two on the continent. It is likely that the flows that pass through the subregion undetected represent a sizeable portion of Europe's cocaine supply.[10]

The Dynamics of Africa's Organized Crime and Narcotics Trade

Transnational organized crime in West Africa takes several forms and includes drug trafficking, advanced-fee and Internet fraud, human trafficking, diamond smuggling, forgery, cigarette smuggling, illegal firearms manufacturing, firearms trafficking, armed robbery and theft, money laundering, and oil smuggling.[11] Of these activities, drug trafficking has perhaps the greatest potential to destroy democratic structures and processes.[12] By focusing on organized crime in Ghana and Nigeria, this section discusses the impact of organized crime on democratic structures and processes in West Africa.

According to the UNODC, "Transnational crime by definition involves people in more than one country maintaining a system of operation and communication that is effective enough to perform criminal transactions, sometimes repeatedly."[13] Today's TOC threat is characterized by at least six trends. TOC groups are (1) increasingly global in reach; (2) involved in multiple forms of criminal activity; (3) expanding their criminal markets to include large-scale financial fraud and cyber crime; (4) willing to protect their illicit activities through violent and ruthless means; (5) linked to international terrorist groups; and (6) devising novel organizational strategies to deter capture. The efficiency with which transnational crimes are sometimes executed presupposes the involvement of some state officials and institutions. In the case of West Africa, transnational organized crime may involve criminals within the region colluding with one another and also with others outside the region—whether elsewhere in Africa or in South America, Europe, or Asia.

There is the need to situate the context within which such activities occur within an understanding of the fragility of the state and its inability to respond to the challenges posed by TOCs. While recent discourse about state fragility has attempted to compare the new postcolonial states of Africa with the more established metropoles, it is crucial to appreciate that the societal disjointedness and frailties that have characterized postcolonial African states also point to the intrinsic structural weaknesses that have made crises and vulnerability key defining elements of the contemporary African state.[14] While it may be true that the fragility of states in West Africa and the weakness of state institutions mandated to combat the drug menace have contributed to the upsurge of TOC in recent times, the complicity—active or passive—of state officials within the regions and outside cannot be ruled out. It must be understood as "part of the highly unpredictable, multi-linear and not unilinear process of state building which entails the ups and downs of establishing and strengthening capacities to discharge the functions of the state, rather than as fixed or final outcomes.... Fragility [must be] approached as [a] process reversal and failure rather than as [an] original or static condition."[15]

Collusion by public officials in trafficking cuts across the Sahelian states of Mauritania, Senegal, Mali, Niger, and Burkina Faso; in West Africa's coastal states, extensive collusion has been found in Ghana, Nigeria, Sierra Leone, Guinea, and Liberia. Furthermore, fragility must be understood as occurring at two potential levels, because it does not constitute a one-size-fits-all model. For example, the January 2004 arrest of an international smuggling gang in Ghana that had imported no less than 675 kilograms of cocaine, with a street value estimated at US$140 million, led to the suspects being released on bail for just US$200,000, causing a public outcry in the press. Both the minister of the interior, Hackman Owusu Agyeman, and the attorney general, Paapa Owusu Ankomah, objected, demanding the incarceration of the suspects.[16]

Another case that suggests the infiltration of drug barons into Ghanaian politics involved a member of Parliament (MP) for the then ruling party, the New Patriotic Party (NPP). In this case, MP Eric Amoateng,[17] together with an accomplice, Nii Okai Adjei, was convicted in a New York district court of conspiracy to transport and distribute heroine, with a street value of over $6 million, to the United States. Although the MP initially strongly denied any wrongdoing, he later admitted to being guilty.[18]

A former head of Ghana's Narcotics Control Board has indicated that certain politicians are influenced by drug dealers.[19] As one investigator noted, more common perhaps is a tendency among some politicians to turn a blind eye to crime, believing that it is preferable to the type of violent conflicts that have destroyed other states in the region. This could be taken to suggest that criminal interests have become so powerful in some countries that they pose a potential political threat.[20]

Another case of political involvement in organized crime in the region concerns the late Maurice Ibekwe, a member of Nigeria's Federal House of Representatives who was arrested for financial fraud, forgery, and conspiracy. He had served as chairman of the House Subcommittee on Police Affairs. However, only in a small number of cases can it be shown beyond reasonable doubt that senior political figures such as Ibekwe were directly involved in organized criminal activities.[21]

The indications from the above examples suggest the infiltration of drug barons into democratic institutions with which they come into contact. In West Africa, among the democratic institutions in danger from organized criminal are parliaments, judicial institutions, political parties, and the executive arms of government. Such institutions are needed for building a democratic culture in any country. But, just as their effectiveness can lead to democratic consolidation, so too can their failure, especially when they are bedeviled with corruption, lead to the failure of the state system and, as a consequence, to a reversal of progress in democracy and development. For instance, a corrupt judicial system that accepts bribes from drug barons is likely to be lenient toward them and allow their business to thrive. In the same way, a government that has been infiltrated by drug traffickers is unlikely to pass tougher laws that can confront the drug trade. The direct involvement of organized criminals (i.e., drug traffickers) in the establishment and control of political parties and their engagement in political processes is likely in West Africa for two reasons: (1) there is an absence of state support for political parties, and (2) there is a lack of effective regulation on campaign financing.

With the increasing level of drug trafficking in West Africa and the involvement of some politicians in it, as the examples illustrate, there is the possibility that a drug baron could take control of political parties and, possibly, a West African government. Should this happen, the institutional capacity, independence, and legitimacy of democratic institutions would suffer at the expense of the parochial interests of criminal elements. Since democratic structures and political processes that lack legitimacy, independence, and effectiveness drive fragility, the already fragile states of West Africa are in danger of further fragility should they not be protected from organized crime.

How Has Organized Crime Come About?

There is a long history of TOC in West Africa, but the threats and challenges posed by organized criminal activities in West Africa have become so pronounced in recent years that experts in the field now characterize TOC groups in Africa as representing particular "African criminal networks" (ACNs). The characteristics of these groups differentiate them from other criminal organizations and give them a distinctive African character. "Although the majority of the criminals engaged in these networks originated in the West African countries of Ghana and Nigeria, the networks have expanded their bases of operations beyond West Africa throughout the African continent."[22] The most succinct characterization of ACNs has been provided by Stephen Ellis, who argues that

> West Africans ... have become significant players in the international trade in illicit drugs. Yet it is hardly possible to identify structured, hierarchical groups staffed by West Africans in this particular field of activity. Successful West African drug [traders] appear to be overwhelmingly individuals who recruit associates only where necessary and generally on an ad hoc basis. They may also be active in other fields of criminal activity, as well as in legitimate business. These characteristics, which are to some extent traditional among West Africans, can be turned to great advantage in modern, globalized markets, including illegal ones.

By expanding on Ellis's characterization, it is possible to provide an explanatory framework within which the activities of such criminal gangs can be located. What is happening with these trading networks is the admixture and exploitation of modern and traditional forms of networks. They use multiple local languages to foil detection and locate their activities within local societies where, because of their social welfare roles, they are perceived as being composed of "big men." Such access to traditional protective mechanisms allows them to be active within the modern economy, where their funds can be laundered and purchase influence. Apart from these characterizations, other critical factors appear to contribute to West Africa's position as a critical intersection for TOC activities.[23] These groups seek out weak entry points within state structures and then exploit institutional fragilities for their own economic and political benefit. According to Eric Pape, "[West African] governments ... are too weak, too corrupt or too consumed by their own problems to enforce laws or adequately monitor their coastlines and airports. Add to that are tens of millions of poor potential 'mules' and the picture becomes all too clear."[24] Similarly, Mark Shaw argues that "the origins of criminal networks from West Africa directly parallel the decline and economic crisis of the ... state in the 1980s. . . . Economic mismanagement, a failed structural adjustment programme, continuous political contestation and on-going and harsh periods of military rule marked the decline of the [West African] state."[25]

However, such characterizations do not provide a full explanatory framework for understanding these groups. For example, it has been argued that "ANCs are non-traditional, socially-cohesive organised crime groups that operate independently and lack a coherent corporate-type structure as seen in other significant illegal drug trafficking groups."[26] If this is so, then what explains the ability of Ghanaian and other West African gangs to compete and conquer territories hitherto thought of as closed to African gangs? Because of the complexity of the layered hierarchies that define these African criminal gangs, their coherence and structure confounds law enforcement officers and analysts who characterize them as "incoherent."

Although it might seem as if the results and the conclusions drawn are concrete, there is a need for caution. ANC activities in West Africa are evolving at such an amazingly rapid rate and speed that any conclusions and deductions made concerning them must be taken as tentative.

What Is the Extent of the Problem?

To attempt to understand the extent of the drug trafficking problem in West Africa, it is imperative to introduce a number of commonalities that may seem to be independent when considered on their own but that are clearly linked when considered collectively. They are the variety of systems that underpin the growth of these criminal groups and their activities— namely, familial, ethnic, cultural, and traditional elements. These systems are bound by a common cultural ethos and have important bearing on why criminal activities continue, in some cases even with the knowledge and tacit support of the local community and the lack of strong intervention by law enforcement agencies. One organized criminal activity in which a cultural approach contributes to understanding the survivability of groups is the trafficking of narcotics in Ghana. Such groups are organized into sophisticated and secretive networks. From a security standpoint, the result is obvious: the more the network goes underground, the harder it is to control and the more it is open to antisocial use by criminal elements.

In the realm of narcotics control, as in all political concerns, there exists a pronounced dualism in West Africa. On the one hand there is a parliamentary and judicial/legal (modern) system, together with all its accoutrements and relevant institutions, including a police force, that have been inherited from the former colonial masters. This is the "official" (modern) system that appears on the surface of things and is increasingly perceived by the populace as alien and corrupt. But on the other hand, there is the "unofficial" (traditional/cultural) system that operates beneath the surface. Throughout West Africa, there are traditional systems of governance, often in the form of taboos, that have various sanctions and systems of institutional support. West Africans are used to shifting from one system to another whenever it is felt to be appropriate.

Legally, only the first exists; the second is barely acknowledged. But the first is embedded within the second. The way the first is interpreted in any given situation depends on its understanding vis-à-vis the traditional system. The power of the second system, of course, arises from the fact that it is embedded in the traditional values and ethical concerns of the people, and its ultimate sanction lies in unseen dimensions, especially those relating to ancestors. Such unseen dimensions include the strong belief in ancestral worship and conception that ancestors—perceived as spiritual protectors—provide a shield against outside and hostile forces. While the efficacy of rituals that bind the physical and the unseen dimensions may be questioned, there is increasing evidence that those who engage in trafficking activities are convinced that having such spiritual protection is critical to the success of such activities. One may be "forced" to observe the first, but one is morally obliged to observe the second.

When it comes to harnessing the active involvement of the local community to comply with law enforcement, therefore, the realm of the latter must be considered and the ramifications of this duality must be examined. Specifically, if an action is considered "criminal" by the first system but is not considered "criminal" by the moral groundings of the second system, the action will not be regarded as truly criminal and people will not respond to it as such. For example, the criminalization of drugs by West Africa's political elites does not necessarily reflect the world view or interests of all the peoples who reside in West Africa.

Table 6.1   Effect of Drug Trafficking on Public Institutions in West Africa

Institution	Negative effect
Judiciary	Corruption, dubious judgments
Police	Corruption
Parliament	Lax laws, ineffective regulatory framework
Political parties	Financing of party activities by traffickers; political support from traffickers
Customs, Excise and Preventive Service	Collusion
Commercial banks	Money laundering, suspicious financial transfers
Central banks	Weak money-laundering regulations

What Sort of State Emerges?

There are different types of states spanning two extreme polarities that can emerge from this sort of impact. At one end of this polarity is a superficially functional state that has all the trappings of well-functioning and responsible public and private sectors. In such cases, the judiciary, police, customs, banks, and legislative bodies will be in place and provide a veneer of transparency and effectiveness. In reality, however, this type of state basically facilitates both the transit and redistribution of drugs and the transfer of illegitimate wealth by using its relatively functional institutions to facilitate such criminal activities (see table 6.1). A classic case is Ghana. The country is democratic and has the requisite supporting institutions and the veneer of functionality. Further, the international community accepts that its democratic institutions are well functioning. In reality, however, according to a 2009 report by the U.S. State Department's Bureau of International Narcotics and Law Enforcement Affairs, interdiction may remain a focus of law enforcement efforts, but "less attention [is] going towards arresting senior members of the narcotics rings or building up cases against local drug barons."[27] The report criticized Ghana's inability to establish appropriate laws dealing with drugs. According to the report, journalists and members of civil society speculate about connections between narcotics trafficking and politicians.[28] The end result, according to Mary Carlin Yates, a deputy commander in the U.S. Africa Command (AFRICOM), is that "8% of the total drug seizures in Europe transited through Ghana."

At the other end of the spectrum sit fragile states that are easily identifiable by their lack of institutional capacity to deliver public goods. Examples of such worst-case-scenario states are Guinea-Bissau and Guinea, where the impact of narcotics contributes to the wayward behavior of public officers and underscores the level of fragility that enables drug barons, with the allure of huge profits from drug trafficking, to control the levers of state authority. Subsequently, officials at all levels of government get involved in drugs and seek the profits that accrue from them.

The Threat of Cyber Crime

While few endeavors have been undertaken in Africa to respond to the challenge of cyber fraud and crime, there are overwhelming reasons why the potential ramifications of this challenge must be understood. This is because cyber crime is both global and local in nature. The most notable of these crimes is the so-called 419 or money-offer scams,[29] a subclassification of advance-fee scams in which the perpetrators are West Africans, primarily Ghanaians and Nigerians, with a global operational reach. In the case of Nigeria, it is estimated that cyber crime is the third to fifth largest industry in the country. The plethora of questions posed by this crime include the following:

- How should African states regulate technology that allows superfast transactions across states?
- What kinds of legal and investigative instruments can be used that cut across sovereign states?
- How can weak states respond to technological threats when the techniques employed by criminals defy the technical security measures that states employ?
- How can response mechanisms be created through national and regional plans to combat cyber crime?

In whichever way one analyzes these challenges, Africa—in terms of its individual states and institutions—is far off from having coherent national, much less regional, responses to these questions and in some instances, such as in Nigeria, Cameroon, and Ghana, to the real challenges posed by cyber crime.

Because of the multiple challenges posed by cyber crime, there is no doubt that "the age of cyber innocence is over."[30] While there is no doubt that the Internet plays a critical role in all aspects of a state's function, it is also clear that this dependency breeds new potential conflicts and new terrains for military, political, and economic crimes. For example, a successful attack on computers that run a country's critical infrastructure—especially that related to electricity, water, oil and gas, financial systems, and communications—would potentially create chaos.

There is no doubt that the cost of cyber-crime attacks in Africa runs into billions of U.S. dollars annually. According to Misha Glenny, "[cyber crime] is the fastest growing sector of criminal syndicates. But it is often impossible to identify if an attack is criminal in nature or has military implications."[31] What then is the nature of this beast that poses such challenges? Cyber crime can simply be defined as any criminal or illegal activity conducted through or against information technology infrastructure (ITI)—that is, any computer or network of computers used to relay, transmit, coordinate, or control communications of data or programs.

There are two well-known types of computer-related crimes commonly conducted against West African organizations and businesses. First are crimes against computers, such as through viruses. These types of crimes are on the increase but are often not reported to official state oversight authorities, as the IT security control systems in most organizations are generally able to deal with such computer threats. Because such threats are not reported or are underreported, full knowledge about their significance and the true impact they have on businesses and economic development is not available. More incentives in the form of policy and programs need to be put in place to encourage data capturing, profiling, and accurate reporting. This will help set up appropriate responses to counter such threats in Africa. However, the biggest challenge with internal IT management in Africa is the high levels of Internet illiteracy among computer users. This adds to the cost of maintaining IT systems in Africa.[32]

Second are crimes in which the computer is used as a tool to commit other crimes. Like crime against computers, cyber crime is also on the increase in most West African countries, a situation which has earned countries such as Nigeria and Ghana the uncomplimentary status of being ranked among the highest Internet crime destinations in the world.[33] In Ghana, nineteen complaints of Internet fraud are reportedly recorded each week. This includes so-called romance scams and business fraud through the use of impersonation and fake credit cards.[34]

In Africa, there are several types of security challenges posed to states by the wrongful misuse of IT infrastructure. They include illegal or unauthorized access, illegal interception (by technical means of nonpublic transfer of data to, from, or within a computer system), data interference (unauthorized deletion, deterioration, alteration, or suppression of computer data), system interference (interference with the functioning of a computer system by inputting, transmitting, damaging, deleting, deteriorating, altering, or suppressing computer data), misuse of devices, ID theft, and cyber fraud. All these IT-related crimes can be place into three broad categories: (1) crimes that target computer networks or devices directly; (2) crimes that are facilitated by computer networks; or (3) crimes whose primary target is independent of networks.

When governments talk about national security, they more often than not are talking about issues related to threats from violent political groups and identifiable parties. However, African states and businesses are not showing enough concern about what is becoming the biggest security threat of the twenty-first century: the threat of cyber attacks, or what has been described as "weapons of mass disruption."[35] While there is a general recognition of the positive uses to which the Internet can be put to, the Internet has also become "an increasingly powerful instrument in the hands of those who want to steal, terrorise and wage war using novel methods."[36] What makes cyber security crucial for government and business engagement is the fact that there is increasing evidence that the Internet is being used by criminal gangs, states, and competing businesses as an instrument of aggression.[37] TOC groups are waging cyberterrorism against states and businesses to steal cash and secrets. In most West African states, particularly the Sahelian ones, such instances of traffickers and terrorists attempting to attack states in the cyber realm is on the increase.

White Collar and Cyber Crimes

There exists a popular misconception about cyber fraud and crime. This misconception is based on the fact that the effects of these crimes are not transparent to society, as in the case of conventional crimes like burglary, assault, and murder. Statistically, however, the indication is that cyber fraud is one of the largest growing segments of criminal activity because of the potential to gain a great deal on the part of the criminal with seemingly little risk of being caught. Additionally, there is almost no possibility of physical harm to the criminal, as in the case of violent crime.[38] The crimes threaten the substantial and growing reliance of commerce, government, and the public on IT infrastructure to conduct business, carry messages, and process information.

In some cases, despite being able to anticipate or detect attacks, the security agencies of most African states are unable to prevent, arrest, or prosecute offenders. These failures are due to the weakness of the security services in some countries, such as in Ghana (*sakawa*), Nigeria (419), and Cameroon (*feymania*),[39] and have contributed to several disturbing trends.

First, there has been a proliferation of urban legends about the prowess of these new forms of transnational crimes, thereby glorifying them. Second, the schemes themselves are masterfully complex, with intricate dynamics. Third, the trade in narcotics and Internet fraud present a profile of the greed, hedonism, and powerful interconnectivity of transnational criminals in Africa. Fourth, those who lead these processes are cosmopolitan and commandeer regional and country-specific teams operating across the region, meaning they are more organized than state operatives. Fifth, these criminal groups function within well-organized structures with standardized rules and practices that their adherents must follow to the letter. Although there is a need to examine these challenges through a security lens, it must also be understood that what these activities represent are the commercialization and industrialization of crime.

It may well be that the now-established *sakawa*s, 419s, and *feymania*s are on the rise because incompetence and complicity among key actors in officialdom precipitates the abetment of such activity. Until the 2000s, many African countries had no policy on information and communications technology (ICT) to guide official responses to Internet fraud.[40] The incidents of 419 scams in West Africa, for instance, have spread from national-level operations to regional syndicated interfaces, with foreign nationals having relocated their activities to neighboring countries. This trend has rapidly intensified, especially among groups in Ghana and Nigeria. According to Calus Von Brazi,

> When 419ers descend unto Accra, they have one main purpose: to withdraw funds sent from far-flung places across the globe. Given that Nigeria has been tacitly and in some cases openly blacklisted as a place to do certain types of business ostensibly due to the 419 scourge, perpetrators of confidence trickery have found a safe haven in Ghana and insofar as easy money is wired to Accra for their nefarious purposes, what better way to enjoy the largesse than by having a Ghanaian passport, fake or genuine, to produce for the collection of [such] easy money?[41]

Inherent in the above statement is an indication that Nigerians are the ones driving the increasing trend in cyber fraud in Ghana. But much as the enterprise is often maneuvered by the giant strides of foreign elements, Ghanaian youth have also developed, over the years, a mastery in the 419 arts and are now developing their own independent capacities and networks, even though they sometimes do so in concert with their foreign partners.[42] The fact that these foreigners are easily able to secure national passports and other such vital documentations of the host state also brings to light the weaknesses in state institutions to effectively perform officially mandated regulatory and oversight responsibilities. This is a major inadequacy facing state institutions that should be addressed without any xenophobic underpinnings and tendencies.

Strategies for Dealing with Security Challenges

Responses to Drug Trafficking

Attempts to stem the tide of organized crime in Africa, especially drug trafficking, have occurred at the national, subregional, and regional levels.

This section examines some of the initiatives that have been undertaken by ECOWAS and the African Union in order to address the challenges posed by organized crime.

Almost a decade ago, during the Twenty-first Summit of ECOWAS Heads of State and Government in Abuja, Nigeria, October 30–31, 1998, ECOWAS issued a declaration titled "Community Flame Ceremony: The Fight against Drugs." Other actions taken by ECOWAS include

- the Resolution Relating to Prevention and Control of Drug Abuse in West Africa (1997);
- Recommendation C/98 on the Establishment of a Regional Fund for Financing of Drug Control Activities in West Africa;
- the Decision on the Establishment of a Regional Fund for Financing Drug Control Activities (1998); and
- the Decision on Establishing the Inter-Governmental Action Group against Money Laundering in West Africa (or GIABA, 1999).

Although such institutional frameworks exist, with the exception of activities undertaken by GIABA, which has been engaged in combating money laundering through its training programs that improve the capacity of member states to respond to the threats of drugs and money laundering, not many practical initiatives have taken place.[43]

Despite its lack of achievements, the ECOWAS Commission continues to show concern with the upsurge of both cyber crime and drug trafficking, and in June 2007, at its Thirty-second Ordinary Session, the Authority of Heads of State and Government expressed serious concern about the expansion in drug trafficking. As a result, the ECOWAS Commission was mandated to take urgent action. To get a fair view of the extent of the problem, GIABA was authorized to determine the scale of the problem and to subsequently prepare ECOWAS's strategy.

As a result of this preparatory work, two initiatives were undertaken: a civil society meeting on drugs was held in Abuja, Nigeria, on October 16, 2008, and the ECOWAS collaborative regional ministerial conference on drug trafficking and control was held in October 2008 in Praia, Cape Verde, and conducted with the assistance of UNODC, the UN Office for West Africa, and the European Union.

An outcome draft document from the conference pledged "to accord drug control the priority it deserves and at the highest level of government . . . as well as at the ECOWAS Commission."[44] In the operative sections of the political declaration, the ECOWAS Commission was directed to establish

- a strong coordination mechanism to forge close links with member-state government and nongovernmental institutions and organizations involved in drug control in order to achieve better coordination in the control of drug trafficking and abuse in the subregion;

- an ECOWAS Drug Control and Crime Prevention Division responsible for the overall coordination of regional initiatives undertaken in the prevention of crime and drug abuse and the treatment and rehabilitation of drug addiction, as well as in the collection and analysis of data on crime and narcotics in the subregion;
- an appropriate structure, under the direct supervision of the president of the ECOWAS Commission, that is responsible for coordinating and monitoring regional initiatives on illicit drug trafficking and drug abuse prevention;
- the Crime Prevention and Criminal Justice Centre to serve as a focal point for mutual legal assistance both among ECOWAS members and nonmembers.[45]
- the Department of Peace and Security, under the Office of the Commissioner for Political Affairs, was tasked with facilitating the formation of the Network of Drug Law Enforcement Agencies/Units within the framework of the West African Joint Operations to coordinate efforts to combat illicit drug trafficking and related TOC in the ECOWAS subregion.

The most important aspect of the new ECOWAS approach is the responsibility of each individual state to address the issue of drugs. In other words, the regional solution will be the result of efforts made at national levels. While Africa's international institutions are good at signing documents, few member states comply with what has been signed. In short, the level of willingness among states to follow through with what they have committed to is low. Thus, in the end, all regional and international decisions and resolutions add up to very little operational action or effective policy implementation. There are several reasons for this: few national government staff members have the technical skill to follow through on state compliance. But more disturbing is the deliberate lack of political will to act. While the actual signing at the international level is usually done quickly, translating such laws into domestic legislation is weak and slow. As a result, what both ECOWAS and AU initiatives have shown so far is that regional policy is largely a reflection of national policies, which thus undermines the transnational cooperation that underlies these institutions. In addition, there is no oversight or monitoring frameworks to bring sanctions against noncompliant or free-riding states.

Aside from ECOWAS, the African Union has undertaken Africa-wide initiatives to try to minimize the potentially negative effects of TOC in Africa. The problem of TOC was placed on the agenda of the Organization of Africa Unity (OAU), the predecessor of the African Union, in the mid-1990s. A first step in this direction was the OAU Plan of Action on Drug Control, which was adopted at the Thirty-second OAU Heads of State and Government Meeting in Yaoundé, Cameroon, in 1996. This Plan of Action was informed by the realization that

> Africa is targeted by drug traffickers who are taking advantage of the socio-economic and political difficulties besetting [the continent] and who are converting the continent into an extension of their worldwide network and are in the process developing markets for drug consumption wherever possible on the continent.[46]

The objectives of this Plan of Action included

- ensuring coherence of AU action in drug control at the national, regional, and continental levels;
- fostering cooperation among countries sharing the same problems, preferably in the same region;
- setting up appropriate institutions to address illicit drug trafficking and illicit drug demand in a balanced, integrated, and timely manner;
- assessing both the supply and demand of illicit drugs and ensuring the capacity of countries to address the problem;
- integrating drug-demand reduction programs into national health and social policy and providing, where not available, infrastructure for treatment of drug addicts and their social integration;
- adopting international drug conventions and legal instruments to deal with the problem;
- evaluating periodically the programs that are being implemented;
- mobilizing resources at the national, regional, continental, and international levels for carrying out the actions identified.[47]

Although there are several processes both at the ECOWAS and AU levels to tackle the trafficking challenges facing Africa in a more concerted manner, these objectives, contained in the 1996 Plan of Action, could not be implemented due to (1) political instability in some countries and regions; (2) limited resources in the context of competing needs and demands regardless of political will; (3) the absence of effective follow-up, monitoring, and mobilization mechanisms; and (4) inadequate institutional capacity at the OAU for drug control.[48]

As a result, this Plan of Action was revised at the first AU Ministerial Conference on Drug Control, in Yamoussoukro, Côte d'Ivoire, in 2002. The Revised Plan of Action placed emphasis on the following key areas: institution building and policy development; information, research, and networking; legal systems and implementation of laws; integrated drug-demand reduction; national law enforcement and control capacities; regional law enforcement and control measures; and international cooperation. Since the revised Plan of Action was to operate from 2002 to 2007, it became necessary to review the Plan of Action again in 2007. Consequently, in 2007, the African Union organized the Third Session of the AU Conference of Ministers for Drug and Crime Prevention in Addis Ababa, Ethiopia. This meeting was "guided by a comprehensive approach in addressing drugs, organised crime, corruption, money laundering, and terrorism issues."[49] The end result of the deliberations was the drafting of a Revised Action Plan on Drug Control and Crime Prevention for 2007 to 2012.

The core objective of the current Plan of Action is "to reverse the current trends of drug abuse, trafficking, organised crime, corruption, terrorism and related challenges to socio-economic development and human security and to achieve tangible improvement in the social and personal well-being of the people of Africa and the communities."[50]

To be able to achieve its objective, the Plan of Action contains seven key priority areas for action from 2007 to 2012:

- ensuring effective continental, regional, and national policy formulation and coordination in the domains of drug control and crime prevention;
- enhancing collaboration, shared responsibility, and harmonized action to address drug trafficking, organized crime, corruption, terrorism, small arms–related violence, and crimes within the community;
- building institutional capacity for the law enforcement, criminal justice, and forensic service systems for the purposes of drug control and crime prevention;
- mainstreaming drug and crime concerns into development strategies;
- advancing regional and national capacity building and training to enhance prevention and care of substance abuse and HIV/AIDS;
- enhancing understanding of the dynamics of drugs and crime for policymaking purposes;
- promoting broad-based responsibility through sports and culture in the service of social development to combat drugs and crime.[51]

These areas will form the basis of action on drug control and crime prevention until 2012, when the plan is likely to be revised again, taking into consideration new developments on TOCs and related crimes. To date, concerted engagement is taking place under several bilateral and multilateral initiatives to combat trafficking. These involve the growing role of the UNODC in supporting West and Central African states in developing national integrated programs to fight TOCs[52]—and the efforts of justice and interior ministers from ECOWAS member states, who adopted in Praia, Cape Verde, two main strategy documents.

These two documents, which were approved at the summit of ECOWAS Heads of State and Government in December 2008 in Abuja, are "The Political Declaration on the Prevention of Drug Abuse, Illicit Drug Trafficking and Organised Crime in West Africa" and "The Regional Action Plan to Address the Growing Problem of Illicit Drug Trafficking, Organised Crime and Drug Abuse in West Africa."

According to ECOWAS, the political declaration provides the political commitment needed from member states and gives new impetus to the ECOWAS Commission in the fight against the drug scourge, while the regional action plan provides the necessary framework for regional and national actions against drug trafficking, with the support and cooperation of development partners. The declaration mandates the ECOWAS Commission to coordinate the implementation of the regional action plan and monitor and report to the summits of heads of state in 2009 and 2010 on the progress made in the implementation of the declaration and of the ECOWAS response action plan.

In addition, it directs the commission to establish a strong coordination mechanism to forge close links with member states, civil society institutions, and organizations involved in drug control in order to achieve better coordination in the control of drug trafficking and drug abuse in the region. Toward this end, the commission is to set up an ECOWAS Drug Control and Crime Prevention Mechanism. As a result of these endeavors, an ECOWAS convention against illicit drug trafficking and abuse was finalized in 2009.

While expressing concern over the alarming surge in drug trafficking in the region and its consequences on the youth, ECOWAS's leaders agreed that only a holistic and global approach can lead to the eradication of the drug menace in West Africa and called for closer cooperation between countries of origin, of transit, and of destination to effectively tackle the scourge.

Responses to Cyber Crime

Most African countries were late in bringing up the issue of cyber crime for public discussion. Their key concern really has been to protect and empower online users by ensuring secured online transactions. Even though much effort has been made at the national and corporate levels in terms of formulating policy guidelines to regulate Internet services, very little has been done at the regional level to strategically coordinate and supervise such activities in Africa. As such, there is no policy direction and position at the regional level to guide national IT policies in Africa. Although the African Union has not yet directed its attention to the impact of Internet fraud on regional integration, building an African brand that will attract both multilateral and bilateral foreign direct investments and other microlevel businesses into the region in the twenty-first century can be undermined by the growth in cyber and other related crimes in the region. It was observed at the Annual African ICT Achievers Awards in 2007 that the apparent lack of collaboration among African governments was the key challenge facing the integration of strategic ICT policy for the region.[53]

There are high-level international initiatives on ICT policies that significantly impact interregional efforts to counter cyber crime. While the International Telecommunications Union's (ITUs) High Level Expert Group (HLEG), for instance, was instituted to develop strategies and guidelines to countries in dealing with cyber crime, the International Multilateral Partnership Against Cyber-Terrorism (IMPACT) works toward forging partnerships among countries in combating cyber crime and building confidence in the use of the Internet. The ITU-HLEG work is specifically designed to assist countries to draft their legislative framework and to fashion out strategies to address the challenges of cyber crime.[54]

At the bilateral level, a few African countries have received support from external partners to develop IT capacity. In 2008, for instance, South Africa was granted observer status to the Information Computer and Communication Policy (ICCP) committee of the Organization for Economic Cooperation and Development (OECD). This was the first time an African country was given that status at the international level in ICT policy.

National legislations on cyber crime, including the South African Electronic Communications and Transactions Acts, provide for the appointment of cyber inspectors to arrest and prosecute fraudsters; however, such measures are not adequate enough to deal with the situation. There is, therefore, the need to build a culture of security to address issues of technological insecurity in the face of rapid technological and socioeconomic challenges. Among such key challenges that require concerted efforts on the part of African countries are high levels of unemployment, illiteracy, and poverty, especially among youth. In Ghana, the government is preparing a legislative bill that will empower security agencies and other organizations to combat cyber crime in the country.[55] Security agencies, especially the police, have complained several times to the government that the absence of a cyber law in the country has frustrated their efforts to fight computer fraud and to prosecute perpetrators of Internet fraud.

Conclusion

African security challenges have manifested, over the years, in both violent and nonviolent ways. Relatively nonviolent challenges such as drug trafficking have significantly contributed to the weakening of many states in Africa. The West African Sahel and coastal regions, for instance, are increasingly becoming the hub of drug trafficking. Apart from the potential of the drug trade to infiltrate and weaken national political organizations and governance institutions in Africa, the menace can also affect the population in general. Such levels of insecurity will put significant pressure on national resources, and thus efforts at ensuring poverty reduction and economic development will come to nothing in the face of rapid globalization.

It is imperative to note that the twenty-first century is an information age and, therefore, should be prioritized as such by African countries. The apparent lack of attention to cyber crime at the continental level needs to be redressed. The attention required in this area should be inclusive of coordinated policies and strategies, targeted programs, and an adequate budget to finance programs in order to achieve the set goal of successfully combating cyber crime. Africa risks losing much desired foreign direct investment from and economic cooperation with its development partners if the problem of cyber crime is not addressed in the short term.

But identifying the key security challenges in Africa is one thing and addressing them is another things. It is now up to African leaders to demonstrate real commitment toward combating drug trafficking and cyber crime if Africa wants to continue to develop democratic governance structures and maintain competitive economic growth.

Notes

1. Antonio Maria Costa, "Cocaine Finds West Africa," *Observer*, March 9, 2008.

2. UNODC, "Drug Trafficking as a Security Threat in West Africa," October 2008, 1 (my italics).

3. Ibid.

4. Cape Verde has had its fair share of attacks. In March 2007, 500 kilograms of cocaine were seized from a container.

5. Ghana, as one of two hubs, serves more as a stockpiling hub for further distribution to other West African countries.

6. In July 2008, a Caracas-registered aircraft flying a false Red Cross flag landed at Lungi Airport, Freetown, with 700 kilograms of cocaine. However, a trial run of a Venezuelan consignment of 2.5 tons of cocaine failed when those loading the drugs onto a plane for a flight to Sierra Leone were arrested.

7. In July 2008, 500 kilograms of cocaine went "missing" while at Bissau airport as soldiers and policemen quarreled about who should take control of the drugs.

8. Joseph Winter, "Africa—New Front in Drugs War," BBC News, July 9, 2007, http://news.bbc.co.uk/2/hi/africa/?6274590.stm.

9. Amando Philipe de Andrés, "Organised Crime, Drug Trafficking, Terrorism: The New Achilles' Heel of West Africa," *FRIDE Comment*, May 2008, 2.

10. "Drug Money 'Tainting Ghana Poll,'" BBC News, October 28, 2008, http://news.bbc.co.uk/2/hi/africa/7695981.stm.

11. Kwesi Aning, "From 'Voluntary' Mechanism to a 'Binding' Process: The ECOWAS Convention on SALW and Ghana," *Journal of Contemporary African Studies* 26, no. 2 (May 2008): 169–81.

12. See Kwesi Aning and Samuel Atuobi, "Security Threats and Links between Trafficking and Terrorism in the Sahel," mimeo, November 2009, 19.

13. UNODC, "Transnational Organised Crime in the West African Region," 2005, 14.

14. Eghosa Osaghae, "Engaging State Fragility in Africa from Below," mimeo, 2007, 4.

15. Ibid., 7. See also M. G. Marshall and R. Cole. Benjamin, "Global Report on Conflict, Governance and State Fragility 2008," *Foreign Policy Bulletin* 12, no. 2 (2009).

16. Kwesi Aning, "Are There Emerging West African Criminal Networks? The Case of Ghana," *Global Crime* 26, no. 6 (December, 2007): 202.

17. Amoateng was arrested in November 2005 by U.S. law enforcement officials.

18. Aning, "Are There Emerging West African Criminal Networks?"

19. UNODC, "Transnational Organised Crime in the West African Region," 7.

20. Ibid.

21. Ibid.

22. This was the definition provided to the conference organized by the Bangkok Country Office and the Joint Interagency Task Force West. See "Notes from the African Criminal Networks Conference," African Criminal Networks Conference, Bangkok Country Office and the Joint Interagency Task Force West, Bangkok, Thailand, May 16–19, 2005, 1.

23. Chris Allen, "Africa and the Drug Trade," *Review of African Political Economy* 79 (1999).

24. Eric Pape, "West Africa: The New 'Drug Triangle,'" *Newsweek International*, August 25, 2005.

25. Mark Shaw, "Towards an Understanding of West African Criminal Networks in Southern Africa," *African Security Review* 10, no. 4 (2001).

26. "Notes from the African Criminal Networks Conference," 1.

27. As cited in Albert Oppong, "Arrest Local Drug Barons," *Daily Graphic*, March 4, 2009.

28. Ibid.

29 Andrew Hathaway, "Ghana, West Africa: The Fraud Zone," *ezinearticles.com*, July 19, 2007, http://ezinearticles.com/?Ghana,-West-Africa---The-Fraud-Zone&id=652324; see also "Nigeria—The 419 Coalition Website," http://home.rica.net/alphae/419 coal/.

30. Misha Glenny, "Cyber Crimes Are Gearing Up in the Cold War of the Web," *Guardian*, June 26, 2009, 24.

31. Ibid., 24.

32. See "Internet Crime Report of 2007," National White Collar Crime Center (United States), www.ic3.gov/media/annualreport/2007_IC3Report.pdf.

33. Ibid.

34. See Ama Achiaa Amankwah, "Ghana: Police Advocate for Laws to Combat Cyber Fraud," *Public Agenda* (Ghana), March 23, 2007, www.cipaco.org/spip.php?article1261.

35. "Cyber Security Risk—The US and UK Are Right to Focus on Internet Dangers," *Financial Times*, June 26, 2009, 8.

36. Ibid.

37. Estonia blamed the Kremlin for a 2007 cyber attack, and when Russia moved into Georgia in 2008, cyber attacks crippled all Georgian government Web sites.

38. Celia Wells, *Corporations and Criminal Responsibility* (Oxford: Oxford University Press, 2001).

39. *Sakawa*, 419, and *feymania* are the names of different aspects of cyber criminality in these respective countries. Stephen Sah, "Two Students Fined for Cyber Fraud," *Mirror* (Ghana), July 18, 2009; see also Claire Chaffey "A Night with Cyber Fraudsters," *Ghanaian Times*, July 31, 2009.

40. See "South Africa: Internet, Cyber Crime to Take Centre Stage at Conference," *allAfrica.com*, December 13, 2008, http://allafrica.com/stories/printable/200806170593.html.

41. Calus von Brazi, "The Nigerian 'Re-invasion' of Ghana (11)" *Ghanaweb*, September 2009.

42. See Amankwah, "Ghana: Police Advocate for Laws to Combat Cyber Fraud."

43. ECOWAS Commission, "ECOWAS Ministerial Conference on Drug Trafficking, Organized Crime and Drug Abuse Prevention in West Africa," October 2008, 2.

44. ECOWAS Commission, "Political Declaration on Drug Trafficking, Organized Crime and Drug Abuse Prevention in West Africa," October 2008, 6.

45. The need for this center's establishment was recognized by ECOWAS as far back as 1999. In Article 46 of the 1999 Protocol Relating to the Mechanism for Conflict Prevention, Management, Resolution, Peacekeeping and Security, the drug threat to the subregion was recognized, but characteristic of ECOWAS and its leaders, nothing was done.

46. OAU, "OAU Plan of Action on Drug Control 1996," 1996.

47. Ibid.

48. African Union, "Declaration on Control of Illicit Drug Trafficking and Abuse in Africa 2002."

49. African Union, "Revised AU Plan of Action on Drug Control and Crime Prevention 2007–2012," 2007.

50. Ibid.

51. Ibid.

52. For example, see the letter dated June 29, 2009, from UNODC to Ghana, in author's personal files.

53. See "South Africa: Internet, Cyber Crime."

54. Ibid.

55. See Amankwah, "Ghana: Police Advocate for Laws."

7

The Middle East

Regional Security Institutions and Their Capacities

Anoushiravan Ehteshami

I n the Middle East, the term "security" is a loaded one, often used to imply its absence rather than to provide evidence of its operational parameters. Everyone talks about security, states are obsessed with it, and regional leaders use it as a carte blanche for covering a multitude of sins in their conduct at home and in their public or foreign policies. It is a fig leaf that tends to serve regime interests. For these reasons, states have developed a highly individualistic approach to security and are usually given to not sharing any aspect of it with other regional actors. This is a region with unique structural characteristics and systematic vulnerabilities, the most salient of which is its "relatively high levels of hard power resources compared to most systems of developing states."[1] In the Middle East, therefore, security is a highly private affair in which the distribution and level of power are arguably "the main system-level factor shaping the security concerns and policies of states."[2] The reasons for this situation are complex and intertwined with the history of state formation in this part of the world.[3] This is a region dominated by an Arab core and imbued with substate identity politics that, since the 1940s, have laced the state system itself. Arab national identity has had to struggle for a middle ground between territorial sovereignty and panterritorial pan-Arabism. The tension between identity and interests has not always been easy to smooth.[4]

One result of this complex and often contradictory relationship has been a lack of trust even between Arab states, which prima facie have so much in common in terms of language and literature, history, culture, religion, and national experience.[5] To add to an already complicated set of relationships, the core non-Arab actors of the Middle East and North Africa (MENA) region (Iran, Israel, and Turkey) are equally loaded with their own historically specific national identities, which often clash with those of the Arab peoples. Israel's national identity is uniquely different from the identity of the Arab world for its reliance on Jewish history and Zionist nationalism; Iran's is distinct for being formed by Shia politics and identity; and Turkey's, though similar to the Arab world's identity in terms of the role of Sunni Islam in it, is potentially threatening for its historical legacy and the secular and pro-Western roots of its post-Ottoman constitution. In this fashion, then, the traditional MENA region can be said to consist of an Arab core of some twenty-two states (and nearly 340 million people) and a non-Arab periphery of three countries (with a total population of around 150 million).

This region has been pressed with competing pressures since its emergence in 1945. By the 1980s, these pressures were as much due to war and conflict and an uneven distribution of national wealth and military power as to ideological reasons. As a result, the region is more recognizable by its "fragmented multipolarity" than its sense of unity of purpose or oneness.[6] Gregory Gause's analysis provides four reasons for the region's systemic problems: "the nature of anarchy in the Middle East," the uneven distribution of power in the region, "the changing nature of state-society relations in the units making up the system," and the poor level of regional economic integration.[7]

Furthermore, despite flashes of autonomous—indeed, anarchical— behavior, MENA remains a highly penetrated regional system that is dangerously exposed to external pressures and forces. The end of the Cold War intensified external pressure and, as Barbara Allen Roberson notes, left the United States as the dominant external actor in the region and as "the sole arbiter in the region's politics"—one "in pursuit of interests that often failed to correspond to those of regional governments or publics."[8]

Yet a number of Arab states, Israel, and Turkey have close military and security links with Western powers. As a NATO member, Turkey is part of the world's most robust security alliance. Although the direct value of the alliance for its core members in the post–Cold War order remains to be tested, NATO does provide Turkey a security niche in the Middle East regional context. Israel, on the other hand, has tried to be as self-reliant as possible in meeting its national security needs, but the country has never been under the illusion that without American help and support it can guarantee its own security.

In the Arab world, Egypt, Iraq, Jordan, Lebanon, and the six Gulf Co-operation Council (GCC) countries have the most intimate security links with the West. Egypt is a major recipient of American military aid and hardware and its forces tend to hold regular exercises with their U.S. counterparts. Jordan is also a close U.S. ally and is reliant on U.S. military and economic support. Similarly, Lebanon relies on the West (in particular, France and the United States) for security assistance but has to manage this relationship against fierce opposition from political forces at home. But it is among the Arab oil monarchies that the most visible security connections exist. The United Arab Emirates, for example, has close links with the United States and France and has signed security pacts with both. Qatar and Bahrain are home to major U.S. deployments, with Bahrain acting as home to the U.S. Navy's Fifth Fleet. In Kuwait and Oman, the United States and Great Britain have a major presence. Saudi Arabia, for domestic reasons, has opted to keep its Western security links at an arm's length, but it remains reliant on American and British hardware and support for its armed forces. In the Maghreb (North Africa), American and French security and military partnerships dominate, though Algeria, Morocco, and Tunisia have thus far failed to find a security modus operandi that serves themselves.

Of all of these relationships, the case of Iraq is perhaps the most complex. It has become a Western partner through a forced change of regime in Baghdad. The new regime continues to owe its livelihood to the support (if not presence) of American military forces. Indeed, Iraq's security remains dependent on American support, and it will be some time before Baghdad is in a position to account for its own security. This forced induced security partnership has major implications for Iraq, particularly in its relationships with its neighbors.

These myriad security partnerships have emerged either as a response to regime vulnerabilities or as a part of efforts to lock some key Arab actors into the West's orbit. Although the Arab states concerned have of course willingly entered partnerships and have themselves often been the instigators of such partnerships, these arrangements do not serve wider regional security concerns. Indeed, the reverse seems to be the case—namely, that "the failure of regional institutions, multilateral or bilateral alliances, and of the regional power balance to give local states security . . . opened the door to acceptance of a heightened role for the non-Arab periphery and for the U.S. hegemon in the region."[9]

Despite the number and intensity of these security and military ties, none of them can be classed as alliances in the strict sense of the word, for the only security alliance impinging on the regional environment is that of Turkey's membership in NATO. Outside of NATO's indirect presence, no other security alliance as such exists in the Middle East.

While a large number of Arab states in the MENA region have forged close security or military links with the West, a number of other Arab states and Iran have made the decision to function outside of the West's security orbit. Indeed, Iran and Syria have positioned their opposition to Western military presence in the region as a virtue and have drawn ever closer together the greater the Western footprint has become. Sudan, Libya, and Yemen are the only other Middle Eastern states without a Western-oriented security structure, even though the latter two have established important security links with several Western countries.

The security picture in the Middle East has gotten even more complex since the passing of bipolar global-power-bloc politics. If anything, enduring regional conflicts, the trauma of 9/11, violent regime change in Afghanistan and Iraq, and the deep impact of the war on terror more broadly has intensified the region's security problems.[10] In the absence of a regionwide security forum or conflict management system, MENA states have tended to set about meeting these intense post–Cold War challenges either unilaterally or through the formation of partnerships among small clusters of states.

But the region harbors other complexities. To begin, the argument that MENA is a regional system does not necessarily mean that its "regionalization" is preordained.[11] Indeed, this is one of the least "regionalized" regional systems of the world when measured by positive economic and market-integration criteria—such as unhindered mobility, the free flow of trade and investment, the presence of an internal market for the subsystem's members, the existence of collective measures to standardize legal and financial management regimes, the formation of a truly regionwide technical secretariat for cooperation, and the establishment of convergence criteria. Many of these features are conspicuous by their absence in the MENA region, despite efforts in the early 2000s to reduce intracountry barriers. External security considerations and judgments aside, it is hard to justify completely the MENA region as a full-fledged subsystem.

Moreover, as the security envelope itself has widened since the end of the Cold War, one has to note (at least for analytical purposes) the emergence of the so-called Greater Middle East, which incorporates Pakistan, Afghanistan, and the Asian republics of the former Soviet Union into MENA. It thus becomes even more difficult to locate a core to the system.

But this is not to suggest that the MENA regional system has grown organically. To the contrary, the broadening of the region has mainly been a product of the growing interdependencies that are increasingly prevalent across the international system. In this particular region, religious, labor, capital, socioeconomic, security, and political networks are the core drivers of its extension eastward. One could argue that the notion of a "greater" Middle East is designed to encapsulate the presence and influence of so-called border states on the subsystem.

By contrast, subregions are much easier to define analytically in the MENA region than the boundaries of the MENA system as a whole. As will be shown, it has been at the subregional level that attempts at institutionalized cooperation have been most effective, though they have not necessarily been particularly successful.

Regional Security Institutions

It is one of the Middle East's ironies that despite its many regionwide and subregional security challenges and conflicts, no regional structure for managing them exists.[12] For sure, the Arab League and its various security-orientated committees articulate Arab views of the Arab-Israeli conflict and the United Arab Emirate's dispute with Iran over Tunbs and Abu Musa, but the organization has no teeth and has failed to show leadership at times of real crisis—such as during Iraq's invasion of Kuwait in August 1990, the overthrow by force of Iraq's government in April 2003, and the July 2006 war in Lebanon. It is partly a result of its inability, for both political and structural reasons, to respond to crises that subregional bodies have tended to emerge.[13] Since the 1970s, three Arab subregional organizations and one major non-Arab organization have appeared on the scene, with very mixed results of success.

Gulf Cooperation Council

The birth of the six-member GCC in 1981 as an organization of oil-rich Arab monarchies has symbolized the region's tendency toward subregionalization. A security organ par excellence, it was created in response to the twin security threats of the Iranian Revolution and the related Iran-Iraq War raging around the Arab monarchies.[14] By European Union standards, the GCC has been far from successful in creating a cohesive unit, or a dominant club, in the subregion.[15] Specifically, it has made little progress toward the creation of a political union (a specific goal of the organization, as exemplified in its charter) or of an integrated market. Vulnerable in both geographic and demographic terms, its success can only be measured in terms of its ability to develop certain unified structures for its members.

On January 1, 2003, a customs union was established by the GCC to standardize customs duties among its members. In accordance with the customs union, Saudi Arabia approved the reduction of customs to 5 percent for goods formerly charged between 7 and 12 percent. In addition, the GCC agreed to the principle of a single port of entry. It was agreed by the members that most related laws and regulations be standardized by the end of 2005. The customs union was a landmark event by regional standards, but even this measure took over twenty years to mature, and only followed slow progress on such agreements as labor mobility.

A key reason for the GCC's slow evolution has been the complex geopolitics of this rather conflict-oriented subregion of unequal powers. Phebe Marr notes that "without cultural or political cohesion, the Persian Gulf comprises countries and societies at varying levels of development and with differing resource bases that share a common body of water of critical importance to all of them."[16] Their diversity, in other words, helps to divide rather than unite the eight countries bordering the waterway. The northern shores of the waterway are dominated by Iran and Iraq, both of which have had their fair share of political anguish over the last five decades. Since 1979, though, their domestic politics have been particularly effective at spilling over borders and destabilizing the entire neighborhood. As Iran's politics have settled down, however, Iraq's politics have again entered a new period of instability. A combination of violence and political uncertainty among the Gulf region's largest Arab actors, therefore, will more than likely further dampen the collaborative tendencies of the states of this strategic waterway—which, of course, will adversely affect the security relations of the wider MENA region. But the GCC can be classified as a regional success story when compared with other subregional organizations.

Arab Maghreb Union

Nearly a decade after the birth of the GCC, another all-Arab subregional organization, the Arab Maghreb Union (AMU), was founded in 1989 for establishing a common market and for managing the economic affairs of the North African states with their more powerful northern neighbor, the European Union. The five-member AMU was meant to forge a common market that would act as a single unit in relations with its geographical peripheries. While looking northward, the AMU was also to play a role in the Organization of African Unity (later renamed African Union), to which its members all belonged. Its successes, however, were limited due to Libya's continuing international isolation, Libya's "Africa first" strategy, the Western Sahara dispute between Morocco and Algeria, and the threat of Islamist militancy arising from the bloody civil strife in Algeria in the 1990s. Issues pertaining to Libya's international policies in particular proved to be a real problem for the AMU from the early 1990s, with Libya effectively turning its back on the AMU when in 1992 its fellow members accepted to impose UN sanctions on it for its involvement in the bombing of Pan Am flight 103 over Scotland in December 1988. The AMU was unable to grow and mature largely because it failed to move from diplomatic integration to the higher level of developmental integration.[17]

Arab Cooperation Council

The Arab Cooperation Council (ACC) followed the AMU with its birth in 1989. The ACC had a security orientation from the beginning and brought under the same umbrella Iraq and three of Iraq's most helpful allies in its war with Iran: Jordan, Egypt, and North Yemen. The ACC became the third all-Arab subregional organization to emerge from the ashes of pan-Arabism, but it barely saw its first birthday as it succumbed to the tensions that arose from Iraq's invasion of Kuwait in 1990. Indeed, by September 1990 the ACC had effectively folded. The birth of the ACC had been enthusiastically engineered by King Hussein, the ruling monarch of Jordan, and Saddam Hussein, the ruling president of republican Iraq. The ACC seemed very different from its neighboring organizations. It was the first subregional organization not to enjoy geographical contiguity. It was also the most geographically diffuse. It was the first to straddle the Arabian Peninsula, the Persian Gulf, and the easterly edges of North Africa. With a combined population of more than 100 million, it promised much in economic terms, but its short life meant that it could not deliver on any of its economic or security-related promises. Indeed, as its untenable position in the 1990–91 Kuwait crisis illustrated, it was again politics and geopolitical complexities that forced the undoing of a promising subregional organization.

Nevertheless, with the birth of the ACC, the Arab world was effectively segmented into three unequal subregional entities. The three organizations encompassed fifteen Arab states, from Morocco in the west to Yemen in the east. The failures of the AMU and the fate of the short-lived ACC speak volumes about the strategic vulnerabilities of the Arab order and its structural weaknesses. It is partly due to the weaknesses of the subregional organizations themselves, as well as to the absence of an Arab hegemon to regulate inter-Arab relations, that the Arabs failed to impose a pan-Arab regional order on the MENA subsystem. In this context, the Arab League is not a champion of regional integration or a panregional body that can impose order on the region. Arab fragmentation is manifested in the Arab League's moribund state.

Economic Cooperation Organization

Post–Cold War politics did, however, open one new window for regionalism in the area. The decision of Economic Cooperation Organization (ECO) members (Iran, Pakistan, and Turkey) to incorporate the Muslim republics of the former Soviet Union and Afghanistan into the organization in the early 1990s created a regional body of more than 300 million blessed with mineral, agricultural, and some significant industrial wealth. It was expected that the founding members of ECO, which was founded in its current form in 1985 and further expanded in 1992, would begin to push this organization as a new economic force in Asia. But weak political structures and a lack of security (interstate and domestic), combined with the dynamism of Asian power balance, dampened the impact of the larger ECO. The ECO continues to function, but this all-Muslim, non-Arab regional organization has little to show for its existence. While the existence of the ECO may have helped bilateral relations among some of its members, it has not, as a rule, created a functional regional bloc to straddle South, West, and Central Asia.

Major Regional Players

The above survey makes the point that the Middle East is now a subdivided region with its subregions acquiring a degree of strategic autonomy. In the Gulf and North Africa, strategic autonomy has produced subregional organizations, with the GCC leading the region in terms of internal coherence and structural cohesion. But subregionalization does not mean that regional problems or crises are less transferable. On the contrary, security issues such as the Arab-Israeli conflict and transnational terrorism routinely transcend geographical boundaries and are today forging a deeper strategic interdependence of the region's security and conflict parameters. Subregionalization does not seem to have halted the transfer of regionwide security issues, though subregions have clearly developed some dynamics of their own. In the Persian Gulf, for instance, numerous international concerns—the relationship between Iran and the GCC states, the state of Iran's nuclear program, the fear of a Shia-dominated Iraq, the political and security situation in Iraq, the nature of the Iran-Iraq relationship, GCC security—are also matters of concern to the Gulf states themselves; all are also of direct interest to the rest of the Arab world and to Israel and Turkey. In this environment, strategic interdependence, one can argue, breeds "insecurity interdependence." Although the larger actors set the scene in the region, they are only rarely able to set the agenda given their inability to act as regional hegemons or to manipulate any regionwide forum. Thus, even if such a forum existed, it would be unlikely that the dominant powers would be able to establish the regional agenda or drive it.

Defining the region's "major" or "critical" players is another complication. This is not an easy task for there is no consensus as to what the criteria for such a status might be—are we defining such actors by population or territorial size, economic muscle, or military might? What makes them "major," one can surmise, is that which also makes them influential players.

In addition to this rather ill-defined category of states, one should also be mindful of the role and impact of what might be called "critical" Middle East states for regional security—that is, those states whose internal dynamics leave a mark on the wider region. These states are significant for their internal weaknesses as much as for their strengths. Critical states are regarded as such because of the ways in which their geography, demography, ethnicity, resource base, and/or other related attributes makes their dynamics relevant to the security of the rest of the region. These states may not be dominant or particularly powerful, but they are major players in terms of their impact and influence.

Broadly speaking, there are only a handful of countries in the Greater Middle East that have the ability to actively shape the geopolitical setting of the area. These "major" players—or key regional security actors— represent a combination of dominant and critical states. They are Iraq, Iran, Saudi Arabia, Israel, Libya, and Pakistan. Algeria, Egypt, Syria, and Turkey are enormously important regional players in their own right, but they are not regional "shape shifters" in terms of being able to dramatically alter the region's security dynamics either through their own power plays or being likely to expose the region to wider insecurities due to their own inherent vulnerabilities.

Iraq

With regard to Iraq, the country's new identity and redefined security parameters have tended to be shaped by a dangerous conflict between the country's Shia majority and the formerly dominant Sunnis. Sunni militants and al-Qaeda have been active in trying to halt the complete transfer of power to the Shia in Iraq and in using Iraqi territory as a place to wage jihad against the United States. The primary focus of the guerrilla operations in Iraq began to shift in the second half of 2003 toward the

Shia community, and these communities have remained a core target of the increasingly exposed Sunni militants. It is a widely held view among al-Qaeda cadres and Sunni militants that the Shia, with the connivance of the United States, are busy implementing their plan for the domination of Iraq and for targeting Sunni Islam's heartland in Saudi Arabia. The terror campaign in Iraq has had a dangerous geocultural dimension that has threatened the stability of Shia-Sunni relations beyond Iraq itself. Iran's ties with its Sunni neighbors in the Arab world have been tested, as has Iran's and Iraq's relations with Sunni-dominated Pakistan, Turkey, and Afghanistan.

Until the launch of the U.S. military's "surge" in 2007, the militant Sunnis' perception of the growing political role of the Shia in Iraq had increased the frequency and intensity of terror attacks on the Shia communities there.[18] These attacks reached a high point on Ashura (Shia Islam's major religious occasion) in early March 2004 (Islamic month of Muharram), with the deadly synchronized attacks on the main Shia shrines in Baghdad and Karbala, which killed at least 170 people and injured hundreds more. The anti-Shia terror campaign in Iraq dangerously resonated in Iraq's Sunni hinterland and stirred greater hostilities between GCC governments and their Shia minorities, as well as between the Shia-dominated states of Iran and Iraq and their neighbors. As a direct consequence of these developments, a clash of religious factions, if not "civilizations," was in danger of being unleashed and engulfing the entire region. Nearly a decade after the war began, this danger still exists and continues to pose a direct threat to regional security.

For a brief period following the occupation of Iraq and "liberation" of its Shia community, voices in Washington began speaking of the need to "free" the eastern Saudi province of al-Hasa province, where the majority of Saudi Shia reside. Neoconservative commentators in particular saw in the war an opportunity to redraw the map of the Middle East. Max Singer, the cofounder of the Hudson Institute, was among those who suggested that Saudi Arabia's strategic eastern oil region should be separated from the rest of the country in an effort to curb Wahhabi extremism.[19] Other Washington insiders, such as Richard Perle, David Frum (President George W. Bush's former speechwriter), and Senator Sam Brownback also recommended that the fight against terror be taken to Saudi Arabia. The message was that the Saudis needed to follow the United States' lead in its antiterror campaign or watch the U.S. encourage the separatist tendencies of the Saudi Shia in al-Hasa.[20] By denying access to the oil, the argument was made, Riyadh could be "tamed" and Saudi fundamentalists would be deprived of the necessary funds to support al-Qaeda.

It was the rather sudden shift of focus in U.S. circles to the geocultural overlap between Persian Gulf oil and Shia communities that alarmed (largely Sunni-dominated) Arab regional actors, as King Abdullah of Jordan, President Hosni Mubarak of Egypt, and several Saudi princes made clear. The West, suggested Mai Yamani, has "woken up to the accident of geography that has placed the world's major oil supplies in areas where the Shi'ites form the majority."[21] It is the liveliness of this geocultural cross section in Western policy terms that petrifies the Arab leaders and fuels their suspicions of the United States' endgame strategy in the region.

Iran

It is in this tense situation that neighboring Iran began to feel empowered and assumed that it could operate with impunity. As the world's only Shia—and expressly Islamist—state, postrevolutionary Iran has been careful not to stray too far from the wider Arab region in its policy pronouncements. It has remained loyal to the Palestinian cause, has developed reasonably cooperative relations with virtually every Arab state that it has relations with, and has ensured that it keeps in close touch with its Gulf Arab neighbors. Yet, the tempo of its domestic politics is hopelessly out of sync with its Arab neighbors. Islamist Iran finds itself in a geopolitical struggle with the United States and its main regional ally, Israel, and as such cannot act as a natural ally of the West in the war on al-Qaeda, or indeed as an ally of Washington's friends in the Arab world. Nevertheless, Iran is destined to play a critical role in the unfolding drama of the region. Asher Susser has noted that in the Gulf region, "Iran is the only regional power of consequence. Iraq is out for the count, and the Saudis are a broken reed."[22]

While the judgment on Saudi Arabia may be somewhat harsh and also premature given Riyadh's proactive diplomacy since 2006, such assessments of Iran would have seemed hardly credible even in the 1990s when oil prices were soft and Iraq was under UN sanctions. Iran was in no state to overtake its influential neighbors, with its weak economy and a hostile Iraq and Afghanistan. But in the wake of the Iraq war, Iran's fast-moving dynamic political system, its relations with Shias outside Iran—in Iraq, Kuwait, Bahrain, Saudi Arabia, Lebanon, Afghanistan, Pakistan, India, and Azerbaijan—and its geopolitical advantages have come to give the leaders of this still structurally weak country a powerful voice in the region.

Saudi Arabia

As already noted, since the fall of the Baath regime in Iraq in April 2003 and the shifting balance of power in the region, Saudi Arabia has shown a real determination to act more directly and even proactively in regional affairs. This shift has grown in significance as Iran has shown a willingness to penetrate core Arab agendas, such as by championing the Palestinian cause, being active in Lebanon, and supporting Hamas and other Arab Islamist movements. Saudi assertiveness has also seemed to be a function of the post-9/11 strains in its close alliance with Washington and of the United States' curtailment of its high-profile military presence in the Kingdom. In addition, the removal of Saddam Hussein as the self-proclaimed leader of the Arab world has opened the door for Saudi Arabia to add political influence to its already considerable and growing economic role and presence. Furthermore, Egypt's demise as the preeminent Arab actor, accompanied by the marginalization of both Iraq and Syria, has paved the way for Saudi Arabia's rise.

Riyadh's confident hosting of the Arab League summit in Riyadh in March 2007, less than five years after the fall of Baghdad to U.S. forces, was designed to send a message of Saudi supremacy across the region. The Arab League fully endorsed the Saudi-sponsored Arab peace plan put forward at the Beirut Arab summit in 2002 and also provided the Saudis the platform to speak on wider Arab issues—from Darfur to Iraq—allowing Saudi Arabia the chance to begin to lead the Arab agenda and to set the tone for Arab positions.

The overriding regional arena of significance to Saudi Arabia is the Arabian Peninsula and the neighboring Gulf region, which Riyadh regards as being of vital importance to its national security and prosperity. Since the 1990s, the Kingdom's political and diplomatic role has been underpinned by an increasingly strong economy—and, more recently, by rising oil prices—that place the Kingdom at the head of the region's league of economic powers. The Kingdom is increasingly prosperous at home, its leadership is confident of its standing, and it is able to exercise its influence on a broad canvass, comfortable that within the troublesome Arab region it is now an unchallenged power. But as it establishes its new place as the preeminent voice in the Arab region, it finds itself having to respond to the challenge coming from Iran. The emergence of a largely acquiescent Arab region has proved to be an insufficient condition for the Kingdom to be able to defend the Arab agenda, or indeed to affirm its own position as the leader of the Arab region. The regional diffusion of power alluded to earlier in this chapter imposes a real cost on Saudi Arabia when it tries to balance its own interests against its growing role as provider of conflict management and mediation in the wider region.

Israel

To the west of Saudi Arabia is the heart of the Arab-Israeli conflict, which is increasingly defined by the policies of its one dominant actor, Israel. Israel has never shied from using its considerable capacity to affect the geopolitics of the region to its own advantage, and Arab weakness merely assists this process. Israel also has been counting on the security fallout from 9/11 and the war on terror to further advance its own interests in the region. With the fall of Baghdad in April 2003, it has been able to do this much more easily than at any time since the signing of the Camp David accords in 1979. Compounded by the collapse of the Soviet Union and Iraq's foreign policy debacles, the Arab world has been unable to find an appropriate response to Israel's supremacy, having to watch from the sidelines Tel Aviv's manipulation of the Arab-Israeli agenda and its ever closer strategic partnership with non-Arab Turkey. Israel therefore has managed to secure for itself a key role in the balancing of forces in the Arab world. But it has not developed a policy of engaging the Arab world for mutual benefit, as its weak response to the Arab peace plan launched by Riyadh demonstrates.

Libya

Libya's emergence from the late 1990s as a nonconfrontational state was completed in 2003–04. By late 2004 virtually all sanctions on the country had been lifted, and with its denunciation of terrorism, support for the anti-al-Qaeda war on terror, and abandonment of all WMD programs, it was set to emerge as a key North African partner of the West, particularly the European Union, in economic and political terms. Its geopolitical position and its hydrocarbon resources will place Libya at the heart of developments in the western side of the Arab world in this century. Its choice of regional partners, therefore, as it frees itself from the shackles of sanctions, will help in the redrawing of North Africa's economic and geopolitical map. Due to its strategic location, Libya's role in the war on terror could certainly overshadow the services of Algeria, Tunisia, and Morocco combined. It could also help in the development of closer economic links between the Maghreb countries, or it could conversely choose to ignore its neighbors by cutting a vertical axis with Europe on the one hand and sub-Saharan Africa on the other. If it were to follow the latter option, the dream of an Arab common market would be in tatters if the market were to lose Libya as a facilitating actor both financially and territorially.[23] Libya may not be dominant, but its geopolitical influence and economic potential make it a critical actor in the region whose policy choices directly affect the well-being of its neighbors and the wider Arab world.

Pakistan

Finally, there is Pakistan and its role on the eastern fringes of the MENA region. Islamabad's role grew immeasurably when it joined the United States' war on terror and assisted the West in its overthrow of the Taliban in Afghanistan and in the military campaign against al-Qaeda. For the Gulf Arab states, Pakistan has been a steady supplier of cheap Muslim labor, cheap manufactured and processed goods, and ready-made military support. In the 1980s Pakistan provided a great deal of logistical and personnel support to Saudi Arabia, as the Kingdom tried to incorporate its massive weapons purchases into its rapidly modernizing armed forces. This military partnership has been kept alive by both parties. But as the Muslim world's only nuclear-weapon state, with close trade and cultural links with the Persian Gulf states, Afghanistan, and some Central Asian countries, the impact of its foreign policy orientation at this crucial juncture in the history of the MENA region is of great importance.

Pakistan is not known for its political stability, however. Muhammad Ahsan explains that in the course of "the past half century this Islamic Republic has had twenty-four heads of state and has adopted three constitutions. Half of its period of existence has been under three periods of martial law, and it has gone to war three times."[24] This analysis of Pakistan's instability was tragically reinforced by the assassination of Benazir Bhutto in 2008 by a suicide bomber and the security chaos that followed. The intense confrontation between the government and the highly militant homegrown Taliban and al-Qaeda forces has since 2008 raised new worries about the stability of Pakistan as a sovereign state. Gulf Arab states in particular are alive to the possibility that the positioning of a highly unstable Pakistan as a close U.S. ally could have serious domestic consequences in both Pakistan and within their own borders. Any instability in Pakistan, or a further consolidation of Salafi Islamist forces in Pakistan, could easily spill over into Afghanistan (and even Iran), and the Arab countries of the Gulf. Pakistan's closeness to the United States, therefore, could worsen the political tensions between regimes and Islamist forces in the eastern Arab world, creating the conditions for further instability in the region.

Pakistan, a real cauldron of instability, is now a close U.S. ally in the war on terror. How the U.S.-Pakistan partnership develops will affect Pakistani politics in the years to come, possibly weakening the secular-leaning and pragmatic forces in this large Muslim country. Radicalization of nuclear-armed Pakistan, however, will destabilize not only Pakistan's partnership with the United States but also its relationships with all of its neighbors. More so now than at any time in its history, Pakistan will directly affect the security of the Greater Middle East should it undergo any radical shift.

Other Important Players

The above is not an exclusivist list, and it has already been acknowledged here that other countries matter too. Several other regional actors in particular have significant geopolitical weight—namely, Algeria, Egypt, Turkey, and Syria. But, in this author's analysis, these states are not seen to be in a position to radically affect the course of developments in the MENA subsystem. Countries such as Turkey have a formidable voice and can bring moral and diplomatic pressure to bear on regional politics, but for various reasons, they are unlikely to shape or affect regionwide security considerations.

As argued, the MENA region has a very mixed bag of state actors, with varying power-projection capacities, hard- and soft-power reservoirs, internal fragilities, and regional reach. There are no "first among equals" in the region, and every state seems to act as if it is in competition with the rest. Countries play for maximum advantage in an effort to deny advantages to the competition and also to ensure that their core interests are not threatened. The mixed power base of these states, coupled with the absence of a regional confidence-building forum, has not helped temper the prevailing "anarchical" approach to security, despite regional and international efforts to create a consensus around some of the core issues in the region— WMDs and nuclear proliferation, the Arab-Israeli conflict, Gulf security, and political violence.

These actors tend to function with an acute awareness of their immediate environment but also demonstrate a full grasp of the interdependencies that now drive the regional security agenda. Security in the Middle East, therefore, is now both local and regional, and as such threats to it are panregional. It would be advisable to sketch some of these security issues before considering the region's capacity to address them in an inclusive and collaborative manner.

Regional Security Issues

As noted, the MENA region is unstable partly because of the nature of the states themselves, the conditions of their birth, the ease with which domestic instability has become an exportable commodity to other countries, the apparent "anarchy" that seems to prevail among the region's state and nonstate actors, the absence of any meaningful consensus on how to take regional agendas forward, and the presence of interstate rivalries that seem to be built on zero-sum competition for the defense of maximalist positions. Many of these points can be demonstrated with a survey of the most pertinent security issues themselves.

Persian Gulf Security

It is remarkable how insecure this strategically important subregion has been over the last thirty years or more. One major revolution, three major wars, externally imposed regime change in one of its core countries, intensive nonstate actor violence, and ethnic and religious sectarian rivalries and violence—none of these events has remotely propelled the Gulf states or the international community to seek a stabilization pack to bring a semblance of order to its interstate relations. Indeed, the greatest external stakeholder in the subregion, the United States, has arguably contributed more to the Gulf's woes over the past thirty years than to its stabilization.[25] In short, the United States' reactive policies seem to have made the situation there worse. From President Jimmy Carter's policy of "prevent any outside force from gaining control," to President Bill Clinton's "dual containment," and President George W. Bush's "preemption," there has been a degree of continuity, if not coherence, between the various U.S. doctrines applied to the Persian Gulf since 1979. Each policy has emerged in response to a unique security challenge. So, while this author accepts that U.S. policies over the last thirty years were informed by the need to establish some order in the subregion, in practice U.S. policies had the opposite effect. Violence and rivalry have intensified.

It is equally possible to argue that this is an overly pessimistic or negative assessment, and that several attempts at making progress on security have been made. Indeed, there have been several attempts at creating a Gulf security forum (the annual International Institute for Strategic Studies (IISS)–sponsored Manama Dialogue, for example), and even the 5+1 group (composed of the five permanent members of the UN Security Council and Germany) has included security in its package of incentives to Iran. But overall the United States has held sway since the early 1970s, having established a significant military presence in the Persian Gulf. At times it has acted unilaterally and at other times, such as during the 1990–91 Kuwait crisis, it has acted multilaterally and in conjunction with its European allies. But these efforts have failed so far largely because of the regional states' own inability to compromise on their key positions.

An example of this inability relates to Iran's nuclear program, which began to rear its head as a major security issue in the Persian Gulf just as the 2003 Iraq war got under way, thus providing a double security problem to the Gulf states. Iraq had been turned from the eastern gateway of the Arab world to a Gulf security vacuum, sucking in outsiders. Al-Qaeda on the one hand and Iran on the other were most active in their interventions in Iraq, increasing the anxiety of neighboring moderate Sunni-led states and their leaders. Neither Shia resurgence in Iraq nor al-Qaeda strength is an appealing prospect for the Gulf monarchies, which fear the activity of both in their own countries in equal measure. But of the two, it is Iran's influence and presence in Iraq that has worried the monarchies most, for if Tehran and Baghdad were to create even a loose alliance of Shia-led countries, it would be composed of more than 100 million people and would control half of the Persian Gulf's oil reserves, allowing the potential to create a dominate bloc in the subregion of the sort that has previously not existed there. Already, Iran has more economic, social, and religiocultural ties with Iraq than at any time since the nineteenth century, and Iran's links to Iraq are much more extensive than those of the Gulf Arab states.

The prospects for an Iraq-Iran alliance is not strong as things stand, for Iraq still retains a very proud Arab heritage that will reassert itself once the country has stabilized. Moreover, Iran and Iraq still have their own border dispute and other bilateral issues to resolve, including the relationship between Najaf (in Iraq) and Qom (in Iran) as the two main holy centers of Shia learning and of religious jurisprudence and guidance. The rise of Najaf could be a challenge for Qom and Iran's political leadership in Tehran, for as things stand Qom's overall endorsement of the *velayat-e faqih* (guardianship of Shia jurist) political system in Iran that Ayatollah Khomeini introduced provides the legitimacy for the country's current religious-based establishment. If Najaf were to counter this, it would be devastating for Iran's leaders, who have relied on religion to justify their system of governance.

Iraq and its rediscovered ties with Iran remain a concern for neighboring countries, but it should be acknowledged that regime change in Iraq has already removed a major threat to Gulf security and has provided the potential for opening a subregionwide dialogue on mutual security. Iran's participation in the annual meeting on Gulf security in Bahrain is a good example of some (albeit unstructured) dialogue taking place. And there is at least one recent example of Iran being forthcoming on regional security matters. The first relates to the proposal put forward by the Iranian deputy foreign minister for Arab-African Affairs (Mohammad-Reza Baqeri) at the IISS-led regional security conference in Manama in early December 2005. At this event, Iran was represented at a high level, indicating the importance that Tehran had attached to security dialogue with its Arab neighbors. Baqeri welcomed the IISS initiative and formally proposed the adoption of a regional security regime, but with the usual caveat that "the security set-up should include a time-table for departure of foreign military forces from the region." In his view, "the increased presence of alien military forces in the region has led to more chaos, strengthened radicalism and terrorism and postponed the growth and development of the region."[26] Of course, Iran's usual cautionary note did not go down well with the U.S.-supported and -armed GCC states. But the Iranian deputy foreign minister also put forward some creative measures for discussion, notably "a governmental and non-governmental war against terrorism, a program to rid the region of weapons of mass destruction and rejection of the theory of regional balance."[27] These were rather general if not vague proposals, but in the context of the meeting were significant signals that Iran was interested in confidence building across the waterway.

Iran's nuclear program, however, is a very different matter and is seen more as a direct security challenge to the subregion if not the wider region. This is a cross-cutting issue that will severely test the strategic interdependence of MENA theaters. Iran's nuclear program is not only a direct challenge to Iran's neighbors but arguably also a direct threat to the region's only nuclear-weapon state, Israel. Since President Mahmoud Ahmadinejad's anti-Israel and Holocaust-denial speeches, the threshold of conflict may well have been lowered, and neither country, it seems, is prepared to resist the securitization of the issue. Both countries' public pronouncements have sounded more like a call to arms than anything else. Despite the efforts of the 5+1 group to find a negotiated solution, the escalation in Iranian and Israeli policies has been palpable since Ahmadinejad's election in 2005. Iran since announced that it had successfully test fired a new generation of surface-to-surface missiles with a range of 1,200 miles, capable of reaching Israel and also southern Europe. Of particular concern has been a system known as Sejil. This new missile uses solid fuel and is said to be more accurate than other missiles in the country's arsenal. Stated Iranian defense minister Mostafa Mohammad Najar at the launch, "[This] missile gives our military force a new capability. It was produced as part of our deterrent policy. It will be for peace and security in the region, and we will only use it against enemies who invade the Islamic Republic." The news of the launch emerged a day after Iranian news media said that the Revolutionary Guards had test fired another new missile, known as the Samen, near the border with Iraq.[28]

These developments were only the latest phase in the ongoing military saber rattling between Iran and Israel. Indeed, the *New York Times* reported in June 2008 that the Israeli Air Force was already practicing for an aerial bombardment of Iranian nuclear targets: "More than 100 Israeli F-16 and F-15 fighters participated in the maneuvers, which were carried out over the eastern Mediterranean and over Greece."[29] Iran's numerous long-range surface-to-surface missile tests in 2007 had gotten their response from Israel. But instead of trying to defuse the situation, the Bush administration used Iran's missile programs as justification for its own military deployments in Europe, in practice creating further confusion and also additional security interdependencies in the region. Iran's missile capacity has been cited by the United States as one reason for an American plan to station an antimissile shield in Eastern Europe, a project that has enraged Russia. In response, Moscow has declared that it would station short-range missiles in its Baltic enclave of Kaliningrad if the United States went ahead with its plan. Thus, the potential military crisis in the Iranian-Israeli relations became hostage to a much bigger, extraregional set of issues, making addressing this at the regional level an almost impossibility.

Returning to the core issue, the fuss of course is not just about the long-range missile proliferation in the region as effective delivery vehicles for conventional and nonconventional warheads, but about the nature of Iran's nuclear program. The stated fear is that Iran is pursuing a two-track nuclear program, with the military program being disguised by Iran's massive peaceful program. The broad assumption is that Iran's extensive industrial and intellectual nuclear know-how will come to serve its military and security needs sooner rather than later. The strategic concern is that by 2015 Iran is likely to have mastered weaponization techniques and could be able to assemble a nuclear bomb. In order to be able to develop such weapons, however, Iran will have to be in a position to produce highly enriched uranium on an industrial scale. Its enrichment efforts have been moving fast since 2005 and the variety and intensity of centrifuges that Iran has used has been taken by the International Atomic Energy Agency (IAEA) as testimony for Iran's wider ambitions.

The logical extension then is that over time Iran will be able to deliver to distant targets a large payload through a wide range of sophisticated surface-to-surface ballistic missile systems. Less directly, there is an equal concern that once Iran has a nuclear weapon it will then be able to dictate its agenda to its neighbors—to become dominant in more ways than one.

Ironically, though, the program grew out of Iran's efforts to deter an aggressive and vengeful Iraq, with its technological breakthroughs occurring in secret in the 1990s, during the so-called moderate administrations of Presidents Hashemi Rafsanjani and Mohammad Khatami, and it has arguably ended up as the ruling establishment's best effort to neutralize American threats to its security. Vulnerable, without strategic allies, and lacking a credible conventional military machine, it can be argued, Iran has felt the need to be able to deter this persistent enemy, and other threats as well, with every means possible. From the Iranian standpoint, the nuclear program is a viable deterrent in this context. However, if Iran's nuclear program results in a confrontation with Israel and indeed accelerates the nuclear programs of Iran's neighbors, its long-term value must be questioned.

In the absence of a regional effort to address the security aspects of Iran's nuclear program, which does remain under IAEA supervision, it should be noted, the onus has fallen on the major powers to try and manage the crisis. While the regional states have welcomed international intervention, the international community's role has meant that a wider regional voice has been absent from the protracted negotiations between Iran and the EU3 (France, Germany, and Great Britain) and later the 5+1 group. The hidden danger in this strategy has been the extraction of the nuclear issue from regional dialogue. While a number of Arab states and Israel have expressed their concerns about this program (in private and also in public), their concerns have been subsumed within the 5+1 negotiations, thus diluting the regional input and impact on the cycle of negotiations that have been taking place since 2003. The 5+1 group has assumed that it acts on behalf of the region in as much as it represents the will of the international community, and yet if one analyzes the incentive packages put to Iran since at least 2006, the regional voice seems to be absent. But there is little doubt that the strategic consequences of Iran's nuclear program are great. Note in this regard the comments of U.S. director of national intelligence Mike McConnell:

> Iran is currently pursuing fissile material. We suspect—although we cannot prove—that Iran secretly desires a nuclear weapon, certainly a nuclear device. If Iran achieves such capability, then the stability of the Cold War that was witnessed between the United States and the Soviet Union or NATO and the Soviet Union would be unlikely to be achieved in the Gulf. And that's going to ... set off an arms race in the Gulf that would be very destabilizing and could have global impact. We are going to be dependent on oil for the foreseeable future. A major portion of it still flows out of the Middle East. And with Iran armed with a nuclear weapon, it would be incredibly destabilizing.[30]

Arab-Israeli Conflict

The Arab-Israeli conflict is in danger of becoming as old as time itself. The dimensions of peace have been self-evident for nearly a generation, and yet the conflict rages on. This conflict is central to the region and through it is set the temperature for relations across the Middle East. Other conflicts do rage on, that is for sure, but none has had the capacity to transcend in the way that the Arab-Israeli conflict has. "The largest, and most important, piece in this multi-dimensional jigsaw [of the Middle East] is the Israeli-Palestinian conflict," notes the sage commentator Philip Stephens. "It is the issue that more than any other shapes attitudes towards the US."[31] And toward the West more generally, it can be added. The problem has been a live issue for successive American administrations for at least sixty years; it is also high on President Barack Obama's list of priorities given that Annapolis 2007 has thus far failed to deliver the Palestinian state that President George W. Bush promised.

The question of the establishment of a Palestinian state and the knot around the other Palestinian issues (refugees, national status, compensation, right of return), coupled with the dispute over the Golan Heights between Israel and Syria, form the crux of the conflict. But unfortunately Saudi-led Arab efforts beginning in 2002 to implement a land-for-peace deal have not broken the logjam, leaving the way open for the conflict to continue to act as a lightning rod for radicalization. Indeed, with the introduction of the Arab peace plan, which has been formally endorsed even by Syria, the face of the conflict has changed into an Islamist-Israeli or an Iranian-Israeli one. Peace with Egypt and Jordan (1979 and 1994, respectively) and Palestinian self-government (post–Oslo Accords in 1993) have gone a long way toward meeting some of Israel's core security concerns, but the lack of peace with some of the front-line actors (such as Syria and Lebanon, for example), together with the monumental failure to establish a viable Palestinian state on the basis of UN Security Council Resolutions 242 and 338, has merely extended the geopolitical frontiers of the conflict beyond the Levant and has left the arena open for more radical forces (Hamas, Islamic Jihad, Hezbollah, Iran) to intervene in an effort to bolster the region's rejectionist tendencies. The restructuring of the Arab-Israeli conflict in this manner is having profound security implications.

Iran is now acting very much as a frontline state in its own right, and through its close and strategic partnership with Syria and Hezbollah, it is able to test Israel's security and also scupper any peace deal that it feels unsatisfied with. In addition, as the West rushed to isolate and punish Hamas for its electoral success in Palestine's elections in January 2006 (and also put pressure on its Arab allies to do likewise), Tehran rushed to support Hamas and extended it not only moral and political support but also financial and allegedly military support. Iran could thus claim that it was the only Muslim country directly and openly supporting the legitimate voice of the Palestinian people. By asserting this moral high ground, Iran also claimed a security stake in the Palestinian-Israeli conflict.

The isolation of Syria for its misdeeds and policies (that is, for allegedly playing a role in the assassination of former Lebanese prime minister Rafiq Hariri, for providing shelter to radical Palestinian groups and their leaders, for supporting Hezbollah, for interfering in Lebanon's internal affairs, for allowing insurgents to enter Iraq through its long border) has helped in pushing it closer toward Iran. The two countries have since 9/11 strengthened their "strategic partnership," and for all of Turkey's efforts since 2005 to broker a deal between Israel and Syria, little strategic headway seems to have been made on that front. Aggressive acts such as Israel's bombardment of an alleged secret Syrian nuclear facility in 2007 merely add new cement to the already well-established security partnership between Tehran and Damascus and further strengthen Iran's hand in this theater.

The unlocking of the Palestinian-Israel door, more than any other effort on the Arab-Israeli front, will help in reshaping the dynamics of the Middle East toward a more secure future. The rejoining of Gaza and the West Bank would make it much more likely that both Syria and Lebanon (Hezbollah, more notably) would yield to international pressure to sue for peace. If the Palestinians have a viable state alongside Israel, what would remain for Iran to do on their behalf? To be sure, Iran's current presence and influence in this theater would be much diminished, and Israel's security much enhanced through such a peace deal. The anti-Israel thrust of the Iranian-Hezbollah alliance would also be checked with the establishment of a viable Palestinian state, as the Palestinian refugees in Lebanon begin to look forward to a new life and an internationally recognized identity. Moreover, the Arab sponsors of peace with Israel would also be given a stronger hand to work toward the deradicalization of their own Islamist forces and the creation of new opportunities for development and partnership. The United States' and the wider West's tarnished image in the Muslim world would also get a makeover if they were seen to be pursuing the agenda of a lasting peace in the Arab-Israeli conflict by lending their considerable resources toward the establishment of a Palestinian state. The first step in making all this possible is the establishment of a viable and well-resourced Palestine, something that Israeli leaders since Prime Minister Yitzhak Rabin have long recognized for themselves.

To enhance the security of the states locked in the Arab-Israeli dispute, therefore, formal regional bodies or institutional arrangements need not be introduced; rather, political will must be injected into Israel and the Quartet (the United States, the United Nations, the European Union, and Russia). Regional institution building will inevitably follow a peace accord as the dynamics of regional relations would change so significantly that it would facilitate and, in fact, require a forum for confidence-building measures. For the moment, the goal of achieving peace needs other things. The only formal institution currently entrusted with this agenda is the Quartet, informally supported by the 2007 Annapolis group of states (essentially the Quartet, plus the Arab League), which agreed to the outline of a peace accord. At this stage of the game, little else is possible or even desirable on this front, for even the Israeli-Syrian track is being pursued informally through Turkey and without formal or informal input from the Quartet or the Arab League. The Arab League, as the Arab states' common regional body, has adopted the formal negotiating position of support for the Arab peace plan. But beyond declarations of intent, the Arab League has never been an implementing body, and despite its many institutions and professional bodies, it has not been allowed or able to grow into a regional governance or security institution. It has been unable to become greater than the sum of its parts.

Conclusions

It has been argued in this chapter that the MENA region, for all its strategic significance, is bereft of any regional security architecture to serve the region or the interests of the many interested external parties. While attempts at subregional structure building have been made, with a degree of focus on security, the experience has been a very mixed one, with some parts of the region doing much better than others. Even where success is evident, such as in the Gulf, the GCC exemplifies the fragmented nature of subregionalization rather than the subregion's strengths. But clearly no regional or subregional body dedicated to the enhancement of security or confidence building has been in evidence in the MENA subsystem. Furthermore, even as the MENA region is a highly penetrated one and therefore exposed to the forces of globalization and also external (particularly Western and specifically American) pressure, it is remarkable how little effort the international community as a whole has devoted to the development of MENA security structures. Fragmented subregional conversations—in the Maghreb (with the European Union) and in the Persian Gulf (through IISS and also through the package of incentives offered Iran)—have indeed taken place, but these have failed to provide any momentum for the creation of viable security dialogue or structures. Moreover, beyond the Quartet (with regard to Israel), little else has tended to tie the Arab and non-Arab MENA actors together, which in turn has encouraged divergence rather than convergence between the various power centers.

In this rather dire state of affairs, the conversation sadly is less about "enhancement" than "establishment." There is currently little institutional base to enhance. Being mindful of the fragmented nature of the MENA regional order, the rubrics of dialogue must be put in place before the agenda of how to meet the many new security challenges arising in the Middle East can be attended. Also, it has been suggested that the establishment of peace between Palestine and Israel will be a precondition for the introduction of any viable security forum in the region. But peace in itself will not remove the many obstacles in the way of MENA security dialogue. Israel's security fears about Iran's aggressive regional role, for example, has to be addressed separately, as indeed does the Gulf Arab states' concerns about Iran's nuclear program, before any substantive progress on security institution building can be made. It should be emphasized that the measures to assure Israel's security have to be adopted beyond the nuclear negotiations between Tehran and the 5+1 group. Multilateral and international efforts will be needed to build any progress on the nuclear issue itself, which cannot proceed without a badly needed and overdue "understanding" between Washington and Tehran. Then, there is Iraq and its future role in the region. Can Iraq emerge as a partner for peace from the ashes of war and the many years of repression and neglect by its neighbors? It is still unclear what a truly independent post-Saddam Iraq will look like, and it will be some years yet before one can see with any certainty the role that Baghdad can play in Gulf security. Given the makeup of its new leaders as (largely) Arabs and (largely) Shias, Iraq is uniquely placed to form a historic bridge between Iran and the Arab world, and with the GCC more specifically. This presents a unique possibility from which the United States will ultimately benefit, because it could in turn directly shape and influence any moves toward building regional security infrastructures.

Nevertheless, there is a glowing silver lining to the MENA region's dark security clouds, and that is the election of a new proengagement American president. Barack Obama's election victory is already testing deep-seated prejudices in the Middle East about America, the efficacy of American democracy, and the mobilizing energies of its democratic institutions. This is good news, and President Obama's success will provide the United States with the moral high ground to lead international efforts at peacebuilding in the Middle East. His declared resolve (now supported in the U.S.-Iraq security pact) to free Iraq of U.S. troops and to help stabilize Afghanistan (and also Pakistan) is very good news as far as the regional states are concerned, but beyond these measures, he will also be expected to deliver the Annapolis promise and to resolve the dispute over Iran's nuclear program. How he deals with the latter, especially in the context of troop reductions in Iraq, is an important one, as America's Arab allies would be loath to see the nuclear issue resolved as part of a "grand bargain" with Tehran. They would be particularly nervous if such a "bargain" were to leave Iran as strong as ever in the region. For the Obama administration, it will therefore be a question of how to manage these many expectations while also keeping the United States on course to advance the cause of conflict resolution. But given Barack Obama's multilateralist instincts he is likely to be looking toward the Quartet and also to America's long-standing Western allies to help build the necessary institutions for peaceful management of conflicts in the Middle East.

A note of caution is necessary, however, for as of this writing, one is struck by the lack of substantive progress being made on any of the MENA regional security agendas President Obama articulated in January 2009 and again reiterated in his Cairo speech in June of that year. America's mounting economic and related difficulties have arguably taken their toll on the president's capacity to engage with intractable regional security problems. In the absence of dramatic improvements on the domestic front, the perception of a hamstrung president unable to mobilize sufficient American and international resources to deal with international problems will only play into the hands of the region's irredentist forces.

Thus, while the Middle East is still in the dark ages as far as regional security institutions and security dialogue are concerned, what is required is dramatic change in the dynamics of the region for it to be able to take the first steps toward inclusive regionalism, albeit at first at the subregional level. Yet, the nature of regional politics is such that without external input no such change is likely to be forthcoming in the medium term. As a highly penetrated regional system, the MENA region's fate is inextricably tied to the fortunes of the prevailing international order, and yet it is the international community that can ill afford an unstable Middle East that continuously fuels global insecurities.

Postscript

Regional security policy in the Middle East and North Africa has been formed—and national interest has been defined—by groups of individuals who have had an iron grip on their respective states.[32] Their absolute control of public space and national interest debates, consistent with their overtly authoritarian rule, has had a strangulating effect on "public policy." So it has been elites and the political regimes that have been serving them who have determined the course of foreign policy, war, and indeed peace. Iraq's two wars against its neighbors did not have popular support, just as Egypt's and Jordan's peace treaties with Israel did not. However, it appears that change is coming, as the plethora of hitherto authoritarian Arab regimes either collapse or adjust (and also redefine) their national priorities in a much more inclusive fashion and more in tune with public opinion. While I do not expect public opinion to begin working against peace, this rather unknown variable will nevertheless affect state policies in the period to come. Let us also remember that new forces are likely to emerge, whose politics and priorities will be less known.

It may unsettle existing assumptions about the region and its regimes, but in the medium to long term the Arab world's emerging democracies—for this is what they are and will be—are going to be well placed to transform and radically improve the discussion about regional security and security governance in the Middle East. After a long wait, the era of "democratic peace" may well be nigh, enabling a look forward to a much more inclusive set of approaches to security and a better understanding of shared destinies. Shared values will become a factor, and open and transparent systems of decision making will help states understand each other better and indeed interact more positively. The region is again changing, but this time with the full promise of better things to come. In the Maghreb and the Mashreq, the emergence of democratic forces will help rewrite regional relations in a new light, but the process will take time and will not be painless or flawless. The Middle East region remains as dynamic as ever.

Notes

1. Paul Noble, "From Arab System to Middle Eastern System? Regional Pressures and Constraints," in *The Foreign Policies of Arab States: The Challenge of Globalization*, ed. Bahgat Korany and Ali E. Hilalh Dessouki (Cairo: American University in Cairo Press, 2008), 101.

2. Ibid.

3. Richard Falk articulates the Middle East strategic predicament as one of being caught in a "geopolitical trap." As a consequence, the Middle East ends up as a "captive region." See Richard Falk, "The Cruelty of Geopolitics: The Fate of Nation and State in the Middle East," *Millennium: Journal of International Studies* 20, no. 3 (1991): 383–93.

4. Michael N. Barnett, *Dialogues in Arab Politics: Negotiations in Regional Order* (New York, NY: Columbia University Press, 1998).

5. Malcolm Kerr, *The Arab Cold War* (Oxford: Oxford University Press, 1970).

6. Raymond Hinnebusch, "The Middle East Regional System," in *The Foreign Policies of Middle East States*, ed. Raymond Hinnebusch and Anoushiravan Ehteshami (Boulder, CO: Lynne Rienner Publishers, 2002), 29–53.

7. F. Gregory Gause III, "Systemic Approaches to Middle East International Relations," *International Studies Review* 1, no. 1 (Spring 1999): 26–30.

8. Barbara Allen Roberson, "The Impact of the International System on the Middle East," in *The Foreign Policies of Middle East States*, ed. Raymond Hinnebusch and Anoushiravan Ehteshami (Boulder, CO: Lynne Rienner Publishers, 2002), 65.

9. Nadia El-Shazly and Raymond Hinnebusch, "The Challenge of Security in the Post-Gulf War Middle East System," in *The Foreign Policies of Middle East States*, ed. Raymond Hinnebusch and Anoushiravan Ehteshami (Boulder, CO: Lynne Rienner Publishers, 2002), 86.

10. Fred Halliday, *The Middle East in International Relations: Power, Politics and Ideology* (Cambridge: Cambridge University Press, 2005).

11. Gause, "Systemic Approaches to Middle East International Relations," 11–31.

12. See Anoushiravan Ehteshami, *Globalization and Geopolitics in the Middle East: Old Games, New Rules* (New York: Routledge, 2007); Raymond Hinnebusch, *The International Politics of the Middle East* (Manchester: Manchester University Press, 2003).

13. Bahgat Korany, "The Arab World and the New Balance of Power in the New Middle East," in *Middle East Dilemma: The Politics and Economics of Arab Integration*, ed. Michael C. Hudson (London: I. B. Tauris, 1999), 36–59.

14. Paul Aarts, "The Middle East: A Region without Regionalism or the End of Exceptionalism?" *Third World Quarterly* 20, no. 5 (1999): 911–25.

15. Abdul Khaleq Abdulla, "The Gulf Cooperation Council: Nature, Origin, and Process," in *Middle East Dilemma: The Politics and Economics of Arab Integration*, ed. Michael C. Hudson (London: I. B. Tauris, 1999), 150–70.

16. Phebe Marr, "The Persian Gulf After the Storm," in *Riding the Tiger: The Middle East Challenge After the Cold War*, ed. Phebe Marr and William Lewis (Boulder, CO: Westview Press, 1993), 109.

17. I. William Zartman, "The Ups and Downs of Maghrib Unity," in *Middle East Dilemma: The Politics and Economics of Arab Integration*, ed. Michael C. Hudson (London: I. B. Tauris, 1999), 171–86.

18. These attacks have continued of course but with different degrees of intensity.

19. This strategy was the main focus of discussions at two Hudson Institute conferences, "Saudi Vulnerability: The Source of Middle Eastern Oil and the Eastern Province," April 2002, and "Oil, Terrorism, and the Problem of Saudi Arabia," June 2002.

20. Ashraf Fahim, "'Liberating' Saudi Shi'ites (and Their Oil)," *Middle East International* no. 722, (April 2, 2004).

21. Ibid.

22. Asher Susser, "The Decline of the Arabs," *Middle East Quarterly* (Autumn 2003): 6.

23. "Libya," declared Muammar Qaddafi at the May 2004 Arab League summit in Tunis, "is currently absorbed in its African space and it is planning to be the bridge between Africa and Europe." It had no intention of turning toward the Arab world. See Dina Ezzat, "Surprise, Surprise," *Al-Ahram Weekly*, May 27–June 2, 2004.

24. Muhammad Ahsan, "Globalization and the Underdeveloped Muslim World," in *Islam Encountering Globalization*, ed. Ali Mohammadi (London: RoutledgeCurzon, 2002), 189.

25. Kenneth Katzman, "US Policy towards the Gulf: The Need for a New Security Architecture," in *GRC Yearbook 2005–2006* (Dubai: Gulf Research Center, 2006), 241–49.

26. See Anoushiravan Ehteshami, "2005: The Year of Crisis in Iran," in *GRC Yearbook 2005–2006* (Dubai: Gulf Research Center, 2006), 349–55.

27. Ibid.

28. *International Herald Tribune*, November 13, 2008.

29. The article further reported that "Mike McConnell, the director of national intelligence, said in February that Iran was close to acquiring Russian-produced SA-20 surface-to-air missiles. American military officials said that the deployment of such systems would hamper Israel's attack planning, putting pressure on Israel to act before the missiles are fielded." Michael R. Gordon and Eric Schmitt, "U.S. Says Israeli Exercise Seemed Directed at Iran," *New York Times*, June 20, 2008.

30. Remarks by Mike McConnell at the 2008 MILCOM Conference and Symposium, San Diego, November 17, 2008.

31. Philip Stephens, "The Choice for Obama Lies on the Road to Jerusalem," *Financial Times*, November 14, 2008.

32. This chapter was written before the 2011 Egyptian revolution. Thus, the postscript was added while the manuscript was in production to allow the author an opportunity to reflect briefly on what impact this and other concurrent events would have on regional security.

8

Israel

Shifting National Security
Challenges and Responses

Itamar Rabinovich

To the analyst or policy planner interested in regional security and regional security structures, the Middle East presents a daunting challenge. As a region, it is characterized by a stark contrast between multiple fault lines and conflicts and scarcity, bordering on absence, of regional institutions capable of regulating and mitigating these conflicts. Furthermore, the Middle Eastern security landscape has been in a permanent state of flux. In the course of the current decade it has been transformed several times by changes in the United States' position and policies in the region, by Russia's return to an activist role in the Middle East, by Iran's quest for regional hegemony and a nuclear arsenal, by Turkey's resumption of a significant role in the politics of the region, by the successes registered by Islamist and jihadist movements, and by the collapse of the Arab-Israeli peace process of the 1990s.

As a major regional power and as a country preoccupied, not to say obsessed, with national security threats, Israel has been pondering the significance of these changes. There is, in fact, no single or uniform Israeli response to them, since Israel's political system and community of national security experts are deeply divided over these very issues.

The roots of this division go back to the June War of 1967—the watershed moment of the Arab-Israeli conflict. On the positive side of the ledger, Israel's spectacular victory created a sense of Israeli invincibility and produced the assets for a territories-for-peace formula with part of the

Arab world. But the same victory gave Israel control over the whole of Mandatory Palestine, triggered a messianic Land of Israel movement, exacerbated the Israeli-Palestinian conflict, and encumbered Israel with control of a large, occupied Palestinian population.

It took several years before the potential for diplomatic settlements inherent in the war's outcome was translated through a lengthy and tortuous process into a peace treaty with Egypt (1979) and through the more ambitious Madrid Process of the 1990s into a Framework Agreement with the Palestine Liberation Organization (PLO) (1993) and a peace treaty with Jordan (1994). A ten-year effort to reach an Israeli-Syrian peace collapsed in 2000, and the relationship between the two countries is formally predicated on the Disengagement Agreement of 1974. During the more than thirty-five years of this intermittent peace process, which began in 1973 following the October war, Israel went through six military clashes of varying scales with its Arab neighbors, dealt with an endemic challenge of terror, and destroyed two Arab nuclear reactors. From this mixed record of peacemaking and ongoing violence, one Israeli school of thought concludes that the durable peace agreements with Egypt and Jordan and the measure of normalization with parts of the Arab world warrant the quest for diplomatic solutions to Israel's national security challenges, while the other school argues that the failure of the Oslo Accords, the ensuing Second Intifada, and the failure of the unilateral withdrawals from Lebanon and the Gaza Strip clearly show that Israel must rely on its own military power to ensure its national security.

Past Israeli Perceptions of National Security Threats— A Brief Overview

During the first nineteen years of its existence, Israel's national security doctrine was predicated on the assumption that the Arab world was determined to destroy the Jewish state and that an Arab military coalition could be formed at any point in order to wage such a war. To that end, the Israel Defense Forces (IDF) were built to be able to wage war on several fronts and to do so on Arab, rather than Israeli, soil. As an ultimate guarantee, Israel also developed a nuclear option.[1]

This phase ended in June 1967, when Israel's stunning victory demonstrated its massive military advantage and hence the futility of Arab hopes for decisive military victory. The war launched by Egypt and Syria in October 1973 was a limited war, designed to regain the territories that they lost in 1967 and to set in motion a diplomatic process that would serve the same purpose.

As noted, the October war led to the launching of a protracted peace process. For the next twenty-seven years, Israel and its Arab neighbors continued to negotiate and fight until the collapse of the peace process in 2000. By the middle of the current decade, Israel came to the conclusion that the deterrence it had established in 1967 was being eroded. Under a slogan of *muqawama* (resistance), Iran and its followers—Syria, Hezbollah, Hamas, Islamic Jihad, and an ill-defined segment of Arab opinion—rejected peacemaking and settlement with Israel as unnecessary capitulation and argued that Israel could be defeated or at least exhausted. Against Israel's conventional military might, they resorted to the full gamut—seeking nuclear weapons, using rockets and missiles, resorting to asymmetrical warfare and terror. Israel has been hard put to contend with these multiple challenges and with a hostile axis that stretches from Tehran to Lebanon to Gaza. Against this backdrop, it is time to take a closer look at Israel's perception of the specific challenges it faces.

Current Israeli Perceptions of National Security Threats

Looking at the next five years, from an Israeli perspective, seven major national security threats can be identified:

Iran

Iran under the current regime represents several national security threats to Israel, to the region, and, to some extent, to the world.[2] Israelis assume that Iran is developing nuclear weapons and medium- and long-range missiles, continues to build a large conventional military force, cultivates Shia constituencies in several Middle Eastern countries, and seeks a hegemonial position in the Middle East. For Israelis, the prospect of a nuclear Iran, particularly when coupled with incendiary rhetoric by apocalyptic Iranian leaders that calls for Israel's destruction, is unacceptable. The emotional responses by the Israeli public and the political system aside, most Israeli national security analysts are skeptical about the possibility of building a stable deterrence against the likes of Mahmoud Ahmadinejad. But these analysts are less preoccupied with the dangers of outright Iranian nuclear attack on Israel as soon as Iran obtains nuclear weapons and delivery systems. They assume that Iran realizes that Israel has a massive second-strike capability. Their concerns are focused on other major consequences and by-products of a nuclear Iran: once it acquires a nuclear umbrella, the Iranian regime is liable to take bolder actions and to undertake greater risks than it has thus far, be it in its immediate environment (Iraq and the Gulf) or in the core area of the Middle East. Should Iran come to posses a nuclear arsenal, several other Middle Eastern and neighboring states (Egypt, Saudi Arabia, and Turkey, to name three) are likely to follow suit. Globally this could deal a final blow to the Nuclear Non-Proliferation Treaty (NPT) regime. In the Middle East, the management of a multipolar nuclear arms race and the maintenance of deterrence on multiple fronts may prove to be impossible tasks. Weapons-grade nuclear material, once available to the current Iranian regime, could conceivably be transferred to nonstate actors to be used against Israeli or other targets without an easily traceable link to Iran.

Iran presents to Israel (and to the region) a conventional challenge as well. Ideologically and politically, it spearheads the camp that denounces Arab acceptance of peacemaking with Israel as capitulation. It supports Syria, Hamas, Hezbollah, and Islamic Jihad in order for them to reject any settlement and promote the notion of "resistance" (directed at the United States, Israel, and the moderate and conservative Arab states). It has in fact, with Syria's help, leaped from the Eastern flank of the Middle East into its core area, building actual bases in Lebanon and Gaza and proving its ability to ignite Arab-Israeli conflicts at will through its Lebanese and Palestinian clients. This camp presents Israel's unilateral withdrawal from Lebanon and Gaza and Israel's unsuccessful second Lebanon war (2006) and unfinished war in Gaza (2008) as vindicating its argument. With the access provided by Syria, Iran projects weapons and training into Lebanon and the Palestinian territories. The changes in Turkey's regional and foreign policies under Tayyip Erdogan's Islamist government have enhanced the power and significance of the "resistance camp" in the Middle East. Several of the national security threats detailed later in this section owe their current significance to Iran.

A Conventional War

The threat of another Arab-Israeli conventional war is currently limited to the Syrian-Lebanese arena (since the signing of an Israeli-Egyptian peace in 1979 and the destruction of the Iraqi Army in 1991 and 2003). Syria was engaged in 2007–09 in an indirect negotiation with Israel. Its official line is that it wants to regain the Golan Heights through a peace settlement, but it has also stated repeatedly that if the diplomatic option does not materialize, it will go to war in order to liberate the Golan. In September 2007, when Israel destroyed the al-Kibar site, it was revealed that Syria had been building with North Korean help a nuclear reactor with a view to producing nuclear weapons. With Iranian support and with greater Russian willingness to provide advanced weapons systems, Syria is upgrading its armed forces in order to be able to stand up to Israel in a military confrontation.

For its deterrence against Israel, Syria relies on three systems of missiles and rockets: Iran's missile system; its own missiles, including Scuds, capable of reaching targets deep in Israel's territory—some of them armed with chemical warheads and many of them in underground silos; and Hezbollah's arsenal of rockets and missiles, which have been replenished by Iran and Syria and in fact doubled in size since the 2006 war.[3]

Rockets and Missiles

The introduction of a whole range of rockets and missiles into the Middle Eastern arena has confronted Israel with a novel set of challenges. Israel was attacked by Iraqi Scud missiles in 1991 and northern Israel has been attacked from South Lebanon during several periods since the late 1970s. But in 2008 Israel's defense establishment came to see the threat posed by missiles and rockets as the single most urgent security challenge confronting Israel.

Iranian missiles. Iran possesses intermediate-range missiles that can reach Israel. These could be used if Iran's nuclear sites are attacked (certainly if they are attacked by Israel and in all likelihood if they are attacked by the United States). They might also be used in the event of another war between Israel and Hezbollah (especially if it breaks out into a war between Israel and Syria as well). To counter such a threat, Israel has been developing antiballistic missile defense systems in collaboration with the United States since the 1990s, but their effectiveness (enhanced recently by a sophisticated American radar system) is yet to be confirmed.

Syrian Scud missiles. (See earlier discussion.)

Hezbollah's arsenal. On the eve of the 2006 war in Lebanon, Hezbollah possessed some 20,000 missiles and rockets; some of them were long and intermediate range, but most of them were short-range Katyusha rockets. The Israeli Air Force took out most of the long- and intermediate-range missiles at the war's outset but was unable to cope successfully with the huge number of Katyusha rockets. A large-scale ground operation that could have put an end to rocket launching into northern Israel was launched only at the war's end and was interrupted by the cease-fire. Consequently, a large number of Katyusha rockets (more than 200 per day) were fired by Hezbollah into northern Israel through the war's last day. This reinforced the sense that the war was not concluded with a decisive victory.

Despite the stipulations of UN Security Council Resolution 1701, which ended the war, Hezbollah's arsenal, as mentioned, has been replenished by Iran and Syria. Furthermore, Israel's military planners know full well that in the event of another war it would be difficult to repeat the early success of 2006 and to immediately neutralize Hezbollah's long- and intermediate-range missiles. In other words, it would be quite safe to assume that at least during the early days of such a war, Hezbollah's missiles would be able to reach targets in the center and even the south of Israel—targets that they failed to reach in 2006.[4]

Palestinian's Qassam and Grad rockets. In the aftermath of Israel's unilateral withdrawal from Gaza and Hamas's victory in the Palestinian elections and take over of the Gaza Strip, Israel has had to face the challenge of short-range, fairly primitive Qassam rockets and somewhat more sophisticated Grad rockets that are fired into neighboring border towns (regularly into Sderot and less frequently into the city of Ashkelon) and smaller rural villages. This has presented Israel with a whole series of challenges: Israel does not possess an effective defense against short-range missiles. Indeed, it is extremely difficult to neutralize rocket launching (as has been the case with the longer-range Katyusha rockets in South Lebanon) given their primitive mechanism, which has no electronic print, and the deployment of such rockets in the midst of innocent civilian population. Ongoing missile attacks from Gaza in 2008 left Israel with very few choices. The government faced strong domestic pressure to relieve the affected Israeli population, but the option of a large-scale military operation in Gaza seemed unattractive. It was argued that it would entail heavy Israeli and Palestinian casualties and international condemnation and that, at the end of the day, Israel would have to choose between staying in Gaza and leaving without effecting a fundamental change. In the end, the Israeli government felt that it had no choice but to respond to the ongoing missile attacks. Although Israel did not suffer major casualties, it paid a heavy diplomatic price for the operation, which was not concluded. The publication of the Goldstone Report, which accused Israel (as well as Hamas) of committing war crimes during the Gaza war, has meant that Israeli decision makers will have a harder time operating against terrorists and rocket launchings embedded in the midst of a civilian population.

It has been a matter of sheer luck that on several occasions the rockets failed to extract a high toll in human life or to hit a strategic target. During Israel's military campaign in Gaza, Hamas intensified its efforts to hit deeper in Israel by using Grad rockets that reached as far as the city of Ashdod and made a habit of also firing at the cities of Beer-Sheva and Ashkelon. Israel was better prepared to deal with the issue than it had been in 2006, but it became clear that without occupying the whole Gaza Strip (and staying there), there would be no military solution to the problem. It has also been realized that without shutting off the Gaza Strip to arms smuggling, Iran and Syria would at some point supply Hamas with larger, longer-range rockets that could reach the Tel Aviv area in the event of a future escalation. Indeed, even when Egypt invested a greater effort than it had in the past, it failed to seal off the Gaza Strip. Smuggling has continued and it should be assumed that at some point Hamas will acquire longer-range and more accurate rockets.

The chain of events described herein has had a significant negative impact on the efforts to negotiate a solution to the larger Israeli-Palestinian conflict. The Palestinian Authority under President Mahmoud Abbas (Abu Mazen) is in control of the West Bank, while Hamas is in control of the Gaza Strip. With a significant Israeli security presence in the West Bank—and with the serious efforts invested by the Palestinian Authority—the area has been quite free of violence, but Israelis—security analysts and the general population alike—are asking themselves whether the pattern now familiar in the Gaza Strip would repeat itself in the event of an agreement and an Israeli exit from the West Bank. Given the area's proximity to Israel's center, it would not take much, or long, for a major crisis to break out. It could be argued that the Palestinian Authority dominated by a secular Fatah would police the West Bank effectively. Indeed, led by Prime Minister Salam Fayyad, the Palestinian Authority, aided by United States security experts, has made significant strides in building a more effective security apparatus. The Fatah movement has also made a partial political recovery, but the Palestinian Authority's ability to defeat a Hamas challenge in the event of a full Israeli departure from the West Bank remains questionable.

Earlier this decade, Israelis believed that a security barrier separating Israel from most of the West Bank would eliminate the suicide bombings that rattled Israeli society in 2001–03 (a fence separating Israel from Gaza was built years ago). Indeed, suicide bombing ceased to be a major issue after 2003 due to the barrier, more effective Palestinian security services, and the efforts of Israel's General Security Services (GSS). But the threat of rockets and missiles being launched above the security barrier removed much of its value as a defense mechanism.[5]

Asymmetrical Warfare

Much of what has been mentioned thus far fits into the concept of "asymmetrical warfare," whether it is used to denote a war between a state and a nonstate actor or a war between a technologically superior army and adversaries that are technologically inferior.[6] Israel has conducted such wars on two fronts. Earlier in the decade it fought a "war of attrition" with the Palestinian Authority, mostly in the West Bank. Once it won this war, the fighting shifted to Gaza. In Lebanon, Hezbollah is a nonstate actor that is stronger than the state and supported by two powerful regional actors. One of the difficulties posed by Hezbollah derives from its multiple identities. It is a political party, an ideological movement, a terrorist organization, an arm of Iran, and an authentic Lebanese Shia movement, with a well-trained and well-equipped small army.

Hezbollah's multiple identities have confounded the Israeli planners and policymakers who have been contending with the organization since the late 1980s. It was one thing to deal with Guerrilla-like attacks on Israeli forces in the security zone in South Lebanon and a whole different matter to discover in the 1990s that radical Israeli actions against Hezbollah prompted Iran and the terrorist wing of the organization to blow up Israeli and Jewish targets on the other side of the globe, in Argentina. Over time, the distinction between the organization and the Lebanese state became increasingly blurred. During the 2006 war some Israeli cabinet members argued that given Hezbollah's creeping takeover of the Lebanese state and the difficulty of targeting Hezbollah, Israel should hit Lebanon's national infrastructure and force the Lebanese state and public to take on Hezbollah or force the international community to come to terms with the fact that Lebanon is a failed state. In the event the prevailing view in Israel held on to the argument that the camp headed by Prime Minister Fuad Seniora was opposed to Hezbollah and its patrons, that the camp had good intentions but no power, and that there was no point in weakening the camp further and penalizing innocent Lebanese civilians.

This debate did not end with the 2006 war and is likely to resume in full if the current lull (produced by the war) is broken. The inconclusive fashion in which the 2006 war in Lebanon was ended is indicative of yet another challenge inherent in the nature of asymmetrical conflicts—the notions and symbols of victory or a war's ending that are associated with traditional warfare do no apply to asymmetrical conflicts.

In the Palestinian arena, Israel faces two very different nonstate actors. In the West Bank, nominal authority is held by the president of the Palestinian Authority, Mahmoud Abbas, who relies on the discredited, emasculated Fatah infrastructure. That group continues to believe in a two-state solution to be negotiated with Israel. But Abbas and his organization lost the elections to the Palestinian legislative assembly and with it the prime ministership to Hamas. Hamas proceeded to seize control of the Gaza Strip, where it is now in charge and whence it conducted an intermittent conflict with Israel. The continuous launching of rockets in the summer and fall of 2008 finally brought Israel to send the IDF into the Gaza Strip—an operation known as Cast Lead. As noted, the operation was a military success but exacted a high diplomatic price from Israel.

Israel's armed and security forces thus face the challenge of engaging in and being prepared for three types of asymmetrical warfare on three fronts—in addition to facing the more conventional challenges presented by Syria and Iran.

The Palestinian Demographic Challenge

The collapse of the Israeli-Palestinian peace process of the 1990s, and the blow thus dealt to the notion of a two-state solution, restored the issue of demographics to the forefront of Israeli thinking and debate on national security. The perpetuation of the status quo would lead in less than two decades to the creation of a Palestinian majority west of the Jordan River. The argument is now frequently made by a variety of Palestinian spokesmen that, given this projection, the "two-state solution" is virtually dead and the Palestinians can sit back, "chip away" at Israel's legitimacy, and at the right time argue for a "one man, one vote" political system that would end in a "one-state solution."

This challenge is exacerbated by the fact that nearly 20 percent of the population of Israel proper are Arabs and that the relationship between that growing minority and the Jewish state has become increasingly strained. It is difficult to establish how the "silent majority" of Israel's Arab citizens view its current status within that state, but the Arab political leaders and intellectuals who speak on its behalf openly reject the status quo. They no longer refer to themselves as "Israeli Arabs" but as "Palestinian citizens of Israel" and argue that Israel should be "dezionized" and become a "state of all its citizens." Even if Israel separates from the West Bank, it will remain with an increasingly estranged and mobilized Arab minority. Coping with this issue through political accommodation is one of the cardinal challenges confronting Israel.

Radical Changes of Policy in Egypt, Jordan, and the Palestinian Authority

Contractual peace with Egypt (since 1979) and with Jordan (since 1994) has become a cornerstone of Israeli national security. Both relationships are stable, but Israeli policy planners must take into account the potential for political and policy changes that could alter the status quo and that would have far-reaching repercussions for Israel's national security. Although Israel does not have a contractual peace with the Palestinian Authority, which has been afflicted by a major crisis, it has an interest in the Palestinian Authority's survival, and the Palestinian Authority's potential collapse is seen by Israel as yet another significant threat to its national security.

Terror

Israel has lived with the challenge of terror since its early days (in fact, well before it achieved statehood), but the scale and significance of this challenge has undergone significant changes over time. In the early 1950s, terrorist attacks launched by Egypt from the Gaza Strip and the West Bank had a devastating effect on the fabric of life in the young Israeli state and played an important role in David Ben-Gurion's decision to launch the Sinai campaign. In the early years of this decade, the wave of suicide bombings contributed to the exacerbation of a major national crisis that was only terminated by Ariel Sharon's defeat of the Second Intifada.

Currently, Israel is coping with active terrorism and terrorist threats from several quarters: Palestinian (Hamas, Islamic Jihad, and groups affiliated with the mainstream Fatah), Lebanese (Hezbollah), and global jihadist (al-Qaeda and its affiliates). It is important to note that the Palestinian and Lebanese terrorist threats are supported, sometimes orchestrated, by two states—Iran and Syria—and are thus part of Israel's conflict with the block led by Iran. With regard to al-Qaeda, it is important to note that Israel has thus far been a secondary target of this organization, which has been preoccupied primarily with the United States and the conservative Arab and Islamic regimes.

The challenge from terrorism is manageable as long as one or more of these groups do not acquire weapons of mass destruction; one or more of these groups do not execute a mega terrorist act on a hitherto unfamiliar scale; and Iran does not acquire a nuclear umbrella or decide to support a massive escalation of terrorist activities.

Regional Security Arrangements

References have already been made to the discrepancy between the richness and complexity of the security challenges facing Israel and, in fact, most Middle Eastern states, and the virtual absence of regional mechanisms designed to deal with them.

Several attempts were made in the postcolonial period to devise such mechanisms for parts of the region. In 1950 an Arab collective security pact was signed as yet another effort to translate the notion of Arab unity into actual cooperation within the Arab state system. In the mid 1950s, the Western powers built the Baghdad Pact as an effort to consolidate cooperation with Turkey and the conservative Arab states against the Soviet Union and Arab radicalism. Turkey itself, as a semi-European state, joined NATO. Later in the 1950s, informal, semiclandestine cooperation was built between Israel, Turkey, Iran, and Ethiopia. These four states shared hostility to and fear of the Soviet Union and its radical Arab allies.

In Israel, this grouping was known as "the alliance of the periphery." The underlying notion was that since Israel could not communicate or collaborate with its Arab neighbors in the core area of the Middle East, it would leapfrog above them and establish a virtual alliance with other essentially conservative actors who happened to occupy a large part of the region's external perimeter.

With the inauguration of an Arab-Israeli peace process in 1973, the notion of security cooperation between Israel and Arab partners became a realistic option, but in the absence of a final status agreement, it remained politically impossible for Arab states to enter into formal or open security cooperation with Israel. In the 1990s, the Bush and Clinton administrations launched and orchestrated the single most ambitious effort to resolve the Arab-Israeli conflict. The Madrid Process, as it came to be called, unfolded along two tracks: bilateral negotiations between Israel and four Arab parties and multilateral talks within five working groups. The multilateral track was designed to facilitate the bilateral negotiation by dealing with final status issues and by painting for the parties the vision of a peaceful Middle East. The Arms Control and Regional Security Working Group held several rounds of discussions and began to deal with such issues as the construction of confidence-building measures and mechanisms, but its deliberations were suspended in 1995 as the peace process ground down to a halt. The legacy, such as it is, of this effort and the academic literature on arms control and security-regime models in the Middle East provide a basis for resuming a serious effort in this field once the political arena undergoes the requisite transformation.[7]

The Arab-Israeli Peace Process

The full-fledged Arab-Israeli conflict is more than sixty years old, with the peace process beginning in 1973. In fits and starts, it produced two peace treaties, a framework agreement with the Palestinian national movement, and a significant measure of normalization with the Arab collective. But the Israeli-Palestinian and the Israeli-Syrian conflicts have persisted and, in certain respects, have been exacerbated over the past two decades, with new challenges having been added by Hezbollah's gradual takeover of Lebanon and by Hamas's growing power among the Palestinians. In earlier decades, when the threats to Israel's national security derived almost exclusively from Arab rejection and hostility, a resolution of the Arab-Israeli conflict could be reasonably expected to lead to the elimination of such threats. Given Iran's current prominence and role in the Middle East, this is no longer the case, but a resolution of the Arab-Israeli conflict could still be expected to yield a dramatic realignment of Israel's national security. But what are the prospects of achieving negotiated settlements between Israel and the Palestinian Authority, between Israel and Syria, and between Israel and Lebanon, and how exactly would such settlements affect Israel's perceptions of its security challenges?

Israel and the Palestinians

The Israeli-Palestinian conflict is the core issue of the larger, more complex Arab-Israeli conflict. The original Arab-Jewish conflict over the right to and control of Mandatory Palestine culminated in the 1948 war. Israel won the war, defeating both the Palestinians and the invading Arab armies, and ended up in control of a territory larger than the one assigned to it by the UN partition resolution of November 1947. The Palestinians ended up without a state and the territory assigned to them in 1947 was partitioned by Jordan (which formally annexed the West Bank), Egypt (which administered the Gaza Strip), and Israel. Some six hundred thousand Palestinians became refugees.

In the aftermath of the conflict, the Palestinian issue was submerged by the larger Arab-Israeli conflict, but two developments restored it to center stage in the 1960s—the establishment of the Arab-states-sponsored PLO in 1964 and the emergence of the authentic Palestinian Fatah in 1965 and the Six-Day War of 1967. As a result of the war, the whole of Mandatory Palestine was brought under a single authority, and the notion of partition and a two-state solution became feasible, at least in theory. In practice, reality was compounded by several developments: "the three nos" of the Khartoum Arab summit, the emergence of both secular and messianic movements in Israel seeking to retain the West Bank and Gaza and the ensuing settlement project, and Yasser Arafat's rise to Palestinian leadership and Arab prominence and his defiant attitude. For twenty-five years, the fierce Israeli-Palestinian conflict raged until the surprising decision by both parties to sign the Oslo Accords in 1993. The Oslo Accords were not a final status agreement but a framework agreement that represented a phased approach to settling the conflict and that provided mutual recognition between Israel and the PLO as the authoritative representative of Palestinian nationalism.

Security issues were an important dimension of the Oslo Accords. Israel maintained overall responsibility for security. The Palestinian Authority built a "strong police force" and an extensive security apparatus. It also took responsibility to prevent terrorist attacks against Israel and Israelis, a responsibility that, for better or for worse, had until then been in the hands of the IDF and Israeli security services. The parties agreed to a five-year transitional period during which the negotiations for a final status agreement were to be completed.[8]

For reasons that fall outside the scope of this chapter, the Oslo process, as it came to be called, collapsed in 2000. The failure of the Camp David summit in July 2000 was followed by the outbreak of the Second Intifada, which turned into a war of attrition between the Palestinian Authority and Israel. Israel's victory in that war was followed in short order by Arafat's death and Abbas's election as his successor, Ariel Sharon's disengagement from the Gaza Strip, Hamas's victory in the Palestinian elections and the formation of a Hamas government, Hamas's takeover of the Gaza Strip and the virtual separation between Gaza and the West Bank, and then by another war of attrition between Hamas and Israel across and over the fence separating the Gaza Strip from Israel, which culminated in operation Cast Lead in December 2008. Through all of this, negotiations continued between the Israeli government of Ehud Olmert and the Palestinian Authority in an effort to sketch, if not complete, a final status agreement.

The contours of such a settlement are quite well-known: Israeli withdrawal from 90-odd percent of the West Bank; a one-per-one land swap for the large settlement blocks that will come under Israeli sovereignty; evacuation of some sixty thousand settlers and their settlements; effective connection between the Gaza Strip and the West Bank; and a de facto demilitarization of the future Palestinian state. No agreement was reached on Jerusalem, on the issue of Palestinian refugees, or on the Palestinian claim of return. In 2009, Olmert offered on several occasions a detailed version of the far-reaching package that he had presented to Abbas.

For the significant body of opinion at the center of Israel's body politic that wants a final-status agreement with the Palestinians and is willing to take the risks and make the concessions that it entails, the advantages offered are clear: such an agreement would consolidate a two-state solution and would resolve the core issues of the Arab-Israeli conflict; it would enable Israel to address in a fundamental way its relationship with the Arab minority in Israel; and it would enable most, if not all, Arab states to normalize their relations with Israel.

But the path of such a final status solution is fraught with difficulties and risks. Abbas may not want or may not be able to offer Israel the finality it seeks in any such settlement, and even if he signs such a deal, he and the secular Palestinian Authority may not have the power to implement it. The West Bank and the Gaza Strip are now two separate authorities, the latter firmly under the control of Hamas. Hamas, which is closely tied to Iran and Syria, is in any event not a partner for a final-status solution. As a radical Islamic movement, it will not recognize Jewish or Christian sovereignty over the territory it defines as a *waqf* (religious endowment). Israel's current Prime Minister, Benjamin Netanyahu, does not accept the position adopted by Olmert in his negotiations with Abbas. During the first months of his tenure—under heavy pressure by the Obama administration—Netanyahu was willing only to offer a vague acceptance of the notion of a two-state solution and to impose a limited ten-month freeze on new construction in Israeli settlements in the West Bank. Although these concessions were seen as insufficient by the Palestinian Authority, they drew a wedge between Netanyahu and the radical settlers and their supporters. And when all is said and done, could Israel rely on a prospective Palestinian state's willingness and ability to keep agreements, force security, and prevent attacks against Israel?

Israel and Syria

Since Yitzhak Rabin jump-started the Madrid Process, Israeli governments have acted as a rule on the assumption that they had to sequence their progression in the peace process—that the Israeli political system would not be able to sustain simultaneous major concessions in the West Bank and the Golan Heights. As a result, all Israeli prime ministers since 1992 (except Ehud Barak, during part of his tenure) have felt that they had to choose between a Syria-first and a Palestine-first policy.

In the 1990s, the Clinton administration and four Israeli prime ministers preferred the Syria-first policy but ended up staying in or shifting to the Palestinian track when the Syrian track proved to be blocked. During most of the 2000s, President George W. Bush and Prime Ministers Sharon and Olmert (in his first year in office) declined to deal with Syria. A change occurred in February 2007, when Olmert authorized Turkish prime minster Recep Tayyip Erdoğan to start mediation with Damascus. Four rounds of indirect talks were held in Turkey. Olmert was quite anxious to seek a swift agreement, but his resignation and the anticipated change of administration in the United States led to a suspension of the indirect negotiation. Olmert's government was replaced by an essentially right-wing government headed by Netanyahu. The nominal position as held by Netanyahu is one of opposition to a full withdrawal from the Golan. But during his previous term as prime minister, Netanyahu conveyed to Syria his conditional willingness to withdraw fully from the Golan as part of a peace settlement. Whether Netanyahu would repeat the pattern of the late 1990s and try to shift from the Palestinian to the Syrian track as his main effort is a matter of speculation.

The preference given to the Syrian track in the 1990s derived from three major considerations: (1) the Syrian-Israeli conflict is "simpler" than the Israeli-Palestinian one—it is essentially "a territorial conflict" as distinct from "a national" one; (2) unlike the disorganized Palestinian political community, Syria is an orderly state with a powerful authoritative government; (3) Hafez al-Assad (in contradistinction to Arafat) was seen as a reliable partner.

Since 2000, two major changes have taken place: Hafez al-Assad was succeeded by his son Bashar, whose personality and capability are still being questioned; and Syria's alliance with Iran has become much closer and has increasingly shifted from an alliance of equals to a patron-client relationship.

The discussion of the pros and cons of an Israeli-Syrian deal has consequently become linked to the Iranian issue. The contours of a prospective Israeli-Syrian settlement were drawn during the negotiations of the 1990s. Israel agreed in principle to a full withdrawal from the Golan in return for a package of peace and security that would meet Israel's criteria. The security arrangements demanded by Israel in the 1990s were designed to compensate it for loss of the Golan's high ground and to minimize the danger of a surprise attack by Syria's large standing army. They included the demilitarization of the Golan Heights, an area of limited deployment well beyond the Golan, and continued Israeli presence in the monitoring station on Mount Hermon. In the present circumstances, the notion of "territories for peace" has been replaced by a new emphasis on "territories for strategic realignment." Israelis are less interested in the development of another cold peace with an Arab neighbor and are rather keen to see Syria disengage from its close partnership with Iran and cease its sponsorship of Hezbollah, Hamas, and Islamic Jihad.

The transition to a direct Israeli-Syrian negotiation and the conclusion of a peace agreement face several major obstacles: Israel and Syria would have to agree on their new border and reconcile Syria's claim to a presence on the shore of Lake Tiberias with Israel's insistence on full sovereignty over the lake. Israel (and the United States) would want an explicit commitment by Syria to a reorientation of its relations with Iran, Hezbollah, and the radical Palestinian organizations, while Syria is likely to seek ambiguity in this matter. Washington may seek to clarify its relations with Tehran before it engages in an effort to draw Syria away from Iran. In Israel, any agreement predicated on a full withdrawal from the Golan and the dismantling of the settlement project that is now forty years old will meet with fierce opposition. In Syria, too, Bashar al-Assad could encounter some opposition from Islamic and pan-Arab critics as well as from elements within his regime who feel that in a state of peace with Israel the Syrian regime may lose its raison d'être.[9]

Israel and Lebanon

Ever since the collapse of Lebanon's traditional political system during the civil war of 1975–76, Israel has contended with a series of security challenges originating in Lebanon's territory: the Beirut-based headquarters of Palestinian terror activities in the 1970s; a virtual mini Palestinian state and military base in South Lebanon in the late 1970s; Syria's military presence and eventual political hegemony in Lebanon; Iran's political and military presence in league with Syria; and the mobilization of the Shia community, initially by Amal Movement and subsequently by Hezbollah. Most significantly, groups and organizations seeking to attack Israel, first Palestinian and subsequently Shia, have used South Lebanon as a base for firing Katyusha rockets into northern Israel and for launching terrorist attacks across the border or by sea.

Over the years, Israel adopted a series of strategies in order to deal with these challenges: two unsuccessful wars (1982, 2006), large-scale raids, the construction of a security zone in South Lebanon maintained by the IDF and a local auxiliary force, and air raids. This was all to no avail. Although temporary solutions were often found, the underlying problems were not resolved.

In the 1990s, most Israeli governments, as well as the Clinton administration, saw the solution to Israel's "Lebanon problem" as part of a larger deal with Syria. Syria held sway in Lebanon and Washington and Jerusalem were willing to recognize that sway, if Syria, after making peace with Israel and building a new relationship with the United States, would undertake to restrain Hezbollah and "allow" Lebanon to make its own peace with Israel. This formula was also acceptable to Syria, but it lost its relevance with the collapse of the Israeli-Syrian negotiation in March 2000. Ehud Barak, Israel's prime minister at the time, then decided to decouple Israel's "Lebanese dilemma" from its relationship with Syria by withdrawing from the security zone to the international boundary and relying from that point on a classic deterrence equation.

During the next few years Hezbollah did stage a number of attacks across the border, but the Israeli government of the day chose either not to retaliate (Barak in October 2000) or to retaliate in a minor way against Hezbollah and Syria (Sharon). The important development of these years was Iran's and Syria's decision to build up Hezbollah's military capabilities and to provide it with some 20,000 missiles and rockets. Sharon chose to ignore this development, but when his successor, Olmert, decided in July 2006 to respond in a major way to yet another provocation by Hezbollah, the second Lebanon war ensued. Unsuccessful as the war was in Israeli eyes, it did restore a deterrence equation, though the border between Israel and Lebanon has been uneasily quiet since the war's end. As mentioned, Hezbollah's arsenal of missiles and rockets has since been replenished, and the organization has continued its gradual takeover of the Lebanese state. The potential of another outbreak of violence is evident, but is there a prospect of a political settlement between Israel and Lebanon?

The territorial issue between Israel and Lebanon is negligible. Hezbollah claims that Israel should also withdraw from the Shebaa Farms and uses this claim as a thinly veiled pretext for continuing its "resistance" to Israel. Israel lays no claims to the Shebaa Farms but views them as Syrian territories that should be restored to Syria if and when peace is made with Damascus. But Lebanon is, in reality, not free to negotiate with Israel. If the Israeli-Syrian negotiation is resumed, a linkage could be reestablished between the two issues, but it is not at all certain that the Obama administration would be willing to recognize a Syrian hegemonic presence in Lebanon, which the Syrians are likely to seek.

A New Middle Eastern Security Arena

During the last few years the Middle Eastern security arena has been reshaped by several new developments.

The War in Iraq

The United States' war in Iraq and the ensuing lingering crisis had manifold effects on regional security in the Middle East. In the immediate aftermath of the toppling of Saddam Hussein, the United States seemed very powerful (two of the by-products were Iranian feelers to Washington and Libya's decision to abandon its nuclear program), but as the United States became bogged down in the postwar crisis, its influence and prestige declined. The fall of Saddam's regime played into Iran's hands and facilitated its drive toward regional hegemony and a weapons-of-mass-destruction arsenal. The United States is now committed to withdrawing its forces from Iraq, but for the time being its massive military presence is an important feature of the region's security landscape. In the coming years, the efforts by several neighbors and other interested parties to shape Iraq's future are likely to be a major issue in the international and regional politics of the Middle East.

Turkey's Increased Role in the Middle East

Turkey's assumption of a more active role in the affairs of the region could become as significant as the activist role played by Iran since 1979. Turkey's continued failure to join the European Union and the consolidation of an Islamist regime have combined to lead Turkey into a role that it had avoided in earlier decades. During much of the twentieth century, the two former imperial powers, Turkey and Iran, played relatively minor roles in the region. The impact of the change in their outlook and conduct (Iran's more so than Turkey) is far-reaching.

Russia's Return

In the aftermath of the Soviet Union's disintegration and the end of the Cold War, Russia was reduced to a ceremonial role in the Middle East. When Vladimir Putin, buttressed by massive oil and gas revenues, decided to reassert Russia's position as a great power, the Middle East was chosen as a significant arena for flexing Moscow's muscle. Technical aid to Iran's nuclear program, refusal to participate in the sanctions designed to check Iran's nuclear ambitions, and arms sales to Iran and Syria were the chief measures calculated to rebuild Russia's position in the region as well as to retaliate for American action in the Caucasus and Eastern Europe that was seen by Moscow as offensive and humiliating.

Exacerbated Security Challenges in Afghanistan and Pakistan

Some of the Obama administration's early decisions have reflected its recognition of the severity of the multiple challenges presented by the Taliban's successes in Afghanistan and by the prospect of further decline in Pakistan's stability. Neither country is part of the Middle East, but crises in both countries and the efforts to resolve them will have important repercussions for the Middle East. The issue of Afghanistan and Pakistan is bound to be a significant component of any American-Iranian dialogue and is going to affect discussion and treatment of nuclear issues in the region. Furthermore, the Taliban's success or failure and the success or failure of Obama's idea of "engaging" the "more moderate" elements among the Taliban will affect the tug-of-war between jihadists and pragmatists in the Middle East.

A New American Policy

In addition to the fresh investment it is making in Afghanistan and Pakistan and its related commitment to withdrawing from Iraq, the Obama administration launched in its first year three initiatives in the Middle East: it sought a dialogue with Iran (without abandoning the position that an Iranian nuclear arsenal is "unacceptable"); it opened a dialogue with Syria; and it assigned high priority to reviving a full-fledged Arab-Israeli peace process with a particular emphasis on the need to resolve the Palestinian-Israeli conflict on the basis of a two-state solution.

If successful, this very ambitious policy could transform the international and regional politics of the Middle East and could lay the ground for a regional security regime. But, as the Obama administration completed its second year and shifted its focus to domestic and economic issues, the prospect of a full implementation of this agenda let alone its implementation in short order was questionable. It became more realistic to think of partial success and a drawn-out process, meaning that the coming period is going to be affected by a great deal of uncertainty. Thus, conservative Arab countries, preoccupied with the Iranian challenge, will be hard put to build an anti-Iranian partnership while the prospect of an American-Iranian dialogue remains an option and U.S. pressure on Iran seems ineffective. The preference given by Obama to improving America's relationship with the Muslim and Arab world led him to assign a higher priority to the effort to revive the Israeli-Palestinian peace process and to distance himself to some extent from Israel and certainly so from Benjamin Netanyahu's government. The security relationship between the United States and Israel and America's ill-defined commitment to Israel's security have not been affected, but the sense of intimacy that was so present during the previous sixteen years has definitely been impaired.

Israel's Present Choices

Israel will conduct itself in this new arena under the leadership of Netanyahu's right-wing government, the product of Israel's February 2009 elections. The new government's right-wing edge was to some extent blunted by the Labor Party's participation in the coalition and Ehud Barak's continued tenure as minister of defense, but of the two schools of thought on Israeli national security mentioned earlier, the Israeli voter opted for the more militant one. It is the conventional wisdom that this school of thought—skeptical of diplomatic solutions and tending to rely on Israel's own military capabilities and actions—is likely to find itself at odds not only with the European Union but also with the Obama administration.[10] This may very well be the case, but Netanyahu is much more likely to try to harmonize his policies with those of the Obama administration. Such an effort would focus on the two main issues that could most affect regional security in the Middle East: Iran's policies and an Arab-Israeli peace process. There are several linkages between the two issues:

- An effective U.S. policy of restraining Iran's nuclear ambitions would lend the United States considerable leverage in dealing with Israel's government over the Arab-Israeli peace process.

- The United States is likely to argue that with palpable progress on the Israeli-Palestinian track, it would be easier for the conservative and moderate Arab states to cooperate directly with the United States and indirectly with Israel in curbing Iran's ambitions.
- Washington's policymakers may well find out that it is easier to move on the Israeli-Syrian track than on the Israeli-Palestinian track and that such progress would be closely linked to Washington's effort to draw Syria away from Iran and into a new, much-closer relationship with the United States. However, it is idle to speculate further in this matter until Washington's initial gambit toward Tehran plays itself out.

Notes

1. See Efraim Inbar and Shmuel Sandler, *Middle Eastern Security: Prospects for an Arms Control Regime* (Portland, OR: Frank Cass, 1995); Zeev Maoz, *Defending the Holy Land: A Critical Analysis of Israel's Security and Foreign Policy* (Ann Arbor, MI: University of Michigan Press, 2006); David Rodman, *Defense and Diplomacy in Israel's National Security Experience: Tactics, Partnerships and Motives* (Portland, OR: Sussex Academic Press, 2005); Gil Merom, "Israel's National Security and the Myth of Exceptionalism," *Political Science Quarterly* 114 (Fall 1999): 409–34; A. Mark Heller, "Continuity and Change in Israeli Security Policy," *Adelphi Papers*, no. 335 (July 2000): 5–84; Uri Bar-Joseph, "Israel's National Security Towards the 21st Century: Introduction," *Journal of Strategic Studies* 24, no. 2 (June 2001): 1–12; Stuart Cohen and David Rodman, "An Exchange on Israel's Security Doctrine," *MERIA Journal* 5, no. 1 (December 2001); David Rodman, "Israel's National Security Doctrine: An Introductory Overview," *MERIA Journal* 5, no. 3 (September 2001); Avner Yaniv, *Deterrence without the Bomb: The Politics of Israeli Strategy* (Lexington, MA: Lexington Books, 1987).

2. See Kenneth Pollack, *The Persian Puzzle: The Conflict Between Iran and America* (New York: Random House, 2004); Uzi Rubin, *The Global Reach of Iran's Ballistic Missiles*, Memorandum no. 86 (Tel Aviv: Institute for National Security Studies, November 2006); Uzi Rubin, "Missile Defense and Israel's Deterrence against a Nuclear Iran," in *Israel and a Nuclear Iran: Implications for Arms Control, Deterrence, and Defense*, Memorandum no. 94, ed. Ephraim Kam (Tel Aviv: Institute for National Security Studies, 2008); Ephraim Kam, *A Nuclear Iran: What Does It Mean, and What Can Be Done?* Memorandum no. 88 (Tel Aviv: Institute for National Security Studies, February 2007); Ephraim Kam, "Changes in Iran's Strategic Posture," *Strategic Assessment* 9, no. 4 (March 2007); Yair Evron, "An Israel-Iran Balance of Nuclear Deterrence: Seeds of Instability," in *Israel and a Nuclear Iran: Implications for Arms Control, Deterrence, and Defense*, ed. Ephraim Kam, Memorandum no. 94 (Tel Aviv: Institute for National Security Studies, 2008).

3. See H. Anthony Cordesman, with the assistance of Aram Nerguizian, *Israel and Syria: The Military Balance and Prospects of War* (Westport, CT: Praeger Security International, 2008); Dani Berkovich, "Wars Aren't Waged in the Summer? How Israel and Syria Might Find Themselves at War," *Strategic Assessment* 10, no. 2 (August 2007); Yiftah Shapir, "The Syrian Army Buildup," *Strategic Assessment* 10, no. 2 (August 2007).

4. See H. Anthony Cordesman, George Sullivan, and D. William Sullivan, *Lessons of the 2006 Israeli-Hezbollah War* (Washington, DC: Center for Strategic and International Stud-

ies Press, 2007); Yossi Kuperwasser, "The Next War with Hizbollah: Should Lebanon Be the Target?" *Strategic Assessment* 11, no. 2 (November 2008); Giora Eiland, "The Third Lebanon War: Target Lebanon," *Strategic Assessment* 11, no. 2 (November 2008); Dani Berkovich, *Can the Hydra Be Beheaded? The Campaign to Weaken Hizbollah*, Memorandum no. 92 [in Hebrew] (Tel Aviv: Institute for National Security Studies, December 2007); Amir Kulick, "The Next War with Hizbollah," *Strategic Assessment* 10, no. 3 (December 2007).

5. See Doron Almog, *The West Bank Fence: A Vital Component in Israel's Strategy of Defense* (Washington, DC: Washington Institute for Near East Policy, 2004); Shlomo Brom, *From Rejection to Acceptance: Israeli National Security Thinking and Palestinian Statehood*, Special Report no. 177 (Washington, DC: United States Institute of Peace Press, 2007); Daniel Byman, "Do Targeted Killings Work?" *Foreign Affairs* (March–April 2006); Anat Kurz, "Seven Years Later: The Israel-Palestinian Conflict—An Interim Assessment," *Strategic Assessment* 10, no. 3 (December 2007); Anat Kurz, "The Israeli-Palestinian Arena: Dynamic Stagnation," in *The Middle East Strategic Balance 2007–2008*, ed. Mark A. Heller (Tel Aviv: Institute for National Security Studies, 2008); Roni Bart, "Israel vs. the Palestinians: Limitations of Dialogue and the Thrust of Force," *Strategic Assessment* 10, no. 2 (August 2007); Ephraim Lavie, "The PA: An Authority without Authority," *Strategic Assessment* 11, no. 2 (November 2008).

6. Avi Kober, "Has Battlefield Decision Become Obsolete? The Commitment to the Achievement of Battlefield Decision Revisited," *Contemporary Security Policy* 22, no. 2 (August 2001): 96–120; Avi Kober, "Israeli War Objectives into an Era of Negativism," *Journal of Strategic Studies* 24, no. 2 (June 2001): 176–201; Avi Kober, "From Blitzkrieg to Attrition: Israel's Attrition Strategy and Staying Power," *Small Wars and Insurgencies* 16, no. 2 (June 2005): 216–40; Uri Bar-Joseph, "The Paradox of Israeli Power," *Survival* 46, no. 4 (Winter 2004): 137–55; Gal Hirsch, "On Dinosaurs and Hornets—A Critical View on Operational Moulds in Asymmetric Conflicts," *RUSI Journal* 148, no. 4 (August 2003); Giora Eiland, "The Changing Nature of War: Six New Challenges," *Strategic Assessment* 10, no. 1 (June 2007).

7. Gabriel Ben-Dor and B. David Dewitt, *Confidence Building Measures in the Middle East* (Boulder: Westview Press, 1994); Alon Platt, *Arms Control and Confidence Building in the Middle East* (Washington, DC: United States Institute of Peace Press, 1992); Emanuel Adler, "The Spread of Security Communities: Communities of Practice, Self-Restraint, and NATO'S Post–Cold War Transformation," *European Journal of International Relations* 14, no. 2 (2008): 195–230.

8. Itamar Rabinovich, *Waging Peace: Israel and the Arabs, 1948–2003* (Princeton, NJ: Princeton University Press, 2004).

9. See Itamar Rabinovich, *The Brink of Peace: The Israeli-Syrian Negotiations* (Princeton, NJ: Princeton University Press, 1998), and the author's forthcoming monograph written for the Saban Center at the Brookings Institution on Washington, Damascus, and Jerusalem; and Eyal Zisser, "It's a Long Road to Peace with Syria: From the Second Lebanon War to Peace Overtures in Ankara," *Strategic Assessment* 11, no. 2 (November 2008). For a negative Israeli view of renewed negotiations with Syria, see Giora Eiland, "Renewed Negotiations with Syria: Currently Not in Israel's Interest," *Strategic Assessment* 9, no. 4 (March 2007).

10. See editorial titled "Being a Partner for Peace," *New York Times*, March 27, 2009.

9

The Imported, Supported, and Homegrown Security of the Arab World

Bassma Kodmani

The Arab world's security predicament lies in the pivotal importance of Arab lands on one hand, and the weak means of control that Arabs have to defend their strategic interests on the other hand. The mere definition of the Arab world as a region can seem like an ideological construct to many foreign observers and policymakers. It is true that the conflict over the Western Sahara between Morocco and Algeria has a life of its own and has little to do with the anxieties that Iraq or Iran, for example, trigger among the monarchies of the Gulf. Nevertheless, there are enough commonalities among Arab societies to consider the Arab world as a relevant frame of reference for regional cooperation: an overwhelming majority of the population is Sunni Muslim and Arabic speaking and has been rooted for many centuries in the same "Arab homeland," which extends from Morocco on the Atlantic Ocean to Bahrain in the Arab Persian Gulf; a shared narrative of history and experience of foreign rule; ideological currents that have swept all Arab-speaking countries before and since independence, with political forces—Nasserite, Baathist, Marxist, and Islamist (both moderate and jihadist)—establishing branches across the Middle East and North Africa; a commitment, at the governmental level, to solidarity in the face of security challenges, which materialized when troops from Morocco, Algeria, Tunisia, and Iraq participated in the various wars against Israel in 1948, 1967, and 1973; and the sustained coordination between the security sectors of all Arab regimes to

221

quell opposition and more recently to fight terrorist networks. As a result, even Arab religious minorities—Shia Muslims and most Christians—consider their "Arabism" as the primary axis of their identity, superseding their "Shiism" or "Christianity." For them, the "linguistic-cultural" variable is the more salient ethnic divide.[1] The Arab League is the most formal expression of this vision of a common Arab fate, even though it is the least significant in terms of effective cooperation.

A distinction therefore needs to be introduced between the region as a strategically relevant framework and the region as a historically and culturally linked geographical area. The former leads to identifying two or three regions—Maghreb, Mashreq, and the Gulf, or the Middle East and North Africa—while the latter refers to a much broader region defined by its historical and cultural continuity and homogeneity. This chapter focuses specifically on the Middle East, which it defines as the Levant (Egypt, Jordan, Syria, Lebanon, Israel, and Palestine) and the Gulf region, where conflict and instability have the greatest impact on international security and the strategic interests of world powers. But it also points to tensions that result from this dual definition of the region when necessary and discusses the competing references for defining the relevant regional framework.

The Middle East maintains a vision of itself as representing an exceptional region that faces unique security challenges due in large part to two factors: the presence of Israel and the presence of vast oil wealth. These two factors weigh structurally on the capacity of the Arab world to manage its own affairs. Almost any minor crisis in the region echoes around the world and impacts international energy security and financial stability, stirs emotions within Jewish and Arab diasporas everywhere, and triggers outside powers' interference, as if the Middle East was too important to be left to Middle Easterners. The people and governments of the region tend to behave accordingly, entrusting their heavy security burden to outside protectors.

Over the last decade, the issue of state capacity became an added source of concern for a growing number of countries. Among the Arab countries, three are characterized as failed states—Somalia, Sudan, and Iraq, ranking first, third, and sixth in the Failed States Index, respectively.[2] As wealth increased over the decades, conflicts multiplied and escalated, with both trends reaching extremes in the decade since 2000. Income from oil has grown to historic levels, while Palestine, Iraq, Algeria, Sudan, and Lebanon are open wounds in the Arab body.

Arabs have had a limited say in shaping their regional order, and this capacity has been further reduced since the end of the Cold War, when Arab countries lost the space to maneuver between the Eastern and Western Blocs. Why is the Arab world such a weak and ineffective player on the world scene and in shaping its own regional order? Why are Iran and Turkey more assertive and active powers in the region than the entire Arab world? Whatever happened to the Arab countries' capacity and will to assert their role as they did in 1956 and in 1973, when they did not win military victories but succeeded in shaking the world order and gained important political assets?

The Arab world is a community with a strong sense of identity, but it has a weak engine to undertake joint action within a regional framework. This chapter will emphasize the common history and strong cultural and social bonds between Arab countries and how this contrasts with a limited capacity to jointly assess risks, organize and mobilize collectively to respond to security challenges, and assert national or regional interests in the face of foreign demands and schemes. Its central thesis is that unless the Arab governments develop a broader, less defensive, and more pragmatic understanding of what security encompasses, not only for the survival of their regimes but for their societies as a whole, there is little chance that they will be able to collaborate in building an autonomous regional capacity to manage conflicts. A second major prerequisite for such a regional framework to operate is the settlement of the major conflicts over which Arab governments do not have absolute control, chief among them the Arab-Israeli conflict.

The various institutional frameworks that exist for managing collective security all seem to suffer from major weaknesses, and none seems adequate to serve the purpose of conflict management, let alone resolution. As a result, temporary ad hoc settings are being experimented with, with some level of success. They bring together all relevant regional and outside players and operate on a pragmatic basis where each player commits to undertaking concrete measures. These ad hoc frameworks offer the most promising prospects so far to address the protracted conflicts of the region. Whether they can be institutionalized and entrusted with a more permanent mission hinges in good part on the governments' willingness to reach a shared understanding of what security priorities are and to commit to setting certain rules and abiding by them. A set of domestic factors, some ideological and others political, resulting from a deep state-society gap, and a set of external factors have weighed heavily on the development of regional capacity to provide security.

The chapter's first section explores the various security narratives in the region and their ideological underpinnings and then identifies existing security challenges, as perceptions determine the way in which those security challenges are addressed. While there may be a large consensus on some challenges, others are a source of profound disagreements. A key question to assess therefore is the extent to which there is sufficient consensus on the assessment of security challenges to forge common conflict management strategies.

The second section examines the conditions for a valid and legitimate regional framework for action. Defining the region is a political and strategic question but also a social and cultural one. Four different and competing frameworks—Arab, Mediterranean, subregional (around the Gulf countries), and Islamic—are analyzed here, including their relevance for addressing security concerns, their legitimacy from societies' perspective, and their capacity. None of these frameworks, as shall be shown, offers serious prospects of building a regional capacity for conflict management.

The third section examines the existing capacity within the region to address threats, mitigate crises, and resolve conflicts. What means are available, what constraints weigh on governments, and what responses have been made to security threats and conflict? The analysis will help understand how informal and nontraditional instruments provide a capacity to mediate conflict. However, when faced with imminent threat, the region relies heavily on outside capacity, primarily from the United States.

The fourth section analyzes the way in which the region relates to new norms and paradigms in the international system. The reluctance to embrace principles such as humanitarian intervention and the responsibility to protect are evident in the way the Arab governments have responded to major crises and brought upon themselves wide criticism from inside and outside the region.

Finally, the chapter reflects on what types of arrangements might work better for building a security architecture for the region.

Fragmented Security Perceptions and Narratives

The Middle East is a strongly integrated region in the global system as judged from its role in the international financial markets and the involvement of foreign powers and of the United Nations in managing crises there. Yet it is only marginally involved as an actual player in contributing to intellectual debates on security challenges, new norms, and mechanisms of international security. Within the Middle East, there is a general reluctance among Arabs—governments, intellectuals, and the public alike—to embrace the post–Cold War international system, to acknowledge that this system requires new thinking about the values and rules that should govern it, and to engage in global debates to define new norms. Such engagement would signal that leaders of the region feel responsible for their security as states beyond the mere survival of the ruling regimes and are able to conceive of a regional security order in which they are actual players.

This is not to say that Arabs are any different from Africans or Asians in their distrust of the international order of the twenty-first century, which they see as being dominated by northern powers who define new norms according to their interests. But the dichotomy between the defensive response of Arab governments to any idea that might challenge their sovereignty on one hand and their reliance on outside powers for their security on the other hand is remarkable.

An Absent Arab Strategic Community

Scholarly work from the Middle East on peace and security is generally poor and in a state of disorientation. There are several reasons to explain this gap:

- There has been a slow shift from the postcolonial and postimperial framework and its ideological underpinnings to a post–Cold war era marked by a major war in the Gulf following the invasion of Kuwait by Iraq. Nationalist visions and Third World solidarities have lost their main champions within governments, but they persist among the scholarly community and shape a certain vision of the world.
- Direct foreign interventions since the end of the Cold War have bred a sense of powerlessness and debility within the strategic community. Conflict management and settlement through internationalization has become the norm. Starting in 1991, the U.S.-led multinational force that waged the war to oust Iraq from Kuwait included a large number of Arab countries. In 2003, the U.S.-led war on Iraq also relied heavily on the support of the Gulf monarchies. Arab leaders and regional organizations seem to have abdicated their responsibilities in the face of major regional conflicts and the direct management of crises by outside powers.
- The majority of Arab countries have become dependent on foreign military protection for their security. The military and security forces are equipped and trained and their doctrines are largely shaped in connection with Western thinking and professional and technical input from key Western partners. Egypt, Jordan, Saudi Arabia, Kuwait, Bahrain, and Oman developed their military forces in full coordination with the United States to ensure interoperability, while Qatar and the United Arab Emirates obtain arms and defense systems from not only the United States but also Great Britain and France.

- The region is both a generator and a victim of terrorism. Its governments work with Western agencies through security and intelligence cooperation to fight terror threats that target national assets, and at the same time Arab societies are a witness to an international debate that seems to make them the epicenter of the war on terror.
- Authoritarianism has led to the creation of a state-society gap, hindering relevant strategic thinking. Arab states have few institutions where security experts can access information from their security establishments to produce independent analysis and offer guidance on strategy and on how to respond to threats of all kinds, from the collapse of states and border disputes to powerful neighbors suspected of hegemonic designs. The security debate remains embryonic or, at best, unstructured and the capacity to anticipate security challenges and formulate concrete policy options is limited. Imminent threats from menacing neighbors, terrorism, or domestic upheavals have led to heavy reliance on outside protection. This reliance on responses from outside in turn inhibits cooperation with neighbors to define regional responses.[3]

A Culture of Hard Security

The global debate on security has seen major shifts in the definition of security, with new concepts emerging after the end of the Cold War. More voices from the developing world have engaged in international debates and articulated alternative visions on new definitions of security and whose security is sought: Is it national or regional security, or is it the security of citizens and that of vulnerable groups? Is it physical or personal security, or integrity of the group or of the community that should guide the research and serve as the central criteria? What is sustainable security and what are the drivers behind it? These new concepts have yet to find their way into the works of Arab scholars.

In the Middle East, a culture of hard security built around concepts of containment, deterrence, counterterrorism, and political violence continues to prevail. Broader definitions of soft security issues have made limited inroads into the debate. This dominant culture of hard security can be attributed to several factors: (1) the ruling elites often come from a military or security background; (2) Israel's understanding of regional security remains built exclusively on military power; (3) armed groups that practice terrorist methods seek to revive the military confrontation with Israel (Hamas and Hezbollah) or challenge Arab governments and confront the West (al-Qaeda and its offshoots across the region); (4) Iran continues to pursue its quest for nuclear capacity and its militant discourse; (5) the United States has increasingly resorted to military action to respond to attacks and challenges to its interests and security, and to shape the regional order.

This culture of hard security shapes the attitudes of Arab governments. With deterrence as the dominant rationale, Arab states focus on the military balance of forces, the regional arms race, nuclear capabilities, and protecting the physical security of their national territory and oil facilities. The rich states of the Gulf seek outside support to deter Iran from pressuring them, intimidating them, or manipulating their vulnerable domestic situations. They look to secure direct U.S. protection, enter security cooperation with European countries, and seek to strengthen ties with Russia and more recently China through major arms deals.

While the end of the Cold War opened the way for an expanded understanding of security to cover threats resulting from poverty, disease, and denial of basic human rights, the attacks of September 11 and the global war on terror encouraged a return to a more traditional approach, one that brought national security back to the center stage, with increased military budgets and expanding security agencies.

Since the Tripartite Agreement of 1950,[4] there has not been one successful attempt at reaching a negotiated agreement on the flow of arms to the region, let alone an arms control agreement between any of the key military powers. Israel continues to expand its arsenal in all types of weapons, while Iraq's nuclear reactor was all but destroyed in an Israeli raid in 1981,[5] and a suspected nuclear site was bombed in Syria in 2007. A military strike against Iran's nuclear sites has been branded as a nightmare scenario. If a negotiation with Iran on its nuclear program reaches some positive outcome, it will be the first time that a negotiation on arms control succeeds in the Middle East.

The State-Society Gap

For most of the twentieth century, the Arab narrative of a common history, culture, religion, and social organization served to shape a strong sense of a common security destiny. This narrative is largely built around a sense of injustice—of wounded pride—a perception of outside powers as arrogant and greedy, fueling strong resentment and vindictive feelings, and a sense of a decline in power and capability in general.

Yet it is important to emphasize from the outset that these perceptions prevail mainly in the densely populated countries of the Levant and North Africa. In the rich but poorly populated Gulf countries, the narrative may be quite different due to their more positive experience with Western powers, specific social and political structures, and higher standards of living. Perceptions are therefore highly fragmented and result in an inability to reach a shared assessment of threats and to pool resources and capacities together.

The politicized elites of the Arab world attribute this fragmentation to domestic reasons and point to the state-society gap that characterizes authoritarian regimes and distorts the concept of national security. With the emergence of juntas that came to power through force, the state became the state of a group, a faction, or a family that manipulates sectarianism and factionalism to control society. A disconnect appeared between security of the state and security of the regime, the latter being based on loyalty and allegiance rather than professionalism and institutions. While this gap is articulated by the scholarly community, public opinion at large does not identify with the official discourse on national security, because it is equated with the security of the governing group rather than of the society. Different social groups are driven toward seeking protection and responses to their needs and concerns from within their religious, sectarian, ethnic, or tribal communities.

Failure to address the challenges of development, unemployment, bad education, sickness, hunger, institution building, social justice, and democracy contributed to making Arab states fragile despite their heavy security apparatuses and reduced the nationalist project of an Arab common destiny to a nostalgic aspiration rather than a project with a plan of action.[6] Furthermore, the "Arab project," as it was called by the nationalists, failed to acknowledge the religious and cultural diversity of the societies. As a result, the advocates of an Arab national security reached an intellectual impasse: how can Iraq, Sudan, Algeria, and the United Arab Emirates remain Arab if they are to become multicultural, develop a federal system of governance, recognize the rights of large minorities, and grant civic rights to masses of non-Arab immigrants?

Security priorities and the identification of enemies and threats are largely fragmented. Bahrain, for example, sees Iran as the most serious threat to regional security, which led it to propose a new regional security arrangement that would bring in Turkey, Israel, Iraq, and all the Arab countries in a common front against Iran, while Oman maintains excellent ties with Iran and is opposed to a unified front against it. Kuwait continues to fear Iraq more than Iran. Egypt makes its decisions on security matters according to its national interest, and Egyptian political and economic elites have grown more inward looking and talk primarily of internal threats to justify its government's regional policy.

Saudi Arabia has a long-standing internal debate within the ruling elite between those who favor a more regionally embedded security approach that seeks to build some common understanding with Iran and Iraq on one side, and those who push for a closer relationship with the United States to ensure the security of the ruling family against all types of threats on the other side. In effect, the Saudi ruling elite dreads both the repercussions of a military confrontation between the United States and Iran, and the prospect of a U.S. deal with the Islamic regime in Tehran that would acknowledge Iran's hegemonic power in the region.

Voices from within the different countries of the Gulf have recently risen to draw attention to sources of domestic instability as a more serious challenge to security than threats from neighbors such as Iran, further illustrating the state-society gap. The concerns over the territorial integrity of Arab states have grown tremendously among both leaders and societies over the last decade due to the destabilization of Sudan, Lebanon, Iraq, and, more recently, Yemen.

The Centrality of the Arab-Israeli Conflict

While many new fears have developed that seem to challenge the vision of the centrality of the Arab-Israeli conflict to the region, this conflict continues to structure the Arab psyche, define the military doctrines of most Arab countries, and shape the Arabs' vision of the world. But this is not a matter of perception only. Objectively, it is at the heart of regional insecurity. Israel represents a security threat in a narrow military definition to each of its neighbors: in Sinai for Egypt, in Lebanon and the Golan for Syria, and in the overall internal stability of Lebanon due to the presence of Palestinian political and armed factions, as well as the powerful Hezbollah movement. Beyond these multiple threats to the national security of Israel's immediate neighbors, the conflict represents a central threat to the region as a whole because it undermines efforts to address almost all other security issues in the region, not least the nuclear ambitions of Iran and possibly other countries. Furthermore, it is the major factor in the radicalization of public opinion and it raises the legitimacy of Islamist movements, moderate and extremist alike.

Iran, Iraq, and the Shia-Sunni Divide

Since the overthrow of the Baathist regime in Bagdad, the threats from Iraq have multiplied. They stem from the chaotic whirlpool of religious and ethnosectarian conflicts, the replacement of a strong central state dominated by the Sunnis with a weak sectarian federal state subject to the influence of the Iranian regime, and the terror networks that have found in Iraq a new base for their activities.

The Sunni-Shia rift has always existed, but since the U.S. invasion of Iraq in 2003, it is perceived by Arab governments both as a major fault line around which strategic realignments are taking place and as a source of instability in the domestic social fabric of Arab countries that have important Shia minorities. Some believe that the divide is artificially inflated by governments to serve two purposes—namely, to exacerbate belligerent attitudes from outside powers toward Iran and to roll back domestic opposition and stifle the debate on internal security challenges. In addition to its role as a natural protector of the Shia communities across the region, Iran is feared as a revolutionary actor that sits at the center of a web of transnational nongovernmental groups through its support to Hezbollah, Hamas, and Islamic Jihad.

The Terrorist Threat

The threat from terror networks has grown tremendously since 2001 as a new generation of jihadists emerged in Afghanistan and settled within Arab borders after the invasion of Iraq. Both countries offer a safe haven for groups to train, organize, and spread across the whole region and beyond. These offshoots of al-Qaeda include members from almost every country of the region, including Saudi Arabia, Syria, Jordan, Palestine, Egypt, Algeria, Morocco, and Tunisia.

Their rhetoric about confronting the West and the "infidels" ruling Muslim states is simplistic and contrasts with their sophisticated methods in launching appallingly lethal attacks. Yet since September 11, 2001, and the mobilization of security apparatuses against these terror networks, Islamist movements in all Arab countries have sought to dissociate themselves clearly from the terrorists acting in the name of jihad. Some, including the radical groups in Egypt, undertook self-criticism and publicly renounced violence.[7] These and more moderate movements are keen to be recognized as part of a peaceful opposition. In more than ten countries, they seek to enter coalitions with other political parties. They also participate in elections wherever they are allowed, as in Morocco, Egypt, Algeria, Jordan, and Yemen, and they formulate political demands through legal means.

To any observer from the region or outside, the distinction between terrorist groups that use religious rhetoric and peaceful Islamist movements that seek recognition as political forces through legal means is now clear. In Egypt, Algeria, Morocco, and Yemen, citizens easily understand and accept counterterrorist measures and controls as long as they feel that these measures are designed to ensure the security of the country, while at the same time the majority resents the suppression of peaceful Islamist movements.

However, two factors continue to blur the distinction between terrorism and political Islam. The first is the use of antiterror laws by authoritarian governments to suppress any form of protest, even when it is expressed in the form of peaceful political demands. The second is the basic disagreement between Israel and Western countries on the one hand and Arab and Muslim countries on the other hand over what constitutes a legitimate use of violence against occupation and how to characterize Hamas and Hezbollah. Nowhere in the Arab world are these two movements labeled as terrorists but rather as resistance movements whose use of force is legitimate as long as Israeli occupation of Arab land is maintained. Leaders from both Hamas and Hezbollah have in effect consistently denounced statements from al-Qaeda leaders and are keen to distance themselves from their provocative calls for jihad against the West. Nevertheless, Israel equates these two movements with terrorism and Western governments formally espoused this position by putting the two movements on their lists of terrorist organizations.

Competing Security Frameworks

An assessment of Arab governments' incentives to engage in sustained cooperation on security matters gives ample reason for skepticism. The Arab world lacks the institutional and political factors that can make it an effective international actor. This section discusses the crisis of existing regional structures to address security concerns of Arab states, the competing frameworks that have emerged over the last two decades, and the key question of their legitimacy versus their efficacy.

The Arab League

The Arab League was created at the initiative of Great Britain in 1945, which encouraged the newly independent Arab states to create a regional framework of their own for political and military cooperation. Its charter includes a joint defense agreement by which Arab states are committed to ensuring Arab collective security, but hardly any Arab official or scholar ever mentions the defense agreement, as it has never been used.[8] The league has strong legitimacy in the eyes of Arab public opinion as the natural space for solidarity but is a very weak framework for managing security issues. There are several reasons for this dichotomy:

- *Reliance on outside powers.* The Arab states see themselves as powerless and rely on the United States for security, or call on the United Nations to play a role when the United States does not assume its role, allowing direct involvement of outside powers in Iraq, Somalia, Lebanon, Sudan, and, of course, Palestine. The key countries of the region are committed to preserving relations with the United States as a priority, which further contributes to disempowering the league.

- *Competition for leadership between the key states.* While this competition was ideological until the 1970s, it eventually came to be based on power politics—such as the race for arms acquisitions and access to nuclear energy—and the capacity to mediate conflicts and assert national influence.

- *Paralysis stemming from the consensus-based decision-making process of the Arab League (in effect, unanimity).* Prospects for reforming the league are dim as this is not a procedural issue as much as an expression of the resistance of Arab governments to cede any portion of their sovereign decision making to a supranational body.

- *Poorly defined terms of relations with its powerful neighbors.* As expressed by Arab League secretary-general Amr Mousa, the league will eventually need to invite Turkey, Iran, and, at a later stage, Israel as observers and perhaps someday as full members if it wants discussions on security to become relevant. Failure to do so has led to constantly enhancing the role of outside powers.[9]

- *A lack of mechanisms for enforcing decisions on commonly held positions.* In 2008, when a large majority of member countries were in agreement to condemn Syria's meddling in Lebanese affairs, the league had no means to coerce Damascus to abide by its decision. The Saudi minister of foreign affairs, Prince Saud al-Faisal, expressed frustration because the Arab League has no "teeth." A nascent discussion took place within the league on the need to adopt some coercive means similar to other international organizations in the event of disruption or failure to implement any of its unanimous resolutions. "Call them sanctions or measures, name them whatever. But if there is unanimity on a plan which is not implemented by one or two states, then there should be deterrent measures, otherwise there will be no seriousness in the Arab action."[10] However, the discussion over such coercive means was not pursued.

There is one area that stands out as an exception where cooperation has been impressive—namely, the joint efforts to fight terrorism. The "war on terror" has provided an opportunity for Arab governments to demonstrate the capacity of their security sectors and their ability to collaborate regionally. But these kinds of achievements are celebrated by the governments only and are seen with much suspicion by the public, as they are often designed to increase the surveillance of the population and have made security institutions more opaque and repressive. The state-society gap goes a long way in explaining the failure of the Arab League to develop an agenda for action.

The Gulf States and the Culture of Vulnerability

The elites of the Gulf countries often express frustration at the Arab League as a functioning regional framework and think that they should not wait for a pan-Arab stance to come out of the womb on issues of vital interest to them. Since they came together to form the Gulf Cooperation Council (GCC), the six Gulf monarchies—Saudi Arabia, Kuwait, the United Arab Emirates, Qatar, Oman, and Bahrain—have developed strong ties among themselves and succeeded in moving toward significant integration of their trade and financial systems. Although they enjoy uneven levels of wealth, they share a homogeneous geographic space, similar social structures, a positive experience of relations with Western countries, and a common sense of vulnerability and desire to protect themselves from the poorer and more troubled neighbors of the Levant. Yet the GCC countries have not shown any serious will to create a joint strategy to face security challenges of any sort, let alone a joint military capacity. The wealthier among them (Saudi Arabia and Kuwait) support the poorer (Oman and Bahrain) and are particularly generous in financing the purchasing of military equipment by the latter for the benefit of building interoperability between their defense systems in accordance with U.S. recommendations. Although the six countries decided to establish a joint military force of 10,000 men in 1982,[11] this force was never built to become a credible operational force.

While insecurity has grown tremendously since the creation of the GCC, the governments continue to lack the capacity to protect their territories and the security of their regimes. Over the last twenty-five years, threats from their two big neighbors, Iran and Iraq, led the governments of the Gulf to develop ever closer cooperation with the United States. In the aftermath of September 11, 2001, this cooperation was expanded and intensified. Gulf leaders see that combating terrorism, ensuring the security of their oil installations, fighting transnational criminal networks, and responding to other security challenges such as narcotics and human trafficking can only be guaranteed through regional and international cooperation with the active involvement of the major oil-consuming nations.

Talk of building a Gulf security system through developing good neighborly relations with Iran is not based on any genuine confidence-building process. The GCC states are extremely nervous about the prospect of a nuclear Iran and have been calling for a nuclear weapons–free Gulf. But in the face of Iran's accelerated nuclear program, a growing number of voices from the GCC countries are suggesting that the best protection is for the United States to extend its nuclear deterrence umbrella to the GCC states. Iran clearly does not believe that a dialogue with its neighbors is likely to provide answers to its vital concerns. It sees itself first as an interlocutor of the United

States and Europe, and only after dialogue with them will it define its policy toward its neighbors. Likewise, the stabilization of Iraq is dependent on a U.S.-Iran deal in which the GCC states have little or no say.

The price for the Gulf countries' reliance on foreign military protection and imported security (some call it trusteeship) perpetuates a culture of vulnerability among its leaders and societies. The GCC is not a credible player without the direct involvement of the United States and is not likely to develop a valid security framework until it defines the terms of its relations with Iran, Iraq, and Yemen.

The Euro-Mediterranean Framework

Initiated in the early 1990s by the European countries of the northern Mediterranean, the Euro-Mediterranean framework was meant to transform the Mediterranean space into a stable partnership between the north and the south. But the Barcelona Process, started in 1995, was more successful in the fields of economic cooperation, trade relations, and development than it was on political reforms and security issues. As of 2008, the partnership was renamed the Union for the Mediterranean, with strong emphasis on soft security and development issues, such as joint projects to address water scarcity and salinity, pollution, ecotourism, and labor migration. Although some European countries would like this framework to serve as a mechanism for a dialogue between Israel and its neighbors, Arab countries have resisted attempts at using the Euro-Mediterranean framework as a forum for discussing hard security issues, and this is likely to remain the case as long as the conflict with Israel is not solved. Likewise, suggestions of an OSCE (Organization for Security and Co-operation in Europe) type of forum where all countries of the Middle East would participate has no appeal to Arab governments or societies that see such a forum as a distraction from their core problem with Israel and its occupation of Arab land.

The Islamic Framework

As in any region, cooperation agreements are most effective when they reflect the beliefs and aspirations of the societies that compose it. The Arab League came into being when nationalist aspirations were high among Arabs. As religiosity developed across the Arab world and as Saudi diplomacy became active in funding states and groups across the Muslim world in the 1970s and 1980s, the Islamic framework began to emerge as an attractive alternative to rethink collective security. Today it has strong resonance among societies and is widely seen as a natural gathering of the Islamic *umma*; it also allows the Muslim world to present itself as a cultural bloc with the potential to establish a balance with the West and to challenge an unjust regional and international order, first and foremost by changing the strategic equation in the Arab-Israeli conflict. However, the appeal of the Islamic framework has increased more as a result of new strategies developed by a combination of states and transnational nonstate actors than by the long-existing intergovernmental Organization of the Islamic Conference (OIC).

Iran's military support for Hezbollah and Hamas, the transmission of its militant discourse by Islamic media channels, and the prospect of an Iranian nuclear capability have given new strategic depth to the Palestinian question in the face of Israel, a depth that the Arab framework had ceased to provide. In addition to Iran as *the* militant Islamic power, Turkey has emerged as a credible and trusted advocate for the Palestinians since Israel's war on Gaza in 2008, a role that has been hugely strengthened by the "Free Gaza" flotilla that was organized by Turkish Islamic associations with the government's support in May 2010.

The more formal Islamic framework represented by the OIC remains for now a loose forum with no institutionalized mechanisms for managing crises. It is also largely perceived as being dominated by the Saudi political and religious establishment and therefore as promoting the Wahhabi trend in Islam and lacking representation of public opinion in Muslim societies. But the OIC has two assets that it can bring to bear: (1) a strong moral standing due to the aspiration of Muslim societies for an Islamic solidarity framework and (2) its economic and financial weight. The latter is unlikely to be used for coercive purposes due to the interdependent interests of key Muslim countries and the West, but in the context of Arab-Israeli negotiations, Muslim countries can play a precious role by providing an overall Islamic blessing to a compromise agreement, particularly on Jerusalem, and by offering Israel major economic, commercial and financial incentives, as they declared for the first time at the summit meeting of the OIC in March 2008.[12]

Informal Means of Conflict Mediation

As the existing regional frameworks provide a limited capacity to manage crises when violent confrontation erupts, Arab governments, when faced with an open crisis, struggle to maneuver within a narrow space between their alliances with outside powers whose interests they are committed to protecting, their need to preserve their own stability, and their need to manage public anger among their societies. In almost every open crisis, they face embarrassment due to their inability to act decisively and suffer a loss of credibility.

Mediation capacity within the region does exist, however, to a certain extent, but it is informal, noninstitutionalized, and nontransparent. Arab governments are able to mobilize important assets to mediate and diffuse conflict before it erupts into violent confrontation. They are often more comfortable mediating crises each on their own and mobilizing their domestic assets and forces that might have connections or yield some influence with certain protagonists. Financial assets and business interests, religious influence, connections between political groups and security agencies, and tribal and family ties are all invisible threads that they activate for mediation purposes.

Financial Means

Money plays an important role in wielding influence and has often proven to be an effective tool in mobilization. The countries of the Gulf make generous donations in various international forums, such as the Paris conferences for the reconstruction of Palestine, Lebanon, and Afghanistan, and in regional forums, particularly the Arab League and the OIC. This financial capability serves the image of the donor country and strengthens its ties with countries of the North, but it is usually sought to serve an international purpose and does not yield visible influence to the donor country. Money is more effective, however, when it is mobilized to serve a national rather than regional policy. Saudi Arabia, Qatar, Kuwait, the United Arab Emirates, Libya, Algeria, and Iraq in the past have all used their financial wealth at one point or another to support certain groups in Lebanon, Iraq, Palestine, or Sudan. Such financial donations are sometimes used to fuel conflict, to cover political differences, or to draw a government into a country's orbit of influence, but they also serve to oil a process to implement an agreed-upon political strategy—whether boosting the resources of the Palestinian National Authority (PNA) to better allow it to resist Hamas or to give it the upper hand; providing support to both the PNA and Hamas to entice them to form a national unity government; or making payments to individual political leaders of Lebanon to entice them to reach a compromise among themselves. Oil wealth is also used to silence opposition and to shape public opinion through support to media outlets, especially TV channels that focus on political news and religious proselytizing.

Other related incentives are frequently mobilized, such as economic support and job opportunities from the rich countries to the poor ones. For example, Saudi Arabia opened its borders to hundreds of thousands of Yemenis and offered them opportunities for work in the Kingdom as a way of alleviating the social and political pressure on the regime in Sanaa.

Money does not provide legitimacy but efficiency. Realpolitik is the driver here and stability and order are the objectives. The only limitation on money as a tool for influence is when money is also available to the opposing party. Iraqi factions, for example, have the financial means to fight one another thanks to oil income, and the Palestinians of Hamas can play Iranian financial support against Saudi support. Similarly, Syria can afford to be deprived of Saudi money when Iran is providing for its needs.

Religious Influence

Although religious influence is not always tied to financial means, Saudi Arabia is in a position to use both and does so to mediate different types of conflicts. It did so successfully in reconciling the two main Palestinian factions and in weighing on the Islamic movement Hamas to reach a compromise with Fatah in Mecca in 2007, and it has been called upon by the United States and the coalition forces in Afghanistan to activate its connections with the Taliban forces that the Wahhabi establishment has developed with the Taliban over the years.

Saudi Arabia takes an active role in seeking solutions for Somalia and Palestine and has helped the Sudanese government reach an amicable agreement with the United Nations for the deployment of UN peacekeeping forces in Darfur. The Saudi government likes to use its means of influence to serve its national agenda of preserving the status quo—that is, the financial, political, and sectarian equilibrium of the region. It makes ample use of its financial capacity to persuade and pressure parties to reach a deal, as it has repeatedly done with Lebanese and Palestinian factions.

Other countries are also able to mobilize Islamic networks, but they do so less regularly. Egypt's religious institution Al-Azhar and sometimes even the Muslim Brothers themselves, despite being an opposition force, are called upon to use their influence in mediation efforts between Palestinians, Jordanians, Sudanese, and others.

Security Agencies

State security agencies offer a diverse means of maintaining connections with certain groups, exerting pressure, and mediating disputes. Egypt is most effective at using the skills of its powerful security apparatus and connections with the security agencies of its neighbors, including Israel, to mediate between parties in a conflict. Egypt's chief of intelligence, General Omar Suleiman, in effect leads Egyptian foreign policy on the most sensitive issues—namely, Israel, the Palestinians, and security cooperation with the United States. It is the Egyptian intelligence apparatus (*mukhabarat*) that brokered the indirect talks between Hamas and Israel that led to a cease-fire and ended the assault on Gaza in January 2009, and it has been brokering talks between Hamas and Fatah, initiating and facilitating a national dialogue to help them reach an agreement on the reunification of the Palestinian polity.

Syria is another player with important mediation capacity thanks largely to its various security agencies. Damascus maintains ties with various militant groups that it hosts on its territory, including Hamas, Hezbollah, Baathist and other groups fighting the U.S. occupation in Iraq, and the Kurdistan Workers' Party (PKK), and it has built a strategic relationship with Iran. These ties have often served as assets that Damascus chooses to deliver in a quid pro quo arrangement, but they may also be assets that Damascus is saving for a grand regional bargain.

These different assets are skillfully combined by other smaller players. Qatar, for example, has specialized in cultivating ties with everyone and using its small size as an asset, as no party can suspect it of pursuing a hegemonic agenda. It is capable of mobilizing its broad network of very diverse relations to convene meetings of opposing factions, offer financial support, and present itself as a neutral broker. Examples include the meetings held in Doha that involved Lebanese factions, Palestinian groups, and Sudanese warring forces. Qatar also maintains close ties with Islamists of all brands, including the most radical ones, by broadcasting their messages through programs on Aljazeera and by offering asylum to the influential Egyptian sheikh Yusuf al-Qaradawi. This allowed Doha to secure Qaradawi's involvement in mediation efforts with radical Sunni Islamists to obtain the release of French hostages held in Iraq in 2007.

Tribal Ties

Tribal relations play a discreet but important role in diffusing tensions, maintaining stability, building alliances, and organizing security across the region. They reflect the strong subnational loyalties that continue to prevail across the borders of the nation-states, though they are hardly mentioned by the media or by governments who leverage them when needed. For example, the commerce between Berber tribes in Morocco and Algeria, the Shummar tribe in Syria and Iraq, and the numerous tribes sitting across both sides of the state borders in the Arabian Peninsula have a life of their own and can be mobilized for security or manipulation purposes. Saudi Arabia relies heavily on intertribal connections first and foremost to ensure its domestic stability but also to secure its border with Jordan, to mediate between Yemeni factions, and to interfere in Iraq. The role of Iraqi tribes in organizing the *sahwa* (awakening) groups that cut across the religious and ideological cleavages of Sunnis and Shias and Baathists and Islamists since 2007 is probably the most recent astonishing example of the significance of tribal relations.

Alternative Regional Security Frameworks

A U.S.-Led Security Order

In the face of an imminent threat or an open crisis, Arab capacity to intervene is limited and reliance on outside support has become the norm. Arab governments are often accused of having no desire for local ownership in managing their security together. They respond positively to calls for participating in peacekeeping operations in remote areas when asked by the United Nations or a U.S.-led multinational force but cannot mobilize the needed political will to collectively deploy peacekeeping forces in a conflict situation that affects their own region.

The Middle East has in many ways become a part of the United States' backyard. The region is organized around the presence of the United States as a full player, not only as a strategic force to protect the region as a last resort but as a party that makes political decisions, cuts deals directly with local groups inside the countries of the region, and ensures security on a daily basis. Examples have multiplied, especially since the end of the Cold War: the United States has supported and armed the Iraqi Sunni tribes of the *sahwa* to turn against the extremist groups that organize the military attacks on U.S. forces; trained security units and cooperated with intelligence agencies across the region, from the Gulf to North Africa, including Yemen, Egypt, Lebanon, and Algeria in the name of the "war on terror"; and actively opposed the Saudi-brokered agreement between Hamas and Fatah in Mecca to form a national unity government, which ended with Hamas's coup to take over Gaza in June 2007.

Any change of government in a key allied country of the United States, such as Egypt, Saudi Arabia, the other Gulf countries, or Morocco, is addressed directly by the United States as a major security issue. Arab societies believe that the United States will always have its say in ensuring a peaceful transition in any given Arab country, in recognizing a new government, or in denying power to forces that Washington deems hostile.

Anti-American feelings have grown accordingly among large sections of the public,[13] which criticize their governments for pursing U.S. interests and for the loss of sovereign decision making. This is especially true in the countries that experienced a struggle for independence from colonial or mandatory powers. Egyptians, Jordanians, and Yemenis resent Washington's heavy-handedness in their domestic affairs, such as in promoting democracy under or fighting terrorism. Religious leaders with their popular militant discourse are largely responsible for giving these sentiments a cultural and religious spin. Hence, Arab governments frequently express a duplicity in their attitudes and actions. For example, in the two wars against Iraq in 1991 and 2003, Arab governments were calling for a diplomatic solution while actively cooperating with U.S. forces to prepare for the war.

Military operations are launched or commanded from U.S. bases in Gulf countries, and the regional base of the U.S. Central Command has been headquartered in Qatar since it was moved from Saudi Arabia in the mid-1990s. Meanwhile, countries that are at peace with Israel—namely, Egypt and Jordan—have enhanced their security cooperation with the United States, Europe, and NATO through joint military exercises, further weakening the prospect of building an autonomous regional capacity. Given this heavy dependence on outside capacity, there is a growing tendency to resort to ad hoc frameworks and informal arrangements where outside powers can bring their influence to bear without arousing criticism about the legitimacy of their participation.

Ad Hoc Frameworks for Grand Bargains

The end of the Cold War is remembered in the Arab world as being marked by the first experience of a multinational coalition, which used military power to oust Iraq from Kuwait in early 1991. This war was followed immediately by the establishment of a multilateral forum to address the Arab-Israeli conflict—namely, the Madrid Conference, which launched the peace process in October 1991. Another interesting model was the short-lived attempt in 2006 to seek a solution to stabilize Iraq by bringing together Arab states with other regional players and outside powers.

Although neither resulted in a successful settlement of conflict, these two ad hoc frameworks seem to provide convenient settings in that they do not require an oath of loyalty from participating states toward the origins, the mission, and the legitimacy of the framework. They are pragmatic settings that allow all participating actors to bring their assets to the table: those who can commit to refrain from using their nuisance capacity, those who can facilitate a settlement, those who have the capacity to coerce, and those who can provide the means to implement a settlement. All participating countries commit to contribute to the resolution of the given issue through concrete measures, such as by controlling their borders, stemming the flow of arms, exerting their influence on some parties, committing to cease manipulating proxies, or providing financial and economic assets. The presence of outside actors is not a contentious issue due to the temporary nature of the framework. Because they allow for the development of bilateral and multilateral tracks simultaneously, these ad hoc frameworks are well suited to secure the multiple responses needed for a settlement.

The forum to stabilize Iraq in 2006 followed the recommendations of the Baker-Hamilton Iraq Study Group report but was suspended soon after it started. The commitment of the Bush administration at the time to work through such a multilateral framework lacked seriousness. Another key reason was the deadlock in the 5+1 negotiations with Iran on its nuclear program. Nevertheless, it seems that the best prospects to secure the right conditions for the reconstruction of a stable political formula and security order in Iraq would be to renew the experience. It would include all Arab and non-Arab neighboring countries, in addition to the full participation of the United States, Europe, and Russia. Through a comprehensive discussion, Syria might be willing to pledge to control the movement of fighters into Iraq; Saudi Arabia would use its influence on the Sunnis to secure their cooperation in a power-sharing arrangement; Iran would do the same with the Shia groups that it controls or can influence; and Turkey would ensure stability at its borders with Iraqi Kurdistan. International powers and the United Nations would need to ensure that any regional agreement is guaranteed internationally and to offer the rewards that the regional players expect in return for their contribution. Syria wants a commitment from the United States to restart negotiations with Israel on the return of the Golan and a similar commitment from both the United States and France to respect Syrian interests and influence in Lebanon. Likewise, Iran would likely pledge to play a constructive role and not pursue a hegemonic scheme if the United States gave it what it wants—namely, the recognition of its right to enrich uranium, the lifting of sanctions, and the recognition of its role as a major regional power.

Similarly, after eight years of unsuccessful efforts by the Bush administration to broker a settlement of the Israeli-Palestinian conflict, an ad hoc structure appears again as the only operational framework to revive the peace process. Arab states, while they have a lot to offer to make a peace agreement successful, know that they do not hold the keys to a solution. The Arab League has consistently tried to push for reintroducing the issue into the United Nations in order to involve all members of the Security Council and to ensure that negotiations would be based on UN resolutions. In the face of U.S. resistance, at least until the election of Barack Obama, they focused instead on pressing the United States to invest serious and sustained efforts into brokering a settlement.

The Madrid Conference of 1991 and the architecture of negotiations that was built on combined bilateral and multilateral tracks of negotiation allowed all players, regional and international, who had something to offer to participate. This structure also offered the needed flexibility to pursue bilateral issues through autonomous tracks and to connect with the other tracks when needed. Attempts at reviving this model are periodically discussed by the members of the Quartet (the United States, the European Union, Russia, and the United Nations). To succeed, the structure would need to include Iran one way or another. The United States, with support from Europe and possibly NATO, could offer the security guarantees that Israel and the newly created Palestinian state expect and Arab governments could offer normalization and trade relations to Israel and financial support for both the Palestinian state and the rehabilitation of Palestinian refugees. Saudi Arabia, Jordan, Egypt, and Morocco, as key Muslim countries, would be able to grant Islamic legitimacy to a compromise agreement on Jerusalem. The Arab plan of 2007 spells out all the measures that the Arab countries are ready to undertake to consolidate bilateral agreements between Israel and the Palestinians, Israel and Syria, and Israel and Lebanon should such agreements be reached.

Today more than ever before, there is a wide international consensus that only through internationalization of the Israeli-Palestinian issue, including direct international presence on the ground, will there be a chance to settle the conflict. As much as they are opposed to the principle of right to intervention, Arab countries have been actively calling for such an intervention. If successful, a grand bargain within such an ad hoc structure might provide the building blocks for a new regional security framework with a more permanent mission.

The Region and New International Legal Norms

The global debate over humanitarian intervention is a good example of how the region refuses to engage in discussions on international legal norms and how this has precluded the scholarly community's efforts at conducting well-informed research and articulating in some constructive manner what the Arabs want and do not want from humanitarian intervention. The knee-jerk reaction from both governments and the public in the Arab world has been to reject outright the very notion of humanitarian intervention for fear that it might be misused or open the door to legitimizing foreign interventions.

Humanitarian Intervention and the Responsibility to Protect

Humanitarian intervention articulated after the end of the Cold War through debates on the "right" or the "duty"[14] to intervene (later replaced with the principle of the "responsibility to protect," or R2P) is seen as a problematic norm by governments and the security intelligentsia alike for several reasons.

First, the principle of humanitarian intervention defines human rights as the overriding paradigm that ought to prevail over all other principles and guide the international order. Arab refusal to endorse it is not based on some cultural or ideological rejection of human rights as a value as much as on the widespread anxiety over the stability, territorial integrity, and national cohesion of states. While the Arab world sees that intervention might save a group or a community in danger, it realizes it creates large-scale destruction for the nation as a whole.

Second, this recent norm introduced by Western powers, without much consultation, as the Arab governments and security intelligentsia see it, opens the door to various forms of manipulation. As one progressive secular thinker put it in a discussion, giving priority to humanitarian law carries the danger of encouraging hard-liners within ethnic minorities to exacerbate tensions deliberately with their governments and to provoke the state into using its armed forces against the minority in the hope of attracting foreign intervention against the state.[15] The argument of the perverse effect of humanitarian intervention (or the "moral hazard," to use the words of Alan Kuperman) is not only set forth by the authoritarian rulers of the region but also by Western scholars and Arab democrats for reasons that cannot be easily dismissed.[16]

Third, the question of which authority decides on humanitarian intervention has occupied a central position in the Arab debate, especially as it took place against the backdrop of the invasion of Iraq. Arab states (just like many other countries of the South) consider that only the UN Security Council is entitled to decide on intervention and must do so under strict conditions and that if the members of the council fail to come to an agreement, humanitarian intervention should simply not take place, whatever the human cost of not intervening. For them, this is preferable to carrying out an intervention on inappropriate legal and political grounds.[17]

Fourth and most importantly, humanitarian intervention is seen as being applied selectively: Arab states and publics claim that the West only invokes human rights violations in the cases of small states or unfriendly regimes, just as the West chooses to punish "rogue states" in order to bring them in line with its strategy.

Whether it is out of nationalism, a desire to keep society under control, or a fear of disintegration of the state, the Arab world remains averse to recognizing the diversity of most societies of the region and granting specific rights to their minorities. The intellectual community has yet to come up with a middle-ground proposition that responds to the intrusive principle of humanitarian intervention without playing into the hands of the region's authoritarian leaders.

Human Security

Human security is an uneasy norm to operationalize and is a challenging concept for authoritarian governments. While it sets the state as the main provider of security, it also puts limitations on its power by challenging the idea that the state is the sole legitimate protector of its population. Massive violations of human rights take on an international scope and open the way for foreign intervention when a population's survival and vital needs are in danger. In fact, the responsibility to protect has imposed itself as a natural corollary of human security. The two concepts were in effect integrated in the final document of the United Nations' world summit in September 2005.[18]

The Arab countries are not alone in questioning the concept of human security. India, China, and many countries of the South consider human security as a concept designed to lay the ground for imposing Western models on the rest of the world. But as in many other debates, Arab experts representing their governments have only marginally been involved in the global discussions. The governments' reluctance to engage stemmed from a combination of lack of trust in the law-making process, lack of self-confidence in their ability to push back foreign schemes, and, most importantly, the governments' fear of losing their exclusive control over their societies. The reluctance is clearly more about preserving the authoritarian nature of their regime than about protecting their sovereignty and territorial integrity.

While the development community has embraced the concept of human security because it builds useful linkages between quality of governance, development, and issues of stability and security,[19] it is treated with suspicion by control-minded governments that see it as a tool for legitimizing foreign intervention.

Three Cases

A brief account of three recent crises and Arab responses to them will serve to illustrate Arab governments' priorities, the regional capacity (or lack thereof) to manage crises, and the way the Arab world relates to new norms in international relations.

Gaza, Egypt, and the Responsibility to Protect

Israel's war on Gaza was the most serious crisis in Egyptian-Israeli relations since the signing of the Camp David Treaty. Over the eighteen months that preceded the attack, the Egyptian security forces had "failed" to stop the smuggling of arms through Sinai into Gaza and the government in Cairo was unable to broker a compromise between the Palestinian factions.

When the attack was staged by Israel, the Egyptian government and security establishment realized that what was at stake was the rank of Egypt among America's allies in the region. It was the second most important recipient of U.S. assistance in the world and had the paramount mandate of protecting Israel's security. A majority in Egypt, from government and society alike, believed that losing this rank was a legitimate national security concern that could not be sacrificed for solidarity with the Palestinians. The Egyptian government was willing to join in the formulation of statements of solidarity by the Arab League, but it was determined to follow its own track of full cooperation with Israeli and American demands for security arrangements on its soil. Egypt's response was to request the deployment of European and Turkish security teams to assist its forces, but the decisive measure that ended the crisis seems to have been the U.S.-Israeli agreement (signed between Israeli foreign minister Tzipi Livni and U.S. secretary of state Condoleezza Rice) to provide technical and military assistance to secure the border from the Egyptian side, though Egypt denies having signed such an agreement.

The crisis served to highlight severe weaknesses on several levels: the absence of crisis management mechanisms within the Arab framework; the priority given to strictly national interests rather than broader pan-Arab security, which was certainly at stake in this situation; and the failure of Arab governments to invoke international norms—in this case, the responsibility to protect—that may have been used to the benefit of the Palestinians.

Iraqi Kurds and Humanitarian Intervention

One case that shaped Arab attitudes vis-à-vis humanitarian intervention is the experience of the Kurds of Iraq. In April 1991, the Security Council adopted UN Resolution 688. Although it was not passed under Chapter VII of the Charter, it was interpreted by the Kurds of Iraq as opening the way for foreign intervention to protect human rights in Iraq and to put the Kurdish issue on the agenda of the international community.

The Kurds of Iraq had suffered under Saddam Hussein's regime and even been gassed with chemical weapons in the town of Halabja, raising limited protest from neighboring countries, which had accepted the Iraqi government's view that the country was at war and needed to defend its national integrity. The Kurds of Iraq came to loathe not only the Iraqi government but Arab nationalism altogether, which made no room for the basic needs of the diverse communities and numerous minorities that compose this imagined pan-Arab nation. They were therefore determined to seek protection and support from outside in order to build a safe Kurdish region in the north that would hold enough assets, mainly oil, and a military force of its own to put them in a position to negotiate with the central government in Baghdad the best terms for an autonomous status within the larger Iraqi entity.

The ambiguity between the protection of human rights and the support for the Kurds' right to self-determination prevailed throughout the twelve years between the 1991 war and the 2003 invasion. While the Iraqi regime and the population of the rest of Iraq were subjected to harsh sanctions, the Kurds received generous support from outside the region to develop a de facto national entity in the north of Iraq. From the protection of the Kurds as a humanitarian issue, the situation shifted to one of their right to self-determination and to choose freely to join in an Iraqi federation. As the Kurdish entity was being built, it seemed to be predetermining the future Iraqi political system by leaving no other option but that of a loose federation.

The case of Iraqi Kurdistan contributed to building suspicion among Arabs vis-à-vis the rights of minorities, the intentions of hostile powers, and the principle of humanitarian intervention.[20] The Kurdish issue continues to be discussed as a regional issue that ought to be managed by the four countries concerned (Turkey, Iraq, Iran, and Syria), with the primary objective of preserving the territorial status quo and the national interests of the states.

Darfur and the Responsibility to Protect

Darfur is the most recent and painful case of Arab rejection of the principle of humanitarian intervention and responsibility to protect since this new principle was adopted by the international community. The crisis raises a set of disturbing questions for which there are no simple answers: Why is the issue of Darfur sidelined in the public debate in Arab countries despite its gravity? What is the level of tolerance among Arab public opinion of violence against civilian populations? Is there no limit of any sort that Arabs see as legitimate to impose on sovereignty? And finally, why are Arab governments protecting Omar al-Bashir's regime in Sudan when they silently acquiesced to the overthrow of Saddam's regime in Iraq?

The consensus among Arab governments is that as sovereign countries, they are responsible for their populations. They therefore treated the Darfur crisis as a Sudanese internal affair and continued to deny the massive human suffering there, hoping that the Sudanese government would handle the crisis alone. The Arab League thus rejected UN resolutions related to sanctions and the deployment of international peacekeeping forces and voted against the proposed UN commission to investigate allegations of genocide.

The failure of the Arab League to take action in the face of an intolerable humanitarian situation resulted in a full transfer of the Darfur issue to the United Nations. When the African Union–United Nations Hybrid Operation in Darfur (UNAMID) was deployed, the Arab League did not contribute any forces and failed to pay the amounts it had pledged for its operation.

The Arab attitude on Darfur is a combination of the usual reflex of protecting fellow authoritarian regimes on the one hand and panic in the face of the risk that Sudan might become another Iraq on the other hand. The precedent of Iraq goes a long way in explaining why Arab countries in the case of Sudan were not persuaded by the mere idea that the international community had a responsibility to protect. As one Sudanese scholar put it, "their position was shaped by the idea of the alleged conspiracy to divide Sudan in addition to doubts over an effective international role, given the developments in Palestine and Iraq."[21]

The Darfur crisis occurred against the backdrop of negotiations over the future of the country and the possibility of secession by southern Sudan following a referendum scheduled in 2011. The fear of a possible collapse of Sudan and its partition remains strong among both Arab governing elites and Arab intellectuals and publics.

Conclusion

The repeated failures to manage crises within an Arab regional framework have led to a transfer of this responsibility to the international level, thus increasing the role of outside powers and postponing the pressing discussion about the need for concrete measures to enhance the indigenous capacity to provide security. The 2003 Iraq War was as equally traumatic for Arab leaders as it was for their societies. It bred a sense of overwhelming disempowerment that left Arab governments in disarray.

The Arab states enjoy a wide range of means to mediate between parties to a conflict, to facilitate dialogue, and to offer incentives and guarantees. Their contribution can be effective to deflect tension before violence erupts. But they appear helpless, divided, and destitute when a crisis breaks out that requires urgent action. The inability to agree on intervention in a conflict by putting together a peacekeeping force, for example, is not so much due to a lack of means as to a deficit of trust among governments and to the persistent fear of creating precedents that might subsequently be used against them.

Arab countries are unlikely to develop a regional capacity at their own initiative. They will need the mothering of the United States for efficacy, the support of all members of the Security Council for legitimacy, and the participation of non-Arab countries of the region for relevancy. While the participation of Israel in a regional security arrangement is unlikely as long as the Arab-Israeli conflict is not settled, the inclusion of Turkey and Iran seems inevitable.

The development of an Arab capacity to manage conflicts and develop a regional security framework, with the participation of non-Arab neighbors when appropriate, hinges on three prerequisites:

1. Arabs should engage in the global debate on changing international norms and break away from the intellectually inhibiting syndrome of falling prey to plans developed outside the region. They need to participate in international debates on security and articulate their vision and ideas rather than remain on the defensive in an attempt to protect their sovereign rights and to run their domestic affairs in isolation from changes in international norms—all while relying on outside protection for their security.

2. Arabs should consider the examples of their non-Arab neighbors. Experience shows that when a government's definition of national interests and national security is broadly shared by its public, it is able to make its case in foreign policy, resist foreign demands, and take initiatives much more effectively than oil-replete but fearful monarchies. Although Arab societies and governments would refuse to view Israel as a relevant model, the government of Turkey, especially since the Justice and Development Party (AKP) was elected in 2002, has developed a highly dynamic and creative diplomacy across the region, as a mediator, facilitator, and advocate of regional cooperation for conflict management. Turkey seems more capable of asserting its national interests and resisting foreign pressure than any of its Arab neighbors. For example, although a member of NATO, Turkey refused to grant U.S. warplanes permission to use its air bases for attacking Iraq in 2003, arguing that this did not serve its national interests and would not be accepted by its public.

    As for Iran, the severe political crisis that followed the presidential election of June 2009 does not seem to have affected its capacity to assert its claim to a full nuclear program. President Mahmoud Ahmadinejad knows his reelection was contested by large sections of the public and part of the political establishment, but he also knows for sure that the national nuclear program has very wide support within Iranian society. Iran's position on its right to enrich uranium has therefore not changed one iota. Because the issue touches on national pride, society is likely to continue to rally behind its leadership. There is little hope that Iran's position on the nuclear issue will be significantly affected by the domestic protests of the summer of 2009. Increased leniency or radicalization of the regime will depend more on the prospects of negotiations with the United States and Europe and on regional considerations than on internal developments.

3. Last but not least, the conflicts that require international involvement must be managed with the direct and sustained implication of the United States and other international powers. Ending the conflict between Israel and its neighbors, reconstructing a stable Iraq, and reaching a compromise agreement on Iran's nuclear program are the three main security challenges that Arab countries cannot address on their own and that will continue to hamper the development of a regional capacity to manage conflict. Even though President Obama kept to his commitment to withdraw the bulk of U.S. troops from Iraq in August 2010, their departure was hardly seen as an end of occupation and was met instead with much anxiety by many Iraqis and most Arab governments over the unfinished job of rebuilding a broken nation that the United States is leaving behind.

While the ad hoc structures proved successful in settling specific conflicts, only after the resolution of those three key security issues will the conditions be created for institutionalizing a regional security architecture and developing a capacity to manage conflicts. Until this happens, it is fair to say that Middle East security will remain inextricably linked to the strategic interests of the United States that require direct U.S. management.

What is needed are policies for sustainable, equitable, and democratic security. Security is not about boosting the safety of a narrow class of ruling elites through increasingly sophisticated and expensive defense and surveillance systems. It is about transforming relations between state and society, and actively involving different sections of society in the debate whose security is sought before deciding on which partners to involve and which equipment to purchase.

Changes are needed not only in institutions but in mind-sets. The visceral distrust of government within Arab societies and the distrust of societies by Arab governments will have to be replaced by a clear understanding that the absence of regional cooperation on security results in ever-growing penetration and manipulation by outside powers and an erosion of sovereignty for every country in the Arab world.

Postscript

Before the sweeping protests that began in early 2011, the Arab world seemed at an impasse.[22] This chapter has emphasized the structural weaknesses of Arab states in developing credible security arrangements, whether at the regional or subregional level. For the Middle East at large, the dilemma of what should come first, democracy or a solution to regional conflicts—first and foremost the Israeli-Palestinian conflict—is beginning to find an answer. Democratic changes will now precede peace.

Countries that have undergone a change of regime will most likely focus on domestic challenges, which are daunting. But domestic changes, particularly in the field of security sector governance, are likely to yield transformations in security perceptions. Bridging the gap between state and society on whose security is sought and developing a more inclusive understanding of security should result in embedding security more in the social fabric of the region. Practically speaking, the aspiration of Arab publics to see the Arab League fulfill its role as a framework for building effective collective security may lead to some progress, though it will probably take time before all countries adjust to this new reality. Security agreements with neighbors and outside partners, including peace treaties with Israel, will cease to mean one leader delivering a whole society. Democratic Arab governments will need to go through the laborious process of marketing any strategic commitments to the approval of their people. In the end, Israel will have the promise of real peace and normalization with its neighbors, something it had given up on because it could avoid paying the necessary price by dealing with autocratic leaders who promised to muzzle public opinion. This minimum price has not changed; it has only become nonnegotiable.

Reconciling governments with their societies will likely result in more assertive foreign policies and, ultimately, in strengthening regional capacity to manage crises. The long-term trend points in the right direction, but many hurdles remain.

Notes

1. Saadeddin Ibrahim, "Ethnic Conflict and State Building in the Arab World," *International Social Science Journal* no. 156 (1998), www.zionalert.com/ecasbitaw.pdf.

2. "The Failed States Index 2009," *Foreign Policy*, June 22, 2009, www.foreignpolicy.com/articles/2009/06/22/2009_failed_states_index_interactive_map_and_rankings.

3. George Perkovich, "Nuclear Developments in the GCC: Risks and Trends," in *Gulf Yearbook 2007–2008* (Dubai: Gulf Research Centre, 2008).

4. The Tripartite Agreement of 1950 was a joint statement issued by the United States, Britain, and France that guaranteed the territorial status quo determined by Arab-Israeli armistice agreements in 1949 and formally placed an embargo on weapons deliveries to

the countries involved in the Arab-Israeli conflict. The "Czech arms deal" of September 1955, by means of which the Soviet Union agreed to sell Egypt $250 million worth of modern weaponry, made irrelevant Western efforts to limit arms transfers to the region and effectively brought the agreement to an end. See www.palestinefacts.org/pf_1948to1967_tripartite_1949.php.

5. Its destruction was completed by a U.S. attack during the 1991 Gulf War.

6. See the interview of Azmi Bishara by Hashem Qasem (in Arabic), in *Al Mustaqbal al Arabi* (The Arab Future) no. 357 (November 2008), www.caus.org.lb/Home/index.php? Lang=en.

7. For an account of how and why the Egyptian jihadist groups renounced violence by the lawyer of the key leaders of the movements, see Montasir al-Zayat, *Al Jama'aat al-Islamyia. Ru'ya Minal Dakhel* (Islamic Groups: A Vision from Inside) (Cairo: Dar Masr el Mahrousa, 2005).

8. Arab countries have reiterated their intention to develop a joint military capacity. In March 1991, after the conclusion of the Persian Gulf War, the six members of the GCC, together with Egypt and Syria, declared their intention to establish a deterrent force to protect Kuwait, with Egypt and Syria providing the bulk of the troops. Kuwait signed a defense pact with the United States shortly after and the Arab force never came to fruition.

9. Amr Moussa advocated for the establishment of a forum for regional cooperation in his opening speech of the Arab League summit of March 2010 in Tripoli and in several public lectures. See "PO: Amr Moussa prône le dialogue arabo-iranien," *Ria Novosti*, March 27, 2010, http://fr.rian.ru/world/20100327/186336852.html.

10. Prince Saud al-Faisal, in a Minister of Foreign Affairs press conference that followed the Saudi decision to boycott the Arab League summit in Damascus, on March 29, 2008, www.mofa.gov.sa/Detail.asp?InNewsItemID=77461.

11. The creation of the Peninsula Shield Force with 10,000 troops was decided in 1982, mainly in response to the Iran-Iraq War, www.globalsecurity.org/military/world/gulf/gcc.htm.

12. The OIC summit in Dakar in March 2008 endorsed the Arab Peace Initiative of 2007 in which all members of the Arab League committed to enter into a peace agreement with Israel and establish normal relations with it once a comprehensive settlement of the Arab-Israeli conflict is reached, www.oic-oci.org/is11/english/FC-11-%20SUMMIT-en.pdf.

13. See the regional public opinion survey titled "Revisiting the Arab Street: Research from Within," Center for Strategic Studies of the University of Jordan, November 2006, www.css-jordan.org/SubDefault.aspx.

14. The "duty to intervene" was an expression used with regard to the Balkans in the early 1990s by several Western politicians and representatives of humanitarian nongovernmental organizations, among them Bernard Kouchner, then head of Médecins sans Frontières (Doctors without Borders).

15. Discussion within the Working Group on Sovereignty and Intervention, the International Institute for Strategic Studies (IISS) and the Gulf Research Center, Dubai, February 2003.

16. "The Moral Hazard of Humanitarian Intervention: Lessons from the Balkans," *International Studies Quarterly* 52, no. 1 (March 2008), 49–80.

17. In a clear attempt to qualify the principle of human rights, a white paper was produced by a group of Egyptian diplomats and scholars and endorsed by the government that stresses the need to reach an international consensus on the norms, criteria, and modalities

of intervention, the irreplaceable role of the United Nations in mandating interventions, and "the necessity of accepting and tolerating cultural, social and economic diversity of states and societies." The document stresses the need to respect the sanctity of borders as enshrined in the charters of both the Arab League and the Africa Union. While it acknowledges that there may be extreme situations where a humanitarian disaster might require outside intervention, it stops short of spelling out what an Arab attitude would be in such cases. The document puts emphasis on preventive measures as the norm and on the prohibition of the use of force as the greatest achievement of the contemporary international legal order during the twentieth century. Mohamed Kadry Said, "Intervention in the Gulf" (white paper presented at the IISS workshop "Humanitarian Intervention: Arab Perspectives," Dubai, May 25–27, 2003).

18. UN Resolution 1674 on the Protection of Civilian Populations in Armed Conflicts, April 28, 2006.

19. UN Development Program (UNDP), *Arab Human Development Report 2009: Challenges to Human Security in the Arab Countries* (New York: UNDP, 2009), www.arab-hdr. org/contents/index.aspx?rid=5.

20. See Saad Eddin Ibrahim, "Minorities' Concerns in the Arab World," in *1993 Annual Report* (Cairo: Ibn Khaldoun Center, 1994). See also the brief reference to ethnic and minority rights in the Arab world in "About Us," Ibn Khaldun Centre Web site, www.eicds. org/english/introduction/about.htm.

21. Haydar Ibrahim Ali, "The Darfur Crisis and the Quest for an Arab Role," in *Gulf Yearbook 2007–2008* (Dubai: Gulf Research Centre, 2008), 307.

22. This chapter was written before the 2011 Egyptian revolution. This postscript was added while the manuscript was in production to allow the author an opportunity to reflect briefly on what impact this and other related events would have on regional security.

10

Play It Again, Uncle Sam

Transatlantic Relations, NATO, and the European Union

Chantal de Jonge Oudraat

Much has been written about transatlantic—that is, U.S.-European—relations. Much of this literature focuses on institutions in general and NATO in particular. Indeed, throughout the Cold War, NATO was central to the transatlantic relationship—it provided tangible proof of the United States' commitment to the defense of Western Europe from both external and internal threats and provided a collective defense mechanism for sharing the burdens of security. With the disappearance of the Soviet threat and the advance of European integration efforts, the rationales for such a commitment became less compelling. Many predicted the demise of NATO and the transatlantic relationship.[1] While this has not yet happened, concern over the future of NATO is justified. It is telling that both France's return to the integrated military structures of NATO and the sixtieth anniversary of NATO, both in April 2009, were for the most part ignored by U.S. and European media. In addition, in the run-up to NATO's anniversary celebration, think tanks on both sides of the Atlantic argued that NATO and the transatlantic relationship would not survive the division among its members in Afghanistan. To many observers, Afghanistan "had become the crucible for the Alliance."[2] In addition, the war in Georgia in August 2008 laid bare deep divisions among NATO allies on how to deal with the alliance's former nemesis—Russia.

There is no question that the tepid response by NATO allies to calls, by the United States and the NATO secretary general, for additional troops in Afghanistan, that the unwillingness of allies to share risks equally, and that the failure of NATO countries to articulate a common Russia policy will have important and long-lasting effects on the alliance and may hasten the organization's demise. That said, to view the transatlantic relationship through the prism of NATO is reductionist and misguided. NATO is no longer the centerpiece of the transatlantic security community, and it is becoming less and less important as time goes by. The barometer of transatlantic relations will be increasingly based on how the United States and the European Union are cooperating.

There are three major reasons why NATO has become a less central player in transatlantic relations. First, the absence of any major security threat in Europe and the improbability that the U.S. and European allies will confront Russia militarily, and vice versa, make NATO as a regional defense alliance somewhat irrelevant. No longer is the survival of Europe premised on the military presence of the United States in Europe. Second, for many NATO allies, global or "out-of-area" activities such as the one in Afghanistan do not involve essential security interests. The inability of NATO to deploy sufficient troops in Afghanistan and the unwillingness of allies to share risks equally attest to this fact. Third, the changing nature of security threats in the twenty-first century, particularly terrorism and the threat of failed and failing states, require whole-of-government responses—that is, they require a mix of social, economic, and military responses. As a military organization, NATO is ill-suited to respond to such threats. Ultimately, the changed security environment has made NATO a less-compelling policy instrument for both the United States and European countries.

The European Union, on the other hand, has since the 1990s steadily put into place dedicated institutional mechanisms and developed military and civilian capabilities to deal with conflict prevention and crisis management. Efforts to develop a security component of the European Union took off with the creation in 1991 of a Common Foreign and Security Policy (CFSP) and the launch in 1998 of the European Security and Defense Policy (ESDP). Finally, in 2010, the union equipped itself with new institutional structures aimed at engendering more effective decision making and enhancing the role of Europe as a global actor.[3] Although European integration efforts are moving in fits and starts and defense efforts remain limited compared to the European Union's economic strength, such efforts have come a long way since 1989 and are on an upward trajectory.

While the United States is a prominent member of NATO—if not the most prominent one—it is not a member of the European Union. American attitudes toward greater European integration and the development of an autonomous European defense capability have seen considerable change from highly skeptical and wariness in the 1990s to reluctant acceptance and embrace in 2009. As Americans have realized that the buildup of European capabilities in the military field is progressing slowly and is not a threat to NATO, they have become less anxious about an EU military capability. In addition, as the political balance of power in Europe has changed—notably through the EU enlargement process—the fear of an anti-American EU caucus in NATO has receded to the background; many new EU members are fierce Atlanticists. Over time, U.S. officials have steadily come to accept the idea that a strong Europe, including a militarily strong Europe, is in the U.S. interest—the United States and NATO cannot be in all places at all times. The development of a serious EU defense force, if done right, could be "a good thing for all concerned—reducing American burdens in Europe, making Europe a better and more capable partner, and providing a way for Europeans to tackle security problems where and when the US cannot or will not get involved."[4] Some U.S. officials have also come to recognize that any hope for developing European military capabilities comes through the development of ESDP, that is, the pooling of European national defense capabilities.[5] Finally, the experiences in Iraq and Afghanistan have made the United States increasingly aware that military power alone is not enough to deal with the many security challenges of the twenty-first century. American policymakers increasingly recognize that contemporary security challenges call for a mix of military and civilian instruments—a mix of hard and soft power. They also recognize that the European Union can make an important contribution in terms of the latter.

NATO's diminishing importance and the European Union's growing role as an international actor require the United States and Europe to redefine their relationship. There are good reasons for a continuing strong transatlantic relationship. First, the overall strategic objectives of the United States and Europe are largely the same—peace and stability, the spread of free markets and democracy, and respect for human rights. Second, there is a great deal of agreement between the United States and most European countries regarding the nature of the threats and challenges in the twenty-first century. The proliferation of weapons of mass destruction, global terrorism, and failed and failing states top the lists of security challenges on both sides of the Atlantic. There is also increasing convergence regarding the importance of stabilizing the Middle East, concern about autocratic tendencies in Russia, and the necessity of dealing with the rise of China. Third, many of the global and transnational challenges cannot be dealt with by one power alone. They require concerted multilateral efforts. Europe and America have a track record of working together and successes to draw on. Together they can help shape norms and practices to deal with these challenges. Fourth, concerted actions in response to such challenges will have greater legitimacy worldwide, particularly if such actions are not seen as the West uniting against "the rest." A 2007 poll by the European Council on Foreign Relations and Gallup based on interviews with 57,000 people from fifty-two countries found that "35% of respondents believed a rise in the EU's global influence would contribute to the world becoming a better place, against 20% who wanted to see its power decline."[6] Fifth, the United States and Europe are the major international donors for humanitarian aid and development assistance. To avoid duplication and waste—or aid working at cross purposes—it is key that policies are coordinated. Sixth, joint U.S.-EU actions should help share operational burdens. In sum, the basis and rationales for a solid relationship between the United States and Europe exist. But partnerships require care, commitment, and periodic readjustments.

The greatest challenge the United States and Europe will face in the years ahead is not that they no longer share a common view of the world and occupy different planets—Mars and Venus—or that they have increasingly diverging interests: the main challenge is that Europe is divided.[7] The recent growth of the European Union has contributed to greater internal divisions. Between 1995 and 2007, it grew from twelve to twenty-seven members.[8] The addition of ten new members in 2004 taxed the union in terms of political cohesion, as well as in terms of institutional capacities. Efforts to equip it with institutions and coherent tools to make it a better organized and more effective international actor for the twenty-first century took close to ten years.[9] The lack of political cohesion and inadequate institutional structures often led to slow and at times incoherent policy responses on the part of the European Union and its members.[10] They also make it irresistible for Americans to adopt a "divide-and-rule" policy, even if a more unified policy toward the European Union would be in the United States' interest.[11]

Transatlantic relations are also challenged because of the huge discrepancy between U.S. and European military capabilities. As a result, Americans and Europeans respond to many international challenges—from Afghanistan and China to Russia and Iran—with different levels of intensity and with different policy preferences.

Finally, transatlantic relations suffer from public disengagement. Neither NATO nor the European Union generates much public interest in either the United States or Europe. Many Europeans see NATO as a relic of the Cold War and an instrument of U.S. dominance, and they question European engagement in Afghanistan. EU member states have a hard time convincing their publics that investments in defense spending are not luxuries but conditions for defending the European *"acquis."*[12] Many Americans see the European Union as an inward-looking, squabbling group of states. Even the informed in Washington "continue to view Europe as comprised of independent nation states, or they see it through the prism of key allies and NATO. Some policymakers still think of the EU as merely a common market ... and fail to appreciate the political, economic, military and security assets that the EU increasingly controls or coordinates."[13] Many in Washington see the European Union as "not a lot more than a trade organization."[14] Unfortunately, many Europeans have a similar uninformed and often negative view of Brussels. Politicians on both sides of the Atlantic have been unable to articulate coherent organizational visions of the future for NATO or the European Union. Not surprisingly, a vision of transatlantic relations also remains wanting.

This chapter first examines recent developments in NATO and the European Union and outlines the challenges these organizations face, paying particular attention to U.S.-European relations. It then examines the obstacles for better cooperation between NATO and the European Union and concludes by arguing that together the United States and Europe can be a formidable force for peace. While European interest in U.S. "strategic reassurance" will continue, the Europeans must, "as time goes by," develop a stronger united voice.[15]

NATO: An "Encore"

Ever since the fall of the Berlin Wall in 1989, NATO has been looking for new missions. Throughout most of the 1990s, there were three main schools of thought on NATO's missions and future. Pessimists believed that, with the end of the Cold War and the disappearance of the Soviet Union, NATO had lost its main mission of collective self-defense—its raison d'être—and they consequently expected NATO would disappear as well. Maximalists advocated that, with the disappearance of NATO's traditional mission, NATO would have to develop new missions and go "out of area" or "out of business." NATO expansion was a key element of NATO's new mission to stabilize countries outside the territory of its members, particularly in the Balkans.[16] Minimalists argued that NATO should focus on its core missions—self-defense and strategic reassurance in Europe—and not get involved in missions or operations outside of Europe.

The pessimist's perspective has receded over time. Few people today think that NATO is on the verge of disappearing. Even so, NATO's member states remain deeply divided between the maximalist and minimalist schools of thought with respect to three issues: missions, membership, and military capabilities.

Most of NATO's new member states are minimalists. They believe that NATO should focus on its core mission of collective self-defense—that is, Article 5 missions. For them, Russia remains a real and growing security concern. Among new NATO members, there is very little support for missions in distant places such as Afghanistan. A June 2008 poll by Pew reported that only 24 percent of Poles supported the deployment of NATO troops in Afghanistan; 65 percent of those surveyed believed that NATO troops should be withdrawn.[17] NATO's new members are open to the possibility of NATO membership for other European countries, such as Ukraine and Georgia, but they do not favor global NATO membership.

The maximalists—led by the United States, the United Kingdom, Canada, and former and current NATO secretary generals Jaap de Hoop Scheffer and Anders Fogh Rasmussen—believe that most of the security threats facing the transatlantic community emanate from outside Europe. They consequently believe that NATO has to adopt a global orientation to deal with these threats. For maximalists, the terrorist attacks of September 11, 2001, ended the debate over NATO's mission. For maximalists, NATO must go "out of area" to deal with the security challenges that migrate around a globalized world. They are eager to turn NATO from a defensive regional alliance into a global intervention force. Many maximalists favor global membership for the alliance. They believe that special partnerships, if not full membership, should be extended to like-minded democracies such as Australia, New Zealand, and South Korea.

NATO's main continental members—that is, France and Germany—straddle the minimalist and maximalist positions. France, which rejoined NATO's integrated military structure in 2009, has a global strategic outlook, but at the same time Paris is focused very much on Europe. Building up Europe's defense capabilities is a priority. France also remains deeply committed to retaining its independent nuclear posture. Finally, although France is the fourth most important troop contributor in Afghanistan, this operation is not a top priority in Paris. As far as NATO membership is concerned, France is definitely a minimalist; it has no enthusiasm for global membership.

Germany has similarly ambiguous positions. Germany is the third-largest troop contributor to the NATO operation in Afghanistan, but it has limited the type of actions German troops can engage in. Berlin also blocks debates in NATO on energy security. Germany is highly dependent on Russia for energy supplies, and it does not want to take actions that would upset Moscow. In terms of membership, Germany like France is a minimalist, and its actions at NATO's 2008 summit in Bucharest were instrumental in stopping the U.S.-led initiative to extend NATO membership to Ukraine and Georgia, which Russia opposed.

When it comes to NATO's military capabilities, all of the alliance's European members are minimalists. The United States has criticized its European allies for years about Europe's lack of investment in real, deployable military capabilities—transport, airpower, and manpower. Most American commentators—both Democratic and Republican—see NATO as an instrument that could and should help the United States with its global undertakings. Most Americans have a maximalist, global conception of NATO and its future. Although the United Kingdom tends to share this view, many Europeans have a minimalist or mixed conception of NATO.

To help overcome these divisions, member states finally agreed that NATO needs to develop and enunciate a new framework—a strategic concept that specifies its missions and roles with respect to challenges ranging from terrorism and the proliferation of weapons of mass destruction to energy and cyber security.[18] This effort was launched in July 2009 with the establishment of a group of eminent persons cochaired by former U.S. secretary of state Madeleine Albright and former CEO of Royal Dutch Shell, Jeroen van der Veer. The group submitted its report in May 2010.[19] The analysis and recommendations of the group were to assist NATO's secretary general in the drafting of a new strategic concept that was submitted to NATO heads of state and government at the November 2010 summit held in Lisbon. The challenge for the NATO secretary general was to find a coherent balance between the minimalist and maximalist positions. NATO was not to return to an exclusively regionally focused organization, nor was it to become an entirely globally focused organization.[20]

Collective self-defense and deterrence (Article 5 missions) continue to be core NATO functions. But even at this more basic level, NATO faces the conundrum that these core functions are, notwithstanding the fears of many new NATO members, no longer perceived by a majority of Europeans as responding to a real security need. Traditional concerns about war in Europe have mostly abated. "Conceived on a national level, there are not many threats to European countries."[21] Javier Solana, the EU high representative for CFSP (from 1999–December 2009) and former NATO secretary general, speaking at the 2009 Munich Security Conference, has argued that security inside Europe is largely completed."[22] This is not to deny that concerns about Russia, particularly after the 2008 Georgia-Russian war, remain vivid, particularly among many countries in the Baltics, the

Balkans, and the Caucasus,[23] but many in Europe believe that these concerns are better addressed through nonmilitary means with the European Union and individual European member states in the driver's seat. Other "in-area" missions, such as homeland security or the strengthening of infrastructures to keep societies afloat when faced with terrorist attacks or natural disasters, may involve NATO, but first and foremost these kinds of challenges will have to be faced initially within an EU context. Similarly, NATO may make contributions to stability, peace, and democracy in Europe and its immediate neighborhood, but the bulk of this task has been handed over to the European Union.[24]

As to NATO's "out-of-area" missions, the difficulties that NATO is encountering in Afghanistan are the direct result of the broader problems described earlier. NATO members have different priorities and perspectives with respect to Afghanistan. For some, this is a mission that is of strategic national interest and at the level of an Article 5 mission; for others, Afghanistan is a peacekeeping and humanitarian mission. As a result, NATO members that are involved in Afghanistan do not have a coherent strategy. NATO's effectiveness and credibility in Afghanistan have been further undercut by the fact that some members are carrying much heavier burdens than others and have placed strict restrictions on what their forces in Afghanistan may or may not do. These caveats, as they are known, are compounding the discord within the alliance.[25] Finally, the Afghan operation has low levels of public support.[26] A January 2009 poll shows that 50 percent of Britons and 52 percent of Germans say that if President Barack Obama calls on EU states to increase their troops in Afghanistan significantly, their country should not send any more soldiers under any circumstances.[27]

There is near consensus among policymakers and experts that unless the United States and its allies can agree on the political objectives they want to achieve in Afghanistan, they are unlikely to turn the corner there. This would have far-reaching—some say, crippling—consequences for the alliance.[28] At the same time, success or failure in Afghanistan depends not only on NATO efforts.[29] Many other international actors are involved in the stabilization and reconstruction of Afghanistan, including the European Union, the United Nations, and the Afghan government itself. It can even be argued that the military effort is a necessary but insufficient element of success in Afghanistan. Currently, all national and international actors involved in Afghanistan are performing at a subpar level.[30]

NATO may be called upon to help address other security challenges, such as those related to nuclear proliferation, energy, or the Internet, but the locus of efforts to manage and address these challenges will be elsewhere—namely, at the level of the United Nations, the European Union, and the United States. NATO would at most have a support function.[31]

In terms of membership, NATO expansion seems to have been halted, despite U.S. declarations that any country has the right to join NATO. It is, indeed, questionable whether NATO's eastward drive has done much to strengthen NATO's core mission, that is, to reinforce and stabilize the security of its members. Richard Betts, for instance, has argued that NATO has overreached in its eastward drive. "NATO's leaders naively thought the age of power politics was over and took in new members without due regard for the strategic implications for relations with Russia." NATO expansion brought the anti-Russia orientation of the organization back to the surface at a time when this was no longer warranted.[32] It is ironic that NATO expansion, made possible because of the fall of the Soviet Union, reinforces NATO's initial raison d'être—that is, strategic reassurance. This is NATO's "encore."[33]

Finally, in terms of capabilities, the 2008 financial crisis has tempered any hope in the near or medium term of serious expansion of European military capabilities.

The NATO summit in November 2010 tried to balance NATO's "in-area" and "out-of-area" missions, straddle the divide between minimalists and maximalists, and clarify the meaning of Article 5, the role of Russia, the future of NATO expansion, and the role of nuclear weapons in NATO's own strategy.[34] While the summit meeting was hailed as a success, the new strategic concept did not break new ground, nor was it able to overcome the divisions within NATO. In addition, interest and support for the alliance in NATO member states remains low.

In sum, NATO is a formidable military organization; no other international or regional organization has the military-planning capabilities of NATO. Unfortunately, NATO is caught up in political struggles of the twentieth century. Even if the political constellations in both the United States and Europe evolve, many of the security challenges of the twenty-first century will require more than a military response. Hence, NATO is on a downward and at best a flat trajectory, and its long-term future is uncertain.

The European Union: Not Yet Ready for a Solo

The European Union has made breathtaking progress over the past fifteen years. Its membership has more than doubled, it has a combined population of almost 500 million, and it has a 22 percent share of world GDP. In comparison, the United States has a 21 percent share of world GDP and

China has an 11 percent share. EU member states are the largest providers of official development assistance, totaling more than 50 percent of all development assistance worldwide. EU member states are also important contributors to the United Nations.

The European Union is not just a formidable economic power and a provider of funds; it is also increasingly a global player in the political arena. Since the late 1990s, it has made progress toward a common foreign and security policy, and it has expanded its capacities to engage in locations outside of Europe.[35]

Within the European Union, the main responsibility for security matters lies with the European Council.[36] The appointment in 1999 of Javier Solana as the secretary general of the General Secretariat of the EU Council and as the EU high representative for CFSP was a big step forward. It provided the union with an identifiable face. In addition, Solana occasionally develops autonomous policy initiatives and thus gives "voice to more than the simple sum of the EU parts."[37] For example, Solana drafted the EU Security Strategy (ESS)—*A Secure World in a Better World*—which was adopted by the council in 2003. It was a major fence-mending effort within the European Union and across the Atlantic after the fallout over the Iraq war and quickly became a "broader consensus-building exercise for the enlarged union."[38] The ESS was a milestone in the development of CFSP in that it provided the union for the first time with a foreign and security policy doctrine.

The document had much in common with the 2002 U.S. National Security Strategy. It identified five main security threats: terrorism; the proliferation of weapons of mass destruction, particularly nuclear weapons; regional conflicts; failed or failing states; and organized crime. Crisis management, good governance, and development aid were considered key tools in dealing with these challenges. The ESS also laid down a strategic objective of working toward an international order based on effective multilateralism—defined by some as a rule-based order and by others as a UN-based order.

In December 2007, the EU high representative for CFSP was invited to examine the implementation of the ESS. The resulting report published in December 2008 reinforced the main thrust of the 2003 ESS. In addition, it highlighted the importance of cyber security, concerns about energy dependence, and the security implications of climate change. The report recognized that the European Union "must be ready to shape events" and become more "strategic" in its thinking. Unfortunately, the report fell short of providing concrete recommendations on how to do so.[39]

The European Security and Defence Policy (ESDP) or Common Security and Defence Policy (CSDP) is the operational arm of the CFSP.[40]

Its parameters were laid down in the 1998 Anglo-French declaration in Saint-Malo. The main objective of ESDP was the development of autonomous military capabilities so that the union could respond to international crises. However, some EU member states, as well as the United States, resisted the development of autonomous defense capabilities. Some European states were afraid that it would result in a decoupling of European and U.S. defense. The United States was afraid that a buildup of autonomous European military capabilities would come at the expense of NATO.[41] The development of military capabilities was also resisted by Nordic EU member states and Ireland. They insisted that ESDP should also have a civilian component and be able to field police, rule-of-law experts, civilian administrators, and civil-protection personnel.

Even though these reservations have not been resolved, the European Union has come a long way since the late 1990s. In July 2010, it was engaged in fourteen missions in Europe, the Middle East, Afghanistan, and Africa. Although most of these missions are relatively small and civilian in nature—they are police or rule-of-law missions—the European Union was also fielding two major military missions, one in Bosnia with 2,500 troops and one off the coast of Somalia with a troop strength of 1,800.[42] In addition, EU member states were contributing some 41,000 troops to NATO operations and over 9,000 troops to UN peace operations.

Admittedly, the European Union could and should do more. With over two million personnel in uniform, the union is able to deploy only about 100,000 troops (5 percent) in out-of-area operations. The 60,000-strong European Rapid Reaction Force, decided on in 1999, remained in 2010 a paper tiger. The European Union has chosen to focus instead on the development of smaller battle groups—groups of approximately 1,500 troops. They became fully operational in January 2007. This means that in theory the union is able to conduct two concurrent rapid-response operations and deploy two battle groups within ten days for a maximum period of 120 days.[43]

That said, further expansion of EU military capabilities is constrained by low levels of defense spending. Only five EU members (Greece, the United Kingdom, France, Bulgaria, and Cyprus) spend over 2 percent of their GDP on defense—the long-time NATO minimum target. Germany, the European Union's economic power house, spends 1.3 percent of GDP on defense.[44] More importantly, defense money in Europe is not being spent effectively. Too much money is being spent on personnel costs and too little on investments in equipment and research and development.[45]

Not surprisingly, the European Union suffers from much of the same problems as NATO does. First, there is great division among member states about policy priorities. EU member states are deeply divided over how to deal with Russia and the United States, what to do about terrorism and energy dependencies, and what role the union should play globally—if at all. Within the European Union the division between maximalist states—the United Kingdom, France, and increasingly Germany—and minimalist states such as Austria, Romania, and Slovenia remains a major obstacle to EU action and the development of EU capabilities.[46] Second, member states are divided over further enlargement. The candidacy of Turkey remains particularly contested among EU member states and is also a point of discord between some European states and the United States.[47] Third, EU defense capabilities are underdeveloped.

The difference with NATO is that within the European Union there is not one obvious leader—there is a group of big countries that matter (notably, France, Germany, and the United Kingdom), but this is far from a coherent group.[48] And many small and new EU member states resent the idea of a European "*directoire*"—that is, a small cohort of states deciding for the union.

Formal high-level relations between the United States and what is now called the European Union were instituted in 1990. These presidential summits represented recognition of the growing political role of what was then called the European Community (EC). However, these summits never really took off and quickly got bogged down in lengthy meetings that were low on substance. U.S. president George W. Bush, after his first EU-U.S. summit meeting in 2001, was so unimpressed that he decided to reduce the annual number from two to one. President Obama has thus far not displayed greater enthusiasm for these meetings, despite the fact that he has expressed great interest in revitalizing the transatlantic partnership and made three trips to Europe during his first six months in office. European unwillingness or inability to help with the closure of Guantanamo, to provide greater support in Afghanistan and Pakistan, and to deal with the 2008 economic crisis in a concerted manner certainly explained Obama's tepid welcome to the EU-U.S. summit in Washington, DC, in November 2009. The fact that he dispatched Vice President Joe Biden to have lunch with Jose Manuel Barrosso, the president of the commission, and Swedish prime minister Frederick Reinfeldt, the acting president of the European Union, was illustrative for many news commentators of the "lost appetite" in the United States for EU summits.[49]

But Europeans themselves also seemed uninterested and showed a lack of policy coordination. During the November 2009 EU-U.S. summit meeting, German chancellor Angela Merkel was in Washington, but for a separate visit. Her visit with President Obama and her address to the U.S. Congress "easily upstaged" the EU-U.S. summit.[50]

As long as Europeans themselves play the "divide-and-rule" game and refuse to present a unified front, transatlantic relations will remain a fetish of nostalgists who believe that "the present is tense and the past perfect"—and they will keep asking Uncle Sam to "play it again." Jeremy Shapiro and Nick Witney in their survey of European attitudes toward the United States and transatlantic relations argue that Europe's lack of voice and its subservient attitude toward the United States is misguided. They encourage Europeans to adopt more robust attitudes as they do in the economic field.[51] That, however, would require Europeans to define a strategic sense of self.[52] Given the political divisions and the lack of investment in the defense sector, this is a tall order.

It will take time for Europe to become the global actor called for in the ESS. Although EU capabilities and willingness to deploy troops will remain a prerogative of each individual EU member state and subject to political domestic constraints, the Lisbon Treaty provides frameworks for like-minded states in the union to move ahead and work toward greater integration in the defense field. These states will ultimately set the standards.[53]

In many other areas—economics, justice, and homeland affairs—the European Union is making policy and is the main interlocutor for other international actors, including the United States. The passing of the Lisbon Treaty, while by no means a panacea, is a step in the right direction.[54]

In sum, European integration proceeds in fits and starts. The rejection of the Lisbon Treaty in the initial referendum in Ireland in June 2008 was clearly a setback to the institutional development of the union, but it did not derail the European project and by the end of 2009 (thanks in part to a second referendum in Ireland in October 2009) all EU member states had ratified it. Further integration will continue on a multitude of social and economic fronts, and the European Union will probably continue to make slow but steady progress on military and security issues. Given the tremendous and unexpected progress the European Union has made in the past fifteen years, one should not bet against its future. Europe, despite its internal divisions, is on an upward trajectory.

NATO and EU Cooperation: Missing Harmonies

Commenting on NATO-EU relations, outgoing NATO secretary general Jaap de Hoop Scheffer remarked, "Our missions, our geographical areas of interest, our capabilities—even our problems and our deficiencies—are increasingly overlapping—not to speak of our memberships. Our definition of the security challenges and the means to tackle them is also increasingly a shared one. . . . But I will leave my office in three weeks' time frankly

Table 10.1   NATO and EU Member States, 2010

NATO	European Union
Albania	
	Austria
Belgium	Belgium
Bulgaria	Bulgaria
	Cyprus
Canada	
Croatia	
Czech Republic	Czech Republic
Denmark	Denmark
Estonia	Estonia
	Finland
France	France
Germany	Germany
Greece	Greece
Hungary	Hungary
Iceland	
	Ireland
Italy	Italy
Latvia	Latvia
Lithuania	Lithuania
Luxembourg	Luxembourg
	Malta
Netherlands	Netherlands
Norway	
Poland	Poland
Portugal	Portugal
Romania	Romania
Slovakia	Slovakia
Slovenia	Slovenia
Spain	Spain
	Sweden
Turkey	
United Kingdom	United Kingdom
United States	

disappointed that a true strategic partnership that makes such eminent sense for both organizations has still not come about, even though many of the old obstacles—the hesitations about ESDP, France's non-integration in the Alliance—have now been lifted."[55]

NATO-EU relations have been rife with turf battles. They occur because not all NATO members are members of the European Union and vice versa (see table 10.1).[56] For example, Turkey, a member of NATO but not of the European Union, has since 2004 blocked formal communications between NATO and the European Union. Turkey objects to Cyprus (an EU member since 2004, with whom it has a long-standing dispute) sitting in on information-sharing meetings between NATO and the European Union. It argues, rightfully so, that according to the EU-NATO agreement of 2002, non-NATO EU members can attend EU-NATO meetings only if they have a Partnership for Peace (PfP) agreement with NATO.[57] Because Cyprus has no PfP agreement with NATO, it cannot participate in such meetings.[58] Conversely, France, Greece, and Belgium argue that discussions between the European Union and NATO should involve all EU members. They are willing to make an exception to this rule for meetings that involve "Berlin-plus" arrangements—that is, on-the-ground operations in which the European Union uses NATO assets, as it does in Bosnia and Herzegovina. The result is that formal EU-NATO meetings can discuss only issues related to Bosnia. Issues such as Afghanistan, Iraq, and counterterrorism are off-limits.[59]

EU-NATO cooperation has also been problematic for the United States. The United States is not a member of the European Union, but it is anchored in Europe through NATO, which for the United States remains the central pillar of the U.S.-European relationship. The United States insists that "any formal communication between the U.S. and Europe with respect to anything involving the military must go through NATO."[60] In practical matters, this has meant that the United States is not prepared to engage the European Union directly when dealing with military-nonmilitary coordination issues. "So voila—there you have it. The U.S. can only talk to Europe through NATO, but NATO cannot talk to the European Union, so the U.S. cannot formally talk to the European Union."[61]

Yet, there are powerful forces to push NATO and the European Union toward cooperation—specifically, limited resources and the global and transnational character of many current security challenges. That said, the track record of multilateral cooperation between and among international institutions is mostly negative. The lack of NATO-EU cooperation should hence not come as a surprise.[62]

There are two main types of obstacles to interorganizational cooperation: political and operational. Internal divisions within both NATO and the European Union compound these problems. The political obstacles have to do with reconciling different mandates and policy priorities. In the case of NATO and the European Union, this has been particularly difficult since both institutions have been searching for new missions. In many instances this has led to competition and zero-sum games. The clash between NATO and the European Union in 2005 over who should coordinate an airlift for AU peacekeepers in Darfur was illustrative in this regard.[63] France's rejoining of NATO's integrated military structure and the more relaxed attitude of the current U.S. administration toward ESDP/CSDP should help alleviate some of these political problems.

That said, ultimately the political problem has to do with inordinate fears in Washington and Paris that they might lose control over the agenda.

In the United States, some officials are concerned that closer EU–NATO cooperation could lead to the development of an EU caucus in NATO, which they argue would decrease Washington's leverage over Europe. The Obama administration seems less concerned about this issue, but bureaucratic behaviors are hard to change. Similarly, in Europe, some officials are concerned that strengthened EU–NATO cooperation could lead to the United States gaining too much leverage over EU foreign and defense policy. Tendencies in Washington to ask Europeans to do more, but without providing them with opportunities for adequate influence over questions of broader strategic objectives, reinforce this paranoia in Europe.

The operational obstacles have to do with reconciling the different managerial cultures and capabilities of the organizations. It is also about reconciling military and civilian cultures and different military doctrines. The military doctrines related to the peace operations of the United States, NATO, and the major European players—such as the United Kingdom, France, Germany, and the Netherlands—are converging, but they continue to have some major differences, particularly with regard to the use of force and notions of "impartiality" and "consent." Such differences are acutely felt in Afghanistan and lead to incoherent responses in the field.[64] Cooperation, on an operational level, was given a boost when NATO and the European Union concluded in 2003 the so-called Berlin-plus agreement, which provides a basis for consultation and cooperation in crisis management and defense planning and in the exchange of classified information. It allows NATO to support EU-led operations in which NATO as a whole is not engaged. NATO is currently seeking a reverse Berlin-plus agreement whereby EU civilian capabilities would be made available for NATO operations. The situation in Afghanistan has shown the importance of such an operational agreement. Unfortunately, such an agreement is currently held up by Turkey, as explained earlier. Operational, including cultural and doctrinal, differences can be managed or overcome if there is overall political agreement on outcomes and objectives.

In sum, obstacles to NATO–EU cooperation are serious—overcoming these obstacles will require greater trust at multiple levels and among a wide variety of actors. In addition, the wealth of European security institutions, including not only NATO and the European Union but also the Organization for Security Co-operation in Europe and the Council of Europe, makes it easy for member states to pass the buck—that is, to delay or avoid making decisions—or to forum shop—that is, to find the organization that will best represent their views.[65] This type of behavior is encouraged when power relations are in flux, as they have been for most of the post–Cold War period.[66] That said, the finite resources of the allies, particularly in view of the 2008 financial crisis, and the immensity of the tasks at hand provide strong incentives for allies to cooperate.

Conclusions

Together, the United States and Europe can be a formidable power for peace and stability around the world. But the changed international security environment, including changed notions of security, requires them to redefine their relationship. The absence of a direct military threat to the European heartland means that the transatlantic relationship no longer needs to be one of Europe blindly following U.S. policy positions, or one in which the United States is always in the driver's seat. The U.S. presence in Europe is mainly to provide strategic reassurance in the unlikely event of a Russian military threat. This is NATO's main residual task. The European Union, while a formidable economic force, has limited military capacity and it and its individual members will hence continue to rely on the United States for its and their ultimate defense needs.

That said, the source of most security challenges to the United States and Europe are to be found outside of Europe. These global and transnational challenges—Islamist extremism, terrorism, nuclear proliferation, failing states, and climate change—require a mix of military and nonmilitary policy responses. They also require international cooperative approaches. Iraq and Afghanistan are reminders that no country, no matter how powerful, can deal with contemporary security challenges by itself. [67]

Europe is a natural ally for the United States and vice versa. First, their overall strategic objectives are largely the same—peace and stability, the expansion of free markets and democracy, and respect for human rights. Second, the United States and Europe are in large agreement about the nature of the security challenges they face. Third, the United States and Europe have established a long and good track record of working together, particularly within NATO during the Cold War, and hence they have a solid basis to build on. The United States and Europe have a better chance of shaping future norms, standards, and governance structures to deal with the challenges of the twenty-first century together than they do alone. Fourth, concerted actions by the United States and Europe may carry greater legitimacy. Fifth, as the two most important donors and supporters of international humanitarian aid and development assistance, it is key that the United States and Europe work together to ensure maximum effectiveness of this assistance and to avoid duplication and waste. This is particularly important in a world of finite resources. Finally, concerted action by the United States and Europe may help share operational burdens.

The problem for both the United States and the European Union is in translating those policy impulses into tangible policy actions.

In 2009, the political leadership on both sides of the Atlantic seemed keen to jumpstart a renewed transatlantic partnership. However, to be successful, such a partnership needs to be followed up by practical actions on the ground. Joint action with respect to Afghanistan and Pakistan is essential, but other security dossiers would also benefit from greater U.S.-EU concerted action—including those related to Iran, the Middle East, Russia, and energy. In addition, conflict prevention and crisis management efforts at the United Nations and multilateral nuclear nonproliferation and climate change initiatives would benefit from greater U.S.-EU cooperation. With all of these dossiers, except possibly for climate change, the ball is in the court of the Europeans. Whether the new EU president and the EU high representative can achieve greater coherence in EU policy, prompt greater action by EU member states, and rekindle popular support among European citizens remains to be seen. But, without greater political unity and action on the European side—transatlantic relations will flounder—and so will NATO.

Notes

1. See, for example, John Mearsheimer, "Back to the Future: Instability in Europe after the Cold War," *International Security* 15, no. 1 (Summer 1990): 5–56; and Steven Walt, "The Ties That Fray: Why Europe and America Are Drifting Apart," *National Interest* (Winter 1998/99): 3–11.

2. See Daniel Hamilton, with Charles Barry, Hans Binnendijk, Stephen Flanagan, Julianne Smith, and James Townsend, *Alliance Reborn: An Atlantic Compact for the 21st Century: The Washington NATO Project* (Washington, DC: Center for Transatlantic Relations, School of Advanced International Studies, Johns Hopkins University February 2009), vii.

3. See the Lisbon Treaty signed in 2007 and entered into force on December 1, 2009.

4. See Philip H. Gordon, "Their Own Army? Making European Defense Work," *Foreign Affairs* 79, no. 4 (July/August 2000): 12. See also Philip Gordon, "Bridging the Atlantic Divide," *Foreign Affairs* 82, no. 1 (January/February 2003). In May 2009, Philip Gordon became assistant secretary of state for Europe and Eurasian affairs in the U.S. State Department.

5. The problem is that the pooling of European military capabilities will go hand in hand with the integration of the European defense industry. Ultimately, this is of course not an attractive proposition for the U.S. defense industry. The intense competition between Northrup Grumman, European Aeronautic Defence and Space Co. (EADS), and Boeing that developed in 2008 around the multibillion dollar U.S. Air Force contract to build 179 refueling tankers is a harbinger of things to come. It was a major setback for Boeing, which had been supplying refueling tankers to the U.S. Air Force for close to fifty years. Further outsourcing to non-American industry will be a very delicate domestic political issue in the United States.

6. Cited in Daniel Korski and Richard Gowan, *Can the EU Rebuild Failing States? A Review of Europe's Civilian Capacities* (London: European Council on Foreign Relations, October 2009), 24–25.

7. Robert Kagan argues in *Of Paradise and Power* that the United States and Europe no longer share a common view of the world and occupy different planets (Mars and Venus). Kagan argues that when it comes to the use of power and military force, Europeans have moved toward a "post-historical paradise of peace and relative prosperity" and "into a self-contained world of laws and rules and transnational negotiation and cooperation." The United States, on the other hand, remains mired in history and engaged in the Hobbesian struggle for survival through the use of power and military force. See Robert Kagan, *Of Paradise and Power: America and Europe in the New World Order* (New York: Alfred A. Knopf, 2003).

8. The 1995 enlargement saw three countries join the union: Austria, Finland, and Sweden. The largest enlargement, however, took place in 2004, when Cyprus, Czech Republic, Estonia, Hungary, Latvia, Lithuania, Malta, Poland, Slovakia, and Slovenia joined. Bulgaria and Romania joined in 2007. Six countries are waiting to be admitted (Albania, Croatia, Iceland, Macedonia, Montenegro, and Turkey). The accession of Iceland and the Balkan countries is relatively uncontroversial. Turkey's accession, on the other hand, is more problematic, even though official accession talks have started. The idea of Belarus, Georgia, or Ukraine one day joining the union is very controversial.

9. Talks about a more coherent institutional structure started in 2001. It led to the drafting of a European Constitution that was defeated by referenda in France and the Netherlands in 2005. Subsequently, the European Council negotiated a new treaty—the Lisbon Treaty—that was signed in 2007 and entered into force on December 1, 2009. In terms of foreign policy, the Lisbon Treaty tries to overcome the duality in EU foreign policy by bringing together the intergovernmental foreign policy, security, and defense tools of the union (that is, the tools of the EU Council) with the supranational foreign policy development tools of the union (that is, the tools of the EU Commission). Under the new rules, the EU high representative for foreign affairs and security policy will have a seat in the council and occupy the post of vice president of the EU Commission. The high representative also heads the European Defence Agency. In principle, this should increase the impact and coherence of the union's foreign policy action. In addition, the Lisbon Treaty led to the creation in July 2010 of the European External Action Service (EEAS)—the equivalent of a European Foreign Ministry and diplomatic service—to support the high representative. In the field of security and defense policy, ultimate authority will remain with individual member states, but the Lisbon Treaty allows smaller groups of states to enter into "permanent structured cooperation" agreements—that is, closer cooperation agreements. The permanent structured cooperation mechanism is in addition to the "enhanced cooperation" mechanism. The latter enables a group of states (at least nine member states) to deepen their cooperation in military crisis management once unanimous approval of the council has been received. Permanent structured cooperation does not have a threshold in terms of numbers of participants. Finally, the Lisbon Treaty provides the union with a single legal personality, which will strengthen the union's negotiating power.

10. Some authors have argued that Europe is allowed this luxury, in part, because it continues to rely on the American security guarantee. They argue that the continued existence of the NATO military command structure encourages free-riding behavior on behalf of the Europeans. See, for example, Barry Posen, "The Case for Restraint," *American Interest* (November/December 2007); and Barry Posen, "A Grand Strategy of Restraint and Renewal" (testimony before the U.S. House Armed Services Committee, July 15, 2008).

11. See Jeremy Shapiro and Nick Witney, *Towards a Post-American Europe: A Power Audit of EU-US Relations* (London: European Council for Foreign Relations, October 2009), 12, and the chapter "Pragmatic America," 41–51.

12. The European *acquis* or *acquis communautaire* stands for the body of law, standards, norms, and principles accumulated by the European Union and applicable to all EU member states. The *acquis* contains over 30,000 legal acts and is continuously evolving.

13. See Leslie Lebl, *Advancing U.S. Interests with the European Union* (Washington, DC: Atlantic Council, 2007).

14. See David C. Acheson (former president of the Atlantic Council of the United States), "Wither the European Union," posted on the Atlantic Council of the United States Web site on June 22, 2006. See also ibid.

15. Jeremy Shapiro and Nick Witney make a similar argument in *Towards a Post-American Europe*. They argue that an "unhealthy mix of complacency and excessive deference towards the United States" lead to "strategies of ingratiation" that fail to secure European interests and does not provide the United States with the sort of transatlantic partner it is seeking.

16. Since 1949 NATO's membership has increased from twelve to twenty-eight countries through seven rounds of expansion: Greece and Turkey in 1952; Germany in 1955; Spain in 1982; the East German Laender (as a result of German unification) in 1990; Czech Republic, Hungary, and Poland in 1999; Bulgaria, Estonia, Latvia, Lithuania, Romania, Slovakia, and Slovenia in 2004; and Albania and Croatia in 2009.

17. See Pew Global Attitudes Project, *Some Positive Signs for U.S. Image* (Washington, DC: Pew Research Center, June 12, 2008). It is ironic to note that had the minimalist position prevailed in the 1990s, the new NATO member states would have never become members of NATO.

18. NATO's last strategic concept had been adopted in 1999.

19. See *NATO 2020: Assured Security; Dynamic Engagement—Analysis and Recommendations of the Group of Experts on a New Strategic Concept for NATO* (Brussels: NATO Public Diplomacy Division, May 17, 2010). The expert group defined NATO's twin imperatives for the future as "assured security" for all its members and "dynamic engagement" beyond the treaty area to minimize threats. The group identified four core tasks for the alliance: (1) deter and defend member states against any threat of aggression; (2) contribute to the broader security of the entire Euro-Atlantic region; (3) serve as a transatlantic means for security consultations and crisis management; and (4) enhance the scope and management of partnerships (pp. 19–21). The report, in trying to respond to both the minimalists and the maximalists, was unable to articulate a new vision of where the alliance would need to go and devoid of any innovative proposals. Its sections on NATO–European Union cooperation were particularly underwhelming. Like the April 2009 NATO summit, the report got very little public attention.

20. For recent discussions on the challenges faced by NATO, see, for example, David S. Yost, "NATO's Evolving Purposes and the Next Strategic Concept," *International Affairs* 86, no. 2 (2010): 489–522; Jens Ringsmose and Sten Rynning, *Come Home, NATO? The Atlantic Alliance's New Strategic Concept*, Danish Institute for International Studies (DIIS) Report (Copenhagen: DIIS, April 2009); Hamilton et al., *Alliance Reborn*; Rem Korteweg and Richard Podkolinski, *New Horzons: Finding a Path away from NATO's De-solidarisation* (The Hague: Hague Centre for Strategic Studies [HCSS], March 2009); Stephen Larrabee and J. Lindley-French, *Revitalizing the Transatlantic Security Partnership: An Agenda for Action* (Guetersloh: Venusberg Group and Rand Corporation, 2009); Richard L. Kugler and

Hans Binnendijk, *Towards a New Transatlantic Compact*, Defense and Technology Paper no. 52 (Washington, DC: National Defense University, August 2008); Klaus Naumann, John Shalikashvili, Lord Inge, Jacques Lanxade, and Henk van den Breemen, *Towards A Grand Strategy for an Uncertain World: Renewing Transatlantic Partnership* (Lunteren: No-aber Foundation, 2007).

21. See Robert Cooper's reaction to Ronald Asmus and Tod Lindberg in, "Rue de la Loi: The Global Ambition of the European Project" (working paper, Stanley Foundation, Muscatine, IA, September 2008), 15.

22. See Solana's speech at www.securityconference.de/Dr-Javier-Solana-Madariaga.246.0. html?&L=1.

23. See, for example, the speech by the president of Estonia, Toomas Hendrik, at the 45th Munich Security Conference.

24. Hamilton et al. have defined two types of NATO functions: "in-area" or "at-home" missions and "out-of-area" or "away" missions. They lament the inordinate amount of attention to "out-of-area" operations and would like to see a recalibration toward "in-area" or "at-home" missions, in particular toward transatlantic homeland security issues. See Hamilton et al., *Alliance Reborn*.

25. The issue of caveats is not an entirely new problem for the alliance. It has also been a problem in Kosovo. In March 2004, when Albanians rioted against Serbs in Kosovo, German troops refused to join other NATO Kosovo Force (KFOR) troops in crowd control. In Kosovo, only 6,000 of the 18,000 KFOR troops were allowed to use force against rioting crowds. See Kristin Archick and Paul Gallis, *NATO and the European Union*, Report RL32342 (Washington, DC: Congressional Research Service, January 28, 2008), 7–8.

26. A June 2008 Pew poll showed that there is little public support in many NATO countries for a continuation of the mission in Afghanistan. In France, 54 percent favored pulling out; in Germany, 54 percent; in Spain, 56 percent; in Poland, 65 percent; and in Turkey, 72 percent. Even in the United Kingdom, 48 percent favored withdrawal. In the United States, 50 percent were in favor of keeping troops as opposed to 44 percent who wanted to see withdrawal. Of the counties surveyed, Australia had the highest level of support—60 percent—for staying in Afghanistan until the situation is stable. See Pew Global Attitudes Project, *Some Positive Signs for U.S. Image*.

27. See the Financial Times/Harris Poll of January 2009, www. harrisinteractive.com. It is interesting to note that, according to the poll, 46 percent of Americans did not believe that President Obama should send more troops into Afghanistan. By August 2009, this number had dropped to 34 percent. Forty-five percent of Americans favor decreasing U.S. forces there, with 24 percent in favor. In an August 19, 2009, ABC News/Washington Post poll, 51 percent of Americans declared the war in Afghanistan not worth fighting for, with 47 percent believing the war was worth fighting for. See Jennifer Agiesta and Jon Cohen, "Public Opinion in U.S. Turns Against Afghan War," *Washington Post*, August 20, 2009.

28. Some observers see Afghanistan as Obama's trap—the iceberg toward which the United States is steering the *Titanic*.

29. It is critical that the United States, its allies, and the Afghan government agree on a division of labor, with clear tasks for NATO, the European Union, the United Nations, other international actors, and the Afghan government. It should go without saying that this division of labor should be based on the comparative advantages of the parties.

30. In March 2011, NATO took responsibility for the military operation in Libya under United Nations Security Council Resolution 1973. But as in Afghanistan, NATO members were deeply divided over the mission and fissures among coalition and NATO partners quickly surfaced.

31. NATO's current mission off the coast of Somalia to combat piracy is an example of a nonessential but useful secondary function NATO is carrying out. Similarly, NATO could assist in the monitoring and patrolling of sea lanes that are essential to energy provision.

32. See Richard Betts, "The Three Faces of NATO," *National Interest Online*, October 4, 2009. Michael Brown made this argument back in the 1990s; see Michael Brown, "NATO at Fifty: Minimalist NATO: A Wise Alliance Knows When to Retrench," *Foreign Affairs* 78, no. 3 (May/June 1999). Russia clearly sees NATO expansion as being directed against Russia. See also note 33.

33. For some NATO members, the 2008 war in Georgia raised serious questions about whether NATO allies would have both the capabilities and the political will to follow through on the defense commitments made to the new NATO members. For Russia, the crisis in 2008 highlighted the inadequacy of European security institutions and gave new impetus to Russian ideas for a new European security architecture—sometimes referred to as Helsinki-2. The first Helsinki accords were signed in 1975 by the members of the Conference on Security and Co-operation in Europe (CSCE), not as a treaty, but as a political binding document outlining measures in the security, economic, and human rights fields that was designed to enhance the security of states in the Euro-Atlantic region—with a geographic range from Vladivostok to Vancouver. In the early 1990s, the CSCE was institutionalized and in 1995 became the Organization for Security and Co-operation in Europe (OSCE). In 2009, the organization counted fifty-six members. Russia pushed for a discussion of a new European security architecture at the OSCE summit held December 1–2, 2010. For more, see Russian president Dmitri Medvedev in speeches in Berlin on June 5, 2008, and October 8, 2008, and during the EU-Russia summit in Nice on November 14, 2008. See also Andrew Monaghan, *Russia's "Big Idea": "Helsinki 2" and the Reform of Euro-Atlantic Security* (Rome: NATO Defense College, Research Division, December 2008).

34. Cognizant of the lack of public support, NATO has also launched a public forum for discussion on its Web site. The Group of Experts in the report *NATO 2020* recognized the importance of public opinion and "telling NATO's story" not just to NATO populations but also to people from non-NATO states.

35. The principles of a more effective foreign and security policy for the European Union were defined in the Maastricht (1992), Amsterdam (1997), and Nice (2001) Treaties and the Lisbon Treaty (2007).

36. The council responsible for foreign and security policy is an intergovernmental body. This is a sector where states have not given up their sovereign national prerogatives.

37. See Antonio Missiroli, "ESDP—How it Works," in *EU Security and Defence Policy: The First Five Years* (1999–2004), ed. Nicole Gnesotto (Paris: EU Institute for Security Studies, 2004), 63.

38. Antonio Missiroli, "Revisiting the European Security Strategy—beyond 2008," European Policy Centre Policy Brief, April 2008.

39. See Sven Biscop, "Odd Couple or Dynamic Duo: The EU and Strategy in Times of Crisis," *European Foreign Affairs Review* 14, no. 3 (2009): 367–84.

40. With the entry into force of the Lisbon Treaty in December 2009, ESDP was relabeled CSDP.

41. In 1998 Madeleine Albright laid down the three "Ds"—that is, the conditions under which the United States would support European defense efforts. They are no decoupling from NATO; no duplication of NATO command structures or alliance-wide resources; and no discrimination against European NATO countries that are not members of the European Union.

42. The military mission in eastern Chad and in northeastern Central African Republic launched in January 2008 with an authorized level of 3,700 troops was handed over to the United Nations in January 2009. For details, see Council of the European Union, www.consilium.europa.eu/showPage.aspx?id=268&lang=en. In terms of civilian capabilities, in theory, the European Union is supposed to be able to call on ten thousand police officers to be deployed overseas. In practice, the union, like other international organizations, has difficulty finding civilian staff for its missions. For more, see Korski and Gowan, *Can the EU Rebuild Failing States?*

43. By 2008, some fifteen battle groups had been established. A battle-group coordination conference is organized every six months to receive offers from member states to populate the standby roster. The problem is that many troops earmarked for EU battle groups are also earmarked for the NATO rapid-reaction force. Avoiding conflicts between such commitments is up to each member state. As of July 2010, no battle group had been deployed in an operation. For more, see Alexander Nicoll, ed., "Europe's Rapid-Response Forces: Use Them or Lose Them?" *IISS Strategic Comments* 15, no. 7 (September 2009).

44. In comparison, the United States spends about 4 percent of GDP on defense.

45. For more, see Nick Witney, *Re-energising Europe's Security and Defence Policy* (London: European Council on Foreign Relations, July 2008); Bastian Giegerich, *European Military Crisis Management: Connecting Ambition and Reality*, Adelphi Paper 397 (London: International Institute for Strategic Studies [IISS], October 2008); and IISS, *European Military Capabilities* (London: IISS, July 2008). It may be noted that personnel costs in the United States are also rising, so this will, in the future, also become a big problem for the United States.

46. See Giegerich, *European Military Crisis Management*.

47. The EU enlargement debate involves two main schools of thought: one sees enlargement as a natural extension of the post–World War II European project, as an evolutionary step in the making of a Europe "whole and free," while the other has a more instrumental view of the European Union and stresses the challenges of enlargement, believing that it will be increasingly difficult to reconcile national interests with an ever-growing number of states.

48. It is important in this context to recall that the European Union is not a state and that the much lauded ESS is not an operational strategic concept. This, of course, also affects EU-U.S. relations.

49. See, for example, Lara Marlow, "Obama Lunch Slight Sums Up Lost Appetite in US for EU Summits," *Irish Times*, November 4, 2009; Ahto Lobjakas, "Lackluster EU-U.S. Summit Highlights Lack of Strategic Depth in Relationship," *Radio Free Europe (RFERL)*, November 4, 2009; and Shapiro and Witney, *Towards a Post-American Europe*.

50. Ibid.

51. Shapiro and Witney, *Towards a Post-American Europe*.

52. See Sven Biscop, ed., *The Value of Power, The Power of Values: A Call for an EU Grand Strategy*, Egmont Papers, no. 33 (Brussels: Royal Institute for International Relations, October 2009).

53. See note 9.

54. On November 19, 2009, the members of the EU Council appointed Herman Van Rompuy (Belgium) as the first permanent president of the EU Council for a once renewable term of two and a half years. Catherine Ashton (UK) was appointed high representative of the union for foreign affairs and security policy and vice president of the EU Commission for a period of five years. Her appointment to the commission was subject to consent by the European Parliament. The high representative will have at her disposal the EEAS.

55. See introductory remarks by NATO secretary general Jaap de Hoop Scheffer at the opening of the strategic concept seminar, July 7, 2009.

56. Canada, Iceland, Norway, Turkey, and the United States are part of NATO, but not of the European Union. Austria, Cyprus, Finland, Ireland, Malta, and Sweden are part of the European Union, but not of NATO. See table 10.1.

57. See the EU-NATO declaration on ESDP, December 16, 2002.

58. Turkey would of course prevent such an agreement. Turkey has no objection to Austria, Finland, Sweden, or Ireland sitting on joint sessions, because these countries have PfP arrangements, and up until 2004 these meetings were allowed to address a wide range of issues.

59. The European Union contributed to this problem by admitting Cyprus into the European Union without a resolution of the Cyprus conflict. The entry of Turkey into the European Union could potentially solve this problem. However, Turkey's admission to the union remains far off.

60. See C. Boyden Gray, U.S. ambassador to the European Union, "Solution to Economic Issues outside NATO's Role," *Washington Times*, February 12, 2009.

61. Ibid. See also Daniel Keohane, "Unblocking EU-NATO Co-operation," *CER Bulletin* no. 48 (June/July 2006).

62. On NATO-EU cooperation, or the lack thereof, see Paul Cornish, "EU and NATO Co-operation or Competition?" (briefing paper for the EU Parliament, October 2006); Thierry Tardy, *The EU and NATO as Peacekeepers: Open Cooperation versus Implicit Competition*, FIIA Report 14 (Helsinki: Finnish Institute of International Affairs, 2006); and Leo Michel and Zoe Hunter, *NATO and the European Union: Improving Practical Cooperation*, A Transatlantic Workshop Summary (Washington, DC: Institute for National Strategic Studies, NDU, March 2006).

63. Suggestions by France that the mission should be co-coordinated from one EU base in Eindhoven—a base also used by NATO planners—were rejected by the United States and Canada. In the end, NATO and the European Union agreed that each organization would run its own airlift operation—NATO out of Mons and the European Union out of Eindhoven.

64. In Afghanistan, the United States and many European countries operate under slightly different military doctrines. For example, for the United States, there is no clear divide between peace operations on the one hand and counterinsurgency operations on the other hand—they are all part of a continuum. However, important allies like the Netherlands and Canada draw sharp lines between such operations. The result is that the latter have a vastly

more restrictive notion of when to use military force. On this issue, see Winrich Kuehne, *Peace Operations and Peacebuilding in the Transatlantic Dialogue: Key Political, Military, Police and Civilian Issues*, ZIF Analysis (Berlin: Center for International Peace Operations, August 2009). EU and NATO officials in Bosnia, Kosovo, and Afghanistan on the whole have good, cooperative local interactions, so even if operational obstacles can be overcome in the field on a day-to-day and case-by-case basis, these doctrinal differences lead to incoherence and friction on the overall strategic level. These differences have their roots in political differences.

65. See, for example, Thomas G. Weiss, ed., *Beyond Subcontracting: Tasksharing with Regional Security Arrangements and Service Providing NGOs* (New York: St. Martin's Press, 1998), 230.

66. The lack of a common EU or NATO policy toward Russia is also part of the problem.

67. Even neoconservatives such as Robert Kagan recognize that "predominance is not the same thing as omnipotence. Just because the United States has more power than everyone else does not mean it can impose its will on everyone else." See Robert Kagan, "End of Dreams, Return of History: International Rivalry and American leadership," *Policy Review* (August/September 2007).

11

Europe's Security

Attitudes, Achievements, and Unsolved Challenges

Alyson J. K. Bailes

The European Union's first-ever Security Strategy, adopted by the European Council in December 2003, famously starts with the words "Europe has never been so prosperous, so secure nor so free."[1] The statement was warranted, in view of Europe's safe emergence from a century of two World Wars and one Cold War, but it was clearly not the whole story. Europe was still facing in 2003, and still faces now, a complex interlayering of threats, risks, and broader challenges in security governance. Like any region of rich states that shares political, economic, cultural, and ethnic ties with other regions, it has to decide not only what to do for its own survival and welfare but also what to do together with its like-minded partners; what to do to help the less fortunate; and what to do for peace, good order, and development in the world as a whole. At present, its response is delivered not only through a range of security-relevant institutions—NATO, the European Union, the Organization for Security and Co-operation in Europe (OSCE), the Council of Europe, and numerous subregional groups[2]— but also by nation-states individually and many kinds of nonstate actors.[3] The task of this chapter is to pick out from such complexity the threads that reveal most about Europe's singularities in security development and the unique pattern of variety among its component states.

As a first attempt to frame the picture, it may be argued that most of the important features of European security can be defined using the prefixes "post" and "schizo." The European Security Strategy (henceforth ESS), for instance, is not only a post–Cold War document but also a "postmodern" document in at least two senses. It speaks for an institutional community with a number of supranational features that moderate or even override traditional sovereignty, and it defines that community's shared interests in what most people would identify as "post-Westphalian" terms.[4] Also very important for understanding European quandaries is the postindustrial phase that most European economies and societies have entered, characterized by reduced reliance on primary production and the extensive privatization and internationalization of strategic economic goods. Schizoid features, meanwhile, exist at the national level—including the composite nature of many European states (Belgium, Switzerland, Bosnia-Herzegovina) and the still important differences of security outlook between them—and at the institutional level—including the number of overlapping security institutions, often without clear demarcation lines. European institutional policies, moreover, do not simply reflect the sum of their member states': compare and contrast Britain's or France's national military behavior abroad with the guidelines they gave to the European Union's common European Security and Defence Policy (ESDP).[5] It is commonplace for a single state to send instructions to its respective NATO and EU delegations that drive them into confrontation with each other. Finally, Europe's whole personality is schizoid (literally "split," or "divided") inasmuch as there is no clear or agreed definition of who is a European and where the continent's boundaries lie. Are Russia and Turkey, for instance, to be included in the study of "European" particularities and if not, why not?

Many analyses that make these points have done so in connection with a debate on European strengths and weaknesses, generally contrasted with the United States. The present chapter's aim is less to judge or compare than to understand, and it does not exclude the hypothesis that weakness could have some security benefits such as risk and cost reduction. In this empirical spirit, the sections below will deal in turn with the prima facie combination of security threats, risks, and obligations facing Europe; then with European national and collective perceptions; and finally with the main spheres and challenges of European security activity, including a critical look at the role of institutions.[6]

Threats and Risks: A Geological Metaphor

The complexity of the European security environment may be pictured as a series of geological strata laid down at different times, yet the strata interact with each other more dynamically than rocks are prone to do. The base rock of interstate military rivalry has been worn down and covered over in the West-West setting by successful integration processes, and in the East-West context (though less reliably) by measures of détente, stabilization, enlargement, and cooperation developed both before and since the end of the Cold War. On top of it comes the sharply defined band of "new" or "asymmetric" threats (terrorism, proliferation) thrown into prominence by the events of September 11, 2001, though they are not equally new to all Europeans nor do they impact equally on all. Other variegated strata, intruding in all periods but especially prominent in twenty-first-century conditions, represent threats to life, welfare, stability, and values from other kinds of violence (internal conflict, social disorder, sabotage, crime) or from nonintentional hazards, such as natural disasters, pollution, and climate change; accidents and infrastructure breakdowns; pandemic disease; and the security impact of energy transactions, economic and financial vicissitudes, including the global crisis starting autumn 2008, and legal and illegal migration. It already takes a very wide and "postmodern" definition of security to accommodate all these different layers and their cross-connections, but opinion polls show that ordinary Europeans often "securitize" other issues even further from traditional warfare, such as economic and social vulnerabilities.[7] To complete the image it should be noted that geological conditions across Europe are not uniform, so that as one approaches the northern, eastern, or southern peripheries, the bedrock of military risk protrudes more openly.[8] It is no accident that the western periphery, free of menacing neighbors, is where most European resources have been liberated for external intervention.

Before getting to the topic of European security exports, however, each of the three main layers of threat types needs some further explanation. The uniqueness of Europe lies in the balance between them, but also in some special features of each.

Traditional Hazards

No continent has seen such dramatic *military* changes as Europe over the last twenty years. At the end of the Cold War in 1989, twenty-three nations belonging to NATO and the Warsaw Pact had 4.5 million armed personnel deployed in the European area;[9] by 2007 the figure was under 3 million.[10] U.S. forces in Europe were reduced over the same period from 326,400 to 96,800 and British forces in Germany went from 69,700 to 21,710. Such figures still fail to portray the quantum leap of history that, over a few months in 1989–90, transformed Europe from a continent divided down the middle into hyperarmed camps and constantly on the edge of nuclear destruction into an open strategic space offering all its nations a free choice of alignment. It took fifteen years for the energies released thereby to produce a clear new political geography, starting with the re-unification of Germany and culminating in the "Big Bang" enlargements of 2004 that brought NATO membership to a total of twenty-six (now raised to twenty-eight by Albania's and Croatia's accession in 2009) and EU membership to twenty-five (now twenty-seven with Bulgaria and Romania). With enlargement's full impact and the scope for further expansion and/or the "deepening" of integration still unclear, Europe has become anything but a status quo community. Many aspects of European strategic hesitancy—especially about anything that risks setting off further chain reactions of change—can be put down to awareness of the many uncertainties already dogging the continent.

At least three crosscurrents have complicated the transition of Europe toward a condition where no two countries are any more likely, or free, to attack each other again than modern France and Germany are. One is the sequence of wars and tense peaces in the *western Balkans*, where ethnic antagonism and separatism combined with some distinctly "premodern" attitudes have shown themselves still very much alive in the recent crisis over Kosovo's declaration of independence. Slovenia, and probably soon Croatia, can be counted as safe within the NATO-EU embrace, but Serbia in its attitudes, and the smaller western Balkan states in terms of governance, are still far from ripe for full integration. In the big strategic picture, this has meant a continued European need for active U.S. military-strategic backup; a containment task for the Europeans themselves; a brake upon the externalization of military priorities; and a still-open challenge for the European Union's transformative powers. This probably also offers Russia's best opening for manipulating events within "core" European territory, if only by political influence in Serbia and blocking tactics on Kosovo.

The second challenge is *Russia* itself and is hard to describe succinctly. It may help to recall that for most of the 1990s, it was not clear whether post-Soviet Russia would be able to hold itself together without resorting to neo-Communism or extreme nationalism; whether Chechnya would remain its only civil war; whether NATO would find the united nerve to integrate all Central Europe; and whether Russia would re-create a Warsaw Pact–like alliance behind the new NATO frontier. This helps to explain why "Russia handling" remained a priority task for Western leaders, and why the incentive for mutually restraining disarmament deals and partnership offers remained cogent,[11] right up to the paradigm shift of 2001. After 9/11, however, the Western strategic focus swung wholesale toward global and functional threats, while Russia remained penned in its own region and was driven more by necessity than any real Western quid pro quo to swallow the NATO-EU "Big Bang" without violence. The further acid added to East-West relations by the United States' post-9/11 military plans for European territory will be mentioned later.

With eight more years having passed and with Chechnya largely "out of sight, out of mind," Russia finds itself stable within its boundaries, rather well protected in its East Asian rear,[12] and with cash reserves from a temporary oil price bonanza that helped it cushion at least the early stages of the 2008 economic shock. At the same time Russia finds NATO-EU territory fencing in its only remaining outlets to the West (the Baltic and White Seas), faces some 45,000 NATO troops in Afghanistan, and sees persistent West-leaning tendencies in its closest former Soviet neighbors—Moldova, Georgia, and Ukraine.[13] It is not necessary to cite the personality of Vladimir Putin in order to grasp why Moscow has been rebuilding its military,[14] continuing its saber rattling over the future of disarmament, actively exploiting its economic strengths (notably as an oil supplier), and using every kind of bullying up to and including military invasion against its smaller pro-Western neighbors. The clear aim throughout is to discourage further Western strategic encroachment and rebuild what Moscow would define as balance and stability (i.e., dominance) in its own backyard. The one card Russia has not been able to play again with much credibility is the threat of active troublemaking in other world regions, where it has now no significant military presence. Indeed, abetting recklessness by countries such as Iran or North Korea would merely threaten its own safety.

Even the August 2008 war in Georgia has not changed the fact that Western Europe's five largest states are now geographically remote from Russian forces, while two of them have major codependencies with Russian supplies.[15] Concern about territorial military threats as such thus tends to be limited to smaller states around NATO and EU peripheries. Yet, in apparent contradiction, the third trend cutting across Europe's post–Cold War relaxation has been a *rebound in many European states' defense spending* from the late 1990s onward.[16] This has been clearest in the case of the large military nations Britain and France, as well as among the Central European states that have entered NATO (and that were given explicit expenditure and modernization targets)—so it cannot be attributed simply to new or persisting territorial concerns. Aside from rising unit costs and investment "bulges" associated with restructuring, increased defense spending most often reflects the pressure to take part in more, and more taxing, armed missions outside the homeland, for reasons to be discussed later. The growing detachment of mainstream European armed effort from purely local balances is tellingly reflected in the fact that no one on the Western side has questioned this as a possible destabilizing factor, a bad example to other regions, or a contradiction with European allegiance to arms control. The new rapid intervention capabilities are seen as linked purely with do-good missions abroad and/or control of nonstate-based threats. The trend has not, however, necessarily been interpreted the same way in Moscow or, for that matter, by some observers (scarred by colonialism) in North Africa.[17]

Nontraditional Hazards

As to the *asymmetrical threats*, all the larger West European states have had historic or twentieth-century experience of native terrorism (and terror attacks during the wars of decolonization), which by 2000 had led them to realize the limits of military suppression, to be interested in political solutions, and to be wary of pitfalls for democracy should the state be tempted into overauthoritarian reactions. In retrospect, the U.S. push, after 9/11, to reimagine terrorism as a monolithic and implacable target of "war" never really displaced this European analysis, but it did help Europeans wake up to what might be called the asymmetrical dangers of integration. The European Union's common market and the "Schengen" common travel space had offered new freedoms to any extremists, and indeed WMD smugglers, who could work from or get inside this huge open playing field. But progress toward an equally transnational mode of law enforcement and intelligence exchange had lagged far behind. Major attacks by terrorists of the new Islamicized and ideologized brand in Spain (March 2004) and Britain (July 2005), among others, have helped sustain a real European effort to make up this time lag through both internal and external cooperation.[18] However, the details of these incidents also pointed to localized features of terrorist motivation and the unsolved challenges of a multiethnic society, while the emerging lessons of Iraq and Afghanistan have reinforced European experts' faith in their own "counterinsurgency" strategies, characterized by more limited and subtle uses of military force. Parallel points can be made about European responses to the threat of WMD proliferation. First, nuclear fears are hardly new for Europe, and second, the European Union's specialized strategy document on the subject advocates addressing the security abnormalities that lead states to want such weapons rather than tackling the WMD factor in isolation through military interdiction or regime change.[19]

The main point to make in brief about the remaining, "softer" challenges to Europe is that they loom relatively higher in the local threat picture than they seem to in the U.S., Russian, or Chinese calculus. This is partly a matter of filling the gap left by Cold War fears and partly the work of effective single-issue lobbies (the Greens have ministers in many European governments!). The publicistic factor can be measured, for instance, in the fact that so many Europeans "know" the dangers of genetically modified foodstuffs while so few currently pay attention to HIV/AIDS, despite mushrooming infection rates just over the Russian border. However, some logical connections can also be seen between worries over climate, energy misuse, disease, and infrastructure and factors such as Europe's dense populations, intensive and sometimes marginal agricultural exploitation, heavy reliance on long supply lines of trade (open to disruption by all hazards anywhere in the world), dependence on sustained growth for social harmony, and—in general—focus on "quality of life" rather than imminent threats to life itself. As a peg for later comments on policy, it may be argued that history, geography, and economic structure all predispose Europeans to feel *interdependent* with people different from themselves for survival among these hazards.

"Europe's Burden" in the World

Interdependence is also a matter of statistics. The European Union is the world's leading exporting bloc with 26.9 percent of the world market, including a 19.5 percent share of nonenergy merchandise trade.[20] Trade creates a higher percentage of all EU states' GNP than it does for the United States. European external investments are valued at $2.2 trillion (33 percent of the world total),[21] and 54 percent of all energy used in Europe comes from abroad.[22] In human terms the continent has several large non-European minorities, including an estimated 13 million Muslims within the European Union,[23] while millions of Europeans travel or reside abroad—with global use of the English, French, Spanish, and Portuguese languages creating cultural and educational ties. Nevertheless, only tiny numbers of European (British and French) military forces are now stationed overseas and even total European deployments on peace missions lag behind the personnel numbers deployed by the United States in one location, Iraq.[24] This *demilitarized* character of external relationships is a fundamental European feature and can best be explained by reference to another "post," the *postcolonial* age that Europe entered during the period from 1950 to 1980.

All large West European powers and some smaller ones once had non-European empires that involved them in extensive force stationing abroad, and in bloody conflicts either with each other or (later) during liberation wars. The final phase of withdrawal took place after 1945 when Europe was focusing both on its own reconstruction (including building social welfare) and on permanent reconciliation through the European Union and NATO. Abandoning imperial traditions was not painless, but it reflected a conscious decision to regroup forces, to multinationalize security, and to resist global Communism on the home front above all. The corollary that Europe would have to work with the rest of the world in the future more by mutual-advantage deals and "soft power" was implicitly accepted fifty years before Robert Kagan developed the latter tag, and was accepted not just by default but for some ethical reasons. European postcolonial "guilt" remains a powerful—though mostly tacit—undercurrent, breeding hesitancy about forceful intervention, *especially on a national basis*, just as it tempts Europeans to think (perhaps wrongly) that they still understand their former colonies' feelings. The implications are wide reaching given that the colonial sphere included the broader Middle East up to the early twentieth century, and South and Southeast Asia for considerably longer. They are seen for instance in the fact that in 2007, an opinion poll showed that 79 percent of all Europeans were willing to send forces for humanitarian work in Darfur, 67 percent for peacekeeping in the Balkans, 66 percent for reconstruction in Afghanistan, and 59 percent for a cease-fire in Lebanon, but only 31 percent to fight the Taliban.[25] To balance this and recall the "schizo" element, it should be added that powerful European *nonstate* actors play far less high-minded roles in former colonial regions, ranging from defense sales and private soldiers to those Europe-based extractive companies that have run into accusations of looting resources and abetting conflict and violence.

The poll just cited also found that when asked what the European Union should do to reduce global threats, the highest number—84 percent—mentioned spending on development aid, followed by 74 percent who hoped to influence other countries by trade (with only 20 percent favoring the use of combat forces).[26] It is well known that Europe includes the world's top aid giver countries in terms of GDP share (Sweden currently gives 0.93 percent of gross national income),[27] but it is also worth noting that a high and increasing proportion of European aid giving goes either through the European Union or through global agencies and charities, thus becoming delinked from national strategic or commercial benefit. Another unique effect of Europe's integration process is that the European Union has a collective trade personality and speaks for all its governments in World Trade Organization talks and in bilateral commercial (including civil air) negotiations, as well as manages a common currency to which sixteen member states subscribe. (It is, however, a mark of the process's flaws that quite different parts of the EU machinery carry out these functions, using different procedures.) Europeans themselves often stress that such post-Westphalian integration methods have so far hardly penetrated into the European Union's Common Foreign and Security or Security and Defence Policies (CFSP and ESDP, respectively), so that much European strategic behavior remains nationally determined. An outsider should, however, be struck by how far the multilateralization trend has invaded nonmilitary spheres of diplomacy. Thus, the mechanisms of the EU-China relationship already decide more key issues than any single state could decide, and the Georgia crisis of August 2008—highlighting the West's weakness when unserious and divided—seems to have boosted a similar shift of approach on EU-Russia relations.

The Subjective Dimension: European National Attitudes

A feature setting Europe apart from many other world regions is that the "modern" process of nation forming has more or less run its course, with boundary changes like the peaceful breakup of Czechoslovakia and dismembering of Serbia almost certainly signaling the last phase. For some decades already, this has allowed some nation-states—most obviously Germany—to develop a national ethos largely based on *avoidance* of (too patent) nationalism, while in other states the national identity is increasingly *subdivided* into that of provinces, some of which play distinct external roles. A given EU citizen may thus have multiple sets of values and ambitions, relating not only to the security behavior of his/her state or even a subsection of the state, but also to Europe's mission as a whole. This makes it harder to offer any simple explanation of European security roles and identities in terms of a clear set of *interests*: the more so as the European Union itself has never used a clear interest-based discourse when drafting collective strategies. These, plus the open-ended nature of European construction, are health warnings to bear in mind when speaking of national differences—as this section must.

Drivers of Difference

One basic source of difference in global outlook is whether a given country had an extra-European empire or not. The countries of Northern and Central Europe did not, but underwent "local imperialism" in early modern history—the Hapsburg Empire, German expansionism, the hegemony of Sweden and its rivalry with Denmark in the North, plus of course forced integration under Soviet rule and the Warsaw Pact in the later twentieth century. Under Europe's current mind-set, this has led to roughly parallel behavior among the former hegemons involved in these parts—Sweden, Austria, Hungary, and Germany (even after reunification). Namely, they play down national assertiveness and use military power only collectively, through NATO, or in "altruistic" neoneutral style (Sweden and Austria). Neighbors formerly occupied by these countries and/or by the Soviets have adopted two main behaviors: going all out for the safe haven of integration (Finland, the Baltics, Hungary), or holding back from it in order not to lose to Brussels what they earlier lost to Big Brother (Norway, Iceland, and the pricklier aspects of Polish attitudes). At the other extreme are Britain and France, who did not share twentieth-century "war guilt" or occupiers' guilt, and who have emerged from decolonization to seek continued worldwide status and influence in good conscience—with the help indeed of some previously colonized partners. Logically enough, these two European nuclear powers are the most robust in external action and the most proactive in Europe's global engagement, while having the most distinctive (if differently revealed) neuroses about submerging themselves in a "federal" Europe.

Europe as a whole has reached a point where nations no longer struggle for strategic power within the region but rather argue over the nonmilitary management of the internal space on the one hand and the choices of external strategic methods and partnerships on the other hand. To take the obvious example, few issues divide European opinions as profoundly as the question of whether to side with U.S. policies in the world. In a 2008 opinion survey, 69 percent of Europeans overall agreed that the European Union should play a leadership role in the world; the lowest level of agreement—in Britain—was still 59 percent. The percentage wanting Europe to work more closely with the United States, however, ranged from 45 percent in Poland to a surprisingly low 26 percent in Britain, an even lower 25 percent in Germany, and 22 percent in Portugal.[28]

This finding may echo the popular view of the "new Europeans" as a natural pro-U.S. caucus, but that was always an oversimplification. Poland and Hungary or Estonia and Lithuania diverge as much in their attitudes as any "older" set of European neighbors, and the new members since 2004 have actually been more interested in swaying the course of EU-Russia relations than EU-U.S. or EU-NATO relations. Rather, at least two divides are at work: (1) between mostly small states on the peripheries of integrated Europe that feel they need the United States because of military vulnerability, and those that are better insulated; and (2) between European states—including quite "old" ones such as Italy and Britain—that share American openness toward the use of force when necessary, and others that have never had military power or have been educated out of it, such as the Germans. The more pro-U.S. group may also be split, for instance, by rebound effects after a failed joint adventure (Iraq syndrome). The resulting complex pattern of more, or less, "Atlantic" sympathies at any given time affects European security attitudes in more than one way. Europeans' natural discourse is heavily influenced by imported U.S. views, which some states embrace because they genuinely agree or are courting U.S. protection, and others reject just because of where the ideas come from. This could explain how a 2007 poll found that 70 percent of Poles but only 42 percent of the French worried about Iranian nuclear capability, even though the two states' natural understandings of proliferation dangers are exactly the other way around.[29]

In the end, views toward the United States or other external factors remain much more conditioned by Europeans' underlying national realities than vice versa. Differences of history have already been mentioned and to these must be added geographical factors that affect political, economic, and ecological threat exposures. Opinion polls regularly show higher German than Spanish levels of concern about Russia and energy dependence—which do not contradict but rather explain Germany's preference for handling Moscow with kid gloves. The British worry more than the Nordics about terrorism and nuclear rivalry, and Italians more than the British about the mafia, while Nordics are more exposed to and concerned about the environment, and so on. Other strong but varying feelings are associated with the degree of multiethnicity in a given society and its experience, or fear, of immigration. German popular opinion's hostility to Turkey joining the European Union, for instance (only 13 percent in favor in 2008 against 27 percent in Britain and 40 percent in Romania),[30] is clearly linked with concern about Germany's large Turkish immigrant population gaining full citizenship. Population patterns as well as geography explain why, in 2008, 56 percent of respondents in both France and Italy expected their own lives to be challenged by Islamic fundamentalism as against just 33 percent in Romania and 29 percent in Poland.[31]

The common perception that large-scale migration and multicultural mixing is linked with crime, job competition, and loss of identity helps to explain much of the last few years' surge of anti-enlargement feeling in Western Europe, as seen inter alia in the French and Netherlands popular "no" votes against a new European Constitution in 2005. Most European states are alert to the risk of conflicts anywhere in a very extended neighborhood creating floods of refugees and asylum seekers, which adds to the urge to avoid conflict in the first place. Most also see permanent migration pressures from places such as North Africa and the Balkans as being driven by economic want and frustration, which leads to an interest in development strategies (rather than plain force or political transformation) for "keeping people at home." The trouble is that Europe as a whole has not yet devoted the high relative priority and the scale of resource input to development aid for its "near neighbors" that this logic would demand.

Another important source of difference is the variation in European national defense and security "cultures," extending to some of the most basic value judgments. The percentage of respondents agreeing that "under some circumstances war is necessary to obtain justice" starts at 62 percent in Britain but falls to 20 percent in Germany, 19 percent in Spain, and 15 percent in Bulgaria.[32] There are further nuances in readiness to intervene abroad: some nations shy away from dangerous actions, some dislike actions far from home, some—like the Nordics—are ready to face considerable risks anywhere in the world so long as the legal base and/or humanitarian motive is strong. Study of which missions countries join also shows varying partialities for working with one institution, or one set of partners, rather than another.[33] European governments weigh risks not just in terms of direct hazard to their troops but also in terms of whether they might be tempted into dishonorable (brutal, neocolonial) behavior, whether home opinion might be thereby alienated from the whole idea of defense, and, conversely, whether other more pugnacious countries might handle things worse without them.

The other obvious limit on possible interventions is whether a country has the necessary resources. This is not just a question of defense expenditure, though the percentage of GDP devoted to this does range from 4.1 percent in Greece to 0.6 percent in Ireland.[34] It also reflects basic military traditions and readiness to reform them and involves questions such as whether states use conscripts or professional armies, how much states are willing to give up traditional territorial defense in favor of outside deployments, whether they are willing to specialize and harmonize with neighbors, and so on. There are crosscutting differences in how widely and confidently countries use their military for internal tasks such as border control, disaster response, and maintaining order, and whether they prefer separate paramilitary forces such as Italy's carabinieri. Roughly speaking, Britain, Denmark, and some Central European states (after joining NATO) have gone furthest in shifting their militaries' profile toward new external tasks and "civil security" duties, while old-style territorial defense remains strongest in the heart of the continent and Scandinavia. France, with a new defense white paper published in 2008, has committed itself strongly to mobilizing more resources for global tasks. Further variations include whether new missions can be launched and financed quickly by executive decision, or whether they are subject to constitutional and parliamentary controls.[35]

Mention of such complexities should underline that Europe's notorious failure to optimize the output—including foreign operational output—of its theoretically huge armed forces pool is not just a result of lack of will,[36] obsession with national sovereignty, or even deficient funds. It reflects the objective difficulty of overcoming huge variations in what defense is

Table 11.1   Measures of Military Effort for Selected EU Member States

Country	Defense spending as percentage of GDP	Material investment per soldier (€)[1]	Deployed forces, as percentage of total forces[2]
(High spending, high deploying)			
United Kingdom	2.5	65,027	19.2 (7.48)
France	2.43	28,381	4.9 (4.25)
Italy	1.81	7,658	3.6 (4.13)
(Low spending, high deploying)			
Netherlands	1.54	26,533	8.0 (4.47)
Germany	1.32	19,297	5.3 (2.80)
Sweden[3]	1.4	79,386	4.9 (3.43)
Ireland	0.52	8,159	7.7 (6.32)
(High spending, low deploying)			
Greece[4]	2.68	10,792	0.9 (1.08)
Bulgaria	2.31	1,741	0.9 (1.25)
(Low spending, low deploying)			
Poland	1.81	6,125	1.9 (2.48)
Portugal	1.58	4,181	2.3 (2.21)
Spain	1.18	20,033	2.6 (2.02)
Belgium	1.14	5,500	2.3 (2.34)

Notes: (1) defined as annual total equipment spending plus R & D spending divided by number of force personnel; (2) deployed outside national territory; (3) Denmark and Norway would fall into a similar category but with much lower "material investment" figures; and (4) Turkey would fall into a similar category.
Sources: Columns 1–3 are European Defence Agency figures for 2006, as cited by Nick Witney, "Re-energising Europe's Security and Defence Policy," European Council on Foreign Relations 2008, text at http://ecfr.eu/page/-/documents/ESDP-report.pdf; figures in parentheses in column 4 are averages for the years 2003–07 and are based on International Institute for Strategic Studies data, from Giegerich, *European Military Crisis Management.*

thought to be *about*, and armed forces *for*, among this set of more than thirty different and deeply rooted national communities. The data in table 11.1 illustrate this further by showing that aside from some obvious over-achievers in defense at the top of the scale and underachievers at the bottom, there is no linear relationship between total defense spending and willingness to face the risks of deployments abroad. Moreover, variations are huge in the level of mechanization and equipment, including ability to transport and sustain one's own forces: a country that can send many soldiers but with minimal matériel is not necessarily pulling its weight for Europe. On the other hand, some of the highest equipment spending (such as Sweden's and Spain's) has more to do with support of native defense industries than operational excellence. Finally, Germany's fairly respectable place in this table recalls the point made earlier that countries are also judged (rightly or wrongly) by the qualitative "hardness" of the tasks they are willing to share.

Convergence and Common Ground

For all this, there are signs that Europeans' security outlooks are gradually converging: the nonmilitary threats that loom larger in post–Cold War conditions tend to affect Europeans more uniformly; the progress of EU integration creates more shared material interests, as well as engages elites in joint strategy making; and key steps forward have been made at moments when Europeans "huddled for safety" in the recent burst of Russian violence or in the face of extreme U.S. actions. The first net result has been to raise the apparent level of security consciousness overall, so that Europeans' concerns in 2007 about international terrorism, Islamic fundamentalism, immigration, and global warming were respectively 16, 15, 14, and 12 percentage points higher than those measured in 2003.[37] Second, the range of threat perceptions is narrowing among the larger West European nations, particularly as German concern over "new threats" rises to join the European mainstream. In the period 2005–07, German concerns about terrorism, Islamic fundamentalism, and immigration grew by 32, 28, and 26 points, respectively; similar upward shifts were seen in Italy and Spain.

When asked in June 2008 if Europeans in general shared some specific values, 61 percent of all Europeans interviewed said "yes" and only 22 percent "no." As many as 37 percent also rejected the idea that the most important values were shared by the whole "West."[38] Such findings offer a practical basis for the post-9/11 theorizing about U.S.-European "Atlantic drift," and also explain why Europeans now talk more confidently about a values divide with Russia. The same surveys, however, suggest that Europeans are less distinctive in the kinds of threats they see than in the level of their agreement over how to handle them. In the Transatlantic Trends findings for 2008, U.S. and European popular gradings of the seriousness of seven key challenges from economic downturn to terrorism were never more than 17 percentage points apart and perceptions about pandemic disease were identical.[39] However, major "output" differences are indicated by the following findings—the message of which makes a good bridge into the final section of this chapter: 83 percent of Europeans but only 70 percent of Americans agree that "economic power is more important in the world than military power";[40] 64 percent of Europeans agree that "globalization makes common rules at world level necessary";[41] and 49 percent of Americans but only 21 percent of all Europeans (including 28 percent of Britons) favor maintaining the "military option" should current diplomacy fail to halt Iran's nuclear progress, with 47 percent of all Europeans but only 27 percent of Americans favoring increased "diplomatic pressure."[42]

Europe as Security Actor: Home and Abroad

Much European analytical writing on security today suggests that institutions are both the determinant and the measure of European effectiveness. This obsession with machinery risks misleading outside viewers and distorting interregional comparisons in several ways. First, as noted earlier, much European security output still comes from nation-states working in purely national or in more-than-European frameworks. Large security "producers" such as Britain and France still tend to treat joint European policies as add-ons to complement more traditional methods, or to address new challenges where national precedents are absent. As also noted, decision making within the European Union's security and defense policies is not (yet) "supranationalized" but works much the same way as in NATO or regional groupings elsewhere. This makes it hard to swing the huge material resources of the European Union as an economic entity behind its politically defined strategic goals, and even joint funding for military deployments is minimal. Thus, if Europeans fail to respond in a given situation as the United States or others might wish, it is not because some abstract "common policy" prevents them but because they do not want or cannot agree to do it. When the multi-institutional pattern of activity seems schizoid, it is because states are playing out their own confusions and mixed purposes, or reflecting different levels in their transition from a "modern" (or "premodern") to a "postmodern" security awareness. When proposed EU advances are struck down in popular referenda, it usually means that the elites have got carried away by an emerging club spirit while the peoples' real needs either remain unreconciled or would have pointed in another direction.[43]

While the ESS highlights "effective multilateralism" both as a principle and policy goal, it is worth noting that European joint efforts abroad have not given highest priority to supporting—or even to monitoring and analyzing—other regions' multilateral processes. While elaborate EU-UN agreements were reached on security cooperation starting in 2003–04, the European Union's record of both sticking together and getting other groups to cohere with it in UN decisions remains weak.[44] Elsewhere, the EU instinct seems to be to handle itself as a quasi-national "pole" and to seek an accommodation first and foremost with the strongest national actor in each region: with the United States rather than the North American Free Trade Area, with Russia and not the Commonwealth of Independent States, with China rather than the ASEAN Regional Forum or Shanghai Cooperation Organization (SCO), and so forth. In regions that lack a single obvious leader, the European Union will work with an institution, such as the African Union, but in regions where there is neither clear leadership nor a respectable institution, it is at a loss—a further clue to poor performance in the "near abroad."

These are all reasons not to focus this all-too-brief final section on institutional analysis. Rather, it will look at the pattern of real European security "outputs" in three interconnected spheres: protection of Europe's own territory, the enlargement and neighborhood issue, and Europe in the wider world.

The Home Territory

The main post–Cold War story has already been sketched above: as the integrated Europe's territory has grown, its traditional defense cover has grown increasingly thin. The withdrawal of most foreign stationed forces and the withering of large multinational units on West European soil has been complemented by the decision not to base foreign forces or nuclear objects on new allied territories in peacetime. As a result, NATO's fundamental commitment to mutual defense has become symbolic and even de-territorialized, as shown by the Europeans' readiness to invoke the guarantee in connection with 9/11 as well as by the new emphasis on allied solidarity *outside* Europe. The story of recent U.S. agreements with Bulgaria and Poland on transit bases for conventional troops, and with the Czech Republic and Poland on installations related to missile defense, is equally telling. Seen from Washington these bases had nothing to do with an East-West defense calculus, although Moscow, with its encirclement psychosis, was bound to see them as such.[45] From the European perspective, the willingness of some Central European states to do such deals outside NATO, thus earning both differential risk exposure and differential U.S. protection, exposes in its own way the decline of a "one-for-all" mentality.

The Georgian shock has prompted a hasty review of the adequacy of common defense—particularly on the sensitive Baltic frontier—and it now looks likely that the next years will witness greater efforts by NATO to demonstrate military solidarity within Europe and to stabilize behavior on *both* sides of the integrated/nonintegrated divide. Such an approach would further highlight the importance of Turkey, as would the demands of a serious Iraq exit strategy and any push to clear away remaining obstacles in EU-NATO cooperation. However, the overall dearth of allied manpower is just one of several factors making it very unlikely that NATO will decide after all to extend collective structures across Central Europe, or to remilitarize Europe's territory generally. Rather, if it tries too hard to reestablish full strategic deterrence, NATO might be drawn down the same path that Russia has been—toward increased reliance on nuclear forces, which would sit ill with President Obama's current efforts to relaunch mutual nuclear disarmament both in Europe and worldwide.

In practice—as confirmed by EU mediation in the Georgia crisis—even in this "hard" security sphere the mantle has passed increasingly to the Europeans themselves and to the nonmilitary strengths that they can or should be able to muster. The hope that EU economic strength, interdependence, and eventual "soft transformation" might eventually restrain Russia is only one topical example. The European Union has always been the only local institution competent to coordinate its members' internal security, border control, and law-and-order policies; to deal with functional dimensions of security from infrastructure and transport to natural disasters and pandemics; and to combat nonstate menaces (terrorism, crime, smuggling, trafficking) by all measures short of military interdiction. It has the competence to create collective policies on energy sourcing and use and on other aspects of managing climate change. It has in effect taken over all responsibility for the peace and eventual full integration of the western Balkans, with the important exception of a NATO military presence in Kosovo. On all these points, including the management of Kosovo's move to declare its independence, Washington (like other great-power capitals) now makes no bones about accepting the EU end of Brussels as its natural interlocutor.

How fast and fully the European Union can grow into these responsibilities is another question. The ESS is notably weak on the internal, territorial management of threat and risk. Collective European reticence about addressing "hard" military security in this setting reflects not only the spread of national differences already discussed—including the presence of six nonmembers of NATO in the European Union—but also the understanding that no one in Europe gains by exposing NATO's limitations or burying NATO before its time. Even in the "softer" dimensions the European Union is too often hamstrung by the diversity of its instruments and institutions, by differences of national structure (notably different degrees of decentralization), and by resistance to internal security harmonization from both ordinary people and elites. Europeans who are sensitive about having their liberties curtailed in the name of security are even less likely to trust Brussels than to trust their own governments to get that balance right. In a distinctive paradox, European armies are much more willing to fight under common command and most European banks are much more willing to accept a common currency, than European policemen, customs officials, and judges are to contemplate stepping outside their national traditions. The European Union's latest attempt at governance reform, the

Lisbon Treaty, which was finally brought into force in December 2009 (and which repackages much of the earlier draft constitution),[46] has introduced some moderately useful measures to pool the union's various funds and staffs for external action, to upgrade the office of the "foreign minister," who commands these resources, and to strengthen political leadership at the level of the European Council. Even leaving aside the doubts about the individuals first appointed to these two latter posts,[47] their effects will hardly touch upon the much knottier challenge of uniting external and internal security governance and wielding economic and societal instruments together with overtly strategic ones.

The Wider Europe and Its Neighborhood

Four things currently stand out about the way the integrated Europe interacts with its neighbors: the complexity and contradictions of NATO and EU "outreach," including enlargement proper; the lack of any stable accommodation with Russia, even twenty years after the end of the Cold War; the weakening of Europe's most inclusive organizations, the OSCE and Council of Europe; and the striking impotence of both European outreach and osmosis toward the east and south of the Mediterranean.

The NATO and EU enlargement processes so far have been demand led: Central European candidate states have borne not only the major financial costs of adaptation but also the burden of clearing up destabilizing disputes with neighbors. The western Balkans are an intermediate case where the European Union itself has to invest heavily in transformation but recognizes a direct strategic imperative to do so. The trouble with both institutions' ambitious partnership and outreach structures—NATO's Euro-Atlantic Partnership (EAP) and the European Union's European Neighborhood Policy (ENP), plus individual partnership and cooperation agreements[48]—is that they stretch to regions of Eurasia where states are far less ripe for change, and where Westerners so far have not been certain whether and why they should take on strategic responsibility. Material transfers have been very small under these programs, particularly when compared with Russia's economic stake in the region or the significance of the petrochemical economy. The West has celebrated self-generated changes such as Georgia's Rose Revolution and Ukraine's Orange Revolution but—as latest events show—has lacked both will and influence either to implant democracy more fully and irreversibly in such countries, or to protect them against Russia's moves (both forceful and insidious) to turn the clock back. In retrospect, expressing the policy challenge of such neighbors as a simplistic one of whether/when to let them into NATO has merely helped the West (and leaders such as Mikheil Saakashvili) to go on dodging the real issues, while sharpening the terms of confrontation with Russia. The Europeans' consequent recoil from the idea of enlargement beyond the Balkans, which was already anathema to most EU public opinion, is likely to be deeper and longer than would otherwise have been necessary and could still provoke serious tensions with the United States.

The Eastern front of enlargement differs from other fronts in that Russia "pushes back" with its own vision of multilateral organization of the post-Soviet space, though it has not been able to make that vision work either. Only Belarus, Armenia, and the Central Asian Republics are now willing to form a military bloc with Moscow, while under the SCO Russia must increasingly share the Central Asian zone of influence with China. The Russians have neither been able to truly pacify Chechnya nor to end "frozen conflicts" further into the Caucasus; and if the reason is that they still hope to manipulate such divisions against the more pro-Western governments involved, that in itself is a confession of weakness. The picture makes most sense if Russia's defensiveness and possessiveness over its "near abroad" is seen not just as a permanent historical reflex, but also as the flip side of its loss of standing in mainland Europe and its inability to find its place in any larger "new West." Moscow may have advanced to the point, with NATO, of having titular equal status in a NATO-Russia Council, but it still has no say in NATO internal decisions—including on enlargement—and has witnessed the United States apparently overturning NATO-agreed restraints. With the European Union, Russia has agreed to build four new common spaces of soft security, human freedom, and economic and scientific development, but it remains shut behind tough trade and migration barriers—it is not even a member of the World Trade Organization yet!—and found itself having to beg for solutions to maintain transit to its exclave of Kaliningrad when the European Union enlarged.

Russia's frustration at these outcomes is comprehensible but can be blamed as much on its own external tactics as on the limits of its internal transformation. Moscow's hectoring has made it hard even for the moderate Central Europeans to act as sympathetic mediators, while the sharpening of antipathies with the Baltic States and Poland has clearly tipped the European Union's overall policy balance toward a willingness to play (nonmilitary) hardball. Putin has consistently pushed threats and divisive tactics beyond the point where they were working, to the point where they only strengthened intra-European and U.S.-European solidarity. In the climate created by Georgia and by an economic crash that has exposed the Russian economy's feet of clay, this syndrome may apply even in the area of a joint EU energy policy where divisions were deepest before. Seen more broadly, the problematic relationship with Russia has neither dominated nor constrained the evolution of total European strategic policies, and still less has handicapped EU relations with other world players such as China. This could only change if the Europeans themselves were to overreact to the latest East-West chill, by misapprehending the real balance of power.

The true casualties of the Russia-West stalemate are the inclusive organizations that played a large part in undermining the earlier Soviet bloc: the OSCE, and to a lesser extent the Council of Europe. The latter's competence to address governance abuses has been sapped by Russia and its remaining allies gaining vetoes within it, but for OSCE the problem is rather that Russia no longer finds it useful to use it for more than grandstanding. In terms of power relations it makes more sense for Moscow to bargain with (both institutions of) Brussels directly than to seek pan-European solutions through Vienna where so few truly "unattached" states are left. From Putin's viewpoint the military checks and balances created in the Conventional Forces in Europe Treaty and other OSCE provisions have failed to constrain U.S. encroachment, and the West has exploited OSCE's "human dimension" to stir up internal change farther East, while blocking enquiries into its own new members' conduct (vide the closing of OSCE missions in the Baltics).[49] President Dmitry Medvedev's suggestion first made in 2008 for a new European Security Treaty, which the Russians fleshed out further in 2009,[50] reflects both this sense that the OSCE has come to the end of the road and perhaps—interestingly enough—second thoughts in Moscow about who will gain by leaving pan-European strategic relations totally unregulated. Clearly Russia would like such a treaty to draw lines around Western enlargement, and just as clearly, the West will not allow this but would insist on importing into any new edifice the OSCE principles of human freedoms and peaceful change. Whether discussions of the new concept can reconcile these two approaches—just as the Helsinki Final Act did when the Conference on Security and Cooperation in Europe, OSCE's precursor, was first created—is an open question that must probably be decided in Washington.

In historical terms, the Mediterranean and North African littoral has always been the region where Europeans were least sure of their role: lying between the space where Europe's own multinational families have flourished, and the zone of durable imperialism. Both NATO and the European Union have in practice invested much more in Eastern outreach than in cooperation toward the Levant and south Mediterranean shore.[51] Both have failed to create more than the most tenuous structural links in the Middle East, or to generate any strong local "buy in" to multilateral approaches for the wider region. Part of the problem is that Mediterranean dialogue meetings of all kinds (including efforts to apply the OSCE *acquis*) are regularly subverted by Arab-Israel tensions; but also important are sundry other local divisions, postcolonial suspicions, and the difficulty of disassociating NATO collective efforts from actions by and attitudes toward the United States. In more substantial terms of strategic need, the region is dominated by nontraditional threats and developmental problems that NATO lacks the competence to address, and that the European Union has hitherto lacked the will and resources to cope with.[52] In civilizational terms, countries south of Turkey seem less open to the European style of internal-plus-supranational transformation, either because their authoritarian structures are too strong or because their national identities are not (yet) strong enough.

During 2008 the story of French president Nicolas Sarkozy's attempt to create a "Union for the Mediterranean" once more underlined the stubbornness of these obstacles. He had originally hoped for a network of north and south Mediterranean states, built on the same concept of shared neighborhood interests as "subregional" groups elsewhere in Europe, but with enough political momentum to boost Middle East peace talks and extend North-South cooperation even into such sensitive fields as nuclear energy. He even spoke of the grouping using "the same goal and the same method" as the European Union itself. Other EU countries, however, were not prepared to surrender the whole Mediterranean agenda to a limited local group of states, nor to redirect budget priorities from the East to the South. Turkey suspected a ploy to divert it from full EU membership, and officials in Brussels pleaded for continuity with the existing Euro-Mediterranean Partnership launched in Barcelona in 1995. In the end, while a summit of all EU members and all other local states except Libya did happen on July 13, 2008, the conclusions were largely a restatement of Barcelona provisions, and promises of new resources were especially noteworthy by their absence.[53]

At a practical level in the last decades, the pattern has been for European states to expect the United States to take the lead in the Middle East and West Asia while feeling free to jointly criticize some parts of Washington's choices (e.g., over Israel), and to divide themselves thoroughly over others (such as Iraq). Again, what is perhaps most striking is how cheaply Europe has gotten away with this limited-liability policy since 1990, leading to the question of what might change in the post-Bush era. Both an Israeli-Palestinian settlement, and a containment solution for Iraq resting on inclusive regional cooperation, would be likely to demand stronger European inputs—but both would create a more Europe-friendly environment and reduce the challenge for Brussels to basically one of resource allocation. (The bargains Europe has been offering Iran already point toward this model.) Alternatively or simultaneously, however, Europe's relations across the Mediterranean could become dominated by migration threats and perhaps Maghrebian conflict triggered inter alia by climate change, which would be likely to boost a common European defense identity while forcing a clearer, "fortress"-style definition of Europe's limits.

Finally: Europe and the Big World

At present, what marks Europe's doctrine about its place in the world is its expansiveness combined with vagueness and lack of follow through. Strategic factors behind the European new-age drive for economic and cultural involvement have been sketched, and Europe's activism in these softer dimensions will clearly be boosted by a will to set its stamp on the handling of the global financial/economic crisis. In the narrower military context, all the European handicaps mentioned herein have not stopped European countries from sending a total of 22,406 persons (in 2007) to the NATO operation in Afghanistan, 12,281 (the same year) to UN operations, and 7,938 (in 2006) to EU military and civilian missions abroad.[54] These numbers are not notably larger than the total number of British, French, and other postcolonial deployments in the late Cold War. The difference is that their basic purpose has switched from the defensive to the transformational, often (in practice) serving emergent European common interests under a gloss of altruism.[55] Such operations are typically just the tip of an iceberg of European humanitarian, economic, and political engagement, including still-significant national security assistance programs.

It has been suggested above that Europeans old and new are hesitantly moving toward common security perceptions, which should logically also discipline and focus the European "export of security." There are already signs, post-Iraq, of clearer European thinking about when it makes sense to do something with the United States; when it is better to seek the same Western goal by other means; and when Europe should chart a different course, possibly with other partners. The deepest uncertainty, however, is not over partner choices or institutional instruments but over whether Europe as an entity wants to be an active power or a passive model: whether it is more important to "do good"—and make things better for itself in the process—or to "be good," and sit tight to preserve itself. Twentieth-century history has pushed toward the cautious choices, sometimes to the point of actual free riding. Already, however, Europeans' caution over military self-assertion contrasts with their readiness to act tough and even make enemies when talking trade and competition, agriculture, or immigration. Twenty-first-century developments in both internal and external security agendas—plus the halting but unidirectional dynamic of the integration process itself—seem more likely than not to encourage more proactive or at the very least more *conscious* European strategic approaches, in a form never seen or possible in history before.

Even a self-aware Europe exploiting its potential to the full will be one of the world's lesser military actors, and an unusually risk-averse one. As such it will not only add to the "multipolarity" of global processes but also make the system more diverse in the nature of its "poles." Europe cannot be another United States or China, any more than it is likely to regress into another Middle East. Its most powerful effects on global evolution are still likely to come from changes that it inspires and mediates in others: whether single nations exploring the benefits of "soft power," or other regions copying the integrationist model. Its greater achievement, in the future as in the past, might simply be that it manages to survive in all its fascinating imperfection, and in all its sometimes inspiring uniqueness.

Notes

1. Text at www.consilium.europa.eu/cms3_fo/showPage.ASP?id=266&lang=EN&mode=g.

2. These are interstate groups such as the Council of Baltic Sea States, Central European Initiative, and Black Sea Cooperation Forum that play existential security roles by building bridges between NATO-EU members and nonintegrated neighbors. They often address "soft" security themes such as emergency response, border management, crime, and disease control.

3. For instance, externally active nongovernmental organizations and charities, business actors, including arms producers and security services providers, media, educational and religious networks, etc.

4. Here understood as a world view that limits and relativizes the role of military force, recognizes important nonstate roles in security process, and defines security desiderata in non-zero-sum terms.

5. The ESDP, focused on military crisis management, was launched by decisions at the Helsinki European Council of December 1999. For a discussion of its normative features (and contradictions), see Alyson J. K. Bailes, "What Role for the European Security and Defence Policy?" *International Affairs* 84, no. 1 (January 2008): 115–30.

6. For factual background and a more straightforward narrative on matters treated thematically in this chapter, the author recommends Andrew Cottey, *Security in the New Europe* (London: Palgrave Macmillan, October 2007).

7. For instance, the European Union's Eurobarometer poll in 2008 found Europeans' top four concerns in their own countries were inflation, employment, crime, and health care (in that order), and their top four concerns for the world were poverty, global warming, terrorism, and conflicts (in that order). Results from Eurobarometer 69 released in June 2008 are available at http://ec.europa.eu/public_opinion/archives/eb/eb69/eb_69_first_en.pdf.

8. This is especially true of the Mediterranean interface with unstable, population-heavy North Africa and the Levantine interface with the Middle East and West Asia. However—as discussed in the next section—there is a persistent and perhaps willful European attention deficit toward these challenges.

9. All 1989 data in this paragraph come from *The Military Balance 1989–90* (London: Brasseys for the International Institute of Strategic Studies [IISS], 1990). Area covered is "from the Atlantic to the Urals."

10. All 2007 data from *The Military Balance 2008* (London: Routledge [for IISS], 2008).

11. The Conventional Forces in Europe Treaty was first signed on November 19, 1990, and updated in November 1999 at the OSCE summit in Istanbul.

12. Thanks to the Shanghai Cooperation Organization, founded in 2002 to manage Sino-Russian coexistence.

13. Russia's only close military allies in the framework of the Comprehensive Security Treaty Organization are Belarus, Armenia, Kazakhstan, Kyrgyzstan, and Uzbekistan, while Ukraine and Georgia have been promised eventual entry into NATO.

14. In 1998 Russian military expenditure, at around US$13.6 billion, was one-third of Germany's; by 2007 it had risen to US$35.4 billion but was still US$24 billion below British spending (data at constant 2005 prices). *SIPRI Yearbook 2008: Armaments, Disarmament and International Security* (London: Oxford University Press [OUP], 2008).

15. They are France, Germany, Italy, Spain, and Britain (in Britain's case this is also because of military withdrawals from the continent). Italy is most dependent on Russian energy among large Western states, followed by Germany.

16. Some noteworthy increases in military expenditure from 2000 to 2005 (in billions of US dollars, constant prices) are: Britain, 47.8 to 59.2; France, 50.4 to 53; Spain, 11 to 12.3; Netherlands, 9.1 to 9.7; Poland, 4.9 to 6.3. These figures are taken from a table in *SIPRI Yearbook 2007: Armaments, Disarmament and International Security* (Oxford: OUP, 2008), 310–16.

17. On the asymmetry of strategic philosophies and hence perceptions that has developed between West and East since the Cold War (plus detailed force data), see the statement by Alyson J. K. Bailes to the OSCE Annual Security Review Conference 2008, published July 3, 2008 at www.osce.org/documents/cio/2008/07/31769_en.pdf.

18. See the chapters by Jörg Monar and Gabriele Porretto in Miriam Gani and Penelope Mathew, eds., "Fresh Perspectives on the War on Terror," Australian National University, July 2008, http://epress.anu.edu.au/war_terror/pdf_instructions.html.

19. Shannon N. Kile, ed., *Europe and Iran: Perspectives on Non-proliferation*, Stockholm International Peace Research Institute (SIPRI) Research Report 21 (London: OUP, 2005).

20. These proportions have only dropped slightly over the last decade. European Commission statistics are available at http://trade.ec.europa.eu/doclib/docs/2008/october/tradoc_141196.pdf.

21. Ibid.

22. European Commission Strategic Energy Review, "Securing the EU's Energy Future," November 13, 2008, http://ec.europa.eu/energy/strategies/2008/2008_11_ser2_en.htm.

23. European Union Monitoring Centre on Racism and Xenophobia (EUMC), "Muslims in the European Union: Discrimination and Islamaphobia," EUMC, 2006, 31. This is a conservative figure; the CIA cites estimates between 14,836,000 and 16,926,000. See Central Intelligence Agency, "The World Factbook," www.cia.gov/library/publications/the-world-factbook/.

24. For details of national and peacekeeping deployments by all European states, see *Military Balance 2008*; and see table 11.1 in this chapter.

25. Transatlantic Trends 2007, www.transatlantictrends.org/trends/doc/Transatlantic%20Trends_all_0920.pdf. Note also that Europe's most willing "go-anywhere" peacekeepers are

the noncolonial Nordics, and EU missions often use a Nordic or Irish commander to signal "clean hands."

26. Ibid.

27. Regerinskansliet (Government of Sweden), press release, April 4, 2008, www.regeringen.se/sb/d/10477/a/102321.

28. Transatlantic Trends 2008, key findings at www.transatlantictrends.org/trends/index.cfm?id=123.

29. Transatlantic Trends 2007.

30. Transatlantic Trends 2008.

31. Ibid.

32. In the United States, only 23 percent *disagreed.* See Ibid.

33. For examples, see Alyson J. K. Bailes, "Motives for Overseas Missions: The Good, the Bad and the Ugly," in *Crisis Management in Crisis?* Research Report 2, no. 40, ed. Susanna Eskola (Helsinki: National Defence University of Finland, December 2008), 73–84.

34. Estimates for 2007 from *SIPRI Yearbook 2007*, table 8.A.4.

35. For more on variables in military "culture," see Alyson J. K. Bailes, "European Defence: What Are the Convergence Criteria?" *RUSI Journal* (June 1999); and Alyson J. K. Bailes, "Differentiated Risk and Threat Perceptions of EU Members and Their Impact on European Security Cooperation," *Dis Politika–Foreign Policy* 29, no. 3–4 (2004), www.foreignpolicy.org.tr/periodicals.html.

36. According to one calculation, only 4 percent of Europe's total armed forces have been deployed on missions abroad at any time in recent years. For more on this, see Bastian Giegerich, *European Military Crisis Management: Connecting Ambition and Reality*, Adelphi Paper no. 397 (London: IISS, 2008).

37. Transatlantic Trends 2007.

38. Eurobarometer 69.

39. Transatlantic Trends 2008.

40. Transatlantic Trends 2008.

41. Eurobarometer 69.

42. Transatlantic Trends 2008.

43. ESDP itself has met rather little popular protest, despite minimal consultation by elites—even with parliaments—because the poll evidence shows that solid majorities in most countries grasp the need for more collective crisis management.

44. European Council for Foreign Relations, "A Global Force for Human Security? An Audit of EU Power at the UN," September 2008, http://ecfr.eu/content/entry/the_european_union_and_the_united_nations/.

45. Zdzislaw Lachowski, *Foreign Military Bases in Eurasia*, SIPRI Policy Paper no. 18 (Stockholm: SIPRI, June 2007), http://books.sipri.org/product_info?c_product_id=339.

46. See http://europa.eu/lisbon_treaty/full_text/index_en.htm.

47. Baroness Catherine Ashton from Britain is the first to take up the "foreign minister" post, and former Belgian prime minister Herman van Rompuy is the first to take on the multiyear chairmanship of the European Council.

48. On EAP, see www.nato.int, and on ENP, see http://ec.europa.eu/world/enp/welcome_en.htm.

49. On the OSCE story, see Pál Dunay, *The OSCE in Crisis*, Chaillot Paper no. 88 (EU Institute of Security Studies, 2006), http:/iss_eu.org/chaillot/chai88.pdf.eu/6.

50. Made in a speech in Berlin, June 5, 2008; see, for example, Judy Dempsey, "Russian Proposal for European Security Treaty Would Sideline NATO," *International Herald Tribune*, July 27, 2008, www.iht.com/articles/2008/07/27/europe/nato.php.

51. Malta and Cyprus are the only "Mediterranean" states included in enlargement and have not joined NATO.

52. For more on these points, see Rosemary Hollis, "The Greater Middle East," in *SIPRI Yearbook 2005* (London: OUP, 2005), http://yearbook2005.sipri.org/ch5/ch5.

53. The summit declaration was published by the French presidency at www.eu 2008.fr/PFUE/lang/en/accueil/PFUE-07_2008/PFUE-13.07.2008/declaration_ commune_du_sommet_de_paris_pour_la_mediterranee.

54. Figures calculated from the SIPRI Multilateral Peace Operations database, www.sipri. org/contents/conflict/database-Intro/.

55. This thesis is argued in Bailes, "What Role for the European Security and Defence Policy?"

12

Russia and Central Asia

Oksana Antonenko

As the world celebrates the twentieth anniversary since the end of the Cold War and seventeen years since the formal dissolution of the Soviet Union, post-Soviet Eurasia is still struggling with many security threats and challenges. These exist on three levels: (1) within many fragile post-Soviet states, which were weakened further by the current global financial crisis and by the authoritarian regimes that have emerged in the majority of post-Soviet states; (2) between regional states, such as Russia and Georgia and Armenia and Azerbaijan, which are currently in a state of unresolved conflict and have no diplomatic ties with one another other; and finally, (3) within the wider region and world, as regional and global threats—from Afghanistan to organized crime—have an impact on post-Soviet states largely due to their location at the heart of the Eurasian landmass, which links Europe and Asia, the South with the North, and developed economies with some of the world's poorest.

Yet despite of all of these challenges, the region still lacks an effective regional security mechanism to address them. The reasons for such a shortage of security capacity are complex and multidimensional and are rooted in a diverse set of factors, including historic links and grievances, limitations on state building and political transition, and the region's lack of capacity to address contemporary challenges with modern strategies and instruments. These structural inefficiencies within the post-Soviet security paradigm stem from the following:

1. Russia is the key regional actor and at the same time the major challenge for regional security policymaking. Russia's residual fears about the West, its nineteenth-century realpolitik approach to the pursuit of international relations in its "near abroad," its fear of democratic changes, and its limited resources (and ideas) to address regional security challenges complicate security relationships in Eurasia.

2. The inherent tension between state-building (which is still under way) and regionalism is to a large extent responsible for the lack of any meaningful regional cooperation in Central Asia, where many regional challenges—from water to Afghanistan—require regional solutions but where regional states are focused on asserting and defending their newly established sovereignty.

3. The failure of security-sector reforms both undermines domestic capacity to deal with security threats and weakens the possibility of finding a regional cooperative solution to regional problems in Eurasia. Under current domestic settings, the military and security services are more preoccupied with propping up authoritarian regimes than with addressing current and rising security threats. Threats are often invented or exaggerated to justify repression. In cases where state intervention is indeed necessary, security sectors lack tools, resources, and ideas for addressing complex modern threats in a strategic manner.

4. Regional states have a distorted view of security priorities and in most cases place little priority on human security, particularly as relates to public health, human trafficking, migration, the environment, and education. As a result, national security policy is defined primarily as security of political regimes, or its leaders, and not of the population. Moreover, unrecognized states and regions closed to international observers, such as a large part of Russia's North Caucasus or Uzbekistan's Fergana Valley, undermines the ability of international players to advance universal values in their policies in Eurasia.

5. Although external engagement in post-Soviet Eurasia by Western and Eastern actors has dramatically increased over the past two decades, such as through a soft form of neocontainment of Russia applied by the Bush administration, a new energy security drive by the European Union, and China's geoeconomic relations with its Central Asian neighbors—it remains limited, nonstrategic, and often geopolitically motivated. At the same time, the war in Georgia weakened the credibility of Western security commitments in

the region and strengthened the perception of a growing security vacuum.

6.   In the past two decades, the engagement of major international organizations such as the United Nations, the Organization for Security and Co-operation in Europe (OSCE), and, most recently, the European Union has added an important but still marginal footprint to the regional security agenda. These organizations have failed to demonstrate the capacity and collective political will to prioritize the resolution of issues of most pressing concern, such as regional conflicts, or to prevent new ones from erupting. The closure of the OSCE and UN missions in Georgia following the Russian-Georgian war in August 2008 indicates a worrying trend that the role of such global institutions will be reduced even further, as Russia and some Western powers continue to disagree on the fundamental principles regulating the resolution of conflicts. In Central Asia, the roles of the OSCE and United Nations will remain much less prominent than other organizations, such as the Shanghai Co-operation Organization (SCO) and the Collective Security Treaty Organization (CSTO). Moreover, the lack of progress on political reforms and endemic corruption are likely to further undermine the value-based organizations' capacity to promote their agendas in Central Asia.

This chapter examines two related case studies that illustrate the limitations on regional security solutions in Eurasia. The first examines the factors that both compel and limit Russia's role as the key security guarantor in Eurasia. The second examines which regional mechanisms exist to address Central Asia's serious security challenges. The chapter concludes with a description of how the post–Cold War security paradigm in Eurasia might be changing as a result of both regional and global forces and what kinds of new frameworks could emerge in its place, particularly with regard to addressing security challenges in Central Asia.

Russia: Drivers and Limitations of the Key Security Actor in Eurasia

As the largest successor state of the former Soviet Union and as the only nuclear power that emerged from the Soviet Union's demise in 1991, Russia is the most powerful and important security actor in the post-Soviet space. It survived a deep economic crisis in 1990s, which prompted Russia's de facto retreat from regional and international affairs, and it has reemerged as a self-declared great power in the early years of the new century and claimed its role as the key regional power in the post-Soviet space. This resurgence is driven by a decade's worth of uninterrupted economic growth (fueled predominantly by the rise of global commodity prices) and the revival of Russia's tradition of a strong, authoritarian, and highly centralized state that was established under the two presidential terms of Vladimir Putin. Russia's oil-export-generated wealth has underpinned its new ambition to play a significant role on the international scene.

In 2010 Russia finds itself at a crossroads. On the one hand, it has shown more interest in exploring a new relationship with the West. The "reset" in U.S.-Russia relations under the Obama administration and the increasingly pro-Western foreign policy pursued by President Dmitry Medvedev as a tool to promote domestic modernization are two examples of this new relationship. On the other hand, Russia continues to exercise utmost sensitivity regarding any Western involvement in its "near abroad" and continues to view its relationship with the United States and the European Union, as well as increasingly with China and Turkey, as one of strategic rivalry and not of strategic accommodation or cooperation.

Russia's security perceptions and its declining domestic capacities to deal with them are likely to determine its future path—that is, whether it will choose to develop a new relationship with the United States and Europe or to continue to pursue its competitive policies, particularly in post-Soviet Eurasia, leveraging its global and regional power by interacting pragmatically with all global powers but forming alliances with none.

Russia's Security Concerns

Although Russia itself has changed significantly in the past decade, its security perceptions have not changed very much at all. Moreover, there are few signs that these perceptions are likely to undergo a significant change as long as the current generation of post-Soviet elites remains in power. If Vladimir Putin, who continues to enjoy popularity and to exercise a significant grip on power despite the formal passing of the presidency to his handpicked successor, Dmitry Medvedev, decides to return as president in 2012, this generation could remain in power until 2024 and beyond.

Russia's threat perceptions fall broadly within three categories. In order of priority, they are (1) the unresolved Cold War legacies in relation to the West; (2) domestic security threats emanating mainly from the instability in the North Caucasus and crime-related threats such as illegal migration and drug use; and (3) regional security threats in post-Soviet Eurasia. In addition to having these prominent concerns, Russia perceives threats from nuclear-weapons proliferation and the possible emergence of a global nuclear multipolarity; the expected impact of global warming on Russia (and its northern regions); and the spread of global pandemics within Russia's largely unreformed public health system. Russia is working with the international community to address these global threats, but it does not view them as vital in the short to medium term. Moreover, Russia is not the key player in resolving any of these challenges, though the Obama administration sees Russia's role as significant on some issues, such as Iran's nuclear program.

Cold War legacies. The first category of Russia's security concerns relates to the security agenda in U.S.-Russian relations, as well as to the post–Cold War European security system and Russia's place in it. Although these concerns are informed by the legacies of the Cold War, for many in the Russian political class, suspicions about the West and, in particular, the United Nations remain central to Russia's security thinking in the twenty-first century. There are two fundamental concerns that shape Russia's security policy.

Russia's first security concern is that the end of the Cold War has not resulted in the creation of a "common security space" between the West and Russia or, geographically speaking, across the European continent, including Russia. Instead, NATO and EU enlargement into Central Europe has simply moved the "dividing line" eastward, excluding Russia from decision-making processes on key European security policies. Moreover, NATO enlargement is seen as advancing the most powerful military alliance in the world close to Russia's borders, while Moscow has no say over NATO policies vis-à-vis Russia itself or the regions that represent the zone of Russia's vital interests. In the mind of Russian decision makers, NATO and EU enlargement have been accompanied by progressively more negative attitudes toward Russia—as represented by the consensus within these organizations, which have been influenced by the inclusion of states that have historic grievances toward Russia, that view it as a threat, and that advocate a policy of neocontainment toward Russia. This perception was reinforced when NATO decided to suspend the NATO-Russia Council in the aftermath of the Russian-Georgian war, thus eliminating the only channel for Russia to communicate its position to NATO and to affect the decision-making process within NATO.

Russia's unhappiness with the evolution of the post–Cold War European security architecture was first expressed by then-president Putin during his famous speech at the Munich security conference. Medvedev went further by proposing in the first month of his presidency the idea of concluding a new European Security Treaty—a Helsinki Two or Helsinki Plus, as it has been referred to by the Europeans—that could address both the old legacies and the new divisions with the objective of creating a common security space from Vancouver to Vladivostok. Medvedev's draft European Security Treaty, which was unveiled in December 2009, did not receive strong support within the Euro-Atlantic region, though it did generate a serious debate on possible ways to enhance Europe's security architecture both to alleviate Russia's sense of exclusion and to boost institutional capacity to address current and future threats.

New NATO secretary general Anders Fogh Rasmussen has signaled NATO's commitment to improve NATO-Russia relations, including through a NATO-Russia collaboration on missile defense. Meanwhile, EU leaders have proposed the creation of a special body to address with Russia certain security issues, including those related to unresolved protracted conflicts in Eurasia. And the OSCE—the most comprehensive regional institution in Europe—launched the Corfu process, an informal initiative tasked with discussing European security architecture, in response to Medvedev's proposals. Yet despite of all this activity, there is still no consensus on possible solutions and little appetite within Europe and the United States regarding a new comprehensive legally binding European Security Treaty as proposed by Medvedev. The Russians, in turn, are skeptical about a pragmatic holistic approach in which more practical cooperation is developed without any overarching strategic treaty-like framework that addresses Russia's fundamental security concerns about further NATO enlargement.

Russia's second security concern relates to the Cold War legacy in U.S.-Russian relations. Russia resented the United States' belief that it won the Cold War and the corresponding image of Russia as a "defeated superpower." It believes that it made as important a contribution as—if not more important than—the United States to the peaceful ending of the Cold War and to the equally peaceful demise of the Soviet Union, which Putin has called the biggest tragedy of the twentieth century. Therefore, Russia is determined to preserve and to restore its legacy as a global power, even if in economic terms it represents only around 2.5 percent of global GDP. The Obama administration's decision to give priority to improving relations with Russia has become an important factor in indulging Russia's ambition to play in the "top league" of international affairs.

The key instrument for Russia to keep up with the United States is in maintaining parity with the United States in terms of nuclear weapons capabilities. This goal has become even more important given that Russia's conventional military power has significantly declined since the end of the Cold War. Therefore, Russia has been reluctant to endorse President Barack Obama's goal of "nuclear zero" and is unlikely to support in the short to medium term more radical cuts in the level of nuclear weapons than those already included in the New START Treaty signed in April 2010. Moreover, Russia seeks ways to limit advances in other U.S. advanced weapons systems, including its missile defense system (assuming it is not based on a joint system with Russia's full participation) and space-based weapons systems.

Russia has strongly welcomed the decision by the Obama administration to change the Bush-era plans for missile defense and to not deploy interceptors and radar in Poland and the Czech Republic, respectively, as agreed between the Pole and Czech governments and the Bush administration. This decision eliminated—at least temporarily—Moscow's concerns that the U.S. missile defense system was directed against Russia and not against Iran as claimed by all recent U.S. administrations. However, the idea of a cooperative U.S.-Russian missile defense system as a part of a global system is still far from being accepted in theory, let alone realized in practice. If it is realized, it would signify perhaps the first major element of a post–Cold War global security architecture that could begin to seriously transform the persisting patterns of U.S.-Russian relations. Such cooperative plans still face very serious political, technical, and financial obstacles between the United States and its NATO allies, let alone between the United States and Russia.

Finally, despite the Obama administration's change of policy, the legacy of the Bush administration has not been overcome, and Russia continues to view the United States as its main rival in post-Soviet Eurasia. The Bush administration's support for the Rose Revolution in Georgia and the Orange Revolution in Ukraine was interpreted in Moscow as a U.S. ploy to install anti-Russian regimes along its borders and to prepare the ground for staging regime change in Russia itself. Russia's response to the U.S. policy came in the form of crackdowns on U.S.-funded nongovernmental organizations (NGOs), a tightening of press freedoms, and the establishment of even tighter controls over the political process, which in effect excluded any pro-Western opposition parties from access either to the media or to the Parliament. Although the Obama administration has retreated from the Bush administration's democracy promotion agenda and declared an era of pragmatic realism in U.S.-Russian relations—predicated on not lecturing Russia about democracy or interfering in any significant way in its domestic human rights problems—Moscow remains suspicious that Washington will continue to use its "proxy" allies in the post-Soviet space to weaken Russia's influence.

Russia successfully worked to weaken those regimes that are most closely allies with the United States, including those of Georgian president Mikheil Saakashvili, with whom Russia fought a war in August 2008, and of former Ukrainian president Victor Yuschenko, who lost an election to a much more pro-Russian candidate, Victor Yanukovich. Moreover, Russia continues to oppose any indications that the U.S. military presence in Central Asia is open-ended and going beyond its narrow objectives of suppressing insurgency in neighboring Afghanistan. Finally, Russia is aggressively—and increasingly successfully—competing with the United States over control of energy export routes from Eurasia. Although the United States will never rely on Caspian oil and gas for any significant share of its energy consumption (if any at all), it views the existence of multiple pipelines, including those bypassing Russia, as important for promoting independence in the region and enhancing the sovereignty of post-Soviet states. In turn, Russia views these projects as politically motivated and directed at weakening Russia and at ultimately putting those post-Soviet states through which the pipelines pass in the position of being able to dictate the terms of Russia's energy exports to Europe, which currently bring and will continue to bring for the foreseeable future, a large share of Russia's budgetary revenues.

The global financial crisis and the election of President Obama had a positive impact on U.S.-Russian relations. The crisis has created the impression that the United States is no longer a dominant hegemon and thus removed Russia's concerns about a U.S.-centric unipolar world. In fact, many Russians now openly talk about the impending demise of the United States as an economic and geopolitical superpower, about its imperial overstretch, and about its loss of authority to promote its model of success to the rest of the world. These views, though greatly exaggerated and representing a form of wishful thinking, have perhaps not very promising implications for Russia, which has itself been severely affected by the financial crisis and which is now facing neighboring China as a new rising superpower. China's rise has many uncertain long-term strategic consequences for Russia, which is destined to play the role of an underdog in any future Sino-Russian strategic partnership.

At the same time, the United States' decision to press a "reset" button on U.S.-Russian relations opened a window of opportunity for Russia to strengthen its global footprint in cooperation with the United States. The "reset" has already delivered important results. It has changed the atmosphere in U.S.-Russian relations, produced the New START Treaty and helped to preserve the Nuclear Non-Proliferation Treaty (NPT) regime, led to much closer U.S.-Russian interaction on Iran, including Russian support for new sanctions on Iran in the UN Security Council, and advanced the negotiations on Russian membership in the World Trade Organization. However, there are doubts about whether this "reset" can be sustained in the longer term—and hence help to decisively overcome Cold War mistrust between the United States and Russia. The risks of it becoming a missed opportunity remains high as both countries, particularly the United States, face strong domestic opposition to the rapprochement and continue to mistrust each other. As a result, they are still unable to find ways to tackle perhaps the most difficult challenge they jointly face—that is, how to find a new modus vivendi in post-Soviet Eurasia, one that can deliver a win-win solution to what has long been a zero-sum rivalry.

Russia's domestic security concerns. Russia's domestic security threats and challenges can be divided into four categories: separatism, terrorism and Islamic extremism, catastrophic accidents (mostly industrial), and crime (drug trafficking, corruption, and organized crime).

The threat of separatism and thus the challenge of preserving Russia's territorial integrity is perhaps the *most significant concern* on the minds of the absolute majority of Russian policymakers and the population at large. There are a number of reasons for this. The first reason relates to the experience of the Soviet Union's collapse, which was unexpected for many and is still viewed by a large share of political elite and commentators as having resulted from a foreign plot. Thus, there is always the thinking that Russia's external enemies are conspiring to destroy Russia itself. The second reason is objective: Russia has too large a territory with too small a population (with negative demographic projections on top of that). This fact makes people nervous about the country's long-term prospects. This size discrepancy would have been perfectly normal—as in the cases of Australia and Canada—if not for two other realities: (1) Russia runs a highly centralized system of governance, meaning regional leaders, who are appointed by Moscow, have little democratic accountability to their populations, and (2) many of these same populations are composed of diverse groups of indigenous peoples aspiring for various forms of self-rule and a say over the choice of their regional leaders. Moreover, the legacy of the Soviet ethnofederal system, in which ethnic groups were given autonomy within a large federal structure, resulted in a number of interethnic conflicts following the Soviet collapse, most of notably in the South Caucasus between Georgia and its two formerly autonomous entities, Abkhazia and South Ossetia, and in the North Caucasus between Russia itself and separatists in the Republic of Chechnya.

The second significant domestic threat is related to terrorism and Islamic extremism. In the mind of most Russians, this threat is closely linked

to the war in Chechnya and to the growing instability in the North Caucasus region as a whole. In his 2009 political essay titled "Forward Russia,"
President Medvedev listed the growing instability in the North Caucasus
as one of the key strategic challenges for Russia's future modernization and
development. In the late 1990s and early 2000s, Russia was a major victim
of terrorism, which was related almost entirely to its war in Chechnya. Following the bloody hostage crisis in a school in the North Ossetian town
of Beslan in September 2004, in which over two hundred children died,
Chechen rebels and their associates ended their high-impact and high-
civilian-casualty brand of terrorism as international public opinion turned
against them. At the same time, Russian security services began to develop
a more sophisticated approach to counterterrorism policies and improved
public security, particularly in Russia's large cities. Despite Russia's decision
in April 2009 to end counterterrorist operations in Chechnya, terrorism
and violence in the North Caucasus has not receded, with most violence
concentrated in Dagestan, Ingushetia, Chechnya, Kabardino-Balkaria,
and Karachay-Cherkessia. Violence is also frequent in North Ossetia and
Adygei Republic.

The third serious domestic security threat in Russia relates to catastrophic accidents, many of which have already taken place as a result of
aging basic infrastructure and a lack of sufficient oversight over safety due
to corruption. The number of such cases, like the August 2009 accident at
the country's largest hydropower station—Sayano-Shushenskaya—in Siberia is projected to increase further as the Soviet-era infrastructure ages
even further beyond its critical level. This weakness can also be used by
criminal and terrorist groups to stage their attacks.

Finally, the fourth domestic security threat faced by Russia relates to
organized crime, which in some cases has merged with state structures due
to widespread corruption. This has made it harder for the Russian government to address the trafficking of people, weapons, and dangerous materials, and the pressing challenges related to the country's very high drug use
and high levels of HIV/AIDs infections. According to the UN Office on
Drugs and Crime, there is a very high prevalence of HIV among drug users in Russia—amounting to almost 37 percent of drug users between the
ages of 15 and 64.[1]

Regional security threats. Since the end of the Soviet Union, Russia has
consistently referred to threats emanating in and from the post-Soviet area
as vital to its security. In August 2008 it demonstrated that it has meant
what it preached all along by showing to the world its unwavering commitment to use force to defend its interests in South Ossetia and to prevent

the likely spillover of security threats from neighboring states into Russia itself. Indeed, while Russia's concerns over NATO enlargement and the U.S. missile defense system in Central Europe are driven by yesterday's or tomorrow's concerns, its concerns in Eurasia are driven by security threats that are real today. Whether one speaks about protracted unresolved conflicts in the South Caucasus or the threat of jihadi terrorism in Central Asia or the implications of Central Asian gas no longer flowing via Russia to the international markets, they all concern Russia directly and, in the view of Russian political elites, could undermine Russia's domestic stability and economic growth and hence deny Russia's ambition of becoming an even more important international actor in the future.

In essence, the importance of the regional threats is based on the fact that Russia views them as directly related to its geopolitical and domestic threats. Russia's concerns over security threats in the post-Soviet space are based around three key assumptions that are a matter of consensus within Russia's political class.

The first assumption is that stability and security in the post-Soviet space is the ultimate test of Russia's power and influence. If Russia is seen as failing to solve problems or letting other players solve them instead of Russia, Russia's hope for being recognized as a major power will be undermined, possibly irreversibly. There is no other region in the world where Russia has such capacity to influence the situation and so many "clients." In short, if it fails to assert its power in Eurasia, it will not be able to do so elsewhere.

The second assumption is that security threats in Eurasia can quickly spread to Russia, with its large immigrant population, ethnic communities, and porous border security regimes. Therefore, Russia prefers to fight and defeat the threat in neighboring regions rather then on its territory. There are a few examples that support this argument. The spread of Hezbut-Tahrir—an underground Islamic network advocating the peaceful overthrow of secular governments and the establishment of the caliphate in Central Asia—spread first in Uzbekistan and Kyrgyzstan and later to Russia itself, affecting many Muslim communities that feel marginalized and ostracized within Russian sociality.[2] Drugs from Afghanistan easily pass through Central Asia and contribute to the extraordinarily high drug rate in Russia and the related spread of HIV/AIDS. Instability in Georgia—both in the early 1990s and in 2008—mobilized support among North Ossetians who live in Russia's North Caucasus, while Georgia's war in Abkhazia in 1993–94 mobilized thousands of volunteers from other parts of the North Caucasus, including over two thousand Circassians who are ethnically related to the Abkhazians. All these mobilizations and movements of armed volunteers over the Caucasus Mountains to Georgia have contributed to instability in the North Caucasus itself. But perhaps the most problematic case for Russia is Ukraine. With around 30 percent of Russia's citizens having relatives in Ukraine or identifying themselves as ethnic Ukrainians, any instability in Ukraine could have a direct impact on Russia.

The third assumption that underpins Russia's fears of insecurity in its "near abroad" is that these threats could undermine the prospects for regional integration in post-Soviet Eurasia by weakening the regional institutions that Russia helped to create after the dissolution of the Soviet Union and in which it plays the central role. These institutions legitimize Russia's claim as the central security player and guarantor in the post-Soviet region and they also act, at least symbolically, as a geopolitical force multiplier in Russia's global force projection ambitions. These regional security institutions include the CSTO (members include Russia, Belorus, Armenia, Uzbekistan, Kazakhstan, Kyrgyzstan, and Tajikistan) and the SCO (members include Russia, China, Kazakhstan, Kyrgyzstan, Tajikistan, and Uzbekistan).

Russia's Capacities as a Regional Security Actor

In the face of these threat perceptions, Russia requires a variety of resources to focus on all three levels of its security agenda—that is, to manage its agenda with the United States and NATO; to address Russia's domestic security challenges, which are set to increase in the coming years; and to manage regional security challenges in Eurasia. All of these tasks require different capabilities and instruments, which contemporary Russia often lacks. First, these tasks require enough economic and military resources to simultaneously address domestic and global security tasks. Second, they require alliances and institutions within which Russia could either seek assurances that its interests are respected (from the United States and U.S. allies) or provide security assurances and guarantees to others (its regional allies in post-Soviet Eurasia). Third, they require a flexible strategy that would allow for pragmatic cooperation with other global and regional players (such as the United States and the European Union) to manage external threats and thus to help create a favorable environment in which domestic security problems could be addressed. Finally, they require confidence about the longer-term prospects for Russia's own development, its evolution vis-à-vis other powerful regional and international players, and its ability to sustain an ambitious foreign and security policy agenda.

On all these issues Russia faces uncertainty that is visible not only to Russia's own decision makers but also increasingly to those in Eurasia. Russia's economic resources and its economic growth projects have been revised by the impacts of the global financial crisis. As a result, for the foreseeable future Russia will not be able to deliver the kinds of financial resources needed to stabilize the economies in its neighborhood—states that have been even more severely affected by the crisis than Russia.

In the military field, Russia is undergoing what its chief of general staff, Gen. Nikolai Makarov, called the country's most profound restructuring in the past two hundred years. The war with Georgia highlighted the real and fundamental limitations on Russia's force projection capabilities, its poor system of military training and command, and its outdated equipment. The reorganization, which was initiated after the August 2008 war, includes the following elements:

- Transforming all units into the category of permanent readiness units that will be fully manned and equipped and undergo regular training.
- Reducing the overall size of the armed forces to 1 million by 2016 (in accordance with President Medvedev's decree on December 29, 2008).
- Altering the top-heavy structure of the armed forces, which has a disproportionately large number of officers (in 2008, the officer corps constituted 32 percent of the entire armed forces), by reducing the overall number of officers from 355,000 to 150,000.
- Improving the effectiveness of the armed forces' command system by transforming it from a four-tier structure to a three-tier structure.
- Transforming ground force divisions into smaller and more flexible brigades that will be able to operate more independently on a specific tactical level within their assigned competence and creating operational commands to reinforce the "joint" command principle across different services.
- Equipping the armed forces with modern weapons and equipment.[3]
- Improving the military education system, including through progressive career training, and the quality of military analysis and research, and transforming the sixty-five existing military education establishments into ten "educational centers."

Although it is still too early to judge whether these reforms are going to deliver the modern and professional armed forces that Russia aims to achieve, the country has already begun a process of breaking down the Soviet armed forces system. If successful, the reforms could create an armed forces that are more interoperable in terms of structure and even equipment (if foreign procurement goes ahead as planned) with NATO forces. This could make it easier for NATO and Russia to cooperate if a political decision to do so is taken in the future.

The plan gives up a large-scale mobilization army that was designed primarily to fight a major war with NATO, in favor of a smaller force geared perhaps to deal with a regional conflict not far from Russia's own borders. At the same time, Russia increases its reliance on nuclear capabilities as a deterrent vis-à-vis the United States. This growing importance of nuclear weapons at a time of increasing disparity in Russia's conventional capabilities vis-à-vis the United States and NATO as a whole will continue to limit Russia's interest in further major cuts beyond those included in the New START Treaty. Moreover, the reforms are likely to create a gap of several years in which Russia will be significantly limited in its capacity to project force abroad and therefore its credibility as regional security provider will be further questioned by regional and external powers concerned about stability in Eurasia. Finally, in its current state of transition, Russia should be particularly concerned about a potential NATO pullout from Afghanistan, which could leave Russia to deal with the regional implications of this decision in Central Asia. Therefore, it is likely that Russia will be more open to the idea of cooperation with the United States and NATO in Central Asia in the coming years to prevent any new outbreak of conflict in Afghanistan after U.S. forces and the International Security Assistance Force (ISAF) begin to withdraw.

In addition to the limitations Russia faces with regard to its economic and military resources, Russia also faces problems with developing effective regional security institutions and in finding a flexible modus vivendi with other global players in post-Soviet Eurasia. Nowhere have these limitations of the post-Soviet security paradigm been so clearly tested than in Central Asia, which faces an increasing number of security challenges and few effective instruments to address them—this, despite a large number of regional and extraregional players (both individual states and institutions) actively engaged in the region.

Central Asia: A Case Study of the Regional Security Deficit Paradigm

The Central Asian region, which comprises five post-Soviet states—Kazakhstan, Kyrgyzstan, Tajikistan, Uzbekistan, and Turkmenistan—is often portrayed as a potential international security problem. However, the region has so far avoided major regional conflict or sustained domestic instability within individual states. Despite this encouraging history, the future might be more challenging for the newly independent states, which have found themselves at the center of geopolitical battles between Russia, China, and the United States, and at the frontline of the major contemporary conflict in Afghanistan. But as the Central Asian region drifts to the margins of the great powers' attention—a consequence of the global financial crisis— the post-Soviet Central Asian states and their nascent regional institutions are struggling to address the growing regional security challenges.

At the time of the collapse of the Soviet Union, many experts warned that the Fergana Valley—a geographically and historically integrated region that is now divided among three states (Uzbekistan, Kyrgyzstan, and Tajikistan)—would become "another Balkans" in terms of its potential for interethnic conflict. They cited as compounding factors the absence of effective instruments for addressing challenges in Central Asia due to alleged weak state capacities to deal with domestic security threats, the perceived failure of regional cooperation, and the limited influence of external actors, which often operated in a zero-sum competition with each other (e.g., the United States and Russia during the Georgia W. Bush and Putin administrations) and hence exacerbated rather than helped to alleviate the shortcoming of indigenous security-management mechanisms.

Indeed, the Central Asian states have experienced serious security challenges. The peak of insecurity in Central Asia occurred during the last years of the Soviet Union. Clashes occurred in Almaty, Kazakhstan, in 1986, and interethnic violence flared between Uzbeks and Meskhetian Turks in the Uzbek part of the Ferghana Valley in 1989 and between Uzbeks and Kyrgyz in the Kyrgyz part of the Ferghana Valley in 1990. Following the end of the Soviet Union, a bloody civil war broke out in Tajikistan in 1992, and the peace treaty there was signed only in 1997. In the late 1990s, the Islamic Movement of Uzbekistan (IMU), together with elements of the United Tajik Opposition (UTO), both found safe haven in civil war–affected Afghanistan, staged several insurgency attacks in the Ferghana Valley—first in Batken region (Kyrgyzstan) and later in Uzbekistan, where large clashes took place with government forces in 1999 and 2000. In Tajikistan, the episodes of internal violence between different regional and ethnic groups and clans persisted until 2001. In the second post-Soviet decade, much attention has been paid to new threats and challenges, including socioeconomic tensions, corruption, and potentially violent nonstate actors (including Islamic radicals).

However, despite the widespread perception from outside Central Asia about the growing gap between regional threats and challenges and the existing regional and external capacities to address them, all regional crises have been either successfully resolved or contained. This conclusion represents a stark contrast to another multiethnic region of the former Soviet Union, the South Caucasus, where the collapse of the Soviet Union triggered several interethnic conflicts with major negative consequences for regional development prospects, for the still incomplete process of consolidation of the newly independent states within internationally recognized borders, and for human security. Even in the case of Tajikistan, which experienced a bloody civil war after the collapse of the Soviet Union, the conflict ended in a comprehensive political settlement, including a form of power sharing between the government and Islamist opposition. This settlement represents the only successful case of conflict resolution in post-Soviet Eurasia (other conflicts in Georgia and Moldova and between Armenia and Azerbaijan, which flared in the early to mid-1990s, have been "frozen" without a political settlement).

In Central Asia, all five states spent the first decade after the collapse of the Soviet Union implementing three parallel "projects"—nation building, regime consolidation, and external balancing. The results of these endeavours gave the Central Asian region its modern characteristics, which are likely to remain entrenched for several generations to come. To begin, nation building led to the formation of five sovereign nation-states, which have never in history existed in this form and within their current state borders and hence had to be created anew out of the ruins of the Soviet Union.

Second, all Central Asian states have evolved toward different forms of authoritarian rule: Turkmenistan and Uzbekistan are the most authoritarian; Kazakhstan compensates for its democratic deficit through activist foreign policy and energy diplomacy; Tajikistan is a state with strong regional identities in different parts of the country and with a delicate power-sharing arrangement; and Kyrgyzstan has fallen victim to persistent political instability, most recently in April 2010 with the political ousting of former president Kurmanbek Bakiyev (who himself came to power in the so-called Tulip Revolution of March 2005, which ousted President Askar Akayev).

Finally, in their foreign policy, all regional states have used their geography and traditions to construct a complex relationship with the outside world. This has helped them to fulfill the objectives of nation building and regime consolidation. Unlike in non-EU Eastern Europe (Ukraine, Belarus, and Moldova) and in the South Caucasus, where the influence of Western institutions and the attractions of European integration helped to stimulate reforms—albeit with varying degree of success—state building in Central Asia has been influenced by an Asian paradigm that rejects any external interference in the internal affairs of newly independent states, even if their weakness threatens stability in the region as a whole.

Following the 9/11 terrorist attacks on the United States, Central Asia suddenly emerged from its landlocked strategic isolation deep in the heart of Asia to claim the international spotlight as the key base for attacks to overthrow the Taliban in Afghanistan. The Northern Alliance—which spearheaded the capture of Kabul from the Taliban with strong support from the United States and its allies, including at that time Russia and Central Asian states—consisted largely of ethnic Tajiks and Uzbeks who traditionally reside in the northern part of Afghanistan. Three Central Asian states—Uzbekistan, Kyrgyzstan, and Tajikistan—offered the U.S.-led coalition against the Taliban access to military bases on their territories and assistance in implementing reconstruction programs in Afghanistan. Cooperation between Central Asian states and the West suffered in 2004 when the Bush administration's support for the Rose Revolution in Georgia and later the Orange Revolution in Ukraine planted the seeds of mistrust among Central Asian authoritarian leaders, who feared U.S. support for popular uprisings inside their own countries. The United States' lukewarm support for the Tulip Revolution in 2005 in Kyrgyzstan, which saw street violence in the overthrow of President Akayev, only reinforced these suspicions. After U.S. NGOs and some politicians criticized Uzbekistan for using excessive violence in putting down demonstrations (which Uzbeks classified as armed insurgency) in Andijan, the Uzbek government asked the United States to close its base in Karshi-Khanabad.

Kyrgyzstan also proved to be a strategic headache for U.S. forces. The Manas air-base facility,[4] located near Bishkek, has been an important hub supporting the war effort in Afghanistan since the U.S. military opened it in December 2001. Since then, Manas's operations have been threatened by political instability more than once. In February 2009, then president Kurmanbek Bakiyev announced that he would close Manas and accept more than $2 billion in emergency assistance and investments from Russia. The later decision to accept an initial $300 million U.S. payment and to renegotiate the rent payment for the facility (along with the decision to rename the facility the Manas Transit Center) suggests on the one hand that Central Asian states have the ability to flip sponsors as and when internal pressures and external rivalries coincide.

On the other hand, an encouraging sign of geopolitical cooperation in the region is witnessed in the effectiveness of the Northern Distribution Network (NDN). As a response to both the United States' declining influence in Central Asia as well as the poor security situation in southern Afghanistan, the United States established in 2008 several new transit corridors to deliver nonlethal goods to its forces in Afghanistan. According to General Duncan McNabb, head of U.S. Transportation Command (TRANSCOM), 80 percent of supplies bound for Afghanistan previously flowed through the port of Karachi and on through Pakistan, but the percentage fell to about

50 percent following the opening of the NDN. Of the total cargo heading to U.S. forces in Afghanistan, 30 percent goes via the NDN and 20 percent by air. Of all nonlethal cargo delivered by surface transport, about 50 percent transits the NDN and 50 percent goes through Pakistan.

The NDN has also become a key component of ISAF's fuel-supply infrastructure. In 2009 its daily fuel consumption increased from 2 million to 4.1 million liters per day, meaning that more fuel had to be imported via Afghanistan's northern borders. According to the Defense Logistics Agency, approximately 40 percent of the fuel contracted by the U.S. Defense Energy Support Center is produced in Pakistani refineries and transported via truck into Afghanistan, while the fuel that is acquired from Central Asia and the South Caucasus (in particular, Azerbaijan, Kazakhstan, and Tajikistan) accounts for approximately 60 percent of the overall contracted volumes and is shipped via the NDN.

However, the success of the northern supply route in equipping ISAF-NATO comes with its own challenges. In December 2009 General Stanley McChrystal, then ISAF commander, stated that "ISAF's Northern Distribution Network and logistical hubs are dependent upon support from Russian and Central Asian states, giving them the potential to act as either spoilers or positive influences." McChrystal's statement pointed not only to the reliance of the United States on Central Asian countries in managing the NDN but also to the risk of overreliance on them. Both the political upheavals in Kyrgyzstan and Uzbekistan's decision in 2005 to close down the U.S. air base at Karshi-Khanabad underline the risks involved. Nevertheless, the NDN will be integral to the implementation of a viable exit strategy for Afghanistan. This will mean increasing the infrastructural capacity of the northern supply routes (therefore reducing dependency on Pakistan) in the near future.

Security Threats

Four categories of security threats exist in Central Asia. The first category relates to the potential for interstate conflict. The probability of these threats manifesting themselves remains relatively small, although in the long run they could become more pronounced. The reasons for such conflicts could include unresolved border disputes, escalation of interethnic tensions in border regions, conflicts over water resources, and spillover from cross-border insurgencies.

The second category of threats are domestic in nature and include internal conflict (e.g., the civil turmoil in Kyrgyzstan in April 2010), clashes with radical Islamist groups (e.g., Andijan violence), and social protests over poor economic conditions that have been exaggerated by the global financial crisis and limited access to international aid resources. Corruption and a lack of security-sector reforms increase the likelihood that even a small incident could quickly escalate into larger clashes and the disproportionate use of force.

The third category of threats relates to challenges originating from Afghanistan, including drug trafficking, which affects the security of all Central Asian states through the spread of criminality, organized crime, and drug addiction. In Tajikistan, for example, the UNODC has estimated that the illicit opiates industry may amount to as much as 30 percent of the country's recorded GDP.[5]

The rise of instability in Afghanistan could also increase the chances of new insurgency attacks in Central Asia originating from bases in Afghanistan as well as the spread of violent radical groups ready to perpetrate terrorist attacks in Central Asia. These risks increased following the opening of the NDN. U.S. military strategists fear that as the volume of cargo delivered along the NDN increases, so too will the risk of exporting Afghanistan's problems into Central Asia. They suggest that bringing Central Asia into the theater of war could lead to an increased threat of attack by the IMU and the Islamic Jihad Union (IJU), groups that have a loyal following in the restive Fergana Valley, which stretches through Tajikistan, Uzbekistan, and Kyrgyzstan. In September 2009, two tankers from Tajikistan delivering fuel to the ISAF were hijacked by Taliban insurgents in Kunduz province in Afghanistan, which borders Tajikistan. After the hijacked trucks stalled while crossing the Kunduz River, German forces called in a U.S. air strike, resulting in dozens of civilian and insurgent casualties. There have since been several battles between Taliban insurgents in Kunduz province and U.S., NATO, and Afghan government forces. In January 2010, there was fighting in a small town in Kunduz province just a few miles from the Tajik border, amid evidence of growing insurgency in the province.

Different policy instruments are required to address such diverse security threats. The situation is further complicated by the nature of the Central Asian states—weak, poor, and authoritarian—as well as by the nature of the threats themselves, which tend to have a cross-border character and require a comprehensive strategy to address them—from education to border security and economic development. From a law enforcement perspective, border security remains central to controlling the narcotics-trafficking industry in Central Asia. For example, along the Amu Darya River between Afghanistan and Tajikistan, the building of new bridges has often been misused by traffickers. According to the UNODC, opiate traffickers, in collusion with corrupt officials, reportedly use the cover provided by legitimate cross-border commerce to traffic growing quantities of heroin into Tajikistan. The vulnerability of Central Asian border security has meant that in all, 95 metric tons of heroin are estimated to be trafficked through Uzbekistan, Tajikistan, and Turkmenistan each year.[6]

The one security threat that is most commonly associated with Central Asia is the threat of Islamic radicalization and the unlawful activities (extremism, terrorism, insurgency) associated with radical Islamic groups. Practically all governments in the region view extremism and radicalization as the key security challenge for their states. This is true for Tajikistan, which has already witnessed a bloody civil war in which Islamists (the UTO) took part; for Uzbekistan, which includes within it major Islamic holy sites and centers (such as Bukhara and Samarkand) and one of the most religious Islamic communities in the Fergana Valley, where in May 2005 hundreds died in unrest in Andijan; for Kyrgyzstan, where due to its less repressive and weak regime many Islamist organizations such as Hezb-ut-Tahrir have recruited many supporters; and for Kazakhstan, where only half of its population is Muslim but where radicalization has spread through economically underdeveloped regions and through extensive labor migration from neighboring states. Turkmenistan is most insulated from globalization due to the extreme repressive and closed nature of its regime. However, given that Turkmenistan has become one of the major routes for drug trafficking from Afghanistan, it is likely that drug money is being diverted to fund Islamist groups there.

There is a dispute among experts in and on Central Asia over the extent to which such emphasis on Islamist radicalization as a security threat is justified. Proponents usually point to insurgencies in Tajikistan, Kyrgyzstan, and Uzbekistan, to continuing incidents of violence (including suicide bombings), mostly against law enforcement officers, and to estimates of thousands or even hundreds of thousands of supporters and members of underground Islamist organisations such as Hezb-ut-Tahrir. For authorities, the threat of Islamist radicalization is also real because it represents a challenge to their political regimes—the only grassroots challenge that they cannot suppress, as they have suppressed legal political opposition. External factors, such as the Internet and the rise of global jihadist ideology, as well as the education of some regional imams in Salafist establishments abroad, have also contributed to the rise of "purist" Islam in Central Asia. For historians, radicalization represents a systemic and not a temporary trend, as witnessed in Western Europe and parts of the Middle East. In Central Asia, radicalization reflects the return of societies from Soviet-made secular models—which were based on a particular education, lifestyle, and relationship between state and society—to traditional models in which regionalism (clan-based society) and Islam are core components. This in the medium- to long-term threatens the viability of secular political regimes. A Gallup poll released in August 2010 found that 85 percent of Tajiks said religion was an important part of their lives, with only 12 percent saying it was not, making Tajikistan first among Central Asian states in terms of religiosity. The transition of Central Asian states into Islamic republics—along the lines of Iran, Afghanistan, and Pakistan—would represent a major geopolitical shift in this strategically important region.

Opponents of the radicalization threat thesis are equally vocal in criticizing constant "abuse" by regional governments. They argue that the threat is being deliberately exaggerated by authoritarian governments in order to enhance their legitimacy and to justify repression. Moreover, they argue that the rise of underground Islamist groups is a direct result of closed political regimes that do not tolerate any opposition and that lead people who disagree with the regime to follow the Islamists by default. The brutality of police and security forces is often responsible for driving the families and friends of those they have targeted to radical underground groups. Moreover, experts argue that even if the large membership in groups such as Hezb-ut-Tahrir is accurate (which some experts dispute), these organizations are essentially peaceful and are legal in a number of Western European states. Moreover, in Central Asia, there is no clear definition of radicalism—many ordinary Muslims who go to prayers every day and grow beards are treated with suspicion by the authorities and often imprisoned. The authorities also control all Muslim clergy and therefore force people to seek informal (underground) leaders among independent preachers. The Office of the UN High Commissioner for Refugees, in a report on religious freedom in Tajikistan, has outlined a number of government abuse and restrictions on religious freedom: in August 2010, for example, Tajik authorities banned the call to prayer in northern Tajikistan during the month of Ramadan. This has only served to fan the flames of radicalism in the country. And finally, due to continuing interstate tensions, it has been suspected that Central Asian states support radical groups in other Central Asian states in order to advance their interests.

Both proponents and opponents of the radicalization threat thesis have a point and, therefore, one should treat statements about the Islamist threat in Central Asia with caution. However, there is no denial that some violence is being perpetuated by radical Islamist groups in and from Central Asia. Several attacks in Central Asia in recent years have been credited to the IMU, including a bombing outside Tajikistan's Emergency Situations Ministry in June 2005 and attacks on Tajik and Kyrgyz border posts in May 2006. In Pakistan's restive tribal areas bordering Afghanistan, IMU fighters continue to participate in battles. Moreover, there is no doubt that many "peaceful" Islamic organizations such as Hezb-ut-Tahrir maintain the strategic objective of establishing an Islamic caliphate in Central Asia.

It is difficult to identify the remedies for addressing the radicalization threat in Central Asia. Clearly, more democratic, accountable, and tolerant governments could have made a huge difference in limiting the appeal of radical Islamic groups. While Tajikistan has been applauded by the international community as a successful example of conflict resolution, reconciliation, and reintegration of former combatants, this model has been rejected by other Central Asian states, all of which have banned Islamist parties from registering and participating in the elections. Even the recent constitutional amendments in Tajikistan itself have limited the powers of the Islamist party in the political process. A key element of the 1997 Tajikistan peace agreement was the promise by Tajik president Emomali Rakhmon to grant to the Islamic Renaissance Party of Tajikistan (IPRT) 30 percent of the seats in government and 30 percent of the ministerial posts. However, the IPRT now holds a mere two places in the sixty-three-seat House of Representatives, as a series of manipulated elections have deprived them of their share.

Furthermore, the strategy of eliminating Islamist groups through arrests and special operations have not been successful, as many people who are subjected to the brutality of the police—often despite being completely innocent—are only too eager to join the Islamists if and once they are released from custody. Lack of security-sector reform within Central Asian states means that the police and security services there remain loyal servants of political regimes rather then effective instruments of deradicalization. Finally, the socioeconomic development of Central Asian states and the elimination of poverty are widely seen as the key prerequisites for reducing the appeal of radical organizations, by offering more young people opportunities to work and study.

Radicalization could, however, represent a real threat to Central Asia if it becomes part of the growing instability in Afghanistan and if Central Asia sees a spillover of violence from there. This spillover effect could be further exacerbated if a viable ISAF-NATO exit strategy from Afghanistan is not worked out. In this case, some regional underground groups could be recruited to join the insurgency, which could target the most vulnerable states—like Kyrgyzstan, Uzbekistan, and Tajikistan. Moreover, radical groups could benefit from growing corruption and criminalization in Central Asia as a result of widespread negative effects from drug trafficking.

Any violence related to suppression of suspected Islamist groups could also provoke interethnic and even interstate conflicts. During the Andijan uprising, which was brutally put down by Uzbek security forces, thousands of residents escaped into neighboring Kyrgyzstan, provoking tensions between the two countries. Tajikistan has accused Uzbekistan of supporting some of its domestic insurgency and Uzbekistan, in turn, has accused Tajikistan of harboring members of the IMU and other groups seeking to overthrow the government of Uzbekistan. The ethnic Tajik population in Bukhara and Samarkand is often seen as disloyal by the Uzbek government, while Tajiks in Uzbekistan claim that their rights to maintain cultural identity are being violated. In the late 1990s in Kazakhstan, tensions between ethnic Kazakhs and ethnic Vainakhs (Chechens), who were moved to Kazakhstan under Stalin's forced resettlement of Chechens from their traditional homeland in the North Caucasus after WWII, sprung forth after Vainakh organizations called for the establishment of an Islamic state in Kazakhstan. Chechens were motivated to do so by their perceived alienation within the traditional Kazakh society. There is also a growing tension between migrants from Kyrgyzstan and Uzbekistan who work in Kazakhstan and the native Kazakh population and authorities, who view migrants as the key reason for the rapid proliferation of radical Islamist groups in Kazakhstan known to be operating in neighboring states. In recent years, Uzbekistan started to reinforce its borders with Tajikistan and Kyrgyzstan, thus interrupting cross-border trade and further increasing tensions between communities on both sides. Kyrgyzstan has in the past accused Uzbekistan's security services of operating illegally on its territory, where ethnic Uzbek communities and refugees from Uzbekistan reside. Indeed, during the turmoil that surrounded Kyrgyzstan in the summer of 2010, Kyrgyz security services accused Islamic groups in the region of taking advantage of "hidden interethnic tensions" between the Uzbek and Kyrgyz populations in the south of the country in order to instigate violence that would disrupt Kyrgyzstan's June 27, 2010, referendum on a new constitution.[7]

Given the lack of trust and any meaningful regional cooperation in addressing regional security concerns among all Central Asian states, it is difficult to see how regional conflicts can be effectively prevented or contained in case of their sudden eruption. The case of Kyrgyzstan proves to be a case in point. The ethnic violence that erupted in southern Kyrgyzstan in June 2010 was rapid. Clashes between Uzbek and Kyrgyz communities in the south were a result of the long-standing frustration of Uzbek exclusion from national-level jobs in the state administration, as well as underrepresentation in the military, the police, and the security services. No regional organization—whether the SCO or the CSTO—was prepared to send in troops to quash outbursts of violence. In fact, the most the CSTO proved capable of was gathering an emergency meeting of member states. The lack of consensus in favor of an intervention among CSTO members—with Belarus and Uzbekistan opposing it—also demonstrated that Russia is no longer able to impose its will on issues related to the use of force. For its part, Russia was neither willing nor able to intervene unilaterally and hence to carry unilateral responsibility for possible failures and unintended consequences.[8] Moreover, many in Kyrgyzstan were reluctant to invite Russian forces, fearing that they could stay for a long time and could help to perpetuate the conflict rather than to resolve it. Russia's peacekeeping history in Georgia's conflict in Abkhazia and South Ossetia did not present a positive model that other countries wanted to see replicated on their soil.

Despite all this, the case of Kyrgyzstan could also be seen as a sign of shifting trends in Central Asia. The fact that ethnic tensions were not manipulated by great powers such as the United States and Russia for their own geopolitical gamesmanship or by Uzbekistan—which demonstrated exceptional restraint and calm—proves that cooperation, not competition, took place during these months. Furthermore, cooperation between the United States and Russia at their April 2010 summit in Prague, where U.S. and Russian officials declared their willingness to pursue cooperation to avert a new round of skirmishes over the U.S. air base at Manas, as occurred in 2009 when Russia put pressure on Kyrgyz authorities to terminate the U.S. lease, and to cooperate in pursuing back-channel talks that facilitated Bakiyev's safe escape into exile, also highlight this emerging shift away from zero-sum based competition in the region. Nevertheless, the point remains that the CSTO failed to bolster its international standing as a security manager in Central Asia.

Institutional Responses to Regional Security Challenges in Central Asia

Central Asia has a number of extraregional institutions that aspire to address its security challenges.[9] None of these are exclusively Central Asian endeavors. All previous attempts to create purely Central Asian organizations failed under the pressure of regional rivalries, the obsessive efforts of leaders to consolidate sovereignty and independence, and a lack of resources. Even if a number of studies clearly show that regional states would benefit economically from regional cooperation and that most regional security problems require multilateral cooperation to address them effectively, the regional states remain reluctant to join any groupings where they are not accepted as agenda-setting regional leaders. The European Union has spent over 2 billion euros over ten years supporting projects geared toward fermenting regional cooperation in Central Asia, with few success stories to report.[10]

Russia-Supported Institutions

In the absence of purely Central Asian institutions, extraregional mechanisms have emerged with the involvement of major regional powers, particularly Russia. The two key extraregional institutions include the CSTO, led by Russia, and the SCO, to which both Russia and China belong as founding members. All Central Asian states with the exception of Turkmenistan, which professes a "positive neutrality" concept, belong to both the CSTO and SCO. Moreover, the two organizations are in some way complementary, as the former is clearly about military security and the latter combines a limited security agenda with a growing economic one. Both organizations can claim some successes in their formative stages—the CSTO helped to preserve and transform post-Soviet military forces into military forces of individual Newly Independent States (although with no major emphasis on reform and modernization), and the SCO, in its preceding form as the Shanghai Five, helped to peacefully settle border disputes between China and all of its Central Asian neighbors. However, in the complex post-9/11 geopolitical landscape of Central Asia, both organizations face an uphill struggle in proving their effectiveness in the future as the security picture in Central Asian becomes more complex and the threat conflict more real.

Collective Security Treaty Organization. The CSTO is a collective security organization founded in 2002 by the Tashkent Treaty.[11] Its predecessor, the Collective Security Treaty (CST), was signed in 1992 within the framework of the Commonwealth of Independent States (CIS). Current members are Armenia, Belarus, Kazakhstan, Kyrgyzstan, Russia, Tajikistan, and Uzbekistan (whereas Azerbaijan and Georgia withdrew in 1999). CSTO's mandate authorizes the collective use of force "in case an act of aggression is committed against any of the States Parties," in accordance with Article 51 of the UN Charter.[12] Article 6 of the treaty states that "Armed Forces can be used beyond the territory of the States Parties exclusively in the interests of international security in strict compliance with the Charter of the United Nations and the legislation of the States Parties to this Treaty."[13]

The concept of the organization rests on the understanding that the Cold War threat is no longer applicable and thus the CSTO seeks to address the threats posed by regional inter- and intrastate conflicts, which could potentially result in "armed confrontation" and "local wars."[14] The CSTO mandate specifies combating the following: "international terrorism and extremism, the illicit traffic in narcotic drugs, psychotropic substances and arms, organized transnational crime, illegal migration and other threats to the security of the member States."[15] Specific military threats that are listed include

- territorial claims against CSTO member states;
- existing and potential hotspots of conflict and armed confrontation, especially those close to the actual borders of the member states;
- the potential threat posed by nuclear and other weapons of mass destruction that are present in the military arsenals of member states;
- the proliferation of nuclear and other weapons of mass destruction, delivery systems, and new military production technologies, combined with efforts of some countries, organizations, and terrorist groups to realize their political and military ambitions;
- the potential threat of destabilization to the strategic environment as a result of the breach of international agreements in the area of arms limitation and disarmament, groundless militarization by other states, and military alliances;
- attempts at outside interference into internal matters of member states and the destabilization of their domestic political environments;
- international terrorism and the politics of blackmail.[16]

The following factors are listed as those that might potentially lead a military danger to escalate to the level of a military threat:

- a military buildup on a member state's border that upsets the existing power balance;
- the creation and training of military factions on the territory of other states, with the intention of using them against CSTO member states;
- the ignition of border conflicts and armed provocations from the territory of neighboring states;
- the introduction of foreign troops into neighboring territories of the member states (unless for peace- and security-keeping purposes sanctioned by the UN Security Council or the OSCE).[17]

On August 1, 2001, at the Yerevan session, the first military component of the CSTO was set up—the Rapid Deployment Forces of the Central Asian Region (KSBR)—aimed at supporting countermeasures for combating international terrorism and aggressive extremism.[18] By 2006 it contained ten battalions (three each from Russia and Tajikistan, and two each from Kazakhstan and Kyrgyzstan), totaling around 4,000 troops. An aviation component stationed at a Russian air base in Kyrgyzstan was added in 2003.[19] The KSBR has since held annual military exercises, each in a different regional location (Kyrgyzstan in 2001, Tajikistan in 2002–03, Kazakhstan in 2004, etc.). These forces were established immediately after insurgencies in Kyrgyzstan and in Uzbekistan (1999, 2000) in order to prepare regional states to respond collectively to such challenges. However, since that time, no such opportunities have been presented, since cross-border insurgencies stopped after the overthrow of the Taliban regime in Afghanistan.

In September 2008, the CSTO announced plans to establish an 11,000-strong regional military force to deal with possible "challenges to the sovereignty" of its member states.[20] This was followed up by the signing of a draft agreement to set up a Joint Rapid Reaction Force (KSOR), intended to respond to the "broadest range of threats and challenges," at the CSTO Moscow session on February 4, 2009 (with each CSTO member state expected to provide a battalion).[21] The agreement on the CSTO's KSOR was finally signed on June 14, 2009. In the words of President Medvedev, this agreement regulates the "most significant, fundamental aspects of this military force's operation [with regard to] its purposes, composition, and the application of the mechanism, ensuring the organisation's member states' collective security. In my view, this will allow our nations to more effectively react to today's major threats of international terrorism, local and cross-border crime, including drug trafficking, and possibly regional conflicts as well."[22] The creation of these forces has been a subject of political controversy, as Uzbekistan refused to join the initiative as a permanent member, claiming the right to take part in some operations on an ad hoc basis. Belarus did not initially sign the documents as a demarche against the imposition of Russia's ban on the import of its milk products, though it later signed them and joined KSOR. In April 2010, KSOR completed a joint command-and-staff counterterrorism exercise in Tajikistan (the Rubezkh 2010 exercises). However, it still remains unclear whether such a force will enhance interoperability or help modernize the national forces of participating CSTO states.

On September 12, 2008, CSTO secretary general Nikolay Bordyuzha announced the organization's plan to create a new Central Asian Group of Forces, in line with Russia's National Security Strategy 2020.[23] According to Bordyuzha, the group may include up to 10,000 personnel drawn from the tank, artillery, and aviation units of five states, as well as from Russian and Kazakhstani naval forces in the Caspian Sea.[24] It is to be tasked with responding to large-scale external threats to the region (that is, to regional conflicts, not to local conflicts as in the case of KSOR), and it has been suggested that the KSBR and KSOR may be subsumed into the new force structure,[25] though these plans have not yet been followed up with practical steps.

In October 2007, the CSTO summit in Dushanbe adopted procedures formally authorizing members to conduct joint peacekeeping operations.[26] Signed on October 6, 2007, the agreement was ratified by the Russian Duma and the Council of Federation in December 2008 and finally signed by President Medvedev on January 6, 2009. According to the agreement, CSTO's peacekeeping activities include "noncombat operations aimed at resolving disputes (in accordance with the UN Charter), in addition to collective action taken using military, police, and civilian staff, for the prevention, containment and cessation of hostilities between states or within the borders of a state, as well as maintaining peace and security."[27] The peacekeeping forces are recruited from member states of the CSTO, which in accordance with their national laws provide an ongoing allocation of peacekeeping units. The peacekeeping units will undergo training using uniform CSTO programs, will be equipped with identical and compatible types of weapons and means of communication, and will take part in regular joint military exercises. Decisions to carry out peacekeeping operations on the territory of any CSTO member state will be taken by the Council on Collective Security, with consideration given to national laws and on the basis of official communications with member states or, where the territory concerned lies outside the CSTO, in accordance with UN Security Council resolutions regarding peacekeeping operations.[28]

According to Secretary General Bordyuzha, CSTO peacekeepers could in theory deploy anywhere in the world, provided they receive appropriate authorization from the United Nations. In practice, the intent of most CSTO governments is to have a force suitable for deployment within the territories of existing member states. According to CSTO agreements, such use would not require the approval of the UN Security Council. The CSTO Secretariat would simply inform UN headquarters of its plans. For example, CSTO peacekeepers could deploy to enforce a cease-fire in a member country experiencing civil strife. Alternately, they could establish a protective barrier along a national border, such as the one between Tajikistan and Afghanistan, which is a common route for drug smugglers. At least some of the member governments might want CSTO soldiers to protect them from domestic challengers, whom they would presumably label as foreign-backed terrorists to legitimize an intervention by the CSTO, whose current mandate addresses defense against external threats.[29]

The CSTO created a working group on Afghanistan in 2005 under the auspices of the organization's Foreign Ministers' Council. Its primary task was to develop recommendations on strengthening Afghan security institutions and improving antitrafficking measures. The March 14, 2005, CSTO statement revealed that the group intends to transform the Channel 2006 antidrug initiative, which is designed to curb trafficking out of Afghanistan, into a permanent regional program. During CSTO's group visit to Afghanistan, the CSTO stated that "the Afghan side is most interested in having their military and law enforcement officers trained in Russia and other CSTO member states, as well as in purchasing Russian weaponry." The CSTO further stated that "Afghanistan's army and law enforcement representatives specifically stressed [a request for] serious assistance in improving the border security of their state, in both technical and personnel training terms."

The CSTO seeks to address cross-border threats. However, its ability to deploy forces to help guard borders has been limited. The withdrawal of Russian border guards from Kyrgyzstan and Tajikistan meant that Russia was no longer influential enough to help strengthen border regimes. In 2007, Secretary General Bordyuzha refused to discuss the request from Kyrgyzstan to bring Russian border guards back to Kyrgyzstan. Similarly, in June 2010, the failure of the CSTO to manage border movement between Uzbekistan and Kyrgyzstan reinforced the limitations of the CSTO's border management capacities.

Russia has long been urging NATO to conclude a treaty with the CSTO on cooperation on all aspects of the Afghan problem. For many years NATO, under pressure from the Bush administration, refused to engage in such cooperation, claiming that by doing so it would recognize Russia's "sphere of influence" in Central Asia and that it preferred to engage instead in bilateral cooperation with Central Asian states. However, such an approach was shortsighted, as it ignored the actual role of Russia in regional security issues and also refused to recognize developments within the CSTO. There are tentative signs that the Obama administration is likely to review this policy and be more open-minded toward engagement with Russia in Central Asia and also with the CSTO. President Medvedev proposed under his new European Security Treaty initiative the development of more formal and regular cooperation between NATO, the CSTO, and other organizations active in Central Asia. The OSCE and CSTO have already established cooperation.

In terms of military capabilities, the CSTO remains very far from qualifying as a new "Eastern NATO." The CSTO's KSBR is far from adequate as a credible security manager. Furthermore, this military cooperation is based primarily on the fact that most of its member states' militaries still have a major link to their Soviet predecessor—the Red Army—in terms of personnel and equipment and, in many ways, training and doctrine. Joint military capabilities have not been deployed and tested in real operations and there are concerns that the level of defense reform in most CSTO states remains poor and that capabilities are thus inadequate for modern threats. The crisis in Kyrgyzstan in summer 2010 demonstrated that CSTO forces are unable to cope with real regional threats for which they were created in the first place.

Shanghai Cooperation Organization. Security has been a core preoccupation of the SCO since its establishment in 2001. The inaugural summit approved the Shanghai Convention on Combating Terrorism, Separatism, and Extremism, under which states agreed to pursue information exchange, extradition, and operational coordination to fight these "three evils."[30] The 2006 Shanghai summit approved a new program for cooperation in fighting terrorism, extremism, and separatism in 2007–09.

The convention laid the foundations for the establishment of the Regional Anti-Terrorist Structure (RATS) and for the development of closer cooperation between security services, law-enforcement agencies, and, to a lesser extent, the militaries of SCO member states.[31] RATS, which is located in Tashkent, was the second of two permanent SCO institutions established in 2003 (the first was the Beijing-based SCO Secretariat). RATS is responsible for information exchange and analytical work among the security services of SCO members. Its staff of thirty includes seven specialists from both Russia and China, six from Kazakhstan, five from Uzbekistan, three from Kyrgyzstan, and two from Tajikistan. Since 2003, RATS has compiled a list of terrorist organizations and key personalities involved in terrorist activity on member states' territories. It has made some progress in harmonizing antiterrorist legislation among member states, yet it has little practical role in addressing either the root causes or managing the consequences of terrorist activities. Moreover, it still plays a minor role in dealing with the key region-wide security concern, drug trafficking.

In addition to participating in the day-to-day activities of RATS, SCO member states also conduct joint antiterrorist exercises. The first took place in 2002 on the Chinese–Kyrgyz border. Primarily including security services, these exercises have offered the first opportunity for Chinese forces to participate in exercises in Central Asia and for Central Asian and Russian forces to enter Chinese territory. In August 2003, five SCO member states—Kazakhstan, Kyrgyzstan, China, Russia, and Tajikistan—conducted joint exercises on the Chinese-Kazakh border, and in 2006 large-scale antiterrorist exercises took place with the participation of all SCO member states. The 2007 SCO military exercises were the largest to date and included an impressive display of military power that seemed to go beyond the SCO's declared terrorism agenda and to have little in common with modern strategies of targeting terrorist groups or insurgencies. The displays appeared to be more a demonstration of power in the context of continuing Western military presence in the region rather than a real reassurance against future terrorist threats.

One role that the SCO could have played is to help translate some of its experience in addressing border disputes between China and post-Soviet states to tackling the existing border problems within Central Asia itself. Many unresolved border disputes represent potential sources of tension and even conflict and obstacles for trade and economic development. Closer ties with Russia helped to some extent to encourage some normalization in Tajikistan-Uzbekistan relations; however, this process is far from complete. The SCO could have played some role in this issue, but Russia is cautious about authorizing anything that could imply some form of long-term presence of Chinese military or other security forces in Central Asia on a long-term basis. Moreover, while keeping the security agenda—where Russia still enjoys greater power than China—among the SCO priorities, Russia is reluctant to empower the organization to such a degree that it could question the need for the CSTO, where Russia remains the undisputed leader. Unlike the SCO, which only established a working group on Afghanistan in 2008 and has achieved few real results, the CSTO has been working on developing a concept of security belts against drug trafficking in Central Asia and on reinforcing joint capabilities, which still remain rather weak and practically untested in real operations. China, on the other hand, is reluctant to see any merger, even on an ad hoc basis, between the SCO and CSTO, perhaps due to the fact that such a union could strengthen Russia's role in the SCO.

Any prospective enlargement of the SCO, which could include any or all of the existing observers (India, Pakistan, Mongolia, and Iran), will multiply security problems within the "SCO area," while further undermining any chances for the creation of meaningful joint mechanisms to deal with them. All current observer states have declared their intention to join as full members, but the SCO failed to reach a consensus on the appropriate procedure for the enlargement. China is concerned that enlargement could dilute the SCO and import new problems into it (like India-Pakistan tensions). At the same time, countries within the SCO are divided on which countries to admit—with China backing Mongolia and Pakistan, Tajikistan backing Iran and India, Uzbekistan opposing Muslim states like Iran and Pakistan, and Russia backing India and to some extent Iran. Even if Mongolia seems to enjoy overall support as the first candidate for full membership, no such membership can be authorized until the overall criteria and procedures for enlargement are developed that would apply equally to all prospective candidates. They feel increasingly frustrated that no such procedure exists and some countries—like India—might even be losing interest in cooperation knowing that it has no prospect of upgrading its status in the near future.

The presence of Russia and China among SCO members is the key reason why the SCO is increasingly taken seriously, although often with caution, by countries in the West and East. Early observers predicted that there would be unavoidable Russian-Chinese rivalry or even conflict over influence in Central Asia. The SCO's ability to regulate this conflict has been, without a doubt, the most powerful testimony of the organization's success to date. However, Russian-Chinese relations within the SCO are becoming increasingly competitive rather than cooperative. As China moves from declarations toward promoting specific projects in Central Asia, including those focused on energy and infrastructure, increasing development loans, and signing contracts for strategic projects in the energy and water management sectors, Russia's role as a regional economic power, inherited from the Soviet Union, is diminishing. At the same time, China has been more cautious than Russia about using the SCO as a tool for anti-Western—particularly anti-US—declarations, preferring instead a quieter but often more effective diplomacy. Indeed, Russia has been the key engine behind the SCO declarations that openly challenge the Western presence and influence in Central Asia—such as those declarations calling for NATO base withdrawal or those declarations in which member states pledge not to take steps that could damage the security of other members. While Russia and China both oppose the U.S. and NATO military presence in the region, China is less concerned about engagement by the European Union and Asian players, such as the Asian Development Bank (ADB). In strategic terms, Russia and China have increasingly diverging views on the future direction of SCO development. Russia is keen to keep the SCO primarily as a security organization, with only a limited economic role focusing on joint infrastructure projects. China wants the SCO to evolve decisively into an economic grouping, which would make it easier for China to implement its business projects in the region, including those in the energy and trade spheres.

Russian-Chinese tensions are likely to grow and Russia will find it difficult to deal with China's rising influence and activism in Central Asia. The SCO is unlikely to help tackle such issues as migration, resource competition, and the increasing economic imbalance between China and its neighbors, including Russia. In this context, Central Asian states will find it easier to advance their interests and balance their relations with one of the two regional superpowers. This happened in August 2008 when Central Asian states appealed for China's support in limiting Russia's pressure on them by recognizing the independence of Abkhazia and South Ossetia.

The Future of Russia-Supported Institutions

Although the SCO and CSTO are both established regional organizations that are likely to continue their existence and even develop further as regional security actors, they remain untested in situations of real crisis. On the one hand, there is concern whether individual states, even members, would like to involve them in a real crisis. Russia, for example, involved neither the CSTO nor the SCO in its war in Georgia or in the June 2010 crisis in Kyrgyzstan. On the other hand, there is concern whether the institutions would even be able to respond to crisis should a major terrorist attack or insurgency take place in Central Asia or an interstate conflict be sparked there or in the South Caucasus.

Even in a more benign environment, there is a real doubt whether the CSTO or even more so the SCO would have the political will or capabilities to support a prolonged peace-support operation. The core purpose of the CSTO will remain preserving post-Soviet military ties, including in training and procurement, but if it fails to move beyond this and prove itself as a real security provider—which will be predicated in many ways on the success or failure of Russia to modernize its military—regional states will progressively lose interest in this organization. In short, Russia has seen promoting "regionalism" in the context of Central Asia's security agenda as a way of preserving post-Soviet military ties and its role as the legitimate and dominant security provider in the post-Soviet space. The SCO, meanwhile, has the challenge of reconciling Russia's waning economic and military strength with China's increasing economic and military strength. In these circumstances, it is possible to envision that Russia might be less enthusiastic about the SCO, particularly as the organization's second role—counterbalancing the West in Eurasia—will grow less important due to either Sino-U.S. rapprochement or Russia's own acceptance of the West in the region, in part, curiously, as a future counterbalance to China. This reality, however, is still only a medium- to long-term prospect. In the short term, the SCO will remain active from summit to summit and increasingly authoritative due to China's interest.

Although the CSTO and SCO have made significant progress in their respective organizational development, they have not been accepted by the international community as core security providers. Neither NATO nor the European Union have so far agreed to establish formal cooperation with CSTO, while the exchange with the SCO is developing as a dialogue with no real cooperation. The argument for nonengagement from those states in the West that are most strongly opposed to cooperation has been both practical and ideological. On the practical side, there is no belief that the CSTO and SCO are capable security organizations—as they have not yet acted collectively to address any problem and Russia itself did not even inform them when it decided to launch its war with Georgia in August 2008. On the ideological side, some Western states, particularly some new NATO members and the United States under the Bush administration, felt that by engaging with the CSTO, the West would legitimize Russia's demand that all security issues in post-Soviet Eurasia be addressed with Russia, not with regional states. The consensus within both NATO and the European Union has been that unless the CSTO develops into an organization that represents first and foremost the interests of smaller regional states, not Russia's geopolitical agenda, it is preferable to engage with CSTO members directly and to bypass Russia.

This has also been the position often expressed by some CSTO members. For example, both Uzbekistan and Kyrgyzstan were adamant that any negotiations on the use of their territory for NATO transit to Afghanistan or for stationing NATO forces for these purposes should be negotiated directly with them and not with Russia or any multilateral organization. At the same time, there are serious internal tensions within both the CSTO and SCO. In the CSTO, a number of states have opposed the creation of collective rapid response forces and resist any idea of their future use on their territory. In the SCO, there are building tensions between Russia and China over whether the organization should evolve more into a security or an economic organization, the latter strongly favored by China as a regional economic superpower and the former by Russia, which still has strong ties with Central Asian states. It appears likely, however, that some form of dialogue between NATO and the CSTO and NATO and the SCO could emerge in the future, as Russia becomes more open to the idea of supporting NATO in Afghanistan and shares the views of Central Asian states that a speedy NATO withdrawal from Afghanistan before core security objectives are achieved would represent a major threat to regional security, including to the security of Russia itself.

Other Extraregional Institutions

In addition to regional security institutions that have been established by Russia, a number of other institutions in which Russia has little or no voice at all are actively seeking to address security challenges in Central Asia.

NATO. NATO has been active in establishing partnerships with regional states in Central Asia since the end of the Soviet Union. In 1994 Kazakhstan, Kyrgyzstan, Turkmenistan, and Uzbekistan joined NATO's Partnership for Peace (PfP) program and in 2002 Tajikistan also joined. The 2004 NATO summit in Istanbul declared special focus on Central Asia and the Caucasus. In 2006 Kazakhstan developed the first Individual Partnership Action Plan (IPAP) among Central Asian states that are members of PfP. It represents an advanced stage of cooperation with NATO. Kazakhstan and Kyrgyzstan have participated in the PfP's planning and review process (PARP) since 2002 and 2007, respectively. This process helps to identify and evaluate forces and capabilities that might be made available for NATO-led peace-support operations. Under PARP, planning targets are negotiated with each participating country and extensive reviews measure annual progress.[32]

Before 9/11, Central Asia was seen by Russia, China, and Euro-Atlantic countries as a potential security challenge. After 9/11, for some countries—including contributors to ISAF—the region became both a potential source of insecurity and a security provider. All Central Asian states condemned terrorist attacks and offered their cooperation to the U.S.-led coalition, including overflight rights, bases, and other assets. When NATO took over the lead of ISAF in 2003, all Central Asian states continued to express their support for the mission.

At present all Central Asian states support ISAF operations. Kyrgyzstan hosted the United States and other coalition members at Bishkek's Manas air base (recently changed into a regional transportation center); Tajikistan's airport in Dushanbe hosts French military aircraft participating in ISAF; Germany uses a facility in Termez, Uzbekistan (and the United States used the Karshi-Khanabad air base in Termez from 2001 until December 2005, when Uzbekistan asked the United States to close it in response to U.S. criticism of its use of force against protesters in Andijan). All Central Asian states also participate in assisting with the reconstruction of Afghanistan. For example, the recent financing of a $165 million project by the ADB of a railway connecting the Afghan border town of Hairatan to the northern city of Mazar-e-Sharif has increased trade with Uzbekistan and increased the speed of freight deliveries across the Uzbek border. Furthermore, trade between Tajikistan and Afghanistan increased by 21.6 percent from 2009 to 2010, according to the Tajik Agency of Statistics.

Finally, Central Asia has proved critical to the supply of cargo for ISAF-NATO troops in Afghanistan. In 2009, Kazakhstan, Tajikistan, Uzbekistan, and Kyrgyzstan each reached agreements with NATO on the transit of cargo for ISAF troops in Afghanistan. In May 2010, the first trial shipment of NATO cargo, consisting of twenty-seven containers of construction materials and food supplies, departed from Riga, Latvia. With an increasing number of attacks on NATO supply trucks along the Pakistan-Afghanistan border (most recently in October 2010), the northern supply routes have reinforced the crucial role Central Asian states play for any ISAF strategy in Afghanistan. Moreover, the NDN has been seen as crucial for NATO involvement in Central Asia and cooperation with Russia and explains why U.S. military strategists are eager to expand the NDN.

For Russia and China, as well as most Central Asian states themselves, NATO operations in Afghanistan have both enhanced their security, by stopping the civil war and eliminating the bases for training terrorists, and served as a source of concern due to the increase in the volume of drug trafficking from Afghanistan and the growing insurgent activity against NATO troops, which is slowly spreading northward and once again threatens the security of Central Asia.

NATO's role in promoting the reform of armed forces in Central Asia has been modest compared with those in some Eastern European and South Caucasus states. However, some successes have been achieved—among them, promoting interoperability with Kazakhstani forces through the Kazakh Battalion and Kazakh Brigade, both of which benefited from NATO training. There is also cooperation on disaster response. Uzbekistan hosted a disaster-response exercise in the Fergana Valley in 2003. NATO also supports the Virtual Silk Highway project, which aims to improve access to the Internet for research facilities in Central Asia and the South Caucasus through a satellite-based network. NATO also supports cooperation among scientists, including a study of the radioactive contamination of selected areas of former Soviet nuclear test sites in Kazakhstan, which is also supported by the International Atomic Energy Agency.

NATO's engagement in Central Asia has been shaped by its needs to support ISAF operations and its interest in promoting defense reform and other security policies that could enhance the independence and security of Central Asian states. Given that none of the Central Asian states have expressed an intention to join NATO, the incentives for such reform have been limited. The bulk of armed forces in these countries remain linked to their Soviet heritage and therefore are more likely to seek closer ties with Russia both in bilateral and multilateral (CSTO) arrangements.[33] Moreover, Central Asian states have used NATO's and the United States' need to secure transit for ISAF through Central Asia as a bargaining chip in order to get both financial (e.g., Kyrgyzstan's demands for payment for the use of Manas) and political benefits (e.g., limited external criticism of human rights records). In the long run, however, Central Asian states have important stakes in NATO's success in Afghanistan, as their security is directly dependent on stability and security there.

European Union. In June 2007 the European Council, under the German presidency, adopted a common strategy toward Central Asia.[34] The decision opened a new chapter in the European Union's relations with this increasingly important region. In December 2006, Frank-Walter Steinmeier, the German foreign minister, identified three areas of strategic interest for the European Union in Central Asia: first, the region's strategic location close to instability in and around Afghanistan, Pakistan, and Iran; second, the region's struggle—so far successfully—to contain Islamist fundamentalism; and third, the region's vast energy resources.

Although the European Union has been active in Central Asia since the end of the Soviet Union and has contributed over 1 billion euros in aid under the Technical Assistance to the Commonwealth of Independent States (TACIS) program, its presence in the region and influence over regional development has been small and clearly disproportional to the actual size of its contribution to such important projects as, for example, the Border Infrastructure Development program and other cross-regional initiatives. The new strategy aims to revise the European Union's approach to the region and to develop new policies that could give the European Union a greater profile and better "value for money" on its assistance.

Moreover, the European Union strives to develop a more coordinated approach that would replace the largely bilateral strategies implemented by a number of EU states with traditionally strong interests in Central Asia. The first step in this direction was the appointment of an EU special representative (EUSR) for Central Asia, who works with all EU institutions and member states to promote a common approach to the region and to raise Central Asia's importance within EU policymaking mechanisms. The recent adoption of the common strategy marks the second important step in EU policy toward Central Asia. This new focus resulted from three powerful trends within the European Union.

First, with the European Union's enlargement, the Eastern dimension has increased in importance within the union. Initially, the European Union focused its efforts on countries in immediate proximity to its borders—in Eastern Europe and around the Black Sea (including the South Caucasus)—including them in its European Neighborhood Policy (ENP). In parallel, the European Union has also sought to develop a special relationship with Russia, which opted out of the ENP in search of an "equal" relationship based on the mutually agreed-upon Four Common Spaces approach. However, it soon became apparent that the enlarged European Union could not limit its engagement to the direct neighborhood only. Therefore, Central Asia, with its vast energy resources and important geostrategic location, has become the subject of a new EU engagement strategy.

Second, the European Union has been developing a new dialogue with Asia, including closer partnerships with Japan and China. Central Asian states, which are gradually redefining themselves as essentially Asian powers (as opposed to post-Soviet states), are seen as part of the union's Asian policy.

Third, energy security is becoming a major source of concern for the European Union. There is a growing perception that EU economies could become increasingly vulnerable to potential interruption of supplies, as happened in January 2009 as a result of the Russian-Ukraine dispute. Central Asia is seen as a region that could help the European Union diversify its sources of energy imports and thus strengthen its energy security.

The approach elaborated in the newly adopted common strategy toward the region marks a major transformation in EU policy for multiple reasons. First, the European Union is developing a more nuanced policy. Until 2006, EU policy was based on the assumption that all Central Asian states faced similar challenges as countries of transition. Therefore, its assistance programs did not take into account the significant specific and varied development challenges faced by each Central Asian. The new strategy acknowledges that major changes have taken place across Central Asian states and that a specific set of priorities need to be developed for engagement with each individual country.

Second, the European Union will begin to closely consult with Central Asian states on its key decisions in the region, including development assistance priorities. In the past, the European Union developed its approach to the region in EU capitals and Brussels.

Third, although the European Union will continue to promote regional cooperation in Central Asia and to encourage countries to implement joint projects, it now recognizes that regional cooperation and integration in Central Asia will be a slow process. Therefore, it now places greater priority on bilateral engagement. To this end, the European Union is planning on expanding its diplomatic presence in Central Asia, moving from one EU Commission office in Kazakhstan for the entire region toward the establishment of EU offices in each Central Asian state. The number of EU member-state embassies in the region will also be increased.

Finally, the European Union has declared that it is prepared to enter into an open and constructive dialogue with regional organizations in Central Asia and to establish regular and ad hoc contacts, such as with the

SCO, the CSTO, and other organizations. Such preliminary contacts have already taken place.

Among the most prominent and successful EU initiatives in Central Asia are the Central Asia Border Management Program and the Central Asia Drug Action Program, which are funded by the European Union and the United Nations Development Program (UNDP) and implemented by UNDP. Moreover, the European Union is promoting cooperation between the border police of Tajikistan and Afghanistan under the Border Management Afghanistan Project. In addition, it promoted the Central Asian Border Security Initiative, which is aimed at strengthening nonproliferation, export control, and border security in all five Central Asian states.

In the long run, however, the European Union will remain a relatively weak actor in Central Asia as compared to its role in the South Caucasus and Eastern Europe, where states understand the union, are attracted by its soft power, and aspire to join it. In Central Asia, there is no such knowledge and interest in the European Union.

Organization for Security and Co-operation in Europe. The OSCE is the only organization that binds Central Asian states with European countries and the United States, and also counts Russia among its members. The OSCE has been present in Central Asia, including through its regional offices, since the end of the Soviet Union and has played an important role in addressing both hard security concerns and a basket of human-dimension issues. The former includes the promotion of border security, and the latter includes the promotion of human rights, the rule of law, civil society, independent media, and, in some cases, election monitoring.

At the OSCE Ministerial Meeting in Madrid in 2007, the organization—for the first time—agreed to help strengthen the border between Afghanistan and Central Asian states. This has led the OSCE to implement a whole range of projects, including training police and customs officers on the Tajikistan-Afghanistan and Turkmenistan-Afghanistan borders, training Afghan border police at the National Border Guard Training Academy in Tajikistan, training police in counternarcotics operations, and monitoring Afghan border crossings in remote parts of northern Afghanistan. The OSCE is also working with Tajik authorities in developing a National Border Strategy for Tajikistan. These efforts are likely to be stepped up after the OSCE summit in December 2010.

Significantly, for the first time in OSCE's history, Kazakhstan chaired the OSCE in 2010. This decision, which overcame the doubts of some member states that expressed concern about the country's democratic credentials, was important as it allowed the most economically developed

Central Asian country to set the OSCE's agenda. It also raised the OSCE's profile in Eurasia and highlighted more the needs of the Central Asian region. It was particularly important because, while under Kazakhstan's chairmanship, the OSCE faced a major crisis in Central Asia in the form of political unrest and interethnic clashes in Kyrgyzstan. Although Kazakhstan played an important role in diffusing the initial crisis by aiding the departure of President Bakiev from Kyrgyzstan in April, cooperating closely with Russia and the United States, the OSCE was unable to prevent interethnic clashes from breaking out in June. The OSCE office in Bishkek sponsored local NGOs to conduct assessments and interethnic dialogue interventions, but those steps were unable to prevent the crisis from escalating rapidly. And only after four days of violent clashes did the OSCE high commissioner on national minorities issue a warning to the OSCE's Permanent Council and fifty-six participating states. When the OSCE decided to send fifty unarmed international police advisers to help local police to reinstate law and order in the southern province of Osh, where interethnic clashes were taking place, the OSCE faced large protests staged by local officials who feared that OSCE deployment could in the long run undermine their territorial integrity and promote separatism in the region, which is largely populated by Uzbeks. The Uzbeks themselves also lacked trust in the OSCE, because it was neighboring Uzbekistan, not the OSCE, which provided them with shelter and humanitarian aid during the most acute stages of violence.

Although the OSCE's inclusiveness and long-standing presence on the ground in Central Asia has made it an influential international actor in Central Asia, its ability to advance Helsinki Principles, such as democracy and human rights, has been limited due to the lack of interest and support from regional governments in such activities.

Conference for Interaction and Confidence-Building in Asia. One extraregional initiative on cooperative security, the Conference for Interaction and Confidence-Building in Asia (CICA), emerged within Central Asia itself. It was initiated by Kazakhstani president Nursultan Nazarbayev at the United Nations in October 1992. Since its 1999 Inaugural Ministerial Meeting, CICA has held regular meetings that bring together ministers and, on several occasions, heads of state from twenty countries, including India, Pakistan, Russia, China, Israel, Iran, Jordan, the United Arab Emirates, Turkey, Kyrgyzstan, Tajikistan, Afghanistan, and Azerbaijan. Given such a diverse composition of members, the organization serves primarily as a mechanism for confidence building and dialogue between states that are often in conflict with one another. Although no breakthrough has been achieved so far, it is an important initiative that shows that Central Asian states can play a role in promoting security in Asia. Kazakhstan's chairmanship in OSCE could bring CICA and the OSCE closer together.

Conclusions: Implications for Regional and Global Conflict Management

The analysis of Russia's security perceptions and those of the Central Asian states, and the role of various institutions dealing with the regional security agenda in Central Asia, offer a number of conclusions that are important for assessing the prospects for the evolution of the regional crisis management system in Eurasia over the next decade.

The first conclusion is that for the foreseeable future Eurasia, including Central Asia, as perhaps one of the more vulnerable regions, will remain a region of insecurity. Stagnation within authoritarian regimes, a continuing economic crisis, interethnic tensions, border disputes, and protracted unresolved conflicts create ample ground for concern. There are also fears that Central Asia will become increasingly insecure after ISAF-NATO forces withdraw from Afghanistan. In addition, future crises may include conflict over water resources, a new civil war in Afghanistan, or even a new wave of terrorism and insurgency in Central Asia. Russia too could suffer from internal instability, all while facing growing challenges in its neighboring states.

The second conclusion is that despite the plethora of extraregional institutions active in Central Asia, including those dominated by Russia (CSTO), Russia and China (SCO), the West (NATO, European Union), and broader pan-European (OSCE) and pan-Asian (CICA) mechanisms, it remains unclear whether these institutions could effectively address both existing and future security challenges in Central Asia. Moreover, many of these challenges remain driven by domestic policies of regional states, which are highly sensitive to any external interference in their domestic affairs. Regional frameworks and institutions have so far been useful in promoting dialogue between regional states to diffuse rivalries among them, to legitimize Russia's ambition as the key regional security player, and to preserve post-Soviet military-to-military ties (CSTO), to reconcile interests between Russia and China (SCO), to provide a framework for Western assistance to Central Asian states (OCSE, European Union, NATO), and to satisfy the new regional ambitions of some Central Asian states (like CICA for Kazakhstan). Yet, as the crisis in Kyrgyzstan in 2010 demonstrates, the security capacity of regional organizations such as the CSTO remains limited. At the same time, however, the lack of intervention in Kyrgyzstan is also related to the fear from the United States and Russia that the events in Kyrgyzstan could destabilize the region as a whole and impact not only bordering states such as Uzbekistan but also U.S. efforts in Afghanistan (particularly since Manas is integral to U.S. supply infrastructure).

The third conclusion is that although Russia continues to view itself as the main security provider in Eurasia, it is no longer seen as such by either the regional players or external actors. In fact, they are concerned that Russia could itself be a source of instability. In Russia, too, more voices are heard within the political elite expressing concern that Russia is losing influence and capacity to affect key negative trends in Eurasia. In these circumstances, it is possible to envision a greater accommodation among key external players and mutual acceptance of the roles played by each of them, provided that the most controversial issues—such as NATO enlargement and democracy promotion—are taken off the agenda. Indeed, the shift away from zero sum–based geopolitical competition in Central Asia was reinforced by putting an end to the bidding war between the United States and Russia over basing rights and instead accommodating shared assessments of the situation (fueled in no part by common security concerns in Afghanistan). This was also highlighted by joint U.S.-Russian threat assessments in Kyrgyzstan and a joint agreement on the future of the Manas facility.

The fourth conclusion is that there is a growing realization in the West that the West needs to find ways to offer Russia a place in the European security architecture. Therefore, discussions over President Medvedev's proposals on a New European Security Treaty, though unlikely to produce a legally binding treaty, are likely to lead to a more ambitious agenda for Russia-NATO and Russia-EU cooperation and to revitalize OSCE as the only truly pan-European organization. It is also likely that a serious dialogue or even ad hoc cooperation will be established between the SCO and NATO and the SCO and the European Union. A dialogue between NATO and the CSTO could also emerge—mostly in regard to Afghanistan—but it is unlikely in the foreseeable future to lead toward real cooperation.

The fifth conclusion is that Russia and the West are no longer the sole players in Eurasia. China is playing an increasingly important role, as are other Asian and Middle Eastern actors. In the long run, Central Asia is likely to gravitate more toward Asia than toward Russia and Europe. This trajectory could present a certain challenge to both Russia and the West.

Toward a New Security Paradigm in Central Asia?

A new security paradigm might be emerging in Europe, and it is in the interests of all external players to help identify and consolidate its tentative trends. There are four major components of this emerging new paradigm that represent a break from the past.

The first one, and perhaps the most pronounced, is *subregionalism*. Today, post-Soviet identity, which united the post-Soviet region into one geopolitical entity, is no longer the defining feature of regional dynamics. Other post-Soviet, historical, and cultural trends are taking over in shaping the trajectories along which these regions will continue to travel. This trend of subregionalism has to be promoted through more robust and ambitious efforts to promote subregional cooperation and institutions, including perhaps some specific issue-based initiatives, such as the Water and Environment Forum for Central Asia or the Turkish proposal for a Stability and Cooperation Platform for the South Caucasus, to build trust in addressing regional conflicts and normalizing interstate relations.

The second feature is the *end of political transition*. Most regional states have transitioned to stable models, although none of them are truly democratic. In the next decade, the end of the critical phase of nation-building projects will likely be seen, a phase that for the past two decades emphasized sovereignty over regional cooperation and helped fuel interethnic and interstate tensions. In this new reality of established state borders and institutions, the emphasis of the international community should be placed on promoting good governance and the rule of law rather than on building capacity and contingency planning against the collapse of states or major interstate conflicts.

The third feature of the new regional paradigm is the *retreat of geopolitics*. Geopolitical rivalries of the past decade are diminishing under pressure of a number of factors: (1) the global financial crisis and U.S. preoccupation with domestic and other regional priorities; (2) the end of active NATO and EU enlargement for the foreseeable future; (3) Russia's declining resources and capacity to exercise its influence in the post-Soviet area (accelerated by the rise of a new generation with no stake or memories in the Soviet past); (4) changes of attitudes within Eurasian states themselves, which reject geopolitical rivalries as a major threat to their stability; (5) the August 2008 war in Georgia, which demonstrated how "costly" geopolitical rivalries can be if allowed to be exploited by regional states; and (6) the increasing emphasis on a common vision of threats among all external actors, which include a wide range of issues from Afghanistan to climate change and was evidenced in the cooperation over the Kyrgyzstan crisis in 2010.

The fourth feature, which is perhaps the most tentative, is the *growth of interdependency*. While the majority of Eurasian states have not benefited from globalization due to their economic weakness, corruption, and closed political systems, they are increasingly aware that in security terms they are increasingly dependent on their neighbors.

In these circumstances it is important to explore how these trends could be brought together in developing a flexible and comprehensive—in terms of engagement of all external powers—model of cooperative security. The term "cooperative security" here follows Barry Buzan's definition of "a set of states whose major security perceptions and concerns are so interlinked that their national security problems cannot reasonably be analyzed and solved apart from one another."[35] One can argue that such a vision for Eurasia is strategically naive. Indeed, there are still many experts who view this vast region through the eyes of Halford MacKinder, who closely associated the very notion of geopolitics with the "heartland of Eurasia."[36] It might still be that geopolitics prevails. But such a scenario does not in any way guarantee that the eyes of the international community will be focused on Eurasia; rather, it would ensure that none of the protracted conflicts are resolved, that regional states continue to exploit great-power rivalries to delay domestic reforms, that the regional strategy for Afghanistan does not succeed, that NATO and EU enlargement will remain blocked by Russia's aggressive opposition, and that the United Nations and the OSCE will be unable to foster consensus to affect change on the regional security agenda.

Russia perhaps has the most to lose from a cooperative security approach. Therefore, it is essential that Russia is brought in as a major player to help shape cooperative approaches together with other global players. President Medvedev's initiative on the New European Security Treaty could be utilized to initiate a process of consultations on the key principles for Russian-Western cooperation in Eurasia, for reinvigorating regional institutions, and for building bridges between Russian-led and Western-led institutions, such as between NATO and the CSTO, and the SCO and the European Union. The United Nations should reemerge as an important actor in Eurasia and leverage all of its capacities, such as the UNDP and the newly established mediation support network. Finally, China should be brought in as an important dialogue partner for any major initiatives on energy security and the stabilization of Central Asia.

As the first post-Soviet generation comes of age, the states of the region face two major challenges. On the one hand, it is important to preserve all of the positive legacies that stem from the centuries of coexistence between the peoples of Central Asia, the South Caucasus, and Eastern Europe, including their cultural, historic, scientific, and human ties. On the other hand, the development of all Eurasian states requires that their progressive elites develop confidence that centuries-long trends of geopolitics and the dominance of major external powers can be overcome for the benefit of their respective security, prosperity, and integration into the global world order—an order in which each of these states has its own distinct interests and responsibilities. For any truly cooperative system to emerge, the initiative must come from the region itself.

Notes

1. UNODC, *World Drug Report 2010* (New York: United Nations, 2010).

2. Roland Dannreuther, "Islamic Radicalization in Russia: An Assessment," *International Affairs* 86, no. 1 (January 2010).

3. According to Russian defense minister Anatoly Serduykov in a speech at the Russian Defense Ministry on March 17, 2009, only 10 percent of all weapons and equipment in the Russian armed forces qualify as modern. Serduykov's plan is for the share of modern weapons in the armed forces to be 30 percent by 2015 and 70 percent by 2020, a very ambitious target given the current state of Russia's weapons and equipment.

4. To demonstrate how important Manas has been to the Afghanistan war effort, by March 2010 it was handling up to 50,000 troops en route to or from Afghanistan each month and refueling the fighter aircraft that patrol Afghan airspace twenty-four hours a day. For more information, see the International Crisis Group policy briefing "Kyrgyzstan: A Hollow Regime Collapses," April 27, 2010.

5. UNODC, *World Drug Report 2010*, 48.

6. Ibid., 49.

7. СНБ Кыргызстана: Погромы на юге организовали Максим Бакиев, узбеки и Талибан, фергана.ру, June 24, 2010.

8. For analysis of CSTO actions during the crisis in Kyrgyzstan, see Deirdre Tynan, "CSTO Indecisive on Kyrgyzstan Intervention," *Eurasianet*, June 14, 2010, www.eurasia net.org/node/61294.

9. The term "extraregional" is used here to refer to institutions that cover the regional states but also other countries outside of Central Asia.

10. See Anna Matveeva, *EU Stakes in Central Asia*, Chaillot Paper no. 91 (Paris: European Union Institute for Security Studies, July 2006).

11. The Charter of the CSTO, Chapter III, Article 7 reads: "In order to attain the purposes of the Organization, the member States shall take joint measures to organize within its framework an effective collective security system, to establish coalition (regional) groupings of forces and the corresponding administrative bodies and create a military infrastructure, to train military staff and specialists for the armed forces and to furnish the latter with the necessary arms and military technology." See www.odkb.gov.ru/start/index_azbengl.htm.

12. Article 4 of the CSTO Charter.

13. Article 6 of the CSTO Charter.

14. The Collective Security Concept of the CSTO.

15. CSTO Charter, Chapter III, Article 8.

16. Ibid.

17. Ibid.

18. Вопросы формирования системы коллективной безопасности, www.odkb.gov. ru/start/index_azg.htm.

19. See www.dkb.gov.ru/start/index.htm.

20. See "Russia-Led CSTO Grouping Adds Military Dimension," Radio Free Europe/ Radio Liberty (RFE/RL), February 4, 2009, www.rferl.org/Content/Rapid_Reaction_ Force_Adds_Military_Dimension%20_To_CSTO/1379324.html.

21. Ibid.

22. See President of Russia, "News Conference on CSTO Collective Security Council Session Results," June 14, 2009, www.kremlin.ru/eng/speeches/2009/06/14/2114_type 82914type84779_217813.shtml.

23. See his interview in *Kommersant*, www.mamf.ru/odkb_mamf/interview/azd.php.

24. Roger McDermott, "New CSTO Military Force Planned," *Eurasia Daily Monitor* 5, no. 181 (September 22, 2008), www.jamestown.org/programs/edm/single/?tx_ttnews%5Btt_ news%5D=33957&tx_ttnews%5BbackPid%5D=166&no_cache=1; *Interfax*, www.interfax. ru/politics/news.asp?id=82399&sw=%EE%E4%EA%E1&bd=23&bm=5&by=2009&ed= 23&em=6&ey=2009&secid=0&mp=0&p=2.

25. McDermott, "New Military Force Planned."

26. "Gendarme of Eurasia: Moscow Takes a Closer Look at Former Soviet Republics," *Kommersant*, October 8, 2007, www.kommersant.com/p812422/r_1/CIS_CSTO_Russia_ Lebedev/Tajikistan.

27. President of Russia, "Dmitry Medvedev signed the Federal Law 'On the Ratification of the Agreement on Peacekeeping Activities of the Collective Security Treaty Organisation,'" January 6, 2009, www.kremlin.ru/eng/text/news/2009/01/211848.shtml.

28. Ibid.

29. Richard Weitz, "Is the Collective Security Organisation the Real Anti-NATO," *World Politics Review*, January 23, 2008.

30. See the Shanghai Convention on Combating Terrorism, Separatism, and Extremism, www.sectsco.org/EN/show.asp?id=68.

31. See SCO, "Executive Committee of the Regional Counter-Terrorism Structure," http://www.sectsco.org/EN/AntiTerrorism.asp.

32. See NATO's information booklet *Partners in Central Asia: NATO Backgrounder* (Brussels: NATO Public Diplomacy Division, November 2007).

33. For a more detailed analysis of Russian and NATO relations with Central Asian militaries, see, for example, Roger McDermott, *Kazakhstan's Defence Policy: An Assessment of Trends* (Carlisle, PA: Strategic Studies Institute, U.S. Army War College, February 11, 2009, www.strategicstudiesinstitute.army.mil/pubs/display.cfm?pubID=904.

34. See "The EU and Central Asia: Strategy for a New Partnership," www.auswaertiges-amt. de/diplo/en/Europa/Aussenpolitik/Regionalabkommen/EU-CentralAsia-Strategy.pdf.

35. Barry Buzan, Ole Weaver, and Jaap de Wilde, *Security: A New Framework for Analysis* (Boulder, CO: Lynne Rienner Publishers, 1998), 12.

36. See the article submitted by Halford John Mackinder to the Royal Geographical Society in 1904 titled "The Geographical Pivot of History."

13

Expanding Circles of Engagement

India and South Asia

Meenakshi Gopinath

South Asia occupies two discrete, even contradictory locations in the contemporary global consciousness. On the one hand, it is seen as a cauldron of interstate and intrastate conflict, ethnic strife, insurgencies, terrorism, low human development indicators, and democratic and governance deficits and as a potential nuclear "flash point." On the other hand, as home to one of every five people in the world and a rich multiplicity of cultures, with an ascendant India poised to engage anew with the world, South Asia presents a prism of possibilities. Much will depend on how India's aspirations to global influence—its diplomatic, strategic, and growth trajectories—will subserve the human security concerns of the region. The leadership it assumes, regionally and internationally, as the world's most populous democracy and potentially third largest economy, will decisively shape the prospects for the resolution of conflict in South Asia.

India's growing strategic and economic importance positions it as an indispensable actor in the making of any new global compact, even as international hierarchies get reconstituted. Consequently, analysts exhort that its engagement with the world requires the shedding of older shibboleths of "third worldism" and of brooding solipsism to craft a proactive assessment of emerging opportunities in an expanded international role.[1] In pursuing commonalities and managing differences globally, India sees

351

the stabilization of its immediate neighborhood as a priority, even as engagement sans entanglement in larger military blocs makes sense for a rising economic power. India will increasingly have to script a role that does justice to its potential.[2] As India stands geopolitically at the vortex of the arcs of "prosperity," "energy," "instability," and "communications," its foreign policy will require both deftness and imagination.[3] India remains a crossroads between West Asia, Southeast Asia, Central Asia, and the Indian Ocean. The situations in the Persian Gulf and Central Asia, the changing power equations in East Asia, a range of maritime concerns like piracy and keeping the sea-lanes free,[4] and the security concerns of the other smaller South Asian states must be sensitively factored into its policy options. India increasingly sees the efficacy of its "global" role linked to the sustenance of democracy in South Asia and the "democratic transitions" effected by national elections between 2008 and 2010 in almost all states of the region—particularly Bangladesh, Afghanistan, Pakistan, Nepal, Bhutan, the Maldives, and Sri Lanka. The manner in which the states of the region balance democratic aspirations with the compulsions of internal security—between "state security" and "people's security"—will largely determine the prospects of regional stability and conflict management. Here, India could play a crucial, facilitative role in helping the countries of the region overcome the anxieties of proximity to a large neighbor.

Consequently, India is in search of a new idiom of strategic reasoning that moves beyond tactics to a sustained engagement in its neighborhood that deftly skirts unilateralism or interventionism and insulates it from charges of "interference" in the internal affairs of its neighbors.

There has been a growing recognition, particularly since the 1990s, that the expansion of democratic values in South Asia is crucial to India's own future as a multiethnic, multicultural nation, especially in the face of the threat of rising religious extremism both within and beyond its borders. The shift to actively promote democratization and political pluralism in the region also reflects India's position that the practice of democracy is not incompatible with Asian values and that India and the South Asian region as a whole can contribute to the enrichment of the democratic idea. The practice of democracy need not be circumscribed by the Western liberal model.[5]

India now seeks a prosperous and peaceful South Asia as integral to its vision of an emerging Asia. To this end, a more proactive effort to build regional ties and an innovative approach are required to provide support to smaller and willing neighbors in need of overcoming their internal political crises to focus on development. Support for democratic transitions in the neighborhood, including facilitating institution building and power sharing among different regions and ethnic groups, is seen as integral to this new thrust of expanding circles of "nonintrusive" engagement.[6] In this new focus, especially on its Western front—in relation to Afghanistan—India has chosen to play this role in concert with the world's "oldest democracy"—the United States.

Analysts locate this emerging strategy in the contexts of the larger macro processes under way in Asia. India, as the second most important dynamo of growth in the region, is seen as a potential "balancer and stabilizer at a time of uncertainties in great-power relations, a force for the growth of democracy and liberal internationalism in Asia and a power opposed to extremism, terrorism, and fundamentalist militant religious moments."[7]

India's real challenge in balancing its potential "big role" with "smart power" comes from its immediate South Asian neighborhood. With the locus of extremism and violence and the "center of gravity" of international terrorism moving toward South Asia, the Indian Subcontinent has been particularly salient to world politics since 9/11.[8] India's neighboring states remain troubled and crisis ridden and deeply affect its sense of security, economic growth, and development. These have long-term regional and global implications that profoundly impact the future role India crafts for itself in a changing world. This is a world where, since the economic meltdown of 2008, the G8 countries are having to contend with the growing salience of the G20, and here too India seems poised to play an influential role.

India's global aspirations will require it to play a more proactive role in both multilateral fora and in confidence-building and conflict resolution processes in South Asia. Balancing both strategic interest and the moral imperative demands the self-confidence to nudge South Asia toward a more equitable power paradigm. It also demands that India cast itself as "facilitator" rather than "looming presence," without ceding "untenanted" space to China in the region. This will require India to fashion a vocabulary that speaks in a different voice as it attempts to "process" peace in the region.

The strength, resilience, and robustness of India's great experiment—that of the world's largest "democracy in the making"[9]—will be judged on the basis of how the Indian state (1) writes the script on security and governance and reconciles and responds to the gaps and seeming contradictions between people's security and what often passes as national security; (2) redefines coexistence in a nuclearized environment; (3) acquits itself as a rising power in the South Asian region with sensitivity and deftness; (4) optimizes efforts to strengthen the region as a whole; (5) calibrates its relationship with China; (6) engages with the United States; and (7) offers at the global level a new vocabulary for a security architecture that moves away from the demonization of Islam.

This chapter examines some of the internal sources of conflict that beset South Asia and India in particular, with the country's complex and combustible mix of economic disparity and ethnic, religious, and ideological fault lines, and analyzes India's attempts at balancing its emerging global role with the imperatives of human security in the region. The evolving trajectory of India's engagement with conflict management is cast against the backdrop of options for supporting the resolution of the Kashmir conundrum, both internally and with Pakistan. The chapter concludes by suggesting that a reconceptualization of security is critical to addressing the conflicts that beset South Asia—and that India's search for a new idiom of leadership is integral to their resolution.

New Security Challenges

The conventional security discourse, a product of the Cold War era, proves inadequate as a methodological basis to evaluate new and emerging threats to security in South Asia, which are a complex amalgam of domestic and external factors and linked indivisibly with the crisis of substantive democracy, equity, and governance.[10] In the case of India, for instance, it has been shown that its losses from terrorism and insurgency have been far greater than those from all its conventional conflicts taken together. Insurgency in Kashmir since 1989, for instance, has resulted in even higher casualties than in the Indo-Pakistan wars. These factors, coupled with corrupt practices, governance inadequacies, and the criminalization of politics, inhibit the capacity of the state to effectively grapple with threats to security.

National security, which was hitherto seen as involving the external dimension—namely, the relationship between sovereign states in an international order—becomes more internally oriented as democratic assertions demand greater transparency and public debate on the security of average citizens. In this scenario, the state's military capabilities become less relevant as a means to achieving the new security needs and aspirations of the citizenry. In addition, the changes in the international system dictate a broadening of the perspectives on national security and a moving beyond realist perspectives. The rise and growing strength of transnational corporations, the World Trade Organization (WTO), the International Monetary Fund (IMF), the World Bank, and international money markets with their astronomical levels of financial flows have put unprecedented pressures on the relative autonomy of states like India and its neighbors.[11]

What is significant for security in India and most countries of South Asia is that the state is neither consistently "protector" nor "predator." It oscillates between these roles depending on which group or interest is negotiating to impact its agenda or seeking access to entitlements or benefits through democratic appeal. It is not open to negotiation by vulnerable categories of citizens. In its attentiveness to some interests, the public agenda is permissively open and vastly inclusionary, while to other, less influential ones, it remains severely exclusionary. The core projects of the state are, it is argued, rendered differentially open to negotiation, and so it is not a problem of too little or too much democracy even in democratic states, but of its selective availability.[12]

The challenges to governance are made even more complex because the state is not always an independent actor in terms of its ability to implement its declared objectives. The constraints that operate with regard to citizens' rights to security are underpinned by factors that place serious limits on the functioning of democracy, namely, economic and social inequalities. While it is universally recognized that the poor are voiceless and largely politically marginalized in the formally democratic pluralist polity, social inequalities are not merely the result of class differences. They also derive from caste, gender, and community and these often overlap with class inequalities. The complexity of South Asian society as it is fractured along several axes—class, caste, gender, and religion—and sometimes along more than one axis simultaneously has created the group characterized as "doubly disadvantaged."[13] These groups—women of minority religions or *dalit* (marginalized caste) communities, tribespeople deprived of livelihoods, "oustees" on account of development projects—constitute a sizable segment whose security needs have been met with a singular lack of responsiveness. Their continued marginalization poses the greatest challenge to national and regional securities.

Borders, Boundaries, and Migrants

The preservation of the sanctity of borders and boundaries still dominates the consciousness of the security elites in India today. Indian prime minister Manmohan Singh's statement in the context of the Indo-Pakistan peace process of making "borders irrelevant" flies in the face of conventional positions. It however reflects the necessity for new paradigms of sovereignty and cooperation in a region that has to engage creatively with processes of globalization and to contain growing terrorism.

As crucial as the struggle between different political forces and imaginations within each country of the South Asian region are the cross-border, panregional implications of various national developments. Both shared histories and geographies make it impossible for any one country to remain unconcerned about developments in its neighborhood. Much of this relates to the bilateral relations the different countries have with India, given its size and centrality, but it also relates to the nature of insurgency, terrorism, cross-border migration, market integration, environmental hazards, climate change, and pandemics, which produce spillover effects with potentially grave consequences. At the South Asian Association for Regional Cooperation (SAARC) summit in 2007, India moved decisively to recognize and accept "asymmetrical responsibilities" for the region.[14]

A critical cross-region problem flows from the *partitions* in the region from the early 1900s, with their typical ruptures, dislocations, and societal struggles that still inform the cartographic anxieties and contribute to interstate and intrastate tensions. The partition of Bengal by Lord Curzon in 1905 along religious lines was the precursor to several others—the partition of the Indian Subcontinent and the birth of Pakistan in 1947; the dismemberment of Pakistan and the creation of Bangladesh in 1971; and the legal existence of "two Kashmirs," one in India and the other in Pakistan since 1948. Pervasive fears about "dismemberment" and "secession" remain even today in India, Pakistan, Sri Lanka, Nepal, and even Myanmar and to some degree in Bangladesh about its Chittagong Hill Tracts. The formalized state order of the postpartition world is constantly subverted by various forms of mobility that refuse to be tamed and territorialized by reasons of state and that persistently "violate" the supposed "sanctity" of borders and boundaries.

The designation "stateless" is now so commonplace that it excites little comment, even as governments grapple with another category of people called "permanent liabilities." The repatriated Tamils of Jaffna and the Eastern Provinces, for instance, have no place to call their own in either India or Sri Lanka; "displaced persons" of erstwhile East Pakistan (now Bangladesh) are still in a kind of limbo in India and live under the constant threat of being declared "infiltrators" or "illegal immigrants." Any number of second-class citizens are to be found in every country of South Asia, and everywhere those in a minority, whether linguistic, ethnic, or religious, are vulnerable.[15] Women and children as refugees in South Asia were estimated to be around 21.5 million at the beginning of 1999.

At the conceptual level, nontraditional approaches to (in)security could interrogate the structures that go "into the making of a territorialized order imposed from above and dictated largely by state-centric spatiality firmly entrenched in hierarchical socio-cultural structures of patriarchy."[16] Rather than circumscribe and tame the spatial in all its diversity, South Asian security could perhaps be better served by acknowledging space as "simultaneity of multiple trajectories," since the "ecospaces" of South Asia continue to challenge the region's geopolitics.[17]

In fact, this "boundary fixation" has imprisoned India and Pakistan in grappling with the legacy of the Radcliffe Line (drawn somewhat arbitrarily and hastily by the British as the territorial demarcation between India and Pakistan to "map" the 1947 partition of the Indian Subcontinent), even as they commit invaluable resources, energy, and lives into guarding disputed boundaries in the inhospitable spaces of the Siachen glacier.

At a policy level, a shift in orientation would better secure South Asia and India in particular, although this may be difficult to do under current configurations of national security sentiment. A new *borderland development policy* is needed where boundaries become irrelevant by treating borderlands as vital areas of cultural exchange and trade. Rather than treating border zones between India and her neighbors as inaccessible, remote, and consequently "secure," they need to be saturated with economic activity with the traffic of goods and people, and linked with excellent infrastructures to the rest of the country. Interlinkages, in this sense, will yield a new security paradigm. A borderland development policy that includes maritime borders will be successful only if borders are nurtured, even if they cannot be settled.[18]

Poverty, Inequity, and Extremism

The deep-seated ambivalence on the part of states and peoples of South Asia to the recurrent cycles of violence and devastation has now become a persistent feature of the region. What appears as the paradoxical reality in the lands of Gandhi, the Buddha, and several Sufi saints is the growing vulnerability of South Asia to extremism, terrorism, and religiopolitical fundamentalism of different kinds.

The specter of terrorism in the region has exacerbated the cartographic anxieties of South Asian states. India's ambitions to big-power status have been constrained by the compelling exigencies of this looming presence that stubbornly defies containment by the conventional weapons of state power. In addition, nearly all of the other states of the region (with the possible exception of Bhutan)—Afghanistan and Pakistan in particular, but also Bangladesh, Nepal, Sri Lanka, and even the Maldives—confront serious threats to security from terrorism, although it assumes different manifestations in different states depending on the internal situations, structural causes, and crises that spawn, support, or exacerbate its reach.

Political movements. India's Prime Minister has cited Naxalism (left-wing extremism) and terrorism as the two big threats to internal security. Naxalites aim for the creation of a classless society. Registering a steady escalation over the last ten years, the Maoist movement has penetrated 160 districts across several Indian states and over 4,000 square kilometers, ambushed around 200 police stations, and is gaining influence. Nine of these states have experienced an average of sixty killings a month since early

2009. In nearly 1,600 violent incidents involving Naxalites in 2006–07, 669 people died. It is estimated that they have over 10,000 armed fighters and around 40,000 full-time cadres with access to about 6,500 weapons, and control a fifth of India's forests. A serious cause of concern is that this movement may be further facilitated by foreign links. The fraternal links of Naxalites with the cadres of the Communist Party of Nepal (Maoist) across the Bihar-Nepal border, it is widely believed, laid the groundwork for the envisioning of a "compact revolutionary zone" in 2001 extending from north Bihar to southern Andhra in India.

Historically, the Naxalite movement was rooted in the problem of poverty and distress facing the marginalized groups, especially in areas that have not seen land reforms. Development (and some conservation) strategies that dispossess tribal and indigenous people and alienate them from forest land, without due regard to an equitable rehabilitation and resettlement process, have exacerbated resentment in these natural resource- and mineral-rich areas, which the Naxalites capitalize on to mobilize cadres around issues of distributive justice. Further, the nexus between corrupt government officials, contractors, and the land and forest mafia divert development funds, leading to high levels of unemployment.[19]

Alienation, underdevelopment, and doubts over the government's commitment to the provision of social security have afforded a support base to Naxal groups. While they operate as underground movements in most parts, they are well entrenched in many areas, especially forest spreads. In the villages scattered through the forest, the Indian state is almost invisible. Policemen, health workers, and officials are never seen, and this vacuum is sought to be filled by Naxalite committees.

Today, however, the movement seems to have changed course drastically. Naxalites actively oppose any form of developmental activity, be it the construction of roads, schools, or hospitals, with the cold-blooded aim of securing their turf. Their sole objective is to keep hammering away at the organs of the state. The movement is explicitly committed to dismantling liberal democratic mores, doing away with elections, closing down the media, and extending sympathy for regional breakaway groups.

Another disturbing development is that local militias have sprung up in opposition to the Naxalites—for instance, the Salwa Judum (Chattisgarh) and the Ranvir Sena (Bihar and Jharkhand, formed by Bhumihar caste landlords). These organizations themselves indulge in violence and extortion and are backed by Indian paramilitary forces, turning the forests into a battlefield and leading local tribal communities to flee from the killing and burning.

A combination of tough action and quiet diplomacy is being seen as a method to tackle the insurgency. How exactly this delicate balance will be struck is difficult to comprehend, especially because the Maoists have not been open to dialogue with the government. In the meantime, thousands of lives are in peril. Whether the war will serve the interests of the desperately poor, whom the Maoists claim to represent, is an open question. From a comprehensive security perspective, eradicating Naxalism is more than a local policing problem. What is required is the *creation of appropriate institutions, systems, and relations*, with the state proactively facilitating people's participation in democratic decision making.

Economic disparity. The closing decades of the twentieth century witnessed in India the creation of a series of people's resistance movements that interrogate prevalent state positions on *security* and *development*. These movements exemplify the political assertion of erstwhile-marginalized sections of civil society that are demanding humane and responsive governance. Focusing attention on the complicity of the state with indigenous elites, and the new inequities of power and privilege unleashed by globalization, they appeal beyond the nation-state to international civil society, invoking issues of human security.

Agroeconomic problems such as those related to crop failure, indebtedness, and macropolicy issues have led to impoverishment among farmers. Often, both the increasing costs of production and falling prices of farm commodities are linked to corporate globalization and trade liberalization, which has added a qualitatively new dimension to the stress on the peasantry.[20] In Nepal, the plight of the peasant farmers and landless workers of the fertile Tarai region has led to serious political alienation from the mainstream. The marginalization of the small shrimp farmers in the Bangladesh economy and the displacement of Pakistan's Punjab province peasants by huge agribusiness land acquisitions (owned by the Foundations of the Armed Forces) also point to the exacerbation of economic inequalities that promote volatility in the region. While India has been at the forefront of G-20 demands for rights to farmers in the Third World, at the domestic level, official agencies in India appear to be in denial of links between free trade and farmers' survival. The introduction of special economic zones (SEZs) as islands of progress with special privileges have exacerbated the politics of gated communities and exclusionary development, leading to violent protests and consequent fierce state crackdowns.

The human security deficit, combined with ethnic exclusions in "democratic" institutions, fueled the thirty-year civil strife and the devastating conflagration between the separatist Liberation Tigers for Tamil Eelam (LTTE) and the state in Sri Lanka. The secession of East Bengal (now Bangladesh) from Pakistan in 1971 was also a result of "internal colonialism" and the exclusion of the Bengali minorities. The ten-year Maoist insurgency in Nepal drew its broad-based support, particularly in the rural areas, by mobilizing the deep alienation of large sections from the lop-sided development priorities of the erstwhile kingdom. Their clout and propensity to earlier subvert parliamentary democracy was the result of the pervasive ethnic, class, caste, and gender inequities of Nepali society. It was only in September 2006 that the Maoists suspended their ten-year-long People's War to join a peace process making common cause with political parties for an antimonarchy struggle for people's democracy through electoral engagement. Their continued intransigence, especially since 2008, within the parliamentary format and the resulting subversion of consensus building further delayed the process of constitution making in Nepal.

Religion, Politics, and Extremism

Religion and politics provide a deadly combustible mix in the states of South Asia. Here, faith touches the lives of people in palpable and sometimes violent ways and appears to provide alternative channels of "succor," especially to the dispossessed. Religious mobilization for short-term political gains has been on the ascendant since the closing decades of the twentieth century in South Asia, witnessing a recrudescence of right-wing religious fundamentalisms. Religiopolitical mobilization has served as a potent tool both to gain legitimacy and at times extraconstitutional space within national boundaries and to "destabilize" unfriendly neighbors. In sum, radical assertions of religiopolitical extremism have often led to chain reactions in neighboring states. This was witnessed during the reprisals against Hindu minorities in Pakistan following the attack on the Babri Mosque by Hindu fundamentalist groups in India in 1992 and the attacks against the Muslims during the Gujarat Carnage in India in 2002. The South Asian region defies the "neat" theoretical characterizations and differentiations between "ideological/ religion-driven" groups and "grievance" groups.[21] In societies like Pakistan, India, Sri Lanka, and Afghanistan, religious terrorism often draws on ethnic identity assertion or resentment against democratic exclusion. South Asia in general is characterized by the overwhelming feeling of insecurity that religious and ethnic minorities experience across the states of the region.

Although Pakistan and Afghanistan are today the epicenter of religious extremist violence, the spillover of the groups that operate with strong regional linkages has not left any state immune. The increasing presence of religion in the public sphere in South Asia appears to belie the long-held premises of the modernization-secularization paradigm. Several Southern Asian countries, with the exceptions of India, Sri Lanka, and more recently Nepal, have accorded a special place to religion in their constitutions.[22]

A close, comparative look at South Asia reveals, ironically, that (except Pakistan, which has been under military rule for more than thirty-two years of its sixty-year history) mass electoral democracy has not seen the containment of religious extremism. Indeed, quite the reverse may be true. Electoral processes in these states, in the absence of a deep secularization and democratization of society, often renders the polity even more vulnerable to religious mobilization. Electoral democracy might in fact provide the context for the legitimation of religious mobilization, as has been witnessed by the ascendancy of the Hindu right-wing Bharatiya Janata Party (BJP) in India; Singhala-Buddhist radicalization in Sri Lanka during the thrity-year conflict with the LTTE; the Bangladesh Nationalist Party (BNP) victory in October 2001 in the parliamentary elections in a coalition with Islamist parties;[23] and the Pakistani military government's support of Hizb-e-Islami leader Gulbuddin Hekmatyar in Afghanistan.

Three major factors are seen as having contributed to the rise and violent assertion of radical Islam on the Afghanistan-Pakistan border: (1) the disintegration of Afghan social structures at the state and tribal levels beginning in 1979 with the revolts against the Communist government of Najibullah and the Soviet invasion; (2) the growing influence of Salafist Islam via the Middle East and the ascendancy of the radical Deobandi and Wahhabi schools as against the moderate Barelvis; and (3) the radicalization of the Pashtuns, the dominant ethnic group along the border that comprises a large part of the population of Khyber Pakhtoonkhwa (formerly the North-West Frontier Province, or NWFP) in Pakistan. The U.S. support to the mujahideen into the 1980s and safe havens provided for them in Pakistan, coinciding with the crumbling of the Afghan education system, witnessed the proliferation of madrassas in Pakistan providing religious-based education to refugees from Afghanistan. The lure of Islamist movements, sparked initially by big-power rivalry in the region, was also symptomatic of a deeper malaise that afflicts the South Asian region—namely, a general breakdown of law and order and the frailties of political governance; the breakdown of interethnic trust and dialogue; a collapse in the sense of control ordinary people feel they have over their lives; and a lack of recourse to justice for the reclaiming of their right to dignity.[24]

In addition, sectarian and religious movements spill over to make border disputes complex and intractable. The history of states offering sanctuary to radical intransigent groups of "hostile" neighbors has only compounded the problems of mistrust. Afghanistan sheltered Baloch nationalists in the 1970s while Pakistan extended refuge and training to the Afghan mujahideen in the 1980s and later supported the Afghan Taliban. Pakistan's military dictator General Zia-Ul-Haq promoted jihad in Afghanistan, funded thousands of Islamic madrassas, armed domestic Islamist organizations, and militarized and radicalized the border region. By supporting Islamist militants among the Pashtuns, the Pakistan government tried to neutralize Baloch and Pashtun nationalism within its borders. In Nepal and India, while Maoist organizations have developed strong ties with each other, some Hindu extremist groups attempt to make space in Nepal's bordering towns. Religious extremism is no longer merely episodic in South Asia. It spreads its tentacles to open up fresh ethnic, subnationalist, and territorial rivalries and affects almost all states of the region. It prompts South Asian states to wage proxy wars against each other, even though all states project their own transnational dangers while claiming to be transnationalism's victims. The deep trust deficit between the countries of the region continues to provide grist to the extremist mill. Here, SAARC can play a more proactive role under the aegis of its antiterrorism protocols and conventions.

The tenacious al-Qaeda and Taliban presence on both sides of the Afghanistan-Pakistan border has not only bedeviled relations between these two countries but also looms through their cross-border networks as a major security threat in South Asia. India sees itself as particularly vulnerable, and the ostensible target of the "thousand-bleeding-cuts" approach of calibrated terror strikes on Indian soil. The alleged tacit support (until recently) of the Pakistan Army for Islamist terror groups like the Lashkar-e-Taiba (LET) and the Jaish-e-Mohammed (JEM), which are essentially based in Pakistani Punjab and engaged in anti-Indian activity focused on Kashmir, has proved to be a double-edged sword. These groups are now known to have developed strong links with Taliban groups both in Pakistan and Afghanistan and pose severe threats to Pakistan's own internal security as well. The blatant and audacious series of terrorist and *fidayeen* (guerrilla) suicide attacks spiraling in October–November 2009 in major cities in Pakistan like Islamabad, Lahore, Peshawar, and above all near the General Headquarters of the Army in Rawalpindi and the Pakistan Aeronautical Complex in Kamra has brought home the imperative to reformulate the Pakistani establishment's strategic approach of "disaggregate" engagement with some terrorist groups. There is a growing sense among sections of the Pakistani elite that the main threat to their society comes from internal extremism rather than from India.[25] India has been at pains to drive home the point that a major shift in the orientation of the Pakistan Army and its powerful intelligence wing, the Inter-Services Intelligence (ISI), is necessary to grapple with the growing challenge of religion-based terrorism in the region.

The Pakistani polity, however, displays an ambivalence toward events such as the storming of the Lal Masjid in Islamabad by terrorists and policies toward the Taliban. Analysts have cited empirical data to show that policies of negotiating with the militants in the Federally Administered Tribal Areas (FATA) were more acceptable than policies of military confrontation. U.S. and other foreign military operations are deeply resented, even when the targets are foreigners seeking refuge in Pakistan from Afghanistan. Determining how the international community and antimilitant elements within the elected Pakistan government might persuade the Pakistani populace to accept the war on terrorism as necessary for Pakistan's own survival remains a vexed policy issue. The Pakistan Army's moral dilemma and declining morale in having waged military operations against its own people adds a difficult dimension. It is argued that while there are extreme crises of civilian leadership in Pakistan and ambivalence about the influence of militant groups, there is little robust evidence to suggest that the strategic elite has made a decision to abandon the use of militants for domestic or foreign policy objectives.[26]

Ahmed Rashid goes further to argue that "a nuclear-armed military and intelligence service that sponsored Islamic extremism as an intrinsic part of foreign policy for nearly four decades have found it extremity difficult to give up their self-destructive double-dealing policies after 9/11, even under the watchful eye of the CIA."[27] Indian analyst Ajai Sahni reiterates that despite the colossal "blowback" of the jihadi-terrorist enterprise that the country is now experiencing, it remains the case that a powerful constituency in the political-military establishment remains sympathetic to and complicit with Islamist extremist and terrorist formations that continue to operate with varying degrees of freedom across Pakistan.[28]

The threat of Islamist militancy looms large in Bangladesh as well, and it has been suggested that Pakistani agencies are implicated in the growth of militancy in India, Nepal, and even Sri Lanka.[29] The blurring of the distinction between Islam as a *religion* and as *nationalism* has enabled these groups to coalesce and establish networks across territorial boundaries to deal with "recalcitrant" or "hostile" states. The Islamist transformation of the Kashmir insurgency, and the gradual marginalization of the indigenous Kashmiri militants by armed groups, made up of veterans from Afghanistan, Pakistan, Uzbekistan, and even Sudan and of other mercenaries, drastically changed the complexion of the conflict in Kashmir from the mid-1990s on. A number of militant groups emerged advocating Nizam-e-Mustafa (Islamic system) as the objective of their struggle, as *azadi* (freedom) gave way to *jihad*. Various Islamist groups like Hizbul Mujahideen, Al Badr, Harkat-Ul-Ansar, Jamaat-e-Islami, Al Jihad Force, Allah Tigers, Harkat-Ul-Mujahideen, and the like emerged on the scene to assert that any solution to Kashmir short of an Islamic caliphate would be unacceptable.[30]

The Taliban were an important external agent fueling Islamic militancy in Kashmir. In addition, Islamist groups like Jamaat-e-Islami and Jamiat Ahle Hadith directed their efforts to eliminate the traditional syncretic social and religious practices in Kashmir that had privileged the inclusive Sufi traditions of Islam. Similar patterns of increasing activity of Islamist militant groups with connections in Pakistan have emerged in Bangladesh, Nepal, Sri Lanka, and even the island state of the Maldives.

South Asian states are deeply implicated in the political, territorial, and religious proxy wars that are being fought in one another's territory. Few states are immune to the growing alliance between religious extremism and political nationalisms in South Asia. The trust deficit between the countries of the region make conflict resolution in this area both urgent and challenging. The "problematic" borders between India and Bangladesh and between India and Nepal, the India-Pakistan conflict, particularly over Kashmir, the Pakistan-Afghanistan conflict over the Durand Line, the Pakistan-Iran face-off over Balochistan and its increasing vulnerability, the India-China territorial disputes, and the final violent denouement of the Sri Lankan conflict with the defeat of the LTTE have all diverted focus from pressing development agendas and legitimated violence as an option for responding to conflict. India as the biggest country in the region needs to assuage the insecurities and threat perceptions of the smaller states and will have to be open to multilateral joint mechanisms to contain the multiple challenges of extremism. Even while there is a growing recognition that the challenges of terrorism and militancy are best tackled collectively, India has conventionally preferred the bilateral route to keep disputes outside of SAARC, a strategy aided by the fact that the SAARC Charter does not provide for responses to bilateral *political* disputes. This may also have served India's ability to leverage its "dominance." Of late, however, in proactively pushing for and adopting the SAARC protocols on terrorism at recent SAARC summits, India seems to have moved far beyond its earlier bilateralism to expanding circles of responsibility for the region as a whole.[31]

Cultures of Militarism and Responses to Terrorism

The failure of the state in South Asia to address the tensions between what it sees as *national security* and the *human security* requirements of increasing numbers of newly articulate groups has spawned *cultures of militarism.*

The 1980s marked the decade when the militarization trend manifested itself. Civilian regimes, unable to tackle politically the rising tide of communalism, casteism, and militant regionalism, came to rely on the police and armed forces to maintain internal stability, and perform such diverse tasks as quelling communal riots, providing relief during natural disasters, maintaining essential services during strikes, and conducting counterinsurgency and antiterrorist operations.

Despite India's constitutional democracy, the Armed Forces Special Powers Act gave almost carte blanche powers to its security forces in the Northeast: it was extended to Punjab in 1983 and Kashmir in 1990. The Terrorist and Disruptive Activities Act (TADA) gave vast powers to the states in 1985. It was made more rigorous (with the burden of proof being shifted to the accused), and its powers extended to the center in 1987. The TADA, which was widely misused and had acquired a distinct anti-Muslim orientation in the 1990s, was revoked in 1995.

Movements with demands ranging from autonomy to independence—in India's Northeastern states of Assam, Nagaland, and Manipur and in Kashmir; in Pakistan's Balochistan, NWFP, and Gilgit-Baltistan; in Sri Lanka among the Tamils; in Bangladesh's Chittagong Hill Tracts; in Nepal's Terrai region; and in Afghanistan's Taliban-controlled areas—reflect the tensions between assertions of ethnicity, religious identity, and the nation-building project. In turn, these movements invariably end up targeting innocent civilians and dramatize their cause by advocating terrorist tactics and being militaristic.

State responses to these movements have tended to demonstrate tactics and strategy that favor militarism over dialogue and reconciliation. The flushing out of terrorists by extensive military operations has required combing operations in which lawful citizens are mistaken for terrorists and suffer from wrongful confinement, torture, rape, and/or custodial death. The excesses of the militants are met with the might of the state, resulting in abrogation of the rule of law and the breakdown of institutions and processes of democracy. The suffering of civilians caught in the cross fire (with women and children as the worst victims) has highlighted the fragility of state structures that treat the failed promise of development as a law-and-order problem. For example, an estimated 60–65 percent of India's military and paramilitary forces are deployed in counterinsurgency operations. The hazards of overreliance on containment as a tool of governance have far-reaching implications for plural societies. The strengthening of such mechanisms outside democratic accountability not only narrows democratic space but also contributes to a brutalization and criminalization of official agencies and institutions.[32]

The real problem arises, as in the case of most South Asian states, when draconian laws, which are enacted to deal with extraordinary contingencies and as temporary measures, become the "paradigm of government." The normalizing of the *deployment* of the military in domestic affairs is a serious concern not just for democratic governance but also for the people's security.

This raises significant questions about terrorism and its containment, which for many countries of the region is a major challenge. The entry of terrorism into the security lexicon as a variable straddling both the domains of the "traditional" and the "nontraditional" reconfigures the notions of conflict and war, with nonstate actors and states in confrontation, subverting all established conventions and boundaries and shared vocabularies and methodologies of combat. With the state having lost control over its monopoly over force, small groups, without countries or uniforms, can cause irrevocable damage. The root of the problem is not any particular religion or ideology, but a fundamental change in the relationship between the state, the market, and the technologies of destruction. Traditional approaches to problem solving have not stemmed the tide.

A new vocabulary that institutionalizes dialogue and conflict resolution techniques and methodologies as central to the security-terrorism conundrum needs to be actively explored. Nontraditional approaches and critical security studies have brought what were considered the "soft issues" of development squarely within the ambit of security. It is time to integrate dialogues on conflict prevention and peacebuilding within the security paradigm. Even now they remain almost discrete domains. The UN initiative to move even the essentially military exercises of peacekeeping toward a peacebuilding trajectory opens important avenues in this regard.

It is crucial for South Asian states to retain their relationships with the international coalition against terrorism (in its operational dimensions) while not being forced on the U.S. bandwagon. India has to be particularly sensitive to the need to develop deeper ties with the Muslim world and also to the potential costs as well as potential benefits of close relations with the United States. In addition, sustained effort should be made to see that labels of "terrorism" and "terrorist violence" are not ascribed to one religious community or caste group. The Joint Mechanism against Terrorism envisaged by the Indian and Pakistani leadership breaks new ground in attempting to evolve new metaphors and mechanisms for borders, boundaries, and issues of sovereignty. It has, however, been held hostage to the trust deficit between the two largest states in South Asia.

The Impasse in Jammu and Kashmir

The Kashmir conundrum remains central to the possibilities for peace on the subcontinent and efforts to build sustainable peace in South Asia. Even today, much of the hostility between India and Pakistan gets enmeshed both symbolically and strategically with the dispute over Kashmir.

The tortuous India-Pakistan relationship—which encompasses wars in 1947–48, 1965, and 1971, the Brasstacks crisis of 1986–87, the Kashmir crisis of 1990, the Kargil conflict of 1999, and the prolonged border confrontation of 2001–02—casts its shadow over the security of the people of the subcontinent. Coming close to the brink of war in 1999 and again in 2001–02, the two countries purportedly held back on the nuclear option following intense U.S. and international pressure.

The Composite Dialogue resumed by India and Pakistan in February 2004 provided the framework for an innovative conflict resolution approach post Kargil. It also marked a decisive shift in India's approach to negotiations, from a short-term tactical militaristic approach to a problem-solving approach that aligns with its self-image as a rising power seeking a place in the sun. Crafting a normative position that simultaneously protected its strategic interests, India began to envision a stable and democratic Pakistan as consonant to this interest. India shed once and for all any adventurist hopes of a dismemberment of its "troublesome neighbor," particularly after the possibility of a terrorist spillover of jihadi or Islamist groups in the event of Pakistan's collapse was made starkly clear following 9/11. The framework marked in a fundamental sense a bend in the road and a genuine willingness to invest in the peace dividend.

Within the Composite Dialogue Framework

The subjects brought to the table reflected a readiness to address all outstanding and contentious issues for a decisive movement forward. The existing "dividers" and potential "connectors" alike were included in the eight-subject menu.[33] India agreed to discuss the Kashmir question purposefully and Pakistan promised to not allow terrorism from its soil. The agreement to negotiate Kashmir in an environment free of violence and terrorism was the principal achievement of the India-Pakistan joint statement of January 4, 2004.[34] The accordion was open to take on board creative ideas and "out-of-box" thinking—as the then president of Pakistan, Pervez Musharraf, put it—on the vexatious question of Jammu and Kashmir.

In attempting to use the opportunity provided by the Composite Dialogue, India and Pakistan came close in secret negotiations to devising a framework for settling their long conflict over Kashmir,[35] but the dialogue was put on hold from March 2007 onward owing to Musharraf's declining popularity, problems in Pakistan, and the chain of events that eventually led to his ouster in August 2008. Khurshid Kasuri, Pakistan's foreign minister at the time, was quoted as saying that the "solution" contained "four big ideas" within which the proposed agreement was discussed. These included demilitarization (the gradual withdrawal of troops from both sides), the granting of special rights to Kashmiris to move and trade freely on both sides of the Line of Control, greater autonomy, and some form of self-governance and a joint mechanism that would link the two Kashmirs, which would consist of local Kashmiri leaders, Indians, and Pakistanis, and that would oversee issues affecting people on both sides of the line.[36] Such a resolution of the Kashmir dispute was to be the cornerstone of a broad agreement representing a paradigm shift that would change the basic nature of India-Pakistan relations.[37] Although India and Pakistan reached substantial understanding on the contested Siachen glacier and, in one of the most significant movements in their bilateral diplomacy, made progress toward a resolution of the Sir Creek maritime boundary dispute,[38] the Composite Dialogue has been frozen since 2008 in the diplomatic chill that followed that year's Mumbai terror attacks.

Beyond Borders: Musharraf's Proposal

The broad pitch for peace had reflected the realization that given the nuclearized environment "war was no longer an option for either side."[39] It seemed to be additionally propelled by Musharraf's own imperatives to be seen as a liberal, modern Islamic leader; to control religious extremism in Pakistan; and to be the architect of a "grand settlement" with India. Musharraf's "out-of-box" articulation in October 2004 for a proposed settlement on Kashmir had underscored a flexible approach, moving away from rigid and hardened positions and even a willingness to "leave behind the UN resolutions," a position that was sensitive to the Indian aversion for a proposed plebiscite. His four-point formula suggested four stages: (1) the recognition of Kashmir as a dispute; (2) the initiation of a dialogue; (3) the shedding of unacceptable solutions; and (4) the securing of a win-win position.

Musharraf's proposal was presented as an attempt to generate focused debate. The formula identified seven regions in Kashmir on which to first focus, two of which are in Pakistan and five in India, on the basis of a combination of factors such as ethnicity, linguistic homogeneity, religious commonalities, geographic proximity, and compactness. As has been shown by Indian scholars, this is not an easy task, because commonalities are difficult to establish in Kashmir, where several differentiated fault lines of ethnicity, caste, class religion, and language combine and collide, often flying in the face of neat labels such as population homogeneity or coherence.[40]

As pointed out by Radha Kumar, the parts of Kashmir that suffered most from the 1949 division in terms of cultural discontinuity are the border regions of Jammu and Azad Kashmir, Kargil, and Baltistan. The people of most of these regions have cross-cutting identities. For example, the Gujjars of Poonch, Rajouri, and Doda may have a common religion with Azad Kashmiris, but their caste and economic activity is better accommodated in Jammu than in Azad Kashmir. The Azad Kashmiris, on the other hand, have a language and culture in common with Jammu, but their Sunni-dominated political order belongs in Pakistan. Despite anger at Pakistan's refusal of their political rights, the people of Baltistan chiefly seek the same status as Pakistan's other provinces. Over the years Shia Gilgit has been adversely affected by sectarian Shia-Sunni conflict in other parts of Pakistan and demographic alteration through Punjabi resettlement. On the Indian side, Jammu and Kashmir comprises a broadly Muslim valley, with a Hindu-majority Jammu and a predominantly Buddhist Ladakh. To speak of a uniform aspiration for freedom or even autonomy is both impractical and fraught. In Pakistan, the Shia communities of Baltistan and Gilgit have other denominations, such as Aga Khanis or Ismailis, and Nurbakshis. Shia-Sunni riots have been endemic and Gilgit was under curfew through much of 2005. "Kashmir" is by no means a monolithic undifferentiated space and defies easy categorization, a fact that has often been overlooked in international discourse.[41]

Musharraf's formula also suggested the need (1) to identify the region of Kashmir on both the Indian and Pakistan side; (2) to seek demilitarization of the identified region; and (3) finally to change the status of the disputed region either under the auspices of the United Nations or a joint control or condominium-type approach.[42]

The idea of "soft borders" gained momentum, even as Prime Minister Singh elaborated in March 24, 2006 (at the launch of the Amritsar-Nankana Sahib bus service), his earlier stated position on the need to make borders irrelevant without redrawing boundaries. By offering a treaty of peace, security, and friendship to Pakistan, Singh took a further leap of faith.[43]

Although Musharraf's proposals are open to varied interpretations, the fact that he was the first Pakistani leader (1) to opt for self-governance in preference to self-determination, or change of borders; (2) to keep UN resolutions aside; (3) to give up plebiscite and independence for Indian Kashmir; (4) to desist from demanding any territory for Pakistan; (5) to reject the communal (religious) criteria; (6) to not demand Kashmir's secession from India; and (7) to encourage Kashmiris' to talk to New Delhi, was not lost on the Indian establishment.[44] There was a recognition in India that it was important to do business with whatever party was in power in Pakistan and could bring the all-powerful army on board. The democratic credentials of the peace brokers were no longer flagged as an important factor for sustaining the dialogue.

The present political leadership in Pakistan has distanced itself from Musharraf's proposals. Since the Mumbai blasts of November 2008 and the subsequent standoff between India and Pakistan, much water has flowed under the bridge. At the UN General Assembly on September 28, 2010, Pakistan's first call in over a decade for a free and impartial plebiscite in Kashmir under UN auspices came as a major setback to the dialogue process. The army chief General Ashfaq Parvez Kayani has not favored building on Musharraf's proposals to resolve the Kashmir issue. Given the renewed violence in the Kashmir Valley in India and recent Pakistani statements, a mutually acceptable overarching solution appears elusive at this stage. Henceforward, small incremental steps in quiet diplomacy, whenever possible, are important.

A significant shift in the Indian articulation has been to see the issue increasingly not just as the problem *of* Kashmir but as the problem *in* Kashmir. There is a growing recognition that issues of regional autonomy within Jammu and Kashmir must be pursued to the extent that local sentiments about identity, fear of dominance, and neglect are addressed. Development initiatives are being followed with greater seriousness, particularly to provide energy, electricity, and better transport, connectivity, and livelihoods to the conflict-scarred region. After decades of disruption, schools, colleges, and universities seem to be functional again. Tourism, the greatest casualty in the post-1980s insurgency and an important pillar of the Kashmiri economy, has received a boost. The iconic image of the militant of the 1990s empowered with the ethical, moral mandate in the struggle for "Azadi" (independence) has also waned, especially among the urban youth. In today's climate, the foreign "guest" jihadi who fights on behalf of the Kashmiris also appears less welcome. There is a recognition that these warriors from outside have ousted or marginalized the indigenous leadership of the movement. With the pan-Islamist jihadi identity's replacement of the Kashmiri identity (Kashmiriyat), the possibility of the Kashmiri becoming irrelevant to his own struggle and of Kashmir becoming irrelevant to its own conflict has become real. There is equally the acknowledgement that the Indian state, in according priority to the "elimination" of "the militant," had given short shrift to the comfort of its own people. Massive investment in development and livelihood opportunities for Jammu and Kashmir is a way to offer the olive branch and to negotiate loyalty.

Within the Boundary: Singh's Initiative

In early 2006, Prime Minister Singh, in an unprecedented confidence-building move to address the human security concerns of the people of Jammu and Kashmir and also to improve relations between the beleaguered state and the central governments, set up five working groups to propose initiatives that best reflected the felt needs and realities on the ground. These groups were headed by eminent persons with an unimpeachable track record of public service who were not affiliated to any political party—two outstanding civil servants, two veteran diplomats, and a retired judge.

The recommendations made by four of the working groups, which focused on confidence-building measures, strengthening cross-line-of-control relations and good governance, and addressing vulnerable groups like women and children affected by militancy, were welcomed as "opening new pathways" by sections of civil society but evoked protests from some political groups that feared erosion of their agendas. The fifth working group, chaired by Justice Sagir Ahmad, which focused on the constitutional status of Jammu and Kashmir and dimensions of autonomy, sparked a furious controversy with the release of its report in December 2009. With political parties across the ideological spectrum jumping into the fray, it was seen as waffling on the crucial issue of autonomy for Jammu and Kashmir, not taking on board the views of the alienated sections of the society and polity, and completely turning a deaf year to sentiments about Azadi and the views of the separatists. Some sections opposed the report for its provalley bias, and for ostensibly ignoring the sentiments of the Jammu and Ladakh regions in the Indian province of Jammu and Kashmir.

Renewed incidents of terrorism and violence, including military reprisals, seem to have further derailed discussions around the sensitive issue of autonomy. Effective implementation of the five working groups' recommendations will depend to a great measure on the new trajectory that Kashmiri aspirations take, the efficacy of "quiet diplomacy" with divergent political groups, and, importantly, the status of the dialogue with Pakistan. The new challenge will also be about engaging rejectionists such as right-wing Jammu nationalists, the All Parties Hurriyat Conference (APHC), and Islamists to forge some consensus. While the recommendations of the working groups offered the prospect of mitigating the day-to-day hardships of the peoples of Jammu and Kashmir, the roundtables of 2007 to discuss the recommendations of the first four working groups was the *first* systematic institutional effort by the Indian government to bring as many stakeholders as possible within Jammu and Kashmir to the table and to initiate a multiparty dialogue. Women were significantly conspicuous by their absence at this table.

The working groups did not duck hard political questions and made some unorthodox and far-reaching suggestions. They called, among other things, for the review and eventual revoking of the Armed Forces Special Powers Act; the strengthening of the state Human Rights Commission; a general amnesty for those on trial for minor offenses; a gradual troop withdrawal (especially from orchards and farming areas); lowering the ominous presence of security forces; the rehabilitation of excombatants; economic and other packages to ensure that young people do not revert to militancy; the vacating of private and public property held by the security forces; special schemes for orphans and widows; employment for Kashmiri Pandits who had to forcibly migrate; full compensation for "illegal" takeovers of property, etc. The recommendation for the establishment of a joint consultative group of ten members from each of the legislatures on both sides of the border, which would exchange views periodically on social, economic, cultural, and trade-related matters of mutual interest, reflects one specific vision of what "joint management" and cooperation in the context of a soft border might constitute. The setting up of an Expert Defense Panel comprising representatives from the state and central government in India to determine the relocation and reconfiguration of troops and to provide periodic review of the Armed Forces Special Powers Act is claimed as a great achievement for the elected governments in meeting an important demand of the people of Jammu and Kashmir.

The opening of the Srinagar–Muzzafarabad bus route, an outcome of intense track-two efforts flagged off on April 7, 2005, was envisaged symbolically as one of the most positive steps in bringing together the people of divided Kashmir and divided families. The devastating earthquake of October 2005 further served to bring people together and facilitate the transport of relief material to victims in Pakistan-administered Kashmir. The agreement to open five points along the Line of Control—Poonch-Rawalkot, Uri-Chakoli, Tithwal-Nauseri, Mendhar–Mirpur, and Uri-Hajipur—for the first time in fifty-eight years was also part of the effort to bolster people-to-people contact. In addition, regular bus links, such as Lahore–Amritsar, Amritsar–Nankana Sahib, Poonch–Rawalkot, and the Munabao–Khokrapar train service and the Karachi–Mumbai ferry service could facilitate further transport and communication links. The memorandum of understanding between the Pakistan Maritime Security Agency and Indian Coast Guard in May 2005 was put in place to help the return of fishermen periodically caught for inadvertently transgressing maritime boundaries and to enhance search operations to control smuggling, drug trafficking, and the like.

There emerged a clearer domestic agenda for Kashmir to quell fundamentalist influences, especially among the *youth*, by developing the economy and building a democratic and secular culture. The revitalization of university campuses through large allocations is part of this thrust, as is greater tolerance and acceptance of local and national nongovernmental organizations (NGOs). The conduct of reasonably free and fair elections since 2002, with unexpected voter turnouts despite boycotts by the separatist conglomerate of the APHC and threats by Islamist fundamentalist groups in Jammu and Kashmir, was read overoptimistically (and mistakenly) by the national government as a waning of militant popularity.

Autonomy Revisited

The nature of "autonomy" that would be offered to the Kashmir territories on both sides remains an open question. India's reasonably successful parliamentary elections in 2004 and 2009 in Jammu and Kashmir, the positive mandate for electoral processes in the Provincial Assembly elections of 2002 and 2008 (despite prepoll violence and threats by the extremists), and an unexpected voter turnout even in 2009, in the aftermath of intrastate tensions and massive protests over disputes around land ownership of a Hindu shrine at Amarnath in Kashmir, are presented as a vindication of the country's position on the democratic space available in Jammu and Kashmir. Average voter turnouts for the Assembly Elections were 44 percent and 60.5 percent in 2002 and 2008, respectively, and between 39.66 percent and 45 percent for the general elections to Parliament from 2004 to 2009. Street protests mobilized largely by separatist groups like the APHC and militant organizations did not seem to translate into votes. This was flagged as declining support for the violence of militancy, despite Pakistan's efforts to stoke the embers through "cross-border" infiltration and terrorism. India argues that Pakistan has done very little to provide autonomy to Pakistan-administered Kashmir and has kept the Northern Areas in constitutional limbo.[45]

Until the close of the twentieth century, the international agenda on Kashmir and the terms of debate were set by Pakistan. India was reactive, responding with fumbling "officialese" or thundering silences. Since 9/11, India has been able to substantially wrest the initiative by shifting the discourse from human rights violations to "cross-border terrorism" and emphasizing the presence of Islamist training camps in Pakistan. There is also focus on the lack of autonomy in Gilgit and the Northern Areas and the inadequacy of democratic arrangements in Pakistan-administered Kashmir. Care is taken to broaden the notion of Kashmiri identity beyond the valley focus that it had acquired in international understanding.

The old formulas of viewing Kashmir through the Pakistan lens as the "unfinished business of partition" are being replaced, with several serious proposals having been offered over the past decade by national and international think tanks and policy experts as possible "solutions" to the Kashmir problem. These include, among others, the Kashmir Study Group

Proposal of 1998 (revised in 2005), the Delhi Policy Group Proposal, the Chenab Formula, the Kashmiri American Council Proposal, the Regional Centre for Strategic Studies (RCSS) Kashmir Group Recommendations, etc. Not all of these are popular with governments, but they serve as pointers in opening the accordion for alternative imaginations on a vexed issue. Equally, the "new voices" on Kashmir look to draw insights from peace-building experiments from other regions of conflict to assess their applicability to Kashmir. These include lessons from Northern Ireland, Aceh, the Ibarretxe proposal for the Basque Region, the Aland Islands Model, the New Caledonia arrangement for autonomy, and the South Tyrol package for the autonomous region between Austria and Italy. These interactions have had the benefit of broadening the parameters of discourse on an issue that was hitherto seen through a very limited lens.

Such interactions between civil society groups and policymakers across the divide have been tacitly encouraged by India. There is a sense that regional, national, and international events have created a window of opportunity that should not be missed and that all that remains is for India and Pakistan to "stop trying to drink soup with a fork and for someone from either side to have the common sense to use a spoon."[46] In moving out of the "partition plus Cold War mode," there is an attempt to examine the requisites for a pragmatic solution. These involve (1) creating conducive environments for "multilogues"; (2) facilitating realistic assessments of prevalent theories and myths; (3) establishing sustainable frameworks for negotiations; (4) accommodating sensitivities on both sides and reducing "preconditions"; (5) recognizing the changed realities of the regional and international environments; (6) injecting more and more confidence-building measures; (7) containing cross-border infiltrations and human rights violations; and (8) committing to demilitarization and demobilization.[47]

President Musharraf's Kashmir proposal in October 2005 suggested that in order to secure a win-win situation, the recognition of Kashmir as a dispute and the initiation of a dialogue were important. The shedding of unacceptable solutions was equally necessary. Consequently, the earlier available options mooted by Pakistan—the plebiscite option, the partition option, the independence option, and the UN-administered option—seem not to be viable at this point. The autonomy option and a collaborative water management option open up "soft-border" possibilities within a future joint management arrangement.[48] In the interim, there is growing acknowledgment and articulation (prompted by civil society initiatives) of the need *within* India to

1. address the people of Jammu and Kashmir as crucial stakeholders and partners in the peace process;

2. sustain a concerted pitch against terrorism;
3. push actively for the cessation of violence by militant groups and the state machinery;
4. set up soft borders to facilitate increased trade and contact among people on both sides of the Line of Control.

For India, the real challenge is to sustain a secular, participatory, and democratic arrangement that also meets the aspirations of the people. At this juncture, the terror attacks of November 26, 2008, in Mumbai not withstanding, the emphasis needs to be on *process*—a *composite* dialogue with Pakistan and a *sustained* dialogue within its province of Jammu and Kashmir. India sees a "secular" solution to Kashmir as integral to its position as a nontheocratic functioning democracy in South Asia, with the competence to integrate citizenship, pluralism, and a national identity. Kashmir becomes the litmus test of its claims of distinctiveness from Pakistan.

In June 2010, the Indian state of Jammu and Kashmir began experiencing its most severe domestic crisis since the beginning of militancy in 1989. The wave of protests once again paralyzed the Kashmir Valley. At the time of this writing, more than a hundred Kashmiris, predominantly young men and boys, had died in clashes with the security forces since the protests began. There is a perceptible lack of governance, and the electoral mandate received by the ruling National Conference has been shortsightedly and insensitively squandered away. The separatist groups, notably headed by Mohammed Ali Shah Geelani, have occupied the ceded political space and seem to call the shots on strikes, protests, and everyday shut downs. The writ of New Delhi does not run. Prime Minister Singh has sought dialogue and reconciliation and has announced an eight-point peace package to respond to frustrated (youth) aspirations, but it seems to have cut little ice with the separatist hard-liners. The strategic aspects of these developments will have implications not only for the Indian state but also for the future of the India-Pakistan relationship. In addition, the implications for the role of the United States as an "honest broker" in the region, especially in light of its engagements in Afghanistan (and its consequent dependence on Pakistan), are immense. The Kashmir Valley is likely to be the crucible in which India's sagacity, diplomacy, and global leadership potential will be stringently and severely tested.[49]

India's "Grand Strategy"

India's increasing salience—along with China—in the emerging security dynamics in Asia and its central role within the strategic fulcrum of the South Asian region position it for greater engagement in today's rapidly changing global order. Indeed, with a population of over a billion, an economy that has grown on average by 6 percent each year over the past two decades and by 8.5 percent since 2004, a more confident technological and military profile since the mid-1990s, and a proven engagement with democracy, India is an "emerging" power to be reckoned with in world affairs.

What gives India's profile added currency is that the world is in flux. The core achievements of the UN system—respect for state sovereignty, the Geneva Conventions, and curbs on military intervention—are all under severe strain. With the attempts to "promote democracy," demolish terrorism, and eliminate WMDs have come the assertions of super-power "hegemonism." India is attempting to position itself as a country that facilitates, with other suitable partners, the construction of a world order that seeks to build a genuinely multipolar international system.

India's strategic choices in this context are defined neither by confrontation nor subordination to the United States. Rather, India's strategy is clearly one of collaboration with the United States and of developing equations with other major powers to "redress the imbalances of U.S. dominance" and to nurture and increase the substance of its relations with important countries opposed to U.S. unilateralism in world politics, such as Russia, China, France, Germany, Brazil, Mexico, and Canada.[50] India's increasing engagement with regional multilateralism through its participation in the Shanghai Cooperation Organization (SCO); Brazil, Russia, India, China Cooperation (BRIC); and India, Brazil, South Africa (IBSA), among several others, including the East Asia Summit (EAS), the Association of Southeast Asian Nations (ASEAN), and the ASEAN Regional Forum (ARF), is indicative of this. Six decades after independence from colonial rule, the prevalent mood in India's metropolitan centers is marked by buoyancy and a new-found confidence—a sense of moving from "limits" to "possibilities." Official discourse today focuses on India's role as an emerging global player, a "responsible" nuclear state, a huge potential market, and a growing knowledge hub in a globalizing environment. Above all, it reflects pride in being an old civilization and a "youthful" nation.

That today 50 percent of the population is below twenty-five years of age opens up enormous possibilities for dynamic change, inclusive development, and progressive governance. Yet the optimization of this "youth divided" is dependent on the sagacity and vision with which India invests in its population. For even today, if you are a Dalit and a woman living in a deeply caste-riven poor belt of the province of Bihar who must walk for miles to fetch water or fodder for survival, the shine of India, sitting at the high table with the powerful among nations, is at best burnished.

India has in the past offered the world alternative visions, through Gandhi's nonviolent resistance and Nehru's nonalignment. A new paradigm awaits articulation for worlds that are in collision. There is a sense that India is positioning itself to play such a role. The interdependence created by globalization, the post–Cold War environment, and the resultant diminishing of the risk of overt conflict between major powers and rival political alliances has proved a favorable context for India. Since 1991, India's quest to expand its sphere of engagement, forge relationships with major powers, and simultaneously seek to improve relations with Pakistan and to initiate border-related confidence-building measures with China and free-trade agreements with neighbors, beginning with Sri Lanka in 1998, reflected a remarkable change in the scale of India's ambitions.

Interestingly, one of the objectives of India's foreign policy has come to be described as rapid and inclusive economic development and poverty eradication.[51] The international situation made possible India's rapid development of relationships with each of the major powers as did India's economic and social transformation. With its engagement with the global economy growing rapidly and with trade in goods and services now exceeding US$330 billion, India's needs from the world have changed, as have its capabilities to achieve them.

Competing Metaphors: Seeking a "Different" Voice

Inevitably, the discourse on "emerging" India or India's rise reflects both the triumphs and ambivalences of its domestic realities and spans a gamut of expectations, concerns, and aspirations. These also include exhortations from parts of the globe outside South Asia, urging a seemingly hesitant India to recognize its potential power and leadership in the region and seize the moment.[52] Predictably, such exhortations do not resonate well with all of India's smaller neighbors.

What is significant is that earlier concerns that "India lacks a tradition of strategic thinking" have receded.[53] Despite India's internal problems, its strategic elite seem confident that India will emerge as a key economic and military player by the end of the second decade of the twenty-first century and will be recognized as such by other great powers.[54]

In this view, India's strategic weltanschauung has shifted from emphasis on "moralspeak" to a realpolitik based on exercising military and economic power—a shift from a belief in the power of ideas to a commitment to the idea of power. India's nuclear tests of May 1998 are projected here as the defining moment of its shift in foreign policy—from its Nehruvian (idealist) moorings to a new phase of realism. The focus is on the imperative to acquire the strength and strategic autonomy to enable it to stabilize an "unfriendly" neighborhood. Deterrence and balance of power are seen as vital for promoting national and international security, as are the economic and "softer elements of power."[55]

In evidence is clearly an impulse to break free of insularity, the solipsistic absorption with Pakistan on Kashmir, border issues with China, and "boxed-in" preoccupations with the ebbs and flows in its most immediate South Asian neighborhood. This "new" role sees engagement with multilateral regimes and regional groupings as vital. Analysts today place India's Look East Policy as the cornerstone of its transition from abstract and frequently "unrealpolitik" views of what constitutes normative behavior. While it is argued that economic growth, maritime capability, and peace and stability in its neighborhood are key goals of India's present behavior as a "normative" foreign policy actor, there is, for the first time, an effort to "marry normative goals and behavior to policies furthering the national interest broadly defined as extending from traditional to human security for its citizens."[56]

Significant voices clamor for a more "masculinist" assertion of India's place in the sun, highlighting the need for it to shed "outmoded" notions of strategic autonomy. As it moves toward becoming the world's third-largest economy and acquires "great-power capabilities," the imperative for it to accept responsibility to shape the international system and share the costs of managing it is underscored.[57] Also critiqued is India's discomfort and nervousness with asserting power and its inability to foreground coercive diplomacy anchored "in military and economic muscle and a trenchant security doctrine."[58]

At the other end of the spectrum is the introspection that is invoked to temper the uncritically heady subscription to the "great-power" metaphor. With 77 percent of India's working population living on little over half a U.S. dollar a day, low human security indices are cited to highlight the gross "mismatch between grandiose perceptions and lived reality," between "robust" GDP growth and pervasive socioeconomic inequities. India, in this view, is a notional and ambivalent power, whose vast and neglected human resource is ill-served by its ruling elite whose short-term objectives trump the larger collective interest. In this view, India's contemporary trajectory of global relevance no longer sits easy with the kind of vision that fostered normative ideals of nonalignment, disarmament, and decolonization.[59]

In attempting to steer course though the conundrums of these colliding positions, Indian foreign policy is today in search of an idiom that reflects a distinctive paradigm of global engagement, in tune with both its aspirations and moorings. The leadership it seeks is prudently tied to an alternative metaphor. The quest is for a new "third way" that looks beyond conventional "hedging," "balancing," and "bandwagoning" (but might contain some of their elements) and that is in many ways reflective of the understated yet confident style of the contemporary political, strategic, and foreign policy leadership in New Delhi.

This is a distinctive shift from past predilections to overtly play hegemon that were so much in evidence during the dismemberment of Pakistan and the creation of Bangladesh in 1971 and that had found expression in the 1980s through India's military operations in Sri Lanka and the Maldives. Operation Pawan involved engaging the Indian Peace Keeping Force (IPKF) in Sri Lanka (1987–90) to disarm the Tamil militants fighting for an independent homeland, and Operation Cactus entailed the intervention of Indian Armed Forces to save the government in the Maldives in 1988 from a coup attempt. Underpinning these operations was a brand of coercive diplomacy projecting India's military capability and unwillingness to countenance "outside interference" in South Asian affairs. The collapse of the peace deal India brokered between the Sri Lankan government and the LTTE, and the subsequent position of Sri Lankan president Ranasinghe Premadasa, which signaled the rather ignominious withdrawal of the IPKF in 1987, pointed to the need to build more acceptable forms of diplomacy in the region.

The leitmotif of the shift best positions policy that engages human security concerns in India's interface with its immediate neighbors and mitigates the threat perceptions of those neighbors. Linking its eastern periphery to Southeast Asia and beyond remains the thrust of India's Look East Policy and ties in with the larger impetus of what former Indian foreign secretary and current national security adviser Shivshankar Menon called India's expanding circles of engagement—that is, spheres of influence that start with the immediate neighborhood and grow to include West Asia, Central Asia, South East Asia, and the Indian Ocean region. Menon went on to identify the key goals of India's foreign policy as first, ensuring a peaceful periphery; second, improving relations with major powers such as the United States, the European Union, Japan, Russia, and China; and third, preparing for issues of the future, namely, food security, water, energy, and environment.[60]

Traversing New Roads

The idea of a neighborhood as one of "widening concentric circles around a central axis of historical and cultural commonalities . . . pursuing a cooperative architecture of Pan-Asian regionalism," with the Indian footprint reaching well beyond South Asia and its interests straddling across different subcategories of Asia, has been articulated as integral to India's emerging geopolitical considerations.[61]

From where India stands today, Cold War concepts like containment have very little relevance. The interdependence brought about by processes of globalization have witnessed major powers coming together to form coalitions to deal with issues where there is a convergence of interests, despite differences. The emergence of a global order marked by the preponderance of several major players has resulted in a "dehyphenation" of relationships, with each major power engaging with all the others in a situation that has been described as "unalignment."[62] These developments have been taken note of by India in fashioning its new multilateralism. The Look East Policy is informed by this understanding. A top foreign policy priority for India is responding sagaciously to China's rise. China's so-called string of pearls strategy is perceived by India as encirclement across the Indian Ocean rim, and tensions remain over China's territorial claims in Arunachal Pradesh (including perceived expansionism vis-à-vis Taiwan). Yet, China is currently India's biggest trading partner. Trade between India and China stood at $61.7 billion in 2010, registering a 43 percent jump in volume from 2009 and a record trade imbalance of $20 billion in China's favor.

The larger concatenation of multiple external security challenges that India faces, and its need to overcome consequent vulnerabilities, has undoubtedly prompted the renewed surge toward strategic space, stability, and strength. An important precondition to greater connectivity toward the East is also the attempt to build a peaceful periphery within which India's transformation can take place.

A major external security threat is seen from nonstate actors and from transboundary effects of the collapse or inadequacy of state systems. There is a palpable sense that India is "located at the centre of an arc of fundamentalist activism, terrorism and political instability."[63] The earlier Bombay blasts of 1992 (a precursor to the more publicized attack of November 26, 2008) are seen as the original act of mass terrorism, akin to the much later 9/11 attack in the United States, but one that did not evoke adequate concern from the global community. Threats are also seen from nuclear-armed Pakistan and China, with which India has yet unresolved disputes and conflicts. In addition, India's anxieties focus on proliferation emanating from and to the region, with fears of WMDs falling into the hands of terrorists and nonstate actors.

The instability of state systems and the collapse of governance in India's neighborhood—in Nepal, in Afghanistan, in Pakistan, and, until recently, in Bangladesh—is seen to provide a breeding ground for terrorists and nonstate actors who also target India. China's growing influence over Myanmar, Nepal, Bangladesh, and lately Sri Lanka and its near preeminence (along with Japan) in Southeast and East Asia has reinforced the impulse in India to strengthen its Look East Policy and to pay greater attention to the maritime security environment.[64]

The security of energy, shipping, and sea-lanes in the Indian Ocean region and potential choke points at Babel Mandab, the Persian Gulf, and the Malacca Strait require concerted management. The Indian Ocean region from East Africa to Southeast Asia is seen as an "area busy with fundamentalist, terrorist and militant, separatist or extremist organizations, and criminal syndicates involved in trafficking in drugs, arms, humans and piracy." Sixty thousand ships, carrying much of the energy resources sent from the Gulf to East Asia, transit through the Strait of Malacca every year.[65] India has coordinated maritime patrolling arrangements with Indonesia, Thailand, and Sri Lanka and conducted joint exercises with the United States, France, Singapore, Russia, and Oman, among others. As a hedge, it has also been forging links with China's own maritime neighbors, including Japan, South Korea, and Vietnam.

India's best periods in history were avowedly those when it was most connected to the world. As it begins to develop its own vocabulary, strategic culture, and doctrine, the portents are that India will increasingly rely on what Joseph Nye described as "smart power" and attempt to open up new spaces for dialogue even within its beleaguered South Asian neighborhood. Smart power combines elements of hard and soft power, but, as is being increasingly recognized in the context of conflict resolution, soft power enables countries like India to project its foundational strengths—democratic and secular aspirations and the desire to forge a civic identity that attempts to transcend the fault lines of language, ethnicity, and religion. This has enormous salience in the South Asian context.

An important aspect of India's strategy is to engage both the United States and China, albeit at different levels of intensity and for very different reasons. Overall, India's preference is for a multipolar Asia that respects its vast political diversity without joining a chorus for uniform democratization in Southeast Asia.

India's determination for autonomy in decision making will not countenance being part of an alliance. India will in all likelihood devise a unique type of arrangement that will not limit it to any one strategic alliance but will allow it to engage with multiple strategic triangular or quadrilateral groupings. There are several unfolding possibilities of strategic linkages with China and Russia, on the one hand, and plausible power equations between the United States, India, and Japan, on the other hand. There are already a whole range of "strategic partnerships" with Russia, France, the United Kingdom, Germany, South Korea, and the United States on civil nuclear cooperation.

India is still not comfortable with notions of collective security and the construction of supranational structures that limit sovereign decision making on national security. It seeks inclusive rather than exclusive arrangements. Nonalignment is unlikely to be formally shed but could emerge in a new incarnation as an input for strategic decision making. It is argued that, contrary to perceptions that India's deepening strategic relationship with the United States is entirely directed against China, India is unlikely to support "either an exclusion of the United States from Asia or a US-led containment of China."[66]

In forging its strategic partnership with the United States and attempting to stabilize its relations with China, India has entered a new domain of strategic engagement that is likely to shape the dynamics of conflict management in the South Asian region. Although new tensions with China have lately reemerged on border issues, there is a careful attempt not to up the ante.

The Growing Salience of India's Look East Policy

India's desire to enhance connectivity with Bangladesh, Myanmar, and beyond to Southeast Asia and to create what it describes as a zone of coprosperity through a network of roads, trade, transport corridors, gas pipelines, tourism, and communication is the avowed aim of its Look East Policy. Bypassing the roadblocks within SAARC, most of which are caused by frequent India-Pakistan standoffs, this policy calls for creating linkages between India and the ASEAN countries and increasing involvement in other regional arrangements, such as the Bay of Bengal Initiative for Multi Sector Technical and Economic Cooperation (BIMST-EC), which has India, Bangladesh, Myanmar, Sri Lanka, Thailand, Bhutan, and Nepal as members; the Mekong-Ganga Cooperation Initiative (MGCI), a cooperative initiative that comprises India and five riparian countries of the Mekong River (Cambodia, Lao People's Democratic Republic, Myanmar, Thailand, and Vietnam); the SCO; trilateral cooperation with Thailand and Myanmar; strategic partnership with Japan; and even the track-two people-to-people Kunming initiative (also known as BCIM), which includes India, China (Yunnan), Bangladesh, and Burma.

Yet in all of these arrangements where China is involved, India has concerns about China aggressively taking over trade when some routes (like the Silk Road or Stillwell's Burma Road) reopen, because such a development could present real challenges in India's Northeastern regions. Here, between maintaining the status quo by keeping borders closed and responding to the contemporary imperatives of opening borders, India is crafting a new approach to borderland issues, as evident in its shifting approach to border concerns with Pakistan (vis-à-vis Kashmir) and China (vis-à-vis the Northeast).[67] The many advantages of opening up the Northeastern region of India to make it the commercial outlet for its Eastern trade have to be weighed against the strategic challenges. India's new multilateralism within its Look East Policy offers spaces for a graduated approach that optimizes economic benefits. But much will depend on the manner in which the classic "security dilemma" with China is grappled and the manner in which trade imperatives are prioritized.

Within ASEAN, over the last decade there has been growing enthusiasm about India's role in security cooperation. Shedding decades of isolationism, India's naval diplomacy expanded in the region, with wide-ranging exercises in the South China Sea. India's emergence as an institutional partner of ASEAN gave greater coherence to the Look East Policy as a cornerstone of a new thrust in its external relations. While the first phase of this policy focused exclusively on economic and institutional partnership, the second phase, at the turn of the millennium, included wider political and security dimensions. India is likely to play an important role in the norm-building and politico-security dialogues of the EAS, to which it was admitted in 2005 despite the known reservations of China.[68]

Historical and civilizational legacies give India a slight edge over China in giving rein to its soft power assets, especially in light of the fear of China in the region. While China will have to continue to be formally treated *both* as competitor and cooperative partner in the region, India will work to enhance its standing with Eastern neighbors through infrastructure improvement, technical transfer, goods and services, aviation, transportation, roads, waterways, and other soft power assets. Importantly, even from within the South Asian frame, for India, the Look East Policy is crucial from a strategic perspective for breaking out of being "boxed in" by South Asian conflicts and for developing greater confidence in its soft power so that it might deploy it more efficaciously in the region.

The Look East Policy is also important for the development of India's troubled Northeast, which in the face of Bangladesh's reluctance to accord transit rights will otherwise become completely cut off. The aim is to convert the Northeast from the periphery of India into the center of an integrated economic and strategic space that links South to Southeast Asia, with India's Northeast being the bridge or the fulcrum of the space.[69] Bangladesh is critical to this strategy. Until there is a sea change in India's relationship with Pakistan on its Northwestern frontier, an important sliver of connectivity with the outside world lies through the East. The transformation of borders into crossings, an important conceptual element of India's Look East Policy, may signal the much-needed shift in vocabulary and idiom that helps craft a new indigenous strategic culture. If India attempts to foster and build a peaceful South Asia as an integral part of emerging Asia, the parameters of conflict management could substantially change and refocus through the wider-angle lens of altered priorities.

Responding to Diversity, Resolving Conflict

Jawaharlal Nehru, in his famous *Discovery of India*, describes Indian civilization as an "ancient palimpsest on which layer upon layer of thought and reverie had been inscribed and yet no succeeding layer had completely hidden or erased what had been written previously."[70] Traditionally, India has used the mantra of *unity in diversity* to describe its approach to the mammoth task of forging a national identity. Perhaps what is needed more today is for the country to revisit its original formulation by poet laureate Rabindranath Tagore of "unity *through* diversity." In fact, assimilation had never been the constitutional recipe—until the BJP sought to alter it, prompted by forces of majority fundamentalism. It learned to its detriment and chagrin that homogenization could not be India's way.

Yet a major challenge today facing the South Asian region in general and India in particular is the management of diversity. There is need to use a "nontraditional" lens to look anew at how issues of identity impinge on security. The religious, ethnic, and linguistic characteristics of civil societies in the region's nation-states overlap with each other. This overlapping results in apprehensions about respective national identities. The challenge is to resolve the contradictions between the nature of civil societies and anxieties about consolidating subnational identities by promoting a democratic citizenship that is integrative and that does not fracture along ethnoreligious lines. Reclaiming the receding secular spaces is especially crucial after the terrorist attacks of September 11 in New York and Washington, DC, and November 26 in Mumbai.[71]

Within South Asia, this would need purposeful affirmative action for religious minorities and marginalized social groups. Fundamentalism and manifestations of terrorism are the price of exclusionist policies that deny access and equity. The answer to the problem of national security in the future may lie not in the acquisition of weapons, or in the mindless deployment of paramilitary forces, but in concerted efforts to overcome the "development deficit," as well as structural and ideological violence and prejudice against marginalized groups. India's secular agenda, which had been somewhat on the wane since the 1980s, needs to be reclaimed and rearticulated in the face of contemporary global discourse. This is bound to have a positive impact on the region in light of anxieties about minority rights across borders.

This agenda may be challenging because the multicultural, multireligious environment of South Asia is rife with discrimination. The 2006 Sachar Committee report that examined issues relating to identity, security, and equity for the Muslim community in India, which accounts for 13.4 percent of the population of the country, irrefutably revealed the profound lack of educational and employment opportunities and the consequently attenuated life choices that confront the majority of Indian Muslims.[72] An ideational shift is required that sees minorities as a resource for multicultural societies rather than as a liability or a challenge that somehow needs to be "managed." This could counter religious fundamentalisms of different kinds. The entire region could, through genuine democratic dialogue and transparent processes of reconciliation, seek to give voice to the progressive, inclusive, and democratic forces of Islam in global partnership. An active engagement in processes and platforms that seriously interrogate the discourse of equating terrorism with Islam is imperative. Institutionalized structures for dialogue and reconciliation are yet to be crafted in South Asia. These can be built squarely into democratization processes rather than be resorted to only during and after overt conflict in ad hoc arrangements, as is the current practice.

The need to pluralize the conception of security, making it more amenable to the noisy yet vibrant arena of democratic debate and ideas, finds resonance for approaches to the transformation and resolution of conflicts and crises in South Asia. The trajectory implicit in Mahboob Ul Haq's evocative articulation of human security has yielded three different conceptions of human security today: one focuses on *human costs* of violent conflict, another stresses *human needs* in the path to sustainable development, and a third emphasizes the *human rights* dimension. From the South Asian perspective, the evolving discourse needs to take on board the emerging factors contributing to peoples' insecurities, including those related to food and water security, livelihoods, displacement and distress, forced migration, human rights, persecution, environmental degradation, natural disasters, pandemics, insurgency, terrorism, and state coercion. It is not difficult to see how these factors are all mediated by power relations and to gauge the intensity of their negative impact on marginalized groups in particular.

Finding new approaches for building a security architecture that addresses the *inequality predicament* and the *democratic deficit* remains a singular challenge for the states of South Asia. Talibanization in Pakistan, Islamization in Bangladesh, the Maoist and Naxalite nexus in Nepal and India, Buddhist radicalism in Sri Lanka, and the sectarian and separatist threats across South Asia cannot be countered without sensitive internal strategies, joint conflict resolution mechanisms, and interstate cooperation.[73] As these violent social movements are present in nearly every South Asian state, and often cross traditional geographical and identity borders, they demand an effective regional response that transcends traditional interstate rivalries and threat perceptions. Here, women and their concerns, hitherto on the margins of the metanarratives of security, can provide some conceptual language for a discourse on security that expands its scope to include not just threats but also empowerment, entitlements, and rights.

Women as refugees, widows, and workers without personal or family security have become markers of the emerging international landscape and markedly so in South Asia. Of the "fleeing people of South Asia," the majority are women.[74] The endemic violence of dislocation and involuntary displacement on account of conflicts and climate change within and between borders and the pervasiveness of camps for "rehabilitation," "resettlement," and even "containment" have fenced out large segments of the region's people from public view and discourse. The growing numbers of these "nowhere" people pose a major impetus to craft more humane metaphors for "security." The internal and interstate conflicts shaping the regional landscape are being fought not only on battlefields but also in homes, communities, cities, and villages. Despite the multiple roles of women in conflict, their voice is seldom heard in the "hard" issue areas of security, foreign policy, finance, and trade.[75] It is important to foreground concerns integral to feminist discourse: its questioning of realism and notions of security as a zero-sum game; its interrogation of the separation of the "public and private" spheres; its critique of war, gendered citizenship, and nationalism; its emphasis on inclusion in democratic arrangements; and its stress on the links between patriarchy, militarism, intolerance, and violence. These are issues integral to the (in)securities of those who constitute roughly half the population in South Asia.

States of the South Asian region are yet to wholeheartedly "engender security," implement the Convention for the Elimination of Discrimination against Women (CEDAW), or engage actively with fashioning a *life-affirming* discourse on security. The countries of South Asia have shown little initiative to include women at the negotiating table—and this should be a key concern for policymakers of the region. The imaginative leveraging of (often informal) extended networks of women for active peacebuilding may be an important route for reversing the pervasive *trust deficit* among countries of the region.

Nontraditional formulations often open up spaces to truly *engender* security. Engendering security goes significantly beyond mainstreaming women's concerns. It shifts priorities from threat perceptions and deterrence vocabularies to a language that cognizes *structural challenges* and *enabling spaces*. Nontraditional formulations of security would inevitably engage with issues of representation (particularly of women), constitutional arrangements, legal frameworks, and women's inclusions and exclusions. These "alternative" formulations break out of the straitjackets of reified discourses, wrest security from congealed definitions, concerns, and elite bastions, and place it squarely within the arena of democratic dialogue and negotiation. The rarefied realm of security establishments could then be touched by the heat and dust of the subaltern (in)securities in the region. India, as the largest democracy, could open up spaces for committed and collaborative engagement around human security concerns that impact the lives of one-fifth of the international community. Its role could prove decisive in forging a solidarity that transcends borders in South Asia.

Conclusion

The complexes and apprehensions generated by asymmetry between India and other South Asian countries in terms of size, levels of technology, and military and economic power have to be addressed through bold initiatives in trade and unfettered *people-to-people contact*. India particularly needs to make purposeful efforts to manage these tensions. Structuring cooperative regionalism and dealing with political and human security problems *within SAARC* in a pragmatic manner will open unforeseen possibilities.

Challenges also come from issues of food security, energy security, conflicts over water and riverine boundaries with neighbors, and issues of environment and climate change. Population flows and a large influx of "illegal" migrant populations from Bangladesh and Nepal (and Sri Lanka) are seen as adding to risks that strain the security of border states and are threatening to significantly alter demographic balances.

As in most countries of the South Asian region, development issues, like adaptation and mitigation for internally displaced people and insurance against pandemics and natural disasters, add to the slew of India's security concerns. Access to clean technologies by developing countries *as global public goods* (on the lines of what was done for retrovirals to fight AIDS) is seen as essential to effectively limit future greenhouse gas emissions. India consequently contests "restrictive" intellectual property regimes and inequitable dispensations in international fora on climate change, asserting that its greenhouse gas emissions are much lower than those of the developed world and that global benchmarks need to be drawn after parity is first established in an uneven playing field.

Multilateralism is today India's declared route for overcoming the deficits that it sees weighted against it. Chief among these are the technology deficit (restrictive technology control regimes), the agricultural deficit (discriminatory clauses of the WTO), and the global decision-making deficit (inadequate representation for India in the United Nations and other major decision-making bodies of the world).

India's unique predicament of living in a conflict-intensive neighborhood and being flanked by two nuclear-armed neighbors calls for an ability to balance diplomacy and defense, restraint and assertiveness. Today, India's default policy options, given its regional context and constraints, rely more on soft power. India's "rise" is not feared and is even encouraged by some international powers, in contrast to China, whose "friendly rising" creates anxieties for countries as varied as the United States, Japan, South Korea, Singapore, Indonesia, Taiwan, Australia, and India.[76]

In finessing the balance between assertiveness and restraint in the deployment of its "smart power," and in steering its course through the unprecedented political and economic opportunities open to it in the second decade of the twenty-first century, India is alive to its fresh imperatives in a fast-changing world. These include developing greater expertise to engage with a multipolar world; to make itself more effective in the Subcontinent and its extended neighborhood in Asia, Africa, and the Indian Ocean littoral; to imaginatively work toward the peaceful reconstruction of the Afghanistan-Pakistan region; to work toward the greater economic integration of South Asia; to reconnect more proactively with the Muslim world to the West of the Subcontinent; and above all to recast and reinvigorate its focus on multilateralism and to create a global footprint.[77] India's emergence as an aid donor to the developing world provides a vital dimension to its leadership metaphor. As India comes to terms with new responsibilities in its neighborhood and the world, the denouement of an emerging grand strategy that creates more space for conflict resolution through multilateralism and diplomatic flexibility is in evidence. There is also a newfound restraint in playing hegemon in South Asia and an attempt to seek greater credibility for a proactive role in this domain. India's membership in the UN Peacebuilding Commission may yet propel it to give fuller rein to the enhancement of its peacebuilding capacities as a foreign policy aspiration.

Prime Minister Singh's statements at Sharm el-Sheikh, Egypt, on the sidelines of the Non-Aligned Movement conference in 2009 underscored India's importance as a "moral force for the equitable transformation of today's world," especially in the context of the "worst economic crisis in living memory" and the need to achieve a comprehensive balanced outcome in ongoing multilateral negotiations, particularly with regard to climate change and decision-making processes at the United Nations and international financial institutions. India's positioning has, of late, been to reclaim normative space within the emerging global order.[78]

Can India help craft a new vocabulary for strategic leadership that helps transcend the monotheism of dominance? To the metaphor of the circle with one defining center, can India counterpose it to the interdependence of the ellipse?[79] Can context sensitivity—once the guiding paradigm of the classical Indian approach to grammar, time and space, music, healing, and indeed rules of behavior—once again inform its systems of meaning? Can the emphasis on interdependent roles and spaces once characteristic of community coexistence across groupings and boundaries once again fashion notions of collective resilience and security? Can flexibility and "flow" soften the reefs of mistrust and the rigidity of borders? On this hinges India's validation, as do the prospects for peace in South Asia.

Notes

The author thanks Amritha Venkatraman and Swapna Kona Nayudu for their research inputs.

1. See C. Raja Mohan, "Learning to Be Happy," *Indian Express* (New Delhi), December 24, 2009.

2. Srinath Raghavan and Mahesh Rangarajan, "Engagement sans Entanglement," *Seminar* no. 605 (January 2010): 66.

3. Terms coined by Rajiv Sikri, *Challenge and Strategy: Rethinking India's Foreign Policy* (New Delhi: Sage Publications, 2009), 12–14, to describe regions strategically salient to India. "Arc of prosperity" refers to the world's largest and most dynamic economies, which account for a significant proportion of global trade; "arc of energy" extends from the Persian Gulf through the Caspian Sea to Siberia and Russia's Far East; "arc of instability" envelops India on all sides—including Pakistan, Afghanistan, Iran, Iraq, Palestine, the newly independent Central Asian Republics, Nepal, Bangladesh, Sri Lanka, and large swathes of India's heartland; the "arc of communication" refers to the North Indian Deccan, which controls the energy flows from the Persian Gulf and sea lines of communication between Europe and Asia and which has become the most militarized region in the world.

4. Elucidated by K.S. Bajpai in "Our Grand Strategy," *Indian Express*, December 31, 2009.

5. For a lucid elaboration of this idea, see Peter R. de Souza, Suhas Palshikar, and Yogendra Yadav, principal investigators, and Harsh Sethi, ed., *State of Democracy in South Asia: A Report* (New Delhi: Oxford University Press, 2008).

6. This is reflected in India's active support since 2007 toward bringing the Maoist movement in Nepal into the mainstream power-sharing and constitution-making exercise, in Sri Lanka's massive reconstruction and development efforts after the defeat of the insurgent liberation movement in 2009, and in the democratic transitions in Bangladesh and the Maldives in 2008.

7. See Sujit Dutta, "The Asian Transition and India's Emerging Strategy," in *Global Power Shifts and Strategic Transition in Asia*, ed. N.S. Sisodia and V. Krishnappa (New Delhi: Academic Foundation, 2009), 19.

8. C. Raja Mohan, "Catharsis and Catalysis: Transforming the South Asian Subcontinent," in *Worlds in Collision*, ed. Ken Booth and Tim Dunne (New York: Palgrave Macmillan, 2002), 205–26.

9. For a lucid elaboration of this theme, see Ramachandra Guha, *India after Gandhi* (London: Picador India, 2007).

10. P. R. Chari, ed., *Perspectives on National Security in South Asia: In Search of a New Paradigm* (New Delhi: Manohar, 1999), 418–19.

11. See Achin Vanaik, "India's Place in the World," in *Wages of Freedom: Fifty Years of the Indian Nation-State*, ed. Partha Chatterjee (New Delhi: Oxford University Press, 1999), 72–86.

12. See Niraja Gopal Jayal, *Democracy and the State: Welfare, Secularism and Development in Contemporary India* (New Delhi: Oxford University Press, 2001), 257.

13. The author owes this characterization to the line of argument developed by Niraja Gopal Jayal in ibid., 239–48.

14. Indian efforts at the April 2009 summit to make the SAARC a more effective regional grouping included the offer of "zero-duty" access to goods from Bangladesh, Afghanistan, Nepal, Maldives, and Bhutan. Pakistan remains the only SAARC country that does not have a free-trade agreement with India.

15. Ritu Menon and Kamla Bhasin, *Borders and Boundaries* (New Delhi: Kali for Women, 1998), 248–49.

16. Sanjay Chaturvedi, "Geopolitics and Gender in the South Asian Spaces" (paper presented at the Women in Security, Conflict Management and Peace [WISCOMP] symposium titled "Revisiting Non Traditional Security," New Delhi, November 2006), 5.

17. Ibid., 3.

18. See Pratap Bhanu Mehta, "Peripheral Vision," *Indian Express*, November 7, 2006.

19. The link between *governance* and *security* is salient here. More political will is needed for the "effective" implementation of initiatives to redress these injustices, such as the Scheduled Tribes and Other Traditional Forest Dwellers (Recognition of Forest Rights) Act, 2006, a landmark piece of legislation that seeks to empower traditional forest-dwelling communities by giving them security of tenure, access to some forest produce, and a stake in the preservation of natural spaces.

20. In 2003, 17,017 farmers in India committed suicide across five major provinces in the country. In August 2006, the Maharashtra government corroborated that 1,864 farmers had committed suicide since 2001 in six districts alone.

21. See, for example, Ted Gurr, *People vs. States: Minorities at Risk in the New Century* (Washington, DC: United States Institute of Peace Press, 2000); and Ian Pitchford, "A Fundamental Difference," in online discussion about Scott Atran, "Genesis and Future of Suicide Terrorism," *Interdisciplines.org*, July 3, 2003, www.interdisciplines.org/terrorism/papers/1.

22. The 2004 Afghan Constitution describes Islam as the state religion, and the Bangladeshi Constitution lost its original secular character and became Islamized in 1997 with Proclamation Order no. 1. There was an attempt in Sri Lanka, through a proposed Nineteenth Amendment, to make Buddhism the state religion. The Islamization program of general Zia-Ul-Haq in Pakistan is also well documented. Islam is the state religion in Pakistan.

23. The newly elected Awami League–led government of Sheikh Hasina Wajed is committed to secularizing the Bangladeshi polity following its massive mandate in the December 2008 election and to reversing the fundamentalist policies of its rival the Bangladesh Nationalist Party (BNP).

24. See Arshi Saleem Hashmi, "South Asia's Growing Vulnerability to Extremism and Terrorism in the Coming Decade: Is There a Way Forward?" *Focus* 27, no. 1 (August 2009): 22–25.

25. David Kilcullen, "Will Zardari Be Curzon's Steamroller," *Asian Age,* July 19, 2009. Former Pakistani president and army chief Pervez Musharraf, who is believed to have been the main architect of the Kargil conflict in 2001 against India, has stated unequivocally in several recent statements that the biggest threat to Pakistan is extremism and terrorism by the Taliban, al-Qaeda, and other extremists in its society. See Pervez Musharraf, "Pakistan and the Perils Within," *Hindu* (New Delhi), July 18, 2009.

26. C. Christine Fair, "Pakistani Attitudes towards Militancy in and beyond Pakistan," in *Saving Afghanistan*, ed. V. Krishnappa, Shantie Mariet D'Souza, and Priyanka Singh (New Delhi: Academic Foundation and Institute for Defence Studies and Analyses [IDSA], 2009), 93–112.

27. Ahmed Rashid, *Descent into Chaos: How the War against Islamic Extremism Is Being Lost in Pakistan, Afghanistan, and Central Asia* (London: Allen Lane, 2008), xxxix.

28. Ajai Sahni, "Encounters in a Nightmare," in *The Great Divide: India and Pakistan,* ed. Ira Pande (New Delhi: India International Centre, 2009), 168.

29. See Kalim Bahadur, "Regional Implications of the Rise of Islamic Fundamentalism in Pakistan," *Strategic Analysis* 30, no. 1 (January–March 2006): 7–29.

30. K. Warikoo, "Islamist Extremism: Challenge to Security in South Asia," *Strategic Analysis* 30, no. 1 (January–March 2006): 38.

31. For more on SAARC's protocols on terrorism and India's engagement, see www.satp.org/satporgtp/countries/India/document/actandordinance/SAARC.htm and www.saarc-sec.org/data/declaration/cooperation/combatingterrorism.rtf.

32. The dramatic nude demonstration by women to protest the alleged custodial rape and killing of a female political activist in the Northeastern state of Manipur, India, in 2006 snowballed into a major conflagration that eventually forced the government to commit to "humanizing" the controversial Armed Forces Special Powers Act.

33. The eight subjects were peace and security, including confidence-building measures; Jammu and Kashmir; Siachen; the Tulbul navigation project; the Sir Creek marshland; terrorism and drug trafficking; economic and commercial cooperation; and the promotion of friendly exchanges.

34. C. Raja Mohan, "India-Pakistan: Ten Questions on the Peace Process," *Economic and Political Weekly* (New Delhi), July 10, 2004.

35. Referred to as the "back channel," the talks were held over several years by special envoys in Bangkok, Dubai, and London. The two principal envoys—Tariq Aziz for Pakistan and S. K. Lambah for India—developed a text on Kashmir called a "nonpaper," because it contained no signatures or names but could serve as a detailed basis for a deal. See "India Pakistan Were Close to Secret Deal on Kashmir: Report," *Agence France-Presse*, February 23, 2009.

36. "Excerpted Interview of Former Foreign Minister of Pakistan Khurshid Mahmood Kasuri, with Karan Thapar," *Hindu,* February 21, 2009. In an interview, Musharraf reiter-

ated and confirmed this, adding that the two countries were close to a solution on Kashmir, Siachen, and Sir Creek. See *Hindu*, July 18, 2009.

37. See "India and Pakistan Were Close to Kashmir Accord," *Indo-Asian News Service*, February 22, 2009, http://in.news.yahoo.com/43/20090222/890.

38. The issue of Sir Creek—an area with varied biodiversity thought to be rich in oil and gas reserves—is one of the least politicized disputes between the two countries, and as a result is considered more amenable to an early settlement. It concerns the demarcation of the India-Pakistan border along a 96-kilometer-long estuary in the Rann of Kutch. Pakistan claims the whole of the creek; India says that the border should run midway through the water channel. At the widest point it means a difference of 10–12 kilometers of territory for both countries.

39. "Excerpted Interview of Kasuri," *Hindu*.

40. See Radha Kumar, *Making Peace with Partition* (New Delhi: Penguin Books, 2005), 115–18. See also B. G. Verghese, *A J and K Primer: From Myth to Reality* (New Delhi: India Research Press, 2006).

41. There is a tendency to equate the state of Jammu and Kashmir with the Kashmir Valley and to see the valley as exclusively Kashmiri Muslim. The "Kashmir issue" consequently is framed as a "territorial dispute" between India and Pakistan and also as a struggle for an independent state by the Kashmiris. What or who is a Kashmiri is still mired in confusion. The province of Jammu and Kashmir, on the Indian side, also represents a plurality with diverse communities such as the Ladakhi Buddhists, the Gujjars, the Bakerwals, and the Kashmiri Pandits, for whom independence may not be an aspiration at all. A lucid elaboration is found in Navanita Chadha Behera, *State, Identity and Violence—Jammu Kashmir and Ladakh* (New Delhi: Manohar, 2000).

42. See Pervaiz Iqbal Cheema, "Sustaining the Composite Dialogue," WISCOMP CT Working Paper II, New Delhi, 2005; and Pervaiz Iqbal Cheema, "Solving the Kashmir Dispute," WISCOMP CT Working Paper IV, New Delhi, 2005.

43. Javed Naqvi, "Indian PM Offers Friendship Treaty: Delinking of Kashmir Sought," *Daily Dawn* (Karachi), March 25, 2006.

44. See A. G. Noorani, "A Working Paper on Kashmir," *Frontline*, February 25–March 1, 2006.

45. The Northern Areas (NA), spread over 72,495 square kilometers, has been described as a "colony" of Pakistan. It was severed from PAK in 1949, was not a province of Pakistan, and enjoyed minimal democratic rights. In May 2004, reflecting the aspiration for real autonomy or provincial status, the Gilgit-Baltistan Thinkers Forum and All Parties National Alliance appealed to the Pakistan Supreme Court to expedite hearings on a 1999 petition, seeking the granting of fundamental rights to the people of NA on a par with citizens of Pakistan. The territory was under direct rule of the federal government through the Ministry of Kashmir and Northern Areas. The military has had a big role in administering the region. A recent package announced by Pakistan—the Gilgit-Baltistan Empowerment and Self-Governance Order 2009—promised a reforms package with maximum autonomy to the people of the region, but without full provincial status.

46. See F. S. Aijazuddin, "The Mulberry Bush of Kashmir," *Dawn* (Karachi), December 13, 2005.

47. See Cheema, "Solving the Kashmir Dispute."

48. Ibid., 10–13.

49. The renewed spate of violence in the Kashmir Valley in India since the summer of 2010 poses serious challenges to the Indian state. Civilian casualties in the wake of military

crackdowns against protesting "stone pelters" has led to arson by irate mobs. The elected government of Omar Abdullah in failing to counter growing alienation or provide effective governance appears adrift. Separatist voices and sentiments have grown more strident and have succeeded in mobilizing citizen anger and disenchantment to their advantage.

50. See J. N. Dixit, "Emerging National Security Challenges for India," *Security and Society* 1, no. 1 (2004): 5.

51. Shiv Shankar Menon, "India's Foreign Policy" (lecture, University of Delhi, January 19, 2009), 8.

52. This was clearly in evidence at the International Institute of Strategic Studies (IISS) Conference in April 2008 in New Delhi. See "International Leaders to Examine India's Rise as a Great Power and Its Impact on Global and Regional Politics," IISS press release, April 3, 2008; "India Needs to Play a Greater Role in Global Issues: Lord Powell," *Press Trust of India*, April 19, 2008; "Interview with John Chipman, Director General IISS," *Indian Express*, April 20, 2008.

53. K. Subramanyam, "Challenges to Indian Security" (KM Cariappa Memorial Lecture, New Delhi, October 28, 2000), 4. Similar positions are reflected in Raja Menon, *A Nuclear Strategy for India* (New Delhi: Sage Publications, 2000), and Verghese Koithara, *Society, State and Security: The Indian Experience* (New Delhi: Sage Publications, 1999), 388–90. An alleged lack of "territorial consciousnesses" is often cited as a historic Indian failing.

54. See Amitabh Mattoo, "Emerging India and the World" (lecture, Jammu and Kashmir Institute of Public Opinion, Jammu, March 7, 2005).

55. Ibid., 8–9.

56. This is lucidly argued by Radha Kumar in *India as Foreign Policy Actor—Normative Redux*, Working Document no. 285 (Brussels: Centre for European Policy Studies, February 2008), www.ceps.eu.

57. C. Raja Mohan, "No Free Rides to Greatness," *Indian Express*, April 19, 2008.

58. Ashok Malik, "The Powers of Pretence," *Pioneer*, April 25, 2008.

59. C. Uday Bhaskar, "India: A Rising Great Power in 2008," *Economic Times*, May 10, 2008.

60. Shiv Shankar Menon, "The Challenges Ahead for India's Foreign Policy" (speech, Observer Research Foundation, New Delhi, April 10, 2007).

61. Shyam Saran, "Present Dimensions of the Indian Foreign Policy," in *Indian Foreign Policy: Challenges and Opportunities*, ed. Atish Sinha and Madhup Mohta, Academic Foundation (New Delhi, 2007), 116.

62. Shiv Shankar Menon, "Inaugural Address on Foreign Policy Dialogue with International Institute for Strategic Studies, London," *Strategic Digest* 38, no. 1 (January 2008): 3–5.

63. See former defense minister Pranab Mukherjee, "India's Strategic Perspectives" (lecture, Carnegie Endowment for International Peace, Washington, DC, June 27, 2005), http://usindiafriendship.net/viewpoints/mukherjee.htm.

64. See Gurpreet Khurana, "China's 'String of Pearls' in the Indian Ocean and Its Security Implications," *Strategic Analysis* 32, no. 1 (January 2008).

65. Mukherjee, "India's Strategic Perspectives," 16.

66. C Raja Mohan, "India's Role in Asian Security: The Eightfold Path," in *Global Power Shifts and Strategic Transition in Asia*, ed. N. S. Sisodia and V. Krishnappa (New Delhi: Academic Foundation and IDSA, 2009), 54.

67. For an excellent articulation of this, see C. Raja Mohan, "Soft Borders and Cooperative Frontiers: India's Changing Territorial Diplomacy toward Pakistan and China," *Strategic Analysis* 31, no. 1 (January–February 2007).

68. India's recognition of the importance of ASEAN in transforming a region that was once known as Asia's Balkans into a principal vehicle for regional integration has impacted India's strategic outlook, causing it to move decisively away from its exclusive focus on its northwestern borders.

69. Rajiv Sikri, "Special Statement, in Indian Foreign Policy and Citizens (Look East Policy)," *Centre for Public Policy Document* (New Delhi), May 7, 2008, 12–15.

70. As cited in Sunil Khilnani, *The Idea of India* (London: Hamish Hamilton, 1997), 150–79.

71. Dixit, "Emerging National Security Challenges for India," 2.

72. See Cabinet Secretariat, "Social, Economic and Educational Status of the Muslim Community of India—A Report," Government of India, November 2006, http://minorityaffairs.gov.in/newsite/sachar/sachar_comm.pdf. See also Ministry of Minority Affairs, "Follow-up Action on the Recommendations of the Sachar Committee," Government of India, December 2009, http://minorityaffairs.gov.in/newsite/sachar/sachar_website-june09.pdf.

73. Arshi Saleem Hashmi, "South Asia's Growing Vulnerability," 25.

74. See Sibaji Pratim Basu, ed., *The Fleeing People of South Asia: Selections from Refugee Watch* (New Delhi: Anthem Press India, 2009).

75. See Cynthia Enloe, *Bananas, Beaches and Bases* (Berkeley, CA: University of California–Berkeley Press, 1990), 197–98. Enloe provides one of the most cogent expositions about the manner in which constructions of the private sphere conspire to exclude women and their concerns from foreign policy and the so-called hard policy areas pertaining to international trade, conflict, peacemaking, etc.

76. See Dhruva Jaishankar, "India's Smart Card," *Indian Express*, January 28, 2009.

77. These prescriptions are persuasively elaborated in C. Raja Mohan, "Diplomacy for the New Decade," *Seminar* no. 605 (January 2010): 55–60.

78. See Siddharth Varadarajan, "India Says Financial Crisis Gives NAM New Relevance," *Hindu* (New Delhi), July 16, 2009.

79. Thomas B. Coburn, "The Difference That Difference Makes," *Beyond the Margins* (New Delhi, March 2003), 3–6.

14

Southeast Asia and Its Evolving Security Architecture

Richard A. Bitzinger and Barry Desker

Southeast Asia can, paradoxically, be regarded as a zone of both relative calm and relative insecurity. On the one hand, the region lacks significant flashpoints—such as can be found in the Taiwan Strait or on the Korean Peninsula—that could lead to a major war. With the resolution of the East Timor crisis, the region is relatively free of open-armed conflict. In addition, the countries of the region are united in a common geopolitical and economic organization—the Association of Southeast Asian Nations (ASEAN)—which is dedicated to peaceful economic, social, and cultural development, as well as to the promotion of regional peace and stability.

On the other hand, Southeast Asia is also beset with a number of security challenges and therefore is also a zone of considerable *potential* conflict. For one thing, the region is an area of high strategic significance, sitting astride many key sea lines of communication (SLOCs) and important chokepoints, which naturally have both economic and military implications. For example, more than half of all global merchant tonnage passes through the various SLOCs in the region, including more than 25 percent of the world's trade and 25 percent of the world's crude oil shipments. In particular, countries such as China, Japan, and South Korea are critically dependent upon energy supplies passing through local waters. Moreover, the South China Sea has grown in salience in recent years, both for economic reasons (oil, gas, and fisheries) and as a strategic operating zone for the Chinese military (especially the People's Liberation Army [PLA] Navy), which sees it as a major jumping-off area into the Western Pacific and Indian Oceans. As China becomes more aggressive militarily in the region, Southeast Asian nations have responded in kind, building up their armed forces.

Despite the existence of ASEAN, many countries in Southeast Asia still harbor considerable suspicions and subcutaneous antagonisms toward one another, due to historical enmities, unresolved territorial claims, and, increasingly, competition for exclusive economic zones (EEZs) in the South China Sea. As a result, the waters around Southeast Asia are becoming more militarized, raising the specter of a potential arms race at sea. Finally, a host of nontraditional security challenges—including terrorism, domestic armed insurgencies, religious extremism (which often drives terrorism and insurgencies), piracy, pollution, climate change, pandemics, natural disasters, etc.—continue to vex the region.

These problems notwithstanding, Southeast Asia has been relatively successful in turning the region into an area of qualified stability, peace, and prosperity. While the countries of the region lack any kind of regional military alliance or even strong military-political links to great powers that could "keep the peace" in the region, they have done a satisfactory job in crafting a unique security system that seems to be working. That said, regional peace and security appears to be based less on any formalized security architectures and more on fortuitousness: the region has not had to deal with any regime-shattering crises. Any major change in the regional security calculus would thus be only for the worse, leaving open concerns that the current structure might be incapable of handling major security challenges in the future.

Challenges to Peace and Stability in Southeast Asia

Challenges to peace, stability, and security in Southeast Asia can be divided into two rough categories: external and internal. The most critical external challenge would be the apparently inexorable rise of China, particularly as a military power, and how this rise might affect Southeast Asia over the long run. Internal challenges include intraregional tensions, a possible regional arms race, local terrorist groups, and insurgencies.

China's Growing Military Potential

Over the past decade or so, the People's Republic of China (PRC) has increased its presence in Southeast Asia substantially. As China's economy has boomed, it has significantly expanded its global trade, importing raw materials (particularly energy supplies) and exporting finished manufactured goods. This has drawn the PRC closer to such strategic waterways as the Malacca and Singapore Straits. Moreover, Chinese investment in and trade with Southeast Asia have grown significantly in recent years, giving Beijing additional incentives to be engaged in the region. At the same time, as the PRC's military might has grown, it has expanded its area of operations beyond continental China and its adjacent waters into the South China Sea and beyond to the Indian Ocean.

Naturally, the countries of Southeast Asian look upon this growing Chinese presence with a certain amount of trepidation. China's growing military activities in the region are cause for some concern, and one may surmise that the ASEAN states would take precautions against a rising China in their midst, including military measures.

The modernization of the PLA and the subsequent expansion of Chinese military power in the Asia-Pacific region have been well documented and need not be repeated here in great detail. It suffices to say that the Chinese have deployed considerable resources and effort into acquiring new capabilities for force projection, mobility, and precision strike. In particular, this has meant deemphasizing ground forces in favor of building up the PLA's naval, air, and missile forces. The PLA Navy, for example, has greatly increased its procurement of large surface combatants and submarines. It has since the late 1990s acquired a dozen Kilo-class submarines and four Sovremennyy-class destroyers (armed with supersonic SS-N-22 antiship cruise missiles) from Russia, as well as a navalized version of the Russian Su-30 fighter-bomber. Just as important, there has been a significant expansion in Chinese naval shipbuilding since the turn of the century. Since 2000, China has begun construction of several new classes of destroyers, frigates, amphibious landing craft, and diesel-electric and nuclear-powered submarines. In addition, rumors persist that the PLA will add at least one aircraft carrier to its fleet within the next seven to ten years.

As a result of these concerted efforts, the military potential of the PRC has expanded considerably over the past decade, and the PLA's recent modernization activities have fueled speculation that China is developing a new military strategy based on power projection and precision strike. China's 2006 defense white paper states that the PLA Navy "aims at gradual extension of the strategic depth for offshore defensive operations and enhancing its capabilities in integrated maritime operations," while the PLA Air Force "aims at speeding up its transition from territorial air defense to both offensive and defensive operations, and increasing its capabilities in the areas of air strike, air and missile defense, early warning and reconnaissance, and strategic projection."[1] Some may interpret these efforts as an indicator of a more aggressive and expansionist China, or at least a PRC more likely to assert its role in the Asia-Pacific region and to use its growing military might to back up its national interests and national security goals.[2]

While such an expanding military capability would most likely be used to attack and defeat Taiwan in the event that Taipei declares independence, and to deter or deny U.S. intervention on Taiwan's behalf, these capacities can also be applied to other areas where the PRC has strong strategic interests, particularly Southeast Asia. This region is one of growing and increasingly diversified significance to Beijing, and China has several territorial, economic, political, and diplomatic concerns that touch on Southeast Asia. These include (1) addressing long-standing disputes over sovereignty issues in the South China Sea, especially the Spratly Islands; (2) securing sea lines of communication to the Indian Ocean and the Middle East; (3) increasing economic ties with Southeast Asia (particularly trade and investment); and (4) legitimizing its own regional security role (and also limiting U.S. influence) through a process of multilateral forums and negotiations.[3]

Consequently, Chinese military assertiveness has been felt as much in Southeast Asia as in other parts of the Asia Pacific. The Chinese have expanded their naval and air presence in the South China Sea and begun to extend naval patrols into the Indian Ocean. For example, the PLA has built a military airstrip on Woody Island in the Paracel Islands in the South China Sea, and it is reportedly constructing a new nuclear submarine base on Hainan Island.[4] The PLA Navy is also building naval facilities in Myanmar and negotiating port access rights with Pakistan. These and other actions have caused some to speculate that the PRC is attempting to develop a network of bases and alliances stretching from southern China to the Middle East, a strategy often referred to as the "string of pearls."[5]

Overall, the PRC's "creeping assertiveness" in the South China Sea and beyond has been cause for considerable concern among the countries of Southeast Asia. Regarding the South China Sea disputes, for example, Beijing's competing territorial claims with several Southeast Asian countries over the ownership or control in the Spratly Islands has led China to be militarily engaged and active in this area for many decades, and this has often led to tension, if not outright clashes. The Spratlys, a chain of coral reefs that barely break the ocean's surface, are adjacent both to major SLOCs and to potentially lucrative maritime natural resources (fisheries, oil and gas deposits). Consequently, several countries in addition to the PRC—including Brunei, Malaysia, the Philippines, and Vietnam—have laid claim to various parts of the Spratlys, and nearly all have attempted to enforce these claims by establishing garrisons and other structures on the islands. This has on occasion led to actual conflict, such as when China occupied and began building on the Philippines-claimed Mischief Reef in the mid-1990s, and when Chinese and Vietnamese naval vessels clashed in Johnson Reef.[6]

In addition, as China's economy continues both to grow and to globalize—with the PRC emerging as a global hub not only for manufacturing but also for research and development and for *outward* direct investments—trade and energy security have become paramount concerns for Beijing. China is now the world's second largest importer of oil (after the United States), and 60 percent (expected to rise to 75 percent by 2015) of its crude oil imports come from the Middle East, much of it passing through the Malacca and Singapore Straits or the Lombok and Makassar Straits. In addition, a quarter of the world's trade also transits through these waterways. Consequently, Beijing is extremely concerned about the continuing openness, safety, and security of these vital SLOCs, which could be disrupted or impeded by an international crisis, terrorist action, or acts of piracy.[7] At the same time, the PRC is uncomfortable with external powers, such as the United States or Japan, maintaining a permanent military presence in these straits. While the PLA Navy is currently unable to project sufficient and *sustainable* sea power into the straits to protect its interests in these waterways, the development of such capacities is certainly a long-range goal of the Chinese. Thus, these straits could certainly become potential zones of conflict.

Finally, lingering historical animosities have contributed to tensions between Beijing and some Southeast Asian nations. For example, bilateral Chinese-Vietnamese relations remain edgy. This is partly a legacy of their brief war in 1979 and partly a result of their ongoing disputes over the Spratly and Paracel groups of islands. Both countries have also been vying for strategic influence in Laos.[8] Additionally, simmering resentment among indigenous Indonesians against their fellow Chinese-Indonesian countrymen (who control much of the Indonesian economy) has occasionally spilled over into Beijing-Jakarta relations (and potentially into other countries in the region with sizable Chinese minorities, such as Malaysia and Vietnam).[9]

Intra-ASEAN Regional Insecurities

While China certainly is a part of the dynamic affecting regional insecurities, it is not the only one, nor is it necessarily the preeminent one. In a larger sense, for example, the regional uncertainties bred by the end of the Cold War have caused many Southeast Asian nations to have an increased concern over regional security and stability. In particular, while the United States has recently increased its presence in Southeast Asia, there remain for some countries lingering concerns about the long-term reliability of America as a strategic partner. This is especially true in Thailand, which saw Washington suspend aid to it in the wake of the country's October 2006 military coup. Other ASEAN countries, meanwhile, are concerned that the United States may try to exploit the global war on terrorism to expand American hegemony. Consider, for example, Indonesian and Malaysian objections to the U.S. Regional Maritime Security Initiative, which they interpreted as an American effort to maintain a permanent military presence in the Malacca and Singapore Straits.[10]

At the same time, the military interests and doctrines of the Southeast Asian nations have changed as well with regard to outward security concerns. During the Cold War, most countries in the region were more worried about separatist movements and communist insurgencies. While terrorism and insurgencies are still major problems in Thailand, Indonesia, and the Philippines—particularly homegrown Islamic-based terrorism—*externally* there has been a move toward a broadening of regional security interests to include economic benefits and other nontraditional goals. In particular, this has led to growing concerns over protecting maritime natural resources (particularly oil and gas reserves and fishing areas), securing regional SLOCs, and countering piracy and trafficking in contraband and humans. Consequently, regional navies, coast guards, and air forces are being increasingly tasked and outfitted with the means to safeguard EEZs, shipping routes (such as the Malacca and Singapore Straits), and other economic interests in the area.[11]

One must also keep in mind that many Southeast Asian states are just as often suspicious of one another as they are of external powers such as China, and that these tensions have also been powerful motivators behind recent national military buildups in the region. Historical bilateral fears and wariness still exist between Malaysia and Singapore, Malaysia and Indonesia, and Thailand and Burma, for example, and these and other suspicions have manifested themselves in a variety of territorial and maritime disputes and clashes over EEZ rights. For example, claimed EEZs in the South China Sea frequently overlap between Malaysia, Brunei, Vietnam, and the Philippines (not to mention China, which claims most of the South China Sea as its own). In addition, competing claims in the South China Sea over the Spratly Islands are just as strong among the various Southeast Asian nations as they are between Southeast Asian nations and the PRC.[12] Other territorial disputes have included the fight between Singapore and Malaysia over the Pedra Branca/Batu Puteh islets and between Indonesia and Malaysia over the Ambalat Sea Block. The 2007 tiff between Singapore and Indonesia over sand and gravel exports only further underscores the lingering distrust that exists within the ASEAN community.[13]

One consequence of continuing intra-ASEAN tensions is the growing concern that the region is on the verge of, if not in the midst, a mini arms race. As already noted, regional militaries are being increasingly tasked with new roles and missions, which has led to an increase in arms procurement—both quantitatively and qualitatively—by many Southeast Asian countries. Coupled with this is the fact that defense budgets throughout the region have been on an upward trajectory for several years. For example, according to data provided by the Stockholm International Peace Research Institute (SIPRI), Malaysia's military budget more than doubled between 2000 and 2008, from US$1.7 billion to US$3.5 billion (in constant 2005 dollars). Over the same timeframe, Indonesian defense spending went from US$2.2 billion to US$3.8 billion, a 70 percent increase; Singapore's defense budget rose by more than 25 percent, from US$4.6 billion to US$5.8 billion; and Thai military expenditures went from approximately US$2 billion to US$3 billion, a 50 percent increase.[14]

Consequently, the region has become a growing market for sophisticated—and increasingly lethal—military and aerospace systems. Malaysia, for example, has bought tanks from Poland, Su-30 fighter jets from Russia, multiple rocket launchers from Brazil, submarines from France, and corvettes from Germany. Indonesia, armed with a US$1 billion export credit from Russia, is buying Su-27 and Su-30 fighters, attack helicopters, corvettes, and land systems. Thailand has acquired Gripen fighter jets from Sweden, antiship cruise missiles from China, self-propelled artillery from France, and assault rifles from Israel. Singapore also casts a wide net when it comes to arms imports, buying American-made F-15SG combat aircraft, Swedish Sjöormen and Västergötland submarines, French Lafayette frigates, and German Leopard 2A4 tanks, as well as surface-to-air missiles from both Russia and Israel.

The acquisition of these new military capabilities has had at least two major repercussions for militaries in the Asia Pacific. First of all, to reiterate, the arms buildup in the region over the past ten to fifteen years has been more than "mere" modernization; these new types of armaments being acquired promise to significantly upgrade the manner in which wars are fought in the region. Certainly, Asia-Pacific militaries are acquiring greater lethality and accuracy at greater ranges, improved battlefield knowledge and command and control, and increased operational maneuver and speed. Standoff precision-guided weapons, such as cruise and ballistic missiles and terminal-homing (such as GPS or electro-optical) guided munitions, have greatly increased combat firepower and effectiveness. The addition of modern submarines and surface combatants, amphibious assault ships, air-refueled combat aircraft, and transport aircraft have extended these militaries' theoretical range of action. Advanced reconnaissance and surveillance platforms have considerably expanded their capacities to see past the horizon and in all three dimensions. Additionally, through the increased use of stealth and active defenses (such as missile defense and longer-range air-to-air missiles), local militaries are significantly adding to their survivability and operational capabilities. Consequently, conflict in the region, should it occur, would likely be more "high-tech": it would be faster and occur across greater distances, yet it would be more precise and perhaps more devastating in its effect.

Second, some Southeast Asian militaries are acquiring the types of military equipment that, taken together, could fundamentally change the concept and conduct of warfare. In particular, those systems related to precision strike, stealth, and, above all, command, control, communications, computing, intelligence, surveillance, and reconnaissance (C4ISR) comprise some of the key hardware ingredients essential to implementing a revolution in military affairs. Bundled together in innovative new ways, they can greatly synergize their individual effectiveness and create new "core competencies" in war fighting. These emerging capabilities, in turn, have the potential to significantly affect strategy and operations on tomorrow's battlefield and hence to alter the determinants of critical capabilities in modern warfare. At the very least, therefore, the countries of the Asia-Pacific region increasingly possess the kernel of what is required to transform their militaries.

At the same time, the introduction of new types of arms and, therefore, unprecedented military capabilities into a region can have many unintended consequences. They can, for example, create or exacerbate arms races that, in turn, could seriously disturb or even destabilize regional or regional military balances, leading to more insecurity and instability in the region. In this regard, the spread of the most advanced conventional weapons could have an adverse effect on regional security environments. Arms races are generally defined as arming actions occurring between two or more participants who already possess a high degree of mutual animosity or antagonism toward each other; whose national military and diplomatic planning is based directly on the capabilities and intent of the perceived adversary; whose defense spending frequently receives large or consistent increases; whose arming focuses specifically on achieving superiority over a perceived adversary; and who, in general, attempt to seek dominance over perceived adversaries in international political-military affairs via intimidation. At the same time, arms races are too often based on negative inferences regarding an adversary's intentions, which can lead to misinterpreting the adversary's actions as bellicose and to discounting positive, benign overtures.

Without necessarily leading to arms *races*, however, these new arms acquisitions can lead to very expensive, and ultimately imprudent, arms *competitions*. Although usually defined as noncataclysmic, "status quo"–oriented rivalries dedicated mainly to the maintenance of military balances, arms competitions can still be disruptive to regional security and can even evolve into arms races. In particular, continued purchasing of advanced weapons platforms may contribute to a classical "security dilemma"—a situation in which actions taken by a country can actually undermine the security and stability that the actions were meant to increase. Arms acquisitions by a state, even if it has no desire to threaten its neighbors, can lead to anxieties and feelings of insecurities in nearby states. Reciprocal responses by neighboring states to "regain" security by buying their own advanced weapons only raise regional tensions further. Even if such tit-for-tat arms purchases do not lead to conflict, they can reinforce mutual insecurities and suspicions and ultimately have a deleterious impact on regional security.

Nontraditional Security Challenges

Up until now, this chapter has mainly concerned itself with *military*-based threats and challenges to security in Southeast Asia. At the same time, the region is confronted by a number of other types of *nontraditional* (although not necessarily new) threats, such as infectious or pandemic diseases, climate change and natural disasters, terrorism, and ethnic insurgencies.

Southeast Asia has long been concerned with the risk of infectious diseases. Dengue fever, for example, is a long-standing health concern to the region and, since it is spread by mosquitoes, one that revisits the area annually and can only be managed, never totally eliminated. Lately, however, pandemic diseases have grown in importance in the minds of both regional health *and* security officials, as

> the risk of infectious disease pandemics is greater than in the past and the global public health response system faces serious analytic and institutional challenges. Infectious diseases have the potential to spread rapidly across national borders and effective response demands rapid and effective coordination between organizations, governments, and experts. . . . Yet the epidemiology of emerging infectious diseases operates in a context of epistemic uncertainty and ambiguity. Information about the number and distribution of cases is rarely complete and little may be known about the disease itself and how it spreads. Confounding signals invariably complicate decision-making. Successful response requires geographically-dispersed networks to develop accurate interpretations of epidemiological information in time-pressured, uncertain and often politicized environments.[15]

The SARS epidemic that hit Southeast Asia in 2003 and the more recent global outbreak of the H1N1 virus brought home to the region not only its vulnerability to pandemic diseases but also the difficulties in crafting national or even regional solutions to dealing with these diseases.

Climate change and natural disasters also contain both long-standing and relatively new security challenges. Of course, the region has long had to deal with tribulations like monsoons (such as Typhoon Morakot, which devastated southern Taiwan in 2009), earthquakes (such as the September 2009 quake in Sumatra, which killed hundreds and left thousands homeless), and tsunamis (particularly the December 26, 2004, tsunami that hit Southeast Asia and killed over 230,000 people, including more than 130,000 in Indonesia alone). Such events have increasingly pressed local authorities to think proactively about national and international disaster planning and risk management, in order to more effectively prepare for relief operations when such disasters occur. On the other hand, global climate change is a much newer phenomenon that can affect regional security in a number of fundamental ways. Rising sea levels (from melting polar ice) affects the very existence of low-lying states, such as Singapore, while perhaps also altering the character of the South China Sea (for example, submerging many islets in the Spratlys, affecting territorial and EEZ claims). Warming or cooling seas could also greatly impact maritime ecosystems, fish stocks, weather patterns, and the like in unpredictable ways.

Terrorism and insurgencies in Southeast Asia are also long-standing security problems, but ones that have taken on particularly new salience in recent years, given the impact that religious radicalism has had on these phenomena and the increasing "globalization" of terrorism through such groupings as al-Qaeda. Jemaah Islamiyah (JI) is the main *transnational* terrorist threat extant in Southeast Asia, but sizable *domestic* terrorist or insurrectionist threats also exist in Thailand and the Philippines. JI is dedicated to the establishment of an Islamic state incorporating Indonesia, Malaysia, Brunei, the Muslim parts of the Philippines, and Singapore. It has operational links to al-Qaeda and the Taliban, and it has coordinated with other Islamic terrorist groups in Southeast Asia, such as the Abu Sayyaf Group (ASG) and the Moro Islamic Liberation Front (MILF), when it comes to recruitment, training, indoctrination, funding, and operations. JI has been responsible for a number of terrorist bombings around Southeast Asia, including the Bali bombings of 2002 and 2005, as well as abortive plots to blow up embassies in Singapore. At its height in the late 1990s, it could count on perhaps 2,000 adherents.[16]

Despite being a transnational organization, JI is operational mainly in Indonesia and, to a lesser extent, in the southern Philippines (through the

ASG). Concerted and coordinated counterterrorist activities by Indonesian, Malaysian, and Singaporean authorities, in the wake of the September 11, 2001 attacks (intensified after the 2002 Bali bombings), have disrupted JI both organizationally and operationally.[17] Expanded maritime patrols in the waters of Southeast Asia have also impeded both the transnational movement of men, money, and arms by terrorist organizations such as JI and acts of piracy in regional waters that in turn helped to fund terrorists.

Thailand's four southernmost provinces are mostly ethnic Muslim-Malay, and Muslim-led insurgencies have been growing in the region, led by two separatist groups, the Pattani United Liberation Organization and the Barisan Revolusi Nasional. From January 2004 to the middle of 2007, more than 6,000 acts of violence are estimated to have taken place in the south, resulting in more than 2,300 deaths. The insurgents have relied mainly on roadside attacks on security forces, bombings of civilian targets, such as banks and shopping areas, and random drive-by assassination attempts on police and local government officials—tactics similar to those utilized by al-Qaeda and JI, sparking rumors that these transnational terrorist organizations are actively supporting local insurgent groups.

Under Prime Minister Thaksin Shinawatra, the response to the south Thailand insurgency was decidedly confrontational. In early 2005, for example, the Royal Thai Army (RTA) reactivated the 15th Infantry Division and deployed it to the Fourth Army in order to bolster the only other combat division in the region, the 5th Infantry Division. In addition, the Thaksin government declared much of the southern region of the country an emergency zone, and empowered security forces to conduct warrantless wiretaps, searches, and arrests; ban public gatherings; censor news; impose curfews; and expel foreign nationals. The crackdown appeared to have little impact, however, and after the 2006 coup, the junta took a more softly, softly approach aimed at winning the "hearts and minds" of the local population, initiating development projects, offering medical services, and deescalating tensions between the armed forces and local civilians. These efforts have also failed to check rising violence, however, and the current military-led government appears to be at a loss as to its next steps.

The Philippines is beset with a number of terrorist, separatist, and insurrectionist groups. These include the MILF, the ASG, and the communist New People's Army (NPA). MILF operates in the southern island of Mindanao and is fighting for the creation of an independent Moro Islamic state. A cease-fire between the MILF and the Philippine government existed from 2003 to 2005, and although this has been broken with sporadic violence—most recently with a bloody attack on government forces in Basilan in 2007—the MILF seems prepared to accept a peace deal with Manila that includes a recognition of the Moro's right to self-determination. The ASG has typically been more obstinate and more violent—kidnapping Americans and other foreigners to hold for ransom and to gain international attention, or bombing the *Superferry 14* in 2004 (reportedly a joint operation with JI that was, incidentally, the country's worst terrorist attack ever, resulting in 116 deaths)—but the group has been weakened by factionalism and is largely confined to the Sulu archipelago.[18] For its part, the NPA has declined significantly in numbers from its peak in the early 1980s, when it had over 25,000 insurgents and was active in 69 of 81 Philippine districts. Today, as a result of party in-fighting, government amnesty programs, and military defeats, its numbers are now less than 6,000, and the NPA controls less than 5 percent of the country.[19]

The Security Architecture in Southeast Asia

The security challenges facing Southeast Asia are considerable. At the same time, the region seems to have crafted a unique security architecture—founded on a growing sense of common security concerns (such as the strategic interplay between economics and security, the growing presence of China in the region, and the idea of shared vulnerability in the face of pandemics, natural disasters, and terrorism/insurgencies) and based on a wide variety of institutions and arrangements—that has been successful in promoting and maintaining relative peace and stability.[20] Some aspects of this architecture are structural and formal (such as the role of ASEAN), while others are the result of initiatives by countries outside the region purposely meant to lower potential tensions involving the region (such as China's more accommodating foreign and security policy regarding Southeast Asia).

The Role of ASEAN

The strongest regional architecture for promoting peace, security, and stability in the region is the Association of Southeast Asian Nations. In 2007, ASEAN celebrated its fortieth anniversary, and it currently comprises ten member states: Brunei, Cambodia, Indonesia, Laos, Malaysia, Myanmar, Philippines, Singapore, Thailand, and Vietnam. ASEAN's security aims are enshrined in its charter, adopted in November 2007, which includes:

- respect for the independence, sovereignty, and territorial integrity of member states;
- peaceful settlement of disputes;
- noninterference in member states' internal affairs; and
- the right to live without external interference.[21]

Figure 14.1 Asia-Pacific Regional Security Architecture

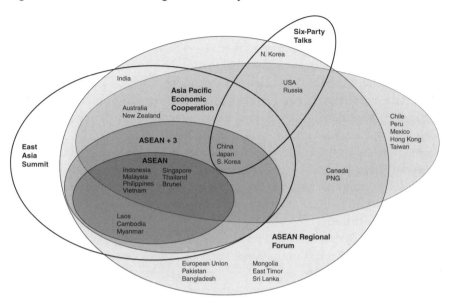

Source: Emmers, "ASEAN's Wider Architecture."

ASEAN is at the center of several regional forums for the promotion of security and good relations within the region and for dealing with actual or potential disputes (see figure 14.1). Premier among these is the ASEAN summit, of which fourteen have been held since its inception, most recently in Thailand in early 2009. The ASEAN summit is a meeting of the member states' heads of government in which they discuss and resolve regional issues. This summit usually includes additional security-building dialogues with other countries outside ASEAN, such as with China, Japan, and South Korea (ASEAN+3), and with Australia and New Zealand. ASEAN+3 was founded in response to the Asian Financial Crisis of 1997–98, with the intent of involving Northeast Asian states in addressing East Asian economic, financial, and nontraditional security issues (such as infectious diseases and transnational crime).[22]

ASEAN also conducts the ASEAN Regional Forum (ARF). The ARF, founded in 1994, comprises twenty-seven countries, including all of the ASEAN members, Australia, Bangladesh, Canada, China, the European Union, India, Japan, North Korea, South Korea, Mongolia, New Zealand, Pakistan, Papua New Guinea, Russia, Sri Lanka, Timor Leste, and the United States. The ARF is "the principal forum for security dialogue in Asia, complementing the various bilateral alliances and dialogues," and it "provides a setting in which members can discuss current regional security issues and develop cooperative measures to enhance peace and security in the region."[23] ARF is basically dedicated to regional confidence building by creating "a sense of strategic community" and encouraging preventive diplomacy and conflict management.

Additionally, ASEAN is the lead organizer of the East Asia Summit (EAS), a pan-Asian regional community-building forum held annually by the leaders of sixteen countries in the Asia-Pacific region: the ten ASEAN member states, Australia, China, Japan, South Korea, India, and New Zealand; notably, the EAS specifically *excludes* the United States. The first EAS was held in 2005, which Russia attended as a guest, and discussion issues have included trade, energy, and climate change. The fourth EAS, scheduled to be held in Thailand in 2009, was postponed due to domestic political unrest there.

In addition to meetings and forums, ASEAN has engaged in some practical initiatives to promote regional security and reduce tensions. In 1995, ASEAN member states signed the Southeast Asian Nuclear-Weapons-Free Zone Treaty. The treaty took effect on March 28, 1997, and became fully effective on June 21, 2001. It effectively bans all nuclear weapons in the region, as well as obligates its members not to develop, manufacture, or otherwise acquire, possess, or have control over nuclear weapons.

Finally, various ASEAN nations, while not engaging in formal alliances, are increasingly working together militarily to support regional security. In particular, Indonesia, Malaysia, Singapore, and Thailand have begun to conduct coordinated naval and aerial patrols of the Malacca and Singapore Straits, while Indonesia and Singapore have also initiated a joint "surface picture" naval monitoring system of the area.[24] Additionally, ASEAN is either central to or a partnering player in both "track-two" level informal security initiatives, such as the Council for Security Cooperation in the Asia-Pacific (CSCAP), and higher level, semiformal "track-one-and-a-half" initiatives, such as the Shangri-la Dialogue of regional defense ministers held every year in Singapore.[25]

Additionally, local academic institutions are playing an increased role in pressing for solutions to regional security challenges, particularly nontraditional challenges. One of these worth noting is the Consortium of Non-Traditional Security Studies in Asia (NTS-Asia), which is directed by the S. Rajaratnam School of International Studies (RSIS) at Nanyang Technological University in Singapore. According to its Web site, NTS-Asia's research agenda includes

- providing an avenue for scholars and policymakers in Asia to discuss and analyze nontraditional security issues in the region;

- encouraging the participation of other scholars in and outside the region on the basis of the principle of inclusiveness and knowledge sharing;
- establishing linkages with institutions and organizations in other parts of the world to exchange information, insights, and experiences in the area of NTS;
- convening regional and international meetings and other collaborative activities for the purpose of consolidating existing researches on NTS-related issues; and
- producing and disseminating publications and, where possible, policy recommendations to relevant governmental and intergovernmental bodies on NTS issues.[26]

The Role of China

While China certainly is a growing regional military power, the impact of which has been felt in Southeast Asia, this has not necessarily translated into a heightened sense of insecurity. In fact, China may even be a *receding* concern in Southeast Asia's security calculus. Much of this has to do with the emergence within the Chinese leadership of a more nuanced and sophisticated foreign policy toward Southeast Asia. While relations between Beijing and some Southeast Asian nations in the past have been poor, even hostile, and while in some cases, such as Vietnam or Indonesia, suspicions of Chinese intent and actions are long and lingering, relations between China and most countries in the region have improved remarkably in recent years and, in fact, have probably never been better. For example, trade between China and Southeast Asia has increased dramatically, and Beijing has become a major investor in and aid donor to such countries as Indonesia, Laos, the Philippines, and Vietnam and maintains close ties to such traditional client states as Myanmar.[27]

Moreover, Beijing had for several years been engaged in a "smile campaign" in Southeast Asia designed to show countries there that it was a nonconfrontational regional player dedicated to a peaceful rise. In a dramatic departure from its earlier belligerent and ham-fisted manner in pressing its national interests, Beijing made

special efforts to assure its neighbors that it is a responsible and constructive partner. It has agreed to codes of conduct where territorial disputes have economic consequence (as in the South China Sea); it has begun negotiations to resolve border disputes that involved important neighbors such as India; it has started to take its nonproliferation obligations much more seriously than before . . . and it has expressed a willingness to shelve active political disputes that cannot be reconciled immediately, so long as none of the other parties involved disturbs the status quo (e.g., Taiwan). In general, China has refocused its energies on expanding trade and cooperation with all its neighbors.[28]

In this regard, PRC became in 2003 the first non-Southeast Asian state to sign the Treaty of Amity and Cooperation with ASEAN. This agreement has been paired with the ASEAN–China Strategic Partnership for Peace and Security, also signed in 2003, and followed up by a Plan for Action agreement in 2004.[29] China is also a participant in the ARF, the ARF Security Policy Conference (ASPC), and the ASEAN+3 meetings.

Nowhere perhaps was this new "play-nice" strategy more evident than in China's handling of the Spratly Islands dispute, at least until quite recently. The situation surrounding the Spratlys has calmed down considerably since the supposed "flashpoint" status of these islets during the 1990s. For much of the first decade of the twenty-first century, the status of the islands was rarely "discussed as a major security concern."[30] To its credit, the PRC had made a concerted effort *not* to let the South Sea issue become a major domestic political football (unlike the Senkaku and Diaoyu Islands dispute with Japan), nor has it seized or occupied additional islands in the Spratlys since 1995. In particular, in 2002, Beijing and ASEAN agreed to a joint Declaration on the Conduct of Parties in the South China Sea, which affirmed the intention of the signatories to peacefully resolve their territorial and jurisdictional disputes and to exercise self-restraint in the South China Sea by refraining from taking actions that would "complicate or escalate disputes and affect peace and stability," such as initiating construction projects on the presently uninhabited islands. In addition, in March 2005, Beijing signed bilateral agreements with the Philippines and Vietnam for the joint exploration for oil in areas of overlapping sovereignty claims. (At the same time, estimates of likely oil and gas reserves in the South China Sea have been revised downward considerably, so there may be much less to fight over than originally believed.) This is not to say that the dispute over the Spratly Islands has been settled once and for all.[31] In particular, recent Chinese claims of "sovereign control" over much of the South China Sea has, temporarily at least, returned the Spratlys dispute to a higher level of concern.

Finally, Beijing has, in general, greatly lowered the tone and rhetoric of its strategic competition with the United States, an action that has gone a long way toward reassuring the countries of Southeast Asia of China's sincerity in pursuing a nonconfrontational foreign and security strategy. Beijing has overall pursued a much more subtle approach toward the United States by not directly challenging the U.S. leadership in Asia, by partnering with Washington where the two countries have shared interests, and, above all, by promoting multilateral security processes that, in turn, work toward diluting or constraining U.S. power, influence, and hegemony in the Asia Pacific and elsewhere.[32]

To be sure, ASEAN nations are not oblivious to the growing (and potentially forceful) assertiveness of China in their neighborhood. As such, these states continue to keep China at a distance politically and militarily even as they embrace it economically and diplomatically. The United States, meanwhile, is still largely regarded as a benign superpower interested in maintaining the regional status quo; indeed, many ASEAN countries have bilateral security agreements with Washington (e.g., Thailand, Philippines) or engage in close if unofficial security cooperation with the United States (e.g., Singapore). This "hedging" strategy will likely continue to define the policy of many Southeast Asian nations toward China.[33]

Conclusions

Southeast Asia is certainly not immune to a variety of security challenges, including the possibility of interstate conflict, regional terrorism, internal insurgencies, and the like. At the same time, many of these challenges are actually less acute than they may appear on the surface. In particular, while the nations of Southeast Asia have considerable grievances with one another—which may appear to have the potential to erupt into conflict— the principles of noninterference and mutual respect, together with an emphasis on economic development (and not doing anything to disrupt that progress) embodied in the ASEAN ideal, have had considerable impact in promoting intraregional peace and stability. Just one example to point out is that Singapore and Malaysia were able to peacefully resolve their sovereignty assertions over the Pedra Branca/Batu Puteh issue through international binding arbitration.

But the current Southeast Asian security architecture is far from perfect. While ASEAN has successfully crafted several structures and institutions for conflict management, security cooperation, and confidence building, most of these have only limited impact on actual security building in the region. The ARF, for example, has lost considerable momentum due to disagreements over what constitutes preventive diplomacy, while any progress within ASEAN+3 is dependent upon China and Japan resolving their complicated bilateral relationship. Additionally, the EAS has never really gained any real traction as a regional security-enhancing initiative, perhaps because it excludes the United States.[34] Consequently, most of these institutions, like ASEAN itself, basically constitute glorified "talking shops," and most of their output consists of highly formalized and lowest-common-denominator declarations and unenforced initiatives. In fact, the whole "ASEAN way" of noninterference in the internal affairs of other states, especially other member states, can be criticized as being inadequate to the task of creating solutions for regional peace and security, as such a refusal to intervene can hobble regional efforts to deal proactively with security challenges, whether terrorism, insurgencies, pandemics, or destabilizing regimes (such as the Burmese junta). In particular, neither ASEAN nor any of its sister architectures have any mechanisms in place to press conventional arms-control arrangements or to create a joint response to possible Chinese aggression in the region.

At present, therefore, most Southeast Asian security structures are not oriented toward or capable of handling many newly arising regional security challenges, particularly nontraditional threats such as pandemics, environmental security, or religious radicalism. Southeast Asian regionalism expert Ralf Emmers has argued that for regional ASEAN-based security structures to truly have an impact, they must overcome their traditionally weak structural capacities and reform themselves to be more relevant and effective by redefining themselves in more functional terms, focusing on specific issues—such as terrorism, climate change, health security, maritime security—and viewing themselves as important venues for substantive cooperation. Additionally, Emmers asserts that any future institution building in the region must take into account (1) U.S. participation; (2) the nature of Chinese involvement; and (3) the role of Japan as a key player. Further, it must recognize that such institutions will only complement, rather than replace, bilateral ties and alliances.[35]

China still remains a low-level threat in many ways, at least at the moment. Certainly the PRC looms large in regional security calculations, and there are many unresolved issues when it comes to a growing Chinese presence in Southeast Asia. Nevertheless, so long as Beijing seems intent on pursuing a "good-neighbor policy" toward the region, the regional security architecture is not directly challenged. At the same time, the ASEAN states will, when it comes to its giant neighbor to the north, likely still keep their powder dry and continue to hedge against any possible renewed Chinese aggression.

Finally, without minimizing the challenges of regional and domestic terrorism, local insurgencies, and piracy, it is worth noting that these threats, too, seem to have been managed reasonably well of late. Piracy in the waters around Southeast Asia, for example, has greatly dropped off in recent years, thanks to concerted and often coordinated efforts by local navies and coast guards (together with global partners). ASEAN states are also cooperating with one another and other countries (particularly the United States) to go after globally linked terrorist groups, such as JI and ASG. As one analysis has put it, terrorism and internal insurgencies in Southeast Asia are at present a "serious but largely manageable security problem."[36]

On the whole, therefore, there is probably more stability in Southeast Asia than might appear. True, regional security architectures are relatively weak and, paradoxically, rigid and formalized. Southeast Asia is at no loss for institutions, initiatives, summits, and resolutions. On the other hand, none of these seem to have much impact on regional security, other than keeping countries committed to the *idea* of multilateral forums for confidence building and conflict resolution. Overall, norms of behavior in the region appear to be dictated by the shared fear that upsetting the security calculus in the region could in turn lead to a worse situation. Consequently, stability and security in Southeast Asia is a function of fortune and delicate balancing. At the moment, there exists no issue in the region so compelling that the local states are willing to disturb the status quo over it. The obvious drawback to such a security structure, of course, is, what will the countries of Southeast Asia do if an issue that cannot be dealt with through benign neglect or mere pronouncements of concern arises?

Notes

1.   *China's National Defense in 2006* (Beijing: Information Office of the State Council of the People's Republic of China, December 2006).

2.   Christopher Griffin and Dan Blumenthal, "China's Defence White Paper: What It Does (and Doesn't) Tell Us," *China Brief*, January 24, 2007.

3.   International Institute for Strategic Studies (IISS), "China, America, and Southeast Asia: Hedge and Track," *Strategic Comments* 11, no. 1 (February 2005): 1.

4.   Office of Naval Intelligence, *China's Navy 2007* (Washington, DC: Office of Naval Intelligence, 2007), 31–32.

5.   Bill Gertz, "China Builds up Strategic Sea Lanes," *Washington Times*, January 18, 2005.

6.   Ian Storey, "China and the Philippines: Moving Beyond the South China Sea Dispute," *China Brief*, August 16, 2006.

7.   Ian Storey, "China's 'Malacca Dilemma,'" *China Brief*, April 12, 2006.

8.   Ian Storey, "China and Vietnam's Tug of War over Laos," *China Brief*, June 7, 2005.

9.   Ian Storey, "Progress and Remaining Obstacles in Sino-Indonesian Relations," *China Brief*, August 16, 2005.

10. IISS, "China, America, and Southeast Asia," 2.

11. Andrew Tan, "Force Modernization Trends in Southeast Asia" (working paper, S. Rajaratnam School of International Studies, Nanyang Technological University, 2004), 28–29, 31–32.

12. Tan, "Force Modernization Trends in Southeast Asia," 30–31.

13. Richard Lloyd Parry, "Singapore Accused of Land Grab as Islands Disappear by Boatload," *The Times*, March 17, 2007.

14. SIPRI Military Expenditure Database, http://milexdata.sipri.org.

15. See www.rsis.edu.sg/nts/programmes.html.

16. Peter Chalk, Angel Rabasa, William Rosenau, and Leanne Piggott, *The Evolving Terrorist Threat to Southeast Asia: A Net Assessment* (Santa Monica, CA: RAND, 2009), 87–103.

17. Chalk et al., *The Evolving Terrorist Threat to Southeast Asia*, 149–65.

18. Ibid., xiii.

19. Ibid., xiv; "NPAs Down to 5,700," *ABS-CBN News Online*, www.abs-cbnnews.com/? StoryId=104670.

20. Ralf Emmers, "ASEAN's Wider Architecture: The Future of the ARF, APT, and EAS" (briefing, September 23, 2009).

21. Lucy Williamson, "South East Asia to Launch Charter," *BBC News*, December 15, 2008, http://news.bbc.co.uk/2/hi/asia-pacific/7783073.stm.

22. Emmers, "ASEAN's Wider Architecture."

23. Australian Department of Foreign Affairs and Trade, "ASEAN Regional Forum," June 26, 2009, www.dfat.gov.au/arf.

24. IISS, "Responding to the Maritime Challenge in Southeast Asia," in *Military Balance 2006* (London: IISS, 2006), 258.

25. Emmers, "ASEAN's Wider Architecture."

26. See www.rsis-ntsasia.org/ourConsortium/introduction.html.

27. Storey, "China and Vietnam's Tug of War over Laos"; Storey, "China and the Philippines"; Storey, "Progress and Remaining Obstacles in Sino-Indonesian Relations"; Robert Karniol, "Country Briefing: Vietnam—Off the Ground," *Jane's Defense Weekly*, December 22, 2005.

28. Ashley J. Tellis, "China's Grand Strategy," *Strategic Comments* 10, no. 9 (November 2004): 2.

29. IISS, "China, America, and Southeast Asia," 1.

30. Ralf Emmers, "What Explains the De-escalation of the Spratlys Dispute?" IDSS Commentaries no. 124, Institute of Defence and Strategic Studies, Nanyang Technological University, December 5, 2006.

31. Emmers, "What Explains the De-escalation of the Spratlys Dispute?"

32. David Shambaugh, "China and Europe: The Emerging Axis," *Current History* 103, no. 674 (September 2004): 246. See also Tellis, "China's Grand Strategy," 2; and Richard Carney and Richard A. Bitzinger, "From Hegemony to Loose Bipolarity: The Evolving Geopolitics of the U.S., E.U. and China," RSIS Commentaries no. 5, S. Rajaratnam School of International Studies, Nanyang Technological University, January 26, 2007.

33. Kuik Cheng-Chwee, "The Essence of Hedging: Malaysia and Singapore's Response to a Rising China," *Contemporary Southeast Asia* 30, no. 2 (2008).

34. Emmers, "ASEAN's Wider Architecture."

35. Adapted from ibid.

36. Chalk et al., *The Evolving Terrorist Threat to Southeast Asia*, xiii.

15

East Asia and Its Evolving Security Architecture

Hitoshi Tanaka and Adam P. Liff

For several decades, East Asia has been relatively free of major military conflict. Remarkable economic growth has facilitated deeper cooperation and widespread interdependence. In this context, throughout East Asia the concept of "security threat" has evolved to include not only traditional security issues but also nontraditional and transnational security issues, many of which are not necessarily directly linked to potential interstate military conflict. Despite an emerging consensus on the gradually changing nature of security threats, however, perceptions concerning matters of degree and exigency continue to differ among nations in the region.

This chapter will examine security challenges in East Asia and the region's approach to conflict management. It will also explore and assess the efficacy of the region's efforts to tackle these challenges. Most current approaches are necessary but insufficient to adequately ensure that nontraditional and transnational security issues do not become serious threats to regional stability. Unfortunately, despite widespread awareness of the severity of existing challenges, East Asia has thus far lacked a cogent and pragmatic vision for a way forward. Failure to tackle these challenges more proactively risks compromising the region's future peace and prosperity. This chapter concludes with a proposal for a new East Asia security architecture.

General Circumstances in East Asia

Before identifying specific security challenges in East Asia, it may be worthwhile to provide a brief overview of the major actors and general circumstances in the region.

China

East Asia is in the midst of a remarkable transformation, the most salient manifestation of which is the extraordinary rise of China. Although most economies in the region suffered steep declines in GDP growth—or even negative growth—during the nadir of the financial and economic crisis that began in 2008, China's economy continued to expand, and in 2010 it surpassed Japan to become the second largest in the world. In addition to its role as a major engine of global economic growth, China has also become a key player in the fields of security affairs, energy, and the environment and is seeking a political standing in regional and global affairs commensurate with its growing economic weight. As will be addressed, China is also in the midst of a rapid military expansion. One of the long-term implications of these developments is a substantial increase in China's global influence.

India

Right next door to China is India, another nation with a billion-plus population whose economy and international political influence are expanding at a brisk pace. Over the past several years, the United States has made a concerted effort to deepen and expand ties with India. For many in East Asia, democratic India is seen as a potential balancer against rising China. This may help to explain why several governments in the region assiduously campaigned for India as well as fellow democracies Australia and New Zealand to be allowed to join the East Asia Summit (EAS) despite opposition from China.

Japan

While much of the attention in the Western press has been focused on the rise of China and India, Japan—the world's third largest economy—is embarking on a substantial transformation of its own.

Over the past two decades, Japan has sought to become a more active player in regional and global affairs. However, its continuing economic struggles have frustrated those efforts. One prerequisite for Japan adopting a more active posture outside its borders in the years ahead is greater political stability at home. Ever since the opposition Democratic Party of Japan (DPJ) took control of the House of Councillors in summer 2007, domestic politics have reached an impasse. It is patently obvious now that political realignment, reform, and strong leadership are sine qua non if Japan is to play a more assertive leadership role in East Asia. The DPJ's landslide victory in the August 30, 2009, general election was a historic event, the full significance of which will not be understood for several years. However, the DPJ's poor showing in the summer 2010 House of Councillors election, in which it failed to gain a majority, leave it an open question whether the DPJ will be able to fully implement its reform agenda and bring long overdue change to Japanese politics.

One issue of growing concern since the mid-1990s is Japanese nationalism. Although the roots of Japan's rising nationalism are overdetermined, perhaps no single factor has been more salient than North Korea, due both to the existential threat posed by its nuclear-weapons and missile programs and the deep-seated antipathy and rancor many Japanese feel toward it because of the abduction issue. How this nationalism evolves in the coming years will have a significant impact on how the rest of East Asia views Japan and, consequently, to some extent determine the kind of role that Japan is able to play in the region.

United States

There is no doubt that America's global influence has experienced a relative decline over the past several years. Some of this has been self-inflicted (e.g., the damage done to America's global image as a result of several U.S. foreign policy missteps during the past decade, the financial crisis, etc.), while some is due to inexorable structural changes occurring in the international system.

Since the end of the Second World War, U.S. policymakers have understood the strategic significance of East Asia and have diligently worked to ensure stability in the region. In the post–Cold War era, the U.S. "hub-and-spoke" system of alliances and security arrangements in the region continues to serve as a guarantor of stability. As economies in East Asia continue to expand and the region becomes increasingly integrated in the years ahead, the significance of East Asia to U.S. interests will only increase. Despite this, Washington's attention during the first decade of the twenty-first century was focused elsewhere, particularly toward the Middle East and South Asia. This trend worried many East Asian leaders, who continue to see America's military presence and engagement with the region as essential for stability and sustained economic growth. Fortunately, the Obama administration came into office with the intention of making East Asia a U.S. foreign policy priority. Despite a few missteps, it has largely kept its word: it has reinvigorated its diplomacy toward the region (e.g., by joining the East Asia Summit) and strengthened alliances.

North Korea

One constant in any discussion of circumstances in East Asia is the matter of North Korea—a small, impoverished nation of only 24 million people that has caused more headaches for policymakers in Northeast Asia and the United States over the past two decades than arguably any other regional issue. North Korea's numerous provocations over the past four years, including two nuclear tests, multiple missile tests, the March 2010 sinking of the South Korean corvette Cheonan, and the November 2010 shelling of Yeonpyeong Island, coupled with the difficulty of restarting the Six-Party Talks, do not bode well for the prospects of denuclearizing the Korean Peninsula. There are also concerns that the forthcoming transfer of power to Kim Jong-Il's son, Kim Jong-un could lead to further provocations and instability on the Korean Peninsula.

Association of Southeast Asian Nations

The member states of the Association of Southeast Asian Nations (ASEAN) have made remarkable progress in recent years in terms of economic growth and subregional political and economic integration. Examples of recent achievements include the ASEAN Charter's entry into force in December 2008, which established the group as a legal entity and committed heads of state to meetings twice a year, and the ASEAN leaders' pledge to formally establish an "ASEAN Community," with free-flowing goods, services, investment, and skilled labor by 2015. Despite these remarkable accomplishments, however, ASEAN nations continue to struggle to achieve sustainable development. Many face widespread governance issues, corruption, and environmental degradation, and widening gaps in economic and human development. Continuing political chaos in Thailand—which resulted in the cancellation and subsequent relocation of the Fourteenth ASEAN Summit several times—and the decision of Myanmar's leading opposition party—Daw Aung San Suu Kyi's National League for Democracy—to boycott that country's first election in two decades have raised serious questions about ASEAN's future course, in particular with regard to the role of democracy.[1] Over the next several years a leadership deficit of sorts is probably in the cards for ASEAN. At present, the long-term implications of these issues for stability in East Asia are unclear.

Russia

Although ostensibly a "Eurasian" nation, Russia's role in East Asian security issues has been limited. Although it is a member of the Six-Party Talks and will begin attending EAS meetings (along with the United States) in 2011, in recent years Russia has been overwhelmingly preoccupied with issues in the former Soviet "sphere of influence," including

NATO expansion and the planned U.S.-led missile defense systems in Eastern Europe. Although the recent resolution of a long-standing border dispute with China has provided Russia with some "breathing room," Moscow has serious strategic concerns about rapidly expanding Sino-Russian economic interdependence and China's growing influence in the Russian Far East. The natural diplomatic alternative is for Russia to engage Japan, but unless it makes a concerted effort to resolve the Northern Territories dispute and sign a peace treaty with Japan, it is unlikely that Tokyo would actively support Moscow's interests in East Asia. However, a recent diplomatic dispute between the two countries following President Dmitry Medvedev's visit to the Russian-held islands does not bode well for such a development. Thus, short of an unexpected development in the regional security situation—such as a major breakthrough in the Six-Party Talks—Russia is unlikely to become a major player in East Asian security affairs in the near future.

Emerging Issue: Regionalism

A final development of note is growing interest throughout East Asia in regionalism and community building. Multilateral dialogue in the region has proliferated at a rapid pace over the past two decades. Several joint statements from ASEAN+3 meetings (that is, meetings of ASEAN nations plus China, Japan, and South Korea)—most notably the 2005 Kuala Lumpur Declaration—and the EAS have demonstrated that the establishment of an East Asia community is a shared goal of nations in the region. The recent explosion of bilateral and multilateral free trade agreements, rising intraregional trade levels (second only to those of the European Union),[2] and widespread governmental support for the expansion of Asian bond markets and currency swap arrangements clearly indicate that regional integration is well under way. It is important to note that progress is no longer limited to market-driven economic and financial integration; rather, in recent years the concept of regionalism has evolved to also include multilateral cooperation in the political and security spheres. This trend is manifest in Southeast Asia, where ASEAN has made remarkable progress in terms of political integration, such as the entry into force of the ASEAN Charter and the decision to form an ASEAN Community.

Security Challenges in East Asia

While a number of developments in the post–Cold War era have allowed East Asian nations to achieve unprecedented levels of prosperity and, generally speaking, the security environment in the region has improved, several traditional security issues remain unresolved. Furthermore, a host of emerging nontraditional and transnational security challenges pose new and growing threats to regional stability.

Improvements in East Asia's security environment over the past several years are attributable to a confluence of factors—in particular, growing economic interdependence throughout the region, which has led to closer economic relations among states and, in turn, a growing appreciation of the inextricable link between regional stability and national prosperity. Although rising nationalism and a number of festering land-border and maritime territorial disputes remain issues of concern, it is unlikely that these tensions will foment open interstate conflict. In a remarkable development, diplomacy across the Taiwan Strait is arguably more constructive now than at any time in the past sixty years. The election of Chinese Nationalist Party (KMT) candidate Ma Ying-Jeou in Taiwan's March 2008 presidential election and the subsequent rapprochement between Beijing and Taipei augurs well for future stability in cross-strait ties. If this trend continues beyond Taiwan's next presidential election in 2012, it could potentially mitigate one of the two greatest threats to peace and stability in East Asia—and arguably the only issue with the potential to give rise to great-power conflict. It should be noted, however, that a major election victory by the (mostly proindependence) opposition Democratic Progressive Party (DPP) in 2012 could have a deleterious effect on the recent improvements in cross-strait ties.

Imminent Security Challenge: North Korea

North Korea's nuclear-weapons program has posed a clear and present danger to peace and stability in East Asia for the past two decades. In order to effectively contextualize current circumstances, it may prove useful to first present a brief overview of the origins of the issue.

First revealed in 1989, North Korea's nuclear ambitions fomented the first North Korea nuclear crisis in 1993–94, an event which pushed the United States and North Korea to the brink of war. Former U.S. president Jimmy Carter's visit to Pyongyang in 1994 helped to defuse the crisis and subsequent bilateral negotiations led to the Agreed Framework that October. This agreement led to a gradual reduction in tensions over the next several years. Beginning in 1998, South Korean president Kim Dae-Jung's "Sunshine Policy," which advocated engagement with North Korea, allowed for a historic North-South summit meeting in June 2000. It was at this meeting that the two sides issued the North-South Joint Declaration calling for economic cooperation, reunification, and humanitarian exchange.

Unfortunately, at the same time that inter-Korean ties were convalescing, North Korea's relations with Japan and the United States were rapidly deteriorating. On August 31, 1998, North Korea abruptly test fired a

Taepodong-1 missile over the Japanese archipelago. This provocative act terrified the Japanese public, strengthened domestic support for a hard-line policy toward Pyongyang, and led the Japanese government to accelerate ballistic missile defense (BMD) cooperation with the United States. In stark contrast to several diplomatic overtures toward Pyongyang in the waning days of the Clinton administration, President George W. Bush came into office in 2001 advocating an uncompromising approach toward North Korea—manifest in the notorious "axis of evil" statement during his 2002 State of the Union address. As a result, constructive dialogue with North Korea ground to a halt during the Bush administration's first term.

In a bid to ease tensions between Japan and North Korea, a summit meeting was held in September 2002 between Prime Minister Junichiro Koizumi and Kim Jong-Il. This meeting culminated in the signing of the Pyongyang Declaration, in which the two sides agreed on a set of basic principles for diplomatic normalization. Kim pledged to extend a moratorium on missile testing, admitted that North Korean agents had abducted Japanese citizens in the 1970s and 1980s, and promised to comply with international agreements on nuclear issues. This salubrious development ushered in a period of relative optimism and within less than a year the first round of the Six-Party Talks was held in Beijing.

Unfortunately, the Six-Party Talks were unable to forestall North Korea's July 2006 missile tests and October 2006 nuclear-weapons test. In the United Nations' strongest censure of North Korea since the end of the Korean War, Security Council Resolution 1718 unanimously condemned the nuclear test and authorized economic and commercial sanctions against the North Korean regime. Resolution 1718 was followed by a resumption of the Six-Party Talks and bilateral discussions between the United States and North Korea in Berlin, two developments which effectively paved the way for the third phase of the fifth round of talks in Beijing and the subsequent release of the Six-Party Joint Statement on February 13, 2007.

Although there was a great deal of optimism immediately following this joint statement—indeed, North Korea blew up a cooling tower in June 2008 in keeping with an earlier agreement—circumstances have since rapidly devolved. North Korea's recent provocations do not bode well for the prospects of denuclearization on the Korean Peninsula. North Korea's second nuclear test on May 25, 2009, essentially nullified the accomplishments of the Six-Party Talks over the past six years. Further complicating an already volatile situation, Kim Jong-Il's declining health has raised concerns about succession and the nature of the impact his death would have on North Korea's future.

Needless to say, twenty years of negotiations with Pyongyang have failed to achieve the international community's basic objective: an end to North Korea's nuclear-weapons program. There are three fundamental reasons why the North Korea issue remains unresolved despite the considerable diplomatic resources that have been dedicated to addressing it.

First, the government of Kim Jong-Il represents arguably the most despotic and reclusive regime in the world. The country's leaders are plagued by a siege mentality that has convinced them that the rest of the world (or at least the United States) is intent on destroying their nation. They see nuclear weapons as the only insurance powerful enough to deter a "hostile foreign power." They neglect their starving people and invest North Korea's limited resources disproportionately into the military, including its nuclear program. Now that North Korea has acquired what seems to be at least a minimally functional nuclear deterrent, it will be very difficult to convince its leaders to denuclearize.

Second, the major powers involved in the Six-Party Talks have differing perceptions of the North Korean nuclear threat. For example, many Chinese do not believe that North Korea's nuclear program poses a direct threat to China's interests. Rather, Beijing is primarily concerned about the possibility of regime collapse in North Korea, a development that it fears could dramatically increase tensions on the Korean Peninsula and potentially trigger a massive flood of North Korean refugees across the Chinese border. In a worst-case scenario, regime collapse could also force a precipitous reunification of the two Koreas. Since this development would most likely result in South Korea absorbing North Korea, many Chinese fear that the loss of a major strategic buffer (a role North Korea has played for more than half a century), together with the possibility that U.S. troops currently stationed in South Korea would be deployed near the Chinese border, would have serious ramifications for China's national security. Additionally, it should be noted that many Chinese see China's experience with economic development since 1978 as a model for North Korea. They take a long-term view of the nuclear issue and see "reform and opening up" as the only practical way to bring the North Korean regime out of its international isolation and eventually achieve peace and stability on the Korean Peninsula. This view is one of the main drivers behind Beijing's efforts to boost trade with North Korea and encourage Pyongyang to implement market-oriented economic reforms.

Although many South Koreans still see North Korea as a conventional military threat, most are not overly intimidated by North Korea's nuclear weapons program. Generally speaking, South Korean leaders are aiming for a "soft landing" in order to minimize the possibility of sudden regime collapse, as abrupt reunification would undoubtedly have a deleterious impact on South Korea's economy. However, it should be stressed that public sentiment in South Korea about its northern neighbor is very complex, particulary in the wake of North Korea's sinking of a South Korean corvette and shelling of Yeonpyeong Island—two provocations that were directly responsible for the deaths of fifty South Koreans.

Of the countries involved in the Six-Party Talks, Japan is probably the country most threatened by North Korea's nuclear program; many believe that if North Korea were to use a nuclear weapon, Japan would be the most likely target. In addition to the existential threat posed by North Korea's nuclear and missile programs, Japanese public sentiment about the abductee issue should also not be overlooked. In fact, the abductee issue is arguably the single greatest factor behind the hard-line posture that Tokyo has adopted toward Pyongyang over the past several years. This approach was manifest most recently in Japan's April 2009 decision to unilaterally reauthorize and strengthen economic sanctions against North Korea.

Although the United States is certainly concerned about North Korea's nuclear weapons program, many—particularly in Japan—fear that the main priority of the United States has shifted from denuclearization to counterproliferation—that is, preventing Pyongyang from sharing its missile and nuclear-weapons technology with other nations or nonstate actors. President Barack Obama's April 5, 2009, speech in Prague in which he called for a "world without nuclear weapons," coupled with U.S. indignation in the wake of North Korea's nuclear weapons test seven weeks later, seemed to evince a clear shift in policy toward a focus on denuclearization. Although the Obama administration's steadfast support of its South Korean ally in the wake of North Korea's recent provocations has reinvigorated the U.S.-South Korea alliance and may deter further attacks, it remains unclear whether the allies' priority is merely containment or also includes denuclearization.

Third, the lack of continuity in North Korea policy between successive administrations in the United States, Japan, and South Korea also represents a major obstacle to solving the nuclear issue. For example, during the first term of President George W. Bush, the United States took a very hard line against the North Korean regime, to the point that there were even less-than-subtle threats that the administration would use military force to remove Kim Jong-Il from power. In contrast, during the Bush administration's second term, the United States was much more open to engagement via both the Six-Party Talks and bilateral negotiations. In Japan the government's approach to North Korea over the past decade has also been inconsistent. This has even been true among successive LDP administrations, whose approaches to North Korea can be summarized as shifting between engagement (Koizumi), a hard-line (Abe), engagement

(Fukuda), and a hard-line (Aso). Meanwhile, in South Korea, the more hard-line "nonnuclear, openness, 3000" policy of the current Lee Myong-Bak administration contrasts sharply with the active engagement and summit diplomacy pursued by his predecessor—the late Roh Moo-Hyun.

The absence of a united front and policy consistency among the five parties has created an environment of indecisiveness, allowing the North Korean regime to effectively exploit policy differences and play governments off one another to great effect. Henceforth, more extensive collaboration among the states involved—as well as greater cohesion and consistency in policy—will be essential.

Long-Term Security Challenge: China

At present, it is clear that China's leaders are focused on domestic concerns and have little interest in overseas adventurism. They believe that internal problems can only be solved by economic development. As long as China depends on trade and an influx of foreign investment and technology to maintain its rapid economic growth, it will continue to seek stable ties with its neighbors and embrace its growing interdependence with the rest of the world. Put another way, for the foreseeable future the likelihood that China will aim to overthrow the U.S.-led Western system—of which it has been a key beneficiary—is minimal. Evidence of China's status quo orientation is manifest in China's attitude toward the U.S.-Japan security alliance, which is now more widely seen as a stabilizing force in East Asia than a major threat to Chinese interests. Although there are signs that China's growing influence and confidence will lead it to play an increasingly assertive and largely positive role in global conflict management concerning issues related to Iran, North Korea, peacekeeping, climate change, and reform of international institutions (e.g., the United Nations, the International Monetary Fund, and World Bank), a number of reasons for concern exist.

The first, and principal, concern relates to China's rapid military expansion and its relatively low military transparency.[3] China shares land borders with fourteen nations—including three nuclear-weapons states (not including North Korea)—and does not enjoy a security alliance with any nation. Given the somewhat precarious geostrategic environment in which China finds itself, it is perhaps understandable that its leaders have taken advantage of rapid economic growth to modernize the People's Liberation Army (PLA). However, given the pace of its military expansion—the PLA budget has increased by double-digit percentages in nineteen of the past twenty years—failure to introduce significantly greater transparency will exacerbate existing concerns about China's strategic intentions and increase the possibility of grave miscalculation.

China's resistance to "reciprocity" in military-to-military ties with the United States and its increasingly provocative behavior in the South and East China Seas have raised questions about China's willingness to observe international norms of conduct and exacerbated fears about its rapidly expanding military capabilities. Recent years have also seen growing concern about the extent to which China's political leadership is aware of and able to control the actions of the PLA. Long a concern of China watchers, the exigency of this issue was made abundantly clear by China's January 11, 2007, satellite intercept test, a provocative and controversial action that China's Foreign Ministry did not publicly confirm until twelve days after the test and six days after it had first been reported in the Western press. The peculiar circumstances surrounding this incident led some observers to suspect that at least some top government leaders had not been informed about the test in advance.

A second set of concerns relates to China's political governance. Despite the gradual liberalization of Chinese society over the past three decades, human rights issues, strict limits on political freedoms, and the absence of significant progress toward major political reform remain troubling. Endemic corruption and issues related to the treatment of minorities (particularly in China's western provinces) have exacerbated these systemic problems. Beijing continues to take umbrage at Western criticism, disparaging calls for greater transparency and political reform as foreign meddling in China's internal affairs. However, it should be noted that the potential impact of China's political governance problems transcends national boundaries. Any major domestic instability would inevitably have an adverse effect on China's economic growth and industrial output, which would in turn have serious ramifications for the regional and global economy and for stability in East Asia. Official Chinese government statistics have revealed a remarkable upsurge in incidents of domestic unrest over the last several years and it seems clear that the only practical long-term solution to stem the tide is gradual political reform. Needless to say, regime collapse, although perhaps difficult to imagine at present, would have a devastating impact on East Asia.

A third set of concerns relates to China's economic governance—in particular, the rapidly expanding gap between rich and poor, the country's very low energy efficiency (as calculated per unit of GDP), and serious and pervasive environmental degradation. Although recent efforts to address these problems—in particular, an exponential increase in investment in alternative energy—should be commended, the government must do much more to mitigate the negative externalities of China's rapid economic development. These problems not only are closely linked to the quality of life of the Chinese people—and thus a threat to domestic political stability in and of themselves—but also have serious ramifications beyond China's borders.

A fourth set of concerns about China's rise has emerged in response to China's foreign policy—in particular, its political, military, and economic ties with and backing of regimes such as those in Myanmar and Sudan. Although China's rise over the past three decades has been mostly peaceful and had a positive impact on the world, its leaders' reluctance to denounce egregious human rights abuses committed by these regimes has frustrated international efforts to provide succor to those in need. This hesitancy has raised doubts about the willingness of China's leaders to act responsibly when doing so runs counter to China's economic interests.

The fifth set of concerns relates to China's growing nationalist sentiment, most clearly manifest in widespread anti-Japanese demonstrations in 2004–05 and anti-Western sentiment (particularly against France) in the run-up to the 2008 Beijing Olympic Games. Since the beginning of China's "reform and opening up" period in 1978, the ideological legitimacy underpinning the Chinese Communist Party's rule has weakened and, particularly since the 1990s, the government has increasingly turned to "patriotic education" campaigns (with Japan more often than not as the target)—both in schools and through the media—as a means to buttress its legitimacy. How this nationalism evolves in the coming years will have a significant impact on how China's rise is viewed overseas.

China's importance as a major engine of the global economy, coupled with the need for its cooperation in tackling a host of regional and global nontraditional security issues such as energy security, infectious disease, maritime piracy, and global warming, ensure that any attempt to contain its rise would be horribly counterproductive. Rather, the world must proactively engage China in a web of rule-based communities to ensure that it adopts the mantle of a "responsible stakeholder" in international affairs. In addition to welcoming China's active participation in extant regional and global institutions, such as the nascent G20, the World Trade Organization, the ASEAN Regional Forum (ARF), ASEAN+3, and the East Asia Summit, new reforms and institutions may also be necessary.

Long-Term Security Challenge: Economic Growth as a Double-Edged Sword

East Asia's economic expansion brings both great opportunities and significant challenges. For example, China and India, representing 1.3 billion and 1.1 billion people, respectively, provide increasingly large markets for global exports and foreign investment as well as a supply of relatively low-wage (and increasingly skilled) labor. However, 2.4 billion people corresponds to roughly 37 percent of the global population and—barring remarkable scientific breakthroughs—further economic expansion and the changing lifestyles that come with increased prosperity will cause serious environmental damage and increased regional and global competition for limited water, food, and energy resources. The international community must expand its efforts to ensure that emerging nations are better able to achieve economic growth in a sustainable manner.

Long-Term Security Challenge: Nontraditional and Transnational Security Issues

At the same time that fears of interstate conflict in East Asia are declining, a host of "twenty-first century" nontraditional and transnational security issues have emerged as threats to peace and stability in the region. These threats—such as maritime piracy, energy security, human and drug trafficking, political instability, WMD proliferation, terrorism, natural disasters, infectious diseases, and environmental degradation—will give rise to a host of novel security challenges in the coming years.

Unfortunately, most measures that are useful for reducing the likelihood of interstate conflict are of limited utility in addressing many of the new threats that the region now faces. At the risk of oversimplification, in the case of traditional threats, stability can be achieved through deterrence. With nontraditional security challenges, however, stability can be achieved only through *proactive* and *cooperative* action. As these nontraditional threats emerge, peace and stability in the region will increasingly *necessitate* joint operations.

The Indian Ocean tsunami in 2004 and Cyclone Nargis in 2008—which together were responsible for the deaths of hundreds of thousands of people—serve as cases in point of not only the serious threat that nontraditional and transnational security issues pose to stability and prosperity in East Asia but also of the difficulty that existing regional institutions have fielding effective responses to these threats. A significant portion of the international community's response to the 2004 tsunami was provided by an ad hoc coalition led by the United States and including Japan, Australia, and India. In the case of Cyclone Nargis, the regional community failed to persuade a member of ASEAN—Myanmar—to accept relief supplies from the international community for several days, during which time tens of thousands of additional lives were lost.[4] The avian and swine influenzas are two more examples of potentially devastating transnational security threats that require proactive and cooperative multilateral responses.

Evaluating the Efficacy of Existing Approaches

While there is no doubt that the existing security architecture in East Asia—based mainly on a web of U.S.-centered bilateral security arrangements—will continue to play an integral role in deterring interstate conflict and preventing the materialization of traditional security threats for the foreseeable future, nontraditional and transnational security issues demand more cooperative and creative solutions. It is clear that current approaches are necessary but insufficient to effectively take on these new challenges.

Although there is a growing awareness throughout East Asia that these nontraditional and transnational security issues pose grave threats to regional peace and stability, very little in the way of functional cooperation has occurred. Existing security institutions in the region are either strictly bilateral (for example, most U.S. security arrangements) or multilateral "talk shops" that rarely, if ever, engage in proactive operations to combat these threats. As the definition of "security" evolves to include these emerging threats, the region's approach to conflict management must follow suit.

This section will present an evaluation of the effectiveness of several existing approaches to managing security issues in the region.

The ASEAN Way

The "ASEAN way" has been a core principle of diplomacy in Southeast Asia since the creation of ASEAN in 1967 and the introduction of the Treaty of Amity and Cooperation (TAC) in 1976. The procedural and behavior norms it encapsulates—consensus-based decision making, the inviolability of state sovereignty, and stringent adherence to the principle of nonintervention—have been remarkably effective at maintaining stability and preventing major interstate conflict in Southeast Asia over the past four decades. Its nonconfrontational approach has simultaneously helped to foster a sense of regional identity and facilitated greater security cooperation in the region.

While it is important to be sensitive to the context in which ASEAN was originally conceived and acknowledge the remarkable contributions that the "ASEAN way" has made to peace and stability in the subregion, it is clear that many of the particular qualities that made it so successful in the past now pose major obstacles to proactive cooperation in order to address emerging nontraditional and transnational security challenges. The current emphasis on behavior and procedural norms—in particular, achieving consensus through conference-based diplomacy rather than action—must be reconsidered. States must be free to engage in coordinated multilateral operations without being held hostage by the veto of a single nation. The norms of noninterference and "quiet diplomacy" cannot be upheld as sacrosanct when the region is faced with a sudden transnational security threat such as a pandemic. Rather, a swift and proactive response is imperative in order to minimize spillover.

The ASEAN Regional Forum

In 1994, East Asian nations established the ARF as a multilateral institution for "regional confidence-building, preventive diplomacy, and political and security cooperation."[5] Unfortunately, the ARF has not had much success over the past fifteen years in bringing states together to engage in concrete security cooperation. Its membership is too large numerically (twenty-seven nations) and geographically (the European Union is a member). It has failed to play a meaningful role when confronted with serious and foreseeable threats to regional stability (for example, the North Korea nuclear issue) and unexpected natural disasters (for example, the 2004 tsunami). When ASEAN/ARF has responded to transnational security challenges, such as the haze issues in the late 1990s, the response has been "too little, too late." Its failure over the years to adequately prevent and respond to major security challenges has led many to question its viability as a framework for establishing and maintaining regional stability.

The ARF's main function is to convene training sessions and support groups, seminars, and meetings. In the past fifteen years, there has been only one example of the ARF carrying out an operational exercise—the Maritime Security Shore Exercise in Singapore in January 2007. It is doubtful whether current plans to set up a "quick-reaction group" (the Friends of the ARF Chair) will succeed in creating a mechanism to facilitate more expedient ARF-centered security cooperation.

In sum, although the ARF provides a very valuable service by facilitating ministerial dialogue, preventive diplomacy, training, and confidence building, its mandate is far too limited. East Asia faces a number of exigent nontraditional and transnational security threats that demand proactive responses. After fifteen years, the ARF has shown that it is unable to take up this challenge.

East Asia and Global Governance

If they are to stay relevant in a rapidly changing world, global institutions must be reformed to more accurately reflect the realities of the contemporary global balance of power and to more effectively address twenty-first century challenges such as climate change. The global order must be re-shaped to incorporate and constructively engage a host of rising powers—most prominently China and India, but also other nations such as Brazil, Russia, and South Africa. Global institutions must also become more proactive.

The UN Security Council is one example of a major global institution that is in desperate need of comprehensive reform. The Security Council's permanent membership is an anachronism, reflecting the global power distribution of 1946 rather than 2011. It must be made more representative; for instance, its membership should be expanded to include major global powers—in particular, East Asian nations such as Japan and India—as permanent members. As East Asia rises, its nations must be given a greater voice in global institutions.

For their part, East Asian nations must proactively contribute to ongoing efforts to consolidate a more stable order in the region. Doing so will not only complement efforts to strengthen global governance but will also be an integral building block of the future global system.

The Way Forward

A New Approach

East Asia is a very diverse region, not only in terms of its various ethnicities and religions but also with regard to its political systems and stages of economic development. This diversity may seem to pose an insuperable barrier to more extensive regional cooperation. However, many of the security challenges that the region faces—particularly in the field of nontraditional security—actually represent functional issues that all nations in the region have a shared interest in cooperatively addressing. The transnational nature of many of these threats became patently obvious with the regionwide swine flu (H1N1) scare in 2009. Continued failure to cooperate effectively in addressing such threats may have catastrophic consequences. In contrast to many traditional security threats, multilateral cooperation in confronting nontraditional and transnational security issues yields benefits that are not zero sum; rather, they serve the interests of all nations. More extensive security cooperation in the region *is* feasible; it merely requires that leaders acknowledge the nature and severity of these threats and decide to act.

There are clear precedents for states in the region jointly confronting challenges and crises. The ASEAN+3 framework grew out of the 1997–98 Asian financial crisis and the realization among governments in the region that multilateral efforts to establish currency stability were necessary in order to ensure regional financial and economic stability. This initiative also laid the groundwork for more extensive cooperation among the ASEAN+3 states and what would ultimately become the EAS in 2005. Other salient examples include the Six-Party Talks—established to address the second

North Korea nuclear crisis—and multinational relief efforts in the wake of the 2004 tsunami.

Going forward, East Asian nations should adopt a functional, action-oriented, and inclusive approach to cooperation. This approach would invite states to proactively cooperate in conducting voluntary and coordinated joint operations to tackle specific challenges. In other words, the aim would not be to create yet another venue in the region to merely discuss these problems; rather, the focus would be on working together to proactively address them. The voluntary nature of these operations would allow states that do not wish to be involved in a particular operation to abstain from participation. However, no state would be able to fall back on the "ASEAN way" and its emphasis on consensus-based decision making to "veto" or otherwise prevent any other nation from participating in these operations.

It is imperative that this cooperative approach be inclusive in nature. Any discriminatory conditions or prerequisites for membership that would exclude certain nations from participation would be counterproductive. East Asia is simply too diverse and participation from as many countries as possible in tackling these issues is too important. For example, values-based or political system–based (for example, "democracies only") approaches are nonstarters.

In the long term, cooperative efforts to tackle nontraditional and transnational security issues will help to resolve the specific problems themselves, and a functional, inclusive approach will also gradually deepen trust among states and establish a norm in East Asia of addressing shared challenges through cooperative action. In time, deeper trust may facilitate closer coordination in addressing more sensitive, traditional security issues. At the very least, it should mitigate distrust and suspicion of one another's intentions, thereby minimizing the risk of threat inflation and/or a disastrous strategic miscalculation.

A New Vision for East Asia's Security Architecture

East Asia is in need of a multilayered and inclusive security architecture to facilitate more extensive multilateral security cooperation in the region. The ideal architecture would aim to forestall the materialization of potential threats to regional stability and, in the event that prevention efforts are unsuccessful, engage states in proactive and joint operations to tackle these threats. It would be predicated on a belief that a functional, action-oriented, and inclusive approach to security will succeed in engaging East Asian states in cooperative actions to address issues of shared concern. This architecture would be centered on three pillars: (1) strengthening and reforming security arrangements and strategic dialogue between the

United States and its partners in East Asia, as well as institutionalizing a mechanism for regular trilateral strategic dialogue among the United States, Japan, and China; (2) laying the groundwork for the Six-Party Talks to eventually evolve into a permanent subregional forum to facilitate multilateral dialogue and cooperation among Northeast Asian states on security issues beyond North Korea's nuclear program; and (3) creating an East Asia Security Forum (EASF) as an institution tasked with bringing states together to tackle nontraditional and transnational security issues through joint operations.

Pillar 1: Bolstering and reforming U.S. security arrangements and institutionalizing U.S.-Japan-China trilateral strategic dialogue. While multilateral joint operations to address functional issues are necessary, for the foreseeable future East Asia will continue to depend on the existing system of U.S. security arrangements in the region as a hedge against future uncertainties. The United States and its partners in East Asia must work to ensure that these security arrangements (in particular the U.S.-Japan alliance) remain robust and continue to function as a powerful deterrent against any potential aggressors. Existing bilateral links should be supplemented by bolstering "minilateral" institutions, such as the fora for strategic dialogue among the United States, Japan, and South Korea, and the United States, Japan, and Australia. These nations must use these minilateral institutions as venues to discuss how the "hub-and-spoke" system of U.S. security arrangements can evolve to better complement a more inclusive regional cooperative security system and to more effectively serve as a public good. The recent trilateral summit between China, Japan, and South Korea bodes well for these efforts. As dialogue and cooperation deepens among East Asian states, the potential for conflict due to disputes over territory or history will decrease.

While existing U.S.-centered security arrangements in East Asia must be strengthened as a security guarantee, the region must also establish new and inclusive mechanisms to facilitate multilateral security cooperation. For example, a more concerted effort must be made to deepen security relations and reduce mistrust among the United States, Japan, and China. With this objective in mind, these three states should immediately institutionalize a mechanism for trilateral strategic dialogue. This framework would complement existing bilateral dialogue, promote military and strategic transparency, and build confidence. It could also be used in the future as a venue for trilateral cooperation to address nontraditional and transnational issues of common concern such as energy security and the environment.

Pillar 2: North Korea and the Six-Party Talks. There is no question that North Korea's recent provocations have frustrated efforts to denuclearize the Korean Peninsula. Nevertheless, the stakes remain as high as ever and the international community must continue to pursue verifiable denuclearization. In order to achieve this objective, the five parties must make a concerted effort to ensure that the obstacles discussed earlier in this chapter do not continue to frustrate progress. In particular, presenting a united front is crucial.

All UN Security Council resolutions regarding the North Korean nuclear program that have been passed up to this point must be implemented with steadfast determination. The UN Security Council must respond swiftly and resolutely to all future North Korean provocations, condemning any further nuclear tests and enacting strong sanctions against Pyongyang. At the same time that the international community actively addresses the proliferation threat, all five parties must also work to bring Pyongyang back to the negotiating table. In addition to resuming the Six-Party Talks, Japan, the United States, and South Korea should also hold concomitant bilateral negotiations with North Korea. For its part, Japan must play a more constructive role in negotiations; its leaders must accept that the abductee issue cannot be resolved outside of a comprehensive settlement between Pyongyang and the other five nations. This comprehensive settlement must include complete and verifiable denuclearization, a concrete road map for normalizing North Korea's relations with Japan and the United States that includes concrete plans for economic cooperation, and a peace regime that formally ends the Korean War and begins reducing tensions on the Korean Peninsula.

Throughout this process, China's role will be particularly crucial. Unfortunately, however, as previously discussed, China's position on the issue of North Korean denuclearization is complex. At the same time that Chinese leaders fear that an excessively hard-line (for example, tough sanctions, etc.) might precipitate the collapse of the North Korean regime, they are also seriously concerned that North Korea as a de facto nuclear state might give rise to a nuclear arms race in East Asia. In particular, China views the prospect of Japan "going nuclear" as inimical to its security interests and completely unacceptable.[6] Further complicating an already messy situation is the increasingly close trade relationship between Beijing and Pyongyang. The effect of international sanctions and the recent sharp decline in South Korea's and Japan's trade with North Korea has basically been negated by a concomitant upsurge in North Korea's trade with China.[7]

A soft landing is clearly in the interest of all states. However, given that Pyongyang sees everything through the mirror of power and incessantly threatens military responses to various "acts of war" committed by the United States, South Korea, and Japan, the parties must always be prepared for the possibility of open conflict. North Korea's attacks on South Korea during 2010 have made the reality of this threat abundantly clear. It is imperative that contingency planning—not only concerning military tactics but also with regard to how to evacuate noncombatants and respond to a possible refugee crisis—be carried out in an earnest and discreet manner.

Once the North Korea nuclear issue has been resolved, Northeast Asia would benefit from the continued existence of the Six-Party Talks as a subregional forum for security dialogue. Although this forum's primary task would be to oversee the implementation of the five parties' comprehensive settlement with North Korea, in time its mandate could expand to cover other security issues and consolidate more stable and constructive political and security ties among the six nations.

Pillar 3: East Asia Security Forum. As previously discussed, East Asia faces a growing number of nontraditional and transnational security issues that pose increasingly serious threats to regional stability. With leadership from Japan, China, South Korea, and the United States, the region should establish an EASF under the auspices of the EAS to proactively tackle these issues. This forum would engage East Asian nations in inclusive, action-oriented, and functional cooperation through joint military-based security operations similar to the Proliferation Security Initiative. Its membership would be limited to the members of ASEAN+6 (that is, the ten nations of ASEAN plus Japan, South Korea, China, India, Australia, and New Zealand) and the United States. The EASF, under the EAS, would have two major objectives (see figure 15.1).

The EASF's first objective would be to bring East Asian states together to jointly address those nontraditional security issues that demand military-based operations, such as those related to nuclear proliferation, natural disasters, terrorism, maritime piracy, and transnational crime. In this sense, the EASF would serve to complement both existing EAS dialogue mechanisms and the ARF, which could be responsible for engaging a much larger group of members in dialogue and preventive diplomacy on traditional security issues. Participation in EASF operations would be voluntary and, as such, not violate the Treaty of Amity and Cooperation's norms of mutual respect for state sovereignty and noninterference. Furthermore, the target of these efforts would not be other states but issues of shared concern: the very nontraditional security threats themselves.

The second objective of the EASF would be to contribute to ongoing efforts in East Asia to deepen inclusive multilateral cooperation. Partici-

Figure 15.1   Proposed Security Framework for the East Asia Summit

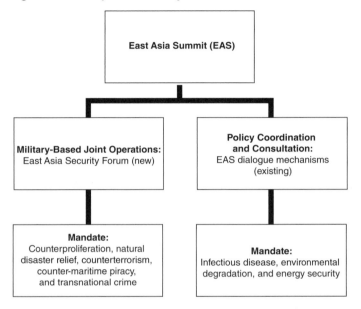

pation in the EASF would help to establish a norm in the region of addressing common challenges in a manner that is cooperative, voluntary, and functional. Given that its mandate would be to tackle nontraditional and transnational security issues, the EASF would function as an effective complement to existing traditional and more deterrence-oriented mechanisms in the region, such as the aforementioned U.S. "hub-and-spoke" system of bilateral security arrangements.

Notes

1.   "Main Opposition to Boycott Myanmar Election," *New York Times,* March 29, 2010.

2.   Based on 2005 data, the level of trade among countries in East Asia has already reached 55 percent, a rate higher than NAFTA (45 percent) and quickly approaching the level of the European Union (60 percent). See Masahiro Kawai, "Toward a Regional Exchange Rate Regime in East Asia," Asian Development Bank Institute Discussion Paper No. 68, June 2007, www.adbi.org/files/dp68.exchange.rates.east.asia.pdf.

3.   China announced a "modest" 14.9 percent increase in its defense expenditures for 2009, which brings the total to 480.6 billion yuan (approximately US$70.2 billion). See "China to Boost Military Spending," *BBC News,* March 4, 2009. In 2010, the government unexpectedly announced a 7.5 percent increase in defense expenditures. It remains to be seen whether this significant drop in the rate of increase is merely a consequence of the global recession or marks the beginning of a long-term trend. See "China's Defense Budget

to Grow 7.5% in 2010: Spokesman," *China Daily*, March 4, 2010, www.chinadaily.com.cn/china/2010-03/04/content_9537753.htm.

4. "Myanmar Faces Pressure to Allow Major Aid Effort," *New York Times*, May 8, 2008.

5. Chairman's statement from the First Meeting of the ASEAN Regional Forum, July 25, 1994.

6. Indeed, North Korean provocations have been the main driver of recent moves to bolster Japan's defensive capabilities through cooperation with the United States on missile defense and the acquisition of spy satellites. Japan may be able to use the "nuclear card" as an effective tool with which to push China to increase pressure on North Korea to denuclearize. It should be stressed, however, that it is highly unlikely that Japan would seriously consider acquiring nuclear weapons. The domestic and international political costs—not to mention the impact on its alliance with the United States—would be extremely high. Nevertheless, if North Korea continues to seek international recognition as a nuclear-weapons state, debates in Japan may become increasingly nationalistic.

7. Trade between China and North Korea reached a record US$2.79 billion in 2008, a 41 percent increase from the year before. See "China, North Korea Trade Boom Despite Rocket Tensions," *Agence France-Presse*, April 5, 2009. In 2008, trade with China represented 73 percent of total North Korean trade. See "North Korea Newsletter No. 86," *Yonhap News Agency*, December 24, 2009.

16

Institutional Mechanisms for Conflict Resolution in South America

Monica Herz

South America has systematically been characterized as a peaceful region,[1] where since the end of the nineteenth century peace has largely prevailed between states. Even though territorial disputes have been abundant in South America,[2] there have been only a few violent conflicts there since the end of the nineteenth century. The War of the Triple Alliance between 1864 and 1870 (Argentina, Brazil, Uruguay, and Paraguay) and the War of the Pacific between 1870 and 1883 (Chile and Bolivia) closed the period of interstate conflicts that started after the independence of South American countries from Spain and Portugal in the 1820s. Formal state apparatuses were consolidated and most remaining boundary disputes were settled peacefully. Throughout the twentieth century, the region witnessed very few instances of interstate war. They include the Chaco War in 1932 (Paraguay and Bolivia), the wars between Peru and Ecuador in 1941 and 1995, and the 1982 war between Argentina and the United Kingdom over the Malvinas/Falkland Islands. Several authors highlight the tendency in the region to seek pacific conflict resolution,[3] and it has become common to hear reference to the peaceful nature of international relations in the region.

Today violence is mostly absent from interstate relations in South America. Countries in the region spend a low percentage of GDP on arms and adhere to arms control regimes. Furthermore, the absence of weapons of mass destruction has been well established in the southern part of the hemisphere. The 1967 Tlatelolco Treaty, which aimed to create a nuclear-weapon-free zone in the whole of Latin America, is fully enforced. The adherence to arms control organizations is widespread and adherence to the Nuclear Non-Proliferation Treaty, the Chemical Weapons Convention, and the Biological and Toxin Weapons Convention is universal. As this author has argued elsewhere, it is unlikely that a security paradox will arise in the region as uncertainty is mostly managed through international institutions.[4]

This chapter looks into the conflict resolution mechanisms constructed in the region that both support this reality, are a result of the historical process that led to its inception, and may be available to deal with the security threats defined by present political debate in South America. It looks into the discourse on and practice of conflict management, the definition of security produced in the region in order to understand the role institutions can play, and the construction and change of institutions on the interstate level.[5] The chapter also investigates the institutional frameworks constructed during the last two decades and the discourses that represent a common agenda for official positions.

Multilateralism in South America

South America is a region of mostly small countries that, following the independence wars of the 1820s, dealt with the disputes between the great powers, first between Great Britain and France and later between the United States and the Soviet Union, over influence and resources. After the end of the World War II, the dominance of the United States was put at the center of the debates on the role and place of South American countries in the world.

In this context, multilateralism has been seen by national elites in South America as a form of protection from the asymmetry of power that marks international relations in the region. A rule-based system and the lawful and peaceful resolution of controversies are seen to preserve the sovereignty of countries that lack significant power resources. The legalist tradition, profoundly rooted in Latin American international culture and also relevant in inter-American relations more generally, is firmly associated with the norm of peaceful conflict resolution and reinforces it. This is part of a wider process of construction of shared meanings and intersubjective structures across the continent. A common language emerged, incorporating standards of legitimacy that emphasize the role of international law and diplomacy. Beth Simmons, for example, notes that there is a "propensity" to "submit to authoritative third-party legal rulings" in the region.[6] Andrew Hurrell, meanwhile, refers to a "diplomatic culture."[7]

It is indeed possible to identify a regional culture largely because of the level of interaction among most regional elites since independence. The history of treaties, organizations, and diplomatic negotiations, particularly since the end of the nineteenth century, reveals elements of continuity regarding practices of peaceful conflict resolution. But the ideas regarding the role of law and diplomacy and the emphasis on multilateral institutions only survive because they are reenacted in discourse and constitute part of the identity of ruling elites in South American countries. Indeed, lately this trend has been reenacted. In 1998, Peru and Ecuador finally settled their boundary dispute after a conflict that left nearly a thousand combatants dead in 1995,[8] and relations between Brazil and Argentina and between Argentina and Chile improved dramatically after the mid-1980s.[9]

These ideas are part of the ongoing building of a complex relationship between the region and the international system, where specificity and Western culture are bound by history. Thus, conflict resolution mechanisms are imported, created, and reinvented in South America.

Challenges for Multilateral Institutions in the 1990s

In the post–Cold War period, the multilateral regional network was revived and redesigned as formal democracy became universal, the pressures of globalization and regionalization became stronger in light of the growing number of issues that were seen to demand international cooperation, and foreign policies and bilateral relations generated an environment favorable to investment in conflict resolution mechanisms. More specifically, the United States opted for a multilateral approach to the region in the 1990s that favored the renewal of the Organization of American States (OAS), Brazil moved toward a foreign policy based on its leadership role in South America, Brazil and Argentina solved their disputes, and Chile opted for the Latin Americanization of its foreign policy.

In addition, the meaning of lawful, peaceful conflict resolution developed in the nineteenth century by the South American elites concerned with their place in the international system of sovereign nation-states was transported to the post–Cold War period, acquiring a new meaning with regard to conflicts with nonstate actors and conflicts regarding control over the state. The actual mechanisms for conflict resolution in the region, which have worked to avoid the escalation of violence between states and within states on several occasions, are nevertheless very limited given the present security environment in the region.

The relevance of institutional mechanisms for conflict resolution in South America has become clear. Tense relations between Venezuela and Colombia,[10] and the violation of Ecuadorian territorial sovereignty by Colombia,[11] are the most recent cases that point to this relevance. The disputes between Brazil and Ecuador over the investments of the Brazilian firm Oderbrecht and the National Bank of Economic Development and between Brazil and Bolivia regarding the production and commercialization of natural gas are examples of international tension generated by the profound social and political changes taking place in Venezuela, Ecuador, Bolivia, and Paraguay. Relations between Brazil and Paraguay have recently been marked by attempts to renegotiate the rules governing the co-ownership of the binational Itaipú hydro complex, and tension between Brazilian soya growers and the new Paraguayan administration are detectable. Argentina and Uruguay have an ongoing dispute about the construction of paper-pulp mills on the Uruguay River.[12]

Crucially, the countries of the region have opted for different paradigms regarding regional cooperation, international intervention, and relations with the United States. Venezuela, Bolivia, and Ecuador have elected left-wing governments with projects to transform their societies and are seeking radical realignments. Colombia has a strategic alliance with the United States, and Brazil, Argentina, and Uruguay are ruled by center-left governments that foster diversified relations in the international arena.

Boundary disputes still exist today and were sources of conflict in the past. The most severe disputes short of war in recent history include the near war between Argentina and Chile in 1978, and the tense relations between Chile, on the one hand, and Bolivia and Peru, on the other, in the late 1970s. The remaining territorial disputes in the region at present are between Peru, Chile, and Bolivia (Chile and Bolivia do not have diplomatic relations); Nicaragua and Colombia; Colombia and Venezuela; and Venezuela and Guyana.[13] The Malvinas/Falklands islands are also a territory in dispute, although this dispute involves an extraregional country, Great Britain.[14]

The war in Colombia is the most dramatic example of an enduring conflict marked by the escalation of violence domestically and repercussions regionally. Colombia has one of the largest internally displaced populations in the world. The International Campaign to Ban Landmines reports that Colombia had the highest number of land mine casualties in the world in 2008.[15] Colombia shares a 1,367-mile border with Venezuela, approximately 1,000 miles each with Peru and Brazil, and smaller borders with Ecuador and Panama. The conflict in Colombia and its associated drug trafficking have led to spillover effects in these neighboring countries.

The tensions on the border between Colombia and Ecuador and between Colombia and Venezuela due to the fight against the Colombian rebels in these areas and the wider dispute between Colombia, Ecuador, and Venezuela over the civil war in Colombia are continuing problems. Furthermore, the social and political transformations taking place in Andean countries generate intrastate conflict and regional tension.

News about South America in recent years has not featured wars and coup d'états, but reports about rampant corruption, gang warfare, drug and arms smuggling, intense urban poverty, and land disputes. Most local law enforcement agencies are poorly funded and equipped and are unable to deal with the level of criminalization sweeping the region. In addition, criminal activity is increasingly transnational, and only regional and international cooperation will allow the threats to individuals, groups, and the state to diminish. The social and economic problems that characterize the region could give rise to international conflicts over resources and migration. The fragility of domestic mechanisms for conflict resolution and of the state apparatuses in general has generated political crises throughout the history of the southern part of the Americas.

This complex reality generates violence, obstructs economic and social development, and affects democratic institutions. The need for regional and international conflict resolution mechanisms is undeniable.

The Definition of Security in South America

Since the end of the Cold War, a debate on the role of regional security mechanisms has been taking place in South America. It has been prompted by systemic changes and processes in the region, such as the transitions toward democracy, regional integration initiatives, the emergence of transnational criminality as one of the region's most pressing security problems, and the specificities of relations among regional countries. The debate on the concept of security developed since the 1980s in the academic and political worlds demands a closer look at the post–Cold War concept of security developed in South America. This debate takes place in both hemispheric and South American contexts.

The multilateral debate on the concept of security and the new demands for security present in the international agenda have taken place largely in the hemispheric context, with the leadership of the U.S. government having been crucial, particularly in the 1990s. The 2003 Special Security Conference that took place in Mexico is considered a reference point for the discussion of security in the Western Hemisphere more widely. Its Declaration on Security in the Americas defines security in multidimensional terms and calls for a flexible security architecture, including different levels of association.[16] Thus, the differences between states and groups of states should be respected. As always in hemispheric fora, the concept of sovereignty was reaffirmed.

During the 2003 conference, the difference in perspectives among the countries of the region became clear. Chile's representatives based their arguments on the concept of human security, Colombia's representatives stressed the threat posed by illegal armed groups, drug trafficking, and terrorism, and Argentinean and Brazilian officials focused on poverty as a threat in itself.[17] The declaration was the result of a process of change that took place since the end of the Cold War and that involved the hemisphere as a whole. The redefinition of the concept of security led to a shift from collective security to cooperative security and the incorporation of an expanded concept of security.[18]

The concept of cooperative security entails a stress on transparency and a focus on confidence-building measures that change relations between states and that prevent certain security dilemmas from developing. Such measures include agreements on prior notice of military exercises, the establishment of mutual confidence or security zones in border areas, rounds of talks between military high commands, and joint exercises.

The expanded concept of security allows for the perception of the interdependence between economic, social, political, and environmental issues and the threats and use of violence.[19] The idea that so-called new threats to security such as drug and arms trafficking, intrastate violence, and the institutional fragilities of states could be tackled in a multilateral context became acceptable. A new normative framework was generated and institutional mechanisms were produced. The definition of who could legitimately claim a need for protection and the dangers in focus were redefined. The protection of objects under threat, although still remaining the responsibility of the state, was a goal seen to be shared and dealt with in the context of intergovernmental forums.[20]

The specificity of the security of the South American region has become increasingly clear to both analysts and regional players. The attempts to create forms of cooperation and association that crystallize this new identity include the creation of the Union of South American Nations (UNASUR), the South American Security Council, and the Bolivarian Alternative for the Americas (ALBA),[21] and the development of a security role for the Common Market of the South (Mercosul) and the Community of Andean Nations (CAN).

The demise of the project for regional integration in the Americas, the need to invest in infrastructural integration in South America,[22] and the choices of left-leaning governments in several countries, which stressed the importance of South American integration in the context of social and political change, gave rise to a restoration of the idea of a South American region with a common destiny and strong common interests. The military dimension of the rapprochement between Brazil and Argentina in the 1980s and between Chile and Argentina in the 1990s and the peace operation experience of South American countries in Haiti since 2004 allowed for a vision of regional cooperation that included the security sphere.

In Haiti, in particular, the cooperation between South American countries is very clear. The level of coordination among South American governments and the participation of South American troops in the UN operation there established a landmark in the history of South American security and the engagement of the region in UN activities. Leadership of the operation has been structured to take this reality into consideration (since 2004, the force commander, deputy force commander, and the head of operations have all been South American). Chilean ambassador Juan Gabriel Valdés served as the UN secretary-general's special representative to Haiti from August 2004 to June 2006, and Brazil and Chile coordinated their efforts to the operation's mandate in 2004 and Argentina and Peru did the same in 2005 and 2006.[23]

Brazilian leadership regarding the definition of South America as a regional base for cooperation and the development of a regional identity has been crucial. Since the government of Itamar Franco (1992–93), Brazil has opted for an emphasis on regional cooperation in South America. As Monica Hirst points out, the foreign policy of the United States toward the region stimulated a differentiation between the subregions of the hemisphere. Hirst cites the creation of the North American Free Trade Agreement in 1994, the preferential regime involving the Caribbean and Central America, the formation of the North Commando in 2002, and, after the attacks of 9/11, the United States' definition of a zone of security that includes Mexico, Central America, and the Caribbean, as all stimulating emphasis on a South American identity.

Institutions Managing Security in South America

Conflict resolution mechanisms have been in place in the Western Hemisphere in general and South America in particular since the end of the nineteenth century, with the OAS and ad hoc groups having taken part in mediation efforts since World War II. Several documents and relevant meetings have incorporated this theme.[24] The institutions that have conflict management responsibilities in South America are either hemispheric in scope, involving South, Central, and North American countries, or are South American or subregional in scope. In some cases, the hemispheric architecture is seen as more suitable for a particular conflict, or is just available, while in others, South American mechanisms are in focus. Some institutions were created during the Cold War environment and have been going through a process of structural change since the beginning of the 1990s, while others have just been created. Ad hoc regional arrangements, such as the Rio Group,[25] the Guarantors of the Peru-Ecuador Treaty,[26] the Summit Meetings of Hemispheric Presidents,[27] the Meeting of Defense Ministers,[28] and the Summit Meetings of South American Presidents have played a relevant role in fostering an environment favorable to peaceful conflict resolution. Two specialized organizations deal with nuclear questions: the Agency for the Prohibition of Nuclear Weapons in Latin America and the Caribbean (OPANAL),[29] and the Brazilian-Argentine Nuclear Accounting Agency.[30] Institutions geared toward economic, cultural, and social integration, such as CAN, Mercosul, and UNASUR, also play a part in the creation and management of a common security agenda.

OAS

The OAS is the most institutionalized and oldest organization in the region that tackles different kinds of security problems. The OAS has had some success in reducing regional tensions and preventing conflicts from escalating.[31] It has functioned as a forum for the discussion of interstate as well as intrastate conflict since its creation. It has also been a major forum for the process of generating regional norms on security, for the peaceful solution of disputes, and for the association between democracy, stability, security, and arms control and the mechanisms to fight transnational criminality. In many instances, the OAS has supported the return to stability or status quo. Negotiations, mediation, technical support, verification, and observation missions are the instruments available to the organization.

After the end of the Cold War, the United States led an effort to re-energize the OAS. Thus, the range of activities in which the organization has been involved has grown notably and new capabilities have been generated. Several institutional changes took place and new agencies were created, such as the Committee on Hemispheric Security,[32] the Unit for the Promotion of Democracy, the Inter-American Drug Abuse Control Committee, and the Inter-American Committee against Terrorism. The OAS has also become active in fostering confidence-building measures and land mine clearing, and has continued its work on the dialogue on border disputes and attempts to prevent conflict. The OAS secretary general also acquired new responsibilities. He or she is now authorized to bring to the attention of the organization's General Assembly or Permanent Council matters that might threaten the peace, security, or the development of member states. The Education for Peace Program was also created.[33]

UNASUR

The recently created UNASUR is the result of a process of coordination among South American countries that has been taking place since 2000,[34] when the first Meeting of South American Presidents took place in Brasilia. Its creation became possible because of the development of the concept of a South American region as described.

At the Third South American Summit on December 8, 2004, presidents or representatives from twelve South American nations signed the Cuzco Declaration, a two-page statement of intent announcing the foundation of the South American Community. The organization, which is modeled on the European Union, is a long-term project that includes even the creation of a common currency. In 2007, its name was changed to UNASUR. The Constitutive Treaty of the Union was signed on May 23, 2008, at the Third Summit of Heads of State. The annual meeting of presidents is the ultimate decision-making forum, with foreign ministers meeting every six months. On December 15, 2008, during one of UNASUR's summits, the South American Defense Council was created. The union has proved to be relevant in intrastate conflict resolution both during the 2008 internal crisis in Bolivia and after the crisis generated by the accord between Colombia and the United States regarding the use of military bases.

Mercosur

On March 26, 1991, Brazil, Argentina, Uruguay, and Paraguay signed the Treaty of Asunción, creating the Common Market of the South (Mercosur). The 1994 Treaty of Ouro Preto gave the body a wider international status and formalized a customs union. Bolivia, Chile, Colombia, Ecuador, and Peru are associate members; Venezuela's full membership has since become a reality.

The Ushuaia Protocol of 1998 establishes that all countries of the organization should be democracies. At the same meeting, the countries declared the intent of the southern cone countries in cooperating in security and defense matters. In 1998, a multilateral mechanism for consultation and coordination for questions of international politics (Foro de Consulta y Concertación Política, or Political Consultation and Concert Forum) was created, thus answering the need for a special foreign minister forum for the subregion. In 2004, when Brazil and its partners in Mercosur became the main component of MINUSTAH, the debate was revived over whether the organization should have a common "military dimension."

Mercosur is geared toward economic integration, but it has a security dimension both as a forum for political coordination and as a mechanism for cooperation in the fight against transnational criminal activities.

Andean Community

The Andean Community was created in 1969 and the membership today includes Bolivia, Colombia, Peru, and Ecuador. Chile is an associate member. The organization is geared toward regional trade integration and political coordination. A free-trade area has been in effect since 1993. Since 2003, social development has been incorporated into the organization's objectives. In 2007, it created the Council of Indigenous People, incorporating into its agenda for the first time an important part of the population and a crucial issue for this part of the world.

The Andean Charter for Peace and Security established a peace zone in the Andean Community.[35] The charter includes several commitments: to ban land mines; to eradicate illicit trafficking in firearms, ammunition, explosives, and related materials; to consolidate the ban on nuclear, chemical, and biological weapons; to have Latin America declared a zone free from air-to-air missiles beyond visual range and medium- and long-range strategic missiles; and to continue the application and the strengthening of various confidence-building measures.

Interstate Violence

The possibility of interstate armed conflict in the Americas is low; nevertheless, as mentioned earlier, interstate disputes are present in South America and conflict resolution mechanisms in this sphere are necessary.

The OAS security structure was designed for collective security operations and for dispute settlement through diplomatic consultation. Chapter VI of the charter endorses the principle of collective security—an attack on one country is considered an attack on all. Regarding conflict between states in the hemisphere, the emphasis lies on peaceful means for the settlement of disputes. Chapter V outlines the procedures to promote this.

When a security threat is detected, either the charter of the OAS or the Rio Treaty may be invoked.[36] There is no established norm regarding which treaty is invoked and in some cases both documents have been used. The political process in each case will determine the selection. The difference in tone between Article 60 of the charter and Article 6 of the Rio Treaty may determine the choice of one or the other. The Rio Treaty indicates that stricter sanctions could be applied. The Permanent Council of the OAS meets and determines whether the request is justified and whether to convene the Organ of Consultation. Frequently, an investigating committee is formed and reports back to the Organ of Consultation. Finally, resolutions may be voted on. Several options are available: sending an observation committee, administering sanctions, or even using armed force. In addition, the special representatives and envoys of the secretary general are sent to engage in preventive diplomacy and mediation in the hemisphere's trouble spots and/or appointed to head OAS electoral observation missions. A look at the organization's sixty-year history reveals that it has had some success in reducing regional tensions and preventing conflicts from escalating.

Regarding the boundary disputes between countries in the Americas, the OAS has proved to be the only regional forum for conflict resolution. In the case of South America, the border tensions tackled by the organization are not specifically linked to territorial disputes. Border tension is present mostly as a result of the spillover effect of the war in Colombia.

An OAS verification commission was created to deal with the tensions between Ecuador and Colombia. Colombia continuously accuses Ecuador of harboring Fuerzas Armadas Revolucionarias de Colombia (FARC) guerrillas and Ecuador, on the other hand, accuses Colombia of violations of its sovereignty as a result of military incursions. The number of Colombian refugees reaching Ecuador has reached 250,000. The border area is extremely vulnerable to violence. The narco-economic activity carried on by competing irregular armed groups, the presence of refugees, the lack of military communication, and the lack of proper presence of state institutions produces a climate of uncertainty.

The severing of diplomatic relations between Colombia and Ecuador after Colombian troops killed Raul Reyes, the FARC commander, on Ecuadorian soil is the latest and clearest example of this tension. The OAS was the forum in which the issue was debated, with the organization adopting a resolution that says Colombia violated Ecuador's sovereignty by launching a military raid into its territory but that avoids a formal condemnation. The resolution also provided for the formation of a commission to visit Ecuador and Colombia to investigate the raid.

Relations between Colombia and Venezuela are marked by tension. The military pact that grants the United States access to seven bases in Colombia,[37] arms procurement in both countries, and the very different ideological stance of the governments currently in power have generated this situation. Furthermore, for many years kidnappings, contraband, and drug trafficking have been common in the border area. In this case, the

OAS has functioned as a forum where the leadership of the two countries can express their concerns, but proper mediation has not been possible.

Arms-control mechanisms play a vital role in security governance; they prevent conflict and may generate the confidence necessary for conflict resolution. This is particularly important because many South American countries have a recent past of conflict or authoritarian rule in which violence was normalized as a means of solving disputes. As a result, conflict brought small arms into areas and taught the practical and psychological skills required for their use. Although institutional mechanisms are relevant to conflict management from an interstate perspective, they can also have a profound effect regarding the use of violence by other actors. The link between the trafficking of small arms and criminality is well established and the preoccupation with weapons of mass destruction is widespread.

The idea of arms control is not explicitly present in the OAS Charter, but it slowly entered the inter-American security environment in the late 1960s and early 1970s. In 1974, eight Latin American governments issued the Ayacuchu Declaration,[38] affirming their support for the idea of arms control, and the Hemispheric Security Committee has taken on this subject.

The Inter-American Convention against the Illicit Production and Traffic of Arms, Ammunition, Explosives and Other Related Materials of 1997 expresses the link between the arms control agenda and the new prominence of the concept of cooperative security mentioned earlier. On June 7, 1999, the OAS General Assembly in Guatemala adopted a landmark Inter-American Convention on Transparency in Conventional Weapons Acquisitions.

The Contadora group, the Ayacucho Declaration, the Treaty for the Prohibition of Nuclear Weapons in Latin America and the Caribbean, and the treaties that ended the nuclear dispute between Argentina and Brazil introduced the confidence- and security-building measures (CSBM) agenda, launched at the 1975 Helsinki Conference, to Latin America. The 1995 war between Peru and Ecuador reminded South American leaders that the pending territorial disputes in the region, a legacy of the nineteenth century demarcation process, could be ignited into an actual exchange of fire. The U.S. government's move in the 1990s toward a more multilateral approach in the region and the democratization of Latin American countries permitted the introduction of the confidence-building agenda. In addition, the concern with the nature of civil-military relations in South America, given the region's history of military intervention in public administration, and the search for new roles and identities for the military led local elites to acquire greater interest in the subject.

In the 1990s, the states in the hemisphere turned to the OAS as a catalyst for confidence building. The emphasis on CSBMs, which encourage transparency of military procedures and the availability of information, replaced the stress on deterrence incorporated in the concept of collective security. The OAS has organized and sponsored conferences on CSBMs that are designed to strengthen military-to-military relations, deal with historic rivalries and tensions, and create an environment that permits the governments of the region to modernize their defense forces without triggering arms race or suspicions from neighbors.

In 1994, a meeting of governmental specialists on confidence-building measures and other security-related issues was held in Buenos Aires. This led to two conferences on the same theme, held in Chile in 1995 and El Salvador in 1998. The Santiago Declaration called on OAS members to accept accords regarding the prenotification of military exercises, to take part in the UN Register of Conventional Arms, to exchange information regarding national defense policies, and to permit foreign observers to be present when military exercises take place. The Declaration of San Salvador expanded this agenda, dealing with political contacts, border cooperation, the exchange of information on national armed forces, the creation of accounting procedures for military expenditure, and the institutionalization of discussions on cooperative security through annual experts meetings. One of the CSBMs proposed by the 1998 San Salvador Conference on CSBMs was the establishment of a common methodology to measure defense expenditures that would facilitate comparison of military spending throughout Latin America. The governments of Argentina and Chile submitted a formal request to the Economic Commission for Latin American and the Caribbean (ECLAC). Following the publication of Argentina's defense white book in 1999, which contained the first-ever public accounting of its military expenditures, ECLAC began data gathering and analysis. ECLAC's common standardized methodology for the measurement of defense expenditures is now available to all nations of the hemisphere as an important CSBM that contributes to disarmament and the lowering of military expenditures. A meeting of experts took place in Miami in 2003, issuing two final documents that are now a reference for the debate on the subject.

The countries of the region have also adhered to CSBMs on a global level, with the OAS having approved the Inter-American Convention on Transparency in Conventional Weapons Acquisition in 1999. This initiative provides a framework for the advance notification of acquisitions of weapons systems covered by the UN register. The data available on the participation of American states in different aspects of the confidence and security agenda attest to the wide involvement of countries in the hemisphere. Among the OAS countries, twenty-six have presented reports on the themes required. Moreover, bilateral arrangements complement this trend, such as the joint operations and training between Brazilian and Argentine forces and between Argentine and Chilean forces. The experience of Latin American armies in Haiti can also be viewed as a confidence-building experience.

The Inter-American Defense Board (IADB) has acquired a new role in this area.[39] Its current programs include clearing mines in Central America, reporting on CSBMs, and developing educational programs on regional security. Resolution 650 (1031/95) of the OAS Permanent Council tasked the IADB with the preparation of an inventory of military CSBMs in the hemisphere. The board also provides a senior-level academic program in security studies for military, national police, and civilian leaders at the Inter-American Defense College. Thus, it is clear that a long process involving hemispheric states, and more particularly the military establishments in the region, has generated a norm regarding knowledge sharing and the diffusion of rules about military activities and arms procurements. This is a change in social interaction that prevents conflict by generating confidence.

The generation of a cooperative security paradigm puts the concept of transparency at the center of interstate relations in the region. The concept has played a particularly relevant role in relations among different military establishments and in changing national security doctrines in the region. The spread of CSBMs creates the right cultural and institutional basis for the generation of verification mechanisms in other areas and for the consolidation of their legitimacy. Although the verification of treaties and confidence-building measures may be treated as two distinct concepts, the availability of information in the security sector is a common denominator and CSBMs "are perceived by some as potent preludes and accompaniments to other forms of arms control in cases of seemingly intractable conflict."[40]

During the 2009 summit of UNASUR in Argentina, the regional tensions generated by the new accord between the Unites States and Colombia regarding the use of Colombian bases by the armed forces of the United States were the focus of debates and negotiations. The deployment of U.S. military personnel in Colombian bases and its implication for the region was included in the agenda of UNASUR, where leaders had the opportunity to voice their concerns and positions. Although the summit failed to produce an explicit declaration rejecting the U.S. bases, it was the forum where regional states were able to reach a minimum common perspective that put pressure on the United States to make clear its position regarding the limits of the agreement. The resolution mentions both the importance of the fight against drug trafficking and terrorism and the respect for the sovereignty of the countries of the region in the case of the presence of foreign military forces. The need to discuss the war in Colombia in a multilateral context was also put forward.

Intrastate Conflict Resolution

Intrastate conflict resolution mechanisms are necessary in the region. Intrastate wars (as defined by the Correlates of War Project) have occurred in twelve South American countries since the 1950s,[41] and violence is present in daily life throughout the continent.

The OAS has helped generate the hemispheric democratic paradigm that associates security and democracy. The new weight given by the OAS to the defense of democracy marked the international landscape in the region in the 1990s.[42] The 1991 Declaration on the Collective Defense of Democracy, often referred to as the Santiago Declaration, called for prompt reaction in the event of a threat to democracy in a member state. Resolution 1080, passed by the OAS General Assembly in June 1991 in Santiago, determines that the OAS Permanent Council should be summoned in case of the suspension of the democratic process in any member state, and thereafter a Meeting of Ministers of Foreign Affairs could be summoned and economic and diplomatic sanctions may be imposed. The 1994 Miami Summit of the Americas set the tone for a growing responsibility regarding the maintenance of democratic regimes in the Americas. In 1997, a reform of the OAS Charter took place through the ratification of the 1992 Protocol of Washington. The agreement strengthens representative democracy by giving the OAS the right to suspend a member state whose democratically elected government is overthrown by force. A new collective identity was fostered, led by the United States, and made possible by the transition of most Latin America countries to democracy in the 1980s. In fact, the OAS relaxed its commitment to the principle of nonintervention in the process of constructing a regime for the preservation of democracy. Finally, in 2001, the Inter-American Democratic Charter was adopted, further institutionalizing the democratic paradigm. This new commitment creates procedures for cases of formal disruption to democracy and for situations when democracy is at risk. It was first formally applied when a coup d'état was attempted against Venezuelan president Hugo Chavez in 2002.

The OAS Unit for the Promotion of Democracy (UPD), now the Department for the Promotion of Democracy, was established in 1991. It provides assistance for the development of democratic institutions and for conflict resolution. During the first years of its activities, the UPD concentrated on the area of electoral observations. Following the First Summit of the Americas in 1994, it got involved in programs for the support of peace processes on the continent. The OAS takes part in electoral observation missions on national and other levels, supporting training, educational, research, and informational programs. Between 1999 and 2009 the organization set up more than fifty electoral observation missions and in 2010 was involved in seven assistance programs.[43] The OAS also promotes national dialogue in countries where political institutions may be facing a crisis—such as Peru and Bolivia—and generates training and educational programs geared toward the generation of a democratic culture.

Since the 1990s, the OAS has also been involved in conflict resolution and national reconciliation. In Colombia, where war has been a reality for decades, the OAS has now established a presence. The OAS Mission of Support of the Peace Process in Colombia was created in 2004 through a Permanent Council Resolution. The mission is present in Bogotá and in several other cities, and it has been supporting the demobilization of paramilitary groups. The scope of the mission is to verify the cease-fire and cessation of hostilities in Colombia, and the demobilization, disarmament, and reintegration of the members of illegally organized armed groups with which the government has already reached agreements.[44]

During the internal crisis in Bolivia in 2008,[45] UNASUR proved to be a relevant forum for conflict resolution. The organization held an emergency summit in Chile on September 15, which was called into session by Chilean president Michelle Bachelet. The meeting resulted in a declaration of support for Bolivia's constitutional government, territorial integrity, and negotiations on crucial issues regarding the federation. A commission, coordinated by its presidency, was set up to accompany the work of a dialogue round table between the government and opposition. It also accepted the proposal of the Bolivian government to send a commission to conduct a "partial investigation" into the violence experienced in the department of Pando. Former Chilean foreign minister Juan Gabriel Valdes has been appointed as UNASUR's special envoy to Bolivia. In this case, the existence of this forum was crucial because, as a purely South American forum, it offered more legitimacy than the OAS. But Dante Caputto, a former Argentine foreign minister and head of the OAS Political Affairs Department, was also present in Bolivia as a personal and special envoy from OAS secretary general Jose Miguel Insulza. The division of labor between the OAS and UNASUR in this sphere has not been established yet, but clearly in some instances, such as the crisis in Bolivia, the need for a forum that excludes the United States can be identified.

The UN peace operation in Haiti, mentioned earlier, is an important example of both de facto peace enforcement and of conflict reconstruction in which South American countries are taking part. Argentina, Bolivia, Brazil, Ecuador, Peru, and Uruguay have sent troops there. The mission is multidimensional and based on a Chapter VII resolution. Its aims are to achieve national reconciliation and allow for the economic and social development of Haiti. The mandate establishes that it should restore a secure and stable environment, promote the political process, strengthen Haiti's government institutions and rule-of-law-structures, and deal with the protection and promotion of human rights. Its activities, supported by military and police deployments, include providing electoral assistance and public security, humanitarian aid, protecting and promoting human rights, managing public services, disarming gangs, and creating the proper conditions for social and economic development.

Taking part in the mission took the level of military and political cooperation in the region to a new level. Today most cooperative military exercises in the region involve peace operation simulations. Thus, dealing with intrastate conflicts outside South America has become a strong stimulus for greater coordination within the region.

Transnational Crime

Drug trafficking and transnational criminal activities in general are currently the most acute threat to states and individuals alike in South America. Criminal networks across Latin America are increasingly organized and effective. South America produces almost all of the world's cocaine,[46] with Colombia, Peru, and Bolivia together producing an estimated 1,000 tons of cocaine annually. The use of South American countries as transit routes, in particular Argentina, Brazil, and Chile, is on the rise. Strategies to counter drug trafficking have often been ineffective, and after more than a decade of sustained effort, cocaine production in the three Andean source countries has not been reduced. Much of this is due to continuous demand from the two largest markets for cocaine, the United States and Europe, and growing markets in Brazil and the Southern Cone.

Drug trafficking threatens the rule of law, and fuels conflict and corruption. Crime rates in Venezuela, Colombia, and Brazil are among the highest in the world. Perceptions of growing crime can fuel popular demand for the use of the military in policing and the introduction of anticrime legislation that reduces procedural protections, eroding human rights gains. Weak law enforcement enables drug trafficking, which, in turn, undermines the rule of law even further. The drug trade also brings in illicit firearms. Money laundering and the fostering of corruption are two other areas where drug trafficking can further undermine both the economy and governance. In this context, the need for the regionalization of the fight against the drug trade is increasingly clear to leaders of most countries.

The countries of South America have generally cooperated with the United States and other Western powers in developing counterterrorism mechanisms. Although the conceptual and legal framework within each of the countries varies greatly—and only Colombia has fully embraced the framework put forward by the United States after the attacks of September 2001—there is wide consensus on the need to mobilize resources and learn from more-developed countries regarding this issue. The OAS and Mercosul have been the most important forums for regional cooperation in fighting transnational criminal activities.

The Inter-American Drug Abuse Control Commission (CICAD) was established by the OAS General Assembly in 1986 as the Western Hemisphere's policy forum on all aspects of the drug problem. The commission is a forum for debate on drug-related problems; it renders support for institution building, develops research through the Inter-American Observatory on Drugs, and establishes standards for state action in this sphere. Alternative development projects are implemented in the Andean countries. Education, prevention, and treatment projects are in place. Training courses on money-laundering operations and, since 1999, a multilateral evaluation mechanism have been making periodic recommendations to member states on improving their capacity to control drug trafficking and abuse and enhance multilateral cooperation. A Working Group in Charge for Preparing a Regional Strategy to Promote Inter-American Cooperation in Dealing with Criminal Gangs was created in 2009 with the mandate of preparing a regional strategy to promote inter-American cooperation in dealing with criminal gangs.

South America is not an area where the presence of terrorist networks is particularly evident; at the time of writing, there were no known operational cells of Islamist terrorists in the hemisphere, although pockets of ideological supporters and facilitators in South America and the Caribbean lend financial, logistical, and moral backing to terrorist groups in the Middle East.[47] As a response, the Inter-American Committee against Terrorism (CICTE) was created in 1999, expanding the OAS's involvement in security issues. The committee deals with cooperation in the fight against terrorism and allows for national authorities to have a proper forum to discuss the sharing of information, the development of activities for training and crisis management, border cooperation, and travel documentation security measures. Programs in eight different areas are being developed at present: airport security, customs and border protection, cybersecurity, legislation against terrorism, port security, terrorist financing, terrorism policy engagement exercises, and tourism security.

Ten days after the 2001 attacks on New York and Washington, the Meeting of Consultation of Ministers of Foreign Affairs approved the resolution Strengthening Hemispheric Cooperation to Prevent, Combat, and Eliminate Terrorism. In 2002, the Inter-American Convention against Terrorism was signed. It seeks to prevent the financing of terrorism, to strengthen border controls, and to increase cooperation among law enforcement authorities in different countries. The committee delivered more than US$5 million in counterterrorism capacity-building assistance in the region. CICTE provided training to nearly 500 port and airport security officials from twenty-nine member states to help meet the requirements of the International Maritime Organization's International Ship and Port Facility Security Code and the International Civil Aviation Organization's new air-security standards. CICTE advised fifteen member states on how to meet the requirements of Security Council Resolution 1373, the thirteen international conventions and protocols relating to terrorism, and the Inter-American Convention against Terrorism, which complements and expands on international conventions and protocols.

Mercosul has also been a part of the regional effort to deal with transnational criminal activity.[48] A general plan for the security of the border region between Argentina, Brazil, and Paraguay and a unified system for the control of money laundering, illicit weapons, terrorism, illegal immigration, car theft, drug trafficking, and smuggling are in place. The conferences of the home secretaries of the Mercosul states, which have been meeting on a semiannual basis since 1997, has given vital impetus to the common fight against organized drug trafficking and the arms trade, international terrorism, and other transnational crimes. The concrete results of this mechanism involve numerous multilateral agreements, a subregional information network that contains data relevant to security, Mercosul's center for police training, and the general plan for regional security passed by the Conference of the Home Secretaries. The institutionalization of subregional security cooperation is already taking place. Beyond the Conference of the Home Secretaries, the Specialized Meeting of Authorities Dealing with Drugs looks into regional drug problems within Mercosul. The Working Group for Counterterrorism has discussed and proposed an agreement on the operative cooperation of police intelligence services in counterterrorism, an agreement on cooperation in the control of transnational criminal activities linked with illegal air traffic, and an agreement on the fight against corruption in the Mercosul border regions.

Regarding law enforcement on the border between Argentina, Brazil, and Paraguay in particular, an ad hoc group, the 3+1 Security Group (Argentina, Brazil, Paraguay, and the United States), has been working to improve the capabilities of these three Latin American states to address cross-border crime and combat money laundering and potential terrorist fund-raising activities.

UNASUR will also likely get involved in operations against drug trafficking, particularly as a reaction to the close ties between the United States and Colombia in this area. On October 6, 2009, ministers responsible for security from the Union of South American Nations agreed to the creation of a South American Council to Combat Drug Trafficking. South American countries are also considering the possibility of establishing a special fund to combat the drug trade. This is only a beginning, but it may indicate a path ahead for much-needed cooperation and leadership in this area.

Conclusion

In South America, conflict resolution mechanisms are available for interstate and intrastate relations at the multilateral level. Norm setting, social spaces for negotiations, mediation efforts, the development of assistance projects and operations, and confidence building occur at the hemispheric, South American, and subregional level. Border disputes, the negotiation of arms control mechanisms and security-building measures, institution building at the domestic level, and coordination for the fight against transnational criminality and terrorism are dealt with in the context of international organizations and the multidimensional definition of security.

The ongoing process of construction of shared meanings and intersubjective structures incorporates the emphasis on diplomacy, legality, and multilateralism that has been important for the region's governing elites since independence. On the other hand, the incorporation of an expanded concept of security and the redefinition of the balance between sovereignty and the transfer of authority and decision-making processes to international forums allow for the production of new forms of conflict resolution, such as those regarding intrastate conflicts and transnational criminality.

The existence of forms of coordination that gather different groups of nations is a positive development given the acutely diverse coalitions of interest possible in the region. The involvement of the United States in particular can be helpful in some cases but hinders conflict resolution processes in other cases, given the features of the international insertion of a great power closely aligned with European powers, Canada, and Japan and the power asymmetry that characterizes the Western Hemisphere.

As seen in this chapter, the OAS is relevant for arms control, confidence building, institution building, the establishment of the democratic paradigm, and the fight against transnational criminality and terrorism. It is also relevant for resolving border disputes and setting the norm for the peaceful resolution of conflict. But the "younger" organizations in the region may play a greater role in the realm of security, particularly in the future. Coordination for the fight against transnational crime takes place in the context of Mercosul and both this Southern Cone organization and the Andean Community play a part in establishing the norm for peaceful conflict resolution and building the region's democratic paradigm. UNASUR has already played a positive role in trying to serve the process of conflict resolution in Bolivia. The changes taking place in the region and the difficulties that result from the different political, social, and ideological processes in the present South American context may require this organization to step in in many more cases.

Although this chapter has focused on how the regional organizations can and do contribute to conflict resolution, it must be clear that the bilateral sphere is crucial for dealing with all the security issues mentioned and that in many cases international organizations or other actors from outside the region have played a relevant role in addressing the issues. More importantly, all of these organizations have to deal with inadequate budgets, legitimacy deficits, and the limitations of intergovernmental organization in general in a region where the concept of sovereignty is fiercely defended by the governing elites.

The existing conflict resolution mechanisms are very limited given the potential conflicts in the region, particularly regarding the spread of transnational criminality and the war in Colombia. The limits of Brazilian leadership, the concern with the protection of sovereignty in this country and others, the tensions between imported political and economic models developed in the West or within the UN context and the reality in South America, the great divisions between South American countries that today mark international relations in this part of the world, and the difficulty of mobilizing resources for common projects explain the absence of more robust and efficient mechanisms. Nevertheless, the plural architecture in the process of constructing these mechanisms is a very positive trend.

Notes

1.   Kalevi Holsti, *The State, War, and the State of War* (Cambridge: Cambridge University Press, 1996); Arie Kacowicz, *Zones of Peace in the Third World, South America and West Africa in Comparative Perspective* (New York: State University of New York Press, 1998); Barry

Buzan and Ole Weaver, *Regions and Powers: The Structure of International Security* (Cambridge: Cambridge University Press, 2002).

2. Jorge Domingues, *Boundary Disputes in Latin America*, Peaceworks no. 50 (Washington, DC: United States Institute for Peace Press, 2003).

3. Kacowicz, *Zones of Peace in the Third World*; Miguel Angel Centeno, *Blood and Debt: War and the Nation-State in Latin America* (University Park, PA: Penn State University Press, 2002.); Benjamin Miller, *States, Nations, and the Great Powers: The Sources of Regional War and Peace* (Cambridge: Cambridge University Press, 2007).

4. Monica Herz, "Building Trust in Latin America," in *The United States and Europe in a Changing World*, ed. Roger Kanet (Dordrecht, The Netherlands: Republic of Letters, 2009).

5. K. M. Fierke, *Critical Approaches to International Security* (Cambridge: Polity, 2007).

6. Beth Simmons, *Territorial Disputes and Their Resolution: The Case of Peru and Ecuador*, Peaceworks no. 27 (Washington, DC: United States Institute of Peace Press, 1999), 213.

7. Andrew Hurrell, "Working with Diplomatic Culture: Some Latin American and Brazilian Questions" (paper prepared for the annual meeting of the International Studies Association meeting, Montreal, March 2004), 2.

8. Monica Herz and João Pontes Nogueira, *Ecuador vs. Peru: Peacemaking Amid Rivalry* (Boulder, CO: Lynne Rienner Publishers, 2005).

9. Brazil and Argentina solved their disputes over water rights and nuclear competition. Chile and Argentina signed the 1984 Treaty of Peace and Friendship that put an end to the Beagle Channel feud.

10. The Colombian government has accused Venezuela of collaboration with the FARC insurgency, while Colombia president Álvaro Uribe's decision to negotiate a new Defense Cooperation Agreement with the United States and to allow U.S. military access to at least seven bases in his country have generated strong reactions from Caracas as well as from other South American capitals.

11. The Colombian government informed the OAS and the Ecuadorian government of the location of FARC rebel camps in Ecuador where hostages were being held and where coca was being grown and processed. On March 1, 2008, the Colombian army attacked a camp in Sucumbios, Ecuador.

12. The two countries have been involved in a dispute over the construction of a paper mill in Uruguay and the ecological consequences of this action. In 2010 a ruling from the International Court of Justice in The Hague opened the way for an understanding between the two countries.

13. Central Intelligence Agency, "The World Factbook," www.cia.gov/library/publications/the-world-factbook/fields/2070.html.

14. Argentina, which claims the islands in its constitution and briefly occupied them by force in 1982 before losing a war with Great Britain, agreed in 1995 to no longer seek settlement by force.

15. See "Colombia," *Cluster Munition Monitor*, www.the-monitor.org/.

16. Special Security Conference, "Declaration on Security in the Americas," OAS/ser.k/xxxviii ces/Dec. 1/03 rev.1, October 28, 2003.

17. See Andrian Bonilla and Marco Cepik, "Seguridad andino-brasileña: Conceptos, Actores y Debates," in *Agenda de Seguridad Andino-Brasileña*, ed. Marco Cepik and Socorro Ramírez (Bogotá: Friedrich-Ebert-Stiftung, 2004).

18. For the concept of cooperative security, see Ashton Carter, William Perry, and John Steinbruner, *A New Concept of Cooperative Security* (Washington, DC: Brookings Institution Press, 1992); Ivelaw Griffith, "Security Collaboration and Confidence-Building in the Americas," in *International Security and Democracy: Latin America and the Caribbean in the Post-Cold War Era*, ed. Jorge Domínguez (Pittsburgh: University of Pittsburgh Press, 1998).

19. Ann Tickner, "Re-visioning Security," in *International Relations Theory Today*, ed. Ken Booth and Steve Smith (Oxford: Polity Press, 1995); Barry Buzan, *People, States and Fear: An Agenda for International Security Studies in the Post-Cold War Era* (London: Harvester Wheatsheaf, 1991).

20. For a discussion of the political process of threat construction, see ibid.

21. The organization, which puts forward a form of international cooperation based on economic solidarity and social development, was launched in 2005 by Venezuela, Cuba, Nicaragua, Bolivia, Honduras, and Dominica.

22. The South American Regional Integration Initiative, created in late 2000 with the participation of the twelve countries of South America, seeks the physical interconnection of the region, energy integration, and changes to legislation, rules, and national regulations that hinder commerce and investment.

23. Monica Hirst, "Los desafíos de la política sudamericana de Brasil," *Nuvea Sociedad* no. 205 (206): 131–40.

24. Pope Atkins, *Latin America in the International Political System* (Boulder, CO: Westview Press, 1999).

25. The Rio Group was established in 1986 from the merger of the Contadora Group (Venezuela, Mexico, Panama, and Colombia) and its support group (Argentina, Brazil, Peru, and Uruguay), which negotiated the peace agreements that ended the Central American crises of the 1980s.

26. A group of four countries (United States, Brazil, Argentina, and Chile) that was established by a 1942 protocol that mediated the negotiations between Peru and Ecuador.

27. Heads of state have met since 1994 to define the economic, political, and security agendas for cooperation in the hemisphere. The first Summit of the Americas took place in Miami in 1994, with subsequent summits held in 1996, 1998, 2001, 2005, and 2009.

28. The Miami Meeting of Heads of State in 1994 established the process. The agenda includes confidence-building measures, the role of the armed forces, the military and the protection of the environment, mine clearing, economic development and political stability, peace operations and narco trafficking, and the production of white papers on defense policy.

29. OPANAL was established by the Treaty of Tlatelolco in 1967 and is responsible for convoking conferences and consultation meetings related to the established purposes, means, and procedures of the treaty.

30. The agency was established in 1991 and is responsible for the administration and application of the Common System of Accounting and Control (SCCC), which is a full-scope safeguards system applied to all nuclear activities covering all nuclear materials in Brazil and Argentina.

31. For an analysis of the history, role, and institutional structure of the OAS, see Carolyn Shaw, *Cooperation, Conflict and Consensus in the Organization of American States* (New York: Palgrave, 2004); and Monica Herz, *OAS Global Governance Away from the Media* (London, Routledge, 2010).

32. The Hemispheric Security Commission was created in 1991, becoming a permanent body in 1995.

33. The program, created in 1999, comprises three areas: education for the promotion of peace between states; education for the peaceful settlement of conflicts; and education for the promotion of democratic values and practices. In August 2005, the Inter-American Program on Education for Democratic Values and Practices was created.

34. Members include Argentina, Bolivia, Brazil, Chile, Colombia, Ecuador, Guyana, Paraguay, Peru, Suriname, Uruguay, and Venezuela.

35. See Andean Community, "CAN Acts, Declarations and Agreements," www.comunidadandina.org/INGLES/documentos/documents/compromiso_lima.htm.

36. The Inter-American Treaty of Reciprocal Assistance, or the Rio Treaty, signed in 1947, provides for mutual defense and defines an attack on one state as an attack on all. Article 6 of the treaty establishes that an Organ of Consultation, which comprises all states, should meet if an aggression against a sovereign state takes place. It should also be responsible for the pacific settlement of disputes.

37. The agreement was signed on October 30, 2009. It is an extension of a standing treaty dating back to 1974 and opens seven bases to U.S. forces.

38. They are the governments of Argentina, Chile, Bolivia, Ecuador, Colombia, Panama, Peru, and Venezuela.

39. On March 15, 2006, the 32nd Special Session of the General Assembly formalized the IADB as an OAS agency.

40. Steve Tulliu and Thomas Schmalberger, *Coming to Terms with Security: A Lexicon for Arms Control, Disarmament and Confidence-Building* (Geneva: UN Institute for Disarmament Research, 2004), 135.

41. They are Colombia, Bolivia, Cuba, Nicaragua, Colombia, Peru, El Salvador, Guatemala, Dominican Republic, Argentina, Chile, and Haiti. See Correlates of War, www.correlatesofwar.org/.

42. Tom Farer, *Beyond Sovereignty: Collectively Defending Democracy in the Americas* (Baltimore, MD: John Hopkins University Press, 1996); Andrew Cooper and Thomas Legler, *Intervention without Intervening? The OAS Defense and Promotion of Democracy in the Americas* (New York: Palgrave, 2006).

43. See OAS, "Misiones de Observación Electoral de la OEA," www.oas.org/electoral missions/.

44. See OAS, "Agreement between the Government of the Republic of Colombia and the General Secretariat of the Organization of American States on Monitoring the Peace Process in Colombia," February 4, 2004, www.oas.org/documents/OEA-Colombia/Convenio OEA-ColombiaE.asp.

45. Since the election of Evo Morales, tension has been growing in Bolivia as the new government tries to implement an ambitious program of change. Other South American countries have direct interest in conflict resolution in this case, as the supply of natural gas can be affected and the conflict could spill over to border regions. President Morales proposed a new constitution that would give the indigenous population living mostly in the east of the country more power, implement a land reform project, and redistribute the revenues from the country's mineral resources. Opposition to the president is concentrated in Tarija, Santa Cruz, Beni, and Pando e Chuquisaca. President Morales signed Bolivia's new constitution into law on February 7, 2009.

46. UN Office on Drugs and Crime, "Coca Cultivation in the Andean Region: A Survey of Bolivia, Colombia and Peru," www.unodc.org/documents/crop-monitoring/Andean_report_2008.pdf.

47. U.S. Department of State, "Country Reports: Western Hemisphere Overview," in *Country Reports on Terrorism 2006* (Washington, DC: U.S. Government Printing Office, 2007), chapter 2.

48. For more on this subject, see Daniel Flemes, "Institution Building in Mercosul's Defence and Security Sector (II): The Common Containment of Transnational Security Threats" (working paper no. 22, Institute for Iberoamerican Studies, Hamburg, Germany, 2004).

17

Security Challenges and Threats in the Caribbean

Hilton A. McDavid

The Caribbean is under a state of light to medium conflict with transnational organized criminal groups. The conflict is exacerbated by the relative power of the criminal gangs, whose financial worth can be greater than national budgets. The violence that these gangs have inflicted led the *Economist* to title a 2008 article "The Caribbean: Sun, Sea and Murder," a play on the Caribbean's well-known tourist slogan "sun, sea, and sand."[1] This conflict came to a head in Jamaica on May 24, 2010, when the government declared a "state of emergency" and deployed the military to retake an area of Kingston known as Tivoli Gardens.[2] This move became necessary after the government issued an arrest warrant for the community leader whose extradition was being requested by the United States, and the residents turned the area into a military-style garrison with blockades, barriers, and obstacles covered by .50-caliber weapons.

The Caribbean benefits from as well as faces challenges that arise from the geostrategic realities of the region. The Caribbean Sea is both a barrier and a bridge: it separates nations, but it also facilitates the flow of illegal commerce and other illicit activities.[3] The Caribbean, because of its geographical position, is considered a prime transshipment location for drugs destined to points in Europe and North America, caught between the world's largest producers of coca and the world's largest consumers. Criminal gangs take advantage of the porous borders to traffic not only narcotics but also arms, ammunition, and, to some extent, people.[4]

The end of the Cold War and the ensuing spread of globalization have also defined the new security environment in the Caribbean in terms of giving rise to new risks and diverse threats, including those related to unemployment; the marginalization of great sectors of the population, particularly in Guyana and Jamaica; terrorism in its various modalities; organized crime; and human rights violations. In addition, the traditional international problem of conventional external aggression remains a possibility in the region given that Guyana has long-standing land-boundary disputes with Venezuela and Suriname, and Trinidad and Tobago, Barbados, and other islands have ongoing maritime-boundary challenges.

As the global security environment, which over the next two decades will feature accelerating and possibly momentous changes in the international system, continues to evolve, so too will its impact on the region. Global developments that will likely affect the Caribbean's security environment include China's economic growth and expansion; the growing rate of technological innovation; the widening proliferation of mass disruption/destruction technologies; the growing power or capacity of nonstate players relative to nation-states; the perpetuation and doggedness of corrosive regional, ethnic, and religious conflicts; and mounting resource scarcity and environmental degradation.[5] Add to this the mounting problems of narco-trafficking, other illicit activities, and natural disasters, and it is apparent that international, regional, and national security have become entwined in an unprecedented fashion.[6]

How to confront this new and emerging environment is an increasingly critical question for the small, developing states of the Caribbean. Since the 1648 Treaty of Westphalia, states have been expected to operate within the parameters of their national laws—the only source of authority empowered to make and enforce law—to treat their citizenry fairly and justly, to contain violent nonstate actors, and to stop illicit acts that reduce law and order both domestically and in the international arena.[7] The current security environment, however, requires multilateral solutions.

Caribbean states have experience collaborating on security matters. For example, the security arrangements for the April–May 2007 Cricket World Cup tournament and the 2009 Summit of the Americas are good examples of cooperation among Caribbean states at the operational and tactical levels. However, a regional strategy to deal with regional threats to the region's stability and overall security is sadly lacking.

This chapter argues that the dimensions of national security from a Caribbean perspective must first be defined before regional security can be discussed. In reconceptualizing national security and regional security in a Caribbean context, the chapter reviews the strategic situation and draws conclusions and recommendations for future research and policymaking. It focuses on the states of the Caribbean Community and Common Market (CARICOM)—Antigua and Barbuda, the Bahamas, Barbados, Belize, Dominica, Grenada, Guyana, Haiti, Jamaica, Montserrat, Saint Lucia, St. Kitts and Nevis, St. Vincent and the Grenadines, Suriname, and Trinidad and Tobago—and reviews the performance of this regional grouping in conflict management.

Current Security Environment in the CARICOM Bloc

To a great extent the overall security order and environment in Latin America and the Caribbean is governed by U.S. national interests and engagement. According to Ivelaw Griffiths, U.S. interests in the Caribbean revolve around democracy, geopolitics, geoeconomics, and geonarcotics.[8] With regard to democracy, the Caribbean has a rich tradition in terms of key democracy variables, such as elections, freedom of the press, and respect for human rights.[9] However, one cannot ignore the dysfunctionalities of corruption and administrative inefficiencies, nor the impact of democratic governance on corruption, poverty, and crime. From the geopolitical perspective, the Caribbean is important to the United States because of its strategic resources (bauxite, oil, and natural gas products and refineries), sea-lanes, and security networks. Geonarcotics refers to the triumvirate of geography, power, and politics of narcotics production and distribution. The critical issues here relate to threats to state security, the extremely high level of conflict within states, and cooperation among nonstate criminal actors.

The unprecedented freedom of movement in the Caribbean facilitates what Max Manwaring describes as "probably the most insidious security problem facing the world and the nations in it today." This security problem, according to Manwaring, "centres on the threats to a given nation-state's ability and willingness to do the following: (1) control the national territory and the people in it fairly and justly and (2) control internal factions or non-state actors seeking illegal violent change within the borders of the nation-state."[10] While providing great economic benefits, this free flow across borders also creates opportunities for miscreants to exploit gaps and weaknesses in governance and sovereignty within and between nation-states. This kind of instability, enhanced by the human destabilizers who exploit them, provides the potential nexus between transnational crime—particularly narco-trafficking with its high reward—and the imminent threats posed by international terrorist networks. There is an obvious need for the countries in the hemisphere to develop a workable and acceptable model to deal collectively and cooperatively with these threats.

Threats to CARICOM Stability

The hemisphere's drug problem has deleterious effects on the small economies of the English-speaking Caribbean. The drug problem is linked to
many kinds of criminality, including systemic or institutionalized corruption. Agents and agencies of national security and good governance
have been severely tainted, besides being negatively impacted politically,
financially, and economically. However, the most critical threat to stability comes from the increase in the number and size of ungoverned spaces
that are being dominated by criminal leaders. This is particularly pertinent
when these criminals are linked to the political structure. For instance,
in Guyana, the use by the government of drug dealers and their gangs to
fight other crimes has led to a perceived dependency by the government
on these criminals for its security.[11] Another important dimension that can
have deleterious effects on the stability of the nation-state is the significant
size of the assets of the leadership of the criminal gangs in relation to the
state's GDP, giving gangs the ability to create instability through armed
insurrection, selective violence, currency speculation, and corruption. As a
rational act, corruption often occurs in situations where official pay is low
and there is opportunity to increase total income by other activities. Corruption will continue as long as the marginal benefits are greater than the
cost expected from the act. Unfortunately, because of the large assets of the
region's criminal networks, the marginal benefits will continue to be much
greater than the costs in the Caribbean.

It is important to point out that state power is not only being eroded by
transnational criminal/terrorist networks but also by legitimate nonstate
actors, including multinational corporations, multilateral and regional organizations, and nongovernmental organizations, which today are playing
much more important roles in the international community than in the
past. For instance, the roles of the United Nations, the World Trade Organization, and the International Criminal Court (ICC) in the world's current security environment are critical factors in national security analysis.
For example, the ICC's March 2009 issue of an arrest warrant for Sudanese
president Omar al-Bashir can be seen as an example of nation-states voluntarily or involuntarily relinquishing powers that have traditionally been
exercised solely by governments.[12] Whatever the source of state-power
erosion, organized crime has taken advantage of it. It has benefited, for
instance, from the reduction in control on trade and has taken advantage
of the free movement of goods, services, and money to make inroads into
fraud and money laundering.[13] In the current security environment, transnational criminal organizations mimic multinational corporations and are
often difficult to distinguish from legal entities.

In the new international security environment, "intermestic" characteristics affect international and domestic security concomitantly and contiguously. These characteristics engender threats that are inextricably linked to each other. For example, there is evidence that drugs are transhipped from Jamaica and that illegal arms are shipped to it. A recent seizure in the country also suggests that cocaine is being transhipped from South America and other Caribbean islands and that marijuana is being exported southward in return. This increases the dependency of countries on each other, which is characteristic of the new international security environment. It is thus critical that the concepts relative to this new situation are understood and defined.

Criminal Gangs and State Sovereignty

In his most recent works on gangs in Latin America and the Caribbean, Manwaring suggests that gang-generated instability amounts ultimately to a "clash of civilizations":

> Rather than trying to depose a government with a major stroke (*golpe* or coup) or in a prolonged revolutionary war, as some insurgents have done, gangs and their allies ... more subtly take control of territory and people one street or neighborhood at a time (*coup d'street*) or one individual, business, or government office at a time. Thus, whether a gang is specifically a criminal or insurgent type organization is irrelevant. Its putative objective is to neutralize, control, or depose governments to ensure self-determined (nondemocratic) ends.[14]

This objective demonstrates a serious political agenda, leads to a clash over the authoritative allocation of values in a society, and defines the insidious nature of the region's insurgency.

With specific reference to Jamaica, Manwaring argues that the behavior and actions of the gangs in that country suggest not a "failed state" but a *failing state* in the process of reconfiguration. Thus, Jamaica appears to be slowly moving toward something like a "criminal state" or a "narco-state."[15] Guyana has had an eruption of gang violence typified by ruthless and merciless killings and though not as organized and disciplined as the Jamaican gangs, the Guyanese gangs can be considered as a major threat to the stability of the state. Of major concern to Trinidad and Tobago, and indeed the region, is the combination of criminal gangs and Muslim groups suspected of having international linkages, such as the Jama'at al Muslimeen and Waajihatul Islaamiyyah.

The consequence of this is that the effective sovereignty of the state and the personal security of citizens are being challenged every day. In fact, the gangs' commercial motives for controlling people and territory demonstrate an implicit political agenda.[16] The growth of criminal violence is weakening state authority, as gangs and criminal syndicates exert control over certain communities. This, in turn, allows arms and drug trafficking to become more prevalent. In Jamaica, the presence and activities of these gangs have reduced the state's ability to deliver political goods such as security, education, health services, economic opportunity, and fundamental infrastructure. Some governments in the Caribbean are increasingly forfeiting their function as provider of public goods, particularly security, to criminal gang leaders and terrorist leaders whom beneficiaries glorify and romanticize as "dons."

Manwaring warns that for sovereignty to be relevant in today's environment, the state and government institutions operating under the rule of law must have a monopoly on the enforcement of laws. As has been seen in Guyana and Jamaica, the powers of the state have to some extent been abridged and negated by the violent, intimidating, and corrupting activities of internal and transnational criminal elements and nonstate actors.

The Development of CARICOM

Over the years, the Caribbean region has responded on a regional basis to these security threats, establishing a number of regional institutions and initiatives. To understand this turn of events, it is useful to look at the historical record in the development of the Caribbean Free Trade Association (CARIFTA) and its evolution into CARICOM, whose secretariat has been housed in Georgetown, Guyana, since its founding at the Treaty of Chaguaramas in 1973.[17] This evolution started with the Guyana-Venezuela border disputes of 1966 and continued onward through various external interventions into the region.

On October 14, 1966, 141 days after Guyana gained independence from Britain, Venezuela invaded Guyana's territory, seizing the Guyana part of the island of Ankoko in the Cuyuni River, the border at that point between the two sovereign nations.[18] The Venezuelan government had reopened its claim to almost 75 percent of Guyana (specifically, to Essequibo County) just prior to Guyana gaining independence on May 26, 1966. Although the Guyanese position was that the matter was settled under the Arbitral Award of 1899, under the Geneva Agreement of 1966, a mixed commission was established with the objective of seeking satisfactory solutions for the practical settlement of the controversy.[19]

At that time, only two other present-day CARICOM countries—Jamaica and Trinidad and Tobago—were independent, and Guyana was without regional support. But, without probably realizing it, the Guyana government developed a national strategy that encompassed all of the elements of national power—diplomacy, information, the military, and the economy—with extremely heavy dependence on diplomacy and information. This approach was dictated by the very small size of the Guyana military, especially when compared to Venezuela.[20] The main and perhaps the only purpose of the Guyana Defence Force was "early warning," that is, to provide information on any further attacks and invasions so that the Guyana government would have sufficient time to get their diplomatic machinery going and to have the Security Council of the United Nations convened to deal with the aggression.

One of the first important diplomatic roles Guyana played at the time was to become one of the main drivers among the anglophone community in the establishment of CARIFTA. Even though it was a trade organization, CARIFTA exerted geopolitical influence as a regional entity and soon evolved into CARICOM. Guyana's diplomatic efforts and achievements were supported by a growing independent CARICOM. Guyana participated as a member of the Non-Aligned Movement (NAM) at the 1970 summit in Lusaka and hosted a NAM foreign ministers conference in Georgetown in 1972. Guyana also was elected as a member of the UN Security Council in 1975–76.

However, Guyana's diplomatic offensive was countered by Venezuela's utilization of the Protocol of Washington, denying the country membership in the Organization of American States (OAS) and accession to international agreements, such as the Treaty of Tlatelolco.[21] In 1991, under extreme pressure from the other CARICOM states, all of which were members of the OAS, Venezuela finally relented and allowed Guyana to join the organization.

Within this context, it is important that the concept of regional security be examined. The lessons of the past must be taken into consideration. In short, attention must be paid not only to the current regional and global threats but also to the territorial disputes that exist within the community, particularly claims on Guyanese territory by Venezuela and Suriname, an ongoing situation in St. Kitts and Nevis that is fueled by a desire of some in Nevis to secede from the federation, and the disagreement between Trinidad and Tobago and Barbados over fishing.[22] CARICOM has intervened with varying degrees of success using the tool of mediation in the internal affairs of member states, most notably in Guyana after the disputed 1996 elections that resulted in the brokering and signing of the Herdmanston Accord in 1998. CARICOM intervention in St. Vincent and the Grenadines following civil and labor unrest, which was to some extent agitated by the opposition, led to the Grand Beach Accord in 2000. While the intervention in Grenada was the only occasion that a military option has been exercised in the region, CARICOM countries at the invitation of the government of Trinidad and Tobago did send troops to assist the country's military after the attempted coup in 1990.

Other developments have affected institutional regional security development. In the aftermath of the Grenada coup in 1979, which brought Prime Minister Maurice Bishop to power, a constellation of twenty-eight groups dislodged the government of Dominica. The coalition of opposition elements paralyzed the economy, forcing the prime minister to capitulate, and ultimately caused elections to be held to legitimize the coup.[23] Some experts believe that the increase in leftist activism in the Caribbean, combined with the closer ties between Grenada and Cuba, heightened the security concerns of the Organization of the Eastern Caribbean States (OECS) and was a major consideration in the formation of its Security and Defence Treaty in 1981, which included OECS members (Antigua and Barbuda, Dominica, Grenada, Montserrat, St. Kitts and Nevis, St. Lucia and St. Vincent, and the Grenadines) and Barbados.[24] This treaty has resulted in the formation of what is called the Regional Security System (RSS), which is a misnomer given the RSS's actual security capability. However, the treaty did facilitate the U.S.-led intervention in Grenada in 1983 and disaster responses driven by non-RSS CARICOM countries such as Guyana and Trinidad and Tobago in the wake of the destruction of Hurricane Ivan to Grenada in 2004.

CARICOM's framework for responding to the grave security threats that the Caribbean's small states and microcountries today face had its genesis during the April–May 2007 Cricket World Cup tournament, when the countries as a group had to satisfy the security requirements as established by the International Cricket Council (ICC).[25] The fulfillment of these requirements was a condition of their hosting the world tournament. As a consequence, the region inherited a sustainable framework that is helping CARICOM direct policy, cooperation, and collaboration in crime and security.

To support the structure that was to be created, the Implementation Agency for Crime and Security (IMPACS) was established, though it now serves more as a coordinating entity for the organizations that evolved as a result of Cricket World Cup 2007. Today, CARICOM's regional security mechanism has four pillars: legislative, border security, intelligence, and security assistance and cooperation. Its legislative instruments include

- a memorandum of understanding for the sharing of intelligence;
- a 2007 immigration (amendment) bill;
- customs (advance passenger and cargo information) regulations;

- a memorandum of intent between CARICOM and the United States on the Advance Passenger Information System (APIS);
- a treaty on security among CARICOM member states;
- a protocol to the treaty on security assistance among CARICOM member states (CARICOM Operations, Planning, and Coordinating Staff [COPACS]); and
- status of forces agreements.

The last three instruments on this list allowed Trinidad and Tobago to host the April 2009 Conference of the Americas with the security assistance of the other CARICOM states. Accordingly, heads of state and their delegations were protected in the twin island republic by military and police deployed from neighboring countries.

Border security has been strengthened through the implementation of APIS and the Advance Cargo Information System (ACIS), which are coordinated by a Joint Regional Communications Centre (JRCC) and the CARICOM Interactive Border Security System (CARIBSECS). CARIBSECS also coordinates and controls the regional and UN "watch lists," the Regional Deportee Database, and the Regional Stolen and Lost Travel Document Database.

Regional intelligence is now, at the strategic and policy level, coordinated by the Regional Intelligence Committee, which consists of the heads of military and police intelligence. However, the Regional Intelligence Fusion Centre (RIFC), which is responsible for the regional security and intelligence mechanisms, such as the CARICOM Intelligence and Sharing Network (CISNET) and the CARICOM Accreditation Watch List System (CAWS), manages day-to-day activities. The RIFC is the focal point for regional and international intelligence cooperation and facilitates joint analyses and threat assessments.

Cricket World Cup 2007 has undoubtedly left the region a legacy of security assets, institutions, mechanisms, and systems and procedures that has resulted in unprecedented levels of multinational, multisectoral, and multiagency cooperation. In summarizing the accomplishments of Cricket World Cup 2007, Col. Tony Anderson, deputy chief of the Jamaican Defence Staff, points to the creation of

- a comprehensive intelligence picture of regional security threats;
- culturally relevant regional security strategies and plans that are developed, managed, and financed by CARICOM;
- upgraded regional border security and intelligence infrastructure that uses technology in an innovative fashion;
- ICT systems designed and implemented by CARICOM resources;

- virtual communication systems that use technology in an innovative fashion to interconnect political, operational, and public-sector stakeholders;
- important new cooperative relationships formed with nontraditional international partners.[26]

Regional Security versus National Security

In order to fully participate—whether collectively or individually—in negotiations on mutual security in the Caribbean Basin, the CARICOM countries must first develop their own national and regional (bloc) security strategies, which begins with identifying and prioritizing national and regional interests. This prioritization should be derived from national interests and must be formulated and implemented concomitant with priorities that distinguish vital interests from others.[27] The listing of these priorities will have the benefit of providing a framework for the systematic assessment of national interests and national security, in addition to being a means for distinguishing among immediate, short-range, and long-range issues.

In discussing national interests and values, one must not be overwhelmed by those of the developed countries. In the Caribbean context, vital interests generally refer to the survival of the nation-state—whether it be from external or internal aggression, or from a pandemic—and should require the coordination of all government ministerial portfolios, especially those of the Ministry of National Security. The small and micro nature of the states of the Caribbean, which have population sizes ranging from 40,000 (St. Kitts and Nevis) to nearly 3 million (Jamaica), result in a peculiar security dilemma.[28]

Regional security in the CARICOM context is here defined as a collective security system based on the credibility and stability of the nations. Like Wilsonian collective security, it can attend to security at all levels,[29] but this, particularly with international or systemic security, will only be possible with a degree of continued involvement with the United States.[30] Perhaps this is an opportunity for the countries to use the leverage that the "new spaces" have created with the conclusion of the Cold War. The major diplomatic front for CARICOM will be the OAS, where CARICOM is the largest voting bloc, representing 14 of the 35 member states.[31] In the OAS, there is no special body like the UN Security Council. Article 64 of the OAS's Rules of Procedures gives each delegation "the right to one vote." And Article 65 stipulates that decisions are taken by the vote of a majority of the member states in both the plenary sessions and the General Committee meetings. The exception to this is rare and occurs only in those cases in which the organization's charter or the Rules of Procedure provide otherwise. In these circumstances it is generally by consensus or two-thirds majority.

In the Caribbean context, regional security should mean not only agreements and protocols for the settlement of border and maritime issues within the regional bloc and with external hemispheric partners but also the inculcation of common values and systems that will support open societies and economies. The states must be willing to eliminate conditions that can lead to internal and external conflicts and adopt regional policies that will deal with common problems in fisheries, forestry, agriculture, and general economic development. A key aspect of CARICOM regional security would be the promotion of greater cooperation in research and industry and of greater commerce within the bloc. A critical component would be the establishment of joint ventures, partnerships, and strategic alliances among firms from different countries.[32]

Taking the Guyana-Suriname disputes as points of departure, encouraging the establishment of joint-venture companies to exploit the mineral resources of the coastal zones of both countries could lead to the production of oil and economic development, while emphasizing the maritime issue would only yield a stalemate. The same can be said for the disputed New River Triangle, which Suriname is claiming from Guyana and where there is the possibility of the exploitation of bauxite and other minerals.[33] Patrick Morgan points out that developing habits of cooperation can achieve widespread benefits and that common achievements would promote expectations of more as the people grow prosperous and healthier and are better educated together.[34]

However, the effectiveness of CARICOM in regional security depends on the use of skilled mediators and conciliators; the current heads of government have a limited and narrow base, with no formal training in mediation. Indeed, it would be more effective to increase the number of trained mediators at all levels of society to expand and enhance governance throughout the region.[35] Also pertinent in the current global and hemispheric security environment is that the United States now has a more cohesive and well-structured partner on its "third border" with which to create a more efficient and effective alliance and partnership.

The "Third-Border" Concept: Opportunities and New Spaces

Any discussion of CARICOM regional security would be irrelevant if U.S. strategic interests were not taken into consideration. However, one of the serious threats to U.S. national security is the American assumption that the United States can continue to fight wars in Europe, Asia, and the Middle East and ignore the criticality of the Caribbean Basin to its homeland integrity and defense. In the current global and hemispheric environment, it is essential that the United States strengthen its cooperation with the CARICOM bloc and expand and adapt the relationship to exercise diligence in the face of the new challenges.

Strategically speaking, the Caribbean is vulnerable to terrorism due to its geopolitical linkages, geographical location, and strategic materials.[36] During the period 1997–2000, Jamaica provided 26 percent of the United States' total bauxite imports and 8 percent of its alumina imports. In addition, three CARICOM countries—Trinidad and Tobago, Suriname, and Barbados—are oil producers, while Trinidad and Tobago supplies 78 percent of the liquefied natural gas consumed in the United States.[37] To some extent, the United States now recognizes this vulnerability, having recently initiated the Caribbean Basin Security Initiative (CBSI), which was formally inaugurated on May 27, 2010.[38]

In advancing hemispheric security cooperation, the key challenges for the United States include overcoming the "lingering suspicion and doubts about its policies and commitment and to help build consensus on a comprehensive vision and strategy for regional security."[39] This approach would undoubtedly produce greater opportunity for CARICOM to improve both its collective security and that of the individual member countries. These opportunities have, in some cases, manifested themselves as new spaces[40]—that is, as freedoms to act without suffering asymmetrical consequences. To be effective, the CARICOM region must establish a common definition of national security and understand the relationships of this definition and the numerous international definitions of national security. The important aspect for CARICOM in dealing with the new spaces is that they must act collectively. Petty interests can create divisions among the member countries and acting independently will deny countries the synergy and bargaining strength that collective negotiations can provide.

The Hemispheric Context

Stephen Flanagan and his colleagues point out that the foundation of the strength of the United States stretches north and south beyond its territorial limits. The geostrategic contribution of the Caribbean is only part of this; the Western Hemisphere as a whole provides approximately 50 percent of U.S. oil imports, as well as significant percentages of the imported electricity and agricultural and manufacturing goods and labor on which the U.S. economy depends. The relationships are already entwined, with the North American Free Trade Agreement (NAFTA) and the Caribbean Basin Initiative (CBI) playing major roles in improving economic and trade integration.[41]

U.S. ties to the hemisphere remain strong and the relationships are generally mutually beneficial. Of critical importance to many of the economies are continued U.S. investments, bilateral trade flows, and remittance transfers. While there have been concerns over China's expanding interest in the hemisphere, Frank Mora, U.S. Deputy assistant secretary of defense for the Western Hemisphere, prefers to characterize this interest as one that presents opportunities rather than threats.[42] Benefits of this interest include contributions to the region's economic development through trade and investment, and assistance and cooperation in the fight against transnational crime. Mora also notes that China's military sales in the hemisphere could assist states in their efforts to more effectively manage their territory and combat threats from arms and human and drug trafficking, but greater transparency of China's intentions and objectives are essential.[43]

The countries of the hemisphere continue to use confidence-building measures both at the government and military level to relieve tensions between neighbors, as was recently seen with Ecuador and Colombia. The same is expected on Colombia's eastern border with Venezuela, and multilateral organizations such as the OAS and the Inter-American Defense Board have pivotal roles in mitigating and attenuating the tensions among countries of the hemisphere.

The Caribbean Basin as the Third Border

As the United States' "southern flank" or "third border," the Caribbean Basin provides some protection to the United States against terrorism and attacks. Two CARICOM countries, Antigua and Barbuda and the Bahamas, contribute to the U.S. military infrastructure. Antigua and Barbuda hosts a satellite-tracking station for the U.S. Air Force and the Bahamas is home to the Atlantic Underwater Testing and Evaluation Center (AUTEC), which is responsible for the research and development of undersea warfare. Another issue of vital concern to U.S. national security interests is the fact that vessels with critical supplies that transit the Panama Canal have to negotiate the Caribbean Sea to and from U.S. East Coast destinations.

Flanagan and his colleagues point out that the U.S. strategy for homeland defense is characterized by "an active, layered defence to deter, intercept, and defeat threats at a safe distance."[44] Mexico, mainland Central America, northern South America (which includes the CARICOM countries of Guyana and Suriname), and the Caribbean archipelago compose the southern geographic approaches to the United States and collectively offer comparable depth to that afforded by Canada to the north. Flanagan and his colleagues also suggest that there is a need for a multidimensional approach to enhancing mutual security in the Caribbean. They call for treating the basin as a geostrategic whole rather than as a series of bilateral relationships. This approach would proceed from the recognition that there is a direct connection between the disruption of entrenched transnational criminal networks and the ability to effectively counter terrorism.

It is thus critically important that the CARICOM bloc be factored into U.S. homeland defense plans. The governments of the CARICOM countries see transnational crime and its deleterious externalities and matters related to immigration as their primary security concerns. Addressing these concerns is consistent with U.S. defense strategy, as there is a strong potential for collusion among gangs, criminal networks, and terrorist groups to advance their separate missions. Indeed, CARICOM governments themselves are highly aware of and sensitive to the role they and their organization can play in U.S. security planning, sometimes more aware than their American counterparts. The recently inaugurated CBSI is an attempt to address these critical matters.

The Caribbean Basin Security Initiative

The CBSI is based on a set of principles to which all the CARICOM countries, the Dominican Republic, and the United States have agreed through a declaration. The nations accept that the unique characteristics of the Caribbean Basin make it vulnerable to multidimensional security threats and recognize the common threats posed by not only transnational crime and narcotics production, demand, and trafficking but also illicit trafficking in small arms and light weapons and humans. The countries have identified areas for cooperation to "substantially reduce illicit trafficking," "advance public safety and security," and "further promote social justice."[45] Their plan of action calls on them to

- "strengthen the commitment and accountability of the Caribbean-U.S. Security Cooperation process at the highest level";
- "formulate strategies, actions, and programs in a consistent and effective manner to advance the mandates set by the Joint Caribbean-U.S. Security Cooperation Partnership and the Declaration of Principle";
- "ensure greater support for implementation at the national, subregional, and regional levels"; and
- "enhance international and inter-agency cooperation."[46]

The problem with these ideals is that for them to become realities, machinery within the CARICOM subgroup has to be established to relate, on

CARICOM's behalf, to the United States and the Dominican Republic. This machinery must provide one voice on behalf of the subgroup. There is a precedence for this within CARICOM; the Regional Negotiating Machinery negotiates trade issues with the European Union, particularly the European Partnership Agreement (EPA).

An integral part of the CBSI, therefore, will be the engagement process. The institutionalization of a framework for security cooperation—the Joint Caribbean–United States Framework for Security Cooperation Engagement—will facilitate engagement through institutional arrangements and instruments; a resource mobilization initiative; review procedures; and reporting procedures.[47] The last item on this list is the key to the success of the CBSI, for CARICOM faces difficulties in coordinating the micro and macro viewpoints of its fifteen small member states. The framework seeks to coordinate these viewpoints through eight entities—namely, the CARICOM Secretariat, the Security Policy Advisory Committee, IMPACS, the RSS, the CARICOM Standing Committee of Operational Entities, the Caribbean Security Coordination Committee Dominican Republic, the Caribbean–United States Security Cooperation Commission, and the Caribbean–United States Ad Hoc Technical Working Groups. With the exception of the last two, these committees have been in existence for some time now.

Conclusion

The January 2010 terror attack on the Togo football team, which was in Angola on its way to participate in the Africa Cup,[48] by the Front for the Liberation of the Enclave of Cabinda (FLEC), an Angolan rebel group,[49] characterizes the world's current strategic landscape. It is one of turmoil and conflicts within regions and states caused by ethnic, religious, and nationalistic differences. This landscape emanates from complex and contradictory forces to which must be added drug cartels and threats from information-age technology. In this new environment, Caribbean national security policy must be designed to meet these challenges, but before this can be done, the region must first understand and conceptualize what national security is from a Caribbean perspective.

CARICOM must adopt a genuinely collective approach to regional security in order to truly have a voice and be heard. The regional security model by definition must include a formal mechanism, similar to the regional negotiating machinery that deals (jointly) with all trade negotiations affecting CARICOM. But in this case, this mechanism would be responsible for managing negotiations pertaining to internal and external challenges and threats to the stability of countries and the region. This machinery should be mandated to negotiate and act on behalf of CARICOM, as the numerous entities identified in the CBSI framework can become a web of disagreements rather than a conduit for good governance and decision making. This regional conflict management and security machinery should be tasked with negotiating, on behalf of CARICOM, the hemispheric security strategy. It should also negotiate, on behalf of any given CARICOM country, territorial and other disputes with non-CARICOM countries. In addition, CARICOM's regional security strategy must focus on economic development, joint development, and the creation of business partnerships rather than on large military expenditures that do little more than create strategic stalemates.

Notes

1. The article was printed in the January 31, 2008, edition of the *Economist*.

2. See "All Out War—As Tivoli Assault Deepens, Casualties Rise," *Gleaner*, May 25, 2010, www.jamaica-gleaner.com/gleaner/20100525/.

3. Statement by Ambassador Glenda Morean-Phillip, inaugural Caribbean–United States Security Cooperation Dialogue, Washington, DC, May 27, 2010, www.caricom. org/jsp/speeches/caribbean_us_security_cooperation_dialogue_morean-phillip.jsp?bcsi_ scan_02AA058D28E26014=0lKYcLrApbXR1rmUy3xHYhcAAABoRj0R&bcsi_scan_ filename=caribbean_us_security_cooperation_dialogue_morean-phillip.jsp.

4. Ibid.

5. Charles Lutes, M. Elaine Bunn, and Stephen Flanagan, "The Emerging Global Security Environment," in *Strategic Challenges: America's Global Security Agenda*, ed. Stephen Flanagan and James Schear (Washington, DC: Institute for National Strategic Studies, National Defense University and Potomac Books, 2008).

6. For instance, Moises Naim suggests that the media's preoccupation with al-Qaeda and terrorism has obscured five other global wars that "pit governments against agile, well financed networks of highly dedicated individuals. These are the fights against the illegal international trade in drugs, arms, intellectual property, people, and money." These wars are being facilitated by global geostrategic trends, with globalization providing rapid flows of both licit and illicit goods, services, and technologies. Moises Naim, "The Five Wars of Globalization," *Foreign Policy* (January/February 2003). Lutes, Bunn, and Flanagan, in "The Emerging Global Security Environment," suggest that under current and foresighted conditions, volatility will likely be the dominant feature for the foreseeable future. They consider globalization to be "an overarching 'mega-trend' altering the world economic, cultural, and security landscape" and opine that "between now and the end of the next decade, volatility will increase as shifts in traditional power structures occur."

7. See Max Manwaring, "The New Global Security Landscape: The Road Ahead," *Low Intensity Conflict and Law Enforcement* 11, no. 2/3 (2002).

8. Ivelaw Griffith, congressional testimony to the Subcommittee on the Western Hemisphere of the Committee on Foreign Affairs, U.S. House of Representatives, December 9, 2009.

9. Cuba and Haiti are notable exceptions to this tradition.

10. Max Manwaring, *Security in the Americas: Neither Evolution nor Devolution—Impasse* (Washington, DC: Strategic Studies Institute, United States Army War College, 2004).

11. A murder squad led by drug kingpin Roger Khan, who is currently indicted in the United States for related charges, executed suspected criminals with the consent of the Guyana government. This is according to evidence given by Khan in a U.S. court. Khan was considered to be a close friend of many members of the government, including President Bharrat Jagdeo. See *Stabroek News*, October 17, 2009, http://www.stabroeknews.com/2009/stories/10/17/justice-done-in-roger-khan-case-%E2%80%93-judge-irizarry/.

12. See Peter Ford, "Global Law Claims New Turf in Sudan," *Christian Science Monitor*, June 10, 2005, www.csmonitor.com/2005/0610/p01s04-wogi.html.

13. Keith Thachuk, "The Sinister Underbelly: Organized Crime and Terrorism," in *The Global Century: Globalization and National Security*, vol. 2, ed. Richard Kugler and Ellen Frost (Washington, DC: National Defense University Press, 2001).

14. Max Manwaring, *A Contemporary Challenge to State Sovereignty: Gangs and Other Illicit Transnational Criminal Organizations in Central America, El Salvador, Mexico, Jamaica, and Brazil* (Carlisle, PA: Strategic Studies Institute, December 2007).

15. Ibid.

16. John Rapley, "The New Middle Ages," *Foreign Affairs* 85, no. 3 (May/June 2006): 93–103.

17. The CARIFTA Secretariat was also located in Guyana.

18. David Granger, *National Defence: A Brief History of the Guyana Defence Force, 1965–2005* (Georgetown, Guyana: Free Press, 2005).

19. Jacqueline Brave-Wagner, *The Guyana-Venezuela Border Dispute: Britain's Colonial Legacy in Latin America* (Boulder, CO: Westview Press, 1984).

20. The current strength of the Venezuelan Armed Forces is given as 111,000 persons, the Venezuelan National Guard as 11,500, and the reserve as 8,000. The military in Guyana is now estimated at 1,100 persons. See "Caribbean and Latin America," *Military Balance*, 108, no. 1 (2008): 55–100. But at the height of the crisis the total strength including reserves would have been approximately 7,000.

21. See Granger, *National Defence*, 57. Under the Protocol of Washington, which established the OAS, membership can be denied to any state whose territory is under claim by a member state.

22. Cedric Grant, "CARICOM: Non-Intervention and Intervention," in *Intervention Border and Maritime Issues in CARICOM*, ed. Kenneth Hall and Myrtle Chuck-A-Sang (Kingston: Ian Randle Publishers, 2006); and Clifford Griffin, "Enhancing Regional Conflict Resolution Mechanisms in the Caribbean: CARICOM and the Failure of Mediation in St. Kitts and Nevis Conflict," in *Governance, Conflict Analysis and Conflict Resolution*, ed. Cedric Grant, R. Mark Kirton (Kingston: Ian Randle Publishers, 2007), chap. 6.

23. Grant, "CARICOM," 44–49.

24. Ibid.

25. The ICC awarded Cricket World Cup 2007 to the West Indies Cricket Board (WICS), which represented teams from Antigua, Barbados, Grenada, Guyana, Jamaica, St. Kitts, St. Lucia, St. Vincent, and Trinidad and Tobago. The ICC and WICS agreed to a Master Security Plan, which evolved into the Regional Security Programme developed through CARICOM. Its overall cost topped $13 million. A Regional Intelligence Fusion Centre and an Implementation Agency for Crime and Security (IMPACS) were established, and

a regional law enforcement team of 400 military and police personnel moved among the venues as needed. The host countries, joined by Dominica, established a "single domestic space" to last throughout the tournament, requiring a CARICOM special visa, so fans could move freely from venue to venue. Its cost—$100—and availability, however, became problematic just before the event began.

26. Anthony Anderson, "Legacy of Cricket World Cup 2007" (presentation, Caribbean Policy Making Seminar, Center for Hemispheric Defense Studies, Miami Hilton, Miami, Florida, May 2009).

27. Sam C. Sarkesian, John Allen Williams, and Stephen J. Cimbala, *US National Security: Policymakers, Processes and Politics*, 4th ed. (London: Lynne Rienners Publishers, 2008), 7.

28. These 2008 estimates come from the Central Intelligence Agency, "The World Factbook," www.cia.gov/library/publications/the-world-factbook/index.html.

29. Patrick Morgan, *International Security: Problems and Solutions* (Washington, DC: CQ Press, 2006), esp. chapter 7, which is devoted to Wilsonian collective security.

30. The United States led the intervention in Grenada in 1983, with support from some Caribbean countries. This action resulted in the stabilization of the country after the prime minister and some members of his cabinet were executed by dissident elements. The United States also intervened in Haiti in 1994 and 2004.

31. All thirty-five independent countries of the Americas have ratified the OAS Charter and belong to the organization. Cuba remains a member, but its government has been excluded from participation in the OAS since 1962.

32. Hilton McDavid, "Regional Security versus National Security," in *CARICOM: Policy Options for International Engagement*, project manager Yolande Collins (Georgetown, Guyana: CARICOM Secretariat, 2009).

33. In June 2000, Suriname dispatched a gunboat to eject the oil exploration rig of CGX Energy Inc., which was then under license by the government of Guyana. It was conducting seismic surveys in the waters of the exclusive economic zone claimed by Guyana and disputed by Suriname. See Cedric Joseph, "Border Controversies and Their Implications for Stability and Security of the Caribbean Community," in *Intervention Border and Maritime Issues in CARICOM*, ed. Kenneth Hall and Myrtle Chuck-A-Sang (Kingston: Ian Randle Publishers, 2006).

34. Morgan, *International Security*, 154.

35. Griffin, "Enhancing Regional Conflict Resolution Mechanisms in the Caribbean," 73–86.

36. Hilton McDavid, "Regional Security versus National Security."

37. Ivelaw L. Griffith, in a panel discussion at the U.S. Army War College 18th Annual Global Strategy Conference, "The Security Landscape in the Caribbean: Problems without Passports," Carlisle Barracks, PA, March 29, 2007.

38. See "Caribbean Basin Security Initiative: U.S. Announces Partnership to Pursue Regional Security, Stability," U.S. Department of State, May 20, 2010, www.america.gov/st/texttrans-english/2010/May/20100524122040ihecuor0.2683331.html.

39. Stephen Flanagan, Leo Michel, James Pryzstup, and John Cope, "Adapting Alliances and Partnerships," in *Strategic Challenges: America's Global Security Agenda*, ed. Stephen Flanagan and James Schear (Washington, DC: Institute for National Strategic Studies, National Defense University and Potomac Books, 2008).

40. Joseph S. Tulchin, "Challenges to Hemispheric Security," (lecture, Research and Education in Defense and Security Studies, October 28–30, 2003, Santiago, Chile).

41. Initially launched in 1983 through the Caribbean Basin Economic Recovery Act and substantially expanded in 2000 through the U.S.-Caribbean Basin Trade Partnership Act, the CBI currently provides beneficiary countries with duty-free access to the U.S. market for most goods. See Office of the U.S. Trade Representative, "Caribbean Basin Initiative," www.ustr.gov/trade-topics/trade-development/preference-programs/caribbean-basin-initiative-cbi.

42. Martin Andersen, "Summary of CHDS and Brookings Institution Conference on Strategic Implications of China's Evolving Relationship with Latin America," Center for Hemispheric Defense Studies, National Defense University.

43. Ibid.

44. Flanagan, Michel, Pryzstup, and Cope, "Adapting Alliances and Partnerships."

45. Inaugural Caribbean-U.S. Security Cooperation Dialogue, Bureau of Western Hemisphere Affairs, U.S. State Department, Washington, DC, May 27, 2010.

46. Ibid.

47. Inaugural Caribbean-U.S. Cooperation Dialogue.

48. See "Togo Withdraws from Football Tourney after Terror Attack," *LittleAbout.com*, www.littleabout.com/news/55862,togo-withdraws-football-tourney-terror-attack-lead.html.

49. The FLEC is a guerrilla and political movement fighting for the independence of the Angolan province of Cabinda.

18

Regional Security and Conflict Management in the Americas

Terrorism from Without, Drugs and Conventional Thugs from Within

John W. Graham

While Al-Qaeda remains a formidable external threat to the Western Hemisphere and most particularly to the United States, terrorist organizations also spring from within the hemisphere. Terrorism as a means to political objectives has been a feature of the internal conflict in Colombia for almost half a century. It has also represented expressions of ethnic fanaticism (the 1985 Air India explosion, killing 389) and individual rage (the 1995 Oklahoma City bombing, killing 168).[1] But organized terrorism, as indigenously incubated networks, is not the major threat to the Americas.[2] By a wide margin, the major threat to the region is the sheer scale and destabilizing power of narcotics-fueled organized crime. Colombia, Peru, and Ecuador, as primary producers of cocaine, are heavily contaminated. Colombia, Mexico, and, more recently, Guatemala are producers and exporters of heroin. Mexico, Central America, and the Caribbean are the main corridors for the flow of drugs into the United States and Canada. Violence, both as a function of the war on crime and gang turf battles, envelops the region. Murder rates in many of these countries are among the highest in the globe and have increased over the past four years. As governments, the judiciary, and security forces are corrupted, the pace of economic development slows, the quality of life is diminished, and many countries are increasingly destabilized.[3]

The chapter first examines the evolution of this conflict over the past twenty-five years and then focuses on the nature and scale of present threats. Remedies are in short supply: the many failures, the few successes, and future prospects are examined.

Shifting Challenges

The classic case of conflict resolution in the Americas of the past twenty-five years is the Esquipulas Agreement,[4] which led to the end of a long and bloody conflict in Central America. Of course, the political landscape has changed enormously since that agreement was signed in August 1987. Colombia aside—and despite the reappearance of Nicaraguan president Daniel Ortega and the fact that even more blood is being spilled violently in this subregion today than during that era—there are no contemporary parallels to that landscape. However, within this story lies a parable.

The agreement, signed by an improbable cast of Central American presidents, not only contained the essence of the formula by which peace would be consolidated but also gained for its leading advocate, Costa Rican president Oscar Arias, the Nobel Peace Prize. Alas, the Nobel Committee blew a golden opportunity to cement the peace process and to instill pride in the presidents' achievement by failing to share the prize with the other four presidents—all of whom played indispensable roles and all of whom had more difficult constituencies than Arias.

Esquipulas was the child of Contadora, the support and mediation group composed of Mexico, Panama, Colombia, and Venezuela. Contadora and its various supporters, including Canada and the Latin Support Group (Peru, Argentina, Brazil, and Uruguay) took the view that while the Cold War had clearly exacerbated the crisis, the roots of the Central American morass were more social, economic, and regional—and that solution required (inter alia) the withdrawal of foreign "advisers." The U.S. view (expressed by Ronald Reagan) was that the conflict was fundamentally an extension of the Cold War. They opposed Contadora and they opposed the premises that underpinned the Esquipulas formula. Increasingly nervous that the five presidents meeting in Guatemala might actually accept terms that Washington regarded as strategically disadvantageous, House Speaker Jim Wright worked with the Reagan administration to produce a more self-serving alternative, which was aimed particularly at the removal of all Soviet bases and Soviet assistance to Nicaragua. U.S. military advisers would be reduced, but not eliminated.

The so-called Reagan-Wright plan landed on the conference table of the five presidents as they were meeting in the small Guatemalan town of Esquipulas. In fact, the prospects of consensus across this politically diverse collection of presidents were not high. Honduran president Jose Azcona had been warned by his leading generals that he would be dead meat if he went along with anything cooked up by Arias and Ortega. As it happened, the five were so mortified that the U.S. government would presume to dictate the terms of a regional compact during their own discussions following four and a half years of painful gestation that they resolved to make peace happen and to make it happen on their own terms.

History in this region offers a range of lessons. Four years earlier another drama engaged the attention of the Reagan government, from which quite a different message emerged. The center of these events was the Eastern Caribbean. The leftist and Cuban-allied government of Grenada was overturned by a group of fanatical Marxist-Leninists who executed Morris Bishop, the prime minister, and most of his cabinet. A small detachment of Cuban troops was on the island. Planning was advanced to use the almost-completed new airport as a staging base for military flights between the USSR and Cuba. Washington and the governments on the Eastern Caribbean were understandably alarmed. The islands were exceedingly vulnerable. Defense forces comprised tiny contingents of modestly armed police constables—some on bicycles. At very high speed, the Reagan government assembled a coalition of countries (Barbados and the Organization of Eastern Caribbean States) to provide international cover for the invasion of Grenada. The purpose of the invasion was the expulsion of the Cubans and the installation of a more congenial interim government pending elections. Although it had its comic opera moments, the mission was swift and successful. Above all, it made sense in the circumstances.[5]

Other vivid examples of conflict management and mismanagement in the last twenty-five years, most of which were clearly marked by success or failure, include the following:

- *Failure in 1991 Haiti.* A coup against Haitian president Jean-Bertrand Aristide by army officers led by General Raoul Cedras succeeded because the government of President George H. W. Bush, quite visibly to the plotters, took no action to stop it.
- *Success in 1993 Guatemala.* Seeking international validation of illegal powers that he had taken to strengthen his internal control, Guatemalan president Jorge Serrano invited the secretary general

of the Organization of American States (OAS) to Guatemala City. The public consultation led by the secretary general emboldened key sectors of the population to resist Serrano's actions (the *autogolpe*), culminating in the bloodless departure of the president.

- *Success in 1994 Dominican Republic.* The OAS, having for the first time in the hemisphere blown the whistle on a manipulated election, engaged in mediation in conjunction with the local Catholic Church. The mediation, empowered by pressure from the United States, caused the government to make concessions to the opposition, thus avoiding open civil conflict.[6]
- *Success in 1994 Haiti.* Backed by UN and OAS resolutions and reinforced by the imminent arrival of three thousand U.S. troops of the 82nd Airborne Division, former president Jimmy Carter, Senator Sam Nunn, and General (ret.) Colin Powell negotiated the bloodless departure of General Cédras and his brutal regime, which had overturned President Aristide two years before.
- *Bad judgment and bad management in 2004 Haiti.* The forced departure of the by then disgraced President Aristide was achieved by the United States with the strong support of France and the *nihil obstat* (tacit declaration of no objection) of Canada, causing the chaos to deepen and lengthen.

The common thread through all but one of these episodes is the role—usually decisive for good or for ill—of the United States. However, the leverage upon which that role depended, while not disappearing, has weakened considerably. With astute stewardship, the authority and credibility of the United States may be revitalized; however, its hegemonic clout is most unlikely to return. Even though the present swing to the left across much of the region may be more cyclical than permanent, the sense of diminished vulnerability to the United States is not expected to change.

The Honduran Muddle

Latin America's most recent coup, which saw the pajama-clad president of Honduras, Manuel Zelaya, rousted out of bed at gunpoint and flown to involuntary exile in Costa Rica in June 2009, illustrates the decline of U.S. leverage and the extent to which the OAS is at times held hostage to pressures from ALBA,[7] the left-wing consortium of states led by Venezuela. Zelaya had flouted his own constitution, apparently to facilitate his candidacy for an illegal second term in office. He sacked the head of the armed forces for failing to comply with orders that the general and the Supreme

Court regarded as unconstitutional. Thereupon, the Honduran Congress, with the support of the Supreme Court and the Supreme Electoral Tribunal, replaced Zelaya with Roberto Micheletti, a civilian who, as interim president, was constitutionally the next in line.

Latin American governments were rattled by the coup. Most sitting presidents have been touched and in some cases burned by coups (*golpes*) in their own countries. As a result, there was unanimous OAS condemnation of the coup and determined efforts to erase the precedent—only the second successful coup in the Americas in twenty years (after Haiti)—and return Zelaya to office. However, under the surface of OAS consensus, a split developed about how vigorously the return of Zelaya should be sought as several members (the United States, Panama, Peru, Canada, and some Caribbean countries), while agreeing that the Honduran military had acted illegally, quietly considered that the generals had responded to "extenuating circumstances." These countries were concerned about the hazards of penalizing—in a manner disproportionate to the crime—one of Latin America's most impoverished countries. They were troubled about the social and political destabilization that would inevitably follow if a route through the impasse were not found. Also exacerbating divisions within the OAS was the view that a coup by a military still subject to elected civilian control is less corrosive of democratic governance than the deliberate erosion of constitutional checks and balances as practiced by the presidents of Nicaragua and Venezuela.

A major confrontation between ALBA and more moderate forces within the OAS took place in Honduras just three weeks before the coup and produced a surprising conclusion. The context was the readmission of Cuba to the OAS, an issue that had dominated the Summit of the Americas two months earlier. The setting was San Pedro Sula, Honduras, where the annual General Assembly of the OAS was meeting. This was probably the most highly charged General Assembly since the inception of the OAS in 1948. While the readmission of Cuba after its expulsion from the OAS in 1962 following the missile crisis was the official issue, ALBA members, especially Venezuela, Ecuador, and Nicaragua, saw an opportunity to open wide a division with the United States and thereby weaken the OAS. The ALBA countries proposed a resolution that would readmit Cuba with no strings attached. In other words, Cuba would be exempted from a robust body of OAS requirements regarding human rights and democratic norms. In the course of two days of heated negotiations, the initiative was resisted initially by Mexico, the United States, Belize, Jamaica, Canada, and Brazil.[8] Eventually, with support for the resolution evaporating, ALBA accepted that Cuba should be readmitted following acceptance of the OAS's human rights and democratic instruments. In the end, the conflict produced a valuable lesson: ALBA does not always win and the OAS need not lose crucial battles. As for Cuba, its government was happy to be used by ALBA for the purpose of removing an anachronism but soon declared that, as the OAS was "totally irrelevant," it had no intention of joining.

The Major Security Threats

At present, neither aggressive ideology nor pressures external to the hemisphere constitute a major threat to the region. In Colombia, as the region's principal guerilla organization, Fuerzas Armadas Revolucionarias de Colombia (FARC), ages and as the American-supported Colombian Army has become more successful, the only remaining armed conflict or civil war in the region with ideological roots has begun to run out of steam.

In Cuba, Raul Castro is not interested in regional destabilization. His priority is to attempt to build prosperity so as to sustain a minimal level of support for his autocratic regime. In fact, he has muted the usual Cuban derogatory language about the United States, apparently wants a settlement with the United States or at least some improved form of modus vivendi, and in 2008 sent out feelers to this effect. President Barack Obama was probably interested, but Cuba is not that high on his agenda and he appears anxious to avoid the antagonism of Republican legislators on nonessential issues.

In Venezuela, Hugo Chavez is not a paper tiger, but he has lowered the volume of his blatant meddling in the area (save Honduras and clamorous objections to Colombia's recent granting of bases to the U.S. military). Furthermore, Obama is not so much fun for him to attack. Chavez also has internal distractions: the highest rate of inflation in Latin America; soaring crime and corruption; and, with lower oil prices, declining national income.

No one knows what fresh contagious paranoia might be sown by the global financial meltdown, but in the Western Hemisphere, the major security threat is neither ideological, nor even militant jihadists. The major threat is the scale and destabilizing power of narcotics-fueled organized crime.

Organized Crime and Corruption: Mexico and Central America

The struggle against organized crime and corruption and its sophisticated technology is not going well. This conclusion applies widely across the Caribbean, including Guyana, and especially to the Caribbean's western shores.

Mexico, Central America, and the islands of the Caribbean (Guyana included) are the main corridors for the flow of drugs into the United States and Canada. There has been talk of Mexico becoming a failed state. Murder rates, already high by international standards, more than doubled from 2007 to 2008.[9] In the four years since Felipe Calderon began his tour as president, 28,000 Mexicans have been killed.[10] That Mexico could move to failed-state category is highly improbable. But destabilization, the extent to which the gangs have penetrated the security apparatus, the impunity with which they operate, the inability thus far of President Calderon to combat the cartels, and the spillover of this crisis down the isthmus and into the Caribbean represent a major threat to hemispheric security. Strategizing about solutions is advanced and the crisis has transformed the levels of Mexican-U.S. cooperation.

The Merida Initiative, introduced by President George W. Bush, is the vehicle for providing much more U.S. security assistance to Mexico and the countries of Central America. The first tranche of the initiative was $465 million, with $400 million marked for Mexico to cover training, technical support, and the purchase of aircraft. Funds were also marked for tracking narcotics flows in and out of neighboring Caribbean states. Another signal of this transformation was the decision taken in 2008, under the auspices of President Bush, to introduce the "gunrunner" program, which tracks the sale of weapons sold in the Southwestern United States—but, as yet, does nothing to limit the sale of weapons that migrate in high volume to Mexican gangs.

Because it specifically reaches beyond the borders of Mexico, the design of the Merida Initiative is considered an improvement on Plan Colombia. Execution, especially the need for adequate funding, is a different matter. Former Mexican foreign minister Jorge Castenada writes that even the stepped-up war against organized crime is "unwinnable" and that the annual commitment by the United States through the Merida Initiative is "woefully insufficient." Castenada is looking for a program on the scale of Plan Colombia ($8 billion over ten years) and a fresh approach to criminal penalties and consumption in the United States.[11] In his book *El Narco: La Guerra Fallida* (Narco: The Failed War), cowritten with Ruben Aguilar, he argues that the key battle must be fought on the U.S. side of the frontier.[12]

Although the penny has taken a long time to drop, Canada is beginning to recognize the threat to its own citizens of increasingly powerful and sophisticated narcotics gangs. In August 2009, Stephen Harper, the Canadian prime minister, announced a project to provide training for the Mexican police by the Royal Canadian Mounted Police (RCMP). This measure forms part of a larger Canadian commitment of up to C$15 million a year to combat crime in the Americas and represents much of the security component of the Conservative government's "Americas Strategy."

Corruption, gang control, and gang impunity are, if anything, worse in Guatemala than in Mexico. Witnesses do not bear witness and the judiciary is either terrorized or bought. Ninety-eight percent of accused murderers walk free. The country's capacity to control many of the fundamentals of governance is dissolving.[13] It is only the smaller scale of Guatemala that drops the country a few notches down as a major regional threat.

El Salvador, on Guatemala's southwestern border, had a well-organized and peaceful election on March 15, 2009. After twenty years of only modestly productive administration, the right-wing political dynasty, Alianza Republica Nacionalista (ARENA), was defeated by the former Communist guerilla organization Frente Farabundo Marti para la Liberacion Nacional (FMLN), now under moderate left-of-center leadership. Astonishingly, no one was killed in partisan collisions. For reasons that are not entirely clear, political competition there has been insulated from gang violence.[14] El Salvador's police force is relatively less corrupt than its Guatemalan and Mexican counterparts. However, the good news stops there. El Salvador's homicide rate (at 48 per 100,000 people) in 2008 was higher than that of either Mexico or Guatemala and rose further still in 2009. For youth (ages 15–24) the murder rate is the worst in the world. (By comparison, the homicide rate in the United States in 2008 was 5.8 per 100,000 people.)[15] As elsewhere on the isthmus, most criminal violence is linked to drug cartel turf battles.

To provide total context, it is necessary to point out that the most common form of violence in Central America, as in Latin America as a whole, is domestic violence, which is linked to psychological and sexual assault.[16]

Organized Crime and Corruption: The Caribbean

Eastward into the Caribbean the situation is better, but not by much. In a 2006 joint text, the World Bank and the UN Office on Drugs and Crime (UNODC) produced a comprehensive and disturbing report on crime in the Caribbean.[17] The report concludes that high rates of crime and violence are undermining growth, threatening human welfare, impeding social development, and inhibiting investment. It highlighted that per capita murder rates in the Caribbean are higher than any other region in the world, slightly worse than those in Colombia and South Africa but not as grim as those in Guatemala and El Salvador. The narcotics industry drives a large part of these statistics. In global terms, the overall Latin America and Caribbean region is responsible for 42 percent of the world's recorded homicides involving firearms and 66 percent of all kidnappings. Another regional distinction—especially for a region that contains only 8.6 percent of the world's population—is that seven of the world's worst rates for intentional homicide are held by Caribbean and Latin American countries.[18]

These high levels of violent crime have obvious impacts on the economy. Many Caribbean states are at the top of the list of the world's most indebted countries and are acutely vulnerable to the swings of international tourism and thus have reduced resilience to the challenges of economic downturn, organized crime, and medical crises. This, in turn, leads to a brain drain, with seven Caribbean countries having among the world's highest rates of emigration of college graduates. In Jamaica, for example, approximately 80 percent of college graduates emigrate, according to the Canadian International Development Agency. Furthermore, increasing amounts of money are being redirected away from productive areas and spent on hiring armed security guards. It is estimated that approximately 4 million persons are now employed in the private security industry throughout Latin America and the Caribbean—some are better armed than the local police, but many have no weapons training.

Concern that crime has become an increasingly attractive vocation for the young is raising questions about why this should be. Part of the answer is, of course, that in societies where there are few career opportunities, the rewards and the macho enticements of crime are perceived to be greater than the risks. Researchers in Jamaica (and more recently in the World Bank) are looking at a complementary cause. In the Commonwealth Caribbean as a whole, males are dropping out of school—leaving an increasingly lopsided social order. Women account for almost 80 percent of university graduates at the University of the West Indies. Alessandra Heineman and Dorte Verner state that "the main risk factor for domestic violence is the lack of education." They note that each additional year of schooling reduces the likelihood of violence by more than 1 percent.[19] Looking for a path out of this destabilizing cycle, experts have concluded that the values and the role model concepts that direct young males to crime are formed in the preprimary years, notably in poor single-parent households, and that by primary school it is too late to reengineer the culture. Potential solutions to seemingly intractable dilemmas are rare. This research argues for much higher investment in and international assistance for preprimary development. Given limited resources, does this mean that some of the funding for tertiary education should be redirected to preprimary? This is a difficult but urgent question that few governments in the region have acknowledged.

Other Security Threats

Inadequate Health Systems

Present challenges call for a definition of conflict management that is sufficiently elastic to include health issues, as they pose increasingly serious risks for regional stability. The following discussion focuses largely on the Caribbean, not because Latin America (especially Mexico) is relatively free of major health concerns but because the Caribbean is the most vulnerable subregion.

The porous virtual border that separates the Caribbean from North America is just as porous for health security as it is for crime security. While health standards in the Commonwealth Caribbean are better than in many areas of the developing world, Caribbean failures and inadequacies constitute a hazardous potential vector because of the magnitude of potential North American exposure. In many areas of the Caribbean, communicable diseases are spiking. Health care systems are incapable of adequate monitoring and compliance with basic standards. Diabetes and cardiovascular figures are rising dramatically and the costs to local health care systems soar accordingly. Bubbling under these concerns is fear of a pandemic, which the Caribbean would be ill-equipped to handle, which would devastate the micro states, and which could easily migrate to North America. While underscoring the gravity of this challenge, the Pan American Health Organization (PAHO) identifies "violence" as the regional pandemic.[20]

The H1N1 (swine flu) pandemic of 2009 highlights this anxiety. Originating in Mexico, the virus followed—with very few exceptions—the most well-traveled flight paths. Both the United States and Canada, in conjunction with PAHO guidance, should apportion increased funding to improve monitoring, regional cooperation mechanisms, and common regional licensing systems, and to more effectively expand medical assistance programs beyond HIV/AIDS to include other chronic diseases. (Canada recently announced an additional C$18 million over four years for this effort, but more is required.) Governments in the region should develop and implement much more aggressive public information programs on hygiene, HIV/AIDS, obesity, and diabetes.

The Arms Build-up

A recent development causing aggravation in the Andean region is the rise of weapons purchases by states. One notable culprit contributing to this trend is Venezuela, whose arms expenditures now average over $1 billion per year. Colombia's armed forces are well equipped with up-to-date weaponry, but they are increasingly overshadowed by Venezuelan firepower, which includes new military aircraft acquired from the Russians. Other states are buying more as well: some to modernize and some, especially in Central America and Mexico, to deal with organized crime. But in many cases, the purchases amount to political trade-offs meant to appease military establishments. In all cases, though, increased military spending means less social spending. The experts in this area have been careful not to characterize the rising purchases as an arms race, saying that while the present situation has the power to intimidate and destabilize, it is more of an arms "build-up."

The Major Players

The two indispensable conflict management players in global terms are the United States and the United Nations. Despite losing the hegemonic clout that it was able to exercise in the last century, and notwithstanding increasing competition from Brazil, the United States unquestionably remains the big player in the Western Hemisphere. The other "big player" on the global field, the United Nations, is not so visible in this region. On a number of occasions over the past quarter century it has played key roles when the regional organization (the OAS) was persona non grata (e.g., in Guatemala) and when it could deploy peacekeepers (e.g., in Haiti), which the OAS is not equipped to do. Nevertheless, despite its many weaknesses, its Washington "centeredness," and its outrageously inadequate funding base, the region has turned more often than not to the OAS for political crisis management.

Since the late 1980s the OAS has played a remarkable role in facilitating the change of political culture from one of authoritarian regimes, punctuated by frequent coups d'état, to one of consistent, if sometimes flawed, democratic governance. In the global context only the European Union can claim such a decisive role in institutionalizing the democratic process. In the Western Hemisphere over the past twenty years, there have been only two successful coups d'état. There has been a correlation between stability and the advance of democratic governance. For about fifteen years— from 1990—the OAS was able to navigate a path between the traditional claims of absolute sovereignty and new rules that commit the hemisphere to condemn the illegal overthrow of governments. All member governments of the OAS (it operates by consensus) endowed the organization with teeth so that governments coming to power through force would be subject to regionwide commercial and diplomatic sanctions.

With the exception of Cuba, all governments of the hemisphere have been elected (more or less) democratically. Unfortunately, the success of the democratic election process has not been matched by other institutional bulwarks of democracy, such as

- healthy political party systems;
- respect for the judiciary, the police, and other security services;
- reformed and adequately and equitably functioning taxation systems; and
- a less than exorbitant disparity between wealth and poverty.

Slippage away from democratic governance is apparent—notably through Chavez's removal of checks and balances and politicization of the judiciary and electoral tribunal. Democratic gains in the region over the past twenty years also received a setback in 2008 with Nicaragua's manipulated municipal elections. With President Ortega seeking to entrench his authority, blatant fraud on this scale has not been seen in the country since the time of the Somozas. By contrast and despite increasingly serious distortions in the preelection playing field, however, the election process on election day in the 2010 Venezuelan elections was relatively transparent.

The OAS: Vexing, Perplexing, and Still Essential

The region's multiple crises should mean more recourse to the OAS, the organization mandated with collective security responsibility. However, just as the region is tired of the old asymmetry, it is showing frustration with the most asymmetrical international organization on the planet—the OAS—and is demonstrating increased interest in alternative fora. The OAS is facing competition. The Spanish founded Ibero-American summits have been meeting annually since 1991. Ibero-American summits exclude Canada, the United States, and the English-speaking Caribbean. Brazil organized a summit, the Union of South American Nations (UNASUR), that excluded the United States, Mexico, and Canada. A long-standing, seldom effective, and almost exclusively Latin American body, the Rio Group, sprang to life in March 2008 when, under the leadership of President Leonel Fernandez of the Dominican Republic, it brokered negotiations that cooled (so far) an incendiary dispute among Ecuador, Venezuela, and Colombia arising from the latter's attack on a FARC base inside the Ecuadorian frontier. It is generally acknowledged that the "accord" would not have happened if the United States had been at the table. Most recently, Mexico chaired a summit meeting in Cancun that created the Community of Latin American and Caribbean States, yet another regional organization that includes Cuba and excludes the United

States and Canada. However, it does not have a permanent secretariat and has little prospect of organizational funding.

The OAS secretary general, Chilean Jose Miguel Insulza, is articulate and energetic but commands reduced authority in the region. In 2010 he was reelected by acclamation for a second term. However, his capacity to defuse political crises has been diminished by perceived poor judgment calls on recent crises in Honduras and Ecuador and by political polarization within the OAS involving frequent Brazilian truculence and the intransigence of ALBA countries.

Five years ago and shortly after his election, Insulza established the Secretariat for Multi-Dimensional Security to collate data, investigate hazards to security, and recommend preventive measures. Inside the organization, this secretariat collaborates with the Inter-American Commission on Drug Abuse (best known by its Spanish acronym CICAD), a much older, very effective, and inadequately recognized instrument of the Inter-American system. Two other regional mechanisms fill out the OAS's magazine of security tools. One is the Inter-American Convention Against the Illicit Manufacturing of and Trafficking in Firearms, Ammunition, Explosives and other Related Materials (CIFTA). Signed in Washington in 1997 and subsequently ratified by almost all member states, it still lacks its sharpest tooth: the United States has not ratified it (nor has Canada). The other— and so far, more useful instrument—is the Inter-American Committee against Terrorism (CICTE), which was established by the General Assembly of the OAS four years before 9/11 with an ambitious mandate. The title may be a misnomer, though, as the CICTE's primary activity is combating conventional crime. Staffed by officers of the OAS, it promotes international coordination and its planning, training, and executive activities engage subregional bodies and the private sector. Key areas covered include financial controls, critical infrastructure protection, cyber/document security, and crisis management. Its border-control segment embraces aviation and maritime security as well as fraud prevention.

Often paralyzed by its own political divisions, the OAS has been unable to adequately address many of the region's new challenges—its consensual system being a strength and at times a debilitating weakness. The OAS has sometimes been and should be the region's principal damage control agency. Often rightly condemned for inaction, it is more often denigrated for its siesta and cigar image. In fact, its record, especially during the period from 1990 to 2002, is better than it gets credit for.

The OAS is the principal delivery system for the Summit of the Americas. The most recent summit, the fifth such forum since 1994, which assembled all of the region's presidents and prime ministers, with the exception of

Raul Castro, was held in April 2009 in Port of Spain, Trinidad. The need for multidimensional action and coordination across the hemisphere against organized crime should have driven this summit. Badly organized and with a mostly jaded set of objectives, it proved a disappointing event—only rescued from disaster by the disarming presence of President Obama. Although not officially on the agenda, Cuba, the U.S. embargo, and the return of the island to normal standing within the OAS dominated much of the inconclusive discussions both behind doors and in public.

Where Next?

The marathon race between organized crime and the authority of government rumbles on, but in terms of control, firepower, resources, and coordination, organized crime has the lead. It is sustained by undiminished consumer demand for narcotics and the weakness of its opponents. In a newspaper article written by Fernando Enrique Cardoso, former president of Brazil and cochair of the Latin American Commission on Drugs and Democracy, described the crisis bluntly: "the war on drugs has failed." Continuing to wage this war "in the same way," he stated, "is ludicrous."[21] Arguing that the criminalization of drug users "drove resources away from treatment and deterred people from seeking help with addiction," Cardoso and his cochairs (former Presidents Cesar Gaviria of Colombia and Ernesto Zedillo of Mexico—all of them hardened veterans of this war) declare that there is an imperative need for "a paradigm shift ... away from repression of drug users and towards treatment and prevention." The war on drugs has not only failed, they argue, but it has also produced fresh monsters. Cardoso notes that one of the unexpected consequences of this war has been the newly developed capacity of criminals to produce synthetic drugs.[22] Another consequence is the slow, corrosive climb in addiction rates in Latin America and the Caribbean. While there are a few signals of pressure for the decriminalization of marijuana, unfortunately there is as yet little appetite for the commission's conclusions in the primary consuming nation, the United States, and only sporadic interest by the other nations of the hemisphere.[23]

A series of investigative articles published by the *Washington Post* in July 2010 exposed major self-inflicted obstacles to the defense of national security in the United States.[24] The reports noted that 854,000 citizens hold top-secret clearances and work inside 1,271 government organizations and 1,931 private companies. The authors of the report describe this new leviathan as having become "so large, so unwieldy, and so secretive" that "it amounts to an alternative geography of America hidden from public view and lacking in thorough oversight." U.S. secretary of defense Robert Gates and CIA director Leon Panetta acknowledged that questions about "whether the government is still in control of its most sensitive activities" are pertinent. The pursuit of organized crime is inevitably overshadowed by the size, complexity, and appetite of this new bureaucratic colossus.

Recent commitments by the United States, the Inter-American Development Bank, and, to a lesser extent, Canada, directed especially to Mexico and its immediate neighbors will provide only limited succor. The failure of the Summit of the Americas in the spring of 2009 to seriously address the region's paramount threat was discouraging. Expectations that a ministerial meeting of the OAS on hemispheric security held later that year in Santo Domingo would redress the weaknesses of the summit proved largely hollow.[25] The secretary general and senior OAS officers reminded delegates that the scale of regional crime and violence is overwhelming; that police education is both inadequate and significantly out of date; that abysmally little is being done about training for senior police management; that there is a major lack of comparative data; and that far too little attention is accorded to community protection. It would be comforting to say that the conference was infused with a new sense of purpose, but this was not the case. Delegations reported several successful initiatives, but with only two exceptions (Paraguay and Chile), no delegation grappled with the central issues identified by the commission cochaired by Cardoso, Gaviria, and Zedillo. The commission itself, cosponsored by some of the most prestigious figures in Latin America, was not mentioned at the conference. The same enervating diffidence about addressing the central issues of drugs and organized crime was evident at the General Assembly of the OAS held in Lima, Peru, June 6–8, 2010.[26]

The need to push the threats posed by the narcotics trade and organized crime up the agenda and to insist on effective interregional coordination is overdue. These are challenges upon which Obama, Chavez, and others from different corners of the political spectrum could make common cause.

Notes

1. Although the Air India crash—the worst mass murder in Canadian history—occurred over international waters, the accused perpetrators and most victims were Canadian.

2. For a discussion of the potential for low-grade terrorism in the Tri-Border Area between Argentina, Brazil, and Paraguay near Iguazu Falls, see Thomas G. Costa and Gaston Schulmiester, *Global Archives* 8, no. 1 (February 2007).

3. Sophisticated organized crime also provides a potential platform for terrorism.

4. The formal title is Esquipulas II Procedures for the Establishment of a Full and Lasting Peace in Central America. The final cease-fire (for El Salvador) was brokered by the

UN secretariat under the leadership of Secretary-General Perez de Cuellar and his special representative, Alvaro de Soto, who mediated the 1992 agreement known as the Chatultepec Accord.

5. Even so, it did not make sense to Canadian prime minister Pierre Trudeau, who was enormously distressed that his friends in the Caribbean had not consulted him and that the Americans had given the Canadian government only oblique advance notice the night before. It was the author's job at the time to interpret the meaning of the message from the State Department and pass it on to the prime minister. John Compton, then prime minister of St. Lucia, subsequently told the author that he had tried to inform the Canadian government but was unable to get through to anyone he knew at the High Commission located in Bridgetown, Barbados.

6. The author was the OAS mediator.

7. ALBA—the Bolivarian Alternative for Latin America and the Caribbean—comprises Venezuela, Bolivia, Ecuador, Dominica, Paraguay, and (precoup) Honduras.

8. As a civil-society observer and representative of the Friends of the Inter-American Democratic Charter and of the Canadian Foundation for the Americas (FOCAL), the author was on the periphery of some of these discussions.

9. Devin Parsons, "The Nature of the U.S.-Mexico Drug War: Equal Responsibility, Unequal Costs," Council on Hemispheric Affairs, June 9, 2010.

10. "Organised Crime in Mexico: Under the Volcano," *Economist*, October 14, 2010.

11 Jorge Castenada, "What's Spanish for Quagmire?" *Foreign Policy* (January/February 2010).

12. Jorge Castenada and Ruben Aguilar, *El Narco: La Guerra Fallida* (Mexico City: Punto de Lectura, 2010).

13. Carlos Castresana, the head of the United Nation's International Commission against Impunity in Guatemala, resigned on June 7, 2010, in protest over the government's appointment of an attorney general who was expected to obstruct his mandate. See Carlos Castresana, "On the Critical Importance of United States Policy Factors," and Jean Daudelin, "Centre for Security and Defense Studies Working Paper" (working paper, Carleton University, Fall 2010).

14. Gang membership in El Salvador is estimated at between 30,000 and 35,000. The figures for Honduras are similar. Alessandra Heineman and Dorte Verner, "Crime and Violence in Development: A Literature Review of Latin America and the Caribbean" (World Bank Policy Research Working Paper no. 4041, World Bank, October 1, 2006).

15. Statistics in this area are not as hard as they could be as a consequence of varying crime definitions across countries.

16. Heineman and Verner, "Crime and Violence in Development."

17. See UNODC and the World Bank, "Crime, Violence, and Development: Trends, Costs, and Policy options in the Caribbean," March 2007, www.unodc.org/pdf/research/Cr_and_Vio_Car_E.pdf.

18. UNODC, "Homicide Statistics, Criminal Justice Sources (2003–2008)," www.unodc.org/unodc/en/data-and-analysis/homicide.html; additional information from Amerigo Incalaterrea, UN Office of the High Commissioner for Human Rights, as reported by EFE, May 14, 2010.

19. Heineman and Verner, "Crime and Violence in Development."

20. Ibid.

21. Fernando Enrique Cardoso, "Former President of Brazil Says Hardline War on Drugs Has Failed," *Observer*, September 6, 2009. The full report of the Latin Commission on Drugs and Democracy is available at www.drogasdemocracia.org/English/.

22. Equally unexpected has been Canada's ranking in the synthetic drugs business. According to the UNODC, Canada is now one of the world's primary producers of ecstasy and amphetamines.

23. Softening of this line, but only on the edges, is signaled by the Obama administration's decision not to enforce antimarijuana laws in states with legalized "medical" marijuana. Cited in Castenada, "What's Spanish for Quagmire?"

24. The first in the "Top Secret America" series of articles by Dana Priest and William M. Arkin was published in the *Washington Post* on July 19, 2010.

25. The OAS's Second Meeting of Ministers of Public Security of the Americas (MISPA II) in Santo Domingo, November 4–5, 2009, was attended by the author in an observer capacity.

26. Security was one of the three central themes of this General Assembly, along with Peace and Cooperation. The author was present as a civil society representative.

19

Security Challenges in Mexico and Central America

Raúl Benítez Manaut and Ricardo Córdova Macías

A new set of emerging transnational security problems—drugs, mounting crime, youth gangs—threaten social and political stability in Central America and have arrested the significant political and security reforms that were undertaken in the late 1980s and 1990s following the termination of civil wars in El Salvador, Guatemala, and Nicaragua. Furthermore, the future stability of the Mexican state, and with it Mexico's democracy, is also in growing jeopardy due to the rising tide of drug-gang-led violence and the use of the army to combat criminal elements.

This chapter discusses the evolution of security sector reform in Mexico and Central America over the last two decades, examines the security issues that are specific to Mexico and Central America and those that are shared between the two, and outlines the main challenges to the region's security agenda.

The Mesoamerica Region: A Definition

Although some authors refer to Mexico and Central America as Mesoamerica, an analysis of economic and development data reveals wide variations between Mexico and Central America and among Central American countries (see table 19.1). In addition, analysis of the evolution of the region's security concerns reveals that the causes and expressions of insecurity in Mexico and Central America have traditionally been different. More recently, however, Mexico and Central America have shared similar security

Table 19.1   Basic Economic and Social Information for Mexico
and Central America

Country	Territory (in sq. kms.)	2009 Population (in millions)	2008 GDP (in millions of USD)	2008 GDP per capita (in millions of USD)	2007 Human Development Index (HDI)	2007 HDI rank
México	1,964,375	109.6	769,256.6	7,092.0	0.854	53
Guatemala	108,890	14.0	23,253.3	1,698.7	0.704	122
El Salvador	21,040	6.2	16,417.4	2,676.9	0.747	106
Honduras	112,492	7.5	10,637.7	1,452.0	0.732	112
Nicaragua	130,373	5.7	5,088.6	896.7	0.699	124
Costa Rica	51,100	4.6	23,441.8	5,188.5	0.854	54
Panamá	75,520	3.5	19,333.1	5,687.9	0.840	60
Belice	22,966	0.3	1,188.9	3,949.7	0.772	93

Note: GDP figures are in constant prices (2000 = 100).
Sources: Comisión Económica para América Latina y el Caribe, "Anuario Estadístico 2009 de América Latina y el Caribe," 79–80, http://websie.eclac.cl/anuario_estadistico/anuario_2009/esp/index.html; *Informe sobre Desarrollo Humano 2009: Superando barreras: movilidad y desarrollo humanos* (New York: UNDP, 2009), 185, http://hdr.undp.org/en/media/HDR_2009_ES_Complete.pdf; United Nations Population Fund (UNFPA), *State of World Population 2009: Facing a Changing World—Women, Population and Climate* (New York: UNFPA, 2009); Instituto Nacional de Estadística y Geografía, http://mapserver.inegi.gob.mx/geografia/espanol/datosgeogra/extterri/frontera.cfm?c=154.

problems (drugs, organized crime, gangs, human trafficking), requiring the creation of mechanisms for cooperation. These security problems have an "intermestic" character, meaning they have both national and transnational dimensions. For example, at Mexico's southern border with Central America, security problems include migration, the presence of organized crime, drug trafficking, and the activities of youth *maras* (gangs). As a result, this chapter refers to Mexico and Central America as subregions that share a set of common security problems.

In the 1990s, the security agenda in Mexico and Central America moved away from one based on Cold War logic. In the Cold War, security was defined by the presence and evolution of armed conflicts and social movements that threatened security. In this sense, the guerrilla movements in Guatemala, Nicaragua, and El Salvador, the U.S. intervention to prevent the "spread of communism," and the multiple efforts to reach negotiated settlements to the armed conflicts were the key issues that defined the agenda. In the case of Mexico, avoiding a revolutionary "contagion" was crucial, and therefore its southern border was militarized. In 1994, the Zapatista movement emerged in Chiapas and positioned itself as a social armed protest on Mexico's southern border. The approach that was given to this movement in Mexico was different; while the conflict was isolated, there was a political negotiation process and increased social investment from the state.[1]

In the 1990s, Central America consolidated peace processes in the form of guerrilla demobilization and demilitarization and, in the context of implementing political reforms, promoted security-sector reforms. Out of these conflicts weak states emerged.[2] In the post-conflict period, one negative result was the emergence of youth *maras*, which governments were slow to identify and respond to and lacked the capacity to address. After the September 11, 2001, attacks on the United States, terrorism was added to the security agenda, as well as organized crime, due to the increasing presence of criminal Colombian and Mexican organizations in cocaine trafficking from Andean countries to the United States.

In Mexico and Central America, these old and new security problems coincided with the processes of democratization. Within the framework of the peace processes in Central America, state reform promoted an institutional transformation of the armed forces, leading to a redefinition of the military's role in the political system, the creation of a foundation for subordinating the military to the constitutionally elected civilian authorities, the development of a national civil police to address public security, and the advancement of democratization.[3] In the case of Mexico, however, democratization has been more complex, because the security apparatus has yet to be reformed and is still supported by the old security architecture built during the twentieth century. In fact, the Mexican government has strengthened the armed forces to confront organized crime.

Security Sector Reform in Mexico from 1990 to 2010

In this section, three topics are analyzed: security-sector reform, cooperation in North America to face common challenges, and key security issues.

Security-Sector Reform

Since the 1980s, the old political system—which dates to the time of the revolution—has been undergoing a crisis in Mexico. This system supported itself on a military institution that had great autonomy from civilian authorities and that served as the cornerstone of stability. Every important policy that was implemented in Mexico's postrevolution years (1929–1946) was developed and supported by the military, including agrarian reform and the foundation of the country's official political party, the Partido Revolucionario Institucional (PRI).[4] During this period, the PRI was a necessary and vital tool for demilitarizing the country's social and political relations in an orderly manner, because the power and influence exerted by the armed forces in the design of the state allowed the military to maintain a high degree of autonomy and to support the creation of a new political elite. This allowed for a harmonious relationship that continued over the following decades.[5]

The end of the Cold War has helped Mexico's democratization efforts, but certain domestic developments have begun to reshape civil-military relations.[6] An active civil society has emerged that has been complemented by parallel processes, including an increased respect for human rights within the state, a reduction in acts of impunity committed by the state's military and police forces, and the construction of a modern political party system. In sum, the reform of the Mexican state has slowly diminished authoritarian-style decision making by reforming the country's economic and political structures and by controlling government corruption.[7]

Following the 1988 electoral process, Mexican civil society and political parties, as well as the international community, began to exert pressure on the government to democratize. The existing authoritarian political regime, based on the hegemonic control of the PRI, was weakened under these demands. The democratization process and the entrance of Mexico into the dynamics of globalization through the North America Free Trade Agreement (NAFTA) led in the 1990s to a redefinition of security threats.[8] New social conflicts, such as the Zapatista uprising in Chiapas, and the rise of "intermestic" problems, such as drug trafficking and organized crime, have had repercussions on Mexico's national security.[9] These security issues present challenges to Mexico's continued democratization. As a result, there has been a process of remilitarization in some parts of the country and within certain state institutions, principally those concerned with law enforcement, justice, and public security.

Due to Mexico's lack of strong government institutions and weak civil society, the armed forces in Mexico have historically played a key role in political leadership, in constructing the state apparatus, and in creating social cohesion. The military was an important factor in the process of national integration in Mexico. However, when instability arose in different segments or regions of the country, such as during the 1985–88 period, when the PRI's power began to decline, the PRI used the military as a mechanism to quell unrest and to support the efforts of other government agencies in maintaining public order. As a result, the political system partially militarized itself as it did after the Tlatelolco crisis in 1968 to control student demonstrations. Thus, the government used the military to control crises, even as the government gradually reduced its budget in favor of social investments and economic development (see table 19.2). Unlike most of the other Latin American countries, the Mexican government did not need U.S. assistance to "contain communism." Hence, military cooperation

Table 19.2   Mexico's Military Expenditures as a Percentage of Total Federal Expenditure by Administration, 1935–94

Period	Administration	Percentage
1935–40	Lázaro Cárdenas	22.03
1941–46	Avila Camacho	18.85
1947–52	Miguel Alemán	10.08
1953–58	Adolfo Ruíz Cortines	7.87
1959–64	Adolfo López Mateos	6.92
1965–70	Gustavo Díaz Ordaz	2.63
1971–76	Luis Echeverría A.	4.86
1977–82	José López Portillo	2.55
1983–88	Miguel de la Madrid	2.33
1989–94	Carlos Salinas de Gortari	3.08

Source: Guillermo Boils, *Los militares y la política en México: 1915–1974* (México City: El Caballito, 1973), 103, and Secretaría de Hacienda y Crédito Público, www.shcp.gob.mx/.

between the two states was very limited during the Cold War. Mexico's political system and armed forces were able to contain the advance of the Left without external cooperation and without interrupting the constitutional order, although human rights violations were committed.

With regard to nuclear weapons, Mexico advocated the Treaty of Tlatelolco, signed in 1967. There are several explanations for why a nuclear-free zone was created in Latin America and the Caribbean. Notably, the elimination of nuclear weapons in Latin America and the Caribbean was strategically favorable for the United States, because it suppressed the possibility of a nuclear arms race in the hemisphere.

In the 1990s, the social function of the military and its institutions was reconfigured, but this has not greatly altered the civil-military pact that has prevailed since the 1940s. During the 1990s, the Mexican state was partially remilitarized through the placement of military personnel in high-level positions within the government's public security forces. This shift occurred primarily under the administration of Carlos Salinas de Gortari which also saw a proliferation of military operations against crime, drug trafficking, and armed movements, such as the Zapatista guerrillas. The events of the 1990s reveal an interesting political dynamic in Mexico: when the country's institutions are able to resolve political conflicts without the use of force, the military repositions and professionalizes itself, allowing the political system to become demilitarized; but when problems of governability emerge, a tendency to partial militarization is produced.[10]

Under President Ernesto Zedillo (1995–2000), militarization occurred both in qualitative and quantitative terms. By 1999, the number of personnel within the armed forces rose to 232,000 and the military garnered 0.60 percent of a significantly expanded GDP. This can be contrasted with defense spending at the beginning of the 1990s, which stood at only 0.48 percent of Mexico's national income. For the first time in the twentieth century, the opposition parties gained a majority in Congress in 1997 and began to demand accountability for the government's actions, including those of the armed forces.

Currently, the constitution outlines three missions for the armed forces, each of which could be invoked to better regulate the armed forces' actions. The first (Defensa Nacional I, or DN-I) is related to the military's preparation for external defense. The second (Defensa Nacional II, or DN-II) serves to guarantee the internal security and social peace of Mexico, and the third (Defensa Nacional III, or DN-III) is connected with the military's protection of the population in cases of natural disasters. Given the present geopolitical situation, DN-I remains purely hypothetical, because Mexico has no external enemies. DN-III, in place since the 1970s, is a well-regarded military mission that has been successfully invoked in many natural disasters in Mexico. As for the activities set out in DN-II, the armed forces are presently confronted with a dilemma: either they will be forced to support a state that cannot sustain its own political stability, which in turn will force the military to intervene to maintain the social order, or they will serve a modernized and reformed state that requires the armed forces to operate in a professional capacity that precludes their political involvement.

The modernization and professionalization of the armed forces will not come about as a result of the military's own actions. Rather, it will be linked to the country's transition to democracy and depends on the ability of other state agencies to solve the country's multiple social conflicts. Only if these processes are successful will the military be able to concentrate on its central constitutional mandate and not on providing social peace and internal security. The failure of the Mexican state to respond to internal conflicts and to correct the country's old power structures has caused an unhealthy overextension of the military's duties into other spheres. Policies that address the root causes of the military's extended engagement will be the only way to keep the army in the barracks. If Mexico wants to modernize and professionalize the function of its armed forces, it will have to address these and other issues that have come to threaten the nation's governability. In the meantime, the challenge of the armed forces is to modernize their combat style, taking into account the human rights of the population.

The end of PRI's hegemony following President Vicente Fox's triumph in 2000 generated many questions about how to redefine the role of the armed forces in Mexico. It also raised a larger debate about the creation of new nonmilitary government institutions and agencies to deal with the country's social issues. As examples from around the world have shown, armed forces that are modernized and professionalized are composed of soldiers who are highly educated, well paid, and adequately trained. They have access to the most advanced technology, equipment, and defense doctrines available. Consequently, it must be said that the Mexican Armed Forces have not gone through the same simultaneous process of democratization and demilitarization that other Latin American militaries (i.e., Argentina, Brazil, and El Salvador, among others) have gone through. The capacity of armed forces to collaborate in humanitarian or peacekeeping missions conducted by either their country of origin or international organizations has become an important characteristic of professionalized forces over the past decade. In the case of Mexico's attempt to modernize its armed forces, there continues to be a contradiction between the armed forces' previous functions under the PRI and their new roles in fighting drug trafficking and assisting in humanitarian operations. This conflict continues despite the use of globally accepted principles of military conduct to professionalize Mexico's armed forces. Nevertheless, globalization has had a positive impact on the doctrines of the Mexican Armed Forces. The new democratic political order of the country has been fully respected, and it now seems unlikely that the Mexican military would ever become "repoliticized."

Another positive effect of globalization has been the armed forces' increased respect for the inherent rights of the population and the decrease in the military's attitude of impunity. Changes to Mexico's military apparatus have also occurred as a result of transnational forces that are slowly influencing the missions, doctrines, and training of its armed forces. For example, the United States has pressured Mexico to be involved in the war against drug trafficking and in instruments of collective security (such as the Inter-American Treaty of Reciprocal Assistance and the Inter-American Defense Board). However, the tendency has been for Mexico to refuse to participate in military operations due to its foreign policy stance of nonintervention. In 2004, when the UN Stabilization Mission in Haiti (MINUSTAH) was created, an important group of Latin American countries, headed by Brazil, Chile, Argentina, and Uruguay, sent troops. The government of Vicente Fox had promised to send soldiers to Haiti, but the military ultimately convinced President Fox not to send them, leading the UN secretary-general to visit Mexico.

In the future, the activities of the Mexican Armed Forces will most likely oscillate between internal and external missions. In the near term, however, their internal operations to maintain public order and social peace in Mexico will not be eliminated. This is due to the slow process of creating civilian institutions—whether professional police, like the Federal Police, or intelligence agencies—that could replace the military's function in policing and intelligence missions. In the end, the consolidation of democratic civil-military relations depends on the reform of the state. There has been a tendency to use state reform as a way to consolidate civil-military relations and to subordinate the armed forces to civilian authorities—specifically, to the president and Congress. The so-called war against drug trafficking, which commits the armed forces to fight drug cartels, could represent an obstacle to advancing democratic governance and could foster conditions under which the armed forces feel less committed to human rights observance.

North American Security Cooperation

In Mexico, reforms aimed at incorporating the country into the globalization process produced uneven results. In the economic sphere, they—specifically through NAFTA—institutionalized the interdependence that the country already had with the economy of the United States and, to a lesser extent, with Canada. In the social sphere, the reforms led to the economic displacement of almost 10 percent of the population, causing substantial migration to the United States and producing changes in the demographic and sociocultural structure of both Mexico and the United States. In the political sphere, the reforms moved the country toward democracy in a zigzag fashion but in an overall direction that would transform the state and society.

The United States, as part of its antiterrorist policies, redefined the structure of its military commands in 2002 and created the Northern Command, which includes the coverage of Canada, Cuba, Mexico, and part of the Caribbean. The Northern Command has its base in Colorado Springs. There, military representatives from Canada and Mexico also converge, facilitating transnational interagency cooperation in terms of defense.

In terms of security, the United States sets the agenda both in U.S.-Mexico relations and in Mexico-Canada relations. After the terrorist attacks in the United States, Canada and Mexico signed agreements with the United States on "intelligent borders" in December 2001 and March 2002, respectively. These agreements are very similar and lay the foundation of what might be called a North American security architecture. In 2005, Mexico, the United States, and Canada signed the Security and Prosperity Partnership in North America, which includes security cooperation in many subjects, including energy security and questions of human security.

Key Issues in the Security Agenda and the Mérida Initiative

At the end of the first decade of the twenty-first century, organized crime and its most polished expression, drug trafficking, became Mexico's main national security problem. This in turn has affected Mexico's relations with the United States and Central America.

One of the main problems in fighting drug trafficking in Mexico is government corruption.[11] This is because the process of governmental modernization is uneven and many institutions are not transforming rapidly. The justice system remains practically the same; police forces, despite many partial changes, have not been able to find a model appropriate for the new conditions in the country, with public insecurity becoming one of the people's main concerns. Some public opinion surveys indicate that for 40 percent of the population, security in the streets is their primary concern.[12]

Because of the inability of the public security and judiciary structures to confront organized crime, the armed forces were obliged to augment their traditional missions. The armed forces are turned to with intensity, because of the threat organized crime represents to stability and governability in the country (see figure 19.1). Mexico's president described the seriousness of the situation when he defined the use of the armed forces as vital and characterized the confrontation against drug cartels as a war:

> Organized crime looks for territorial control. It will be a no-holds barred war because there is no possibility to coexist with the drug trafficker. There is no return; it's them or us.... The key element in the stage we are living through is an expression of political will. That, in my judgment, we are missing. Nevertheless, an in-depth strategy cannot be ruled out—a strategy that always requires, in my opinion, a constant revision. The strategy focuses on two horizons: the first, in the very short term, consists of repositioning the state's authority and power through the mobilization of public forces and the army. We cannot lose territories; there are federal entities in which authority has been infringed. Military and police massive operations, which we have carried out, evidently do not eradicate criminal activity, but they permit the state to strengthen, recuperate, and assume the rule of law over its own territory.[13]

Thus, bilateral cooperation between Mexico and the United States increased gradually because of a sort of security need. However, the respective national policies were formulated first, and only then was the bilateral agenda configured.[14] Toward the end of the twentieth century, some authors argued that the bilateral agenda was already "narcotized," as the problem of drug trafficking became an increasingly critical subject. Because of that, Mexico has committed to cooperate with the United States through the Mérida Initiative. For Mexico, two important factors contribute to this

Figure 19.1   Assassinations Attributed to Organized Crime in Mexico by Year, 2001–09

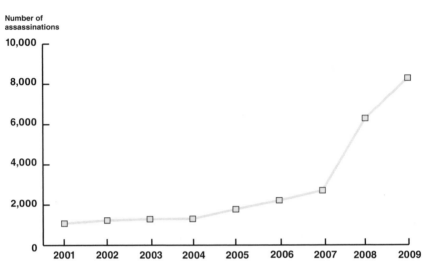

Source: Drug Violence in Mexico: Data and Analysis from 2001–09 (San Diego, CA: Trans-Border Institute, University of San Diego, February 2009).

security threat: the consumption of drugs in the United States, and the commercialization of weapons in the United States.[15]

In short, the Mexican government recognizes that drug-related organized crime has transnational dimensions and that the fight against it must therefore be carried out at the same level. This is another of the paradigms of Mexican national security: that global problems must be solved with transnational strategies. The Mérida Initiative is therefore an expression of Mexico's willingness to cooperate with a foreign country over a phenomenon that is expressed throughout its national territory. In this respect, Mexico follows the path of the international community and, indeed, has signed the great majority of international instruments linked to the fight against organized crime, including the United Nations Convention against Transnational Organized Crime of December 2000 (or Palermo Convention), which also includes two additional protocols against migrants and firearms trafficking.

At the level of international cooperation, the signing of protocols and conventions is very important. However, this is not enough, because it needs to provoke a spillover effect toward justice, police, intelligence, and even public security and military structures. In the case of Mexico, practically all the existing protocols have been signed at the global and hemispheric level. Problems appear with the harmonization of national laws over the commitments acquired and especially with their instrumentation.[16] As a result, Mexico has needed to ask for the United States' support in fighting drug trafficking through the Mérida Initiative.

The Mérida Initiative explicitly proposes to prevent drug trafficking from Mexico to the United States and firearms trafficking from the United States to Mexico, as well as the circulation of persons involved with these activities, and to limit the financial resources linked to them. Due to the nature of drug-trafficking routes in the Western Hemisphere, the Mérida Initiative also involves Central American and Caribbean states. The proposal includes delivery of inspection equipment, ion scanners, canine units for customs control, communication technologies, technical assistance and training for justice institutions and witness-protection programs, and surveillance helicopters and planes. This initiative is linked to the United States' National Southwest Border Counternarcotics Strategy, implemented along the U.S.-Mexico border.[17] In 2008 and 2009, the Mérida Initiative provided nearly $1.3 billion to Mexico, Central America, and the Caribbean to combat organized crime and reform security institutions.[18]

Security Sector Reform in Central America from 1990 to 2010

Turning to Central America, in this section four topics are discussed: the armed conflicts, the peace processes, security-sector reform, and the key issues in the security agenda.

Armed Conflicts

In the 1980s, Central America witnessed three internal armed conflicts in Nicaragua, El Salvador, and Guatemala. They had a significant impact on the region, causing its accelerated militarization. In addition to these internal conflicts, growing interstate tension arose between the countries in the region because of "the threat the Sandinista government perceived from its neighbors" and the way "Nicaragua's neighbors interpreted the Sandinista revolution as a potential threat themselves."[19] Central America became one of the main areas of East-West confrontation in the Cold War.[20]

These armed conflicts had enormous consequences in terms of lives lost and social and economic costs, and they had a profound impact on the countries' political systems. The decades-long war that Guatemala went thru (1960–96) left a total of 150,000 people dead, 50,000 missing, and 1 million internally displaced, with another 100,000 becoming refugees.[21] In the Salvadoran conflict (1980–92), an estimated 75,000 died, meaning that 1 out of 66 Salvadorans died in the war.[22] It has been calculated that the armed conflicts caused nearly $1.6 billion of direct and indirect damage, while the Salvadoran government estimates that the total cost of the peace agreements reached $2.4 billion.[23]

Peace Processes

Both national and international peace initiatives were developed during the 1980s for Central America.[24] The most important international effort came from the Contadora Group, which included participation from the Mexican, Colombian, Venezuelan, and Panamanian governments. This was a diplomatic initiative that sought to promote peace and democracy in the region in the period between 1983 and 1986. Although it failed in its purpose to promote peace, the Contadora Group "did have an important effect: it presented an alternative vision of security to the discussion, linking the crisis to a lack of democracy and socio-economic inequalities."[25]

The next diplomatic initiative toward peace and democracy in the region was structured around the Central American presidents who met in San Jose and signed on August 7, 1987, the Esquipulas II Agreement.[26] Esquipulas opened space for the promotion of "internal reconciliation," reinforcing the need for a "democratic opening" and respect for human rights. In this sense, the Esquipulas II Agreement created the conditions for a regional détente and progress in democratization.

Esquipulas II Agreement also created a favorable environment for the conclusion of the conflicts in the area, allowing each of the countries with internal armed conflicts to develop their own negotiation processes. Each of them responded to the specifics of their own national situation. This trend was bolstered by the fall of the Berlin Wall in 1989, which ushered in a new international era. In this new context, Nicaragua developed its process around the 1988 Sapoá Agreements, while El Salvador and Guatemala subsequently developed national processes that were mediated by the United Nations.[27]

The Nicaraguan negotiations focused on the demobilization of irregular groups, addressing the demands of the demobilized, whose primary concerns were security and access to resources, particularly land, and promoting democratization. However, after the signing of the agreements and the start of demobilization, difficulties in fulfilling all the government promises for demobilization created a crisis. The presidential elections that took place on February 25, 1990, became an important milestone in the Nicaraguan transition, because the ruling Frente Sandinista de Liberación Nacional (FSLN) accepted its defeat, thus reaffirming the process of democratization. The signing of the Protocol of Procedure of the Transfer of Executive Power both allowed for the change of government and provided stability to the political process.

The case of El Salvador is a classic case of a military stalemate,[28] where neither the guerrillas nor the army could be defeated. In the initial stage, all the efforts and negotiation proposals had a tactical nature in which the parties to the conflict sought to improve their positions with the aim of a military solution to the conflict. The break from the tactical negotiation approach and the shift to a strategic negotiation came when both parties concluded that winning the war in military terms was not possible. This was the turning point after which all the conditions for a politically negotiated solution to the conflict underwent the greatest development. The dialogue/negotiation process can be divided into two periods. The first phase of this process, characterized as a phase of dialogue without negotiation, began with the first meeting between President Napoleón Duarte and the Frente Democrático Revolucionario-Frente Farabundo Martí para la Liberación Nacional (FDR-FMLN) in La Palma in October 1984 and ended with the military offensive of November 1989. The second phase, characterized as time-concentrated and intense, began on April 4, 1990, when an agreement to begin negotiations under the mediation of the United Nations was reached. This phase lasted until January 16, 1992, when peace accords were signed in Chapultepec Castle in Mexico City.[29] The peace accords ended the armed conflict, promoted an important demilitarization process, and established the foundations for the democratization of the country's political regime. The economic and social problems were marginally addressed in the peace negotiations, which instead focused on demilitarization and the promotion of political reform.

In the case of Guatemala it should be noted that, "with the start of the transition, the conflict did not know previous peace agreements, nor military or political ties. The transition itself was not the result of negotiations forced by adverse political conditions for the armed forces or losses of any nature in the military field. On the contrary, the predominant perception among members of the Guatemalan army was that the war was won and resolved militarily and, as a result, they were not willing to lose at the political negotiating table what they had already won on the battlefield."[30] This fact had a profound impact on the peace negotiations. The final stage of negotiations between the government of Guatemala and the Unidad Revolucionaria Nacional Guatemalteca (URNG) took place between 1990 and 1996, during which sixteen agreements were signed between the parties, including the Agreement on the Strengthening of Civilian Power and on the Role of the Armed Forces in a Democratic Society, signed September 19, 1996. The final peace agreement and the implementation timetable were signed in Guatemala City in December 1996.

Security-Sector Reform

The peace processes in Nicaragua, El Salvador, and Guatemala promoted historic security-sector reforms that allowed for an important process of demilitarization and laid the foundation for the subordination of the armed forces to constitutionally elected civilian authorities. In sum, the security-sector reforms generated by the peace process focused on three main areas: (1) reducing the size of the militaries and their budgets, (2) separating the institutions in charge of defense and public security, and (3) redefining the doctrines of the armed forces.[31]

The focus on reducing the size and budgets of the military led to significant results. In Nicaragua, which saw the largest army demobilization in Latin America, the size of its armed forces dropped from 86,810 men in 1990 to 14,084 in 1996,[32] and then to 12,187 in 2002.[33] In El Salvador, the size of the armed forces went from 63,175 in 1992 to 31,000 in 1993,[34] and then to 15,500 in 2003. In Guatemala, the armed forces decreased in size from 46,900 in 1996 to 31,423 in 1998,[35] and then to 15,500 in 2004. These countries witnessed an associated reduction in their national defense budgets. In El Salvador, the percentage of the national budget assigned to national defense fell from 13.7 percent in 1992 to 3.8 percent in 2004.[36] In Nicaragua, the national defense budget was reduced from $177 million in 1990 to $31 million in 2002.[37] In Guatemala, the budget assigned to the army in 1999 stood at 0.68 percent of GDP, but by 2005 it had been reduced to 0.33 percent of GDP.[38]

Furthermore, El Salvador purged members of the armed forces and investigated the violence of the past through an ad hoc commission and a truth commission. The officers mentioned in the reports of the commissions were removed from their positions. Guatemala created a similar mechanism—the Commission for Historical Clarification in Guatemala—to study the historical truth of the armed conflict period. The reports of both the Salvadoran and Guatemalan commissions contributed to greater knowledge about the events that occurred during the period of armed conflict and the authorship of those events, but their findings had no judicial implications.[39] Nicaragua did not utilize such mechanisms.

The focus on separating the institutions in charge of defense and public security led to important constitutional reforms in El Salvador (1992) and Nicaragua (1995), and this separation was part of Guatemala's peace agreement. The purpose was to draw clear boundaries between the armed forces, whose role under the Ministry of Defense is to defend the sovereignty and territorial integrity of the states, and the police, whose role under the Ministry of Interior is to ensure public security.

In addition, El Salvador and Guatemala dissolved all previous security forces, with both creating a National Civil Police (PNC). However, faced with fast-increasing crime rates, both El Salvador and Guatemala pushed for rapid deployment, sacrificing quality for quantity in the PNC. They also faced problems in reeducating policemen.[40] These factors, coupled with weak internal control mechanisms and limited resources and policing equipment in both countries, has affected the ability of the police to deal with criminal activity and violence, which in turn has presented important challenges for the states. In the past few years, two specific problems have been reported in the case of Guatemala that weakens the work of the police: corruption and a constant change in leadership, as reflected in the changes of the ministers of interior and the national directors of the PNC.[41] As Douglas Kincaid states with regard to El Salvador, "The principal problem affecting security in El Salvador in recent years undoubtedly has been the increase in criminal activity and non-political violence. Although reliable statistics on crime are scarce, especially for comparing current levels with those of wartime or prewar years, a generalized sense of crisis has emerged."[42]

As a result of this rise in crime and violence, governments have decided to use the armies to support the PNC in operations to combat crime, which in turn has generated a debate about the army's participation in public security tasks. This concern focuses on the potential impact such a strategy might have on the progress achieved to date on the separation of defense and public security. The rise of crime and insecurity has also led to the privatization of public security, expressed both through a proliferation of guns in private hands and through increases in the number of private security agencies operating in the countries. In El Salvador, for example, before the signing of the peace accords, there were only ten private security agencies in the country. Within three years, this figure had risen to eighty. In Guatemala, meanwhile, the figure rose from 40 in 1997 to 114 and in 1999.[43] This has opened a debate about the need for regulation and control of these agencies by the state.

The focus on redefining the doctrines of the armed forces led to the elimination of functions that had been assigned to the armed forces in the past, such as internal security. This has left the armed forces with a primary mission of defending state sovereignty and territorial integrity.[44] In a historical perspective, this redefinition of the mission of the armed forces represented a major advance in limiting its scope, especially because armed forces in Central America had existed as a kind of "supra-institution" that stood above all other state institutions and that weighed heavily on the political process.[45] Today, the civilian leadership needs to define precisely the specific types of missions that should be assigned to the armed forces.

Key Issues on the Security Agenda in Central America

At the beginning of the twenty-first century, the main security issues that Central America faces are violence, crime, drug trafficking, gangs, and a general sense of insecurity. Latin America and the Caribbean have the highest recorded murder rates in the world after sub-Saharan Africa,[46] meaning that Central America is the most violent of those regions not affected by intense political violence.[47]

The situation of Central America "is very serious indeed," with the United Nations Development Program (UNDP) estimating that 79,000 Central Americans have been murdered between 2003 and 2008.[48] "The average homicide rate for the seven countries of Central America is a little more than three times the world average and seven points above Latin America. But El Salvador, Guatemala, Honduras, and Belize have a more serious problem—between three and six times more serious—than Panamá, Costa Rica and Nicaragua. The first group is above the average of Latin America and Mexico, and is even worse than a proverbially violent country like Colombia. . . . The second group of countries (Panamá, Costa Rica, and Nicaragua) do not reach the Latin American average, but they are above the world average."[49] Making matters worse, from 2000 to 2008, there has been an increase in homicide rates in all Central American countries, albeit with different levels of magnitude (see table 19.3).

Similarly, in terms of nonhomicidal violence (assault, rape, kidnapping) and crimes against property (robbery, theft, fraud), El Salvador, Guatemala, Honduras, and Belize are classified as countries with high criminality; meanwhile, Panama, Costa Rica, and Nicaragua are classified as countries with low criminality—that is, as countries with medium or low rates of homicide and moderate, stable, or declining rates of nonhomicidal violence and crimes against property.[50]

The most recent study about the economic costs of violence in Central America was carried out by Carlos Acevedo for the National Council for Public Security of El Salvador. He estimates that the direct and indirect costs of the violence in Central America amounted to $6.5 billion in 2006, equivalent to 7.7 percent of the GDP for the region.[51] "In absolute terms, the costs are higher for Guatemala (US$2,291 million) and for El Salvador (US$2,010 million), and lower for Costa Rica (US$791 million) and Nicaragua (US$529 million). In relative terms, the situation changes based on the size of each economy. On the one hand is El Salvador, where violence imposes a cost close to 11% of GDP; on the other hand is Costa Rica, where costs are 3.6% of GDP. In Honduras and Nicaragua, the costs of violence are 9.6% and 10% of GDP, re-

Table 19.3   Central America: Homicides per 100,000 Inhabitants, 2000–08

Country	2000	2001	2002	2003	2004	2005	2006	2007	2008
Belize	19	25	30	24	27	28	31	30	32
Costa Rica	6	6	6	7	7	8	8	8	11
El Salvador	45	40	39	40	49	62	65	57	52
Guatemala	28	30	32	37	38	44	47	45	48
Honduras	—	—	69	65	35	39	46	50	58
Nicaragua	9	10	10	12	12	13	13	13	13
Panama	10	10	12	11	10	11	11	13	19

Source: UNDP, *Informe sobre Desarrollo Humano para América Central 2009–10*, 69.

spectively. In Guatemala, the relative weight of the costs of violence is lower (7.7% of GDP), even though it is the country with higher costs in absolute terms."[52]

Another factor included in the security agenda in Central America is the large presence of *maras*,[53] particularly because they "are a complex, heterogeneous, and evolving phenomenon in Central America."[54] Miguel Cruz identifies ten factors associated with the emergence of the gang phenomenon: processes of social exclusion, a culture of violence, fast and disorderly urban growth, migration, community disruption, drugs, troubled family life, the adverse influence of friends and gang members, the dynamics of violence, and the difficulties of constructing a personal identity.[55] Other observers emphasize its transnational character. For instance, Wim Savenije states that these organizations "create transnational structures and therefore cannot be isolated or understood in the context of a single country . . . with local branches maintaining links and communication with each other."[56]

The governments of the countries of the northern triangle—Guatemala, Honduras and El Salvador—have promoted "iron-fist" plans and enacted special antigang legislation to face the problem of youth gangs. However, the legality of some aspects of legislation has been called into question, and policies as a whole have not delivered on their promise. Making matters worse, the weaknesses of the security and justice systems have generated a sense of impunity. According to a report by IDHAC, "about nine out of ten newly reported crimes go unpunished."[57]

Another factor linked to this problem of violence and crime in the Central American region is the abundance of weapons. With an estimated 3 million firearms circulating in Central America, two out of three are believed to be illegal.[58] Finally, organized crime, particularly as relates to drug trafficking, significantly contributes to the levels of violence and insecurity for three principal reasons:

Table 19.4   Public Perceptions of Main Problems in Central America by Country and Percentage, 2004 and 2006

	Guatemala		El Salvador		Honduras		Nicaragua		Costa Rica
	2004	2006	2004	2006	2004	2006	2004	2006	2006
Economic problems	51.1	32.3	60.5	45.6	74.1	42.6	82.7	67.4	49.1
Crime, violence, insecurity	38.9	50.9	31.5	44.9	18.4	35.6	3.2	4.5	21.3
Corruption	4.3	3.5	1.4	0.6	2.4	10.0	5.5	9.3	7.1
Others	5.6	13.2	6.6	8.9	5.1	11.8	8.6	18.8	22.5
Total	100	100	100	100	100	100	100	100	100

Note: Approximately 1,400 people were polled in each country.
Source: Latin American Public Opinion Project, Vanderbilt University, 2004 and 2006.

1. Mexico and Central America link the main production centers (the Andean countries) to the main consumption centers (United States). "They are mainly transit countries, but they also have become places of production and consumption."[59]
2. Due to the fight against drug trafficking being waged by Colombia and Mexico with the support of the United States, the drug cartels have been moving to Central America and particularly to Guatemala.[60]
3. Technical and budgetary problems, a shortage of human resources, and a lack of coordinated policies make it difficult for some Central American states to control their maritime areas, air space, and land borders.[61]

Collectively, these factors contribute to high perceptions of insecurity among the citizens of many Central American countries (see table 19.4).

This is especially troubling because of the effect these statistics and perceptions have on Central America's young democracies. A study by Orlando J Pérez, for example, found that crime-based victimization and the perception of insecurity significantly affects the support for democracy. He further notes that both El Salvador and Guatemala's perception of insecurity increases support for authoritarian values.[62] A recent study that looked specifically at the Salvadoran case similarly found that crime-based victimization reduces trust in the political institutions of the system and interpersonal trust within the society, leading to the erosion of social capital.[63]

Mexico–Central America Security Relations

The problem of insecurity in Mexico and in Central America has transcended borders. Economic disparities, internal social problems, varying security policies, corruption, and weak justice systems contribute to making the security situation complex. It is exacerbated by the geography of the region, which allows for porous borders.[64]

Mexico's southern border witnesses a high inflow of narcotics and migrants and all kinds of smuggling. In order to have better border control, Mexico has signed cooperation agreements with Guatemala and Belize that are similar in nature to the ones signed between Mexico and the United States.[65] But the difficult geographical conditions of the region, the deficient reach of security and intelligence institutions, and corruption constitute obstacles to real border protection.

Nevertheless, the border problem is just one of the more visible effects (and contributors to) the region's insecurity. In this context, Mexico's southern border is a mosaic of illegalities, where human, arms, and drug traffickers abound, as well as all kinds of smugglers. Thus, national problems complement and contribute to the general sense of insecurity. Specifically, Mexico's institutional weaknesses and problems have favored the expansion of both criminal networks in the Central American region and the transmigrant population, which suffers at the hands of traffickers and corrupt authorities.[66] The United States provides the demand for drugs and the financing for this illegal commerce, as well as the weapons supply that feeds all common and organized crime in Mexico.

Conclusions and Challenges

In Mexico, the rise of the power of drug traffickers has put into question the government's capacities to impose the rule of law. Another factor that threatens democracy and governability is that the government has opted to define the conflict as a "war" and to employ the armed forces as a tool.[67] State reform of the justice and police system has been slow and the government strategy does not emphasize prevention-focused social policies. In addition, effective mechanisms are necessary for the accountability, supervision, and control of armed forces with respect to human rights. There are regions and cities in which violence and homicide is very high, such as Ciudad Juárez, which registered a rate of 190 homicides per 100,000 inhabitants in 2009, the highest rate in the world. Mexico faces a great challenge in the drug trafficking cartels' power. However, there has been a movement in Mexico away from a "nationalistic" national security, which prevailed in the past, because Mexico has recognized that external help is needed, such as through the Merida Initiative. The starting point was the recognition that drug trafficking is a transnational Mesoamerican problem and that battling it requires cooperation among Colombia, Central America, the Caribbean, Mexico, and the United States.[68]

In the Central American countries, a combination of policies that focus simultaneously on control, prevention, and rehabilitation is required in order to address the subregion's security problems; at the same time, the institutional capacities of the police and the justice, intelligence, and penitentiary systems must be strengthened to allow for greater interinstitutional coordination. Beyond the national domains, some initiatives have been developed in terms of cooperation at the Central American level. In the last few years, some instruments of regional security have been approved, some with a more doctrinal character, such as the Democratic Security Framework Treaty (1995), and others with a more technical operative reach, such as the Treaty for Mutual Legal Assistance in Criminal Affairs (1993) and the Constitutive Agreement for the Central American Commission for the Eradication of Production, Traffic, Consumption and Illicit Use of Narcotics and Psychotropic Substances (1993).[69] Nevertheless, the transnational nature of some of the subregion's security problems pose a challenge for advancing greater levels of cooperation both within Central American and among Central America, Mexico, and the United States.

Another important aspect related to the security agenda is the need to respect the human rights of migrants. Central Americans who employ Mexican territory to get to the United States are victims of criminal groups all along the way, as well as victims of corrupt government employees, who extort them. This has been pointed out by international NGOs such as Amnesty International: "Every year, tens of thousands of women, men and children travel through Mexico without legal permission as irregular migrants. More than nine in every ten are Central Americans, mostly from El Salvador, Guatemala, Honduras or Nicaragua. The vast majority are headed for the US border in the hope of new life far from the poverty they have left behind. Their journey is one of the most dangerous in the World."[70]

The problems of security in the twenty-first century in Mesoamerica are both domestic and international. This means that the problems and actors are transnational and that the fight against them should be transnational, too. In the case of drug trafficking, the production-transportation-consumption chain leads criminal actors to have partners in every country of the region. Addressing such issues in a joint manner imposes new challenges on the governments. It is necessary for them to improve their own justice, police, and intelligence systems and to increase their level of intergovernmental cooperation. Doing so will improve the effectiveness of border security policies, eradication efforts, policing and intelligence initiatives against cartels, anti-money-laundering strategies, and preventive policies in health and education. Not doing so will increase the risk that these new security problems will weaken governance and undermine the consolidation of democratic processes.

Notes

1. John Womack, Jr., *Rebellion in Chiapas: An Historical Reader* (New York: New Press, 1999).

2. Edelberto Torres-Rivas, "Los caminos hacia la democracia política en América Central," in *A Challenge to Democracy: Political Parties in Central America, Panamá, and Dominican Republic*, ed. Diego Achard et al. (San José: BID, IDEA, OEA, and PNUD, 2004).

3. For an overview of the peace processes in Guatemala and El Salvador, see Dinorah Azpuru, Ligia Blanco, Ricardo Córdova Macías, Nayelly Loya Marín, Carlos G. Ramos, and Adrián Zapata, eds., *Construyendo la democracia en sociedades posconflicto: Guatemala y El Salvador, un enfoque comparado* (Guatemala: International Development Research Centre, 2007).

4. The country's official political party was founded in 1929 as the Partido Nacional Revolucionario (PNR). It was renamed the Partido de la Revolución Mexicana (PRM) in 1938 and the PRI in 1946.

5. Regarding the role of the armed forces in Mexican politics, see David Ronfeldt, ed., *The Modern Mexican Military: A Reassessment* (La Jolla, CA: Center for U.S.-Mexican Studies, 1984).

6. Roderic Ai Camp, *Mexico's Military on the Democratic Stage* (Santa Barbara, CA: Praeger Security International, 2005), 37.

7. Andrew Selee and Jacqueline Peshard, eds., *Mexico's Democratic Challenges: Politics, Government, and Society* (Washington, DC: Woodrow Wilson Center Press, 2010).

8. Joseph S. Tulchin and Andrew D. Selee, eds., *México's Politics and Society in Transition* (Boulder, CO: Lynne Rienner Publishers, 2003), 16.

9. Laurie Freeman and Jorge Luis Sierra, "Mexico: The Militarization Trap," in *Drugs and Democracy in Latin America: The Impact of U.S. Policy*, ed. Coletta A. Youngers and Eileen Rosin (Boulder, CO: Lynne Rienner Publishers, 2005), 264.

10. Raúl Benítez Manaut, "Chiapas: Crisis and Disruption of Social Cohesion—Challenges for Negotiations in the Twenty-First Century," in *Human Security, Conflict Prevention and Peace*, ed. Moufida Goucha and Francisco Rojas Aravena (Santiago, Chile: United Nations Educational, Scientific and Cultural Organization, 2003), 209.

11. Selee and Peshard, eds., *Mexico's Democratic Challenges*.

12. *Cultura política de la democracia en México: 2006* (Nashville, TN: Vanderbilt University and Americas Barometer, 2007), 72, www.americasbarometer.org.

13. Jorge Zepeda Patterson, "Entrevista a Felipe Calderón," *El Universal*, February 27, 2009.

14. See Tony Payan, "United States International Anti-Narcotics Policy: Lessons from Mexico" *National Security Studies Quarterly* (April 1997): 71–90.

15. "Felipe Calderón: le consommateur américain, responsable du narcotrafic," *Le Monde*, March 5, 2009.

16. José Borjón Nieto, *Cooperación internacional contra la delincuencia organizada trasnacional* (Mexico: Instituto Nacional de Ciencias Penales, 2005).

17. U.S. State Department, "The Merida Initiative: United States-Mexico-Central America Security Cooperation," 2007.

18. U.S. Government Accountability Office, "Status of Funds for the Mérida Initiative," GAO-10-253R, December 3, 2009.

19. Gabriel Aguilera Peralta, "La problemática de seguridad en Centroamérica en la situación de post-crisis," *Revista Fuerzas Armadas y Sociedad* 6, no. 3 (July–September 1991): 21–35.

20. For an overview of the Central American conflict from the perspective of international politics, see William LeoGrande, *Our Own Backyard: The United States in Central America, 1977–1992* (Chapel Hill, NC: University of North Carolina Press, 1998); G.W. Sand, *Soviet Aims in Central America: The Case of Nicaragua* (New York: Praeger, 1989); Mary Desjeans and Peter Clement, "Soviet Policy toward Central America," *Proceedings of the Academy of Political Science* 36, no. 4 (1987); Peter Sherman, "The Soviet Challenge in Central America," *Proceedings of the Academy of Political Science* 36, no. 4. (1987); Robert S. Leiken, ed., *Central America: Anatomy of Conflict* (Pergamon Press, 1984); *Report of the National Bipartisan Commission on Central America* (Washington, DC: U.S. Government Printing Office, 1984).

21. See the 1998 Recovery of Historical Memory Project report titled "Guatemala: nunca más." In addition, the Commission for Historical Clarification estimated that 200,000 people either died or went missing in Guatemala. See Commission for Historical Clarification, "Guatemala: Memoria del silencio, Vol. 1," 1999.

22. Mitchell A. Seligson and Vicent McElhinny, "Low-Intensity Warfare, High-Intensity Death: The Demographic Impact of the Wars in El Salvador and Nicaragua," *Canadian Journal of Latin American and Caribbean Studies* 21, no. 42 (1996): 60.

23. Ricardo Córdova Macías, "Las relaciones cívico-militares en Centroamérica a fin de siglo," in *Pasos hacia una nueva convivencia: Democracia y Participación en Centroamérica*, ed. Ricardo Córdova Macías, Günther Maihold, and Sabine Kurtenbach (San Salvador: Fundación Guillermo Manuel Ungo [FUNDAUNGO], Instituto de Estudios Iberoamericanos de Hamburgo, and Instituto Ibero-Americano de Berlin, 2001), 317–80.

24. For a review of the peace proposals in this period, see Ricardo Córdova Macías and Raúl Benítez Manaut, eds., *La Paz en Centroamérica: Expediente de documentos fundamentales 1979–1989* (Mexico: CIIH-UNAM, 1989).

25. Peralta, "La problemática de seguridad en Centroamérica en la situación de post-crisis," 21–35.

26. For an overview of the Esquipulas process, see Enrique Gomariz, ed., *Balance de una esperanza: Esquipulas II un año después* (San José: Universidad para la Paz, 1988).

27. For an overview of the peace process in Nicaragua, see Rose J. Spalding, "From Low-Intensity War to Low-Intensity Peace: The Nicaraguan Peace Process," in *Comparative Peace Processes in Latin America*, ed. Cynthia J. Arnson (Stanford, CA: Stanford University Press, 1999). For an overview of the Salvadoran peace process, see Ricardo Córdova Macías, *El Salvador: las negociaciones de paz y los retos de la postguerra* (San Salvador: IDELA, 1993). For an overview of the peace process in Guatemala, see Dinorah Azpuru, "Peace and Democratization in Guatemala: Two Parallel Processes," in *Comparative Peace Processes in Latin America*, ed. Cynthia J. Arnson (Stanford, CA: Stanford University Press, 1996); Gabriel Aguilera, Rosalinda Bran and Claudinne Ogaldes, *Buscando la paz: El bienio 1994–1995,* Colección debate no. 32 (Guatemala: Latin American Faculty of Social Sciences [FLACSO], 1996); Edelberto Torres-Rivas, *Negociando el futuro: La paz en una sociedad violenta. La negociación de paz en 1996,* Colección debate no. 36 (Guatemala: FLACSO, 1997); Susan Jonas, *Of Centaurs and Doves: Guatemala's Peace Process* (Boulder, CO: Westview, 2000).

28. For more on the thesis of the military stalemate in the Salvadoran case, see Raúl Benítez Manaut, *La teoría militar y la guerra civil en El Salvador* (San Salvador: UCA Editores, 1989).

29. In regard to the particular case of El Salvador, see Córdova Macías, *El Salvador: las negociaciones de paz y los retos de la postguerra.*

30. Rodolfo Cerdas Cruz, "Contribución al estudio comparativo de las relaciones cívico-militares en Centroamérica," mimeo.

31. For a discussion on security sector reform within the framework of the peace process in Central America, see Córdova Macías, "Las relaciones cívico-militares en Centroamérica a fin de siglo," 317–80; P. Williams and Knut Walter, *Militarization and Demilitarization in El Salvador's Transition to Democracy* (Pittsburgh, PA: University of Pittsburgh Press, 1997); A. Douglas Kincaid, "Demilitarization and Security in El Salvador and Guatemala: Convergences of Success and Crisis," *Journal of Interamerican Studies and World Affairs* 42, no. 4 (2001): 3–42; Ligia Blanco and Adrián Zapata, "Contribución del proceso de paz a la construcción de la democracia en Guatemala," in *Construyendo la democracia en sociedades posconflicto. Guatemala y El Salvador, un enfoque comparado,* ed. Dinorah Azpuru et al. (Guatemala: International Development Research Centre and F & G Editores, 2007); Bernando Arévalo de León, "Civil-Military Relations in Post-Conflict Guatemala," *Revista Fuerzas Armadas y Sociedad* 20, no. 1, (2006): 63–108; Mark J. Ruhl, "The Guatemalan Military Since the Peace Accords: The Fate of Reform Under Arzu and Portillo," *Latin American Politics and Society* 47, no. 1 (2005): 55–85.

32. Roberto J. Cajina, *Transición Política y Reconversión Militar en Nicaragua, 1990–1995* (Managua: CRIES, 1996).

33. Roberto J. Cajina, "Reconversión de la Defensa en Nicaragua: Asimetrías e Incoherencias," *Security and Defense Studies Review* 2 (2002).

34. Humberto Corado Figueroa, "Los procesos de desmovilización de las fuerzas armadas," in *Desmovilización, Desmilitarización y Democratización en Centroamérica,* ed. Francisco José Aguilar Urbina (San José: Fundación Arias y Centro Internacional para los Derechos Humanos y el Desarrollo Democrático, 1994), 147.

35. United Nations Verification Mission in Guatemala (MINUGUA), "Situación de los compromisos relativos al ejército en los acuerdos de paz," May 2002.

36. Based on Ricardo Córdova Macías, Carlos G. Ramos, and Nayelly Loya Marín, "La contrucción de la democracia en El Salvador (1992–2004)," in *Construyendo la democracia en sociedades posconflicto: Guatemala y El Salvador, un enfoque comparado,* ed. Dinorah Azpuru et al. (Guatemala: International Development Research Centre and F & G Editores, 2007).

37. Roberto J. Cajina, "Reconversión de la Defensa en Nicaragua: Asimetrías e Incoherencias," 298.

38. MINUGUA, "Asesoría del fortalecimiento del poder civil," November 15, 2004, 18.

39. The Salvadoran Truth Commission issued its report, "From Madness to Hope: Twelve-Year War in El Salvador," on March 15, 1993, and the Commission for Historical Clarification issued its report, "Guatemala: Memory of Silence," on February 25, 1999.

40. In the case of Guatemala, of 8,400 PNC officers in late 1998, "75 percent were so-called *reciclados* (personnel previously with the National or Treasury Police) and 25 percent were new recruits." Kincaid, "Demilitarization and Security in El Salvador and Guatemala," 49.

41. MINUGUA, "Informe al Secretario General," August 30, 2004.

42. Kincaid, "Demilitarization and Security in El Salvador and Guatemala," 45.

43. Charles T. Call, *Sustainable Development in Central America: The Challenges of Violence, Injustice and Insecurity,* Working Paper # 8 (Hamburg: Institut für Iberoamerika-Kunde, 2000).

44. However, this issue was left pending in the case of Guatemala due to the rejection of the Popular Consultation of May 16, 1999, which affected the constitutional reforms arising from the peace accords.

45. For more on the political role of armed forces, see Williams and Walter, *Militarization and Demilitarization in El Salvador's Transition to Democracy.*

46. "Statistics on Homicides, Suicides, Accidents, Injuries, and Attitudes towards Violence," Pan American Health Organization, Washington, DC, 2003.

47. Central America averaged 29.3 homicides per 100,000 inhabitants in 2004, while the world average was 9, the European average was 8, and the Latin American average was 25. See UNDP, *Informe sobre Desarrollo Humano para América Central 2009–2010: Abrir espacios para la seguridad ciudadana y el desarrollo humano* (Colombia: UNDP, October 2009).

48. Ibid., 68.

49. Ibid.

50. Ibid., 85–86.

51. Carlos Acevedo, *Los costos económicos de la violencia en Centroamérica* (San Salvador: Consejo Nacional de Seguridad Pública, 2008).

52. Ibid., 13.

53. For more on *maras*, see José Miguel Cruz, "Los factores asociados a las pandillas juveniles en Centroamérica," in *Exclusión Social, Jóvenes y Pandillas en Centroamérica*, Temas de Actualidad no. 3 (San Salvador: FUNDAUNGO and Programa Latinoamericano del Woodrow Wilson International Center for Scholars, 2005); José Miguel Cruz, ed., *Street Gangs in Central America* (San Salvador: UCA Editores, 2007); U.S. Agency for International Development, Bureau for Latin America and Caribbean Affairs, "Central America and Mexico Gang Assessment," 2006; Ana Arana, "How the Street Gangs Took Central America," *Foreign Affairs* 84, no. 3, (May/June 2005): 98–110; Centro de Estudios y Programas Interamericanos (CEPI) "Pandillas juveniles trasnacionales en Centroamérica, México y los Estados Unidos: Resumen ejecutivo," (Mexico: ITAM, 2007); Marcela Smutt and Jenny Lissette E. Miranda, *El fenómeno de las pandillas en El Salvador* (San Salvador: FLACSO Programa El Salvador, 1998).

54. UNDP, *Informe sobre Desarrollo Humano para América Central 2009–2010*, 106.

55. Cruz, "Los factores asociados a las pandillas juveniles en Centroamérica."

56. Win Savenije, "La Mara Salvatrucha y el Barrio 18st," *Foreign Affairs* (in Spanish) 4, no. 2 (April/June 2004): 42.

57. UNDP, *Informe sobre Desarrollo Humano para América Central 2009–2010*, 235.

58. Ibid., 169.

59. Raúl Benítez Manaut, *La nueva seguridad regional: amenazas irregulares, crimen organizado y narcotráfico en México y América Central*, comentario marzo (FRIDE, 2009).

60. See Ken Ellingwood, "Mexico under Siege: Drug Violence Spilling into Guatemala," *Los Angeles Times*, June 4, 2009.

61. UNDP, *Informe sobre Desarrollo Humano para América Central 2009–2010*, 103.

62. Orlando J. Pérez, "Democratic Legitimacy and Public Insecurity: Crime and Democracy in El Salvador and Guatemala," *Political Science Quarterly* 118, no. 4 (Winter 2003–4): 627–44.

63. Ricardo Córdova Macías and José Miguel Cruz, *Cultura política de la democracia en El Salvador, 2008: El impacto de la gobernabilidad* (San Salvador: FUNDAUNGO, IUDOP, Vanderbilt University, PNUD, and BID, 2008).

64. Natalia Armijo, "La frontera sur: La frontera abierta" (paper presented at the seminar "México: La Seguridad Nacional en la Encrucijada," El Colegio de México, September 25–26, 2007).

65. Secretaria de Relaciones Exteriores, "Celebran México y Guatemala reunión del Grupo de Alto Nivel de Seguridad Fronteriza (GANSEF)," Mexico, April 3, 2008, www.sre.gob.mx/csocial/contenido/comunicados/2008/apr/cp_088.html.

66. Interview with National Immigration Institute Commissioner Cecilia Romero in *El Faro* (San Salvador), September 15, 2009; "La crisis de derechos humanos en la frontera sur de México," Due Process of Law, Washington, DC, August 2008, www.dplf.org.

67. Felipe Calderón "La guerra al crimen organizado," in *Atlas de la Seguridad y la Defensa de México 2009*, ed. Raúl Benítez Manaut, Abelardo Rodríguez Sumano, and Armando Rodríguez Luna (Mexico: CASEDE, 2010), 17, www.seguridadcondemocracia.org.

68. Armando Rodríguez Luna, "La Iniciativa Mérida y la guerra contra las drogas: Pasado y presente," in *Crimen organizado e Iniciativa Mérida en las relaciones México-Estados Unidos*, ed. Raúl Benítez Manaut (Mexico: CASEDE, 2010), 66.

69. See Laura Chinchilla, "Estabilidad social y seguridad ciudadana en Centroamérica," mimeo.

70. Amnesty International, *Invisible Victims: Migrants on the Move in Mexico* (London: Amnesty International Publications, 2010), 5.

Part III

Conclusion

20

Regional Security through Collective Conflict Management

Chester A. Crocker, Fen Osler Hampson, and Pamela Aall

W hen we began this project, we expected that the chapters written by experts from the regions themselves would confirm the
view that regions are different, with widely varying interest in
and capacity for conflict management. What we hoped for was a deep and
nuanced analysis of those differences, along with a strong sense of how
perceptions of global security change from place to place. The chapters in
this book far exceeded our expectations, both in their individual contributions to our understanding of global and regional security and conflict
management, and in their collective impact. Regions have indeed tried to
create their own kind of peacebuilding, a self-help effort that has produced
modest but stable structures in some areas, grand mansions in others, and
underresourced shacks built on shaky foundations in still others. The preceding chapters bring into sharp relief the different ways that various regions define security, identify threats to that security, and construct conflict
management responses to address those threats.

All of this confirmed our initial perceptions. To our surprise, however, we
also found evidence of a new way of building, one that not only continues
the practice of self-help conflict management but that also involves many
different types of institutions acting together. Building on and borrowing
a term from earlier work on interinstitutional collaboration in the field of
peacekeeping, we call this peacebuilding collaboration "collective conflict

management." This concluding chapter will summarize the security challenges, examine the conflict management differences, offer some thoughts on why regions have chosen to strengthen cooperation in this field, and assess the effectiveness of regional peacebuilding. It will then look at the concept of collective conflict management, examining whether there is a trend toward collective responses to conflict and security challenges. The chapter argues that while it may be too early to identify a new approach, it is possible to identify new patterns of cooperative international behavior that combine conflict management capabilities at both the regional and global levels and that may provide an appropriate model for global conflict management in the twenty-first century.

The Global Security Environment

The security environment that regions have faced since the end of the Cold War is characterized principally by its complexity. No longer is international security dominated by two competing superpowers and complemented by the United Nations, a global security institution whose charter reflects the era of interstate war in which it was drafted. No longer is international security "indivisible" as it was in the period when the ideological and political rivalry between the United States and the Soviet Union defined not just their interests but also the interests of those countries who were allied with or opposed to each.

If the Cold War represented a Manichean struggle between two competing political systems, today's world is much more disaggregated. International security has become divisible—broken into many parts—as people, governments, and regions attempt to address a wide range of security challenges and threats. These threats are often generated within individual societies but spread across borders to their surrounding environment, and at times become impacted by unhealthy regional dynamics. To further complicate the picture, today's security threats may encompass a whole series of social and environmental factors, such as pandemic disease, piracy, illicit trafficking, and environmental degradation along with traditional military challenges. In addition, they occur in a time of bewildering connectivity and advancing political complexity. The world has become a multicentric system in which the United States will share the space with China, India, Brazil, the European Union, and other centers of political and economic power and influence.

The Center for International Development and Conflict Management at the University of Maryland, which tracks global trends in armed violence, points out that, although there was a steady decline in the number of active conflicts around the globe immediately following the end of the Cold War, the trend appears now to be reversing itself with a resurgence of armed conflict and violence in many countries.[1] Furthermore, many of the peace agreements that were concluded in the 1980s and 1990s to end sectarian strife have failed. Since 1982, the number of "significant" terrorist attacks—those that have involved "loss of life, serious injury, or major property damage"—has risen steadily, as the horrific attacks on the United States on September 11, 2001, and more recently in Baghdad, Islamabad, Kabul, Mumbai, and elsewhere all too tragically lay bare.

The changes in the regional and international security environment test the world's capacity to hold in check potentially devastating threats to peace. International governance systems and institutions, constructed out of the ruins of the Second World War and the Great Depression, lag behind the steepening curve of globalization. Major powers and major international security bodies have scrambled for politically sustainable and doctrinally coherent strategies. Their search for answers has produced familiar policy catchphrases—for example, "failed states," "cooperative security," "loose nukes," "post-conflict stabilization and reconstruction," "the responsibility to protect," "genocide prevention," and "the war on terrorism"—aimed at generating the political will for action.

These phrases, however, served to identify symptoms or reflect specific agendas rather than set direction, and the preceding chapters show that regional actors do not always agree with the normative and policy responses that arise from these phrases. In a world where threats to international security can be global, transnational, or local and at times can operate at all levels, there is no clear assignment of responsibility for dealing with these threats and little sign of an emergence of a global consensus on which powers or institutions should be responsible. To further complicate the picture, today's international system, as Gilles Andréani points out, is a mixed system, or a mixture of systems: hegemonic, multipolar, democratically cacophonic, and potentially confederal. It is a multicentric stew in which different centers of power, influence, and political and economic attraction cooperate and compete as they see fit.

In addition, as the security environment grows in complexity, the nature of the global response has also changed. The post–World War II proliferation in the number of global, regional, and subregional institutions dedicated to security and stabilization has led to confusion about role sharing and to unequal burden sharing. There is more than a haphazard quality to those instances where the international community has intervened. This is compounded by continuing moral and legal double standards in selecting cases for intervention, including the fact that very few if any cases where intervention has actually occurred have been prompted by the "responsibility to protect" (R2P) or other human security precepts and norms. International cooperation and capacities for conflict management and prevention continue to be thwarted by a lack of clear concepts, guidelines, and mutually satisfactory arrangements (including legal frameworks) for international, regional, state, and (benign) nonstate actors to work together. When interventions of the peacemaking, peace enforcement, or peacebuilding varieties have occurred, international actors have generally tended to pay inadequate attention to regional dynamics when addressing the needs of one state or territory. In addition, with the attention of major global actors focused on Iraq and Afghanistan, many other conflicts in the world either have been "forgotten" (e.g., Western Sahara) or are simply excluded from international treatment or consideration because of the sensitivities of key regional (or great) powers and a general unwillingness to tackle them.

This is the current security environment, at least from the global perspective. However, when security and conflict management are viewed from a strictly global perspective, we may obtain a grand sweep at the expense of the individual characteristics and response capabilities of different regions. Barry Buzan and Ole Waever give a succinct criticism of the typical scholarly "tradition of finding one dominant story to impose on the whole international system." The remedy, they argue, is to recognize that "there are distinct stories at several levels with none holding the master key to a full interpretation."[2] As is evident from this volume, much is happening at the regional level, although these conflict management initiatives do not necessarily resemble each other in form, function, or objective. Under these circumstances, a critical question is whether these various regional capacities will join with each other and/or with international and other actors to form new models of multilateral conflict management. In order to examine this question, this chapter will look next at the differences in regional patterns and the significance of these differences for conflict management.

Regions' Diverse Patterns of Response

The chapters of this book show that the evolving patterns of security and conflict management are quite diverse. Paul D. Williams and Jürgen Haacke suggest that the dimensions of variation are several, including the regional political structure, the presence or absence of hegemons, the domestic political mind-set toward conflict and its sources, and cultural attitudes toward security and the use of force.

Differences in Regions

Regions differ at the most elemental level of definition. The geographical scope of many of these cooperative arrangements tends to be somewhat ill-defined and it is clear that "regional" is a spongy concept that may bear little relation to geography, culture, or even formal state boundaries. Although sub-Saharan Africa and South America are sometimes viewed as distinct regional entities because they are clearly delimited by geography, the same cannot be said about Europe, the Middle East, Southeast Asia, or Northeast Asia. In these areas, the concept of a distinct "region" is blurred by competing, if not rival, perceptions of the boundaries of the region itself because of culture, religion, politics, history, and the self-identification of states and other subnational entities and groupings that make up the region. Many regional organizations also offer few clues about the scope of the region through their membership. For example, the Organization for Security and Co-operation in Europe (OSCE) has a membership that spans the globe from Vladivostok to Vancouver despite the obvious "European" orientation and focus of this organization and its mandate.

Regions also differ in their institutional capacity for conflict management. Europe, for instance, is replete with institutions—in this region, the European Union, the OSCE, the European Parliament, the Council of Europe, and NATO are only the most prevalent. Africa also has a complex structure of regional organizations, from the African Union to the African Peer Review Mechanism and the Economic Community of West African States, which operates with various degrees of capacity. In many cases, regional actors are developing at the regional level fresh approaches that derive from the specific history, culture, political requirements, and concrete capacity constraints of the region. Other regions suffer from weak institutional capacity, a lack of basic political coherence, inadequately trained personnel, and insufficient resources to deal with their ongoing and emerging security challenges or to engage effectively in the various kinds of conflict prevention and management activities that may be warranted or considered desirable. In other cases, regional powers sometimes find themselves torn between their priorities as conflict parties and as conflict managers (that is, as third parties), as the experiences of France, Russia, the United States, and India demonstrate.

Another important dimension of variation is the degree of regional interest in interacting with global institutions and major powers in the region's security problems, and the level of the region's readiness to accept support and assistance in conflict management tasks from extraregional sources. Regions pose different demands or questions of the central, global powers. Some may say, "Leave us alone," while others may say, "Help us break the regional logjam or, at a minimum, don't make things worse"; others may plead, "Please don't disengage and go away"; and some voices may ask, "Does anyone out there really care about us?"

For instance, some regions, such as the Caribbean, Africa, and Central Asia, are receptive to capacity-building initiatives by powerful global actors. Others—Southeast Asia and the Middle East, for instance—show either resistance to or ambivalence about this prospect. Meanwhile, there is uneven interest on the part of the international community. While the Middle East and northern Asia continue to dominate both headlines and political circles, other regions with long-enduring conflicts (Mindanao in the Philippines, the Western Saharan conflict) receive less attention and conflict management support. Furthermore, many states continue to worry about intrusions into their sovereignty and may actively thwart the development of new institutional capacities for cooperation. In spite of globalization, the enduring rivalries and competition between states is a continuing feature of our Westphalia-based interstate system and an obstacle to political initiative, cooperation, and collective action. Regionalism, however defined, can become hostage to such rivalries; interregional cooperation can be inhibited by them.

As the preceding chapters illustrate, there are major differences in the degree of regional autonomy from or dependence on global mechanisms and power centers. Dependence may not be visible on the surface because there is a tendency to take for granted the stability and predictability of the core of the international system and great power relationships. Stability and continuity at the global level provide the essential context within which regions can develop their security doctrines and conflict management capabilities. If the core system breaks down or becomes increasingly incoherent or unable to master its central tasks—for example, in controlling WMD proliferation or adapting peacefully to the rise of newly powerful actors—this will affect the world's regions.

Differences in Regional Organizations

Regional organizations generally vary along two dimensions: structure and function. The formal regional institutions and security arrangements discussed in this book can be roughly classified into four broad groups: (1) dialoguing or general political and cultural associations, such as the Association of Southeast Asian Nations (ASEAN), the Shanghai Cooperation Organization, or the Organization of the Islamic Conference (OIC); (2) political organizations that have a broader collective security focus or mandate but that do not have military forces at their disposal, such as the

Organization of American States (OAS), the Council of Europe, or the League of Arab States; (3) economic and political organizations such as the European Union and the African Union, which have developed expanding mandates and capabilities for collective action that extend into the foreign policy and security realm; and (4) regional security organizations that provide for the collective defense of their members, such as NATO, but that also operate "out of theater" and increasingly engage in a wide variety of security functions that go beyond their traditional mandate and role (e.g., counterinsurgency, counterterrorism). At present, NATO is the only example of this last category and is in a class by itself.

In terms of function, this book is filled with examples of organizations that have formal mandates for either the provision of security or conflict management or both. However, it is also important to recognize that in terms of regional organizations there is often a gap between the mandate and what the organizations actually do. The de jure mandates of formal regional institutions sometimes bear little relationship to their de facto role in life and their institutional mandates can evolve with the addition of new members and/or the adoption of new roles and functions, as the cases of the European Union, ASEAN, and the Economic Community of West African States (ECOWAS) illustrate. As the global tectonic plates of power and authority shift (or erode), the pressure to change roles and adapt to their changing security environment also increases. This pressure is clearly apparent in the case of NATO, which some argue should live up to its greater potential as an alliance and become a new hub of a globe-spanning web of regional cooperative undertakings.[3]

The traditional institutional "hierarchy" between regional institutions and arrangements and the United Nations as envisioned in the UN Charter is also evolving. It is becoming at once both more "flat" with the erosion of traditional political hierarchies and more deeply interconnected. The framers of the UN Charter originally foresaw a clear institutional link between the United Nations and regional arrangements in the maintenance of international peace and security. Although the charter assigns key responsibility for international security to the UN Security Council, Chapter VIII of the UN Charter looks forward to the "existence of regional arrangements or agencies for dealing with such matters relating to the maintenance of international peace and security as are appropriate for regional action."[4]

The use of regional agencies for resolving regional disputes traditionally has been viewed as the first line of defense according to Articles 33 and 52 of the charter, and the United Nations itself can refer disputes to regional organizations for mediation and arbitration (Article 52). Regional actors can also engage in collective self-defense in the event of an armed attack pending action by the Security Council, but the arrangements allowable under Article 51 do not fall within the purview of Chapter VIII. However, Article 53 of the UN Charter regarding the use of regional arrangements for enforcement actions under UN authority has also been interpreted flexibly, especially in recent years. The Security Council, for example, gave its retroactive blessing to the military actions of ECOWAS, but it never formally sanctioned NATO's use of force in Kosovo or the "allied" invasion of Iraq.

A related issue revolves around more general international expectations of how regional institutions will carry out their functions. In the 1960s and 1970s, for example, many looked to regional institutions to promote greater levels of social, economic, and political integration among their members, the assumption being that greater level of integration would advance the cause of peace.[5] Later, this focus came to include flows of investment and trade across borders, economic pressure groups, elite socialization, and other processes that were viewed as critical to the integration process and the formation of a shared political, economic, and security community.

With the end of the Cold War, attention has shifted to the role that international institutions, including regional arrangements, can play in generating new norms to inform, guide, shape, and regulate the behavior of their members. Traditional prohibitions against intervention in the internal affairs of states began breaking down, allowing some regional organizations to be more active in the advancement of democratic and human rights norms. In Latin America, for example, as both John W. Graham and Monica Herz argue, the principles of sovereignty and nonintervention, which were the cornerstones of the inter-American system, have been relaxed and modified to allow the OAS to play a greater role in the defense of democratic principles and the advancement of human rights. The Santiago Declaration, incorporated in OAS Resolution 1080 of 1991, has served as the basis of OAS prodemocracy interventions in Peru, Haiti, the Dominican Republic, Guatemala, Paraguay, and elsewhere.

Even so, the embrace of human rights and democratic norms and principles is by no means uniform across regions. In the case of ASEAN, for example, most of its members actively shun what they see as Western bias in definitions of human rights and democracy. Good governance, in an Asian context, does not necessarily mean that there is widespread acceptance of rights-based liberal democracy. Thus, in the ASEAN and wider ASEAN Regional Forum (ARF) context, regional security cooperation has typically centered on a more traditional security agenda of confidence building, nuclear nonproliferation, peacekeeping, and military cooperation and exchanges of information. Similar reservations are also to be found in the Middle East and North Africa, where there has been no official endorsement of evolving norms and principles in the United Nations system and elsewhere to advance the concept of human security.

In the late 1990s and early twenty-first century, attention shifted yet again to the promise (and performance) of regional institutions and arrangements in conflict management and prevention at both the intrastate and interstate levels, including their role in offering "good offices," negotiation, and mediation. Because regional groupings are typically united by geography, history, language, or culture, some argue they may be better suited to addressing local security challenges by being more sensitive to the interests and needs of local interests than "outsiders" like the United Nations or coalitions of great powers. Regional actors are also more likely to have a greater stake in the resolution of conflicts because of concerns about conflict escalation and the implications for regional stability. Some observers view regional arrangements as the preferred instruments of preventive diplomacy and conflict management because of their proximity to the sources of conflict and understanding of local conditions.[6] At the same time, there remains a more critical stance toward "regional task sharing" that underscores the fact that regional organizations are typically biased toward state actors—which thereby limits their utility in civil conflicts—and that recognizes the danger of regional organizations being captured by local hegemons.[7]

Differences in Openness to Civil Society Participation

It is against the background of this evolution that nongovernmental organizations (NGOs) have become more salient as instruments of conflict management. This is partly because there may be resistance to external official intervention on the part of the governing party that might legitimize opposition or rebel groups, especially in the case of failing but not necessarily completely failed states. This resistance derives from concerns about the loss of sovereignty; concerns about a further weakening of the political legitimacy and authority of those in power; and concerns about the potential escalation of stakes resulting from the intervention of an external actor. Where the challenge is to gain entry into a conflict and initiate dialogue with the parties, a nonofficial problem-solving approach where the third party provides "good offices" in a low-key setting that is removed from the political spotlight is often desirable. Increasingly, practitioners and scholars are coming to recognize the capacity of qualified NGOs to foster personal relationships, develop trust, provide training, and build supportive constituencies for dialogue. The importance of building a broad base of constituents for peacebuilding within conflict societies has also been recognized. Without popular support, peace agreements can break down under the sheer weight of public repudiation. Engaging NGOs and civil society groups has increasingly become a significant ingredient in conflict management efforts.

It must be emphasized, however, that the world's regions are very unequal in their openness to civil society and NGO participation in conflict management. In regions where the bias in favor of states and governments is clearest, the scope for action by international and regional NGOs is narrowed accordingly. International NGOs in the conflict management and capacity-building space have experienced mounting restrictions and official (or officially inspired) push back in parts of Africa, the Middle East, Central Asia, and the former Soviet Union. This uneven pattern is another illustration of the regional variations identified in this study.

Why Do Countries Choose to Act on a Regional Basis?

The countries that compose regions vary on many dimensions—including in their perceptions of threats, their foundations on which to build conflict management institutions or initiatives, their barriers to conflict management cooperation, and their willingness and ability to reach out to each other in regional cooperation or to global institutions in a more multilevel form of cooperation. Taken together, these elements define the regional capability for conflict management. Table 20.1 captures in broad-brush strokes these differences as reflected by the preceding chapters.

The question remains, however, of what makes countries in a region want to cooperate and to be willing to cede some decision-making authority to either regional partners or global institutions in order to achieve greater conflict management capacity. Our first impulse is to say that cooperation is dependent on robust governmental institutional capacity to bear the costs and reap the benefits of cooperation. This kind of cooperation is expensive in terms of monetary and human resources and in terms of the time and political capital required to create and implement joint policies. However, when we compare regional responses along these two axes—preferences toward maximum protection of state sovereignty or toward regional/global cooperation, and national/regional capacity to organize and cooperate for common purposes—the widespread patterns of variation are nonetheless still evident.

While one might expect that areas with weak institutional capacity prefer (out of fear of outside interference) not to cooperate, we find that some do cooperate (Africa and the Caribbean, and to a degree Southeast

Table 20.1 The Sources of and Obstacles to Collective Conflict Management by Region

Region	Security threats	Collective conflict management building blocks	Barriers to collective conflict management	Cooperation with others within the region	Cooperation with others outside the region
Regional characteristics	• internal and identity based • external • traditional • nontraditional	• economic interdependence • democratic norms • culture of cooperation • negotiation tracks • regional institutions	• low levels of economic interaction • sovereignty addictions • autocratic regimes • enduring regional rivalries • financial and institutional capacity deficits • absence of shared threat perception	• receptive • unreceptive	• receptive • unreceptive
Middle East	• internal and identity based • traditional	• negotiation tracks	• all of the above	• weakly receptive	• receptive, albeit unevenly throughout the region
Africa	• largely internal and identity based • nontraditional	• strengthening democratic norms, emerging culture of cooperation, and regional institution building	• pockets of autocracy • resources and institutional capacity deficits • some regional rivalries	• receptive	• receptive
South Asia, Southeast Asia	• all • internal and external	• democratic norms • economic interdependence • negotiation tracks • regional institutions	• all • sovereignty addictions • some regional rivalries	• unreceptive • receptive	• unreceptive • receptive

(continued on next page)

Table 20.1 The Sources of and Obstacles to Collective Conflict Management by Region (continued)

Region	Security threats	Collective conflict management building blocks	Barriers to collective conflict management	Cooperation with others within the region	Cooperation with others outside the region
Northeast Asia	• external • traditional	• growing economic interdependence • negotiation tracks	• sovereignty addictions • enduring regional rivalries • institutional and capacity deficits • weakly shared threat perceptions	• variable receptive	• partially receptive
South America	• internal • some external	• all	• some autocratic regimes (democratic populism) • some regional rivalries	• receptive	• partially receptive
Central America, Mexico, and the Caribbean	• nontraditional	• weak regional institutions	• low levels of economic interaction (& development) • financial and institutional capacity deficits • political resistance and some autocratic regimes	• receptive	• receptive
Europe	• internal • nontraditional • external (new)	• all	• few	• highly receptive	• receptive
Eurasia	• all	• all	• all	• unreceptive	• unreceptive

Asia), and some do not (the Middle East, Eurasia, and South Asia). Equally, we find that certain countries with a strong national institutional capacity—for example, India—prefer to maintain their national sovereignty, while other countries—for example, in Europe—prefer to cooperate, at least in the security area. These preferences, of course, are often issue dependent and can change rapidly and should not be taken as fixed over time. They do indicate, however, that the desire to join with others can be found both among strong, more developed states and among weak, less developed states.

We also find that a country's history as a colony of another state does not serve as a good predictor of whether or not it seeks cooperation. Here again, some areas with colonial pasts—South Asia, the Middle East—have historically resisted cooperation with others, while the former colonies in the Caribbean and Africa have sought it out. Other variables—such as whether or not there is a regional hegemon or the degree to which there is political or economic dependency on another part of the world—also do not consistently point to positive attitudes toward interregional or extraregional cooperation.

One driver may be the absence or uneven presence of global assistance and support to fill the "security gap."[8] The suggestion here is that regional capacity and ownership of conflict management roles evolve to fill a vacuum. A related driver may be the perception by regional actors that they have specific and unique attributes, skills, and cultural insights that more distant, external bodies or states lack. Regional expertise and perceived legitimacy can also play a role in the emergence of this driver.

In some regions, there may be evidence of another driver: that an incompatibility is developing between the doctrines and normative priorities of global actors and regional states. For example, it is unlikely that the SCO and the OSCE would place the same degree of emphasis on governance norms in approaching the challenges of combating terrorism and maintaining border security in Central Asia. African peacekeeping missions could be encountering a parallel dilemma: UN and Western agencies and NGOs may have one set of conditions for achieving a legitimate "exit" from military operations, while African leaders may have quite a different one that reflects the realities of patronage and "wealth sharing" in many societies.[9]

Additional drivers of regional innovation and capacity building are to be found in reactions at the regional level to perceived global "interventionism" (under whatever guise) and the assertion by external parties (official or nonofficial) of the need to act on behalf of "universal" values that may not, in fact, be so universally admired or respected. When major powers seek to project their priorities into distant places, privileging a single issue such as nonproliferation or terrorism or corruption, there will be regional pushback and an "opening" for local/regional initiatives. If, as Nigel Quinney's account suggests, there is tentative evidence of a regional conflict management culture in some regions, it will be important to understand the basis for the emergence and development of such cultures. The extent to which the driver is shared experience and perceptions of legitimacy, shared interests, political preferences, or a common appreciation of what is possible needs to be evaluated.

The best explanation we can offer is that cooperation on conflict management arises when there is a widespread perception of a common threat and general agreement on (or convergence toward) conflict-management norms, or in less theoretical terms, agreement on how to proceed in the face of security challenges and specific conflict management needs. For instance, the fear that democratically elected governments could be overthrown by coups in Latin America led to the adoption in 1991 of OAS Resolution 1080, which enshrined the Santiago Declaration. The desire to keep both China and the United States at arms' length—but still to engage them—led to the development of ASEAN, "the ASEAN way," and the spin-off institutions, the ARF and Council for Security Cooperation in the Asia Pacific (CSCAP). The European Union members share a concern—at least up to a certain point—about instability in Africa and the Middle East and agree that development aid, capacity-building support, and modest peacekeeping assistance are the best means that they have to address these instabilities. In these cases, consensus may have emerged as the result of the influence of leading states but was rarely imposed by a hegemonic actor. Collaborative conflict management seems to be based on patterns of limited consensus, although like many cooperative arrangements, there are always a couple of countries willing to set the agenda and bear a larger share of the economic and political costs of cooperation.[10] Accordingly, it is possible to imagine that, as more regions come of age in the modern international system, their leading states will define responses to security challenges, but that intraregional differences of interest and tacit "agreements to disagree" over security threats and conflict management activities will limit and shape the trajectory of concerted policy.

Is the Regionalization of Conflict Management Capacity Effective?

We finally come to the question of effectiveness. When countries join together on a regional basis to manage conflicts, either inside the region or (in the case of NATO and the European Union) abroad, are they able to deliver peace or at least enhanced security? Even more, do regional groupings have special qualities that make them the agency of choice in the task of making peace or responding to regional threats?

The answer that grows out of the collection of chapters in this book is ... it depends. It depends on the strength of the commitment to act regionally, but it also depends on the nature of the conflict. When global actors have an interest in a conflict's trajectory—as in the Iraq and Afghanistan conflicts—regional actors tend to be marginalized. When one of the conflict parties is against outside involvement in a peacemaking effort (the example of Kashmir comes to mind), regional participation could be counterproductive. The advantage that regional actors have over all other outsiders is their deeper and more nuanced familiarity with the conflict, its players, and dynamics, as well as their strong interest in the outcome of the conflict management initiative, especially in cases where the conflict has leaked over borders. Their disadvantage grows out of that same familiarity and the same strong interest.

This is a frustratingly limited conclusion to draw from such a rich menu of examples as are presented in this book, but it also highlights the problem of focusing on effectiveness in this field. As of yet, there is not a gold standard for conflict management against which to measure all peacebuilding initiatives. However, the sheer volume of activity on a regional basis reflects both the real desire by regions to participate in their own conflict management efforts and the lack of leadership at the global level. The DIY peacebuilding approach grows as much out of a desire to create conflict management capacity as it does out of the lack of alternatives, the result of living in a world where the big "construction firms"—the United States and the United Nations—are otherwise occupied. Under these circumstances, a more interesting question than "is the regionalization of conflict management capacity effective?" would be "are there mechanisms that could allow regional engagement to maximize its strengths and minimize its weaknesses?"

Toward a Concept of Collective Conflict Management

The answer to the above question lies, as so much else in this narrative does, on changes that are happening in the international system. The concept of conflict management is changing. Approaches that depend on only one institution, country, or region seem to be a thing of the past. Rather than focusing purely on the regional aspect, it may be useful to think of the regional parameters of conflict management in the more expansive terms of the growing network of formal and informal institutional arrangements that operate across national, subregional, and regional boundaries. These networks have the capacity to shape conflict management strategies and responses at all three levels—the local, the regional, and the global. When the political environment is supportive, networks of conflict managers can help to develop effective engagement strategies of negotiation and mediation that support and reinforce each other. They also have a key role to play in supporting peace processes from their inception to their conclusion, including the implementation of a formal peace settlement. What may be emerging in certain places are what could be termed conflict management "coalitions" that can include governments, intergovernmental institutions at both the global and regional levels, eminent persons, and nonofficial groups.

From a cross-regional perspective, as many of the essays in this volume also demonstrate, the actual form and shape of these crosscutting networks varies from one region to another. Some regions, like sub-Saharan Africa, are more open and receptive to the support and engagement of global or external actors than others. For those that have generally tended to operate as self-help systems where there is a desire to keep outsiders at bay, such as Southeast Asia, the challenge may be to encourage greater receptivity to external sources of support and engagement, recognizing that such support must be sensitive to (and perhaps even modified to accommodate) local cultural norms and traditions of conflict management. This includes the provision of donor support and external assistance directed at strengthening the conflict management capacities of local and regional entities that are underfunded or face other kinds of capacity or leadership deficits.

In order to grasp what is happening, we would like to build on the concept of collective conflict management (CCM), developed by Joseph Lepgold and Thomas G. Weiss in the 1990s to describe collaborative actions by states to counteract "breaches of the peace" through a variety of collective actions from cease-fire monitoring to military intervention.[11] The definition and the phenomenon were closely tied to the explosion of internal conflicts in the 1990s and the role of what was termed "the international community" in responding to those conflicts. Through our examination of regional conflict management, we found evidence of the same interest in working collaboratively in responding to conflict, but on an expanded scale, no longer tied to decisive action by the United Nations or a powerful state to organize the response. Today's CCM describes an emerging phenomenon in international relations in which countries, international and regional/subregional organizations, and nonofficial institutions or private actors address potential or actual security threats by acting together to (1) control, diminish, or end the violence associated with the conflict through combined peace operations and/or mediation, conflict prevention, and avoidance; (2) assist, where appropriate, with a negotiated settlement through peacebuilding and other reconstruction efforts and measures; (3) help to deal with the political, economic, and/or social issues that underlie the conflict; and/or (4) provide political, diplomatic, and economic guarantees or other long-term measures to improve conditions for a sustainable peace.

Current CCM is a relatively new pattern of cooperation in international affairs with no organizational center or universal rules of the road. As a result, the practice of these various coalitions may be very different, depending on who is practicing and what the circumstances of the conflict are. A defining feature of these relatively cooperative ventures is that they span global, regional, and local levels in terms of their institutional membership or actor composition. Many CCM ventures also typically involve a combination of public (intergovernmental) and private (nonstate) partners.

There are no universal rules of the road or consistent principles behind CCM. The practice or application of CCM by various organizations or coalitions may also be different and range, as noted earlier, from combined/joint peace operations to peacemaking, peacebuilding, and conflict prevention. In one sense CCM follows the traditions of collective defense and collective security (see table 20.2).[12] However, unlike collective defense and collective security, which involve formal obligations to undertake joint action in response to the actions of an aggressive state, CCM involves improvised strategies of collective action often in response to diverse security challenges ranging from "traditional" security threats such as the outbreak of civil war or regional conflict to "nontraditional" threats such as organized crime, piracy, kidnapping, arms trading, narcotrafficking, and conflict-related commodity rents. Faced with such problems, states or regions seek remedies where they are available—from international agencies, regional organizations, bilateral official or nonofficial partners, or joint "neighborhood watch" initiatives.

CCM is informal, improvised, ad hoc, and opportunistic. Pragmatism reigns, sometimes at the expense of the norms embodied in formal charters or alliances. CCM choices are also shaped by national preferences and regional security cultures or norms. They are also influenced by a convergence of threat perceptions at the regional level. Stated in less theoretical terms, many CCM undertakings are make-do arrangements to deal with specific security challenges and immediate conflict management needs.

Table 20.2 Differing Approaches to Conflict and Security Management

	Actors	Security threats	Forms of cooperation	Degree of institutionalization	Patterns of leadership
Collective defense	State signatories to a treaty, which is rooted in a multiparty alliance	Military threat from the outside	Formal and rules based	High	Centralized, hegemonic
Collective security	State signatories to a treaty, which is collective, supported by an organization, and does not draw lines to leave anybody out	Any military threat to one or more of the members of the organization	Formal and rules based	High	Centralized, oligopolistic
Collective conflict management	Informal coalitions or networks of state, intergovernmental, and nonstate actors	External or internal, traditional and nontraditional threats	Ad hoc, on a case-by-case basis, evolutionary, and open structure	Low	Diffuse, shared, pragmatic, and ad hoc (and opportunistic)

Cases of CCM

Consider the following example of CCM, which has both military and broader political and legal elements. In 2009, in response to escalating attacks by pirates on ships and merchant vessels transiting the Gulf of Aden and the Indian Ocean off the Horn of Africa, a combination of intergovernmental, regional, state, and private actors mounted a collaborative effort to address this threat. Combined efforts to deal with piracy have involved joint, ad hoc naval coordination among key NATO, EU, and Coalition Maritime Forces; a major parallel role of the private sector, especially among those companies whose ships transit these waters; the critical cooperation of Kenya in handling captured pirates; and the impact of more effective efforts by distinct nonstate Somali entities. Although there is no unified command structure among the three naval contingents, there has been extensive coordination at the tactical level to deal with Somali pirates.

Another positive development is improved efforts by merchant shipping lines to protect their own vessels. Up to 70 percent of pirate attacks are now being defeated by merchant ships' crews themselves. As a consequence, pirates face significant risks and less likelihood of reward if they attack merchant ships. While Kenya has agreed to prosecute pirates who are apprehended, other regional states lack the necessary legislation or political will to cooperate with international efforts to provide legal support for direct naval action against pirates.

At the end of the day, naval operations are ultimately no substitute for greater efforts to tackle the sociopolitical and economic challenges within Somalia. However, even here there has been some modest progress as a result of encouraging political developments in the autonomous regions of Somaliland and Puntland. It is also now recognized that security-sector reform is necessary, particularly in terms of building regional "brown-water" naval and coast guard capacities. This does not mean that the threat has diminished. However, there is something of an evolving cooperative network of global, regional, state, and nonstate actors to address the piracy problem.[13]

Another example of CCM in both a reconciliation/peacemaking context and within a regional and international context that is changing is in Jammu and Kashmir, where a wide variety of civil society groups and policymakers have attempted to create a constructive space for ongoing dialogue and discussion to reduce tensions between India and Pakistan. As Meenakshi Gopinath points out in her chapter, "the old formulas of viewing Kashmir . . . as the 'unfinished business of Partition'" is being replaced by serious dialogue at a time of great regional tension. These efforts have been led by a wide variety of national and international think tanks and policy experts such as the Kashmir Study Group, the Delhi Policy Group, the Regional Centre for Strategic Studies, and the Kashmiri American Council, all of which have broadened the discourse at the official level in ways that have generally been positive and constructive. Official diplomacy has also been reinforced by civic engagement at the local level as various women's groups have mobilized to end violence by promoting reconciliation and bridging religious, ethnic, and linguistic divides. What is significant about these developments is that they have been occasionally encouraged by the Indian and Pakistani governments in a pragmatic quest to establish a sustainable framework for dialogue and negotiation.

The Dubai Process—a cross-border CCM venture facilitated by Canada—offers another illustration of the kinds of networks that are spawned to deal with today's complex security challenges. Major, long-standing disagreements between Afghanistan and Pakistan over the issue of the Durand Line (which constitutes the de facto border between the two countries) have for many years thwarted any kind of dialogue or security cooperation between the two countries on a wide range of border problems, including the cross-border movement of insurgents; the absence of proper infrastructure and customs management at key, legal border-crossing points (Waish-Chamam, Ghulam Khan, and Torkham); the smuggling of duty-free goods between Afghanistan and Pakistan; the illicit cross-border flow of narcotics; and illegal migration.

This initiative was developed when then Pakistani president Pervez Musharraf threatened to mine the border in response to pressure from the international community to assume greater responsibility for controlling the country's borders. Canada, a longstanding champion of the anti-personnel landmines treaty, stepped in to suggest an alternative approach to dealing with the myriad problems in the disputed border region. Since 2007, in keeping with the 2007 Potsdam Statement by G8 foreign ministers and the foreign ministers of Afghanistan and Pakistan (and the Pakistan-Afghanistan Joint Peace Jirga), the two countries have met on a regular basis under Canadian auspices in a series of technical, working-level workshops to discuss Afghanistan-Pakistan border management cooperation. The five working areas of what is now referred to as the Dubai Process (named after the Persian Gulf Emirate where the first meeting took place) include customs, counternarcotics, management of the movement of people, law enforcement in border areas, and government-to-people connections through social and economic development. The meetings are now part of an internationally recognized process that not only promotes dialogue between Afghan and Pakistani officials but also advances cooperation in each of the five areas. Importantly, the process has engaged and mobilized a wide range of partners and stakeholders not only in the two countries but also at the international level, including the U.S. Border Management Task Force in Kabul and Islamabad, the United Nations Office on Drugs and Crime, the International Security Assistance Force Regional Command South, the World Bank, the United Nations Assistance Mission in Afghanistan, the Office of the United Nations High Commissioner for Refugees, the International Organization for Migration, other organizations working on border management, and key donors such as Germany and Denmark.[14]

The 2003 Liberian peace talks offer another illustration of a CCM undertaking because of the many international, regional/subregional, and local actors and institutions that supported negotiations to end a bloody and protracted civil war between President Charles Taylor and his National Patriotic Party and two rebel groups, the Liberian United for Reconciliation and Democracy and the Movement for Democracy in Liberia. The negotiations, which took place in Ghana, were mediated by former Nigerian president General Abdulsalami Abubakar under the auspices of a subregional entity, ECOWAS. ECOWAS, which sent peacekeeping troops into the country during the civil war in the 1990s, had a main interest in ending the conflict, because the Liberian conflict threatened neighboring ECOWAS members, notably Sierra Leone, Guinea, and Côte d'Ivoire. Other international and regional actors participating in the negotiations were the United States, the European Union, the International Contact Group on Liberia, the African Union, and the United Nations. In addition, among the key parties attending the talks were Liberian civil society organizations, which maintained constant pressure on the negotiating parties in both Ghana and Liberia to reach an agreement. These groups represented interreligious interests, human rights, women's rights, and legal interests. Many had even risked their lives by traveling through Côte d'Ivoire to reach the talks in Ghana. Among the most forceful was the 150–200 member team from the Women of Liberia Mass Action for Peace group, which, at one point, even barred delegates from leaving the room during the course of negotiations until they had reached an agreement.[15]

We find evidence of similar patterns of CCM cooperation in contemporary peace operations. An especially interesting example has evolved in Sudan's violence-torn Darfur. Initially, the African Union fielded the African Union Mission in Sudan (AMIS) with considerable financial and logistical (airlift and training) support from NATO and the European Union. But the problem was larger than AMIS could handle. Various UN agencies, including the UN Development Program, and the government of Japan launched capacity-building initiatives to bolster AMIS. In 2007, the

UN Security Council authorized the creation of a hybrid peace operation known as the UN/AU Mission in Darfur (UNAMID), where up to 22,000 uniformed troops and police have operated under a UN mandate with UN financing ($1.8 billion in 2010), a joint AU/UN special representative (Nigeria's Ibrahim Gambari), and a blue-helmeted African force commander as well as a jointly appointed police commissioner. UNAMID's replacement of AMIS was a recognition of the African Union's capacity constraints, the political sensibilities of the host government, and the severe challenges of the mission mandate.[16] Some of this evolution has involved "rehatting" a largely African force, but the change brought a major upgrade of logistics and command and control arrangements. UNAMID's political guidance comes from the joint special representative liaising with both Addis Ababa and New York, an arrangement that succeeded the earlier twinned matchup of "joint special envoys" from the United Nations and African Union. To round out this mosaic, the United Nations and the African Union deploy separate special envoys in support of implementation of the 2005 Comprehensive Peace Agreement of the North-South Sudan conflict, and the 10,000 troops and police of the UN Mission in Sudan (UNMIS) serve in a conventional—not a hybrid—UN peace operation.

The Philippines' International Contact Group (ICG), established to support the peace talks between the government of the Republic of the Philippines (GRP) and the Moro Islamic Liberation Front (MILF), provides another example of CCM. The ICG's assignment is to assist a Malaysian-led mediation process, to build trust between parties, to help to monitor compliance to agreement, to provide expertise, and to conduct research on matters of interest to the peace talks. Unlike the antipiracy example, however, this group is not the result of third parties joining together to increase security and provide conflict management, but of an agreement between the parties to the conflict—the GRP and the MILF—to seek additional external support and participation in the reopened talks in December 2009. The country members of the ICG include the United Kingdom, Japan, and Turkey. The OIC, while not a member of the ICG, has ties to this group through Turkey. In addition, OIC member Malaysia leads the mediation, while fellow OIC members Brunei and Libya participate in the International Monitoring Team, which monitors the cease-fire between the GRP and MILF.

Interestingly enough, the GRP and MILF also asked two NGOs, the Asia Foundation and the Centre for Humanitarian Dialogue (HDC), to be on the ICG and requested that the HDC act as the secretariat for the group. The Asia Foundation has a long history of engagement in the Philippines and in Mindanao, the governance of which is critical to the peace talks. HDC's involvement in the Philippines is more recent and has focused on the conflicts between the government and the Communist rebel group, the New People's Army. Its contribution lies in the fact that it specializes in mediation and facilitation and can draw on its experience from other conflicts. Presumably, the addition of the ICG to the existing Malaysian-led mediation process will also add to the transparency of the process. While it is too early to assess the effectiveness of this complex new structure, the fact that the parties sought assistance from this diverse set of countries and institutions shows recognition that this seemingly intractable conflict needed a variety of talents and perspectives to help it toward resolution.

As noted earlier, although the OAS is the most institutionalized organization for dealing with security problems in the Western Hemisphere and, as Monica Herz observes, the most important regional forum for conflict management and resolution, its work is complemented by a wide variety of subregional and ad hoc groupings and entities such as the Rio Group, the Guarantors of the Peru-Ecuador Treaty, the Summit Meetings of Hemispheric Presidents, the Meeting of Defense Ministers, and the Summit Meeting of South American Presidents—all of which have contributed significantly to "fostering an environment favorable to peaceful conflict resolution." CCM norms are also reinforced by two bodies that deal with nuclear matters—the Agency for the Prohibition of Nuclear Weapons in Latin America and the Caribbean and the Brazilian-Argentine Nuclear Accounting Agency. As Herz argues, regional economic cooperative endeavors such as the Common Market of the South, the Union of South American Nations, and the Andean Community also help foster a common security agenda. These arrangements underscore the importance of formal institutional mechanisms and confidence-building instruments in the CCM equation because they contribute to legality, transparency, and widespread political "buy-in" from members through direct institution-to-institution partnerships.

Formal regional organizations can also serve as the launch pad for a wide variety of CCM ventures of the more informal variety that extend beyond the direct membership of the organization. For example, ASEAN has established several forums for the promotion of security and good relations within the wider Asia-Pacific region and to deal with ongoing or potential disputes. Among these are the ASEAN summit of member states to discuss and resolve regional issues and tensions, security-building dialogues with countries outside of ASEAN, such as with China, Japan, and South Korea (ASEAN+3) and with Australia and New Zealand, the ARF, which is composed of twenty-four countries and which, as Richard Bitzinger and Barry Desker note, is "basically dedicated to regional confidence building by creating 'a sense of strategic community' and encouraging preventive diplomacy and conflict management." The explosion of bilateral and multilateral free-trade and economic partnership agreements in the Asia-Pacific region is also underpinning the CCM enterprise in constructive ways by deepening the bonds of cooperation through rapidly growing levels of economic interdependence. At the same time, ASEAN and its outreach adjunct bodies have some potential to serve as a forum for airing and debating divisive issues and for bringing balancing pressure to bear when a powerful state appears to be acting in a threatening manner toward neighbors, as Chinese officials have experienced.

CCM and Regional Conflict Management

It is an open question whether CCM is a transitional practice—a halfway house to more formal, binding forms of cooperative action—or a step backward because of the failure of existing institutions of conflict management to address collective security challenges. It is also important to recognize the limitations of CCM, especially in the context of regional, state, and nonstate actor interactions. Many nongovernmental organizations have expressed unease at being co-opted by official institutions and military authorities in conflict zones like Iraq and Afghanistan. Some NGOs specializing in conflict management, like the Crisis Management Initiative run by former Finnish president Martti Ahtisaari, have gone so far as to design communication systems for specific conflict locations so that military and civilian/NGO partners can work more effectively together. But when it comes to developing general "rules of engagement" between state-based and nonstate actors, governmental and intergovernmental authorities will have to respect the special nature (and limitations) of NGOs and not infringe on their independence and ideals. The NGOs, in turn, will need to decide whether to accept the constraints of operating in insecure locales and relying on others for security and physical survival.

There is also great diversity in CCM practices and choices. National preferences and regional "security cultures" are two variables that seem to influence both. But it also matters a great deal whether powerful regional hegemons assert themselves regionally in order to shape their environment. And, not least, it matters whether external, extraregional states are available to help out as conflict management partners. Emerging patterns of cooperation clearly remain in flux. For instance, as noted earlier, peace and security appear more divisible today than during the great geopolitical struggles that characterized the twentieth century. European norms shape much of the regional security agenda of the members and would-be members of Europe's institutions, but they do not shape the security agenda of regions/countries beyond this geographic zone. The United States may be able and willing to impose itself directly on decisions taken in some regions but not in others. UN norms such as the "responsibility to protect" rest uneasily on the most fragile consensus. Unlike the earlier versions of CCM in the 1990s, the unifying "prism" generated by these core power centers is only experienced selectively. To some degree, then, CCM—as it unfolds in individual regions—may be partly a response and partly a reaction to the perceived shortcomings of external policy and doctrine.

Understanding CCM and the complex interaction between regions and the global system requires some additional work, at both the conceptual and practical levels. Some of the key questions to be explored in further development of the concept of CCM include: (1) Is there an external security umbrella that shapes the calculations of regional actors (e.g., in Europe, Northeast Asia, parts of Africa, and the Caribbean)? (2) Is there a balance between the demand for and supply of "imported" security and conflict management assistance? (3) Are links with outside security "exporters" a source of consensus or polarization within the region, and do these links form a part of regional arrangements and norms? (4) Do regional states act in ways suggesting that they are dependent on outsiders or are they assertive in increasing regional autonomy? (5) Are global security actors such as the United Nations and the G-8 or G-20 members acting consciously to build regional capacity for CCM or do their policies create divisions and obstacles to concerted regional action?

More generally, if "free riders" are a problem in highly organized, formal institutions, how can this not become an even more severe problem in the case of improvised arrangements between different types of actors, as in the cases mentioned above? Will CCM face the challenge of having its apparently free-form and spontaneous activity descend into a race to the bottom and a net reduction in available capacity as resources and capabilities become diluted? The answers to such questions will illuminate additional issues at the core of a potentially emerging CCM "system."

CCM also brings with it orchestration challenges. With the growing involvement of a wide variety of state and nonstate actors in conflict management processes, the challenges of effective coordination generally tend to grow greatly—if not exponentially. As more and more players take the stage, it becomes increasingly difficult to orchestrate the process, maintain coherence, ensure that different players are not working at cross-purposes, and ultimately determine who can—or should—take the lead. As we have argued elsewhere,[17] multiparty conflict management is a reality of the present era that requires its own special brand of leadership and diplomatic skill set.

If regions are to "come of age" as conflict managers, shaping their own destiny rather than being externally shaped—and we recognize that this is a big "if"—it is not too soon to explore how this trend will impact regional security arrangements in the years ahead. We do not foresee an age of autarchic self-sufficiency in the world's regions. Rather, we conclude that CCM could become more common and take a wide variety of forms. We anticipate that conflict management arrangements will increasingly be task- and situation-determined, improvised within less formal mandates or rules, and developed spontaneously in response to the needs and interests of those who participate. In a sense, regions will be the "test beds" from which new patterns of collective action and new protonorms may emerge. Often, we would expect that such improvised arrangements would have a finite life span, serving only as long as they served some purpose and garnered the interest and support of "members." This, after all, has been the experience of contact groups and ad hoc coalitions of "friends" that become involved in conflict management processes.

We doubt, however, that it will be quite as simple as this picture implies. As conceived here, CCM takes place because participants have a problem and want to do something about it. Consequently, it has something of the quality of a "neighborhood watch," which is only as effective as its membership wishes it to be. There will be tension—and even conflict—between regional action and the rules of global institutions as well as international law (especially human rights law and laws of war). There will be sectors such as counterproliferation, counterterrorism, and antipiracy where the programs and policies of cooperating partners need to be harmonized or justified in terms of such rules, laws, and norms. However, there is growing recognition of the need for improved communication and coordination at the interinstitutional level between global institutions and major regional and subregional organizations. As UN secretary-general Ban Ki-moon noted in remarks to the Security Council in early 2010, regional bodies are "part of a new landscape—one in which the problems we face are so complex and interlinked that no-one can work in isolation, and no-one can afford to do without the benefits of cooperation and burden-sharing."[18] He could have been describing CCM. Regions, in all their differences and similarities, strengths and weaknesses, will play a critical role in whether these new collective conflict management ventures will succeed.

Notes

1.   Joseph J. Hewitt, Jonathan Wilkenfield, and Ted Robert Gurr, *Peace and Conflict, 2010* (College Park, MD: Center for International Development and Conflict Management, University of Maryland, 2010).

2.   Barry Buzan and Ole Waever, *Regions and Powers: The Structure of International Security* (Cambridge: Cambridge University Press, 2003), 26.

3.   Zbigniew Brzezinski, "An Agenda for NATO" *Foreign Affairs* 88 no. 5 (September/October 2009): 2–20.

4.   For a discussion of the evolution of the relationship between the United Nations and regional organizations, please see Rodrigo Tavares, *Regional Security: The Capacity of International Organizations* (London: Routledge, 2010).

5.   Karl Deutsch, *Political Community and the North Atlantic Area* (Princeton: Princeton University Press, 1957); Leon N. Lindberg, *The Political Dynamics of European Economic Integration* (Stanford: Stanford University Press, 1963); Joseph S. Nye, Jr., *Pan-Africanism and East African Integration* (Cambridge, MA: Harvard University Press, 1968); Joseph S. Nye, Jr., *Peace in Parts: Integration and Conflict in Regional Organization* (Boston: Little, Brown, 1971).

6.   Carnegie Commission on Preventing Deadly Conflict, *Preventing Deadly Conflict: Final Report* (New York: Carnegie Corporation, 1997); Connie Peck, *Sustainable Peace: The Role of the UN and Regional Organizations in Preventing Conflict* (Lanham, MD: Rowman and Littlefield, 1998).

7.   Jacob Bercovitch and Richard Jackson, *Conflict Resolution in the 21st Century* (Ann Arbor: University of Michigan, 2009).

8.   Charles Call and John Schmitt, "Explaining Civil War Recurrence" (paper presented at the annual meeting of the International Studies Association, "Exploring the Past, Anticipating the Future," New York, February 15, 2009).

9.   Alex de Waal, "Mission without End? Peacekeeping in the African Political Marketplace," *International Affairs* 85, no. 1 (January 2009).

10. I. William Zartman, "Conflict Management as Cooperation," in *International Cooperation: Extents and Limits of Multilateralism*, ed. I. William Zartman and Saadia Touval, 161–181 (Cambridge: Cambridge University Press, 2010).

11. Joseph Lepgold and Thomas G. Weiss define collective conflict management as "a pattern of group action, usually but not necessarily sanctioned by a global or regional body, in anticipation of or in response to the outbreak of intra- or interstate armed conflict. CCM includes any systematic effort to prevent, suppress, or reverse breaches of the peace where states are acting beyond the scope of specific alliance commitments, the traditional means of international security cooperation." Joseph Lepgold and Thomas G. Weiss, eds., *Collective Conflict Management and Changing World Politics* (Albany, NY: State University of New York Press, 1998), 5. The same definition appeared in Joseph Lepgold, "Regionalism in the Post–Cold War Era," in *Regional Conflict Management*, ed. Paul F. Diehl and Joseph Lepgold (Lanham, MD: Rowman and Littlefield, 2003), 12.

12. Collective defense and collective security are defined as follows: "Collective security is one type of coalition building strategy in which a group of nations agree not to attack each other and to defend each other against an attack from one of the others, if such an attack is made. The principal is that 'an attack against one, is an attack against all.' It differs from 'collective defense' which is a coalition of nations which agree to defend its own group against *outside* attacks. Thus NATO and the Warsaw Pact were examples of collective defense, while the UN is an attempt at collective security." See the University of Colorado's International Online Training Program on Intractable Conflicts, www.colorado.edu/conflict/peace/treatment/collsec.htm.

13. One account summarized the 2009 CCM picture this way: "Three large coalitions of naval forces conduct counter-piracy patrols in the vast area: Combined Maritime Forces

of NATO (Operation Ocean Shield); the EU's NAVFOR Somalia (Operation Atalanta); and Commander, Naval Forces U.S. Central Command in Bahrain, serving as Commander Maritime Force for Combined Task Forces 151, which was led in recent months by Pakistani, Australian, Singaporean, and United Arab Emirates flag officers. Still, with only two dozen patrol ships on station, all manner of small ship or casual dhow can and do evade land-based and now sea- and air-based surveillance efforts. Nevertheless, in 2009, the combined maritime operations of NATO and allied forces disrupted 411 pirate operations of 706 encountered; delivered 269 pirates for prosecution under prevailing legal interpretations to Kenya and other jurisdictions (of whom 46 were jailed); and killed 11 pirates. The combined operations also destroyed 42 pirate vessels; confiscated 14 boats, hundreds of small arms, nearly fifty rocket-propelled grenade launchers, and numerous ladders, grappling hooks, GPS receivers, mobile phones, etc." Robert I. Rotberg, *Combating Maritime Piracy*, Policy Brief #11 (Boston: World Peace Foundation, January 2010).

14. See Government of Canada, "The Dubai Process: Bilateral Cooperation Workshops," www.afghanistan.gc.ca/canada-afghanistan/news-nouvelles/2009/2009_04_03.aspx?lang=eng; and Government of Canada, "Minister Cannon Attends Kabul International Conference on Afghanistan," http://news.gc.ca/web/article-eng.do?m=/index&nid=548449.

15. Priscilla Hayner, *Negotiating Peace in Liberia: Preserving the Possibility for Justice* (Geneva: Henry Dunant Centre for Humanitarian Dialogue, 2007), http://fr.hdcentre.org/files/Liberia%20Report.pdf.

16. See United Nations, "Protecting Civilians, Facilitating Humanitarian Aid and Helping Political Process in Darfur," www.un.org/en/peacekeeping/missions/unamid/.

17. Chester A. Crocker, Fen Osler Hampson, and Pamela Aall, eds., *Herding Cats: Multiparty Mediation in a Complex World* (Washington, DC: United States Institute of Peace Press, 1999); and Chester A. Crocker, Fen Osler Hampson, and Pamela Aall, *Taming Intractable Conflicts: Mediation in the Hardest Cases* (Washington, DC: United States Institute of Peace Press, 2004).

18. Secretary-General Ban Ki-moon, "Remarks to the Security Council on Haiti and on Cooperation between the United Nations and Regional Organizations," January 13, 2010, www.un.org/apps/news/infocus/sgspeeches/statments_full.asp?statID=698.

Index

United States
Institute of Peace Press

Since its inception, the United States Institute of Peace Press has published over 150 books on the prevention, management, and peaceful resolution of international conflicts—among them such venerable titles as Raymond Cohen's *Negotiating Across Cultures;* John Paul Lederach's *Building Peace; Leashing the Dogs of War* by Chester A. Crocker, Fen Osler Hampson, and Pamela Aall; and *American Negotiating Behavior* by Richard H. Solomon and Nigel Quinney. All our books arise from research and fieldwork sponsored by the Institute's many programs. In keeping with the best traditions of scholarly publishing, each volume undergoes both thorough internal review and blind peer review by external subject experts to ensure that the research, scholarship, and conclusions are balanced, relevant, and sound. With the Institute's move to its new headquarters on the National Mall in Washington, D.C., the Press is committed to extending the reach of the Institute's work by continuing to publish significant and sustainable works for practitioners, scholars, diplomats, and students.

Valerie Norville
Director

About the
United States Institute of Peace

The United States Institute of Peace is an independent, nonpartisan institution established and funded by Congress. The Institute provides analysis, training, and tools to help prevent, manage, and end violent international conflicts, promote stability, and professionalize the field of peacebuilding.